LAWYER BARONS

This book is a broad and deep inquiry into how contingency fees distort our civil justice system, influence our political system, and endanger democratic governance. Contingency fees are the way personal injury lawyers finance access to the courts for those wrongfully injured. Although the public senses that lawyers manipulate the justice system to serve their own ends, few are aware of the high costs that come with contingency fees. This book sets out to change that, providing a window into the seamy underworld of contingency fees that the bar and the courts not only tolerate but even protect and nurture. Contrary to a broad academic consensus, this book argues that the financial incentives for lawyers to litigate are so inordinately high that they perversely impact our civil justice system and impose other unconscionable costs. It thus presents the intellectual architecture that underpins all tort reform efforts.

Lester Brickman is a professor of law and former acting dean at the Benjamin N. Cardozo School of Law at Yeshiva University, where he teaches contracts and legal ethics. He has written extensively on legal ethics, and his writings have been widely cited in treatises, casebooks, scholarly journals, and judicial opinions. Brickman is a leading authority on contingency fees, and his writings on that subject are the basis for a proposal – examined in this book – to realign the contingency fee system with its policy roots and ethical mandates.

Lawyer Barons

WHAT THEIR CONTINGENCY FEES REALLY COST AMERICA

Lester Brickman

Benjamin N. Cardozo School of Law

CAMBRIDGE
UNIVERSITY PRESS

CAMBRIDGE UNIVERSITY PRESS
Cambridge, New York, Melbourne, Madrid, Cape Town, Singapore,
São Paulo, Delhi, Dubai, Tokyo, Mexico City

Cambridge University Press
32 Avenue of the Americas, New York, NY 10013-2473, USA

www.cambridge.org
Information on this title: www.cambridge.org/9780521189491

First published 2011

Printed in the United States of America

A catalog record for this publication is available from the British Library.

Library of Congress Cataloging in Publication data
Brickman, Lester, 1940–
    Lawyer barons: what their contingency fees really cost America / Lester Brickman.
        p.   cm.
    ISBN 978-1-107-00122-0 (hardback) – ISBN 978-0-521-18949-1 (pbk.)
    1. Lawyers – Fees – United States.   2. Torts – Economic aspects – United
    States.   I. Title.
    KF310.C6B75   2011
    347.73'77–dc22   2010043979

ISBN 978-1-107-00122-0 Hardback
ISBN 978-0-521-18949-1 Paperback

In memory of Teddy. Twice taken from me before our time.

Contents

Foreword: Sorting Out Our National Liability Crisis

Richard A. Epstein

The Liability Crisis

Lester Brickman is a man with a mission: to expose the waste and fraud that permeate the system of tort liability as it has grown over the past forty years in the United States. Brickman is not alone in this crusade. Philip Howard has also noted the powerful resistance that the trial bar has posed to any medical malpractice reform. But Brickman offers a broader critique that extends to all phases of the liability system and the procedural engines that drive it forward. Owing to its breadth and detail, Brickman's crusade strikes fear in the hearts of those who profit from the system. That crusade provokes a genuine sense of unease on the part of many Americans who like to believe that the principles of justice and institutions that administer them both work well in their country, as in many cases they do. Yet the signs of real doctrinal and institutional decay are everywhere, at least to those who care to look and who know where to look. Brickman both cares and knows. More unusually, he is prepared to break polite social conventions to speak out against the dominant social elites that are all too comfortable with the current overheated system of liability.

It should be evident from the briefest perusal of his work that Brickman is an indefatigable researcher who understands that the keys to unlocking the secrets of the tort system cannot be easily gleaned solely from the formal tort law that continues to speak, as it has always spoken, in the traditional language of strict liability, negligence, proximate cause, assumption of risk, and contributory negligence. To analyze these conceptions, a large academic industry seeks to prove by a thousand theorems the efficiency of a tort law system crafted from these materials. After all, it is sensible, almost tautological, to insist that the purpose of the law is to minimize the sum of the costs of accidents, the cost of their avoidance, and the cost of administering the system. Although the legal precepts to do this are available, however, they are not easily put into a harmonious whole. As is said commonly about music, the notes may be the same, but the melodies are not. So too beneath the constancy in legal terminology lurk the enormous twists and turns in both tort doctrine and practice over the past forty years that have fueled a massive expansion of tort liability – which is, in terms of the dollars at stake, greater than any and all previous transformations of tort law during the previous thousand years.

At the global level, we sense this in our bones because the level of litigation has gone up in areas like product liability and medical malpractice by close to a thousand-fold relative to its sleepy days of the 1950s. By degrees, the law was quietly transformed during the 1960s, leading to a full-scale crisis by the 1970s. I became acquainted with this as a young law professor when I was summoned as a consultant to a meeting of the American Insurance Association in 1976 to address the various issues associated with this first iteration of the tort crisis. What was so astonishing for that neophyte to learn was that *no one* in the insurance industry had yet to develop any real expertise in product liability because the field had long been regarded as an underwriting backwater. I was told that the important lines of insurance had been in such areas as workers' compensation, automobile, and occupier's liability. Product liability was something of an orphan that no one chose to price separately – at least until the large verdicts in the early 1970s started to roll in. The source of perplexity was even greater because the expansion in tort liability took place at a time when technological advances in the workplace and elsewhere had started to drive accident rates downward, which should have been reflected in a lower level of tort liability and lower premiums to reflect the decline in both the frequency and severity of accidents. Yet it was quite clear that the trend lines were moving in the opposite direction. It first happened with machine tools, but slowly it spread to other product lines like drugs, chemicals, and asbestos, the extensive use of which promised a long succession of high-risk, big-ticket tort suits that were being blessed ever more by the legal system.

My AIA job at that time was to see if I could isolate the source of the shift in legal rules and do something to propose statutory reforms that could do something to staunch the flow. It took a lot of talking and thinking to come up with the drivers of this transformation, which doctrinally seem easy to identify in retrospect. All of the elements of the plaintiff's basic case were expanded, and all the potential lines of defense were contracted. Oddly enough, the one point that did not seem to make all that much difference was the adoption of a strict liability standard for defective product, which was accomplished in the Restatement (Second) of Torts in the mid-1960s. Rather, the key changes were the new and expanded definitions of defect, which allowed virtually every choice in design and warning to be attacked after the fact as defective, and recalibration of defenses so that manufacturers were held to anticipate and guard against extensive forms of misconduct by product users.

In the fullness of time, these turned out to be anything but small shifts. In the area of machine tools, which started the progression to the modern view, the older view took the position that if a worker knew the equipment with which he worked, he took the risk of obvious conditions because of his ability to alter behavior to minimize their effects. But in the new iteration, the drumbeat was that even obvious conditions could be treated as defective so long as the jury could think of some design change that could – or could not – obviate the danger without impairing the operation of the equipment, which opens up litigation to the fevered enthusiasms of the plaintiff's expert witnesses. Similarly, this one-two punch took its toll in other kinds of litigation. Thus, the definition of a defective cigarette underwent a parallel transformation. In the 1960 Restatement, the definition of "defect" covered cigarettes laced with cyanide or other impurities. Over the next generation, the new expanded definition treated all tobacco products as defective because of their potential to cause harm. Conversely, assumption of risk in tobacco could no longer be established by the common knowledge that cigarettes posed a threat to health (which I have known since I was nine years old in 1952, when our family in unison persuaded my late physician father to quit smoking).

We are not talking of small shifts. However, we need to get some explanation as to what drove this puzzling transformation. It should seem evident that advances in technology have raised safety to all-time highs, which has necessarily reduced the levels of injury far below what they were in earlier times. The two numbers just do not mesh. Better performance and fewer injuries should lead to a reduction in the size of the tort law, not to its massive expansion. We need to find an explanation for this inversion, and Brickman supplies it. The main driver is the contingent fee system, whose payment arrangements for lawyers are the fee tail that wags the tort dog. A second driver is the procedural class action. In many ways, Brickman runs against the grain. It is worth spelling out both arguments in some detail.

Contingent Fees

At first look, the initial response is to ask this question: What is there not to like about the contingent fee system? Individuals generally do well at business with which they have had some experience. Markets are generally rational. Public institutions are generally sensitive to the functions they discharge. The contingent fee offers the injured party a way to handle the risk that is associated with litigation. Quite simply, everyone needs an agent in navigating treacherous waters, which is what injured persons or the estates of dead persons are required to do.

On this sunny view, the contingent fee is simply a rational response to the vicissitudes of modern life. People are better at buying electronic equipment than new homes. And they are better at buying new homes than suing to recover damages for accidents. Human beings, as we all too well know, cannot function as infallible rational agents, especially in times of stress. They have cognitive limitations, and in times of pressure their decision-making capabilities are always compromised. So these people follow a rational strategy that dominates all other kinds of fee arrangements. They pay the lawyer out of the winnings of their lawsuit. That way, they are protected against a lawyer who runs up the bill without providing services of real value; they no longer have to make each and every strategic decision; and they retain some right to decide whether or not to settle the suit in question. So the parties gravitate to arrangements that outperform the ordinary fee-for-service contract, which leaves plaintiffs exposed to a lawyer running up a bill, and a lump-sum payment, which leaves the lawyer with little or no incentive to work a case hard. It is for reasons such as these that many, perhaps most, academics defend the contingent fee system that Brickman sets in his crosshairs.

It is critical for the skeptical reader to pay close attention to the massive amount of evidence that Brickman amasses to expose the soft underbelly of this story. To his great credit, Brickman does not go into rigid and futile denial about the potential benefits of the contingent fee arrangements, which continue to work well in small-stakes cases like routine traffic accidents. He chooses instead to show that the contingent fee contract is not immune to the types of deficiencies that influence all sorts of other contractual arrangements, only more so.

To put his point in perspective, it is useful to understand how the modern law and economics movement thinks (or at least should think) about contract arrangements. The original presumption is properly set in favor of contractual freedom. The explanation normally is that rational actors do not enter into agreements that leave them worse off than they were before, so that in the ordinary case voluntary agreements produce mutual gains between the parties. These gains are *augmented* in the usual case by the *positive* externalities in third parties who, quite simply, have greater opportunities for advantageous exchange as other individuals increase their wealth. It is for this reason that the market in ordinary goods and services tends to outperform a whole variety of regulatory schemes that give the power to the government to set minimum terms and maximum prices, both of which drive reputable sellers from the marketplace and clear a path for fast operators to take over an impoverished marketplace.

Yet this set of observations does not clinch the case for contractual freedom. Rather, it only creates a rebuttable presumption that all is well in the land of free contract. There are three major threats to this grand synthesis, however, all of which have real bite in the law that governs contingent fee arrangements, even though they are in fact in tension with one another. The first of these is the question of whether one side to the contract is able to take advantage of the other because of differential knowledge or experience. In dealing with competent adults, the presumption is generally set against drawing that inference. The second is whether the contract takes place in an environment with limited entries that protect service providers from competition. The third is whether the contract enables the plaintiff and his or her lawyer to take unfair advantage of third persons who are not privy to their arrangements. In one sense, it is hard to see how the first of these concerns cohere with the second two. How is it that the clients who are exploited by their lawyers eagerly sign up to joint arrangements that allow them to exploit the vulnerable positions of third parties – in this instance businesses, governments, charities, and other organizations that the plaintiffs' bar targets. The answer to that question is this: All of these defects do not arise in all cases, but each of them is of sufficient importance in some fraction of cases that it requires some recounting.

Plaintiff Competence

Starting with the first of these concerns, Brickman's central point is that the success of a contingent fee depends on the choice of the correct baseline against which it is measured. In those cases where the prospects are for zero recovery without hard work, taking a percentage of each dollar may make sense. But it is quite a different kettle of fish in a case where the defendant has already made a firm offer of settlement before the contingent fee arrangement is made. In these instances, taking a cut out of first dollars makes no sense to the client because she is worse off than with just taking the deal. Brickman leads with the example of Mary Corcoran whose husband was killed by the defendant's freight train. The railroad put an offer of $1,400,000 on the table. With a 25 percent contingent fee offer, starting with first dollar would leave her worse off if the lawyer litigated a settlement at anything less than $1,866,670, even if we ignore the risk of failure and the additional personal expenses needed to make the settlement work. He then relates that the lawyer who reviewed the case, Thomas Demetrio, took no fee when he found that the settlement was fair, but that the local small town lawyer Joseph B. Dowd, who referred the case to Demetrio, insisted that he get the 40 percent of the contingent fee that Demetrio had ceded to him. Dowd won in court, which only shows how the pitfalls of contingent litigation make it hard for a client to get legal advice as to which lawyer to see and why. One simple reform could stop this. Require all contingent fees to be a percentage of the take above the defendant's final firm offer. At this point, more plaintiffs will settle out quickly. Why pay a steep contingent fee on the overage when you could lose everything in litigation? This is precisely the driving force behind Brickman's "early offer" proposal, which is designed to protect plaintiffs from this form of advantage taking.

The Collusion Risk

Brickman's second concern with the contingent fee also harps at the theme of exploitation, that is, its excessive fees. In principle, contingent fee lawyers should earn more per hour in successful cases to make up for the cases that don't work out as well as they might. But that risk has to be properly calibrated to take into account the smallness of those risks in many cases. When Brickman reports average fees in key cases that are multiples of what good hourly lawyers earn – where the top of the distribution is around $1,000, which ain't hay, as they say – someone has to look to see whether some barriers to entry block the ordinary operation of the market and, if so, what to do with them. Brickman thus enters into an extensive discussion of "effective hourly" rates that in toxic torts and airline crash litigation can hit between $2,500 and $5,000 per hour, and in mass torts between $20,000 and $30,000 per hour.

Where are the barriers to entry that prevent competitive forces from bringing figures down? Brickman then identifies the various prohibitions on alternative fee arrangements, such as selling claims outright to third persons, including nonlawyers, and limitations on bar admissions in certain states that could help account for the difference. He also notes the price rigidity in contingent fees, which counts as some evidence of a less-than-open market under standard antittrust doctrine. Moreover, for all we know there may be other restrictions in, for example, the selection of class action lawyers that could influence the process. Brickman also goes at great length to dissect the evidence put forward by others to show the competitive nature of this market. It is extremely difficult to quantify all the relevant variables, but with time I have become persuaded that the persistence of high fees in the face of low risks suggest that the system is indeed out of whack in some serious way. The high rates do not seem to be necessary for making a proper risk adjustment, given that most cases settle out in these areas. A larger market should perhaps bring some form of relief. Maximum limitations on contingent fees might help as well, but as usual the issue is difficult because those limitations could easily reach the routine automobile cases where the system seems to work fairly well. Reform prospects on this front today seem uncertain at best, however.

Litigation as Aggression

The most powerful and urgent portion of this book, however, does not deal with client relations or with market structures. Rather, it deals with the use of litigation to achieve private ends. It is too easily forgotten today that litigation is a form of aggression, as is the resistance to litigation. In these circumstances, the contingent fee lawyer does his client a great service by pushing hard on whatever would allow the case to settle for its maximum value. Part of that package is taking advantage of every legal advantage that the law gives to the plaintiff on matters of principle or proof. On this issue, the key insight is that the contingent fee system *magnifies* both the strengths and weaknesses of the tort system. If the substantive claims were correct, and the evidence sufficient unto the case, the contingent fee would force the defendants to recognize the costs that their errors inflict on others, which in turn would satisfy the twin goals of compensation and deterrence. But if questions of doctrine and proof are not well handled by the legal system – and emphatically they are not – neither the loyal nor the greedy contingent fee lawyers should be expected to surrender any of the advantages that the legal system gives them. Their job is to play the game under the rules, not to redesign them during the course of play.

On the state of the legal rules, the evidence is disturbing. In general, I think that too many modern judges have all sorts of theories as to why defendants should be held liable and all too few reasons as to why they should not. To give perhaps the most egregious example of the doctrinal blunders, consider the tort doctrine of foreseeable misuse, which allows individuals who have acted in reckless disregard of their own safety to recover from manufacturers who did not protect them sufficiently against their own foolishness. The same can happen with third-person misconduct, in which a drug company can be held responsible when its product has been maladministered by a physician's assistant in ways that manifestly contravene the detailed warnings provided. Too often, product liability law seems to assume that there is always some, any, stronger warning that would have done the trick. Too many eminent courts never ask the question whether a little downstream prudence would have helped.

The most conspicuous version of this unfortunate situation is the recent case of *Wyeth, Inc. v. Levine*, a 2009 decision of the U.S. Supreme

Court. One difficulty in the case was that the court refused to give conclusive effect in state tort actions to the FDA-approved warnings that
had been used without incident for more than fifty years. The significant back story, however, is that the underlying tort action arose because
a physician's assistant disregarded every safety warning given with the
drug Phenergan. The drug injection had to be in a vein and at low pressures. The physician's assistant injected into an artery at high pressure
and didn't stop to notice her blunder. So the plaintiff musician lost her
arm to gangrene, exactly what the warning noted would happen. A
cheap settlement with the doctor and his assistant enabled them to testify against Wyeth, which was saddled with a $6 million verdict.

It is upside-down law for which the blame should be placed not only
on the plaintiff's lawyer who won the case, but on the Vermont Supreme
Court that bought into such dangerous tort law reasoning. Yet when
courts think that risk sharing is the dominant end of the tort law system,
it is very hard to conjure up the backbone to throw any plaintiff out of
court. It is ironic that whereas excessive medical malpractice liability
contributes between $50 billion and $75 billion in costs to the health care
system, we have instances in which obvious cases of malpractice are not
deterred because of the ability of health care providers to enter into strategic settlements to stick drug companies with the bill for the manifest
incompetence of the doctors and other health care providers.

The second problem that is exacerbated by the contingent fee is, if
anything, more reprehensible. Lots of the claims that are filed are fraudulent, which requires the cooperation not only between lawyers and their
clients but the assistance of a large cast of characters that includes physicians, crew bosses, and street runners, each in for a piece of the take.
In some instances, judges like Janis Jack come down tough on a slew of
bogus claims that are brought by a single law firm. Often these firms rely
on all-too-eager experts who fabricate scientific evidence at startling
rates. Dealing with this problem is no small task to say the least. And
the sad part is that for every judge, like Janis Jack, who is tough on these
cases, there are others who are all too lenient. There is little question

that the contingent fee makes it easier for lawyers to bring fabricated suits. So in the second-best world in which we live, it is much harder to be comfortable with a system that produces such egregious results in mass tort situations, even if it works admirably in other less-charged cases.

Class Actions

The same analysis can be made of the second great driver of modern tort litigation, which is the class action aggregation device. As a matter of principle, there is much to commend class actions in a variety of contexts. These are strictly needed to prevent the improper diversion of funds from corporations and other voluntary organizations. The shareholder that mounts the successful attack on the transfer sees the transaction unwound and the misappropriated property restored to the corporation. He gets his fees from the corporation itself, that is, from the other shareholders that benefited from the transfer. Unless that coercive mechanism were in place, only a few crusaders would be prepared to foot the entire bill to vindicate the interests of the group.

But the class action aggregation plays out entirely differently when the issue turns to various kinds of tort actions, including many suits brought for consumer fraud under state consumer protection and unfair trade statutes. At this point, the astute plaintiff's lawyer is able to bring countless individuals' claims together in a single action. The commonality of the cases, however, would be impossible to achieve if each individual plaintiff had to show how he or she were injured by the improper practice of the defendant. So many courts just remove the requirement of individual reliance, often by using weird theories that provide plaintiffs refunds of the purchase price for products that they say were improperly sold, even if they were successfully used. Refund actions for all cigarettes or drugs sold can easily add up to billions of dollars. Some courts have stopped the game, but others have been willing to let it go forward. Guess which courts get the business? As Brickman points out, the passage of the Class Action Fairness Act in 2005 has been instrumental in cutting back on these abuses in national class actions. But even single-state classes can easily mount to large dollars if allowed to go forward on exotic legal theories. Once again the judges who are too easy on liability matters are often too easy on the critical class action rulings as well.

Conclusion

Even this brief introduction should give some indication of the serious nature of the various problems that currently beset our tort system. What is truly striking about Brickman's book is the tenacity with which he tracks down just about every scrap of available evidence on a particular problem and melds it all into a compelling narrative that reads as a coherent whole. But there is no reason to take my word for it. All that is necessary is for the curious reader to dive in on page one and read through to the grim finale. Anyone who finishes the journey will quickly conclude that tort reform belongs back on the national agenda.

Acknowledgments

I am indebted to my colleagues Alex Stein and Stewart Sterk, who provided invaluable assistance with technical economics issues. My colleague, Arthur Jacobson, played a critical role in the publication process, and I am especially indebted to him for his generous assistance and support.

Over a period of two decades during which the themes of this book were being honed, I have greatly benefited from the efforts of at least a score of research assistants. Among these, Alan Blutstein, Mellissa Steedle Bogad, Amy Gilday, William Hanes, Sara Klein, Alex McTague, Andrew Pak, Tamir Pakin, Jonathan Rohr, Alyse Rosenberg, Evan Wilson, and Timothy Yip made substantial contributions.

The research librarians at the Cardozo Law School, Norma Feld, Beth Gordon, Kay Mackey, Kim Ronning, and Peter Walenta, have never failed to hunt down even the most obscure source material that I have requested. I have also benefited from the Project on Legal Ethics in the Tort System at the Cardozo Law School, which underwrote research and editing assistance, and from the considerable efforts of Erika Siu, program director for the project. I also wish to express my appreciation for the assistance of the Manhattan Institute, Larry Mone, president, and Jim Copland, director of its Center for Legal Policy, for their support during the editing process and marketing of this book. Finally, I would like to acknowledge the strong support I have received from John Berger, senior editor at Cambridge University Press.

LAWYER BARONS

Introduction

ON OCTOBER 11, 1998, A FREIGHT TRAIN STRUCK AND killed Michael Corcoran as he worked on a Union Pacific track bed in Illinois. Soon afterward, a railroad representative offered his widowed wife, Mary, a $1.4 million settlement. Mary, a 46-year-old former waitress, did not know how to judge whether the settlement offer was fair. An experienced lawyer could advise her, but at what price?

The answer may surprise and even enrage you.

The following spring, Mary visited Harpoon Louie's, a bar in Winthrop Harbor, Illinois, to reminisce about her husband with the regulars. Joseph P. Dowd, a small-time lawyer who had heard about the accident, happened to be at the bar also. He introduced himself to Mary and offered to take her case and refer it to a big-time lawyer. He would later explain his motivation for doing so: "Somebody gets run over by a train and killed and leaves a wife and two children. That's a good case."

Mary gratefully accepted Dowd's offer to help. She told him she wanted to retain one of the top personal injury firms in Chicago, Corboy & Demetrio, because her father had gone to school with one of the partners. Dowd arranged a meeting with Thomas Demetrio, and Mary agreed to pay the firm "25 percent of any sum recovered from settlement or judgment" with Dowd to receive 40 percent of that attorney's fee. She had no idea – because her lawyers did not tell her – that their fee would include a big slice of the $1.4 million that the railroad had already offered her.

After two years of effort, the Corboy & Demetrio lawyers concluded that they could not improve on Union Pacific's $1.4 million offer. They recommended that Mary accept it and then did something lawyers almost never do. Because they couldn't improve Mary's settlement offer, they waived their fees.

Not so Joe Dowd. He demanded $140,000, his 40 percent share of the $350,000 fee that the big-time lawyers waived. Mary balked. Could Dowd really charge her $140,000 for attending a few meetings, making a few phone calls, and reading a file? An Illinois trial court said yes. An appeals court concurred and added that Mary should have protected herself by including a provision in Dowd's retainer agreement stating that the lawyer would only get a percentage of the value he *added* to the settlement offer.[1] Alas, Mary did not realize that she needed a lawyer to negotiate a lawyer's fee.

Failing to point out to an unsophisticated client that the agreement she was being asked to sign would entitle the lawyers to 25 percent of her $1.4 million settlement offer – even if the lawyers did not add one penny to that amount – surely was a deceptive act. If an Illinois business had engaged in similar conduct, it would have been subject to suit under both the Illinois Consumer Fraud Act and the Uniform Deceptive Trade Practices Act.[2] Virtually all states have enacted similar statutes that lawyers have turned into weapons of mass extortion aimed at pharmaceutical companies, large retailers, and other businesses (as described in the second section of Chapter 11). Why didn't these acts protect Mary Corcoran? Simple: Under state court rulings, lawyers are exempt from these legislative protections for consumers;[3] they are instead subject to disciplinary regimes set up by state supreme courts. However, according to the Illinois courts, what Mary Corcoran's lawyers did was perfectly fine.

Alas, what happened to Mary Corcoran is not uncommon. Similar fleecings take place hundreds of times a year – perhaps even thousands.[4] Nor are the Illinois courts' decisions approving the fee and how Dowd "earned" it an aberration. It is the law of the land in all fifty states that victims of wrongful acts, called torts,[5] are fair game for one-sided bargains dictated by personal injury lawyers – a law promulgated by lawyers, for lawyers, enforced by judges who are lawyers, and heartily endorsed by the ethics committee of the American Bar Association (ABA) in an advisory opinion notable for its blatant self-interest and disingenuous analysis.[6]

Instead of being protected by her lawyer and the courts, Mary Corcoran fell prey to a powerful force. Over the past fifty years, this force has (1) shaped our civil justice system to best serve the interests of lawyers while providing a cumbersome, inconsistent, and unpredictable system for compensating injured persons; (2) created perhaps the most powerful regulatory regime in the land – one that dwarfs federal and state regulatory agencies; (3) empowered lawyers and courts to hold the fate of entire industries in their hands and extract billions of dollars in what are, effectively, ransoms; (4) inflated medical costs due to auto accidents by at least $30 billion annually; (5) empowered lawyers, in collaboration with judges, to usurp legislative authority and engage in policy making for profit; and (6) led to a litigation explosion.

This force, of course, is the contingency fee. The incentives created by contingency fees are so powerful that the U.S. Treasury bars lawyers (and others) preparing tax returns from charging contingency fees out of fear that their use would lead to corrupt practices and cost the U.S. government billions of dollars in lost revenues. Even so, of all of the elemental forces shaping our legal and political systems, this force – enveloped in stealth sheathing and largely flying below our radar screens – is the most underappreciated. Though well known to lawyers, its workings and effects are only dimly understood by most of the public.

If you are injured and want compensation, you may process a tort claim on your own. It is desirable (and sometimes essential), however, to hire a lawyer in cases of serious harm. Lawyers, like all professionals, want to be well paid for their services. The contingency fee is the way personal injury lawyers finance access to the courts for most of us who are wrongfully injured and want to seek compensation. In a contingency agreement, tort lawyers lend their services to injured persons, typically advancing litigation costs, including filing fees, court reporter charges, and expert witness fees. In exchange, tort lawyers charge a standard percentage of the recovery, usually one-third (or more) plus reimbursement of their expenses. American lawyers spend more than $100 million annually on thousands of ads in the Yellow Pages, on billboards, late night television, and the Internet trumpeting the mantra, "no fee unless you win." If you win, however, you will end up paying your lawyers at least one-third of your award plus expenses.

Even if your lawyer does not add any value to your claim, you will likely still fall victim to a scheme that is a routine part of contingency fee practice. When an injured person hires a lawyer to pursue a tort claim, even if the claim already has substantial value at the time the lawyer was hired, the lawyer assigns the value of the claim as zero and applies the contingency fee to the entire recovery. I call this scheme, which snared Mary Corcoran, the "zero-based accounting scheme." Even in the absence of a pre-retention settlement offer, the very fact that a contingency fee attorney agrees to represent a client on a contingency fee basis indicates – as a court has noted – that the cause of action "had value in the very beginning."[7] Stephen Gillers, a leading legal ethics professor at New York University School of Law, concurs that "most personal injury cases – certainly most that lawyers are willing to accept – have some value" and questions why "the plaintiff's lawyer [should] get a full contingent fee for 'recovering' this amount."[8] The plain answer is: They do so because they can.

Because of these and other artifices and a greatly expanded tort system, tort lawyers' profits have risen prodigiously to levels far beyond what is necessary to create sufficient incentives for lawyers to provide access to the civil justice system. Lawyers justify their fees by saying that they bear the risk of losing the case. Indeed, by chasing down business through advertising and aggressive outreach, some lawyers appear to be among our society's quintessential entrepreneurs. They invest and put at risk time and capital, sometimes amounting to millions of dollars, in exchange for a percentage of an uncertain recovery. Professional athletes, rock stars, hedge fund managers, and CEOs enjoy huge earnings. Why not lawyers? How can we say that their returns are excessive, so long as the field of play is level and they play an honest game?

But in fact, the field of play is tilted; the deck is stacked; the game is fixed. Many lawyers charge for entrepreneurial risks they don't actually bear. By careful case selection, they prevail in the substantial majority of the cases they accept. Despite the limited risk, their share of damage awards routinely amounts to one-third or more.

Lawyers can charge for these phantom risks because they use positional advantages to shield themselves from market forces. They charge standard contingency fees, even in cases where there is no meaningful liability risk and a high probability of a substantial recovery. They benefit from enormous economies of scale in class actions and other large-scale litigations but do not share these benefits with their clients. They take advantage of complex state and federal regulatory systems, conceived of and applied by lawyers. They use their influence, if not control, over ethics rules to advance their self-interest. When ethics rules appeared to require lawyers to adhere to heightened fiduciary standards rather than the *caveat emptor* rules of the marketplace when bargaining with clients over fees, lawyers simply changed the rules so that they do not apply to the fee-bargaining process – as the Illinois court emphatically pointed out to Mary Corcoran.

Lawyers further exploit the bar's arcane ethics rules, such as those prohibiting business structures that encourage price competition, to extract unearned profits. They use the bar's monopoly over the practice of law to prevent competition from nonlawyers. They appear to be entrepreneurs when, in fact, they mostly are what the great economist Adam Smith called "rent seekers."

Economists use the term "rent" or "economic rent" to mean something different than a monthly payment to the landlord. Economic rent encapsulates any positional gain that exceeds opportunity costs: an earning, unrelated to productivity, realized by manipulating the legal environment or by taking advantage of a dominant position in the market.[9] This rent is the difference between the rent seeker's actual price and the price he would charge in a fully competitive environment. The investment in rent seeking may produce lucrative returns but does not generate benefits for society as a whole as does trade and production of goods and services. In layman's terms, economic rent is *unearned* financial gain. Unlike mere profit seekers, who extract value by offering a better product at a lower price, rent seekers often bypass the market and lobby the government for advantages that markets cannot confer. Oil companies seek rents, or unearned gains, for instance, when they lobby for tax breaks. Farmers who seek price subsidies, labor unions that seek government mandates for above-market wages, and automakers who seek protective tariffs are rent seekers, too.

Personal injury lawyers, though they ideally serve a socially protective function, are rent seekers. They extract rents in a variety of ways. First, lawyers have entrenched their position as monopolistic producers of legal services. For example, they use unauthorized practice of law statutes to keep out competition from those who would charge less, such as insurance adjusters who could provide effective but much less expensive claim settlement services were they able to market these services to the public. Second, tort lawyers also extract rents by inhibiting price competition. Virtually all tort lawyers in a community charge identical contingency fee percentages – usually 33⅓ percent of the plaintiff's recovery and 40 percent in mass tort cases – allowing them to collect fees that can amount to thousands of dollars an hour. They enforce this anticompetitive strategy through ethical codes that preclude the establishment of business structures that could foster price competition. A third form of rent-seeking behavior is the collaborative enterprise of tort lawyers and lawyer-judges to expand tort liability and lawyers' profits. This envelope-expanding litigation imposes significant costs on the economy by increasing uncertainty and the difficulty of doing business.

Some degree of rent seeking, however, may be beneficial to tort clients. Because these clients cannot monitor their lawyers' behavior, they have to rely on the incentives created by the contingency fee. A too-low contingency fee yields an insufficient incentive for the lawyer to invest the requisite time and litigation costs to maximize a recovery. The outcome may be a lower net recovery for the client than if the contingency fee were higher. The optimal contingency fee, then, is one that minimizes both lawyers' rents and underinvestment in claims.[10]

Most rent-seeking behavior by tort lawyers, however, does not redound to a client's benefit. Consider what Joseph Dowd did in securing a substantial positional gain. He used the bar's monopoly over the practice of law to extract substantial unearned profits from Mary Corcoran. She was forced to pay a contingency fee just to know whether the settlement offer she received was fair – a fee that would come entirely out of the money she had been offered as a settlement *before* she had a lawyer.

Tort lawyers' rent-seeking behavior is not limited to the abusive fee practices that tort victims like Mary Corcoran fall prey to. Both the rent-seeking activity of tort lawyers and the rents thus obtained raise a far greater basis for concern. This is the same concern that we face in reforming our health care system – the effects of financial incentives on doctors and other service providers and how those effects impact national policy.[11] Just as we must factor in doctors' financial incentives in determining how to reform the health care system, we must also take lawyers' financial incentives into account in deciding how to reform a civil justice system that allowed Mary Corcoran to fall prey to her lawyer's avarice – a civil justice system that has generated profits from contingency fees, as measured by lawyers' effective hourly rates, that have soared to unimaginable heights.[12] It is beyond cavil that at some level of lawyers' profitability, the financial incentives to litigate perversely affect our civil justice system. Too-high incentives in the form of greatly increased effective hourly rates distort the objectives of the tort system and impose other social costs. One such effect is substantially higher volumes of tort litigation, which are not justified by increased levels of injury or the need to induce potential injurers to increase investment in product safety. Despite these effects, most legal scholars have largely ignored the role of increased profitability of tort litigation in contributing to dysfunctional wealth transfer.[13] Unlike these scholars, Stuart Taylor Jr., a leading legal journalist, has focused on the issue with laser-like intensity. Surveying the legal landscape, he laments "how often plaintiffs' lawyers pervert our lawsuit industry for personal and political gain, under the indulgent eyes of judges, without rectifying any injustices, at the expense of the rest of us."[14]

Profits from contingency fees also account for the vast expansion of the range of acts that can give rise to tort liability. A modern-day Rip Van Winkle who awoke after a decades-long slumber would be amazed to learn of the many new ways that he could be held liable to others. Similarly, a large manufacturer can awake one morning to learn its very existence was at risk because the legal system had retroactively decreed that *all* of the millions of products it sold over the past twenty-five years are legally defective.

Over the past fifty years, expanded tort liability and higher profits have driven higher levels of litigation. This has led to a veritable litigation explosion. The more we *can* resort to courts, the more we *do* resort to courts. A litigious society benefits lawyers and judges by expanding their regulatory powers but with a high social cost.

The consequences of this legal rent seeking are thus profound. Contingency fees have empowered lawyers to shape our civil justice system in ways that further their financial interests to our detriment. The contingency fee is the "key to the courthouse" for most persons wrongfully injured, but whereas the public senses that lawyers manipulate the civil justice system to serve their own ends,[15] few are aware of the formidable costs that come with the benefit. This book, which distills over twenty years of my research on contingency fees, sets out to change that.[16]

If, after reading this book, you come away with the message that this is just another attack on "greedy" trial lawyers, then I have failed in my essential purpose. Trial lawyers are greedy but so too are CEOs, hedge fund managers, bankers, actors, doctors, teachers, airline mechanics, oil and drug companies, politicians – to name but a few – as well as you and I. What distinguishes trial lawyers from the rest of us is the positional advantage that judicial control over the practice of law and use of contingency fees has enabled them to attain. If you want to be titillated by tales about greedy trial lawyers or, for that matter, about companies that "put profits over people," you are well supplied by cottage industries dedicated to those pursuits. If you want to understand how contingency fees distort our civil justice system and endanger democratic governance, then read on.

My intent in this book is fourfold: (1) to demonstrate how contingency fees have empowered lawyers to shape our civil justice system in ways that further their financial interests while relegating the interests of the public to secondary importance; (2) to point out a compelling need to provide the same scrutiny now focused on our havoc-wreaking financial institutions on the costs imposed by the financial incentives for tort and class action lawyers to file lawsuits; (3) to show how fundamental allocations of power between the branches of government have been recast by contingency fee lawyers in collaborative efforts with judges to enlarge both the scope of liability of the tort system and the role of judges in allocating resources; and (4) to offer politically feasible corrective measures that are protective of both consumers of legal services and of society. My goal is to bring about reform of the civil justice system by exposing the corrupting influence of powerful financial incentives and the seamy world of contingency fees that the bar and the courts not only tolerate but, in some ways, protect and even nurture.

I come to the subject of contingency fees not only as a scholar of lawyers' ethical obligations but as a critic of mass tort litigation. These perspectives make me distinct from most torts scholars. I have been teaching legal ethics since the outset of my teaching career in 1965. In the mid-1980s, I developed a specialized interest in ethical issues raised by lawyers' fees. In several articles, I challenged the use of the nonrefundable retainer – an upfront, nonrefundable fee charged by matrimonial, criminal, and bankruptcy lawyers often amounting to thousands of dollars, which a lawyer would entirely keep even if the next day the client decided not to proceed and the lawyer had not yet done any work. Relying on this scholarship, New York's highest court outlawed the use of nonrefundable retainers,[17] and many other state supreme courts have followed suit.

By the late-1980s, I had begun to delve into lawyers' contingency fee practices. In a 1989 article in the *UCLA Law Review*,[18] I criticized the practice of charging standard one-third contingency fees in cases where there was no meaningful contingency or risk. I likened charging contingency fees in the absence of risk to *Hamlet* without the Prince of Denmark. Based on this article and others that followed, I developed a public profile as a critic of lawyers' fee abuses and have been a key participant in the ongoing battles to reform contingency fee practices.[19] In the ensuing twenty-plus years, I have been a keen observer of contingency fee practices and of lawyers' behavior. I have studied those practices, investigated them, debated them, written about them, and developed critical data about how this system works, who benefits, and how. In addition to my writings on contingency fees, I have focused my research on mass torts and have published articles on fraudulent claim generation driven by contingency fees in such mass tort litigations as asbestos, silica, fen-phen (the diet drug), silicone breast implants, and welding fumes. Here, too, I have acquired a reputation as the leading expositor of mass tort fraud. I have poured the sum total of this experience into this book.

Though contingency fees have been hotly debated among legal experts over the last several decades, this is the first book that analyzes the costs imposed by contingency fees and challenges the view of torts scholars that tort lawyers' profits, though great, are socially beneficial. Contrary to a broad consensus in contemporary legal scholarship, I argue that the level of financial incentives available to lawyers to litigate distort the objectives of our civil justice system and impose other unconscionable social costs.

In the chapters that follow, I explore just how profitable the contingency fee has become, why profits have burgeoned, and how the quest for these profits produces behavior that we would condemn in most other spheres of life. I explain the quirks of history that legitimized contingency fees in the United States while other countries, notably Great Britain, banned them. I show that what began as the poor client's "key to the courthouse" has become, for many lawyers, the key to great wealth. I describe the incredible wealth transfer created by this dynamic and outline its destructive effects on our society. I contest the arguments used by lawyers to defend their gaudy profits; show how they increase their profits by restraining price competition – efforts that are augmented by ethics rules that elevate the interest of lawyers above those of consumers of legal services; and I explore the worrisome impacts on policy making and governance. Along the way, I reveal how:

- Over the past forty-five years, due largely to contingency fee financing, tort lawyers have increased their incomes in real terms by more than 1,000 percent. In specialty areas, such as products liability, medical malpractice, airline crash litigation, and mass torts, lawyers can realize effective hourly rates of thousands of dollars an hour – even as much as $30,000 an hour. In the litigation against tobacco manufacturers brought by states' attorneys general who partnered with contingency fee lawyers, these rates reached $100,000 an hour.

- The ability of lawyers to use positional advantages to garner billions of dollars in unearned fees is intimately intertwined with the profession's self-regulatory status – a status that flows from state supreme courts' self-appointment as the exclusive regulator of the practice of law.

- Armed with greatly increased and often unearned profits, tort lawyers have engaged in collaborative efforts with judges to significantly increase the scope of liability of the tort system over the past fifty years.

- Contrary to the denials of many legal scholars, contingency fee pricing has, in fact, unleashed a litigation explosion, unjustified by any rising level of injury. Indeed, while most accident rates have been consistently declining during the past forty-five years, both tort

system costs and the volume of tort litigation, properly counted, have
been increasing.

- Contingency fees provide financial incentives for lawyers to drive up
  "pain and suffering" damages and to cause their clients to incur unnecessary medical expenses as a way of increasing their fees. These same
  incentives drive some lawyers to screen hundreds of thousands of potential mass tort litigants and to hire technicians and doctors to generate
  largely phony medical reports in support of the claims generated.

- Under the impetus of contingency fees, lawyers and lawyer-judges
  have made class actions one of the most powerful regulatory forces in
  our society and one of the greatest wealth-producing mechanisms ever
  invented. Whereas many class actions seek to redress injury, many
  more serve as ATM machines for lawyers. Rent-seeking lawyers have
  been instrumental in creating a legal system that empowers them to
  scoop up thousands of consumers into a class action and, by the sheer
  force of numbers, threaten the economic viability of all but a handful
  of the nation's largest corporations. Even the fate of an entire industry can be at stake in a class action.

- The effects of superprofits generated by contingency fees are not
  confined to the tort system – these profits also impact our electoral
  and policy-making processes. Tort lawyers recycle a portion of their
  profits from contingency fees into the political process and justly
  boast of their record of turning back threats to their prosperity. No
  longer content to just play defense, tort lawyers are seeking to take
  advantage of the current political climate to pass legislation to further expand the tort system and their profits – expansions that will
  impose additional burdens on business and drive up the cost of goods
  and services for all of us.

- The quest for contingency superprofits has led lawyers in collaborative efforts with judges to use the courts to secure outcomes that are
  indistinguishable from legislative acts and administrative rule making. This "regulation through litigation" dilutes our democratic form
  of government by exempting large areas of policy from legislative

control. In effect, lawyers are using their positional advantages to convert policy making into a highly profitable enterprise. When public policy making is thus removed from legislatures, so too is political accountability and public participation in the process.

I conclude with some detailed proposals for reform of this broken system. Among these, I spotlight what has become known as the "early offer" idea, which I conceived with Jeffery O'Connell of the University of Virginia Law School and Michael Horowitz of the Hudson Institute. By enforcing traditional but long-dormant ethical rules, this proposal would direct lawyers to apply their contingency fees only to the value they add to tort cases. Although perhaps not the "stake through the heart" that some tort reformers demand, I believe that the "early offer" proposal is the most reasonable and politically feasible way to protect the Mary Corcorans of this world from their lawyers' avarice and to add order and balance to our system of civil justice. I cap off the proposals with some thoughts on how we, as citizens, can begin to change the power structure that courts have created to elevate lawyers' interests over that of all other groups in society.

NOTES

1. My account of these events is based on Steven Lubet, *Dispiriting the Law*, 25 Am. Law., 146 (2004); Adam Liptak, *Ethical Question Raised On Legal Fee From Widow*, N.Y. Times, Aug. 28, 2004, at A8; and *Corcoran v. Northeast Ill. Reg. Commuter R.R. Corp.*, 345 Ill. App. 3d 449, 803 N.E. 2d. 87 (Ill. App. 2003).
2. 815 ILCS § 505/2 and 815 ILCS § 510/2, respectively.
3. *See infra* Chapter 10, note 24, and Appendix J.
4. *See* Lester Brickman, *Effective Hourly Rates of Contingency-Fee Lawyers: Competing Data and Non-Competitive Fees*, 81 Wash. Univ. L.Q. 653, at 660–62, n.14 (2003) [hereinafter Brickman, *Effective Hourly Rates*].
5. America is a "common law" system, meaning that judges have largely formulated our civil justice laws over the course of many centuries. Our civil justice system has three main branches: property, contracts, and tort. Property law regulates how different forms of property are created and transferred. Contract law enforces obligations that people have voluntarily assumed. Tort

law is different: It imposes duties on all of us not to engage in conduct that harms others and provides for a system of redress for those who are injured.

6. *See infra* Chapter 3, note 9.

7. *Kenseth v. Comm'r of Internal Revenue*, 114 T.C. 399, 413 (2000).

8. STEPHEN GILLERS, REGULATION OF LAWYERS 173 (8th ed. 2009). Attorneys also recognize this – this is why they actively seek out these lucrative claims in order to apply their standard one-third contingency fee charges to the entire recovery. So do lenders, to whom tort attorneys turn when they need to finance long-term litigation. These loans are made in anticipation of the lawyers receiving a big pay day. As one law firm stated in a letter to its lender: "Thank you ... for recognizing that contingent fees make the best collateral and have substantial value prior to case resolution." Advertisement in TRIAL, Apr. 2008, at 44.

9. *See* Robert Tollison, *Rent Seeking: A Survey*, 35 KYKLOS 575, 577 (1982).

10. Bruce L. Hay, *Contingent Fees and Agency Costs*, 25 J. LEGAL STUD. 503, 510 (1996).

11. Consider the costs we bear for unplanned hospital readmissions: One in five Medicare patients discharged from a hospital are readmitted within a month and one in three within three months – adding $17.4 billion to our health care costs in 2004. Proposals to curb these costs include paying bonuses to hospitals with low readmission rates and penalizing those with high rates. However, these proposals, as noted in a recent *New York Times* article, are doomed to failure because hospitals do not hospitalize patients; doctors do. "And doctors currently stand to gain little from lowering readmissions. In fact, they will lose revenue. As is often the case in our health care system, doctors' incentives do not serve broader social goals." Sandeep Jayhar, *To Curb Repeat Hospital Stays, Pay Doctors*, N.Y. TIMES, Dec. 1, 2009, at D6.

12. We have no way of directly measuring tort lawyers' profits. In this book, I use *effective hourly rates* as a surrogate measure of tort lawyers' profits. By that, I mean tort lawyers' gross incomes from contingency fees, divided by an estimate of the time devoted to representation. Lawyers' gross revenues do not equate with profits, because lawyers must deduct overhead costs, such as rent, secretarial expenses, and library costs. A rough rule of thumb is that overhead amounts to one-third to one-half of revenue. Because I focus on changes in effective hourly rates over time as a measure of increased profits, I do not consider overhead costs.

13. *See* George L. Priest, *Lawyers, Liability and Law Reform: Effects on American Economic Growth and Trade Competitiveness*, 71 DENV. U. L. REV. 115 (1993) [hereinafter *Priest, Lawyers, Liability and Law Reform*] ("[T]he previous literature has largely ignored the major influences on substantive law that might be traced to the wide variation across the major common-law jurisdictions in the rules setting financial incentives for litigation."). A few commentators have

noted the effect of financial incentives on the tort system. *See, e.g.*, John Fabian Witt, Toward a New *History of American Accident Law: Classical Tort Law and the Cooperative First-Party Insurance Movement*, 114 HARV. L. REV. 690, 699–704 (2001) (discussing the role of contingency fees in the initial development of tort law as America's primary accident compensation system); ROBERT A. KAGAN, ADVERSARIAL LEGALISM: THE AMERICAN WAY OF LAW 3, 100 (2001) (explaining that the "American [civil justice] system is shaped more by an exceptionally large, entrepreneurial, and politically assertive legal profession, and less by national ministries of justice.").

14. Stuart Taylor Jr., *Lawsuits That Benefit Only Lawyers*, NAT'L J., May 17, 2008, at 17.

15. Polls consistently show that public confidence in the civil justice system has significantly eroded. Sixty-seven percent of Americans believe that the (largely) lawyer-induced increase in the propensity to sue is changing society for the worse. *See* Nationwide poll of voters conducted by Communications Center, Inc., commissioned for Common Good, Sept. 2007; results published in Fact Sheet: The Effects of the Civil Justice System Across Society, distributed at a Brookings Institution forum on "The Boundaries of Litigation," Apr. 15, 2008.

    Other polling results are equally worrisome: 83% agree that the legal system makes it too easy to make invalid claims; only 16% trust the legal system to defend against a baseless claim, 55% strongly agree and another 32% agree somewhat that many people use the justice system like a lottery; 56% believe that our civil justice system is in need of fundamental change; and 88% agree (62% strongly and 26% somewhat) that we need more judges who will turn back frivolous lawsuits. Harris Interactive, "Public Trust of Civil Justice," 2005, published in Fact Sheet, *id.*

16. Most scholarly writing on contingency fees is based on economic theory and includes complex mathematical equations. In this book, however, after introducing the concept of rent seeking, I explain, in a nontechnical way, how contingency fees negatively impact our civil justice system. Instead of "rent," I mostly use the terms "unearned profits," "excessive profits," and "windfall fees," depending on the context. I also identify the ways in which lawyers use their positional advantages to extract unearned gains.

17. *See Matter of Cooperman*, 83 N.Y.2d 465 (N.Y. Ct. App. 1994). My research assistant and later colleague, Larry Cunningham, was a coauthor of these law-changing articles and the amicus brief we filed in the New York Court of Appeals.

18. Lester Brickman, *Contingent Fees Without Contingencies: Hamlet Without the Prince of Denmark?*, 37 UCLA L. REV. 29 (1989) [hereinafter Brickman, *Contingent Fees*].

19. For example, an article in the *American Bar Association Journal* about my successful efforts to reform the tax code to require reporting of payments to tort lawyers referred to me as "a conservative pit bull chewing on contingency fee abuse." Terry Carter, *Keeping 'Em Honest*, A.B.A.J., Aug. 1997, at 28. One academic critic of my scholarship has contended that law professors' self-interest alone should lead them "to hold pro-lawyer views," Charles Silver, *A Rejoinder to Lester Brickman: On The Theory Class's Theories of Asbestos Litigation*, 32 PEPP. L. REV. 765, 766 and 776 (2005), whereas I seem to "display a bias in [my] public statements ... [against the interests of] attorneys." *Id*. at 766. He went on to ascribe to me (and others), a share of responsibility for the low esteem in which the bar is held. *Id*. at 769, 778. I responded that "as academics and as ethical role models for our students, law professors have an obligation that trumps any purported self-interest," and that the bar's "low esteem is not due to criticisms of various practices of lawyers and the bar but rather to the practices which are the subject of those criticisms." Lester Brickman, *A Rejoinder To The Rejoinder*, 32 PEPP. L. REV. 781, 790–91 (2005) (citation omitted).

1 The Origin of the Contingency Fee

MOST OF US WHO ARE WRONGFULLY INJURED AND WANT to seek compensation need to hire a lawyer. Lawyers, however, are expensive. To proceed, we would need a way to finance the cost of hiring a lawyer. Four methods of financing tort litigation merit consideration.[1]

First, the government could provide financing. As early as 1495, England began subsidizing access to the courts for those who were impecunious and injured.[2] The English system of government subsidies – later called "legal aid" – eventually proved both costly and inadequate, and in 1990, the British government instituted a "conditional fee" system, allowing lawyers to finance access by charging an "uplift" of up to double their regular fee if the suit were successful in exchange for the same amount of downward adjustment of the fee if the case was lost. The English "double or nothing" conditional fee, often referred to as a "a success fee," however, is a far cry – incentive-wise – from the American contingency fee system, which ties lawyers' fees to the amounts recovered. Even so, English solicitors have done quite well under this system. The expectation was that the uplift would reflect the degree of risk that the lawyer was assuming so that upward adjustments would be balanced by downward fee adjustments. In fact, downward adjustments have been infrequent because solicitors carefully select the cases in which to charge a conditional fee and rarely suffer a loss.[3] To induce clients to agree to the uplift, some solicitors simply exaggerate the litigation risk. The net effect is that solicitors have increased their fees by undertaking a largely phantom risk[4] while drastically driving up England's National Health Services' costs to settle negligence claims.[5]

In the United States, both government and private financing of access to civil legal services exist for those at the low end of the income scale. Under pressure from tort lawyers, however, neither federally funded Legal Services nor privately funded Legal Aid are permitted to file tort actions. Injured persons who are income eligible for representation must hire private lawyers to seek compensation.

A second method – which most commentators agree would be the most efficient and market-oriented structure for financing tort litigation – authorizes lawyers to compete with one another to buy the right to a tort claim from the injured party or his representative, and then prosecute it on their own behalf.[6] This financing method would have the added advantage of generating a competitive pricing structure, which would deprive tort lawyers of the monopoly profits they now enjoy at the expense of their clients. However, as I will point out, for precisely this reason the legal profession has promulgated ethical rules prohibiting bidding on tort claims.[7]

A third method is a further elaboration of the second financing system. Instead of confining tort claims purchasers to lawyers, this method allows anyone to buy a tort claim. In response to the creation of a market for tort claims,[8] large-scale claim-buying entities would likely form. Obvious candidates include insurance companies, labor unions, health care providers, and for-profit entrepreneurial ventures. Economies of scale would enable these entities to obtain compensation more efficiently than plaintiffs' lawyers. They would also buy claims that lawyers are unwilling to undertake because they are too small to be profitable.[9] Although creating a market for tort claims would benefit tort victims, it would be a losing proposition for most tort lawyers. Less tort litigation would also be harmful to defense lawyers because much of the claim process would be handled by in-house counsel for the large tort claim-purchasing entities. Not surprisingly, state supreme courts have largely prohibited the sale of tort claims.

The fourth method – a uniquely American invention and the method that lawyers most favor – is for lawyers to self-finance by charging a contingency fee.[10] This method is used to finance virtually all tort litigation in the United States. When using a contingency fee, lawyers agree to lend their services to the client in exchange for a percentage of any recovery. Thus, the contingency fee is a joint venture that functions to hedge risk: The client's exposure to loss is limited or eliminated by the lawyer's assumption of the fee risk, but the client's potential gain is also limited by the lawyer's fee. The lawyer's percentage of recovery is both payment for services rendered – including interest for deferral of the payment until the case is resolved – and a premium for having assumed the risk of no recovery or a recovery that insufficiently compensates the lawyer.

In our civil justice system, the contingency fee is vital to the vindication of important legal rights. It has been called the "key to the courthouse" because it enables accident victims, other injured persons, and persons deprived of legal rights to finance access to counsel and the courts, which would not otherwise be feasible.[11] Even parties who can afford to pay lawyers on an hourly basis mostly prefer the contingency fee because they shun the risk of having to pay their lawyer even while losing the case.

Although contingency fees are regarded as "intrinsically evil" and are illegal in most countries,[12] most of these countries provide universal health care, thus obviating, at least in part, the need for compensation systems for wrongful injury.[13] In England, contingency fees are illegal because they violate the ancient and venerable law against champerty – the selling of an interest in litigation in return for a share of the proceeds to someone who litigates a case at his own risk and expense.[14] This prohibition was first enacted in 1275[15] in response to the practice of powerful landowners using litigation as a form of warfare. Instead of using armed knights to forcibly take possession of another's land, they hired one of a handful of sergeants – the first courtroom pleaders – to file suit to gain ownership of land or other valuable assets belonging to others – a strategy known as "oppressing the possessors."[16] This wealthy nobility also attempted to intimidate the local juries to vote in their favor by packing the place of trial with their supporters who would wear the noble's colors. The prohibition against champerty and related forms of financing (called barratry and maintenance), which encouraged litigation, stemmed from a view that litigation was a vice and a threat to the king's peace.[17]

In addition to prohibiting financing methods that facilitated litigation, the English adopted a rule to discourage litigation that can be traced back to Roman origins.[18] This "English Rule" as it has become known – sometimes referred to as "loser pays" – provides that the losing party in a litigation has to reimburse a major part of the prevailing party's legal costs including attorney fees.[19]

Though we inherited the English legal system at the time of our independence, we have developed a fundamentally different attitude toward litigation. In our system, litigation came to be protected, even encouraged, as a way to effectuate the First Amendment right "to assemble and petition government [including courts] for redress of grievances." The resort to the courts in the second half of the twentieth century to secure civil rights for African Americans and the protections that the U.S. Supreme Court provided for that litigation are notable examples of how our jurisprudence veered sharply from the English attitude toward litigation.

In the United States, contingency fees were originally banned in many states because they fostered litigation and violated the prohibition against champerty that we inherited from England.[20] It was only in the mid-nineteenth century that contingency fees gained the legitimacy that later led to their widespread use. This process was facilitated by adoption of the Field Code, which revolutionized lawyer fee regulation, an undecipherable U.S. Supreme Court decision, and America's Industrial Revolution.

Though lawyers' fees today are subject to some statutory and judicial regulation, lawyers are mostly free to charge what the market will bear. It was not always so. In the beginning, we followed the English practice, under which the court applying customary rates set both the fees that a prevailing party in litigation could recover and the fees that a solicitor could charge his client.[21] In the New World, however, distrust of lawyers, coupled with a populist preference for reposing decision-making competence in elected legislatures, led to fee setting by legislatures rather than courts.[22] An example of the depth of this mistrust is chronicled in the 1770 Grafton County, New Hampshire, census report to George III:

> Your Royal Majesty, Grafton County ... contains 6,489 souls, most of whom are engaged in agriculture, but included in that number are 69 wheelwrights, 8 doctors, 29 blacksmiths, 87 preachers, 20 slaves[,] and 90 students at the new college. There is not one lawyer, for which fact we take no personal credit, but thank an Almighty and Merciful God.[23]

From the very beginning of colonization until the mid-nineteenth century, strict statutory regulation of lawyers' fees was the rule in America, not the exception.[24] Perhaps the first attempt in the New World to regulate attorney fees occurred in 1658, when Peter Stuyvesant, in response to abuses alleged to have been committed by various court officers, prohibited lawyers from charging excessive fees.[25] Stuyvesant's proclamation was said to have reduced the fees charged for various legal services by 50 to 85 percent.[26]

Although the original English laws in the Colony of New York (the Duke's Laws) made no particular reference to attorney fees, by 1693, the New York Colonial Assembly had published a catalogue of permissible fees.[27] However, attorneys usually ignored the fee limits and charged their clients what the market would bear. As a result, the Assembly promulgated another act in 1709, reestablishing a fee schedule and providing for severe punishments for lawyers who charged in excess of the prescribed amounts.[28] The bar exerted such enormous pressure on the colonial government that the act was repealed in December of the same year.[29]

The next year, the governor and council issued another ordinance regulating attorney fees that raised fees slightly above the rates authorized by the 1709 act but omitted the severe penalty provisions.[30] This manifestation of the bar's political power was a precursor of things to come. A shortage of attorneys in relation to the degree of commercial activity in eighteenth-century New York – which the bar fostered – also contributed to upward pressure on fees.[31]

Lawyers in the other colonies were also beset by societal attempts to regulate their fees and were largely successful in resisting those efforts. In 1787, after years of public anti-lawyer sentiment, the Massachusetts legislature twice tried and failed to pass an ironclad fee schedule.[32] In 1777, Pennsylvania installed a new fee schedule that, because of inflation, doubled the fees previously set in 1752.[33] There is considerable evidence, however, that lawyers ignored the new fee schedule.[34]

When New York emerged as a state, it followed the English Rule. Like the other former colonies, New York extensively regulated lawyers' fees. Through 1813, New York enacted several "fee bills" that prescribed what attorneys could charge ("fees") and the litigation costs recoverable by the winning party, which included attorneys' fees ("costs" taxable to the losing party).[35] Thus, the fee bills purported to declare that the specified recoverable costs were the full measure of the lawyer's compensation.[36] New York fee bills after 1813, however, no longer controlled what courts could allow as recoverable costs but continued to prescribe what fees attorneys could charge their clients.[37]

Despite express statements in some fee bills that lawyers could not charge their clients more than the statutorily authorized amount, lawyers did precisely that. In *Adams v. Stevens & Cagger*, the court construed away the express language in the fee bills stating that the limits set

> ... have always been considered as merely fixing the rate of allowance of taxable costs, as between party and party ... [and not] as limiting the amount which the counsel was to receive from his own client, for trying or arguing his cause. [38]

In addition to disregarding the fee bills, lawyers responded to the fee restraints in other ways. For example, one of the fee bills stated that a lawyer could charge two dollars for "[p]ursuing and amending interrogatories" and one dollar for "drawing a demurrer or joinder in demurrer."[39] Thus, lawyers' incomes became a function of court filings, and "the prominence and practice of a lawyer was judged by the number of writs [filings] he sued out, or to which he appeared."[40] Because a lawyer's compensation depended on "the number or length of the proceedings," the fee bills encouraged "multiplication of the processes."[41] The proliferation of pleadings and proceedings that ensued, coupled with the inordinate procedural complexities that resulted from the dual systems of equity and law (which often denied meritorious claimants victory because of their archaic insistence on obsolete formalisms),[42] led to the demise of the system of pleading cases in court.

Under the leadership of David Dudley Field, the New York legislature was compelled to adopt a new code of civil procedure in 1848 – the Field Code.[43] This code was then adopted by many other states, virtually verbatim, and ultimately became the model for the federal rules of civil procedure. Field believed in free markets, and included a provision repealing the fee bills[44] and providing that lawyer and client were free to negotiate fees.[45] However, based on a lawyer's oath that he added to the Code, this did not mean that he meant to legitimize contingency fees. One of the eight duties included in the oath was "not to encourage either the commencement or the continuance of an action or proceeding, from any motive of passion or interest."[46] Of course, the contingency fee did just that. Field did not otherwise address the use of contingency fees in his Code. Ironically, however, by repealing the legislative fee bills and declaring that fees would thereafter be set by bargaining, the Field Code dealt the champerty prohibition a lethal blow. Furthermore, because this provision was included in the civil procedure codes that many other states adopted, the Field Code helped to legitimize contingency fees throughout the states.

Adoption of the Field Code inadvertently contributed to the atrophy of the English Rule in America. As indicated, at the time of its independence, America inherited the English Rule that the prevailing party in litigation was entitled to reimbursement of his legal fees and costs from the losing party. The English "loser pays" rule was implemented by a judicial taxing clerk who determined the reasonable amount that the losing party would have to pay to the prevailing party as reimbursement. At the time the Field Code was adopted, "loser pays" remained the prevailing rule in the United States. Indeed, maintaining the status quo, the Field Code specifically provided that the process of taxing costs to the losing party, including attorneys' fees, would continue as a matter of fundamental fairness – the losing party having caused "a loss to his adversary unjustly ... should indemnify him for it."[47] Furthermore, it allowed the prevailing party to recover higher attorney fees than previously recoverable.[48] Professor John Leubsdorf, the leading scholar on the subject, asserts that although the amounts allowed were consistent with what some clients were paying their attorneys, "elite lawyers charged far more."[49]

Because maximum fees were set by statute, attorney fees were easy enough to calculate when they were awarded to the prevailing party. However, by the time the Field Code was enacted, lawyers were already ignoring the statutory limits and charging market rates.[50] The Field Code's insistence that statutory approximations of prevailing party's attorney fees should continue to be taxed against the losing party was trumped, however, by lawyers who raised their fees to levels that far exceeded the reimbursement levels. Over time, the disparity between the repealed fee-bill limits that were the basis for setting reimbursement rates and market rates became so substantial that the reimbursement levels approached the trivial.[51]

In *Alyeska Pipeline Serv. Co. v. Wilderness Society* (1975),[52] the U.S. Supreme Court attributed the formal demise of the English Rule in the United States to the 1796 case, *Arcomble v. Wiseman*.[53] However, this is a misattribution. *Arcomble* rejected a $1,600 allowance for attorney fees, stating: "The general practice of the United States is in opposition to it; and even if that practice were not strictly correct in principle, it is entitled to the respect of the court, till it is changed, or modified, by statute."[54] If the Court was stating that the general practice was not to award prevailing parties recoupment of some part of their attorney fees, it was incorrect. What was true, however, was that as the disparity between what lawyers charged and the amounts that courts allowed to prevailing parties as reimbursement of their attorney fees grew, the practice of including attorney fees as part of costs awarded to prevailing parties simply atrophied.

These statutes, practices, and decisions ultimately led to the replacement of the English Rule with its opposite: a rule that each party is responsible for his attorney fees unless otherwise provided by contract or statute.[55] Much later, both a name and a policy justification for the rule would emerge.[56] It would be called the American Rule, and scholars and courts would justify its ability to protect access to courts by eliminating any possible penalty for instituting litigation.[57] Had the English Rule not met its unintended demise and if losing parties had to reimburse even a share of prevailing parties' attorney fees, the tort litigation spigot might never have opened to the point of becoming today's torrent.

One more historical phenomenon helps to explain how the contingency fee became what it is today. In the decades following the enactment of the Field Code, America went through the Industrial Revolution, leading to an increase in industrial accidents. Working-class plaintiffs with severe injuries, however, had no means of hiring lawyers to recover compensation. At about this time, there was a large influx of European immigrants into the United States. Those who sought to become lawyers mostly attended night law schools that catered to working-class students. Looked down on by the bar, these lawyers discovered that they could get business representing working-class clients who could otherwise not afford to hire them by charging contingency fees. Judicial acceptance accelerated as these developments took hold, and by 1881, the contingency fee was said to be an "all but universal custom of the profession."[58] In 1884, the U.S. Supreme Court gave contingency fees its imprimatur.[59]

The leaders of the American Bar Association (ABA), which reflected the views of establishment lawyers, were opposed to the influx of foreign-born lawyers. Even so, the ABA grudgingly approved of contingency fees. As part of its first code of ethics, the ABA adopted Canon 13 in 1908, allowing lawyers to charge contingency fees but adding the caution that contingency fees "should be under the supervision of the court, in order that clients may be protected from the unjust charges."[60] Mary Corcoran would have been protected from the "unjust charges" of her lawyer had she lived a hundred years earlier. However, by 1994, the ABA had done an about-face. In an advisory opinion, the ABA Standing Committee on Ethics and Professional Responsibility held that contingency fee lawyers could charge for risks that did not exist.[61] What had changed in the interim was that the contingency fee had become a multibillion-dollar industry. Under this impetus, the unjust had become the just.

NOTES

1. A fifth method, which is separately developed in detail, allows for awarding the prevailing party both the legal costs incurred and a reasonable attorneys' fee to be paid by the losing party. In the United States, this "fee shifting" is usually the result of federal legislation that seeks to provide lawyers incentives to represent persons seeking to vindicate civil rights, employment discrimination, and environmental protections. In England and most European countries, this is a fundamental part of their civil justice systems.

2. *See* Scott L. Cummings, *The Politics of Pro Bono*, 52 UCLA L. REV. 1, 10 n.36 (2004) (Beginning in 1495, an *in forma pauperis* law in England allowed an indigent person to bring suit without incurring court costs and provided for free appointed counsel. This law was later repealed and legal aid was replaced under the Rules of Court in 1883. Legal assistance for the poor has since gradually evolved over the following century under various other statutes until the modern Legal Aid Act of 1999); *see also* Joan Mahoney, *Legal Services: Green Forms and Legal Aid Offices: A History of Publicly Funded Legal Services in Britain and the United States*, 17 ST. LOUIS U. PUB. L. REV. 223, 226–29 (1998).

3. *See* Michael Zander, *Export/Import: American Civil Justice in a Global Context: Eighth Annual Clifford Symposium on Tort Law and Social Policy Article: Will the Revolution in the Funding of Civil Litigation in England Eventually Lead to Contingency Fees?*, 52 DEPAUL L. REV. 259, 262, 265 (2002) [hereinafter Zander, *Civil Litigation in England*].

4. *See* Report to the Lord Chancellor by Sir Peter Middleton, GCB, Review of Civil Justice and Legal Aid, Sept. 1997, at xii–xiii, xvii–xviii (quoted in Colleen P. Graffy, *Conditional Fees: Key to the Courthouse or the Casino*, 1 LEGAL ETHICS 70, 85 [1998]).

5. Despite the great disparity between the incentives created by the English "conditional fee" and the American "contingency fee," English lawyers representing clients suing the National Health System (NHS) are largely responsible for a spiraling up of the NHS's costs to settle negligence cases. These costs are expected to exceed 800 million pounds in 2009 – a 60% increase from five years earlier. Sam Lister, *Lawyers growing rich on NHS negligence*, TIMES ONLINE, Dec. 18, 2009, *available at* http://www.timesonline.co.uk/tol/life_and_style/health/article6961087.ece. Lawyers' fees, increased by use of "success fees," accounted for almost half of the damages paid in 2008. In more than one in five cases, legal costs exceeded the damages paid to clients; in some cases, lawyers were getting ten times as much as their clients. *Id.* The moral of this story is that financial incentives – even though quite modest when compared to the American contingency fee – can have enormous social costs.

6. *See, e.g.,* Bruce L. Hay, *Contingent Fees and Agency Costs*, 25 J. LEGAL STUD. 503, 513 n.20 (1996) [hereinafter Hay, *Agency Costs*]; Marc J. Shukaitis, *A Market in Personal Injury Tort Claims*, 16 J. LEGAL STUD. 329, 331 (1987).

7. *See* MODEL RULES OF PROF'L CONDUCT (2006) at R.1.8(j) [hereinafter MODEL RULES]; Rudy Santore & Alan D. Viard, *Legal Fee Restrictions, Moral Hazard and Attorney Rents*, 44 J. L. & ECON. 549, 551–56 (2001); Shukaitis, *id.* at 329–30. Prohibitions against bidding for clients are typically in the form of ethical rules prohibiting providing financial assistance to clients, see Chapter 6, § C(1), paying anything of value to anyone for recommending a lawyer, see MODEL RULES, *id.* at R.7.2(c) or operating for-profit lawyer referral services, see Chapter 6, § C(2).

8. *See* Robert Cooter & Stephen D. Sugarman, *A Regulated Market in Unmatured Tort Claims: Tort Reform by Contract*, in WALTER OLSON, ED., NEW DIRECTIONS IN LIABILITY LAW 174–75 (1988).

9. As Samuel R. Gross of the University of Michigan Law School has concluded:

Claims buyers might also be able to consolidate claims for particular types of accidents, or claims against particular defendants or particular insurance companies, especially if a secondary market in claims emerges. Consolidation could reduce the transactions costs of tort claims enormously. For example, if Global Claim Buyers has accumulated 2,000 tort claims for which Universal Insurance is financially responsible, the two companies will never have to bargain over each case separately. All they will need to do is negotiate over damage schedules, cost estimates, and discounts for factual uncertainty – and perhaps actually investigate a small sub-sample of cases to check on the reliability of the information the other side provides. Ultimately, even the most unpredictable disputes can be compromised when they are reduced to probabilistic estimates of the likely outcome and combined with a large number of other cases.

See Samuel R. Gross, *We Could Pass a Law ... What Might Happen if Contingent Legal Fees Were Banned*, 47 DePaul L. Rev. 321, 326 (1998).

10. A number of countries permit some form of contingency fee; however, these are not based on a percent of the recovery as in the United States. Countries that allow a limited form of contingency fee include Australia, Canada, Indonesia, Japan, and New Zealand. Though some Canadian provinces allowed contingency fees more than one hundred years ago, they have been rarely used. Loraine Minish, *The Contingency Fee: A Re-Examination*, 10 Manitoba L.J. 65, 69 (1979).

11. *See* Philip H. Corboy, *Contingency Fees: The Individual's Key to the Courthouse Door*, 2 Litig. 27 (Summer 1976).

12. *See* W. Kent Davis, *The International View of Attorney Fees in Civil Suits: Why is the United States the "Odd Man Out" in How it Pays its Lawyers?*, 16 Ariz. J. Int'l & Comp. Law 361, 381–82 (1999). In England, both solicitors and barristers are prohibited from using contingency fees by the Solicitors Act and by both the Inns of the Court and the General Council of the Bar, respectively.

13. *See* Kagan, Adversarial Legalism, *supra* Introduction, note 13, at 26–33.

14. *See Kennedy v. Broun*, 13 C.B.(N.S.) 677, 143 Eng. Rep. 268 (Ct. C.P. 1863). For the history of the doctrine of champerty, see Max Radin, *Maintenance by Champerty*, 24 Cal. L. Rev. 48 (1935); Percy H. Winfield, *The History of Maintenance and Champerty*, 35 L.Q. Rev. 50 (1919).

15. Statute of Westiminster I (1275), 1275 Chapter 53_EDW_1.

16. *Slyright v. Page*, 74 Eng. Rep. 135, 154 (K.B. 1589). A related practice was to aid those with claims on the property of others, thus stirring up lawsuits.

17. *See* Max Radin, *id.* at 48, 68 (stating that the English adopted the medieval and Christian tenet that litigiousness is a vice).

18. *See* Goodhart, *Costs*, 38 Yale L. J. 849 (1929).

19. 3 W. Blackstone, Commentaries on the Law of England 399–401 (London, 1765–69).

20. *See, e.g., Holloway v. Lowe*, 7 Port. 488, 490–92 (Ala. 1838); *Scobey v. Ross*, 13 Ind. 117, 124 (1859); *Thurston v. Percival*, 18 Mass. (1 Pick). 415,416 (1823); *Backus v. Byron*, 4 Mich. 536, 538 (1857); *Key v. Vattier*, 1 Ohio 132, 152 (1823); *Martin v. Clarke*, 8 R.I. 389, 403 (1866). Nonetheless, there are a number of reported cases in which noted litigators such as Henry Clay and Daniel Webster provided their services on a contingency fee basis in the early- to mid-1800s. *See Clay v. Ballard*, 9 Rob. 308 (La. 1844); *Contingent Fees*, 59 Cent. L. J. 401–02 (1904) (referring to a contingency fee agreement entered into by Daniel Webster in a will dispute). Contingency fees were also used in

many land claim disputes. However, whereas some jurists regarded contingency fees with approval, *see* Peter Karstan, *Enabling the Poor to Have Their Day in Court: The Sanctioning of Contingency Fee Contracts, A History to 1940*, 47 DePaul L. Rev. 231, 235, 237–38 (1998), the dominant view was that they were illegal.

21. *See* Arthur L. Goodhart, *Costs*, 38 Yale L.J. 849, 853–55 (1929).

22. These laws prescribed both the fees that lawyers could charge clients and the amounts that prevailing parties could collect from their adversary as reimbursement for their attorney's fees. *See* John Leubsdorf, *Toward a History of the American Rule of Attorney Fee Recovery*, 47 J.L. & Contemp. Prob. 9, 12 (1984) [hereinafter Leubsdorf, *American Rule*].

23. E. Norman Vesey, *The Role of Supreme Courts in Addressing Professionalism of Lawyers and Judges*, in Prof'l Law. 2, 8 (1997) (quoting 1770 Census Report).

24. I Anton-Hermann Chroust, The Rise of the Legal Profession in America 153 (1965) [hereinafter I Chroust].

25. *See* I Charles Z. Lincoln, The Constitutional History of New York 458 (1906) ("It is then provided that the officers enumerated shall serve the poor gratis for God's sake, but may take from the wealthy the fee specified.") (quoting proclamation issued by Peter Stuyvesant).

26. I Chroust, *supra* note 24, at 153.

27. *Id.* at 159.

28. *Id.* at 159–60 ("That if any Lawyer Or Attorney shall take or Exact any more or other fees than is Limited in This Act or Refuse to Serve any person for the aforesaid Fees not being Retained by the adverse party Shall forfeit Fifty pounds Currant money of this Colony and for Ever be Debarred from Practicing in any Court within This Colony.") (quoting I Colonial Laws of New York 1638–53, at 653 [1894]).

29. *Id.* at 160.

30. *Id.*

31. As early as 1695 an act was passed that prohibited a litigant from hiring more than two attorneys because the litigant could otherwise "fee" or hire all of the available attorneys and deprive the opponent of counsel. Lawrence M. Friedman, A History of American Law 87 (1973).

32. Maxwell Bloomfield, American Lawyers in a Changing Society 1776–1876, at 56 (1976).

33. I Chroust, *supra* note 24, at 257.

34. Despite the statute, the governor of Pennsylvania required in 1792 that: [A]ll attorneys "entitled to demand or receive fees" were required to "transmit to the governor of the commonwealth a particular statement of the several services for which they are entitled to demand and receive fees ... and of the

fees ... which they respectively charge and receive ... for the performance of their respective duties, together with the several particulars." *Id.* (quoting ch. 1648, § 1, 14 STATUTES AT LARGE OF PENNSYLVANIA 1682–1801, at 329 [1909]). The purpose of this demand was to allow the legislature to collect reliable data about the actual fees that attorneys were charging so that it could draft a new and perhaps more realistic act for regulating fees. *Id.* The lawmakers must have concluded that the prior regulations were not being observed. Otherwise, the legislature would not have needed to ask attorneys what they were actually charging for their various services.

35. *See* 1813 N.Y.Laws, ch. 83 ("[N]o officer ... shall exact, demand or ask, or be allowed any fee greater than prescribed.").

36. *See Davenport v. Ludlow*, 4 How. Pr. 337, 338 (N.Y. Sup. Ct. 1850) (referring to function of fee bills prior to repeal).

37. *See, e.g.*, 1840 N.Y.Laws, ch. 386, §§ 1–4, at 11–41.

38. 26 *Wend.* 451, 455–56 (N.Y. 1841).

39. 1840 N.Y. Laws, ch. 386, §§ 2–3.

40. HENRY W. SCOTT, THE COURTS OF THE STATE OF NEW YORK 217–18 (1909).

41. FIRST REPORT OF THE COMMISSIONERS ON PRACTICE AND PLEADING, NEW YORK CODE OF PROCEDURE, tit.X, at 205 (1848) [hereinafter FIRST REPORT].

42. FLEMING JAMES, JR. & GEOFFREY C. HAZARD, JR., CIVIL PROCEDURE § 1.6, at 17–18 (3d ed. 1985).

43. *See* FIRST REPORT, *supra* note 41, at 204.

44. Though this repeal provision was certainly an expression of his free-market principles, there may have been a political goal as well. *See* FIRST REPORT, *supra*, at 204–06. Because lawyers had invested heavily in the formalistic pleading system and would have had to devote considerable time to learning a new pleading system, many no doubt opposed Field's proposal. It is possible that the price for their political acquiescence was the abolition of the fee bills.

45. 1848 N.Y. LAWS, Ch. 379, tit.10, §258.

46. CODE OF CIV. PROC. N.Y. § 511 (1850) (repealed).

47. *See* FIRST REPORT, *supra* note 41, at 206, 208 tit.X ("The losing party, ought however, as a general rule, to pay the expense of the litigation. He has caused a loss to his adversary unjustly and should indemnify him for it ... [including] fees of attorneys, solicitors and counsel in civil actions ... [which] may be allowed to the prevailing party ... by way of indemnity.")

48. 1848 N.Y. LAWS 262, 263; 1840 N.Y. Laws 2.

49. *See* Leubsdorf, *American Rule, supra* note 22, at 68.

50. *See* 26 *Wend.* 451 (N.Y. 1841).

51. *See* Leubsdorf, *American Rule, supra* note 22, at 20–22.

52. 421 U.S. 240, 249–50 (1975).

53. 3 U.S. (3 Dall.) 306 (1796).

54. *Id.* at 306.

55. 421 U.S. 240 (1975).

56. *See* Arthur L. Goodhart, *Costs*, 38 YALE L.J. 849, 856 (1929).

57. *See* Leubsdorf, *American Rule, supra* note 22, at 28.

58. *Current Topics*, 13 CENT. L. J. 381 (1891); *see also* Chapter 8, notes 19–25.

59. *Taylor v. Bemiss*, 110 U.S. 42 (1884).

60. 33 A.B.A. REP. 80, at 579 (1908).

61. *See* ABA Comm. on Ethics and Professional Responsibility, Formal Op. 389 (1994).

2 How Profitable Are Contingency Fees?

THE CONTINGENCY FEE IS THE ENGINE THAT DRIVES OUR tort system, including personal injury and class action litigation. Contingency fees provide the incentives for lawyers to represent tort claimants and earn a return on their investment of time and capital. Those who write about contingency fees focus on clients' incentives to pursue claims.[1] A claimant's decision to sue, they say, is based in large measure on the expected returns, net of legal fees, and other costs.[2] Based on this presumption, these scholars calculate how varying incentives affect clients' behavior. This emphasis on clients' incentives is misplaced. For the most part, it is lawyers' incentives – not clients' – that matter. At any moment, thousands of would-be clients are seeking representation. Lawyers, however, will only accept a fraction of these claims. A lawyer decides whether to accept a case based on its potential profitability – a function of the litigation risk, the anticipated recovery if the case is successful, and the amount of time and capital that the lawyer will have to invest.

There is no widely accepted measure of the profitability of tort litigation. Rather than wrestle with that formidable task, I indirectly measure profitability by calculating changes in lawyers' "effective hourly rates." I use this term to mean the amount of fee income obtained by contingency fee lawyers, divided by the amount of time devoted to all representations. This measure accounts for the time spent on losing cases but not overhead (office rent, secretarial and paralegal services, and equipment), which generally accounts for between one-third and one-half of a lawyer's gross income. Although the data required to directly calculate tort lawyers' effective hourly rates does not exist, there is a surrogate. Using data on automobile accident litigation published by the Joint Economic Committee of the Congress, I calculate that attorneys in auto tort litigation received effective hourly rates averaging $325 in 2001 – two-and-one-half times insurance defense lawyers' average hourly rates at the time.[3] Whereas auto accident litigation is the most prolific source of tort litigation – accounting for about 60 percent of tort claims filed in court[4] – it is also the least profitable. The higher the percentage of auto accident cases in a lawyer's caseload, the lower that lawyer's income compared to lawyers with lower percentages of auto accident claims in their portfolios.[5] Effective hourly rates of lawyers specializing in product liability and medical malpractice – where average verdicts are approximately twenty-eight times higher than those in auto accident cases[6] – as well as those in airline crash litigation and class actions, are multiples of those of auto accident lawyers.

Herbert Kritzer, a professor at the University of Minnesota Law School, has arrived at a different outcome. He concludes that tort lawyers' effective hourly rates are substantially the same as those of defense lawyers who charge hourly rates.[7] Kritzer's data is integral to tort reform opponents' arguments against rolling back some of the enormous expansions of the tort system in the past fifty years. I have studied Kritzer's empirical data and have identified several weaknesses.[8] The first is that some key conclusions regarding lawyers' incomes are based on state bar association surveys to which only three to four dozen lawyers out of the thousands practicing in that state responded. Moreover, the surveys were not limited to lawyers who solely or primarily did tort cases. This flaw is significant because lawyers who restrict their practices to tort cases earn higher incomes than general practice lawyers who occasionally do tort cases.

Furthermore, the data is unrepresentative because many of the conclusions are based on a survey of Wisconsin lawyers.[9] By most measures,

Wisconsin is one of the least litigious states in the country, and its tort lawyers rank toward the low end of the contingency fee income scale.[10] You would as much seek out Wisconsin data as indicative of tort system trends as you would for trends in illegal immigration, pollution, women's fashion, or real estate.[11]

Finally, the data is unreliable. One example of this flaw is data showing that Wisconsin tort lawyers' effective hourly rates are higher than tort lawyers in Michigan and Ohio. This is highly implausible. With the exception of certain "magic" jurisdictions where tort lawyers reign, the more urbanized an area, the greater the volume of tort litigation and the greater the income of its tort lawyers. That is why tort lawyers' incomes in more urbanized Michigan and Ohio are – contrary to Kritzer's data – substantially higher than in more rural Wisconsin.[12]

As noted, my own calculation of the effective hourly rate of tort lawyers in auto accident litigation understates the rates realized by many tort lawyers. Calculating a more representative income level is difficult because information on tort lawyers' incomes is sparse – perhaps intentionally so. Indeed, we know far less about tort lawyers' earnings than we do about earnings of other professional groups.[13] Consider a comparison of baseball and the tort system. The former is a private enterprise; the latter a governmental function. Yet we know far more about the earnings of baseball players than we do about the earnings of tort lawyers who play a central role in the tort system – itself a core component of our civil justice system.[14] Because society pays for the direct costs of the tort system (and also, arguably, for the indirect costs in the form of higher insurance costs and product prices) and has an abiding interest in the efficient and effective operation of that system, it is virtually axiomatic that society is entitled to the full panoply of information about the operation of the tort system, which includes the quantum of contingency fees that clients pay to lawyers to access the system. That is a closely guarded secret, however.

I contend that lawyers specializing in aggregative litigation, including class actions and mass torts, realize effective hourly rates of $5,000 to

$25,000 per hour; that the upper tier of contingency fee lawyers, who specialize in product liability, toxic torts, and airline crash litigation, are realizing $2,500 to $5,000 per hour[15]; and that in some mass tragedies with no litigation risk, lawyers pocket fees of $20,000 to $30,000 an hour.[16]

Surely a public interest is implicated when lawyers obtain fees of this magnitude.[17] Richard Abel, a torts scholar at the UCLA School of Law, is a champion of the rights of tort victims and a staunch opponent of attempts to reign in tort liability. He has called the "fees pocketed by the most successful plaintiffs' personal injury lawyers ... obscene [and] not necessary to ensure adequate legal representation."[18] These effective hourly rates, however, reflect more than just egregious overcharging of tort claimants. They also generate excessive levels of tort litigation, as well as produce other adverse effects on the operation of the tort system.[19]

As evidenced by numerous statutory schemes, American policy strongly favors the public's right to have access to critical information about the functioning of government. For example, states require governmental bodies to hold their meetings in a forum open to the public.[20] These "sunshine" laws reflect the premise that public knowledge of agency decision making is, as stated in the Pennsylvania Constitution, "vital to the enhancement and proper functioning of the democratic process and that secrecy in public affairs undermines the faith of the public in government and the public's effectiveness in fulfilling its role in a democratic society."[21] Public access to information about lawyers' fees is also vital to the proper functioning of markets.[22]

Contingency fees provide a type of stealth sheathing that hides information about tort lawyers' income from public view and obscures the effect of inordinately high contingency fees on the tort system. Contingency fee practitioners have been effective in keeping this vital information out of the public domain. They rightfully perceive that if their earnings or hourly rate equivalents were known, the public would demand tort reform. This is why higher-earning contingency fee lawyers do not participate in bar-sponsored surveys of lawyers' incomes or cooperate in efforts to produce reliable information about effective hourly rates. These lawyers also oppose efforts to generate knowledge about income for public scrutiny. This attitude was evident when, after learning that tort lawyers were the only occupational group with substantial earnings for which no record (such as a W-2 or a Form 1099) was provided to the IRS, I urged the Ways and Means Committee of the U.S. House of Representatives to remedy the inequity. Unsurprisingly, President William Clinton, who received millions of dollars in campaign contributions from tort lawyers, objected.[23] In a rare legislative defeat for tort lawyers, the proposal nonetheless became law. It requires that insurance companies and other payers of settlements and judgments to tort attorneys submit IRS Form 1099 to notify the IRS of the amounts they paid that year to tort lawyers.[24] Unfortunately, the IRS – which does not have a clue as to the potential significance of this data – has failed to capitalize on this potential treasure trove of information by requiring that the 1099s be filed electronically. Without electronic filing, it is virtually impossible for the IRS to compile and publish aggregate data that could be used to provide tort lawyers' gross contingency fee incomes.

To overcome the dearth of data on contingency fee incomes, I have used the inflation-adjusted increase in a long-term compilation of jury verdicts to measure the increase in profitability of tort litigation over the past five decades. This calculation is based on the fact that, while more than 95 percent of tort cases are settled, settlement values are informed by trial verdicts; that is, lawyers and insurers make jury verdicts the basis for the "going rates" they use to settle the vast majority of cases.[25] Moreover, there have been no appreciable changes in lawyers' win rates or the number of hours they devote to their practices over the past five decades.[26] Because contingency fee lawyers continue to charge a standard percentage of judgments and settlements – and this has also not appreciably changed in the past fifty years – increases in tort lawyers' incomes and effective hourly rates roughly correspond with increases in tort verdicts.[27] Using this approach, I have calculated the inflation-adjusted effective hourly rate of the contingency fee bar to have increased by 1,000 to 1,400 percent over the past forty years.[28] It is hard to grasp the enormity of a real 1,000 to 1,400 percent increase. In the aggregate, tort lawyers' incomes from contingency fees have grown to Fortune 500 levels, ranging from $50 billion to $55 billion in 2006.[29]

Jury Verdict Research (JVR) compiled the more than 40-year span of jury verdict data that I used. I have relied on the JVR data to show *changes* in jury verdicts over time.[30] Because of criticisms of the data,[31] I crosschecked the accuracy of my conclusion using two other completely independent methods. In one, discussed previously, I calculated the effectively hourly rate of plaintiffs' lawyers in auto tort litigation.[32] In the other, discussed in Appendix A, I calculated tort lawyers' effective hourly rates in 1960 and compared that to the results from the JVR data. Both methods yield results that are consistent with my calculation based on JVR data.

Professor Alex Tabarrok of the economics department at George Mason University challenges this calculation of the increase in tort lawyers' income.[33] He concludes that "real income for [all] lawyers has increased by only 59 percent since [the] 1960s"[34] – that is, by less than 1 percent a year. Tabarrok's data, however, is not limited to tort lawyers, and as a result, the conclusions he draws from that data miss the mark. I present a detailed analysis of Tabarrok's methodological errors in Appendix A.

When confronted by the disparity between Tabarrok's calculations and my own, I checked the validity of my calculation by devising an alternative way to calculate the increase in tort lawyers' effective hourly rates over time. I used several data sources to determine the average net annual income of contingency fee lawyers in 1960. From there, I determined their gross income by estimating an overhead component.[35] Dividing that gross income by the estimated number of hours worked per year, I calculated that the hourly rate of tort lawyers in 1960 was $6.68 (in 1960 dollars),[36] or $40 per hour (in 2001 dollars).[37] Although this appears to be quite low at first blush, it is important to note that the tort world in 1960 was as different from the contemporary tort world as the Sahara Desert is from the Amazon basin. In 1960, lawyers bemoaned their economic fate: "no fortunes are [to be] made in the practice of law ... only a living."[38] Tort lawyers, who were at the lowest end of the lawyers' income scale, fared even worse, according to the leading survey of lawyers' incomes in the 1960s.[39]

An increase of 1,000 percent of the 1960 $6.68 hourly rate yields an effective rate of $400 per hour in 2001; a 1,400 percent increase translates into an effective rate of $560 an hour. This is consistent with my calculation that tort lawyers' effective hourly rate from auto accident litigation – which is at the low end of the income totem pole – was $325 in 2001 dollars.[40] A recent study of Texas tort lawyers supports the validity of this calculation. The study found that tort lawyers' incomes correlate inversely with the percentage of auto accident litigation in their portfolios and that the median income of the top quartile of tort lawyers exceeded the bottom half by 55 percent.[41] Applying that to my previous calculation for auto accident litigation yields an effective hourly rate of $500 for lawyers who do minimal auto accident litigation – an inflation-adjusted increase of more than 1,100 percent above the effective hourly rate calculation for 1960.[42] This is roughly consistent with my calculation. A 1,000 percent increase of the effective hourly rate in 1960 translates into an effective hourly rate of $560 in 2001. Moreover, the Texas study does not capture any of the enormous fees – running into the thousands and tens of thousands of dollars an hour – which lawyers collect from high-end products liability, mass tort, and class action litigation.

NOTES

1. *See, e.g.*, Eyal Zamir & Ilana Ritov, *Neither Saints, Nor Devils: A Behavioral Analysis of Attorneys' Contingent Fee* 5 (2008) [hereinafter Zamir & Ritov, *Behavioral Analysis*], *available at* http://papers.ssrn.com/abstract=1085985; Charles Silver, *Does Civil Justice Cost Too Much?*, 80 Tex. L. Rev. 2073, 2088 (2002) [hereinafter Silver, *Civil Justice*] (contending that clients' claiming rates are a function of the amount of legal fees).
2. *See* James R. Posner, *Trends in Medical Malpractice Insurance*, 1970–1985, 49 Law & Contemp. Probs. 37 (Spring 1986).

3. *See* Brickman, *Effective Hourly Rates*, *supra* Introduction, note 4, at 122–26.

4. *See* Steven K. Smith et al., Bureau of Justice Statistics, U.S. Dep't of Justice, NCJ–153177, Tort Cases in Large Counties, at 2, tbl.1 (1995) (reporting that a study of 378,314 tort cases disposed of by state courts in a one-year period ending in 1992 in the nation's seventy-five most populous counties indicates that auto torts accounted for 60.1% of the tort cases); *see also* Dan Miller, et al., Econ. Comm., 105th Cong., Auto Choice: Impact on Cities and the Poor 4–5 (Comm. Print 1998); Ins. Research Council, Paying for Auto Injuries, App. 1, tbl.4–4 (1994) [hereinafter IRC, Paying For Auto Injuries] (showing that the majority of tort claims filed in state courts are automobile claims).

5. *See* Stephen Daniels and Joanne Martin, *It Was the Best of Times, It Was the Worst of Times: The Precarious Nature of Plaintiffs' Practice in Texas*, 80 Tex. L. Rev. 1781, 1789 tbl.4, 1794 (2002).

6. Thomas H. Cohen, Bureau of Justice Statistics, Tort Trials and Verdicts in Large Counties, 2001, at 4 tbl.4, *available at* http://www.ojp.usdoj.gov/bjs/pub/pdf/ttvlc01.pdf (last visited Sept. 24, 2008) [hereinafter Tort Trials and Verdicts 2001]. Effective hourly rates of lawyers specializing in medical malpractice litigation have to take into account that the win rates at trial are about one-half those in auto accident litigation.

7. Herbert M. Kritzer, The Justice Broker: Lawyers and Ordinary Litigation, 137–143 (1990); Herbert M. Kritzer, *Seven Dogged Myths Concerning Contingency Fees*, 80 Wash. U.L.Q. 739, 761–72 (2002) [hereinafter Kritzer, *Seven Dogged Myths*]. Kritzer is widely cited for that proposition. *See, e.g.*, Charles Silver & Frank B. Cross, *What's Not To Like About Being a Lawyer?: A Life of Counsel and Controversy*, 109 Yale L.J. 1443, 1444 n.5 (2000); Ted Schneyer, *Empirical Research with a Policy Payoff: Market Dynamics for Lawyers Who Represent Plaintiffs for a Contingent Fee*, 80 Tex. L. Rev. 1829, 1830–31 (2002); Stephen C. Yeazell, *Re-financing Civil Litigation*, 51 DePaul L. Rev. 183, 206–07 (2001), [hereinafter Yeazell, *Civil Litigation*].

8. *See* Brickman, *Effective Hourly Rates, supra* Introduction, note 4, at 664. Kritzer has responded to my critique. *See* Herbert Kritzer, *Advocacy and Rhetoric vs. Scholarship and Evidence in the Debate Over Contingency Fees: A Reply to Professor Brickman*, 82 Wash. U. L.Q. 477 (2004).

9. *See* Kritzer, *Seven Dogged Myths, supra* note 7, at 741. Kritzer justifies this reliance on the ground that "there is a high probability that the general picture the Wisconsin data provides is applicable to many, if not most, areas of the country." Herbert M. Kritzer, *The Wages of Risk: The Returns of Contingency Fee Legal Practice*, 47 DePaul L. Rev. 267 (1998) [hereinafter Kritzer, *The Wages of Risk*].

10. *See* Brickman, *Effective Hourly Rates, supra* Introduction, note 4, at 679–85.

11. The focus of tort litigation in recent years has been in such jurisdictions as the District of Columbia, Texas, Florida, West Virginia, New York, California, Rhode Island, New Jersey, Illinois, and Pennsylvania.

12. Brickman, *Effective Hourly Rates*, *supra* Introduction, note 4, at 670–75.

13. *Forbes Magazine* noted that in preparing its annual surveys of the top lawyers, by income, tort lawyers were "less than forthcoming about what they earned." FORBES, Nov. 6, 1995, at 10.

14. Indeed, the tort system has been referred in an American Bar Association report as a "mirror of morals and a legal vehicle for helping to define them." ABA SPECIAL COMM. ON THE TORT LIAB. SYS., TOWARDS A JURISPRUDENCE OF INJURY: THE CONTINUING CREATION OF A SYSTEM OF SUBSTANTIVE JUSTICE IN AMERICAN TORT LAW, 12–1, 12–5 (1984).

15. For discussion of a "top tier" of tort lawyers and how their fees exceed those in lower quartiles, see Brickman, *Effective Hourly Rates*, *supra* Introduction, note 4, at 687 n.112.

16. A case in point of fees of this magnitude that were mostly unearned is a 1989 Alton, Texas, school bus tragedy. A Coca-Cola Bottling Company truck collided with a school bus resulting in twenty-one deaths and additional injuries. Dozens of lawyers descended on the community to sign up the Hispanic parents of the children. The cases promised extremely lucrative returns and absolutely no risk. Consider how Coca-Cola's advertising campaign that "things go better with Coke," would have contrasted with the national publicity attendant at a trial involving claims of wrongful deaths of twenty-one school children. That would have been disastrous to the company's image. Thus, even if the company could have reasonably contested liability, it almost certainly would not have done so. To cash in on this manna from heaven, lawyers promised the parents signing bonuses: $5,000 cash, a new house, and a new GMC Suburban van. *See* Paul Marcotte, *Barratry Indictments: DA Claims Four Texas Lawyers Solicited Bus-crash Clients.* A.B.A. J., July 1990, at 21. A $150 million settlement and contingency fees ranging from 30%–45% yielded attorney fees of more than $50 million. *See* Tony McAdams, *Blame and The Sweet Hereinafter*, 24 LEGAL STUD. F. 599, 607 (2000); James Pinkerton and Glen Golightly, *The Spoils of Tragedy; Profiting on Disaster*, HOUSTON CHRON., Aug. 2, 1992, at A1; Lisa Belkin, *Where 21 Youths Died, Lawyers Wage a War*, N.Y. TIMES, Jan. 18, 1990, at A1. Of particular note was the settlement of seventeen of the twenty-one death claims for $4.5 million each with contingency fees of 40% yielding fees of $1.8 million per claim. Most of the attorneys collecting these fees did little work, not even participating in the settlement negotiations. I conservatively estimate that these attorneys pocketed at least $25,000 to $30,000 per hour in these totally riskless cases. *See also* Lester Brickman, *On the Theory Class's Theories of Asbestos Litigation: The*

Disconnect between Scholarship and Reality, 31 PEPP. L. REV. 33 (2003–04) [hereinafter Brickman, *Asbestos Litigation*]; Lester Brickman, *On the Relevance of the Admissibility of Scientific Evidence: Tort System Outcomes are Principally Determined by Lawyers' Rates of Return*, 15 CARDOZO L. REV. 1755, 1773 (1994); Andrew Blum, *Megafees in Baltimore Megacase*, NAT'L L.J., Aug. 29, 1992, at 2 (mass consolidation of 8,555 asbestos cases estimated to have yielded – from settlements alone – $100-$125 million in fees); Peter Passell, *Challenge to Multimillion-Dollar Settlement Threatens Top Texas Lawyers*, N.Y. TIMES, Mar. 24, 1995, at B6 (settlements resulting from the Phillips Petroleum case yielded a law firm a "$65 million fee [which] translates into almost $20,000 an hour, a windfall in a case where tens of millions in compensation was a foregone conclusion."); D. Ralles, *84.5 Million Offered in Tainted Water Case*, ARIZ. REPUBLIC, Feb. 26, 1991, at 1A (settlement yielded $33.8 million in attorneys fees, most likely producing rates of return in excess of $30,000 per hour); *see also* Brickman, *Contingent Fees, supra* Introduction, note 18, at 33 n.12, 77 n.186.

17. Politicians and the media are paying close attention to the huge increases in recent years in corporate CEOs' earnings. If that attention is justified as a matter of national concern – as it certainly is – then tort lawyers' earnings merit even greater scrutiny. Society has an obvious interest in the operation of the tort system – a system that is driven largely by lawyers' profits.

18. *See* Richard Abel, *General Damages are Incoherent and Incalculable, Incommensurable, and Inegalitarian (But Otherwise A Great Idea)*, 55 DEPAUL L. REV. 253, 324–25 (2006) (footnotes omitted) [hereinafter Able, *General Damages*] ("The obscene fees pocketed by the most successful plaintiffs' personal injury lawyers, who virtually monopolize the cases with the highest general damages, are not necessary to ensure adequate legal representation. First, lawyers themselves have worked long and hard to make sure that the market for legal services is seriously imperfect: Entry barriers are high (especially to the provision of services by nonlawyers), and restrictive practices dampen intraprofessional competition. Britain allows nonlawyer claims agents to market their services freely to the injured and negotiate settlements with tortfeasors and their insurers. Second, there are many other possible fee arrangements: fee shifting (perhaps not perfectly symmetrical), legal insurance (ex ante and ex post, perhaps with premiums recoverable from the defendant), and state subsidy (on the theory that the deterrent effect of damages creates a public good).")

19. An example of the legislative concern for the effects of the financial incentives created by contingency fees is the action of the New York Legislature, which enacted sliding-scale caps on attorney's fees in medical practice actions "purposely reduc[ing] the percentages of the plaintiff's award to be allocated to attorneys ... 'to diminish the distortion of such high [attorney's fees] awards

on the system' (1985 NY SESS. LAWS ch. 194, Exec. Mem., at 3022)." *Yalongo by Goldberg v. Popp*, 84 N.Y.2d 601, 607 (Ct. App. 1994).

20. *See, e.g.*, N.Y. PUB. OFF. LAW §§ 100–111 (McKinney 2002); OHIO REV. CODE ANN. § 121.22 (West 2002); 65 PA. CONS. STAT. §§ 701–16 (2001).

21. 65 PA. CONS. STAT. § 702 (2001).

22. For this reason, the Securities and Exchange Commission (SEC) has mandated that any company making a public offering of securities "[f]urnish a reasonably itemized statement of all expenses in connection with the issuance and distribution of the securities to be registered [including attorneys' fees]." SEC Registration Statement and Prospectus Provisions, 17 C.F.R. § 229.511 (2002). The instructions included in 229.511 indicate that legal fees "shall be itemized separately." *See id.* The SEC explains on its Web site that the purpose of these disclosure provisions "is to require companies making a public offering of securities to disclose material business and financial information in order that investors may make informed investment decisions." *See* U.S. SEC. & EXCH. COMM'N, DESCRIPTIONS OF SEC FORMS, http://www.sec.gov/info/edgar/forms/edgform.pdf (last visited Dec. 18, 2008). A substantial attorney fee may indicate to investors that a lot of heavy legal lifting had to be done to purchase a lawyer's stamp of approval – and that the reason for this should be carefully pursued before purchasing a security.

23. *See* Peter Passell, *Economic Scene: Washington May Tighten up on Reporting of Fees By Trial Lawyers*, N.Y. TIMES, Jan. 25, 1996, at D2 ("After Republicans proposed [a bill requiring lawyers to report settlement amounts], President Clinton did not include this seemingly innocuous revenue raiser in his own budget ... Representative Bill Archer, a Texas Republican who is chairman of the House Ways and Means Committee [wrote:] 'Your omission [President Clinton] would appear to indicate a special preference by the White House on behalf of trial lawyers'.")

24. I.R.C. § 6045(f) (2000).

25. *See* Stephen Daniels & Joanne Martin, *It Was the Best of Times, It Was the Worst of Times: The Precarious Nature of Plaintiffs' Practice in Texas*, 80 TEX. L. REV. 1781, 1803 (2002) [hereinafter Daniels & Martin, *Plaintiffs' Practices*].

26. *See* Brickman, *Effective Hourly Rates*, *supra* Introduction, note 4, at App. B.

27. *Id.* In some jurisdictions, notably New York, jury verdicts are subject to meaningful judicial and appellate court review that can result in reducing verdicts. Sustained jury verdicts would therefore be a more accurate metric. This data, however, is generally not available in a compiled form.

28. *Id.* The surrogate data I use does not include punitive damages or class actions. Taking this into account, effective hourly rates have probably increased closer to 1,400% than to 1,000% over the past forty years. *Id.*

29. This is based on 2002 data compiled by the Tillinghast division of the Towers Perrin Company, which provides consulting services to the insurance industry. Tillinghast estimated that plaintiffs' attorney fees were 19% of tort costs. *See* Tillinghast TOWERS PERRIN, U.S. TORT COSTS: 2003 UPDATE at 17 (2004) [hereinafter TILLINGHAST 2003]. Tillinghast further estimated that 14% of tort costs went for defense costs, 22% for economic loss, 24% for noneconomic loss, and 21% for administration. *Id.* In 2006, Tillinghast concluded that tort system costs were $247 billion. *See* TILLINGHAST, TOWERS PERRIN, 2007 UPDATE ON U.S. TORT COSTS TRENDS 14 (2007) [hereinafter TILLINGHAST 2007]. Applying the Tillinghast 19% estimate yields plaintiffs' attorney fees in tort cases of $47 billion in 2006. This calculation, however, does not include fees in workers compensation cases, aviation accident cases, cases in which uninsured punitive damages are awarded, shareholder litigation, and the fees generated by the 1998 settlement between tobacco manufacturers and various states' attorneys general, which will total more than $15 billion and are currently being paid at the rate of $500 million per year. My estimate of $50 billion to $55 billion is based on the Tillinghast data and my own very conservative estimate of contingency fees generated by these omitted areas.

30. Whereas JVR has acknowledged that its database is not systematically collected nor comprehensive and is biased to the upside, *see infra* note 31, it maintains that it has used the same system of data collection since 1961 and that its "numbers nevertheless accurately reflect trends." Rachel Zimmerman & Christopher Oster, *Assigning Liability: Insurers' Missteps Helped Provoke Malpractice "Crisis,"* WALL ST. J., June 24, 2002, at A1.

31. JVR data has been severely criticized by tort system expansionists because it is not comprehensive and much of it is supplied by plaintiffs' lawyers. *See, e.g.*, Michael J. Saks, *Do We Really Know Anything About the Behavior of the Tort Litigation System – And Why Not?*, 140 U. PA. L. REV. 1147, 1158 (1992) [hereinafter Saks, *Do We Really Know Anything*]; Stephen Daniels & Joanne Martin, *Jury Verdicts and the "Crisis" in Civil Justice*, 11 JUST. SYS. J. 321, 326–28 (1986).

32. *See supra* notes 3–5.

33. *See* Alex Tabarrok, *The Problem of Contingent Fees for Waiters*, 8 GREEN BAG 2d 377 (2005) [hereinafter Tabarrok, *Waiters*]. This article appears to be an adaptation of chapter five of a book that he and Eric Helland have published. ERIC HELLAND & ALEXANDER TABARROK, JUDGE AND JURY: AMERICAN TORT LAW ON TRIAL, ch. 5 (2005) [hereinafter HELLAND & TABARROK, JUDGE AND JURY].

34. Tabarrok, *Waiters*, at 377.

35. The gross income can be calculated using the following formula: Gross Profit = (Net Profit)/(1-Overhead). *See* Daniel J. Cantor, *Ethics and Economics in Hourly Fees* 50 A.B.A. J. 951, 953 (1964).

36. The precise steps I followed in this calculation are set out in Appendix B: Calculating Tort Lawyers' Effective Hourly Rates in 1960.

37. This calculation was done using a table of inflation conversion factors compiled by Robert Sahr of Oregon State University. According to the table, the inflation conversion factor to convert 1960 dollars to 2001 dollars is 0.167. Dividing $6.68 by 0.167 yields $40. *See* Robert Sahr, *Inflation Conversion Factors for Dollars 1965 to Estimated 2013, available at* http://oregonstate.edu/dept/polisci/fac/sahr/sahr.htm (last visited Dec. 1, 2005).

38. *See* Jackson L. Boughner, *Let's Throw Out the Reasonable Fee Schedules*, 48 A.B.A. J. 252, 253 (1962); Ethel S. Barenbaum, *Attorney's Fees–More Matter With Less Art* (pt. 1), Pac. Law., Dec. 1962, at 22 [hereinafter Barenbaum, *Attorney's Fees*].

39. *See* Robert I. Weil, Economic Facts for Lawyers; Resurvey Shows Dramatic Changes in Pennsylvania Practice, 6 Law Econ. & Mgmt. 373, 378 (1965) ("Plaintiff lawyers, a large group, fared less well [income-wise] on the whole" than attorneys practicing in other fields of law including "corporations," "probate, trust and wills," and "patent, trademark and copyright law."); *see also* Comm. on Econ. of the Bar, Benchmarks for Your Practice, 17 J. Mo. B. 13, 13 (1961) (showing that non-timekeeping lawyers, which included tort lawyers, earned less on average than timekeeping lawyers); Samuel H. Morgan, *By Our Bootstraps – A Story of Economic Improvement*, 49 Ill. B.J. 622, 626 (1960).

40. *See* Brickman, *Effective Hourly Rates, supra* Introduction, note 4, at 691.

41. *See* Daniels & Martin, *Plaintiffs' Practices, supra* note 25, at 1789 tbl.4 (2002). The study classified tort lawyers into four tiers based on income. The top quartile of lawyers devoted considerably less time to automobile accident cases than the bottom tier of lawyers; auto accident litigation comprised 51.2% of the caseload of bottom-tier lawyers, whereas it comprised only 14.7% of the caseload of top-tier lawyers. The bottom two tiers had a median income of $112,500, whereas the top tier had a median income of $175,000, 55% higher than the median income of the bottom half.

42. To calculate the effective hourly rate of top-tier lawyers, the 55% increase must be applied to the $325-per-hour rate (calculated for auto accident litigation), representing an effective hourly rate of $504 per hour. This figure represents an increase in effective hourly rates of more than 1,160% since 1960.

3 Are Contingency Fee Profits "Reasonable"?

I N VIRTUALLY ALL STATES – NEW YORK AND CALIFORNIA BEING notable exceptions – state supreme courts exercise nearly exclusive control over the practice of law. In some states, this power is conferred by a specific provision in their constitutions. In most states, however, state supreme courts claim the exclusive authority to regulate the practice of law simply by fiat.[1] The courts use this purloined power to fend off regulation of lawyers by state legislatures and to advance lawyers' interests in a variety of ways.

As part of their exercise of control over the legal profession, states' high courts have promulgated codes of ethics, which are typically adaptations of model codes of ethics drafted by the American Bar Association (ABA). The ABA adopted its first code, the Canons of Ethics, in 1908. As noted, Canon 13 recognized the validity of contingency fees, provided they were reasonable in light of the risk borne by the lawyer.[2] In 1963, the ABA replaced the Canons of Ethics with the Model Code of Professional Responsibility. In 1983, the ABA extensively redid the Model Code and titled the new version, The Model Rules of Professional Conduct. Today, every state but California has adopted, through judicial approval, the Model Rules in full or in substantial part. The ABA has extensively modified its code since 1983, and state supreme courts have adopted many of these modifications, albeit with changes. These successor codes of ethics continue to limit lawyers' fees to "reasonable" amounts and list eight factors that are to be considered in determining whether a fee for the performance of a legal service is reasonable. The principal factors are the time and labor involved; the level of skill required; the fee customarily charged; the experience and reputation of the lawyer; and the results obtained.[3]

The eighth factor – "whether the fee is fixed or contingent"[4] – is not, however, a model of clarity. It purports to allow lawyers to charge higher fees if the fee is "contingent" on securing a recovery. This eighth factor, then, is a restatement of the requirement set forth in Canon 13 that the lawyer must actually bear a risk for a contingency fee to be reasonable. As U.S. Supreme Court Justice Harry Blackmun stated: "lawyers charge a premium when their entire fee is contingent on winning... The premium added for contingency compensates for the *risk* of nonpayment if the suit does not succeed."[5] Thus, the ethical validity of a contingency fee – which is designed to yield a higher fee than an hourly rate or fixed fee – is that the lawyer is assuming a risk of nonpayment.[6]

Not all tort cases involve a meaningful risk of nonrecovery, however. A quintessential example is the motorist sitting in his car at a red light when another motorist rear-ends him. In this case, there is no liability risk, and the amount of recovery will depend on the severity of the injury, available insurance, and the offending driver's assets. The fact that the amount of the recovery is not fixed at the time of the engagement does not import any meaningful risk into the process. The lawyer can eliminate even the remotest risk by determining the availability of insurance before the client signs the retainer agreement. Even so, in the vast majority of cases, when the injured motorist hires a lawyer to bring a tort claim, the lawyer will insist on charging a standard contingency fee of one-third or more of any recovery. Thus, in addition to the zero-based accounting scheme (charging the client for representation as if the claim had no value before retaining counsel), tort lawyers pad their fees by charging clients a risk premium for nonexistent risk. Moreover, although contingency fee lawyers routinely charge for phantom risks, the courts and the bar have explicitly and implicitly given lawyers a free pass to charge standard contingency fees in such cases.[7] The Illinois courts' approval of Dowd's substantial "contingency fee" for little work and assuming zero risk in the case of Mary Corcoran is a prime example.

The premium that lawyers charge for assuming risk is a substantial component of the contingency fee. Because the ethical codes mandate that a lawyer can only charge a contingency fee if she is assuming risk, it follows, *a fortiori*, that if risk is present, the risk premium must be proportionate to the risk (which includes the anticipated resources that will be put at risk). Nonetheless, in actuality, risk premiums do not vary. As I discuss in Chapter 4, lawyers charge standard contingency fees – usually one-third – and almost never deviate, even though cases in their portfolios may reflect widely varying risk or acute differences in the projected costs of providing the representation. As a result, lawyers charging standard contingency fees are routinely overcharging at least some claimants whose cases involve no meaningful risk of a low or non-recovery. Indeed, many tort lawyers openly assert that they do not accept cases where there is meaningful risk. Even though unearned and unethical overcharges in these cases can rise to thousands of dollars an hour,[8] an ABA Committee that renders advisory opinions on legal ethics condones this violation of the ABA's own ethics rule – an opinion that I have described in an article subtitled "Money Talks, Ethics Walks" as blatantly self-interested and disingenuous in its analysis.[9]

Tort lawyers and supporting scholars have advanced two arguments – both based on false premises – in support of the practice of lawyers routinely overcharging some clients. The first is the cross-subsidy argument, which legitimates fee overcharges because they subsidize other contingency fee litigations, enabling more litigants to gain representation.[10] In other words, a few must sacrifice for the greater good. This argument fails for two reasons. First, even if the "rob Peter, pay Paul" rationale were a valid depiction of a lawyer's practices, it is inconsistent with a lawyer's fiduciary and ethical obligations to deal fairly with each client and charge each a reasonable fee.

Second, although taking from Peter to pay Paul always meets with the approval of Paul,[11] it is instructive to consider the true identities of both parties in the contingency fee context. Peter is the client paying a windfall fee to the lawyer in a case without meaningful risk. Paul, at first blush, is the subsequent client who gains representation at the expense of Peter. When Paul is unmasked, however, he is properly identified as the attorney – the repeat beneficiary of increased contingency fee litigation – who not only charged Peter an unearned windfall fee but, whenever possible, subsequent clients as well. There is simply no empirical evidence to support the proposition that lawyers use their windfall fees to subsidize anyone except themselves.

The second argument that tort lawyers and their supporters advance to justify overcharging some clients is the "win some, lose some" argument. Lawyers argue that their profits from tort litigation are not excessive and that clients with "easy" cases are not being overcharged because lawyers' winnings have to be offset by losing cases. In effect, they focus on lawyers' aggregate incomes rather than the fee in any single case.

The underlying assumption in both of these rationales is that lawyers accept all – or even most – cases. In fact, they carefully screen potential clients and generally limit the cases they accept to those where the predicted return will at least equal their opportunity costs.[12] As a result of this intensive screening process, lawyers reject approximately two-thirds of those seeking representation.[13] For example, Stephen Z. Meyers, cofounder of the law firm Jacoby & Meyers, which "all but abandoned" a practice oriented toward middle-class needs in favor of a "more lucrative" contingency fee practice, has stated that their storefront offices reject more than 80 percent of personal injury claims and other types of contingency fee cases.[14]

To further control risk, lawyers assemble portfolios of carefully selected cases to produce a reliable income stream.[15] For each matter brought to them, tort lawyers assess the litigation risk, the settlement value, the amount of time they will have to devote to the matter, and the money that they will have to advance. Though these are not mathematically precise calculations, tort lawyers' determinations of whether to take a case are essentially an estimation of the effective hourly rate the case will produce, the litigation risk they will have to assume, and the risk level of the cases currently in their portfolio. Typically, lawyers reject the large majority of would-be clients because the projected return on their investment is insufficient. Once they have accepted a case because of its anticipated profitability, lawyers adjust their level of investment in each case in their portfolios depending on unfolding events.

Any portfolio of cases may be evaluated in terms of levels of risk – a measure that is analogous to the "beta" measure of stock portfolios. If a prospective case appears likely to generate a high reward but is also high risk, the decision whether to add the case to the portfolio is a function of the level of risk of the current portfolio (as well as the lawyer's own level of risk tolerance). The more that a portfolio includes "cash cow" cases, that is, cases where there is no meaningful risk and where, by charging standard contingency fees, lawyers are able to "milk" the "cash cow" to provide a steady stream of windfall fees, the more lawyers are willing to accept a higher risk case, provided the potential reward is sufficient to compensate for the risk. If the portfolio, however, has few cash cows, a lawyer is less likely to take on that same higher risk case. It is the stream of revenue from cash cow cases that provides tort lawyers with the requisite capital to invest in new litigation opportunities.[16]

Lawyers' careful case selection typically results in very high success rates – in the 70 to 90 percent range according to available but sparse data.[17] Indeed, a survey of plaintiffs' lawyers determined that although the participating lawyers' ex ante appraisal of their likelihood of success was mostly in the 70 to 90 percent range, in fact, they prevailed in 91 percent of their cases.[18] "Win some, lose some" is therefore a misleading term and does not support overcharging a significant subset of clients.

Careful screening before accepting a case does not eliminate all risk. Even "sure winners" can come unhinged when adverse facts later emerge or anticipated assets prove nonexistent. Moreover, tort lawyers may take on some high-risk cases for which the anticipated award does not justify the high risk; even when they prevail in these litigations, they may not recover the time and money that they invested. These cases, however, are investments to expand the tort envelope and thus future litigation opportunities.

Acknowledging that tort lawyers do assume some risks, however, does not justify tort lawyers' failure to be forthcoming with regard to the effectiveness of their case screenings. This lack of candor has successfully misled the public into believing that tort lawyers face substantial risks in their practices. Even scholars who write about contingency fees have been snared by this misinformation.[19] The effectiveness of lawyers' screening procedures – which tort lawyers and many torts scholars fail to acknowledge – is further attested to by the rise of numerous entrepreneurial ventures that provide nonrecourse financing to tort claimants in exchange for what often amounts to a significant share of the recovery. (Nonrecourse means that the loan does not have to be repaid unless there is a sufficient recovery). For this business model to flourish – as it has – lawyers must prevail in a very high percentage of the tort cases that the entities invest in. In fact, win rates in these cases are very high and have led some courts to strike down these loans as usurious, because the effective interest rates range from 50 percent to nearly 300 percent. These courts reject the argument that because of the nonrecourse feature, litigation financing is an investment, not a loan, and therefore not subject to usury laws. Instead, the courts consider the nonrecourse provision merely pretextual, and they reason that litigation financing is a loan because there is no risk involved.[20] But if, as these courts conclude, there is no risk, then what justification is there for lawyers charging a substantial risk premium in the form of a standard contingency fee in these cases?

NOTES

1. *See* Charles W. Wolfram, *Lawyer Turf and Lawyer Regulation – The Role of the Inherent-Powers Doctrine*, 12 U. ARK. LITTLE ROCK L. REV. 1 (1989–90); Thomas Alpert, *The Inherent Power of the Courts to Regulate the Practice of Law: An Historical Analysis*, 32 BUFFALO L. REV. 525 (1983).

2. Canon 13 provided that a "contract for a contingent fee where sanctioned by law, should be reasonable under all the circumstances of the case, including the risk and uncertainty of the compensation, but should always be subject to the supervision of a court, as to its reasonableness." A.B.A. REP. 700 (1933).

3. ABA MODEL RULES OF PROF'L CONDUCT R.1.5 (2006) [hereinafter MODEL RULES].

4. MODEL RULES, *id.* at R.1.5(a)(8).

5. *Pennsylvania v. Delaware Valley Citizens' Council*, 483 U.S. 711, 735–36 (1987) (Blackmun, J. dissenting).

6. If a lawyer could ethically charge a contingency fee absent any realistic risk of nonrecovery, then the mere fact that he called his fee a contingent fee – and thereby raised his fee beyond what a fixed or hourly rate fee would have yielded – would be considered a factor attesting to the reasonableness of the higher fee. This would be an absurd result.

7. *See* Lester Brickman, *Contingency Fee Abuses, Ethical Mandates and the Disciplinary System: The Case, Against Case-by-Case Enforcement*, 53 WASH. & LEE L. REV. 1339 (1996) (discussing ABA Comm. on Ethics and Professional Responsibility, Formal Op. 389, 1994) [hereinafter Brickman, *Disciplinary System*].

8. For discussion of a "top tier" of tort lawyers and how their fees exceed those in lower quartiles, *see* Brickman, *Effective Hourly Rates, supra* Introduction, note 4, at 660–61 n.14, 687 n.112.

9. ABA Comm'n on Ethics and Professional Responsibility, Formal Op. 389 (1994). *See* Lester Brickman, *ABA Regulation of Contingency Fees: Money Talks, Ethics Walks*, 65 FORDHAM L. REV. 247 (1996) [hereinafter Brickman, *Money Talks*]; *see also* GEOFFREY HAZARD & WILLIAM HODES, THE LAW OF LAWYERING (3d. ed. 2005) § 8.6 (criticizing Formal Op. 389 on the grounds that it fails to "come to grips with the practical realities of the contingent fee as charged on a routine basis today," which is that "in the vast majority of cases standard contingent fees are charged without any discussion with the clients; furthermore where the result is an unreasonably high fee, clients usually do not realize that it is such and therefore do not complain.") So much for the exhortation in the preamble to the ABA Model Rules of Professional Conduct that the lawyers' code of ethics is intended to be "in the public interest and not in furtherance of parochial or self-interested concerns of the bar." MODEL RULES OF PROF'L CONDUCT, Preamble (2006) [hereinafter MODEL RULES].

10. *See* HERBERT M. KRITZER, THE JUSTICE BROKER: LAWYERS AND ORDINARY LITIGATION 260 (1990) ("The client who turns out to have a very good case cross subsidizes the client whose case turns out to be a dog.").

11. *See Thoughts on the Business of Life*, FORBES, Apr. 23, 1984, at 176 (quoting George Bernard Shaw).

12. *See Boccardo v. United States*, 12 Ct. Cl. 184, 187 (1987) (recognizing the use of a screening process by numerous law firms to weed out those cases that are financially impractical based on the likelihood of success).

13. Herbert M. Kritzer, *Seven Dogged Myths Concerning Contingency Fees*, 80 WASH. U. L.Q. 739, 755 (2002) [hereinafter Kritzer, *Seven Dogged Myths*].

14. Randy Kennedy, *Groundbreaking Law Firm Shifts its Focus to Personal-Injury Cases*, N.Y. TIMES, May 12, 1995, at A29.

15. *See* Brickman, *Effective Hourly Rates, supra* Introduction, note 4, at 98, n.152.

16. This point is driven home by a suit brought by a law firm against a client for nonpayment of its hourly rate fee. In addition to its fee, the firm was seeking "consequential damages," that is, damages for the lost opportunities the firm suffered because the client failed to pay. These lost opportunities, the firm said, were the contingency fees it did not earn because of the tort cases that the firm could not take on because it lacked the necessary capital as a consequence of the client's failure to pay what he owed. *See Stuart v. Bayless*, 964 S.W.2d 920, 921 (Tex. 1998) (The court denied the consequential damage claim because of its remoteness.). It is, of course, not just lawyers who base their decision of whether to make a new investment involving risk on the amount and security of the cash flow from their current portfolio of investments. Stephen Ross heads the Related Companies, one of the largest real estate firms in the country. The firm's holdings of luxury developments and its investments in low-income housing generate, not just rental income, but also extensive tax credits. According to an article in the *Wall Street Journal*: "This massive low-income housing operation throws off a river of cash ... that runs fairly steadily through real-estate boom and bust." *See, e.g.*, Alex Frangos, *Affordable Housing Empire Fuels Developer's Upscale Aims*, WALL ST. J., Aug. 22, 2006, at A1. As explained by a corporate official, "The consistent stream of fee income from the affordable side enables us to take on larger scale [riskier] market-oriented projects." *Id.*

17. *See* Brickman, *Effective Hourly Rates, supra* Introduction, note 4, at 734–36. By "success rate," I do not mean how often lawyers prevail at trial but rather how often they receive contingency fees in the cases they accept. The vast majority of legal claims are settled. Only a small percentage of claims, approximately 1%–4%, are resolved by trial. Win rates for tried cases vary according to the type of litigation. *See* Thomas H. Cohen, *Tort Bench and Jury Trials in State Court* (2005), Bureau of Justice Statistics Bulletin, Nov. 2009, *available at* http://bjs.ojp.usdoj.gov/content/pub/pdf/tbjtsc05.pdf (4% of all state tort cases were resolved by jury and bench trials in 2005); Administrative Office of the United States Courts, Federal Judicial Caseload Statistics,

March 31, 2009, U.S. District Courts-Civil: Table C-4 Cases Terminated by Basis of Jurisdiction and Nature of Suit, *available at* http://www.uscourts.gov/ judbus2009/ appendices/C04Sep09.pdf (Of the tort cases terminated in U.S District Courts from March 31, 2008 to March 31, 2009, less than 1% were disposed of by trial.)

In state courts, plaintiffs prevailed in about half of the cases tried (51.6%), broken down as follows: auto accident cases – 64.3%; asbestos product liability cases – 54.9%; medical malpractice – 22.7%; other products liability – 19.6%. *See* Cohen, *id.* at 4. In federal courts in 2002–03, plaintiffs prevailed in 47.7% of the cases that were tried; the win rate for product liability cases was 33.5% and for medical malpractice, 36.7%.

18. *See* James H. Stock & David A. Wise, *Market Compensation in Class Action Suits: A Summary of Basic Ideas and Results*, 16 CLASS ACTION REP. 584, 588, 590 fig.2 (1993).

19. *See, e.g.,* Herbert M. Kritzer, *Rhetoric and Reality ... Uses and Abuses ... Contingencies and Certainties: The Political Economy of the American Contingent Fee* 37 (Wis. Inst. For Legal Studies, Working Paper No. 11–8, 1995).

20. Further commentary on nonrecourse litigation financing is set forth in Appendix H.

4 How Tort Lawyers Have Increased Their Profits by Restraining Competition

N THE NEXT THREE CHAPTERS, I EXPLAIN HOW TORT LAWYERS have been able to increase their inflation-adjusted effective hourly rates by considerably more than 1,000 percent in the past forty-five years. The simple and most direct reason is that lawyers engage in anticompetitive behavior to restrain price competition. In the next chapter, I explain why the market has failed to correct the absence of price competition, and in Chapter 6, I discuss the ethical rules adopted by the bar that are designed to enforce restraints on competition. In subsequent chapters, I discuss other ways tort lawyers have increased their profits, including vastly enlarging the scope of liability of the tort system and increasing the amounts of damages awarded.

A. How Competitive Is the Contingency Fee Market?

It is an article of faith among proponents of tort system expansion that tort lawyers compete with one another on the basis of price and thus are not overcharging consumers. For example, when contingency fee rates in New York dropped from 50 to 33⅓ percent in the early 1960s, Marc Galanter, a torts scholar at the University of Wisconsin Law School whose writings in support of tort system expansion are widely cited,[1] concluded that this drop was a result of "the increase in supply of lawyers serving individual clients, the increased competition ushered in by the demise of fee schedules, the advent of lawyer advertising, and a gradual increase in the sophistication of clients."[2] However, as I explain later in this chapter, in 1960, when long-prevailing contingency fee rates were 50 percent, New York courts promulgated a rule that essentially limited contingency fees to one-third.[3] That is why the standard percentage dropped from 50 to 33⅓ percent. Competition had nothing do with it.

Other pro-tort expansion scholars, such as Professors Ted Schneyer, Charles Silver, and Herbert Kritzer, have also advanced the view that the market for contingent-fee-financed tort-claiming services is "highly competitive."[4] The evidence is emphatically to the contrary. It is true that contingency fee lawyers compete with one another for clients with lucrative cases. They do not, however, compete on the basis of price – not even in mass tort litigations, in which they may represent hundreds or thousands of individual claimants and obtain contingency fees that mount up to millions of dollars.

In two recent mass tort litigations, a handful of judges took extraordinary steps to reject exorbitant contingency fees despite the scholars' claims that these fees were a product of a highly competitive market. The first litigation, involving 8,000 individually represented claimants, alleged injuries caused by the antidepressant, Zyprexa, and failure to provide adequate warning of risks[5]; the second, involving 4,000 individual lawsuits, alleged defective implantable defibrillators.[6] Professors Charles Silver and Geoffrey P. Miller criticized the judges' rulings, which capped the fees in these litigations somewhat below the 40 percent contingency fee percentages provided for in most of the individual retainer agreements.[7] In the *Zyprexa* settlement, Judge Weinstein justified the cap, stating that the individual fees failed to reflect that "much of the discovery work [which] would normally have [been] done on a retail basis in individual cases has been done at a reduced cost on a wholesale basis by the plaintiffs' steering committee."[8] The steering committee is compensated for its work by an assessment leveled against the other plaintiffs' lawyers in the litigation.[9] Silver and Miller strongly objected to the fee caps and the lack of empirical justification advanced by the courts. Although acknowledging that the stated reason "that aggregation reduces lawyers' costs by generating economies of scale ... is plausible,"[10] they concluded on the basis of economic theory that the lawyers had undoubtedly already discounted their fees and that the courts were unfairly ordering what amounted to a second discount. In their words, "lawyers compete for clients in competitive markets ... [and this] *should* cause lawyers to pass the benefits of scale economies onto clients without any prodding from judges ... because the market for legal services is highly competitive."[11]

Silver and Miller then take the fee-capping judges to task for failing to advance empirical justification for capping the fees. Instead, the judges should have "quantif[ied] the extent to which prices [fees] were inflated ... requir[ing] testimony from an expert economist or accountant."[12] To support their assertions that the market is competitive and that clients can use the Internet to comparison shop (presumably on the basis of price), Silver and Miller refer to a Web site: "An Attorney for You, http://anattoneyforyou.com ... ([Web site] enabling consumers to obtain offers of representation from competing firms)."[13] This Web site, however, merely directs potential claimants to the Web sites of other lawyers who are seeking to amass large numbers of mass tort clients, with no mention of competitive pricing. Thus, whereas firms do compete for this very lucrative business, they carefully avoid doing so on the basis of price.[14] Silver and Miller's reliance on economic theory – that a competitive market *should* cause lawyers to discount their standard fees because of economies of scale and *should* force lawyers to price their services efficiently – does not satisfy the standard to which they hold the judges. Though Silver and Miller criticize the judges because "[t]hey invent numbers,"[15] they themselves provide no empirical evidence of *any* fee discounting from the prevailing 40 percent to reflect the cost savings from these aggregated procedures' huge economies of scale. Further, there is no discussion by Silver and Miller of whether the prevailing 40 percent fee in mass tort litigations (which is nearly double what would be awarded if these were class actions) is justified by the anticipated effort

and the litigation risk assumed. Lawyers charge 40 percent fees in mass
tort litigations, some of which generate hundreds of millions of dollars
in fees, because they can and because other lawyers competing for this
business do so as well.

U.S. Federal District Court Judge Elaine E. Bucklo put it plainly:
"[T]he market for contingent legal services especially among consumers is highly uncompetitive."[16] Even state supreme courts, which have
advanced the interests of lawyers at the expense of consumers of legal
services, have acknowledged the need for caps on contingency fees
because they are unrestrained by competition.[17] Judges' understanding
of the lack of price competition is confirmed by a number of other indicia, including the bar's maintenance of uniform contingency fee rates,
the lack of any economic justification for these uniform rates, and the
use of referral fees to capture monopoly profits. In the sections that follow, I discuss how each of these indicia evidences the absence of a competitive market for tort lawyers' services.

B. How Uniform Pricing Overcharges Clients

The dominant feature of the market for personal injury litigation
financed by contingency fees is the standardization of fees. In mass tort
litigation, as noted, the 40 percent fee is common. In individual personal
injury litigation, the standard fee is typically 33⅓ percent, though in
some communities, it is 40 or even 50 percent.[18] In addition, the standard
fee sometimes varies according to the stage of the proceeding. A typical variable percentage is 33⅓ percent if the case settles before trial, 40
percent if a trial commences, and 50 percent if the trial is completed.[19]
Whereas downward deviations from the standard one-third fee exist,
they are comparatively rare. Lawyers charge standard contingency fees
even when they are presented with tort claims in which liability is clear,
damages are substantial, and the lawyer anticipates devoting only modest
amounts of time to generate an acceptable settlement offer. These fees
often amount to thousands of dollars an hour.[20] In the world of contingent fees, the more lucrative the claim, the more inflexible the pricing.

An illustrative example is the aftermath of an underground steam pipe explosion that spread asbestos across the Gramercy Park area of New York City in 1989. After initially denying the presence of asbestos, the owner of the steam pipe, Con Edison, acknowledged its responsibility. Once the presence of asbestos was confirmed, hundreds of residents in the immediate area were forced to leave their apartments for several months and to abandon virtually all of their possessions.[21] Shortly after the explosion, lawyers descended on locations where displaced residents were being housed.[22] By then, the utility had admitted liability, projecting it at $30 to $40 million. The claim process largely consisted of documenting additional living costs, the value of abandoned personal possessions, and the like – pretty much what any insured home owner would do when asserting a claim in the event of a fire. Nonetheless, the lawyers charged the standard 33⅓ percent contingency fee. In these representations, not even economies of scale were shared with claimants in the form of discounted fees.[23] The Bar Association of the City of New York provided free legal counseling for displaced residents. I urged the Association that, as part of their pro bono services, it encourage affected residents to bargain for lower percentages than the standard one-third "contingent" fee. I further suggested that the Association issue an advisory opinion stating that fees in excess of 10 percent were presumptively unreasonable in light of the purely administrative nature of the claim process and the complete absence of risk. The Bar Association did not act on either recommendation.

The *Con Ed* case is not an aberration. Overcharging tort clients is routine[24] and virtually never results in a sanction.[25]

It is both a consequence of an uncompetitive market for tort-claiming services and an indictment of our civil justice system that whenever an egregious act of medical malpractice resulting in grave injury occurs, a tort lawyer will obtain a million-dollar or multimillion-dollar fee.[26] The lawyer will claim this fee irrespective of the effort she exerts or the value, if any, that she adds to the claim. Even if she adds no value to the claim, she will, as part of the zero-based accounting scheme, still collect her million-dollar fee, as Mary Corcoran learned to her dismay.

Because contingency fee percentages are standard, they do not reflect differences in risk, anticipated costs, or returns on the lawyer's investment. A lawyer who represents a severely injured claimant, where the settlement value of the claim is $10 million or more, charges the same standard contingent fee as when she represents a less severely injured claimant, where the settlement value is only a tenth or twentieth as much and the liability risk and the anticipated effort is substantially the same. The higher-valued claim will usually yield a substantially higher effective hourly rate because pricing is inflexible and does not vary on the basis of differences in risk or the cost of production of services.

Case selection further facilitates lawyers to overcharge tort clients. As noted, they carefully screen claims – a process that is so effective that the limited data we have indicates that they prevail mostly by way of settlement in 70 to 90 percent of the cases they accept.[27] If the market for lawyers' services were competitive, the percentages lawyers charge would roughly reflect the likelihood of success in each case.[28] In fact, differences in the likelihood of success have no impact on the contingency fee. With few exceptions, price is unrelated to risk.

Uniform pricing of contingency fee services does not, in and of itself, prove that the market for contingent-fee-financed tort claiming is uncompetitive. Uniform pricing can occur in a competitive market. First, the uniform price may be an equilibrium price – that is, the price at which the quantity of the goods or services supplied equals the quantity demanded. When price lies above this equilibrium, sellers must decrease the price in order to increase demand, thereby enabling sale of a quantity of the goods or services for which profits cover output costs. Likewise, when price lies below the equilibrium, demand exceeds supply, and sellers will increase price until they reach the equilibrium price.[29] There is considerable evidence, however, which I review later in this chapter, that the standard contingency fee rate is not an equilibrium price.

Uniform pricing may also be an efficient response in a competitive market. As Saul Levmore, dean of the University of Chicago Law School, has observed:

> Those people who understand markets ... realize that competition often generates uniformity that works to the advantage of buyers and sellers. Uniform percentage fees also may be desirable products of competition. They entail low bargaining costs, they align the interests of lawyers and clients in contexts in which clients have difficulty monitoring lawyers' behavior, and they enhance client confidence by equalizing lawyers' incentives across caseloads.[30]

The real estate brokerage market is a typical example for which uniform pricing may be an efficient response in a competitive market. In this market, the standard contingency fee is a commission of 6 percent of the sale price of the house.[31] If commission rates were individualized, home owners would worry that their broker might devote greater efforts to selling the homes of owners who had agreed to pay higher commissions. Standard pricing of brokers' services is an efficient way to reduce these agency costs – that is, the costs to principals (home owners) of monitoring the efforts of real estate brokers.[32] In addition, uniform pricing of brokerage services may minimize transaction costs by displacing more costly individualized bargaining and by reducing search costs.

Nonetheless, there are several reasons why the economic justifications for uniform pricing in real estate brokerage do not similarly translate to contingency-fee-financed tort services. First, because tort lawyers allocate their time and capital among the cases in their portfolio as if they were charging differential contingency fee rates, uniform pricing does not reduce agency costs. When contingency fee lawyers assemble their portfolios of cases, they estimate how much time will be needed and how much capital will have to be advanced for litigation costs in each case. Thereafter, lawyers constantly reevaluate their portfolios and rearrange their investments going forward. A lawyer who discovers that a contingent fee case that he accepted is insufficiently remunerative – either because of a mistake in judgment or newly discovered information – has incentive to shirk or settle quickly and cheaply.[33] Lawyers thus devote less time and capital to cases that have depreciated in value. Conversely, they allocate additional time and capital to cases that appear more profitable than initially anticipated. As a consequence, they are able to recoup the vast majority of the expenses they advance.[34]

As part of this process, contingency fee lawyers are constantly reevaluating their portfolios' expected returns and updating their estimates of the effective hourly rate for each case by considering: (1) the amount of time required to generate a settlement or take the case to trial; (2) the settlement or trial value of the case (which takes litigation risk into account); (3) the lawyer's share thereof (a function of the uniform percentage charged); and (4) the advances for litigation costs that will be required.

Whereas some contend otherwise,[35] this evidence demonstrates that lawyers do not devote uniform efforts to advancing their clients' interests. Although contingency fee uniformity affects the calculation of the estimated effective hourly rate value of each case, its effect on minimizing agency costs is marginal.

C. Price Rigidity in the Face of Highly Variable Production Costs

In competitive markets for uniform or easily substitutable goods or services with little variation in costs of production, prices gravitate toward an equilibrium point.[36] The market for tort-claiming services, however, differs from this model because there is enormous variation in the costs of production and the rates of return. One claim may present substantial risk and a need for a high investment level but offer high reward possibilities. Another may present identical risk and reward probabilities but require only a modest investment. Still another may involve little or no risk, a need for little investment, and promise of high reward, thereby generating an anticipated windfall fee. In a competitive market, the prices charged for these services would vary on the basis of differences in production costs and anticipated rewards.[37] Not so in the market for tort-claiming services, in which price rigidity is the norm.[38]

D. Referral Fees as Indicative of Rents: A Product of Uniform Pricing

The way that lawyers divide profits when a second lawyer is brought in to take over the case provides further substantiation of the lack of a competitive market for pricing of tort lawyers' services. Many lawyers vigorously seek out tort clients whom they have no intention of representing. Instead, they sell these claims to other lawyers higher up on the food chain. In the jargon of the trade, this is termed "referring" a case. Usually, the referring lawyer, like Mr. Dowd, does nothing more for the client. Nonetheless, he is paid a "referral fee," which typically ranges from 30 to 50 percent of the contingency fee realized by the performing lawyer.[39] In fact, tort lawyers, especially in large-scale litigations such as mass torts, maintain an exclusive and active secondary market in tort claims in which they buy, sell, and trade claims in exchange for referral fees or services, such as providing access to critical documents or conducting a trial.

The amount of the commission for a referral is unique to tort litigation. In the business world, typical commissions for brokering the sale of a small business range between 10 and 12 percent.[40] Were contingent fee pricing subject to competitive forces and were lawyers allowed to purchase claims in the secondary market, they could be expected to share some of the saved commission costs with claimants who bypass the referring lawyer. Despite the substantial savings realized from this disintermediation, performing lawyers who routinely pay 30 to 50 percent of their fee to a referring lawyer just as routinely refuse to discount their standard rates when the claimant comes directly to them.[41] The fact that performing lawyers are charging enough to pay a commission of such magnitude is further evidence that the standard contingency fee is not an equilibrium price but one that generates substantial unearned income.[42]

The existence of a uniform price for tort services – which is not justified by economic efficiency – and the rigidity of that uniform price in the face of highly variable production costs is evidence of a market failure.[43] In the next chapter, I explain why the market has failed to correct this economic anomaly.

NOTES

1. *See, e.g.*, Marc S. Galanter, *Anyone Can Fall Down a Manhole: The Contingency Fee and Its Discontents*, 47 DEPAUL L. REV. 457 (1998) [hereinafter Galanter, *Contingency Fee and Its Discontents*]; Marc S. Galanter, *Reading the Landscape of Disputes: What We Know and Don't Know (and Think We Know) About Our Allegedly Contentious and Litigious Society*, 31 UCLA L. REV. 4 (1983); Marc S. Galanter, *The Day After the Litigation Explosion*, 46 MD. L. REV. 3 (1986).
2. Galanter, *Contingency Fees and Its Discontents, supra*, at 470.
3. *See* 22 N.Y.C.R.R. § 603.7(e) (McKinney 2002); *Gair v. Peck*, 6 N.Y.2d 97, *cert denied*, 361 U.S. 374 (1960) (upholding appellate division's fee-limiting rule as within the power of the court).
4. Professor Ted Schneyer of the University of Arizona Law School, writing for a symposium convened for the specific purpose of creating scholarship critical of the Brickman-Horowitz-O'Connell "early offer" proposal to reduce windfall fees (described in the Introduction and elaborated on in the Conclusion at § B(3)), relies on Galanter for the proposition that "today's legal services is competitive enough to keep excessive fees to a minimum." Ted Schneyer, *Legal-Process Constraints on The Regulation of Lawyers' Contingent Fee Contracts* 47 DEPAUL L. REV. 371, 376 (1998). This mirrors the words of Stuart Speiser who, decades earlier, stated that "[c]ompetition among highly qualified tort lawyers all over the country keeps fees at reasonable levels." Stuart M. Speiser, LAWSUIT 569 (Horizon Press 1980); *see also* Charles Silver, *Does Civil Justice Cost Too Much?*, 80 TEX. L. REV. 2073, 2088 (2002) [hereinafter Silver, *Civil Justice*]; Herbert M. Kritzer, *The Wages of Risk: The Returns of Contingency Fee Legal Practice*, 47 DEPAUL L. REV. 267, 307–09 (1998) [hereinafter Kritzer, *The Wages of Risk*].
5. *In re Zyprexa Prods. Liab. Litig.*, 451 F. Supp. 2d 458, 477 (E.D.N.Y. 2006).
6. *In re Guidant Corp. Implantable Defibrillators Prods. Litig.*, MDL 05–1708, 2008 WL 3896006 (D. Minn. Mar. 28, 2008).
7. Charles Silver & Geoffrey P. Miller, *The Quasi-Class Action Method of Managing Multi-District Litigations: Problems and a Proposal*, 63 VAND. L. REV. 107 (2010) [hereinafter Silver & Miller].
8. *In re Zyprexa Prods. Liab. Litig.*, 424 F. Supp. 2d 488, 490 (E.D.N.Y. 2006).
9. I am not addressing Silver and Miller's criticism of the "tax" that the lawyers in each litigation were forced to pay to the steering committee lawyers

to compensate them for doing most of the actual discovery and settlement negotiations.

10. Silver & Miller, *supra* note 7, at 137.

11. *Id*. at 137–38 (emphasis added). They go on to state:

> When news breaks of a possible mass tort, advertising lawyers shift into high gear, referral networks activate, and competition for clients begins.... Potential clients can easily use the internet to find law firms willing to handle ... [these kinds] of cases. They can also comparison shop by allowing multiple firms to compete for their cases...
>
> As a matter of economic theory, then, scale economies (*if they exist*) provide no justification for fee cuts. Market pressure *should* force the lawyers competing for products liability cases to price their services efficiently.

> *Id*. at 138 (emphasis added).

In a prior article, Professor Silver had a more positive view of the existence of economies of scale in aggregate litigation. Instead of questioning scale economies – "if they exist," he and a coauthor asserted that "plaintiffs can substantially reduce their per capita litigation costs" in aggregated litigations and that "[t]hese savings ... can be divided among plaintiffs, making all of them better off than they would be if they sued alone." Charles Silver & Lynn A. Baker, *Mass Lawsuits and the Aggregate Settlement Rule*, 32 WAKE FOREST L. REV. 733, 744–45 (1997). These substantial economies of scale lead to a higher "probability of winning" and "more favorable settlements," *id*. at 746, factors that should lead the lawyers to reduce their fees from that which they would have charged solo litigants to reflect the lowered litigation risk and probability of higher settlements.

12. Silver & Miller, *supra* note 7, at 138 (citations omitted). They go on to state:

> Yet, when concluding that lawyers' fees were hundreds of millions of dollars too high [these] judges ... considered no evidence of this type – or any other. They appear to have thought that a court exercising its inherent power needs neither a sound methodology nor competent evidence when cutting fees. This cannot be right. The efficient price for legal services is an empirical matter, and judges cannot properly resolve empirical matters by means of armchair speculation. *Id*.

13. *Id*. at 113.

14. *See* Jeffrey O'Connell, Carlos M. Brown & Michael D. Smith, *Yellow Page Ads as Evidence of Widespread Overcharging by the Plaintiffs' Personal Injury Bar – and a Proposed Solution*, 6 CONN. INS. L.J. 423 (1999–2000) (reporting a survey of yellow page phone advertisements that indicates that virtually no price competition exists among attorneys who charge contingency fees. In fact, just a single ad out of the 1,425 studied, or 0.07%, gave any indication whatsoever that the advertising attorney would be willing to bargain with potential clients with regard to the fee that would be charged). *Id*. at 426–27, 430. Over

the course of thousands of advertisements by contingent fee lawyers costing hundreds of millions of dollars, no contingent fee lawyer has published an advertisement indicating that he charges less. In fact, it is a common practice among contingent fee lawyers to have the contingent fee percentage included on a preprinted standard retainer agreement used by that lawyer and to then fill in the client's name, address, and a brief description of the nature of the claim on blank lines in the agreement before having the claimant sign it. *See, e.g.,* DAVID CRUMP & JEFFREY B. BREMAN, THE STORY OF A CIVIL CASE: DOMINGUEZ V. SCOTT'S FOOD STORES, INC. 8 (3d ed. 2001) (a law school text listing a model contingency fee agreement in a tort claim, which includes a preprinted portion in which the contingent fee is: "ONE THIRD (1/3) ... [of] amounts received in settlement ... and FORTY (40 percent) per cent ... if ... collected ... after suit is filed"). Most consumer organizations, for example, the Consumers Union, publisher of Consumer Reports might be expected to represent consumers' interests in the tort claiming process by focusing public attention on lawyers' anticompetitive practices and taking the lead in seeking redress in the political arena, but fail to do so, perhaps because of their close ties to plaintiff lawyers.

15. Silver & Miller, *supra* note 7, at 110.
16. *See In re Synthroid Marketing Litig.*, 201 F. Supp. 2d 861, 875–77 (2002); *see also* Richard W. Painter, *Litigating on a Contingency: A Monopoly of Champions or a Market for Champerty?*, 71 CHI.-KENT L. REV. 625, 656–59 (1995) [hereinafter Painter, *Litigating on a Contingency*]; Gillian K. Hadfield, *The Price of Law: How the Market for Lawyers Distorts the Justice System*, 98 MICH. L. REV. 953, 999 (2000).
17. For example, the Florida Supreme Court, in justifying adoption of a cap on contingency fees, stated: "[T]his Court expressed its belief, (possibly, its hope) that lawyer advertising would create greater public awareness regarding attorneys' fees and services and that competition would provide a self-regulator on fees... [S]uch does not appear to be the case." *See The Florida Bar Re Amendment to the Code of Professional Responsibility (Contingent Fees)*, 494 So. 2d 960, 961 (Fla. 1986); *see also* Mark A. Franklin, Robert H. Chanin and Irving Mark, *Accidents, Money and the Law: A Study of the Economics of Personal Injury Litigation*, 61 COLUM. L. REV. 1, 22 (1961) (because the assumption that competition would prevent abuses in setting contingent fees was not borne out, New York's Appellate Division, by rule, found it necessary to set limits on contingency fees).
18. *See* Brickman, *Effective Hourly Rates, supra* Introduction, note 4, at 657 n.11.
19. *See Miss. State Bar v. Blackmon*, 600 So. 2d 166, 176 (Miss. 1992).
20. *See* Brickman, *Effective Hourly Rates*, *supra* Introduction, note 4, at 660 nn.14–15.

21. *See* Mirey A. Navarro, *Gramercy Park's Refugees Long for Home*, N.Y. TIMES, Oct. 6, 1989, at B1 (reporting that Con Edison projected costs for explosion cleanup and reimbursements to displaced Gramercy Park area residents to be in the $30 to $40 million range following the August 19, 1989, steam pipe explosion that spewed cancer-causing asbestos throughout the neighborhood); *see also* David E. Pitt, *Con Edison Takes Blame in Steam Blast*, N.Y. TIMES, Sept. 9, 1989, (Saturday, Late ed.) § 1, at 25 (recounting the three deaths caused by the accident, as well as the estimated 176 pounds of asbestos that were sprayed over Gramercy Park).

22. *See* Daniel Wise, *Lawyers Gear Up to Handle Asbestos Claims; Experts Say Personal Injury, Property Claims Look Good; Outlook Grim for Psychic Trauma*, N.Y.L.J., Sept. 18, 1989, at 1 (stating that shortly following the explosion, "[i]n the race to sign up clients, some lawyers descended upon Gramercy Park 'like locusts' ... peddling their ability to recover the 'sun, moon and stars'").

23. Fee bargaining occurred in only one instance of which I am aware. In that case, a lawyer who was among the victims assembled a group of other victims to join with him in securing legal services. He negotiated a discounted fee for his group.

24. A State Farm Insurance Company adjuster with forty years of experience stated: "Over the years I witnessed many examples of attorneys charging their client (people with a claim against State Farm) a contingency fee of one-third or more when State Farm had already or would have offered to pay that client all that State Farm was obligated to pay under the policy of insurance in force." Affidavit of Will B. Graham, *Bond v. Maynard*, No. 03CV165925 (13th Jud. Cir. Ct., Calloway County, Mo., May 6, 2003). A Texas physician, writing the Senate Judiciary Committee, which was holding hearings on contingency fee abuses, described the plight of his friends, Gilberto and Rosario Alvarez. The Alvarez' daughter was involved in an uncontested medical malpractice action. According to the physician, the attorney handling the low risk case "did virtually no work," yet received 40% of the Alvarez' damage award of $400,000. *See* Brickman, *Effective Hourly Rates, supra* Introduction, note 4, at 661 n.14. The Alvarez' lament is reflected in an e-mail I received a few years ago from a husband whose wife had been severely injured in an auto accident, asking for my assistance in finding a tort attorney who would not overcharge them: "On March 2nd this year [2003] my family was hit head on by a snow plow pickup truck that crossed into our lane. My daughter and myself were injured [*sic*] but my wife is paralyzed from the waist down and is still in rehabilitation at [a New Jersey hospital]. There is no issue of the other drivers [*sic*] culpability, [*sic*] there was a witness [*sic*] and he pleaded guilty to the summons for failure to keep to the right. He is well insured with a commercial policy. How do

I find an attorney that will work for time and expenses. [*sic*] I have resources to pay. All attorneys that I have contacted to date will only work on a contingency basis." (E-mail from a claimant to Lester Brickman, June 22, 2003, 10:45:43 EST, on file with author.) My advice was that he should deal directly with the defendant's insurance company and seek a settlement offer. Then take that offer to tort lawyers in his community and see if any would agree to represent him on the basis of a contingency fee to be applied against whatever the lawyer was able to add to the offer. I then added that his chances of success in finding a lawyer who would agree to this were low.

25. *See generally* Brickman, *Disciplinary System*, *supra* Chapter 3, note 7.

26. For an example, *see* Brickman, *Contingent Fees*, *supra* Introduction, note 18, at 32–33. For discussion of the frequency of million-dollar fees, *see* Brickman, *Effective Hourly Rates*, *supra* Introduction, note 4, at App. F.

27. *See supra* Chapter 3, note 17.

28. *See* Murray L. Schwartz & Daniel J. B. Mitchell, *An Economic Analysis of the Contingent Fee in Personal Injury Litigation*, 22 STAN. L. REV. 1125, 1139–40 (1970). ("Under competitive conditions the same percentage fee would not be charged for both [high value and low value] cases.") Other factors would also be important in setting the percentage including the value of the claim, the amount of lawyer time that would be necessary, the amount of litigation expenses that the lawyer would have to advance and thereby put at risk, the lawyer's workload, and whether a quick settlement, even though for a modest sum, was in the offering.

29. *See* BEGG ET AL., ECONOMICS 32–34 (4th ed. 1994).

30. Saul Levmore, *Commissions and Conflicts in Agency Arrangements: Lawyers, Real Estate Brokers, Underwriters, and Other Agents' Rewards*, 36 J. L. & ECON. 503, 505–06 (1991) [hereinafter Levmore, *Commissions and Conflicts*]. *See* Charles Silver, *Control Fees? No, Let the Free Market Do Its Job*, NAT'L L.J., Apr. 18, 1994, at A17.

31. *See* Patrick Barta, *Home Rules*, WALL ST. J., Oct. 6, 2001, at R12.

32. *See* Levmore, *Commissions and Conflicts, supra* note 30, at 505, 509 n.12; Owen R. Phillips & Henry N. Butler, *The Law and Economics of Residential Real Estate Markets in Texas: Regulation and Antitrust Implications*, 36 BAYLOR L. REV. 623, 641, 649 (1984) [hereinafter Philips & Butler, *Real Estate Markets in Texas*] (noting that though brokerage commissions are uniform, "[i]t is difficult, nevertheless, to embrace the conclusion that uniform prices are sufficient proof of the existence of collusion," and that "it is not in the interest of one firm to lower prices if it knows that rival firms would follow to maintain their market share [thus it] is in each broker's interest to maintain the status quo"). Others, however, see the existence of such uniform pricing as indicative of collusion among real estate brokers. *See* Bruce M. Owen, *Kickbacks Specialization, Price Fixing, and Efficiency in Residential Real Estate Markets*, 29 STAN. L.

REV. 931, 946–48 (1977) (multiple listing services enable real estate agents to share information, and this facilitates maintenance of uniformity of prices by price-fixing and collusion).

33. To be sure, ethical codes require that lawyers zealously advance their clients' interests; shirking is unethical. In reality, however, shirking is commonplace and is only the subject of disciplinary proceedings when a lawyer does it repeatedly and also engages in other egregious behavior that attracts the attention of disciplinary counsel.

34. There is empirical evidence to support this view. In a series of federal tax cases, the Fifth Circuit Court of Appeals analyzed the degree of recovery of litigation expenses that contingency fee lawyers had advanced. *See, e.g., Burnett v. Comm'r*, 42 T.C. 9, 12 (1964), *remanded*, 356 F.2d 755 (5th Cir. 1966), *cert. denied*, 385 U.S. 832 (1966). The *Burnett* court noted that "although reimbursement [of litigation expenses advanced] was tied to the recovery of a client's claim, assistance was granted only to those whose claims would in all probability be successfully concluded." *Id.* at 760. The record revealed that the firm recovered over 96% of the total litigation expenses that it had advanced for all of its cases. *Id.* at 759. To recover such a high percentage, a firm must invest far more capital (and presumably time) proportionately in those 70% or more of cases in which it prevails than in the 10% to 30% in which it does not prevail.

Other firms' experiences are comparable. *See, e.g., Monek v. Comm'r*, 25 T.C.M. (CCH) 582, 584 (1966), in which a lawyer recovered approximately 98% litigation expenses advanced and *Canelo v. Comm'r*, 53 T.C. 217, 218 (1969), aff'd 447 F.2d 484 (9th Cir. 1971) in which there was a 90% recovery. In *Boccardo v. Comm'r*, 56 F.3d 1016 (9th Cir. 1995), the record indicated that the plaintiff firm had prevailed in 70% of their cases but recovered 80% to 90% of all expenses advanced including expenses advanced in cases in which they did not prevail. There is additional evidence in support of the proposition that lawyers differentially invest in cases based on the perceived likelihood of success. *See, e.g.,* Web site of Advocate Capital, Inc., http://www.advocatecapital.com (Advocate Capital provides loans to lawyers to cover litigation expenses, using the "case as collateral"). Advocate Capital requires lawyers to repay loans even if the case is lost; however, the Web site implies that this should not be overly burdensome on attorneys, citing their "experience that a minimal amount of money is invested in cases that are ultimately abandoned." *Id.*

35. Professor Charles Silver argues that "a lawyer who manages a portfolio of similar matters has an incentive to invest equally in each." Charles Silver, *Preliminary Thoughts on the Economics of Witness Preparation*, 30 TEX. TECH L. REV. 1383, 1394 (1999) (italics omitted).

36. *See* BEGG ET AL., ECONOMICS, *supra* note 29, at 32–34.

37. *See* Schwartz & Mitchell, *supra* note 28.

38. The degree of price rigidity maintained by contingency fee lawyers stands in
     stark contrast with the practices of real estate brokers. As noted, real estate
     brokers charge a standard contingency fee: a 6% sales commission. If that
     rate represents an equilibrium price that, on average, provides reasonable
     compensation to brokers, then a projected rate of return that is substantially
     higher than the added transactional costs of negotiating a more individualized
     bargain should result in negotiation of a lower price. On the other hand, if law-
     yers' uniform contingency fees are not an equilibrium price but are, instead,
     a collusively maintained price designed to generate economic rent, then we
     would expect lawyers to reject bargaining out of the standard rate even when a
     substantial rate of return, disproportionate to risk, is anticipated. Both expec-
     tations are borne out by industry practices.

     In the case of expensive homes, brokers charge a lower rate, 5% and even 4%,
     instead of the standard 6% brokers' commission. *See* Hannah Fons, *Banishing
     The "B-Word": Your Broker as Selling Partner*, THE COOPERATOR, Nov. 2002, at
     18, 19. This reflects the fact that sellers have or can acquire substantial knowl-
     edge of the market value of the home they are selling and therefore the price
     they will be paying the broker. It also reflects the recognition that the increased
     compensation from selling an expensive home for a standard commission may
     not be justified by any increased amount of work to be done by the broker.
     Accordingly, the parties bargain for an individualized rate reflective of the
     specific elements of those transactions. In the comparable case for tort lawyers,
     that is, in which the lawyer's expected return is substantial because of the seri-
     ousness of the injury, the amount of insurance or assets available, the absence
     of meaningful liability risk, and the likelihood of settling the claim without the
     need for a substantial time expenditure, clients who lack that knowledge but
     who nevertheless attempt to secure a lower contingency fee, are easily rebuffed.
     Even when clients have knowledge about the value of their claim and how much
     time will likely be required, they are no match for lawyers who will conjure up
     all sorts of phantom risks as justification for insisting on the standard rate. *See
     supra* Chapter 5, notes 4–5.

     Even real estate brokers' standard commissions of 6% have succumbed to
     competitive pressure. Many brokers have slashed their fees by 25% or more. *See*
     Jay Ramano, *Under 6% What Do Sellers Get?*, N.Y. TIMES, Dec. 8, 2002, at RE5.
     Beyond the traditional, full-service brokerage firms, a number of companies
     now advertise that they offer their services at a variety of commission levels,
     fixed charges, or some combination of the two. The levels of service vary widely,
     and may or may not include use of the local multiple listing services (MLS).
     The Internet has added to the competitive pressures. Discount real estate
     brokerages have been operating on the Web for years. However, their growth
     has been severely restricted in part because they generally do not have access

to the exclusive listings that members of the National Association of Realtors share. *See* Patrick Barta, *Realtors Pressured to Cut Commissions: Low-Cost Competitors Gain Ground, Undercutting Traditional 6% Fee; a Cash Rebate for Buyers*, WALL ST. J., Nov. 12, 2002, at B1. However, a Web site has been created that has gained access to MLS by hiring local brokers who join local realtor associations and thus qualify for access to the MLS. This site typically charges sellers no more than 4.5% in commission. Patrick Barta, *Home Rules: Real Estate Listings on the Web are Loosening the Grip Realtors Have Long Had on the Market*, WALL ST. J., Oct. 29, 2001, at R12.

By contrast, lawyers' standard contingency fee rates remain unaffected. Unlike competitive markets that often feature price and quality advertising by suppliers of goods and services, tort lawyers never advertise their prices, let alone offer "discounts" from the standard rate. Moreover, if contingency fee lawyers were threatened with the kinds of competitive pressures as are now affecting real estate brokers, instead of cutting prices, they would simply adopt ethical rules to bar or, at least, deter any practice that would generate price competition – a subject I address in Chapter 6.

39. *See, e.g., Matter of Fuchsberg & Fuchsberg*, N.Y. L.J., Oct. 3, 2003, at 21 (indicating that a well-known New York plaintiff law firm routinely pays a 50% referral fee). Andrew Blum, *Big Bucks, But … Cash Flow a Problem*, NAT'L L.J., Apr. 3, 1989, at 1 (indicating that preeminent personal injury law firm pays out 28% of its gross fee income to referring lawyers).

40. *See* Henry Jackson, *Small-Business Brokers' Gift*, ORLANDO SENTINEL, Apr. 28, 1997, at 20.

41. This refusal may be less a matter of greed than sound business practice. A lawyer who depends on referrals for a significant part of her business will not want to be seen as competing with the lawyers who sign up clients and refer them up the chain. Referring lawyers would retaliate by referring their clients to other lawyers.

42. Payment of referral fees is a phenomenon largely confined to contingency fee lawyers. Hourly rate lawyers do not pay referral fees to other lawyers who refer clients to them (though they may reciprocate by referring clients to lawyers who have sent them clients). The difference in business practice is accounted for by the rents that contingency fee lawyers obtain. The market for hourly rate fee services is, by comparison, quite competitive.

43. *See* Painter, *Litigating on a Contingency, supra* note 16, at 657–59 (arguing that in a competitive market the contingency fee charged by attorneys should vary based on differences in the size of claim, the level of risk, the amount of time devoted to the case, as well as the skill of the attorney, and that "a competitive market in which fees consistently are the same percentage of judgment or settlement (for example, 33 percent) would be unusual").

5 Why the Market Has Failed to Correct the Absence of Price Competition

A. Lack of Transparency

Freely competitive markets are characterized by the presence of many comparable producers of goods or services with prices that are published and readily discovered. Consumers are fully informed and register their personal preferences through choices based on that perfect information. Information about the prices charged by service providers must be easily available in terms that are meaningful to consumers; that is, the units in which the prices are stated must convey sufficient information to enable consumers to make price comparisons.[1] In addition, consumers must be able to determine the relative quality of the service providers vying for their business so that they can make informed price/quality tradeoffs in selecting a provider. Producers respond to the consumer demand for information by campaigning aggressively to provide it – an effort that epitomizes interfirm competition. To diminish incentives for existing firms to collude,[2] it is also necessary that firms be able to freely enter and exit the industry.

Though the market for tort claiming hosts many producers, virtually all of the other components of a competitive market, particularly perfect or even adequate information, are absent. Awareness of price in the tort market requires knowledge of the value of claims. This is so because consumers pay a contingency fee for a lawyer's service by exchanging a share of their claims. The fairness of the price depends on the value of the claim being exchanged, which is itself a function of the risk undertaken by the lawyer. Most tort claimants, however, have little knowledge of the value of their claims, the risk the lawyer is assuming, the amount of time the lawyer anticipates will be required to produce an adequate recovery, or the litigation costs that he will have to advance. Tort lawyers, on the other hand, are experts in the valuation of claims, the risk involved, the estimated time required, and the funds that they will need to advance. This asymmetry of information redounds to the lawyer's benefit and disadvantages the consumer when bargaining over the price of the service.[3] If risk and anticipated effort is so low that charging a standard contingency fee will likely lead to a windfall for the lawyer, he does not, as a matter of practice, share that information with the client.[4]

It might seem incongruous to contend that claimants lack knowledge of the price of lawyers' services when contingent fees are standard. But despite knowing that the lawyer is charging one-third of the recovery, consumers of tort claiming services have no basis on which to determine the fairness of the fee. This is because they are unable to estimate the lawyer's effective hourly rate, as such a calculation requires estimates of the value of the claim and the amount of time required to produce an acceptable settlement or to take the case through trial. Here, too, it is in lawyers' self-interest not to make such disclosures, as that information might induce clients to seek to bargain for lower fees. Even after settlement, tort claimants are usually rebuffed when they attempt to learn how many hours their attorneys devoted to their matters. A typical tort claimant, paying a standard one-third fee, has no idea, ex ante, of the amount he actually is agreeing to pay – let alone of the effective hourly rate that the lawyer is charging – and does not know – and cannot determine – the effective hourly rate he actually paid ex post.[5]

The fee-bargain playing field tilts decidedly in favor of lawyers because of these imbalances in knowledge. A claimant seeking representation faces a daunting task in overcoming this information asymmetry because tort lawyers do not engage in price advertising, let alone competitive price advertising.[6] Claimants entering the market quickly learn – if they did not already know – that virtually all lawyers charge the same contingent fee percentage and that lawyers will not bargain over the fee.[7] The signal is clear: Attempts to obtain lower prices will be rebuffed. Furthermore, most tort claimants are unsophisticated one-time users of legal services and lack experience in negotiating fees with lawyers.[8]

Claimant search costs are further magnified by deceptive information about risk that standard contingency fees convey. To be sure, many tort claims involve considerable risk and some insufficient reward. As noted, however, attorneys carefully screen these claims and reject about two-thirds of would-be clients, including most claims denominated as high risk.[9] This enables lawyers to charge premiums for assuming the very risks that they have substantially cut out of their portfolios. To justify their substantial fees in cases in which they are assuming little or no meaningful risk, contingency fee lawyers may deliberately exaggerate the risk they are undertaking, confident that the client will be unable to ever prove any such duplicity. By collectively maintaining a substantial uniform rate, tort lawyers are sending deceptive signals to potential tort claimants that all contingency-fee-financed litigation is high risk. If the case involves high risk and insufficient reward, the lawyer simply declines to take the case. If the lawyer believes it will generate a substantial effective hourly rate, the lawyer presents the claimant with his standard contingent fee agreement form. If the client correctly believes that her claim presents a low or nonexistent risk and seeks a lower percentage fee, however, the lawyer insists on the standard rate because it is the standard rate.[10] Because all lawyers charge the same rate, it is necessarily "fair" and comparison shopping is unnecessary and, indeed, futile.[11]

Standardized contingency fees also deter consumers from seeking out "discount" lawyers because they may be perceived as providing low-value services. Most tort victims are unable to monitor their lawyer's behavior and have to rely on a lawyer's personal incentive to maximize the recovery. Thus, a lawyer offering a cut rate may appear to be signaling that she intends to devote less time to the representation than required to obtain a substantial percentage of the maximum settlement value of the claim. Or she may be perceived as signaling her intent to seek a quick settlement offer less than the maximum settlement value and to then induce the client to accept it by portraying it as the best obtainable offer.[12] Finally, a discount lawyer may appear to be inferior in quality and therefore obtain a substantially lower settlement offer than the maximum settlement value of the claim. In sum, the consumer, who can neither monitor the lawyer's efforts nor evaluate the quality of the lawyer, has reason to be concerned that if she hires the price cutter, she may end up with a lower net recovery.[13]

Thus, due to the intended lack of transparency and the related deleterious effects, the market for tort claiming services is not competitive. Another element working against market competition is the uniform contingency fee that is, as discussed hereinafter, enabled by the concerted actions of tort lawyers.

B. Uniform Contingency Fees: A Product of Lawyers' Concerted Actions

Lawyers maintain a uniform pricing structure because they perceive that it is in their self-interest to do so. A law firm that considers undercutting the standard price would recognize that if it did so, other firms might also lower their prices and, as a consequence, both aggregate and individual income would fall.[14] This provides a strong incentive for concerted actions to maintain a uniform price.[15]

The argument that lawyers are acting in concert to fix the price of tort claiming services is open to a number of objections. A collusive pricing system maintained by a few corner gas station owners is easily policed by the owners. Prices are posted and deviations are instantly identified. Thousands of lawyers operating in the low-visibility confines of their offices, however, cannot be nearly so sanguine that other players are maintaining the standard price. According to standard economic theory, oligopolists are "torn between the desire to collude, thus maximizing joint profits, and the desire to compete, in the hope of increasing market share and profits at the expense of rivals."[16] In the standard supply-demand curve, the demand curve slopes from left to right; that is, the lower the price, the higher the quantity demanded.[17] If one member-firm increases output by undercutting the standard price, consumers will substitute its services for those of the firms maintaining the (higher) standard price. This increase in demand will yield a rise in the price-cutting firm's profits at the expense of those maintaining the standard price, thus creating a strong incentive to stray from the tacit agreement. Thus, economists would predict that some lawyers would charge less than the standard price, expecting to increase their volume of sales sufficiently to generate higher profits. In addition, lawyers who operate more efficiently or who are able to obtain higher settlements would also bid prices down, driving out less-efficient and less-competent lawyers. That contingency fee lawyers do not deviate from standard contingent fee pricing is, therefore, under standard economic theory, an indication that the standard price is a competitive-market-derived equilibrium price and that lawyers who charged less would not be able to compensate for lower prices with sufficient increased volume to generate higher profits.[18] I dissent. As I have previously argued in this chapter and develop further in the next section, standard contingency fees are not the product of a competitive market.

C. How the Standard Contingency Fee Became the Standard

If the standard one-third fee were a competitive-market-derived equilibrium price, we would expect to find historical evidence of price fluctuation, both up and down, as the price moved toward the equilibrium point. The historical evidence, however, does not demonstrate any such pattern of fluctuation. For most of the nineteenth century, contingency fees were often moderate and risk-reflective – in the 5 to 25 percent range.[19] Later, in response to the increased demand for representation during the Industrial Revolution, lawyers raised their contingency fee percentages, which quickly climbed to 50 percent and higher. Courts then promulgated an arbitrary dividing line between 50 and 50.1 percent (and higher) contingency fees. They reasoned that if the lawyer owned more than 50 percent of the claim, the fee arrangement would amount to champerty[20] and be impermissible. Although the difference between 50 and 50.1 percent in an election or in stock ownership is significant, in the case of contingency fees, the difference is one-tenth of 1 percent – nothing more. Nonetheless, based on the concern that fees greater than 50 percent made the profession appear greedy, courts essentially capped contingency fees at 50 percent.[21] In many jurisdictions, lawyers simply charged the maximum allowed. This occasioned severe criticism by the public and some lawyers.[22] In response, states and courts, despite the strenuous opposition of tort lawyers, further capped contingency fees through statutes and rules, especially for medical malpractice litigation, driving the rates to between 25 and 50 percent, with most hovering at the one-third level.[23] Typically, these rules and statutes established sliding scales, applying the largest percentages to the initial amounts of recovery and smaller percentages to additional increments; some simply set a maximum percentage.[24]

The available historical evidence shows that the one-third (and higher) standard rate is a political determination and represents a balance of power between attorneys, courts, legislatures, and, least of all, clients. Markets did not set this standard – regulators did by establishing maximum contingency fee rates, which lawyers transformed into minimums. The result is the standard rate, which varies from 33⅓ to 40 percent, depending on the jurisdiction. In my judgment, had regulatory regimes not intervened to cap contingency fees at 50 percent or lower, the standard contingency fee would likely have risen to the 60 to 75 percent range.

D. The Political Dimension of the Tort System

In addressing the issue of whether contingency fee pricing is competitive, legal scholars – most of whom support an expanded tort system – reject my conclusion that standard contingency fee rates are not the product of a competitive market. As noted, they advance arguments primarily based on standard economic theory. I have previously reviewed and rejected these arguments, including: (1) if uniform pricing generated substantial rents, some lawyers would undercut the standard price in order to increase volume and profits[25]; (2) because economic theory provides that "prevailing prices [for contingency-fee-financed tort litigation] should ... be efficient," then therefore they are[26]; and (3) uniform pricing of contingency fees is not the result of a market failure but is attributable to such phenomenon as assortive matching.[27] These arguments are invoked to buttress the claim that the existence of uniform pricing does not justify regulation to ensure that clients are charged a competitive fee.[28] The academics who reject the conclusion that there has been a market failure, however, have not advanced credible reasons for the persistence of uniform contingency fees.[29]

One of the more artful attempts to reject my explanation of a market failure and justify the existence of uniform contingency fees is offered by Professors Eyal Zamir and Ilana Ritov of the Hebrew University of Jerusalem.[30] First, they argue that the one-third rate is "plausibly" determined by "ordinary economic factors, such as supply and demand."[31] They then argue that "focal points" and "status quo in bargaining" – that is, the rule that in bargaining, people tend toward mathematical simplicity and bargaining norms – account for the "distinctive uniformity" of contingency fee rates.[32] Thus, the focal point of one-third – as opposed to another percentage – is more conducive to mathematical calculation, and if past bargains relied on the one-third rate, then maintaining the status quo results in a "reduction of confrontations in bargaining [which] is particularly important in relational contracts."[33]

Zamir and Ritov then argue that the "standard rate [of one-third] endures in the market thanks to a process of assortive matching, that is, the process through which plaintiffs with very strong cases contract with the very best lawyers, second-best cases are handled by second-best attorney, and so forth."[34] Because cases of differing strength are "matched" with lawyers of differing skill sets, the prevailing rate – which they say has been determined by the market forces of supply and demand – is uniform across the board.

Contrary to Zamir and Ritov's statement that "ordinary economic factors" account for the standard one-third fee, I have offered a variety of arguments to show that the origin and maintenance of this standard fee is not the result of a competitive market. Rather, it is principally the product of political considerations and regulation by courts and legislatures. Supply and demand *least* accounts for the origin of the standard one-third fee, which tort lawyers help maintain by the promulgation of ethical rules to enforce anticompetitive behavior and inhibit price competition.

Zamir and Ritov's "assortive matching" is an attempt to describe the referral system by which lawyers seek out lucrative tort clients whom they have no intention of actually representing. Instead, they refer these clients to higher-level lawyers who will actually try the case or negotiate a settlement. For signing up these clients, the referring lawyers are typically paid 30 to 50 percent of the contingency fee realized by the performing lawyers. This referral system, as I explained, is evidence that referring lawyers are rent seekers, using their positional advantages to cut themselves in for a substantial portion of the contingency fee, which they have not earned by their productive efforts. Moreover, the fact that lawyers are willing to pay an astonishingly high commission of 30 to 50 percent of their standard one-third (to 40 percent) fee for the referral is compelling evidence that the standard contingency fee includes an unearned and excessive profit component.

Finally, there is no persuasive basis for the claim that the standard one-third fee endures because of the referral system ("assortive matching"). In a widely differentiated market for tort services, there is no economic basis for lawyers who primarily do slip-and-fall and auto accident cases to charge the same percentage fee as those who specialize in products liability litigation, medical malpractice, or mass torts. It is equally implausible that a competitive market would result in standard contingency fees when there are wide variations in litigation risk, the anticipated costs (in time and money) for the production of services, and the projected returns on lawyers' investments. "Assortive matching" also fails to explain why a lawyer charges the same contingency fee in a $10 million case as she does in a $1 million case, when the added value in the former is solely a function of the higher level of injury or the greater availability of defendants' assets, and there is no commensurate additional effort anticipated.

Other scholars also reject the existence of a market failure and advance arguments against regulation of contingency fees based on the deterrence value of the tort system. They contend that the tort system is an effective and efficient distributor of injury avoidance costs and a deterrent to unsafe corporate behavior. Though the empirical evidence is contrary and at least casts much doubt on this proposition,[35] numerous articles incorporate those propositions as fundamental premises.[36] In the view of these authors, the tort system is a bulwark that holds back a tide of egregious corporate behavior that would otherwise engulf the polity. However, that bulwark can only be maintained if tort lawyers receive "substantial fees." Otherwise, says Stuart Speiser, "there will be no plaintiffs' bar capable of carrying on the fight to balance the scales of justice."[37] And that would lead, according to Professor Carl T. Bogus of the Roger Williams Law School, to fewer "[l]awsuits [that] shine light on dark corners, exposing corporate wrongdoing."[38] Thus, the argument is two-fold: (1) acknowledging that some tort lawyers are overcharging their clients could be an impetus for regulatory reforms that would undermine this bulwark; and (2) by allowing more egregious corporate behavior to go unpunished, that conduct would proliferate.

This view may also partly explain why most torts scholars align with tort lawyers in opposing most tort reform proposals. Tort reform is seen as limiting lawyers' fees – leading to less exposure of corporate wrongdoing and potentially stripping away protections created by the tort system's expansion of the scope of liability. Thus, the tort system and its reform have a political dimension. Torts scholars and tort lawyers mutually reinforce one another's interests within this arena.

Campaign contributions confirm this political alliance. Tort lawyers, as a class, are among the largest single-issue contributors to political campaigns and provide a significant portion of the Democratic Party's funding.[39] Profits from tort cases that are redistributed through the political process support the Party and its office holders' attempts to advance policies and positions that many torts scholars espouse. Tort reforms and regulatory actions to curb abusive fee practices would diminish this flow of capital. This political reality may subtly influence some scholars' views.[40] Based on contributions of politically active law professors in the top-ranked law schools, Democratic-leaning law professors outnumber their Republican-leaning counterparts by five to one.[41] Tort lawyers as well as judges funnel millions of dollars annually to legal academics for their services as special masters, trustees, expert witnesses, and consultants, mostly in the areas of mass torts and class actions, thus solidifying the proclivity of law professors to support an expanded tort system.[42] The dominant view of scholars that tort lawyers are earning reasonable profits from contingency fees set in a competitive market may therefore be influenced by this political dimension.

NOTES

1. *See generally* James D. Dana Jr. & Kathryn E. Spier, *Expertise and Contingent Fees: The Role of Asymmetric Information in Attorney Compensation*, 9 J. L. ECON. & ORG. 349 (1993).
2. *See* BEGG ET AL., ECONOMICS 32–34 (4th ed. 1994).
3. *See In re* Joint E. & S. Dists. Asbestos Lit., 129 B.R. 710, 864 (E.D.N.Y. 1991) ("Contingent fee clients are often unsophisticated and infrequent consumers who may not be in a financial position to pursue an alternative [fee] arrangement.").
4. As Derek Bok, a former president of Harvard University has observed: "There is little bargaining over the terms of the contingent fee. Most plaintiffs do not know whether they have a strong case, and rare is the lawyer who will inform them (and agree to a lower percentage of the take) when they happen to have an extremely high probability of winning. In most instances, therefore, the contingent fee is a standard rate that seldom varies with the size of a likely settlement or the odds of prevailing in court." *See* DEREK BOK, THE COST OF TALENT: HOW EXECUTIVES AND PROFESSIONALS ARE PAID AND HOW IT AFFECTS AMERICA 140

(1993) [hereinafter BOK, THE COST OF TALENT]. If the client questions whether the fee is justified in light of clear liability or the amount of damages of the claim, the lawyer uses his superior knowledge to fend off the attempt to bargain over the fee, for example, by exaggerating risk in order to justify the high price implicit in the standard contingent fee. *See, e.g., In re Rappaport*, 558 F.2d 87, 88 n.3 (2d Cir. 1977); *Rohan v. Rosenblatt*, CV 930116887S, 1999 LEXIS 2231 (Conn. Super. Ct. Aug. 13, 1999) (attorney's representation that suit would be necessary to collect the proceeds of a $100,000 life insurance policy on the client's deceased wife "had no factual basis"; therefore, former client prevailed in suit to recover $33,333.33 fee paid); *Robinson v. Sharp*, 201 Ill. 86, 92 (1903) (finding that lawyer aroused "serious [mis]apprehensions"); *In re* St. John, 43 A.D.2d 218, (1974); *Haight v. Moore*, 37 N.Y. Super. (5 Jones & Spencer) 161, 165–66 (N.Y. Super. Ct. 1874); *Ransom v. Ransom*, 70 Misc. 30, 41–42 (N.Y. Sup. Ct. 1910), rev'd, 147 A.D. 835 (1911); *Kickland v. Egan*, 36 S.D. 428 (1915); *Nugent v. Moody*, 271 S.W. 266 (Tex. 1925); *Committee on Legal Ethics v. Tatterson*, 352 S.E. 2d 107, 114 (W. Va. 1986) (lawyers "misrepresented the difficulty in obtaining the ... proceeds"); cf. *United States v. Blitstein*, 626 F.2d 774 (10th Cir. 1980), cert. denied, 449 U.S. 1102 (1981); *Wunschel Law Firm, P.C. v. Clabaugh*, 291 N.W.2d 331, 336 (Iowa 1980); *Renegar v. Staples*, 388 P.2d 867 (Okla. 1963); *see also* Brickman, *Contingent Fees, supra* Introduction, note 18, at 65; Brickman, *Effective Hourly Rates, supra* Introduction, note 4, at 653, n.13.

5. Over the years, I have received many calls and e-mails from tort claimants seeking advice in cases where despite being told by their lawyers that their case was risky and would require extensive effort, in fact, a settlement was reached in a matter of a few weeks or months. These callers believe they were hornswaggled by their lawyers who deliberately exaggerated the risk and the amount of lawyer effort required. Most state that they were rebuffed when they asked their lawyers how much time they devoted to the matter. One standard answer they received is: "I don't keep time records." Those who persisted got the brush off with an answer such as: "I devoted substantial time to the matter." Those who still persisted, however, were threatened with suit by the lawyer unless they agreed to endorse the settlement check made out jointly to both lawyer and client so the lawyer could deposit the funds into his trust account and then withdraw his fee. When these clients call, they ask me whether there is anything they can do. Should they, for example, complain to the lawyer disciplinary body? My standard answer to these twice-victimized clients is the following: "Lawyer disciplinary agencies have no interest in these fee disputes. You have been mulcted by the legal profession, and you have no realistic recourse." *See generally* Brickman, *Disciplinary System, supra* Chapter 3, note 7.

6. *See supra* Chapter 4, note 6.

7. *See Kenseth v. Comm'r*, 114 T.C. 399, 422 (identifying "a standardized form contract prepared by … [the attorney who] would have declined to represent … [the client] if he had not entered into the contingent fee agreement."), *id.* at 444 (2000) (Beghe, J. dissenting) ("a contingent fee agreement in all significant respects amounts to a 'contract of adhesion'"); *Gisbrecht v. Barnhart*; 533 U.S. 789, 812 (2002) (Scalia, J. dissenting) ("[I]t is uncontested that the specialized Social Security bar charges uniform contingent fees … which are presumably presented to the typically unsophisticated client on a take-it-or-leave-it basis.").

8. *See supra* note 3.

9. *See* Brickman, *Effective Hourly Rates, supra* Introduction, note 4, at App. H.

10. *See* Vonde M. Smith Hitch, *Ethics and the Reasonableness of Contingency Fees: A Survey of State and Federal Law Addressing the Reasonableness of Costs as They Relate to Contingency Fee Arrangements*, 29 LAND & WATER L. REV. 215, 245 (1994). ("Often clients accept whatever rate an attorney suggests merely because it *seems* to be the 'going rate', and thus they do not realize that they are being overcharged.")

11. In fact, the Massachusetts Supreme Court stated that the standard contingency fee that a lawyer charged in a no-brainer case – amounting to more than $1 million – was fair because that was what the other tort lawyers in the community charged. *See* Lester Brickman, *A Massachusetts Debacle: Gagnon v. Shablom*, 12 CARDOZO L. REV. 1417, 1429–30 (1991).

12. *See* Brickman, *Money Talks, supra* Chapter 3, note 9, at 247, 283–87 nn.128–48.

13. *See* Rudy Santore & Alan D. Viard, *Legal Fee Restrictions, Moral Hazard and Attorney Rents*, 44 J. L. & ECON. 549, 550 (2001) [hereinafter Santore & Viard, *Legal Fee Restrictions*].

14. *Cf.* Owen R. Phillips & Henry N. Butler, *The Law and Economics of Residential Real Estate Markets in Texas: Regulation and Antitrust Implications*, 36 BAYLOR L. REV. 623, 641, 649 (1984) [hereinafter Philips & Butler, *Real Estate Markets in Texas*].

15. By "concerted actions," I do not mean that lawyers meet together, clandestinely or otherwise, to agree on a uniform price. Rather, I mean that lawyers act in the same manner as do gas station owners on adjacent corners who recognize that if any of them lower the price, the others will respond by lowering their prices. The ensuing "gas war" will lead to lower profits for all of the adjacent owners. To avoid such mutually destructive behavior, adjacent gas station owners are likely to consciously collude with one another by maintaining at least near price uniformity. Lawyers maintain a uniform price for the same reason; that is, it maximizes revenue for all lawyers. Effective collusion over price is aided by control over the practice of law that courts have reposed in themselves. *See* CHARLES WOLFRAM, MODERN LEGAL ETHICS, § 2.2.3; Charles W. Wolfram,

Lawyer Turf and Lawyer Regulation – The Role of the Inherent-Powers Doctrine, 12 U. ARK. LITTLE ROCK L. REV. 1 (1989). That control is used to restrain price competition – a subject I address in Chapter 6.

Contingency fee lawyers may also be aided in acting in a concerted fashion to maintain standard contingency fee pricing by inertial social forces. "Path dependence," an economic theory, postulates that some remediably inefficient social systems persist because of information and public choice costs. *See* Stephen E. Margolis and S.J. Liebowitz, *Path Dependence*, in PETER NEWMAN ED., THE NEW PALGRAVE DICTIONARY OF ECONOMICS AND THE LAW 17, 19 (1998). However, the empirical evidence advanced in support of this theory is weak. *Id.* at 21–22; *see also* Oona A. Hathaway, *Path Dependence in the Law: The Course and Pattern of Legal Change in a Common Law System*, 86 IOWA L. REV. 601 (2001).

Another explanation is based on a theory that law has an "expressive" function; that is, "that law influences behavior independent of the sanctions it threatens to impose" by providing "a focal point around which individuals can coordinate their behavior." *See* Richard H. McAdams, *A Focal Point Theory of Expressive Law*, 86 VA. L. REV. 1649, 1650–51 (2000). This theory may help to explain the persistence of standard contingency fee pricing. In a number of states, maximum contingency fees, usually one third, are set by statute or court rule. *See* Robert L. Rossi, ATTORNEY'S FEES, at § 2:10, 114–20 (2d ed. 1995). Because there is standard pricing, that maximum fee is also, in reality, the minimum fee. Thus, the legal expression of a maximum fee "provide[s] a focal point for coordinating individual action," by contingency fee lawyers; that is, it signals to lawyers that by acting in a coordinated fashion, they can maintain the maximum fee as the standard fee. McAdams, *A Focal Point Theory of Expressive Law, id.*, at 1666. "[T]he state can focus attention on one of several equilibrium solutions to a coordination game by commanding or merely recommending that individuals coordinate around that solution." *Id.* at 1663. "Each [lawyer] selects the salient strategy [of uniform contingent fee pricing] because they expect the other[s] to do the same and each has an interest in doing what the other[s] do." *Id.* at 1668.

16. *See* BEGG ET AL., ECONOMICS, *supra* note 2, at 162.

17. *See id.* at 35.

18. In addition to the structural impediments and ethical restrictions discussed *infra* that inhibit price competitive behavior, tort lawyers may also be reluctant to deviate from standard pricing out of concern that they will be ostracized by fellow tort lawyers. In addition to peer group approval concerns, lawyers may also fear that courts and disciplinary bodies would not look kindly on such fee "cheating" and would use their discretionary authority to punish them in more tangible ways.

19. *See Wylie v. Coxe*, 56 U.S. 415 (1853) (the first Supreme Court opinion to approve a contingent fee; though there was considerable risk, the contingent percentage was only 5%). In *Wright v. Tebbitts*, 91 U.S. 252 (1875), in which there was also considerable risk, the contingent percentage was 10%. In *Stanton v. Embrey*, 93 U.S. 548 (1876), the Court noted that the usual contingent fee was 20%–25%, *see id.* at 549, though in the matter before it, the fee was 5%. *See id.* at 556. In a will contest fraught with uncertainty, the contingent fee was 5%. *Schomp v. Schenck*, 40 N.J.L. 195 (1878) (plaintiff lawyer testified that the usual contingent fee for collection suits was 5%). In a personal injury action against a railroad, the contingent fee was 20%. *Benedict v. Stuart*, 23 Barb. 420 (N.Y. App. Div. 1856). Higher percentages were also charged. *See, e.g., Bayard v. McLane*, 3 Del. (3 Harr.) 139 (1840) (66%).

20. *See supra* Chapter 1, text at notes 14–17.

21. *See* Brickman, *Contingent Fees, supra* Introduction, note 18, at 30 n.1; *see also* ROBERT H. ARONSON, ATTORNEY-CLIENT FEE ARRANGEMENTS: REGULATION AND REVIEW 92 (1980).

22. *See* REPORT OF COMMITTEE ON CONTINGENT FEE, in 1907 NEW YORK STATE BAR ASSOCIATION 121; ANN. REP. OF SPECIAL COMMITTEE ON DESIRABILITY OF JUDICIAL REGULATION OF CONTINGENT FEES FOR 1937–38 TO THE ASSOCIATION OF THE BAR OF THE CITY OF NEW YORK 294 (1938):

    [T]he amount of the contingent fee … has become in the large majority of cases … 50 percent of the recovery…. For the first two or three decades after the legalization of the contingent fee, percentages were moderate, [*sic*] fifteen per cent. or twenty per cent. of the recovery was considered reasonable. This has grown until forty per cent is common, fifty per cent is not unusual, and sixty per cent has been known to have been charged.

    Id.

23. In New York, lawyers battled furiously to maintain 50% rates. After attempts by the New York legislature to cap tort lawyers' fees were successfully opposed by lawyer legislators, a New York intermediate appellate court promulgated a rule in 1960 essentially limiting contingency fees in personal injury cases to one-third. *See* 22 N.Y.C.R.R. § 603.7(e) (McKinney 2002); *Gair v. Peck*, 6 N.Y.2d 97, cert denied, 361 U.S. 374 (1960) (upholding the appellate division's fee-limiting rule as within the power of the court). The court's action infuriated tort lawyers who worked feverishly to overturn it. In opposing a legislative effort by tort lawyers to repeal the rule, the *New York Herald Tribune* in an editorial in 1960 stated that the court had "found that most of the lawyers in 150,000 contingency fees cases each year were hauling down 50 percent of amounts recovered for themselves. This, incidentally, seems to be pretty much the national picture." N.Y. HERALD TRIB., Mar. 23, 1960 (quoted in Note, *A Study of Contingent Fees in the Prosecution of Personal Injury Claims*, 33 INS. COUNSEL J. 197, 203 [1966]). In a rare loss for the lawyers, the rule prevailed.

Lawyers have devised ways to circumvent the rule, however, by allying with out-of-state lawyers to take the lead in settling mass tort claims.

24. *See, e.g.*, CAL. BUS. & PROF. CODE § 6146(a) (2002) ("MICRA") (limiting contingent fees in medical malpractice actions to 40% of the first $50,000 recovered, 33% of the next $50,000, 25% of the next $500,000, and 15% of any amount of recovery over $600,000); CONN. GEN. STAT. § 52–251c (b)(2001) (limiting contingent fees in personal injury, wrongful death, or damage to property claims to 33% of the first $300,000, 25% of the next $300,000, 20% of the next $300,000, 15% of the next $300,000, and 10% of any amount exceeding $1,200,000); FLA. STAT. ch.73.092 (2002) (capping contingent fees in eminent domain proceedings to 33% of any benefit up to $250,000, 25% of the benefit between $250,000 and $1,000,000, and 20% of any benefit exceeding $1,000,000); OKLA. STAT. tit.5 § 7 (2003) (limiting contingent fees to 50% of the net recovery); TENN. CODE ANN. § 29–26–120 (2002) (limiting contingent fees in medical malpractice cases to 33% of all damages awarded); TEX. LAB. CODE ANN. § 408.221 (Vernon 2002) (limiting contingent fees in workers compensation cases to 25% of the plaintiffs' recovery); WIS. STAT. § 655.013 (1986) (limiting contingent fees in medical malpractice cases to 33% or 25% of the first $1 million, depending on whether the liability is stipulated within a statutory deadline, and 20% of any amount over $1 million); WIS. STAT. § 102.26(2) (1993) (limiting contingent fees in workers compensation cases to 20% of disputed benefits). In social security cases, fees are typically limited to no more than 25% of back benefits up to a maximum of $4,000. *See* 42 U.S.C. § 406(a)(2) (2006).

25. *See, e.g.*, Bruce L. Hay, *Contingent Fees and Agency Costs*, 25 J. LEGAL STUD. 503, 513 n.6 (1996); Saul Levmore, *Commissions and Conflicts in Agency Arrangements: Lawyers, Real Estate Brokers, Underwriters, and Other Agents' Rewards*, 36 J. L. & ECON. 503, 505–06 (1991); Rudy Santore & Alan D. Viard, *Legal Fee Restrictions, Moral Hazard and Attorney Rents*, 44 J. I. & ECON. 549, 550 (2001).

26. *See, e.g.*, Charles Silver & Geoffrey P. Miller, *The Quasi-Class Action Methods of Managing Multi-District Litigations: Problems and a Proposal*, N.Y.U. Law & Econ. Research Paper No. 147 (Feb. 2009), *available at* http://www.ssrn.com/abstract=1352646.

27. *See, e.g.*, Zamir & Ritov, *Behavioral Analysis, supra* Chapter 2, note 1, at 6, 9, 36.

28. *Id.* at 36.

29. *See, e.g., id.* at 36–41.

30. *Id.*

31. *Id.* at 44.

32. *Id.* at 6, 44–45.

33. *Id.* at 45 (footnotes omitted).

34. *Id.* at 6–7.

35. *See* Chapter 8, § A.

36. *See, e.g.*, Arthur R. Miller, *The Pretrial Rush to Judgment: Are the "Litigation Explosion," "Liability Crisis," and Efficiency Clichés Eroding Our Day in Court and Jury Trial Commitments?* 78 N.Y.U. L. REV. 982 (2003); Marc Galanter, *An Oil Strike in Hell: Contemporary Legends About the Civil Justice System*, 40 ARIZ. L. REV. 717 (1998); Michael J. Saks, *Do We Really Know Anything About the Behavior of the Tort Litigation System – And Why Not?*, 140 U. PA. L. REV. 1147 (1992).

37. Stuart M. Speiser, LAWSUIT 570 (Horizon Press 1980).

38. Carl T. Bogus, *Introduction, Genuine Tort Reform*, 13 ROGER WILLIAMS UNIV. L. REV. 1, 6 (2008).

39. *See* Appendix I, Political Contributions by Tort Lawyers and the U.S. Chamber of Commerce.

40. Tort scholars' fidelity to a pro-tort expansion agenda may sometimes lead them to misinterpret data or misstate facts. *See* Gary T. Schwartz, *Empiricism and Tort Law*, 2002 U. ILL. L. REV. 1067, 1076 (2002). For example, one of the leading scholars advancing the pro-tort expansion agenda, Marc Galanter, coauthored an article in which he used the Ford Pinto case as support for an expansive punitive damages regime. *See* Marc Galanter & David Luban, *Poetic Justice: Punitive Damages and Legal Pluralism*, 42 AM. U. L. REV. 1393, 1436–38 (1993). Professor Gary Schwartz, who is squarely planted in the middle ground between pro-tort expansionists and pro-tort reformers, thoroughly debunked the claims of pro-tort expansionists with reference to the Ford Pinto case. *See* Gary T. Schwartz, *The Myth of the Ford Pinto Case*, 43 RUTGERS L. REV. 1013 (1991). Professor Schwartz criticized Galanter's account because it "invents facts about the case that are simply absent in the record of the case or in the court's opinion." Schwartz, *Empiricism and Tort Law*, at 1077.

41. A study of law professors' campaign contributions found that 74% contribute primarily to Democrats and only 16% do so to Republicans. *See* John O. McGinnis et al., *The Patterns and Implications of Political Contributions by Elite Law School Faculty*, 93 GEO. L.J. 1167, 1169–70 (2004–05); *see also* John O. McGinnis & Matthew Schwartz, *Conservatives Need Not Apply*, WALL ST. J., Apr. 1, 2003, at A14.

42. Tort lawyers also sponsor law school conferences – including those by the American Association for Justice's Roscoe Pound Institute – that seek to advance the AAJ's agenda. *See, e.g.*, Symposium, *of Litigation in America*, 47 DEPAUL L. REV. 227 (1998) (designed to generate scholarship in opposition to the "early offer" proposal that I and others have advanced; the proposal is reviewed in the Conclusion at §A); Symposium, *Genuine Tort Reform*, 13 ROGER WILLIAMS U. L. REV. 1 (2008).

6 Impediments Imposed by the Bar to Price Competition

EVEN THOUGH THE ANTICOMPETITIVE BEHAVIOR AND market failures addressed in Chapters 4 and 5 largely account for the lack of price competition, they do not sufficiently explain the persistence and pervasiveness of uniform contingency fee pricing. Absent additional factors, we would expect some tort lawyers to compete by advertising below market rates. We would also expect a variety of other market-based solutions to arise that would lead to price competition. In this chapter, I consider the bar's policies to prevent the rise of market mechanisms that would facilitate price competition.

To be sure, all occupational groups – not just lawyers – seek to limit price competition.[1] One of the most common strategies for professional groups is to prohibit business structures that would likely promote price competition under the guise of ethical rules. For example, the American Medical Association (AMA) long maintained that "it was unethical for physicians to join partnerships or other professional relationships with [nonphysicians] unless ownership remained solely in the hands of the licensed physicians."[2] These restrictions were justified in that they preserved the independent decision-making power of doctors and maintained high standards of medical care.[3] When this rule came under attack in 1975, a federal court of appeals rejected the AMA's justification and found that the restrictions "had the purpose and effect of restraining competition by [nonphysicians], and restricted physicians from developing business structures of their own choice."[4] Lawyers have an identical anticompetitive rule and justification, which appellate courts have upheld. If doctors sat on appellate courts, the outcomes might well be reversed.

The story of lawyers' use of ethical rules to restrain price competition begins more than 150 years ago. From the earliest days in the New World, lawyers fought to free themselves from legislative price regulation and to establish market-based pricing.[5] Once they achieved the right to freely negotiate prices with their clients, they sought to insulate themselves from market forces by restricting entry to the profession, banning competition from outside the profession, prohibiting the outright purchase of tort claims, and adopting ethical rules to preclude price competition, including rules prohibiting lawyers from providing financial assistance to tort clients and from engaging in the brokerage of lawyer services.

A. Barriers to Tort Market Entry

The legal profession's control over the market for tort claims is the beginning of any analysis of the impotency of market solutions to counter the lack of price competition.[6] This control is part of the broader monopolistic power that the profession exercises over the practice of law.[7] Technically, it is not lawyers qua lawyers who regulate the market for tort claims; rather, it is state supreme courts that have arrogated to themselves exclusive control over the practice of law.[8] One manifestation of this phenomenon[9] is that tort claimants who wish to sell a percentage of their claim to finance their pursuit have a limited market. Nonlawyers cannot be purchasers.[10] Many states – by rule or statute – prohibit the sale or assignment of tort claims or categorize such sales as illegally champertous.[11] All tort claims sellers are channeled to one class of purchaser – the lawyer-oligopsonist, thus insulating contingency fee lawyers from competition from nonlawyers for the purchase of tort claims.[12]

B. The Prohibition Against the Outright Purchase of Tort Claims

In a competitive market for contingency fee lawyers' services, attorneys would bid against each other for the right to a client's legal claim. Most commentators agree that this is the most efficient method for providing-tort representation.[13] This would enable injured parties to realize most of the initial value of tort claims because lawyers would be willing to pay some injured persons substantial sums for being hired on a standard contingency feebasis. Bidding for tort claims, however, is unethical – a prohibition that serves to protect lawyers from having to effectively disgorge some of their monopoly profits. State courts, which are protective of lawyers' interests, do not allow lawyers to either purchase tort claims or bid for clients.[14] Indeed, most state supreme courts have precluded the creation of a market for tort claims by prohibiting the sale of tort claims to anyone.[15] Whatever the historical bases for these restrictions, they are maintained today largely to inhibit price competition and to prevent tort-claim-purchasing entities from competing with lawyers.[16]

C. The Use of Ethical Rules to Preclude Price Competition

From 1887, when the first lawyers' code of ethics was adopted, to the present, restraint of price competition has been a central feature of the bar's ethical regimes.[17] The anticompetitive tone of these codes was set by David Hoffman, a leading American lecturer on law in the mid-nineteenth century. His Resolution XXVIII provided: "I shall regard as eminently dishonorable all underbidding of my professional brethren."[18] The United States Supreme Court, however, has interceded to strike down the bar's anticompetitive rules to limit price competition, including the use of mandated minimum fee schedules, prohibitions on advertising, and the prohibition against groups (such as labor unions) hiring lawyers to provide legal services to their individual members.[19] Despite the Court striking down these anticompetitive rules, many restraints on competition endure in the form of ethical rules.[20] Of particular concern are restraints

on financing tort claimants, business practices, and organizational structures that would facilitate price competition.

1. Prohibitions Against Providing Financial Assistance to Clients

Lawyers are permitted but not required to advance litigation costs, such
as filing fees, transcript costs, and expert witness fees. The ethical rule
requiring that clients remain liable for these advances, irrespective of
the outcome of the case, was largely ignored, and in 1983, the rule was
changed to allow repayment to be contingent on success of the claim.[21]
Providing financial assistance to clients (such as loaning them money
for living expenses), however, is a different kettle of fish. The ethical
rule here, which applies virtually exclusively to tort lawyers, prohibits
them from financially assisting their clients at any point in the litigation
process.[22] The ostensible purpose of these prohibitions is to protect clients from being enticed into selecting lawyers on the basis of offers of
subsidized living costs rather than other more "appropriate" criteria.[23]
It is not clients whom the prohibition seeks to protect, however. In the
absence of such a ban, lawyers would use offers of financial assistance,
based on the anticipated value of the claim, to bid against one another.[24]
This would negate the effects of the zero-based accounting scheme
(applying the contingency fee to the entire recovery even when the claim
already had substantial value at the time the lawyer was retained) and
drive down effective contingency fee rates. Indeed, for some high-value,
low-risk claims, lawyers would be willing to pay clients signing bonuses
as high as hundreds of thousands of dollars in exchange for the right to
represent them and charge a standard contingency fee.

2. Prohibitions Against Brokerage of Lawyers' Services

If the contingency fee market were truly competitive, the legal practice
equivalent of mortgage brokerages would likely emerge. Mortgage brokers serve as intermediaries between borrowers and banks, facilitating

the lending process by evaluating the borrower's financial circumstances and recommending and obtaining the lowest bank mortgage loan rates available to the lender.[25] Economies of scale enable them to obtain discounted mortgage rates from banks and other lenders, which they pass on to borrowers, thereby underselling the very same banks and lenders.[26] They derive income primarily from commissions paid by the lending banks as well as fees paid directly by the borrowers. In a competitive-contingency-fee personal injury market, we would expect a similar structure to emerge: the for-profit lawyer-broker.

The hypothetical "The Personal Injury People, Inc." (PIP) is an example of such a structure. Seizing on the public's recognition of the law profession's high degree of specialization and the public's paucity of knowledge about the quality of individual contingency fee lawyers, PIP would advertise that it will evaluate personal injury claims, and if it concludes that a claim has value, it would use its specialized knowledge to refer the claimant to the right attorney – one who is not only competent but whose specialty is appropriate for the case. In this hypothetical model, PIP would not charge the claimant a fee for this service; instead, PIP would collect a fee from the law firm to which the matter is referred – usually a percentage of the fee that the firm charges against the recovery. Typically, these referral fees are at least one-third of the referred lawyer's fee, though they can be as high as 50 percent. If the referred lawyer charges a standard one-third fee, and the referring lawyer's referral fee is one-third, then PIP's commission would amount to one-ninth of the recovery; if the commission were 50 percent, then that would amount to one-sixth of the recovery. To induce business, PIP may further advertise that it will rebate a portion of its fee to the claimant if there is a successful outcome, thus undercutting the standard price. More ominously from the perspective of the bar, if PIP's business model proved successful and it led to the formation of other contingent-fee-lawyer brokerages, PIP would likely seek to maintain or enlarge its market share by bargaining with some of the law firms to lower their standard contingency fee rates for PIP customers because of the volume of business supplied. If it succeeded in doing so, PIP might further advertise that it not only secures high-quality, specialized personal injury representation, but that PIP customers pay below standard contingency fee rates. Furthermore, they could assure consumers that by monitoring the lawyers selected, PIP will guard against reduced efforts. Thus, PIP's business model would likely lead to price competition and some amount of discounting from standard rates.

To ward off such price competition, the bar has promulgated ethics rules that effectively prohibit for-profit "lawyer referral services" (the term the bar uses to refer to PIP's brokering of lawyers' services). Additional restriction on not-for-profit lawyer referral services assure that they pose no threat of price competition.[27] Under the banner of ethics rules, the bar has declared the PIP model, R.I.P.[28]

D. The Use of Unauthorized Practice of Law Statutes

Lawyers also use statutes and rules prohibiting the "unauthorized practice of law" (UPL) to restrain price competition and prohibit insurance companies from entering settlement agreements with accident victims who have not retained lawyers. Lawyers argue that the purpose of UPL laws is to protect the public from incompetent nonlawyer providers. However, there has never been a groundswell of consumers demanding that they be protected from nonlawyers who provide low-level "legal" services at low cost. Moreover, there are no studies supporting the conclusion that nonlawyer service providers have harmed the public. To the contrary. Virtually every commentator who has written on the subject decries these anticonsumer laws, which are intended to and do drive up the cost of legal services.[29]

Consider how Jack Jones, an insurance adjuster, could provide an efficient service to accident victims. Jones has worked for several insurance companies, settling auto accident, slip-and-fall, and other such claims. After twenty years he decides to set up his own claim adjustment business, advertising that he will evaluate the merits of accident claims and negotiate a settlement with the insurance company for a fee of 10 percent of the settlement. If no acceptable settlement is offered, he will charge only $100 for his efforts. Jones is likely to do at least as well in most cases in which damages are less than $50,000 – and better in some – than would a lawyer, and he charges less than a third of what lawyers charge. So why don't we see Public Insurance Claims Adjuster signs sprouting up, as for example, they do in Europe?[30] Because the Bar has deemed this the unauthorized practice of law, lawyers are able to charge more by blocking competition from those like Jack Jones, who would charge less.[31]

Lawyers also seek to use UPL laws to prevent insurance companies from settling claims with accident victims unless they hire contingency fee lawyers. Recall that the Union Pacific Railroad offered Mary Corcoran $1.4 million to settle her claim arising out of the death of her husband. This offer was the result of a corporate policy to try to reach an early settlement of accident claims. Within a few days of an accident, railroad employees contact the injured person or the family of those killed to initiate discussion of settlement. Many of the offers of settlement are accepted, as was the case, ultimately, with Mary Corcoran. This policy, however, has not sat well with the torts bar. Each such settlement is a loss of a one-third or more contingency fee that tort lawyers would have received. Moreover, the railroad's offers of settlement make it likely that, had these victims been represented, lawyers could have collected their fees with little risk or investment. In addition, of course, using the zero-based accounting scheme, they would have applied their percentage fee to the entire recovery – not just to the amount by which they augmented the value of the claim.

Seeking to protect the positional advantages available to tort lawyers to extract these unearned profits, an Arkansas lawyer brought suit against the Union Pacific Railroad, seeking class action status for the approximately 300 persons who settled personal injury or wrongful death claims with Union Pacific between 1992 and 2005.[32] The suit alleged that offering settlements to unrepresented persons constitutes the unauthorized practice of law and violates the Arkansas Deceptive Practices Act. In 2008, an Arkansas state judge certified the class, allowing the suit to go forward.[33] The judge agreed with the lawyer's argument that those who settled were being cheated because if lawyers had represented them, the settlements would have been higher.[34] The clear intent here is to prohibit the railroad from settling any injury cases unless the claimants are represented by a lawyer. But it isn't claimants' interests that the lawyers are seeking to protect; it is lawyers' interests in their contingency fees. As for the claim that if lawyers were involved, settlements would be higher, it is belied by Mary Corcoran's experience. To be sure, lawyers would extract higher settlement offers in some cases, but simply acknowledging this without further explanation is deceptive. What the lawyer bringing the suit and the judge did *not* say is that represented claimants would end up with a *net* benefit. After payment of lawyers' fees and the higher medical care costs that lawyers induce, higher settlements would leave a substantial number of claimants worse off than if they settled their claims without hiring a lawyer.

Fortunately, the Arkansas Supreme Court reversed the class certification in 2009, finding that an individualized factual inquiry was necessary with regard to each class member, and therefore, their claims were not suited for class treatment.[35] However, the court did not reject the lower court's characterization of Union Pacific's early settlement policy as the unauthorized practice of law.

An even more stunning example of how lawyers have sought to use their effective control of the legal system to protect unearned gains – especially those realized through the zero-based accounting scheme – is how the bar put the kibosh on the Allstate Insurance Company's attempt to control accident costs. In the mid-1990s, Allstate instituted a program[36] based on the "early offer" proposal that I describe in the Conclusion at Section B(1). When Allstate learned that one of its insureds caused an accident, it sent a letter to the injured party, stating: "[Allstate] would like to share with you what you can expect during the processing of your claim" and indicating that it was sending an agent to discuss settlement of the claim.[37] Included was a brochure, "The Role of Attorneys in the Claim Process," in which Allstate posed a number of questions and answers. The key element was a subtle suggestion that the claimant not hire a lawyer until Allstate had a chance to make a settlement offer. Then, this paragraph appeared:

> If I don't get an attorney now, can I still get one later? You may hire an attorney at any time in the process. In each state, there is a time limit (generally no less than one year following the accident) for taking legal action against Allstate's policyholder. Before you decide to see an attorney, you may wish to seek an offer from Allstate first. If an attorney believes he or she can achieve a higher settlement, you can then see whether the attorney is able to accomplish that. And, you may wish to hire an attorney on the condition that the contingent fee apply only to the settlement amount in excess of what Allstate offered to you without the attorney's assistance.[38]

Allstate's purpose was clear. By making early settlement offers[39] before the injured party had hired a lawyer, it could lower its cost of settling claims. As discussed in Chapter 15 Section B(2), hiring a lawyer results in greatly inflated medical expenses, which benefit the lawyer and the doctor but not the client. Often, after subtraction of the one-third fee and the higher medical costs, there is no net benefit to the represented client; there may even be a net loss. Early settlements often generate substantial savings for responsible parties because they minimize lawyer-induced medical care costs and save on defense costs.

How did the bar react to this attack on its unearned fees? Despite the fact that Allstate was offering the same advice that an Illinois court said Mary Corcoran failed to heed, state attorneys general, bar associations, and others filed at least fifty-six lawsuits against Allstate in twenty-two states, contending that Allstate's practice was fraudulent, deceptive, illegal, and the unauthorized practice of law.[40] According to the rule of lawyers, explaining whether or when an individual may want to hire an attorney is legal advice and, therefore, is the practice of law. Only a lawyer is authorized to give advice as to whether and when you need to hire a lawyer. So Allstate was found guilty of engaging in the unauthorized practice of law, fined, and ordered to stop sending out its brochure. The lesson is plain. Don't mess with lawyers' fees, no matter how excessive.[41]

It is important to note that Allstate did not advise injured persons not to hire an attorney, but only to first hear the company's offer and then take the matter to an attorney to see if it was fair. Recall that Mary Corcoran did just that, but she did not have the benefit of the strategy – suggested by Allstate – that she negotiate a fee based on the value the attorney added to the claim. And, not having received the Allstate brochure, how would she know to negotiate a value-added fee? Well, by consulting a lawyer. But the lawyer she consulted, of course, gave her no such advice. Instead, he victimized her by having her sign a standard retainer agreement, cutting him in for a share of the offer that was already on the table. The states that went after Allstate did so to preserve lawyers' ability to do just that.

NOTES

1. *See* Deborah Rhode, *Why the ABA Bothers: A Functional Perspective on Legal Codes*, 59 TEX. L. REV. 689, 702 (1981) ("A principal force animating any occupation's efforts at self-regulation is a desire to minimize competition from both internal and outside sources.").
2. AM. ANTITRUST INST., CONVERGING PROFESSIONAL SERVICES: LAWYERS AGAINST THE MULTIDISCIPLINARY TIDE (Feb. 9, 2000), *available at* www.antitrustinstitute.org/books/multidisc.cfm.
3. *Id.*
4. *Am. Med. Ass'n v. FTC*, 638 F.2d 443, 449 (2d Cir. 1980), *aff'd by an equally divided court*, 455 U.S. 676 (1982). To forestall price competition, the optometry profession adopted an ethics rule barring its members from establishing offices in commercial locations (shopping centers) and from "engaging in the 'corporate practice' of optometry" – a prohibition that the Federal Trade Commission successfully challenged. *Michigan Optometric Ass'n*, 106 F.T.C. 342 (1985); *American Academy of Optometry, Inc.*, 108 F.T.C. 25 (1986). Anticompetitive ethical rules are not limited to the health care industry. Before the U.S. Supreme Court upheld a challenge to the restriction, the National Society of Professional Engineers maintained an ethics rule "barring members from engaging in competitive bidding." *National Society of Prof. Engineers v. U.S.*, 435 U.S. 679, 694–96 (1978). The association claimed that allowing

competitive bidding would promote cost-cutting measures and thus potentially endanger public safety. *Id.*

5. I Anton-Hermann Chroust, The Rise of the Legal Profession in America 159 (1965).

6. I use the terms "lawyers' control," "bar control," and "legal profession's control" interchangeably to refer, *inter alia*, to control over the practice of law exercised by courts, bar associations, disciplinary boards, and lawyers through collective actions to restrain price competition.

7. *See* Benjamin Hoorn Barton, *Why Do We Regulate Lawyers?: An Economic Analysis of the Justifications for Entry and Conduct Regulation*, 33 Ariz. St. L.J. 429, 483 (2001); Derek A. Denckla, *Nonlawyers and the Unauthorized Practice of Law: An Overview of the Legal and Ethical Parameters*, 67 Fordham L. Rev. 2581 (1999).

8. *See* Charles W. Wolfram, *Lawyer Turf and Lawyer Regulation – The Role of the Inherent-Powers Doctrine*, 12 U. Ark. Little Rock L. Rev. 1 (1989–90); Thomas Alpert, *The Inherent Power of the Courts To Regulate The Produce of Law: An Historical Analysis*, 32 Buffalo L. Rev. 525 (1983).

9. Other manifestations include entry restrictions and market-division strategies designed to limit competition within the profession. *See* Roger Cramton, *Delivery of Legal Services to Ordinary Americans*, 44 Case W. Res. L. Rev. 531, 551–52 (1994). In addition, ethical provisions prohibiting the aiding of the unauthorized practice of law and fee splitting also seek to preserve lawyers' monopolistic control over the dispensation of certain services and, as well, to maintain lawyers' primacy over other professional groups.

10. *See* Adam Scales, *Against Settlement Factoring? Market For Tort Claims Has Arrived*, 2002 Wis. L. Rev. 859, 897 (2002) (stating personal injury litigation constitutes "a very odd market – one with only a single buyer ... [and] usually only one seller").

Rules prohibiting the sale of tort claims are a subset of common law rules against alienation of choses in action. *See, e.g., Karp v. Seizer*, 132 Ariz. 599 (1982); J. B. Ames, *The Inalienability of Choses in Action*, in Lectures on Legal History 210 (1913); Walter W. Cook, *The Alienability of Choses in Action*, 29 Harv. L. Rev. 816 (1916); Jeffrey O'Connell & Janet Beck, *Overcoming Legal Barriers to the Transfer of Third-Party Tort Claims as a Means of Financing First-Party No-Fault Insurance*, 58 Wash. U. L.Q. 55 (1980). The persistence today of vestigial remnants of these prohibitions in the form of restrictions on the assignability of tort claims owes more to its utility as a means of precluding price competition in the tort claiming market than fidelity to tradition or policy. *See* Max Radin, *Maintenance by Champerty*, 24 Cal. L. Rev. 48, 66, 72, 78 (1935).

11. *See* MODEL RULES OF PROF'L CONDUCT, R.1.8 cmt.6 (2006) [hereinafter MODEL RULES] (explaining that the provisions of the Model Rules that prohibit lawyers from acquiring a proprietary interest in a subject of a pending litigation "has its basis in common law champerty and maintenance"); *see also* Michael Reese, *The Use of Legal Malpractice Claims as Security Under the UCC Revised Article 9, 20* REV. LITIG. 529, 534–35 (2001) (indicating that the UCC's prohibition of assigning security interests in a personal injury claim is a remnant of common law rules against maintenance and champerty). Because lawyers are able to, in effect, purchase a one-third (or more) share of tort claims via a contingency fee arrangement, only lawyers are permissible purchasers of tort claims.

12. *See* Patrick T. Morgan, Note, *Unbundling Our Tort Rights: Assignability for Personal Injury and Wrongful Death Claims*, 60 MO. L. REV. 683, 705 (2001) (restricting the partial sale of tort claims via contingent fee arrangements creates an uncompetitive marketplace for tort claims sellers).

13. *See, e.g.,* Bruce L. Hay, *Contingent Fees and Agency Costs*, 25 J. LEGAL STUD. 503, 513 n.6 (1996); Rudy Santore & Alan D. Viard, *Legal Fee Restrictions, Moral Hazard and Attorney Rents*, 44 J. L. & ECON. 549 (2001); Saul Levmore, *Commissions and Conflicts in Agency Arrangements: Lawyers, Real Estate Brokers, Underwriters, and Other Agents' Rewards*, 36 J. L. & ECON. 503, 522–23 (1991) ("[T]he optimal arrangement between lawyer and client from the perspective of reducing agency costs would be for contingency fee lawyers to "bid for clients, with the winning lawyer naming the highest x and receiving a standard percentage [such as 80%, for example] above x."); Marc J. Shukaitis, *A Market in Personal Injury Tort Claims*, 16 J. LEGAL STUD. 329, 331 (1987) [hereinafter Shukaitis, *Market in Tort Claims*]; Kevin M. Clermont & John D. Currivan, *Improving on the Contingent Fee*, 63 CORNELL L. REV. 529, 596–97 (1978).

14. *See* MODEL RULES, *supra* note 11, at R.1.8(j); Santore & Viard, *Legal Fee Restrictions supra*, at 551–56; Shukaitis, *Market in Tort Claims, supra*, at 329–30. Prohibitions against bidding for clients are typically in the form of ethical rules prohibiting provision of financial assistance to clients, see infra Section C(1), paying anything of value to anyone for recommending a lawyer, see MODEL RULES, *supra* note 11, at R. 7.2(c) or operating for-profit lawyer referral services. For a detailed discussion of the ethical rules prohibiting for-profit lawyer referral services, see Lester Brickman, *The Market for Contingent Fee-Financed Tort Litigation: Is It Price Competitive?*, 25 CARDOZO L. REV. 65 (2003) [hereinafter Brickman, *Contingent Fee Market*].

15. *See, e.g., TMJ Hawaii, Inc. v. Nippon Trust Bank*, 153 P.3d 444 (Haw. 2007); *North Bend Senior Citizens Home, Inc. v. Cook*, 623 N.W.2d 681 (Neb. 2001); *Beaty v. Hertzberg & Golden, P.C.*, 571 N.W.2d 716 (Mich. 1997).

16. Hay, *Agency Costs, supra* note 13, at 513 n.6; Santore & Viard, *Legal Fee Restrictions, supra* note 13, at 550; CHARLES WOLFRAM, MODERN LEGAL ETHICS 507 (1986); Samuel R. Gross, *We Could Pass a Law ... What Might Happen If Contingent Fees Were Banned*, 47 DEPAUL L. REV. 321, 325–28 (1998); Radin, *Maintenance by Champerty, supra* note 10, at 66.

17. The first lawyer's code of ethics was adopted in 1887 at Albany, New York. H. DRINKER, LEGAL ETHICS 23 (1953). In the same year, the Alabama bar also adopted an ethics code. ALA. STATE BAR ASS'N CODE OF ETHICS (1887).

18. DAVID HOFFMAN, A COURSE OF LEGAL STUDY 752–75 (2d ed. 1836).

19. *See Bates v. State Bar*, 433 U.S. 350, 384 (1977) (holding that a rule prohibiting lawyers from advertising violates the First Amendment); *Goldfarb v. Virginia State Bar*, 421 U.S. 773, 793 (1975) (ruling that minimum fee schedules violate antitrust laws); Kenneth L. Penegar, *The Professional Project: A Response to Terrell and Wildman*, 41 EMORY L.J. 473, 477 (1992) (stating that the bar's traditional anticompetitive practices included minimum fee schedules and prohibitions on advertising).

20. Though the focus of this chapter is on the use of ethical rules to preclude price competition in the contingency fee bar, defense lawyers also invoke such rules for anticompetitive purposes. For example, insurance companies have been forcing defense lawyers' fees down by limiting legal defense costs through billing and litigation management guidelines. Defense lawyers have struck back at these fee-depressing actions by invoking various sections of the Model Rules of Professional Conduct in an attempt to declare such guidelines as unethical. In at least one instance, a state supreme court has concurred. *See In re* Rules of Prof'l Conduct and Insurer Imposed Billing Rules and Procedures, 2 P.3d 806 (Mont. 2000). A number of bar associations have also opined in favor of defense lawyers' attempts to limit the ability of insurance companies to mandate practices that have the effect of limiting lawyers' fees. *See* Amy S. Moats, Note, *A Bermuda Triangle in the Tripartite Relationship: Ethical Dilemmas Raised by Insurers' Billing and Litigation Management Guidelines*, 105 W. VA. L. REV. 525 (2003).

21. *See* MODEL RULES, *supra* note 11, at R.1.8(e) (1983).

22. *See id.*; MODEL CODE OF PROF'L RESPONSIBILITY DR 5–103(B) (1983). For a detailed analysis of the origins of the rules prohibiting financial assistance to clients and of the policies cited in support of the rule, see James E. Moliterno, *Broad Prohibition, Thin Rational: The "Acquisition of an Interest and Financial Assistance in Litigation" Rules*, 16 GEO. J. LEGAL ETHICS 223 (2003). For a sympathetic treatment of advancement of living expenses, see Jack P. Sahl, *The Cost of Humanitarian Assistance: Ethical Rules and the First Amendment,* 34 ST. MARY'S L.J. 795 (2003). For a detailed discussion of

states' rules regulating payment of living costs advancements to clients, see Brickman, *Contingent Fee Market, supra* note 14, at 119 n.179 (2003).

23. *See Attorney Grievance Committee v. Kandel*, 563 A.2d 387, 390 (Md. 1989) ("An important public policy interest is to avoid unfair competition among lawyers on the basis of their expenditures to clients. Clients should not be influenced to seek representation based on the ease with which monies can be obtained."); *In re Carroll*, 602 P.2d 461, 467 (Ariz. 1979) ("[T]he practice of making advances to clients, if publicized, would constitute an improper inducement for clients to employ an attorney ... [B]etween a lawyer who offers such an agreement and a lawyer who does not, the client will choose the lawyer who offers the lesser financial obligation.").

24. *See, e.g., Attorney AAA v. The Mississippi Bar*, 735 So. 2d 294, 299 (Miss. Sup. Ct. 1999) (restrictions against providing financial assistance to clients "are rationally related to the legitimate interest of the state in avoiding bidding wars"); *Mississippi Bar v. Attorney HH*, 671 So. 2d. 1293, 1298 (Miss. 1996) ("[U]nregulated lending to clients [to provide financial assistance while a tort claim is being pursued] would generate unseemly bidding wars for cases."); Kentucky Bar Association, Op. E-375 (1995) (reaffirming the state's ban on advances for living and medical expenses after noting that "dropping the time-honored rule will invite bidding by lawyers for clients"); *see also* Brickman, *Contingent Fees, supra* Introduction, note 18, at 107 n.317 (1989).

25. *See* Robert Buss, *Use Caution in Picking a Mortgage Broker*, CHI. TRIB., Nov. 13, 1998, at 2G (stating that mortgage brokers act as middlemen during the real estate loan process, taking borrowers' applications, shopping them around to various lenders seeking the best loan terms, and finally collecting a commission for a successful matchmaking). For how mortgage brokers operate, see Edwin McDowell, *A Booming Business in Selling Money*, N.Y. TIMES, Dec. 2, 2001, at § 11, 1; Jane Bryant Quinn, *Mortgage Shopping Still Wise for Home Buyers*, CHI. TRIB., Dec. 17, 1990, at Bus. 9. The business of brokering home mortgages arose in the aftermath of the deregulation of the home mortgage industry. *See Brokers Look for the Best Deal*, EVENING POST (Wellington, Australia) (predicting a rise in the number of mortgage brokers in Australia, as has occurred in the United States, due, in large part, to the deregulation of the banking industry).

26. *See* Kenneth R. Harney, *Citicorp Arouses Mortgage Bankers' Ire*, BARRON'S, June 27, 1988, at 81.

27. For a detailed discussion of the ethical rules prohibiting for-profit lawyer referral services, see Brickman, *Contingent Fee Market, supra* note 14.

28. *Requiescat in Pace* (rest in peace) is a prayer for the repose of a dead person.

29. *See, e.g.*, CHARLES WOLFRAM, MODERN LEGAL ETHICS, § 15.1.1 (1986); Charles Wolfram, *The ABA & MDPS: Context, History and Process*, 84 MINN. L.

REV. 1625 (2000); Deborah L. Rhode, *Policing the Professional Monopoly: A Constitutional and Empirical Analysis of Unauthorized Practice Prohibitions*, 34 STAN. L. REV. 1 (1981–82).

30. In the Netherlands, for example, nonlawyer "claims agents" can represent the interests of personal injury victims. See Niels J. Phillipsen & Michael G. Faure, *Fees for Claim Settlement in the Field of Personal Injury: Empirical Evidence from the Netherlands*, 1 J. EUROPEAN TORT LAW 75, at n. 15 (2010).

31. One court has gone even further by declaring unconstitutional a detailed legislative scheme that regulated and licensed insurance adjusters to negotiate property loss claims of policyholders against their insurance companies. See *Professional Adjusters, Inc. v. Tandon*, 433 N.E. 2d 779, 883 (Ind. 1982).

32. TRIAL, July 2008, at A19.

33. *Vickers v. Union Pac. R.R.*, No. CV-05–5–2 (Ark. Lafayette County Cir. Ct. Apr. 11, 2008).

34. *Id.* at ¶¶ 13, 37.

35. *Union Pac. R.R. v. Vickers*, No. CV-09–5–2 (Ark. Sup. Ct. May 7, 2009).

36. John Budlong, *Domino Strategy*, TRIAL, June 2001, at 20 (discussing Allstate's Claims Core Process Redesign).

37. *See* Allstate letter (on file with the author).

38. Allstate, The Role of Attorneys in the Claim Process, circa 1995 (on file with the author).

39. Allstate's "early offer" practice is modeled after a proposal that I and others advanced (the Brickman-Horowitz-O'Connell "early offer" plan), which is mentioned in the Introduction and laid out in further detail in the Conclusion at § B(1).

40. *See, e.g., Commonwealth of Pennsylvania v. Allstate Ins. Co.*, No. 1009 M.D. 1998 Commonwealth Ct. of Pa. (Apr. 2, 2001); *In re Unauthorized Practice of Law Complaint v. Allstate Ins. Co.*, Case No. 001–97, W. Va. State Bar Com. on Unlawful Practice (Sept. 22, 1997). In Pennsylvania, West Virginia, and other states, Allstate's distribution of the brochure was found to be unlawful because it constituted the unauthorized practice of law.

41. This massive assault on the Allstate Insurance Company is part of a concerted effort by tort lawyers and their political supporters to soften up the insurance companies and make them more amenable to settle cases on terms favorable to plaintiffs and their lawyers. The American Association for Justice (AAJ), the trade association of the tort lawyers, has issued a report titled, *"The Ten Worst Insurance Companies in America: How They Raise Premiums, Deny Claims and Refuse Insurance to those Who Need it Most." See* www.justice.org/docs/ TenWorstInsuranceCompanies.pdf. AAJ's mission is "to put insurance companies on the defensive by exposing how they put profit over policyholders." *Allstate is worst insurer for consumer, new AAJ report finds*, TRIAL, Sept. 2008,

at 12. This populist tactic seeks to capitalize on the public's negative perceptions of insurance companies. It is undeniable that insurance companies often
adapt intransigent settlement positions to delay – if not deny – valid claims. But
the AAJ is seeking to force insurance companies to be more pliable across the
board. Lawyers' profits will increase, but so too will the cost of insurance for
most consumers.

7 The Effects of Incentives Created by Contingency Fees

TO THIS POINT, I HAVE ARGUED THAT TORT LAWYERS USE anticompetitive practices and ethical rules to obtain unearned profits. In this chapter, I explain how contingency fees affect lawyers' behavior. In Chapter 8, I shift my focus from the atomistic level to a broader examination of the effects of contingency fees on our civil justice system. Some of these effects contribute to public welfare, but others are perverse and diminish public welfare.

Contingency fees generally align the interests of lawyers with the interests of their clients because the size of the lawyer's fee depends on the amount of the client's recovery.[1] Nonetheless, contingency fees may also induce lawyers to recommend that clients accept inferior settlement offers when the additional investment of time required to raise the offer would result in diminishing effective hourly returns. This reflects the fact that a contingency fee lawyer, like any entrepreneurial investor, tailors her effort to the size of the expected reward.[2] Thus, a contingency fee lawyer who will earn $100,000 if she prevails and nothing if she loses will, in most cases, expend proportionately more effort than a lawyer who will only earn $10,000 if she prevails.[3] Raise the stakes from $100,000 to $1 million, however, and it is unlikely that the lawyer's effort will continue to increase proportionately with the increased stake. When stakes reach $10 million, the additional effort expended will likely be considerably less than ten times the effort when the stakes were $1million.[4] As the stakes increase even more, the

107

increased incentive to prevail may induce other consequences beyond additional effort.[5]

In this chapter, I consider some of these "other consequences." To begin, I reprise some of the literature on the potential dangers of lawyers having a direct personal interest in the outcome of the litigation. The first danger I address is that lawyers will resort to "undesirable" practices to obtain fees. I then draw an analogy between stock options for corporate executives – and their perverse effects – and contingency fees for lawyers to illustrate the potential dangers of "too high" incentives. I continue with an explanation of the ostensible versus real reasons for prohibiting contingency fees in criminal representation. Further, I identify fraudulent practices induced by contingency fee profits and specifically address why lawyers engage in "ambulance chasing" and the modern day equivalent, litigation screenings. I conclude the chapter by arguing that the question of whether contingency fees induce frivolous litigation is itself frivolous because it detracts from the focus on the improper incentives created by contingency fees.

A. "Undesirable Practices"

Financial incentives are the foundation of our capitalist economy. When these incentives induce social harms, we react by enacting legislation and establishing regulatory commissions to tame unbridled capitalism. The financial incentives unleashed by contingency fee financing of tort litigation fill a vital social need – access to the civil justice system – but they also distort the civil justice system and impose costs on both individual consumers and society.

Recognition that contingency fees are potentially corrupting extends as far back as Roman law and has continued ever since.[6] For example, in a series of lectures delivered while at the University of Pennsylvania in the 1850s, George Sharswood, one of the leading voices of the American legal profession in the mid-nineteenth century, observed that:

> a [contingent fee] contract changes entirely the relation of counsel to the cause. It reduces him from his high position of an officer of

the court and a minister of justice, to that of a party litigating his own claim. Having now a deep personal interest in the event of the controversy, he will cease to consider himself subject to the ordinary rules of professional conduct ... be tempted to make success, at all hazards and by all means, the sole end of his exertions ... [and become] blind to the merits of the case.[7]

B. Stock Options and Contingency Fees

Stock options create some of the same incentives as contingency fees and serve as a useful illustration of how profit incentives can actually produce perverse effects. In recent years, stock options for corporate executives have been heralded as "the simplest and most effective method of aligning th[e] interests [of CEOs and shareholders]."[8] By tying executive compensation directly to the performance of the company's stock, corporations create financial incentives for corporate officers to manage the company in ways that maximize the stock price to the benefit of all shareholders.[9] Recent corporate scandals, however, demonstrate that these stock options over-incentivize some executives and motivate them to manipulate stock prices by creating short-term profits, which later expose the company to enormous losses. As characterized by one commentator, "[h]ighly incentivized executives ... lied about corporate profits and assets to keep stock prices up long enough for them to sell their shares."[10] In doing so, the executives often made millions while the shareholders and rank-and-file employees who invested in 401(k) plans watched their savings disappear.[11] The moral of this story is that excessive financial incentives – in any form – can produce perverse outcomes.[12]

C. The Prohibition of Contingency Fees in Criminal Representation

From the beginning, contingency fees were prohibited because of fears that the financial incentives to maximize their clients' recoveries would tempt advocates to act unethically. Though the billions of dollars in fees generated by tort litigation during modern times have muted these criticisms,[13] the concern that contingency fee incentives may generate unethical and possibly illegal action is nonetheless reflected in a variety of our policies.

The ethical rule prohibiting contingency fees in criminal cases is ostensibly justified on liquidity concerns and conflict-of-interest grounds; in fact, the actual basis for this prohibition is the fear of unleashed incentives caused by contingency fees.[14] First, this ban is justified because "legal services in criminal cases do not produce an asset (called a *res*[15]) with which to pay the fee."[16] This justification is inadequate,[17] however, because there are criminal cases in which there is a *res*. For example, the government may seek to take away assets that are allegedly the product of the criminal enterprise; a successful defense can leave the defendant in possession of a substantial *res* from which to pay the contingency fee.[18] There are also cases in which a defendant may be blocked from inheriting an estate or recovering life insurance proceeds unless he is acquitted in a related criminal prosecution.[19] The implausibility of the *res* rationale is further illustrated by the fact that there is no prohibition on civil attorneys charging contingency fees in cases without a *res*.[20]

Another justification for the ban is that contingency fees would create a conflict of interest for criminal defense attorneys. Consider the example of a retainer agreement that provides that a fee is only payable in the event of an acquittal. The lawyer may have a financial interest to recommend that the defendant accept or reject a plea bargain offer, even if that is not in the best interest of the defendant.[21] By structuring retainer agreements to account for various possible outcomes, however, including plea bargains and conviction of lesser offenses or mixing contingency fee elements with hourly rates or set fees, conflicts of interest can be minimized. An outright ban is overkill if this ostensible justification were the actual justification. Indeed, if we were so concerned about conflicts of interest created by fee arrangements, we would restrict or prohibit defense attorneys from the common practice of charging a flat fee up front.[22] When the attorney receives the entire fee up front, he may have an incentive to devote less time to the case or seek a plea bargain as quickly as possible.

Some scholars suggest that the absolute prohibition of contingency fees in criminal prosecutions reflects a concern that criminal defense attorneys are less ethical than their civil counterparts.[23] There is, however, no evidence to support this view.[24] The real reason for the prohibition is our fear of the effects of unleashed incentives on our criminal justice system. Our society puts greater importance on the process of determining guilt or innocence in a criminal prosecution than the outcome of a civil proceeding. So although we recognize that some lawyers will act unethically or illegally if the financial stakes are high enough,[25] we are more willing to tolerate a risk of unethical or illegal lawyer behavior in civil cases than in criminal cases.[26]

A similar concern underpins the U.S. Treasury's prohibition against tax practitioners charging contingency fees for preparing original tax returns or for providing advice in connection with positions taken in such returns[27] – a provision that the Treasury has recently extended.[28] As in the case of contingency fees in criminal representation, the concern is that contingency fees would give lawyers "too high" an incentive to go "too far," resulting in significant losses of tax revenue.

D. Fraudulent Practices

Fraudulent schemes abound because of their profitability and the proliferation of wealth in our society. The legal profession has its own share of fraud, though there is no data indicating that lawyers have any greater (or lesser) propensity to engage in fraud than other occupational groups. Lawyers' fraud takes many shapes. Embezzlement of client funds probably accounts for a majority of defrauded funds. Fraudulent practices associated with contingency fees simply reflect the fact that the transfers of vast sums of money in the tort system provide abundant opportunities for dishonest lawyers.

One such recurring fraudulent activity involves staging phony auto accidents to collect from insurance companies. Medical insurance fraud is another recurrent theme.[29] In another typical scam, the lawyer pays a "capper" to bring in potential plaintiffs who sign standard contingent fee agreements. The lawyer then sends the client to a medical provider – often a chiropractor – who submits a claim to an insurance company. The medical provider receives the medical portion of the insurance settlement, the lawyer takes the contingency fee, and the client receives the remainder. The medical provider then kicks back nearly 50 percent of his share of the settlement to the lawyer in exchange for referral of the patient. Another scheme involves contingency fee lawyers bribing insurance company adjusters to obtain faster and higher settlement awards.[30] Still another scheme occurs when lawyers scan police band radios for accidents and dispatch "runners" to the scene. They hand out leaflets with phone numbers and encourage passengers to say they suffered from back and neck injuries, which are subjective in nature and therefore hard to disprove.[31]

Finally, no account of contingency-fee-inspired fraud can neglect the efforts of Morris Eisen, whose personal injury firm was once among New York City's top ten. Eisen was sentenced to five years in prison for numerous frauds against the city. Among his schemes were bribing a witness to falsely testify about an event (the accident took place while the witness was in jail), enlarging a pothole before photographing it, using a scaled-down ruler to make a pothole appear larger in a photograph and taking a sledgehammer to a new tire rim to create evidence of dents.[32] In one year, Eisen's firm grossed $20 million in contingency fees.[33]

Even though it accounts for hundreds of millions of dollars in illegitimate payments, fraud is only a minor factor in toting up the costs of contingency fees.

E. "Ambulance Chasing"

"Ambulance chasing" occurs when tort lawyers use "runners" or other agents – such as nurses or ambulance drivers – to solicit legitimate accident victims or their families. This practice, which originated more than eighty years ago, violates ethical rules prohibiting lawyers from paying agents to solicit business.[34] Some runners receive illegal payments totaling more than $450,000 per year[35] – a sure signal that contingency fees are generating super profits. The profit potential has inspired new creativity. After the August 1987 crash of a commercial airline flight in Detroit, a man posing as a Roman Catholic priest, Father John Irish, appeared at the scene to console the families of the victims. Father Irish "didn't offer Mass or give a priestly blessing."[36] Instead, he "hugged crying mothers and talked with grieving fathers of God's rewards in the hereafter ... Then he would hand them the business card of [a] Florida attorney ... urge them to call the lawyer, and disappear."[37]

Lawyers engage in ambulance chasing to capture windfall fees in personal injury cases. Many of these cases pose no meaningful risk and are unlikely to require any substantial investment of time in order to obtain a settlement. The practice, which occasionally generates significant sanctions for lawyers,[38] is universally condemned.[39] The condemnations are mostly for show, however.[40] The ostensible reason for the public condemnation is that the practice takes advantage of accident victims who may be suffering ill effects of the accident and thus may not be fully cognizant of what they are doing.[41] As stated in a rule adopted by the Florida Supreme Court to prohibit the solicitation of accident victims and their families within thirty days of the incident:

> There is potential for abuse inherent in direct solicitation by a lawyer of prospective clients known to need legal services [because a] prospective client often feels overwhelmed by the situation giving rise to the need for legal services and may have an impaired capacity for reason, judgment, and protective self-interest. Furthermore, the lawyer seeking the retainer is faced with a conflict stemming from the lawyer's own interest, which may color the advice and representation offered the vulnerable prospect.[42]

This rationale, however, does not survive analysis. Contingency fee rates are the same regardless of how the client comes to retain a lawyer. Accident victims may have been induced to hire lawyer A, who solicited them, instead of lawyer B, whom they might have hired had they not been rushed to a decision by the solicitation. But there is no indication that accident victims are induced to sign more onerous retainer agreements with lawyer A than lawyer B because all lawyers in that community charge the same contingency fee percentage. In fact, the prohibition is in place for two reasons. First, as a way of restraining trade: If ambulance drivers and hospital employees were allowed to realize the fair market value of their access to those in need of legal assistance, those costs would be borne by tort lawyers, thus diminishing their profits. Second, ambulance chasing focuses unwanted attention on unjustifiable profits from contingency fees. Rather than acknowledge that charging standard contingency fees in cases without meaningful risk is an abusive fee practice, the legal profession condemns the practice of sole practitioners paying agents to sign up tort victims.

For similar reasons, the legal profession prohibits in-person solicitation of accident victims. On its face, this prohibition appears to be aimed at a pernicious practice: lawyers taking advantage of vulnerable accident victims. Here too, however, the prohibition more often serves as a way of singling out the bar for special privileges and for diverting attention from abusive fee practices. Consider the leading case of *Ohralik v. Ohio State Bar Assn.*,[43] in which the United States Supreme Court upheld the right of a state supreme court to promulgate a blanket prohibition of in-person solicitation of clients by lawyers irrespective of whether the client was disadvantaged by the lawyer's actions. Concerned about the low esteem of the legal profession, the Court carved out a special exemption for rule making by the legal profession from the protections accorded to commercial speech that apply to all other professional regulation.[44] This special treatment also allowed the Ohio Supreme Court and bar to ignore certain seamy conduct by Albert Ohralik, a lawyer, which is all too prevalent in the profession, by finding that he had violated Ohio's antisolicitation rule, when in fact that was among the least of his transgressions.

On February 2, 1974, two young women, Carol McClintock and a passenger in her car, Wanda Lou Holbert, were in a serious automobile accident.[45] The driver of the other vehicle – who was responsible for the accident – was uninsured. McClintock's policy provided for $12,500 of uninsured motorist coverage. On February 13, 1974, while at the Post Office, Ohralik learned about the accident[46] and proceeded to the hospital where McClintock was undergoing treatment for her injuries.[47] While at the hospital, Ohralik reviewed with McClintock the legal merits of her claim and the need for proper representation and obtained her oral consent to represent her.[48] Two days later, he obtained her signature on a retainer agreement.[49]

Ohralik then drove directly to McClintock's parents' house, where he reviewed the insurance papers with her parents – a conversation he secretly recorded.[50] He also obtained the address and directions to Holbert's home.[51] Holbert – who was eighteen years old at the time – admitted Ohralik to her home, where he advised her that he represented her friend McClintock and that he had a "tip" for her: that she had a substantial legal claim for her injuries and that he could provide her with the legal services necessary to capitalize on her claim.[52] He persuaded Holbert to orally engage him as her attorney in the matter.[53] Again, Ohralik had a concealed tape recorder and recorded the conversation.[54] The following day, Ohralik telephoned Holbert in order to formalize the client-attorney relationship.[55] However, Holbert's mother answered the phone and unceremoniously advised him that his services were not desired. Ohralik protested that it was not she but her daughter, a competent consenting adult, who was his client.[56] No formal document was ever signed.

Over the next few days, Ohralik contacted the other driver and McClintok's insurance carrier, seeking payment of the uninsured motorist coverage. McClintock attempted to reach Ohralik but was unable to contact him. Though in a body cast, she had a friend drive her to Ohralik's home.[57] Following that meeting, McClintock decided to terminate her relationship with Ohralik and retain another lawyer. Ohralik, despite receiving a letter terminating his services, maintained he was owed one-third of the $12,500 payment to be made by the insurance company.[58] Later, Ohralik filed suit against McClintock for $4,166.66 and also filed for an injunction to prevent the insurance company from paying McClintock. McClintock was forced to settle Ohralik's claim and paid him $4,100.[59]

Holbert also terminated Ohralik less than a month after Ohralik secretly recorded his conversation with her in which she agreed to retain him. Holbert testified that she was unable to obtain payment from the insurance company due to Ohralik's involvement. Ohralik demanded $2,466.66 and threatened suit if she did not pay. As evidence of a binding agreement with Holbert, Ohralik produced the surreptitious tape recording of his conversation with her. Nonetheless, he eventually abandoned his claim because the contract "[originated] in a controversy."[60] Holbert retained other counsel to pursue her claim, and McClintock sought the help of an attorney to file her complaint against Ohralik.

Charging Ohralik with a violation of the antisolicitation rule allowed the Ohio Supreme Court to avoid having to come uncomfortably close to condemning commonly used tort lawyers' tactics. For example, Ohralik charged a standard contingency fee, one-third, in a case where there was no issue of liability. Indeed, given the medical bills, lost wages, seriousness of the accident, and clear culpability of the other driver, McClintock's claim for the full policy limit of $12,500 was never in doubt. There was no meaningful contingency. Charging Ohralik with an ethical violation because he charged a patently unreasonable one-third fee, however, would have focused attention on the routine practice of tort lawyers' charging standard contingency fees in cases where there is no issue of liability and the presentation of the claim for full policy limits is mostly an administrative procedure. Better from the profession's point of view to charge Ohralik with in-person solicitation than to condemn a common practice of tort lawyers.

Second, Ohralik secretly taped his conversation with his intended clients – indicating that he was aware that, at best, they were reluctantly consenting to retaining him. This transgression was amplified when Ohralik refused to be terminated by both accident victims after he had used door-to-door sales techniques to sign them up. Ohralik followed up this egregious act by sending letters to State Farm and filing motions with the intent to coerce his clients to pay him – a clear violation of his fiduciary obligation.

Finally, Ohralik sued McClintock for one-third of her recovery and threatened to sue Holbert as well. McClintock's decision to pay Ohralik one-third of her recovery, which was done after she retained other counsel and incurred another fee, simply reflects the reality of how most tort clients fare when they have disputes with their lawyers. Had McClintock not settled, she would almost certainly have met the same fate in the Ohio courts as Mary Corcoran met in the Illinois courts.

F. The Modern Form of Ambulance Chasing: Litigation Screenings

Ambulance chasing, even as part of an organized ring, is penny ante when compared to its modern incarnation – the "litigation screening."[61] In a litigation screening, potential litigants who have been exposed to, ingested, or were implanted with harmful products are solicited through mass mail, television, Internet, and newspaper advertisements, providing "1-800" telephone numbers. These Internet Web sites purport to provide medical information about toxic exposures, drugs, or specific diseases, but the information is often "overwhelmingly biased and misleading."[62] In fact, many of these sites are actually "fronts" for law firms to which visitors are referred. Potential litigants are invited to a strip mall, motel room, union hall, or lawyer's office, where a doctor or medical technician administers tests and, in some cases, performs a cursory physical examination in order to generate medical evidence of an illness or injury. The "medical evidence" – which serves no medical purpose – is solely used for litigation purposes.[63]

Lawyers hire doctors – often through the screening companies – who are willing to mass-produce mostly unreliable and arguably fraudulent medical reports in exchange for fees ranging into the millions of dollars. Some of these litigation doctors provide thousands, even tens of thousands, of medical reports to advance the scheme to mass-produce litigants.[64] I estimate that lawyers have spent around $1 billion to sponsor screenings in the asbestos, silica, fen-phen (diet drugs), silicone breast implants, and welding fume litigations, garnering fees of $13 billion to $14 billion.[65] Each of the service providers involved in a screening – the paralegals, litigation doctors, medical technicians, employees, and owners of the screening companies – are acutely aware that if the screenings do not generate enough litigants, the lawyers will simply hire others who can do the job more effectively. Indeed, the market for litigation screenings is highly competitive. Only those doctors and screening companies that produce the "right" results can expect to generate substantial fees.

In nonmalignant asbestos litigation, the "right" results are staggering. Clinical studies of the effects of occupational exposure to asbestos on pulmonary health demonstrate that approximately 40 of each 1,000 exposed workers contract asbestosis.[66] Nonetheless, litigation doctors – who generate the majority of the medical reports prepared for asbestos litigation – find approximately 550 out of 1,000 screened workers have asbestosis.[67] Settlement values for these cases have ranged from $30,000 to $150,000.[68] Thus, at $50,000 per claim, the "excess" diagnoses have generated $25 million per 1,000 workers screened – a tidy sum when you consider that approximately 700,000 potential litigants participated in asbestos litigation screenings.

Litigation screenings violate the same ethical rule as does ambulance chasing, namely that prohibiting lawyers from paying someone to recruit clients for them. In litigation screenings, lawyers pay screening companies to round up thousands of potential litigants who must sign a retainer agreement with the law firm that is sponsoring the screening in order to be screened. Nonetheless, the routine and widespread practice of paying screening companies to solicit hundreds of thousands of clients for lawyers incurs no disciplinary response.[69] One explanation for the failure to condemn this practice is that, whereas ambulance chasing generates mere millions of dollars in fees, litigation screenings generate billions of dollars. The failure of the bar, disciplinary agencies, courts,[70] and prosecutors to sanction, let alone condemn, the practice of litigation screenings is a measure of the powerful influence exerted by lawyers, armed with vast profits from tort litigation. Once again, the take-away here is that when billions of dollars of fees are at stake, money talks and ethics walks.

G. The Incidence of Frivolous Litigation

Tort reform proponents often claim that contingency fees encourage "frivolous litigation."[71] Tort reform opponents counter that, to the contrary, contingency fee lawyers have strong financial incentives to bring only "meritorious" claims.[72] Both opponents and proponents agree that this issue – whether contingency fees promote frivolous litigation – is one of the main planes of battle in the tort reform wars.

The "meritorious" versus "frivolous" debate also plays out in the context of tort reform proposals. Those who favor an expanded tort system and therefore reject tort reforms – such as adopting the English Rule ("loser pays"), caps on damages or lawyers' fees, shortening statutes of limitation, collateral source offsets, eliminating or restricting joint and several liability, and strengthening venue requirements – also argue that these proposals deny victims with meritorious claims access to the legal system.[73] A typical example appears on the editorial page of the *New York Times*:

> [P]roposals ... requiring a losing plaintiff to pay the defendant's legal fees, sharply curtailing contingency fees for lawyers and recklessly attacking punitive damages ... [would] discourage ... legitimate but risky [lawsuits] .... Similar arguments apply to contingency fee arrangements by which lawyers get a percentage of the winnings, but only if they win .... [These proposals] fail ... to distinguish between meritorious and meretricious suits.[74]

It is undeniable that contingency fee financing of tort litigation has resulted in an expansion of the scope of tort liability – a subject I address in Chapters 9 and 10. It has also resulted in a vast increase in the volume of tort litigation, as I set out in Chapters 11 and 12. But do contingency fees induce higher amounts of frivolous litigation? To answer this question, we need a clear definition of what constitutes frivolous and meritorious litigation. Unfortunately, there is no clear definition.

Neither side in the debate bases its arguments on identifiable empirical evidence. This absence becomes evident when we attempt to define the terms "meritorious" and "frivolous." We can define meritorious claims as either (1) claims that have resulted in jury verdicts; or (2) claims that appear worthy of compensation regardless of jury verdicts. Relying on jury verdicts is dubious, however, because they are highly variable. Studies have shown that two (or more) juries deciding the same case may reach different outcomes.[75] For example, in a Texas multiparty product liability case, five different juries reached substantially different verdicts after hearing the same facts.[76] Cass Sunstein, a Harvard Law School professor and liberal icon, has observed the irrational and unpredictable nature of juries and concluded based on empirical studies of cognitive biases, that jury awards are "erratic, unpredictable, and arbitrary."[77] In addition, using a jury verdict to determine a claim's merit necessarily confers approbation of verdicts that defy rationality or have been thoroughly discredited by medical science.[78]

Instead of defining a case as meritorious based on jury verdicts, we might rely on expert assessments. Experts, however, would either offer predictions of probability of success based on previous jury verdicts or define merit by using a complex cost/benefit calculus based on policy goals. In the former case, different panels of experts, however, would often reach different conclusions as to the probability of success. The latter would require identifying and securing widespread agreement to a set of policy goals and then, for each tort claim, determining which outcome most achieves those policy goals. We can agree on the need to provide access to courts to redress inflicted harms; we can further agree that any legal system that provides for compensation for injury must have a way of drawing the line between the compensable and the noncompensable. Even experts drawing this line, however, will disagree as to where.

The meritorious claim is, therefore, a normative – not a descriptive – term. It expresses a set of policy preferences. Attempts to define claims on a scale of merit will necessarily founder on disparate social policy shoals. In this context, the concept of the meritorious claim is dubious at best and contributes little to the tort reform debate.

Most tort reforms will deprive some number of claimants of access to courts, and some of these claimants would have prevailed had their cases gone to trial. That, of course, is precisely the purpose of tort reform: to curtail tort litigation. If the *New York Times* editorial page and other opponents of tort reform followed the logical consequences of their arguments, however, they would not only oppose tort reforms – as they do – but would also espouse policies to increase the number of claimants who are provided access to courts because some of them would prevail at trial. The most efficient way to increase access is to make it *more profitable* for lawyers to take cases. And the best way to increase lawyers' profits is to raise the standard contingency fee from its current level. Raising the standard contingency fee will raise the volume of litigation to a multiple of its current volume, as well as increase the number of jury verdicts in favor of plaintiffs. If the definition of the meritorious claim is that a jury has found in favor of a plaintiff, then more meritorious claims will have been brought. Indeed, the only way to assure the highest level of meritorious litigation would be to raise contingency fee rates to 100 percent. Lawyers presumably would then rebate part of their fees to claimants in order to induce them to assert claims.

Like the meritorious claim, frivolous claims are in the eye of the beholder.[79] Here too, there is little consensus.[80] To be sure, a minute fraction of tort (and contract) claims – which are *totally* without any legal or factual basis – can properly be deemed frivolous. It is rare, however, that a lawyer cannot find *some* merit in a claim, even if it is gossamer thin.[81]

Truly frivolous suits are so rare as to be tangential to the debate over whether contingency fees promote frivolous litigation. What does drive the debate is the normative judgment that many tort claims are being filed that should not be brought. These claims are then denominated as frivolous.[82]

Some use the term frivolous to describe litigation with a very low probability of success.[83] However, so long as a claim has more than a zero probability of success, there is no legitimate basis for terming the claim frivolous.[84] Lawyers will bring claims with a low probability of success if they think that the claim will be profitable – that is, if the reward potential is high enough to compensate for the low probability of success or if winning the case would stretch the tort envelope, paving the way for additional similar filings.[85]

A third use of the term frivolous applies to mass tort litigation in which lawyers have filed a mass of mostly bogus claims in a "plaintiff-friendly" jurisdiction with the expectation that defendants will be forced to settle the entire set of claims without the plaintiffs having to prove their case. These bogus cases are generated by litigation screenings – which I have previously discussed – using litigation doctors who manufacture thousands and tens of thousands of diagnoses for money. There is little sense, however, in calling these cases frivolous. Hundreds of thousands of these bogus cases generated by screenings have yielded settlements in the range of $30 billion to $40 billion and $13 billion to $14 billion in contingency fees for lawyers.[86]

Those who criticize tort litigation because there is too much frivolous litigation are simply expressing a political view that the amount of tort litigation is excessive. Those who oppose tort reforms because that would deny some access to courts to press meritorious claims are also expressing a political view that the current level of tort litigation is too low or, like the baby bear's porridge in the Goldilocks fable, is "just right." Thus, whether there is too much or too little litigation is mostly a function of one's political calculus. As a matter of policy, tort litigation where there is no actual injury, or where the social benefits are outweighed by the social costs, can be deemed excessive or perverse. Denominating this litigation as frivolous, however, does not serve any useful policy function. Indeed the terms frivolous and meritorious add little to the debate on the effects of contingency fee financing of tort litigation.

NOTES

1. *See* Murray L. Schwartz & Daniel J.B. Mitchell, *An Economic Analysis of the Contingent Fee in Personal Injury Litigation*, 22 STAN. L. REV. 1125, 1125 (1970). This alignment, however, is less than perfect. *See* Brickman, *Contingent Fees, supra* Introduction, note 18, at 47–48.
2. *See* Herbert Kritzer et al., *The Impact of Fee Arrangement on Lawyer Effort*, 19 LAW & SOC. REV. 251, 267, 273–74 (1985).
3. *See* Ronald Braeutigam et al., *An Economic Analysis of Alternative Fee Shifting Systems*, 47 LAW & CONTEMP. PROBS., Winter 1984, at 173, 183–84 (the lawyer's incentive to invest increases with the stakes).
4. The lawyer may, however, increase her financial investment in the case by advancing more litigation costs, for example, to secure higher priced expert witnesses.
5. The essence of the potential threat posed by contingency fees is captured by Walter Olson: "The ethical rules of many professions share a common underlying principle: If temptations are allowed to get out of hand, many will yield. To put it in raw dollar terms, if under system A people can grab $1,000 by telling a lie, and under system B they can grab $1 million by telling the same lie, more people – not all, but more – will tell the lie under system B." *See* Walter K. Olson, *Sue City: The Case Against the Contingency Fee*, POL'Y REV., Winter 1991, at 47.
6. *See* James A. Brundage, *The Profits of the Law: Legal Fees of University-Trained Advocates*, 32 AM J. OF LEGAL HISTORY 1, 1 (1988). Brundage indicates that medieval writers generally considered contingency fees both immoral and illegal but that the very frequency with which writers disapproved of the practice probably indicates that they were not unknown in medieval legal practice. *Id.* As early as 1244, English statutes prohibited the use of contingency fees in London. *See* PAUL BRAND, THE ORIGINS OF THE ENGLISH LEGAL PROFESSION 67, 93 (1992). More recently, in 1979, a royal commission established in England to consider replacing government-funded legal aid rejected the American contingency fee system for fear that if "the lawyer has a direct personal interest in the outcome of the case, [it] may lead to *undesirable practices* including the construction of evidence, the improper coaching of witnesses, the use of professionally partisan expert witnesses (especially medical witnesses), improper

examination and cross-examination, [and] groundless legal arguments, designed to lead the courts into error and competitive touting." *See* Michael Zander, *Will the Revolution in the Funding of Civil Litigation in England Eventually Lead to Contingency Fees?*, 52 DePaul L. Rev. 259, 262–63 (2002) [hereinafter Zander, *Civil Litigation in England*].

7. Honorable George Sharswood, *An Essay on Professional Ethics*, 32 Rep. ABA 160–64 (1907).

8. Charles M. Yablon and Jennifer Hill, *Timing Corporate Disclosures to Maximize Performance Based Remuneration: A Case of Misaligned Incentives*, 35 Wake Forest L. Rev. 83, 85 (2000) [hereinafter Yablon & Hill, *Timing Corporate Disclosures*]; *see also* The American Bar Association, Task Force on Corporate Responsibility, *Preliminary Report of the American Bar Association Task Force on Corporate Responsibility*, 58 Bus. Law. 189, 193 (2002–03).

9. Margaret M. Blair, *Directors' Duties in a Post-Enron World: Why Language Matters*, 38 Wake Forest L. Rev. 885, 903 (2003) [hereinafter Blair, *Duties in a Post-Enron World*].

10. Blair, *Duties in a Post-Enron World, supra*, at 889.

11. *See Stock Options – Sailing into Troubled Waters?* (Oct. 2002), *available at* http://www.watsonwyatt.com/asia- pacific/pubs/execcomp/ articles/ oct02/2002_10_01.asp.

12. See Mark A. Sargent, *Lawyers in the Perfect Storm*, 43 Washburn L. Rev. 1, 8–13 (2003); *Remember When – Recollections of a Time When Aggressive Accounting, Special Purpose Vehicles, Asset Light Companies and Executive Stock Options Were Positive Attributes*, 11 Am. Banker. Inst. L. Rev. 1 (2003); Yablon & Hill, *Timing Corporate Disclosures, supra*, at 86–88 (outlining recent studies on the actual incentives and effects created by stock option compensation); Blair, *Duties in a Post-Enron World, supra*, at 904. One such outcome is the backdating of stock option grants to increase CEO profits at the expense of shareholders. See David Reilly, *Street Sleuth: FASB Appears in a New Light on Stock Options – Some Companies That Opposed Expensing Rule are Caught Up in U.S. Probe on 'Backdating'*, Wall St. J., Aug. 14, 2006, at C1 (backdating options to a time when the share price was lower than the date the option was actually granted, resulting in an instant paper profit).

13. For consideration of the powerful impact of the profits from contingency fees on ethical rules, see Brickman, *Money Talks, supra* Chapter 3, note 9, at 247, 250–59; Lester Brickman, *Contingent Fee Market, supra* Chapter 6, note 14, at 118–25.

14. *See* Model Rules of Prof'l Responsibility (2006), at 1.5(d)(2) ("A lawyer shall not enter into an arrangement for, charge, or collect … a contingent fee

for representing a defendant in a criminal case."); MODEL CODE OF PROF'L RESPONSIBILITY (1983), at DR 2–106(C)(1).

15. A *res* in this context is simply an asset from which the fee is to be paid, such as the recovery in a tort case.

16. MODEL CODE, *supra*, at EC 2–20(2). *See* Pamela S. Karlan, *Contingent Fees and Criminal Cases*, 93 COLUM. L. REV. 595, 601 (1993) [hereinafter Karlan, *Contingent Fees and Criminal Cases*].

17. *See, e.g.*, Karlan, *id.*; Peter Lushing, *Criminal Law: The Fall and Rise of the Criminal Contingent Fee*, 82 J. CRIM. L. & CRIMINOLOGY 498, 530 (1991) [hereinafter Lushing, *Criminal Law*]; Brickman, *Contingent Fees, supra* Introduction, note 18, at 40–41.

18. See Karlan, *Contingent Fees and Criminal Cases, supra*, at 603.

19. *See, e.g., United States v. Murphy*, 349 F. Supp. 818 (E.D. Pa. 1972); *Schoonover v. State*, 543 P.2d 881 (Kan. 1975).

20. *See, e.g., City of Riverside v. Rivera*, 477 U.S. 561, 575 (1986) (allowing plaintiffs' attorneys to recover fees from losing parties in a civil rights action under 42 U.S.C. § 1988 regardless of the amount of monetary relief granted to the plaintiffs).

21. See Lushing, *Criminal Law, supra*, at 517.

22. *See* Karlan, *Contingent Fees and Criminal Cases, supra*, at 612 ("If the perverse incentive created by flat fees fails to justify a per se ban, then it is hard to see why the perverse incentive created by contingent fees justifies one.").

23. *See* CHARLES WOLFRAM, MODERN LEGAL ETHICS, § 9.4.3, at 536–38 (1986); Karlan, *Contingent Fees and Criminal Cases, supra*, at 608; Lushing, *Criminal Law, supra*, at 526.

24. *See* Karlan, *Contingent Fees and Criminal Cases, supra*, at 611 ("It is worth considering whether a civil litigator faces opportunities and incentives for a greater amount of subornation. In a large number of criminal cases, the defendant presents no witnesses of his own. Instead, he merely puts the prosecutor's case to the test.").

25. *See* Eugene R. Gaetke, *Lawyers as Officers of the Court*, 42 VAND. L. REV. 39, 59–60 (1989) ("Presumably the drafters of the *Code* [of Judicial Conduct] intended this restriction to further the judicial system's interest in preventing illegal or otherwise unsavory conduct by counsel that might be encouraged by a contingent fee in criminal defense work."); Karlan, *Contingent Fees and Criminal Cases, supra*, at 621–26.

26. *See Baca v. Paddila*, 26 N.M. 223, 228–29, 190 P. 730, 731–32 (1920) (presenting the theory of tolerating overzealousness and distinguishing what is at stake in criminal versus civil cases); *see also Peyton v. Margiotti*, 156 A.2d 865, 867 (Pa. 1959) ("A proper [contingent] fee in a civil suit, where the client is not taken

advantage of, is valid.... In criminal cases the rule is stricter because of the danger of corrupting justice.").

27. 59 Fed. Reg. 31,253, 31,525, 31,527 (June 30, 1994); see also Treas. Dep't, Regulations Governing the Practice of Attorneys, Certified Public Accountants, Enrolled Agents, Enrolled Actuaries, Enrolled Retirement Plan Agents, and Appraisers Before the Internal Revenue Service, Circ. No. 230 (Rev. Apr. 2008).

28. 31 C.F.R. § 10.35(a), (b)(4), (b)(7) (2007).

29. For example, more than 175 California lawyers were investigated for engaging in medical insurance fraud scams in which they received kickbacks from medical providers. See Richard C. Reuban, *California Scheming*, A.B.A. J., Feb. 1996, at 26. The investigation, code-named the "Medlaw Project," may have been the "largest lawyer sting by U.S. law enforcement officials," and just the first four indictments may have involved "more than $100 million in potential fraudulent medical claims." *Id*. The Medlaw task force secured the convictions of more than fifty lawyers, medical providers, and administrators for the payment of kickbacks from medical providers to attorneys. 2003 NCFIA Program Schedule "bio" of Daniel S. Linhardt.

30. Daniel Wise, *Probe of Tort Settlement Scheme*, N.Y. L.J., Oct. 7, 1994, at 1.

31. Sometimes the runners offered passengers money ($50 to $100) to come to the doctor or lawyer's office. The New York City Transit Authority suspects that it pays out tens of millions of dollars each year in fraudulent claims of this nature. See Joseph P. Fried, *Transit Authority Moves to Control False Claims*, N.Y. TIMES, Oct. 29, 1993, at B4. Another type of claim is the urban phenomenon of pedestrians who board municipal buses that have just been involved in accidents in order to file claims for injury. In a sting operation in New Jersey, bus accidents were staged and filmed. Many of those who later filed claims from the accident were not on the bus but rather came to the scene and climbed on after the accident had occurred. Some were never on the bus at all. Some of the undercover "passengers" on the buses agreed to be treated, and were subsequently taken to chiropractors or physicians who provided ten-minute massages and heat treatments three times a week for fifteen weeks. The doctors charged between $4,500 and $6,000 for this unneeded care and often padded the bills with other treatments that were either unnecessary or never actually took place. Hundreds of thousands of dollars of claims resulted from the operation. See Peter Kerr, *"Ghost Riders" are Target of an Insurance Sting*, N.Y. TIMES, Aug. 18, 1993, at A1; *see also* JEFFREY O'CONNELL, THE LAWSUIT LOTTERY: ONLY THE LAWYERS WIN 211 (Free Press 1979) (referring to a case in Boston where "240 persons filed claims for a collision between a streetcar and a truck – but the streetcar had a top capacity of 68"); Kerr, *Insurance Sting, id*., at A1; Greg Steinmetz, *Ex-Cop Hunts Down Petty Insurance Cheats*, WALL ST. J., Dec. 28, 1993, at B1.

32. *See* Nina Bernstein, *No Holds Barred for Guilty Lawyer*, NEWSDAY, Feb. 11, 1992, at 7; Deborah Pines, *Eisen Loses Appeal of* Rico *Convictions*, N.Y. L.J., Aug. 18, 1992, at 1.

33. See Daniel J. Popeo, *The Fraud Tax: The Cost of Hidden Corruption in America's Tort Law*, LEGAL BACKGROUNDER, Mar. 27, 1992, at 5.

34. *See The Solicitation of Accident Cases*, 63 AM. L. REV. 135, 136–39 (1927) (discussing the long-standing practice of using "runners" to solicit clients for lawyers); Burnele V. Powell, *The Problem of the Parachuting Practitioner*, 1992 U. ILL. L. REV. 105 (1992) (discussing the phenomenon of the "parachuting practitioner" – lawyers who solicit clients at mass accident sites). The indictment of the Milberg Weiss law firm for allegedly paying off named plaintiffs in securities class actions alleges a modern form of ambulance chasing. *See* Editorial, *The Milberg Weiss Indictment*, N.Y. SUN, May 19, 2006, *available at* http://www.nysun.com/article/33031; Julie Creswell, *U.S. Indictment for Big Law Firm in Class Actions*, N.Y. TIMES, May 19, 2006, at A1; Peter Elkind, *The Fall of America's Meanest Law Firm*, FORTUNE, Nov. 3, 2006, at 155.

35. *See* Bruce Schultz, *"Runners" Fill Legal Coffers, Negative Image of Lawyers*, BATON ROUGE ADVOCATE, Nov. 20, 2000, at 1A.

36. Christopher Scanlan, *Preying on Disasters – Priest-Imposter Sought after Detroit Crash*, ST. PETERSBURG TIMES, Sept. 19, 1987, at 1A.

37. Matt Beer, *"Priest" at Crash Site Recommends Lawyer*, NAT'L L.J., Oct. 5, 1987, at 3.

38. *See, e.g., Fla. Bar v. Barrett*, 897 So. 2d 1269 (Fla. 2005) (increasing a sanction for an attorney who hired an ordained minister as a "paralegal" to bring in new clients from the emergency area of a hospital); *In re Anis*, 599 A.2d 1265 (N.J. 1991) (ordering public reprimand of an attorney who solicited the families of victims of the crash of Pan American Flight 103).

39. *See, e.g., In re Anis*, 599 A.2d 1265, at 456 ("The form of solicitation ... is so universally condemned that its intrusiveness can hardly be disputed.").

40. Despite widespread evidence of ambulance chasing, the number of disciplinary prosecutions approaches the infinitesimal. In the period 2002–2007, only 62 out of 1.3 million licensed attorneys were disciplined for ambulance chasing. Anita Bernstein, *Sanctioning the Ambulance Chaser*, 41 LOYOLA L. REV. (2008).

41. *See* The 1996 Aviation Disaster Family Assistance Act, which is designed to protect and assist victims and their families in the aftermath of aviation accidents inside the United States by, inter alia, prohibiting the unsolicited communication concerning a potential action for personal injury or wrongful death by lawyers, their agents, or potential parties to related litigation undertaken before forty-five days following the date of accident. 49 U.S.C. § 1136(g)(2) (2006). Giving teeth to this provision is an enforcement mechanism allowing civil actions for its violation

by either the National Transportation Safety Board or the Attorney General. *See* 49 U.S.C. § 1151 (2006). The U.S. Supreme Court upheld the Florida rule against a First Amendment challenge by an attorney and his referral service. *Fla. Bar v. Went For It, Inc.*, 515 U.S. 618 (1995).

42. Rules Regulating the Florida Bar, R. 4–4.7, cmt. (2006).

43. 48 Ohio St.2d 217, 357 N.E.2d 1097 (1976), aff'd, 436 U.S. 447 (1978).

44. In upholding the Ohio Supreme Court's decision to discipline Ohralik for violating the court's antisolicitation rule, the U.S. Supreme Court accorded the bar special treatment. The Court had held that commercial speech that is not false or deceptive is entitled to First Amendment protection. That would seem to cover in-person solicitation that was neither false nor deceptive. Indeed, in a later case, the Court stated that it would review with "special care" any "blanket prohibition against truthful, nonmisleading speech about a lawful product" and that the prohibition would "rarely survive [such] constitutional review." *44 Liquormart, Inc. v. Rhode Island*, 517 U.S. 484, 504 (1996). Nonetheless, in *Ohralik*, the Court upheld just such a "blanket prohibition" on commercial speech. Only the legal profession has been singled out by the Court for this special treatment. For example, in *Edenfield v. Fane*, 507 U.S. 761 (1993), the Court expressly refused to apply *Ohralik* and struck down to a rule promulgated by the Florida Board of Accountancy that barred in-person solicitation by CPAs. In distinguishing *Ohralik*, the Court held that a lawyer is a "professional trained in the act of persuasion" and thus more likely to take advantage of a client than an accountant. *Id.* at 775. Taken at face value, the Court appears to be saying that the public needs more protection from lawyers than accountants. But the real reason for the Court's greater deference to the legal profession's rule – even when the rule conflicts with the First Amendment – appears to be concern about the public's low opinion of lawyers. This is a concern that the Court, made up entirely of lawyers, extends to no other profession. See *Florida Bar v. Went For It, Inc.*, 515 U.S. 618, 625–34 (1995); Michael Dorf, *Can the Legal Profession Improve Its Image?: Americans Believe Lawyers to Be Necessary But Dishonest, Survey Finds* (April 17, 2002), available at http://writ.news.findlaw.com/dorf/20020417.html (survey concluded that Americans believe that 39% of lawyers are dishonest, 60% believe lawyers are overpaid, and 48% of the wealthiest Americans believe lawyers do more harm than good); Leo J. Shapiro & Associates, Public Perceptions of Lawyers Consumer Research Findings, Section of Litigation of American Bar Association 9–13 (April 2002), available at http://www.abanet.org/litigation/lawyers/publicperceptions.pdf. (Americans say that lawyers are greedy, manipulative, corrupt, and do a poor job of policing themselves; only 19% of consumers express confidence in lawyers or the legal profession; 73% of consumers believe lawyers are corrupt.)

45. *Ohralik*, 48 Ohio St. 2d at 217.

46. *In re Albert Ohralik* (Board of Commissioners on Grievances and Discipline of The Sup. Court of Ohio) (findings of fact and recommendation) Mar. 1978, at 1 [hereinafter *Findings*].
47. *Ohralik*, 48 Ohio St. 2d at 217.
48. *Findings, id.*, at 2.
49. *Ohralik*, 48 Ohio St. 2d at 218.
50. Brief of Relator, Ohio State Bar Ass'n at 2, *In re Albert Ohralik*, No. 229 (Mar. 15, 1976).
51. *Ohralik*, 48 Ohio St. 2d at 218.
52. *Findings*, id., at 3.
53. Brief of Relator, Ohio State Bar Ass'n at 2, *In re Albert Ohralik*, No. 229 (Mar. 15, 1976).
54. *Ohralik*, 48 Ohio St. 2d at 219.
55. *Id.* at 218.
56. *Id.*
57. Transcript of Carol McClintock testimony at 97, *In re Albert Ohralik*, No. 229 (Dec. 30, 1975).
58. Affidavit of Plaintiff Albert Ohralik at 2, *Ohralik v. McClintock* (filed Mar. 23, 1974).
59. *Ohralik*, 48 Ohio St. 2d at 218.
60. *Id.*
61. See Lester Brickman, *The Use of Litigation Screenings in Mass Torts: A Formula for Fraud?*, 62 SMU L. Rev. 1221 (2008) [hereinafter Brickman, Litigation Screenings].
62. *See* The Center for Medicine in the Public Interest, *Insta-Americans: The Empowered (and Imperiled) Health Care Consumer in the Age of Internet Medicine* Jan. 5–6, 2008 (reporting that a study of Web sites providing medical information showed that this "online real estate was dominated by [Web sites] paid for and sponsored by either class action law firms or legal marketing sites searching for plaintiff referrals" and that the information provided were often "overwhelmingly biased and misleading").
63. One of the largest asbestos screening enterprises, Most Health Services, which has screened more than 400,000 potential litigants, acknowledged that it provided no health services. Instead, it said that "the sole purpose ... of [t]he screening process ... is collecting evidence for future asbestos litigation." Brief of Appellants at 19, *In re Asbestos Prods. Liab. Litig.*, Nos. 98–1166 and 98–1165 (3d Cir. 2000), quoted in Mem. In Support Of Motion For Case Management Order Concerning Mass Litigation Screenings at 5–10, *In re Asbestos Prods. Liab. Litig.* (No. VI), Civ. Action Nos. MDL 875, 2 MDL 875 (E.D. Pa. 2001) (describing in detail, including references to depositions and exhibits, the operation of Most Health Services, Inc., a screening company).

64. In asbestos litigation, approximately twenty-five doctors have accounted for the majority of the hundreds of thousands of medical reports generated in the course of litigation screenings. CRMC Response to Amended Notice of Deposition Upon Written Questions at ex.D, *In re Asbestos Prods. Liab. Litig.* (No. VI), Civil Action no.: MDL 875 (*Arbuthnot et al. v. Ford Motor Co. et al.*, Mar. 2, 2006).

65. *See* Brickman, *Litigation Screenings, supra* note 61.

66. See Lester Brickman, *Disparities Between Asbestosis and Silicosis Claims Generated by Litigation Screenings and Clinical Studies*, 29 CARDOZO L. REV. 513–566, 588–89 (2007) [hereinafter Brickman, *Disparities*].

67. *Id.*

68. Brickman, *Litigation Screenings, supra* note 61, at 1231.

69. *See* Lester Brickman, *Ethical Issues in Asbestos Litigation*, 33 HOFSTRA L. REV. 833 (2005) [hereinafter Brickman, *Ethical Issues*].

70. The notable exception is U.S. District Court Judge Janis Jack who, in 2005, found that the 10,000 claims of silicosis had been "manufactured for money." *In re Silica Prods. Liab. Litig.*, 398 F. Supp. 2d 563, 635 (MDL 1553, S.D. Tex. 2005).

71. See, e.g., George J. Zilich, *Cutting through the Confusion of the Loss-of-Chance Doctrine under Ohio Law: A New Cause of Action or a New Standard of Causation?*, 50 CLEV. ST. L. REV. 673, 699 (2002–03) ("Frivolous litigation is a cost of contingency fees and the American Rule, which generally prohibits recovery of legal fees by the prevailing party in litigation."); Mimi Marchev, *The Medical Malpractice Insurance Crisis: Opportunity for State Action*, NAT'L ACAD. FOR STATE HEALTH POL'Y, at tbl.2 (July 2002) (listing sixteen states that have implemented tort reform in the form of limiting attorney contingency fees based on the argument "that attorneys' fees are often excessive, take away from the victims compensation, and encourage attorneys to bring frivolous suits."); Eric Peters, *Slick Lawyer Would Damage Kerry*, THE AUGUSTA CHRONICLE (Georgia) Mar. 6, 2004, at A06 ("Personal injury lawyers ... often win hundreds of millions of dollars in contingency fees in what any reasonable American would describe as frivolous lawsuits.").

72. *See, e.g.*, Alexander Tabarrok, *Give the Lawyer His Cut*, FORBES, Aug. 3, 2005, at 42 ("Despite the cry of tort reformers, contingency fees are good for the legal system. They weed out bad cases."); Michael J. Saks, *Do We Really Know Anything About the Behavior of the Tort Litigation System – and Why Not?*, 140 U. PA. L. REV. 1147, 1191–92 (1992).

73. *See* OFFICE OF TECHNOLOGY ASSESSMENT, IMPACT OF LEGAL REFORMS ON MEDICAL MALPRACTICE AWARDS 29 (1993) [hereinafter OTA] ("[R]estricting [lawyers'] fees ... might ... discourag[e] ... attorneys from taking on meritorious cases whose expected financial returns are low.").

74. Editorial, *Bashing Lawyers*, N.Y. TIMES, Feb. 15, 1992, at A20.

75. *See* Shari Seidman Diamond et al., *Juror Judgements About Liability and Damages: Sources of Variability and Ways to Increase Consistency*, 48 DEPAUL L. REV. 301 (1998) (describing a study in which participants watched the same videotape of a products liability trial; 51% found for the plaintiff and the other 49% for the defendant); *see also* Chapter 15 for discussion of the unpredictability of economic damage awards. *But cf.* Neil Vidmar, *Medical Malpractice Lawsuits: An Essay on Patient Interests, The Contingency Fee System, Juries and Social Policy*, 38 LOY. L.A. L. REV. 1217, 1237–38 (2005) [hereinafter Vidmar, *Medical Malpractice Lawsuits*] (studies comparing jury verdicts with the opinions of judges and neutral medical experts show a high level of correspondence).

76. *See* KAGAN, ADVERSARIAL LEGALISM, *supra* Introduction, note 13, at 127.

77. *See* Cass R. Sunstein et al., *Assessing Punitive Damages*, 107 YALE L.J. 2071, 2074 (1998) (concluding, based on an empirical study, that although "people's moral judgments are remarkably widely shared," they "have a great deal of difficulty in mapping such judgments onto an unbounded scale of dollars," resulting in "erratic, unpredictable, and arbitrary awards, [and] possibly even meaningless awards").

78. Juries, for example, have ruled that millions of dollars be paid to women claiming that they had an autoimmune disease caused by silicone breast implants, despite the fact that the epidemiological data indicate no causal relationship. *See* David Bernstein, *The Breast Implant Fiasco*, 87 CAL. L. REV. 457 (1999) [hereinafter Bernstein, *Breast Implant Fiasco*]; *In re Silicone Gel Breast Implant Prods. Liab. Litig.*, 1994 WL 578353 (N.D. Ala. Sept. 1, 1994) (approving a thirty-year compensation program for current and latent injuries that medical science indicates are not caused by silicone breast implants). In one of the early such litigations, a Houston, Texas, jury awarded Gladys Laas $5.2 million for an autoimmune disease that she claimed was caused by her silicone breast implants. *Laas v. Dow Corning Corp.*, No. 92–16550 (Tex. Dist. Ct., Harris County, 157th Dist. Feb. 15, 1995). The scientific evidence, however, was entirely to the contrary. *See* Brickman, *Litigation Screenings, supra* note 61, at 1266–77. One of her attorneys pleaded with the jury to rise up and exclaim: "[w]e believe you, Gladys Laas, when you tell us what happened to you." Quoted in Bernstein, *Breast Implant Fiasco, id.* at 496. The jury did believe, finding against Dow Corning, the manufacturer of the implant, not on the basis of scientific evidence, but because Ms. Lass had "a couple of years to retire" and was "having to have help with her housework." *Id.*

Two jurors in that case who were interviewed for the PBS television program Frontline revealed how uninterested the jury was in the most significant piece of scientific evidence that existed at the time of the trial:

Narrator: How did the jury reach its verdict? Two jurors agreed to talk to us. We asked if they were satisfied that silicone caused Gladys's disease?

Jose Ramirez: No.

Judy Sorensen Nauman: No.

Narrator: Was there any evidence that the implants hurt Gladys? Did the evidence prove that the implants were actually harmful?

Judy Sorensen Nauman: No, there isn't enough evidence -

Jose Ramirez: No, there isn't.

Judy Sorensen Nauman: – for that.

Narrator: But what about the prestigious Mayo Clinic study that Dow Corning had pinned their hopes on? Did that figure much in the deliberations?

Judy Sorensen Nauman: Uh-uh.

Jose Ramirez: No.

Judy Sorensen Nauman: That didn't really impress me that much. Uh-uh.

Jose Ramirez: I don't think we went over that during the deliberations, either.

Narrator: So why, then, did they award Gladys such a large sum of money?

Jose Ramirez: She had a couple of years to retire. We added that up. That went into the – the $5 million.

Judy Sorensen Nauman: She's having to have help-

Jose Ramirez: Yeah.

Judy Sorensen Nauman: – with her housework. She can no longer cook. Her husband's having to do a lot of the cooking. They used to travel a lot and go on vacations-

Jose Ramirez: Yeah.

Judy Sorensen Nauman: – and they can't do that anymore.

Jose Ramirez: The future medical bills.

Judy Sorensen Nauman: I mean, it's just – you know.

Jose Ramirez: All those added up together.

Judy Sorensen Nauman: Her life has been changed, both of them.

Frontline: Breast Implants on Trial (PBS television broadcast, show 1412, Feb. 27, 1996) (transcript at 9–10), quoted in Bernstein, *Breast Implant Fiasco, id.*, at n.190.

79. *See* DEBORAH L. RHODE, IN THE INTERESTS OF JUSTICE: REFORMING THE LEGAL PROFESSION 120–23 (2000); *see* also Robert G. Bone, *Modeling Frivolous Suits*, 145 U. PA. L. REV. 519, (1997) [hereinafter Bone, *Modeling Frivolous Suits*] (arguing that claims can be unmeritorious but not frivolous where the defendant likely did not commit a wrong but where the plaintiff has a high likelihood of success because of a favorable jury).

80. *See* Bone, *Modeling Frivolous Suits, id.* at 520 (stating that remarkably little is known about frivolous litigation, that no clear explanation has been given as to why frivolous suits are filed, and that no consensus exists as to what constitutes a "frivolous suit"); Carl Tobias, *The 1993 Revision of*

Federal Rule 11, 70 IND. L. J. 171, 196 (1994) (numerous courts have encountered difficulty defining the term frivolous and articulating consistent standards for identifying cases that fall under its guise); David B. Wilkins, *Who Should Regulate Lawyers?*, 105 HARV. L. REV. 799, 866 (1992) (noting the "definition of frivolous is notoriously vague"). *Cf.* Warren F. Schwartz & C. Fredrick Beckner III, *Toward a Theory of the "Meritorious Case": Legal Uncertainty as a Social Choice Problem*, 6 GEO. MASON L. REV. 801 (1998) [hereinafter Schwartz & Beckner, *Toward a Theory of the "Meritorious Case"*] (There is no strong intuition about what constitutes a meritorious claim, and there is no widely accepted method for approaching this question.).

81. Examples of claims that meet the "totally without merit" standard include those for which the statute of limitations for bringing a claim has expired; or the basis for the claim is a lawyer's misreading of a statute; or where the legal argument put forth in support of a claim is the same as that which courts in that jurisdiction have rejected previously; or where the losing party seeks to relitigate the exact claims. *See, e.g., Willhite v. Collins et al.*, 385 F. Supp. 2d 926 (D. Minn. 2005) (describing repeated attempts to relitigate a failed land boundary claim that had been held to be barred by *res judicata* and collateral estoppel); *see also* Bone, *Modeling Frivolous Suits, supra* note 80, at 533 (defining frivolous claims as those filed by a plaintiff when he knows that the facts establish complete [or virtually complete] absence of merit as an objective matter on the legal theories alleged, or those that are filed by a plaintiff without conducting reasonable investigation, which if done would put the case in the first prong of this test); Tobias, *The 1993 Revision, supra*, at 199 (the term frivolous should connote that the legal contention is meritless or groundless). Even these examples, however, may include nuances that elevate them from the truly frivolous to the merely fantastical.

82. *See* Bone, *Modeling Frivolous Suits, supra* note 79, at 531 (recognizing that suits are labeled frivolous, not simply based on the merits of the case, but to express a normative judgment that the suit should not be brought).

83. *See* Charles M. Yablon, *The Good, the Bad, and the Frivolous Case: An Essay on Probability and Rule 11*, 44 UCLA L. REV. 65, 67 (1996) (Claims that have been challenged in the past years as violations of Federal Rule 11 were not zero-probability cases, but rather those that the plaintiff's lawyer reasonably believed had a low [between 10% and 30%] chance of success.); Chris Guthrie, *Framing Frivolous Litigation: A Psychological Theory*, 67 U. CHI. L. REV. 163, 186 (a frivolous case is simply a case in which the plaintiff has a low probability of prevailing at trial) [hereinafter Guthrie, *Framing Frivolous Litigation*]; Schwartz & Beckner, *Toward a Theory of the "Meritorious Case," supra*, at 801 (noting that the term frivolous is employed to convey that it is socially undesirable for a case with too little chance of success to be brought).

84. *See* Charles Silver, *"We're Scared to Death": Class Certification and Blackmail*, 78 N.Y.U. L. Rev. 1357, 1392–95 (2003) (noting that a low-probability claim with high damages could be considered to have the same "value" as a high-probability case with low damages).

85. Lawyers who have a steady stream of income from carefully screened cases are financially enabled to take a case that has a low probability of success provided there is sufficient potential of receiving a large return. *See* Guthrie, *Framing Frivolous Litigation, supra* note 83, at 208.

86. *See* Brickman, *Litigation Screenings, supra* note 61, at 1266–77.

8 How the Quest for Profits Influenced the Development of the Tort System

I N CHAPTER 7, I FOCUSED ON HOW CONTINGENCY FEES influence lawyers' behavior at the atomistic level. Now I shift to a more systemic examination of how a financing system based on lawyers' quest for profits has shaped the development of our tort system. The theme of this chapter is that because our tort system has been shaped by a profit motivation, it fails in its essential purposes. It neither efficiently compensates the injured nor effectively deters the production of unsafe services and products. By way of illustration, I consider both the inefficiency of medical malpractice litigation as a compensatory system and its ineffectiveness in deterring malpractice.

A. The Deterrent Effect of the Tort System

Ideally, a tort system should compensate wrongfully injured persons and reduce future injuries by deterring wrongful conduct. By that measure, however, our tort system falls woefully short. It does not efficiently compensate wrongfully injured persons, accounts little for improvements in product safety, and begets substantial costs such as the practice of "defensive medicine," which is discussed later in this chapter. To begin, there are huge transaction costs. Almost 50 percent of the payments by insurance companies for auto accidents ends up in lawyers' pockets; transaction costs are even higher in other tort cases, averaging close to 60 percent.[1] Imagine going to an ATM machine and withdrawing $100 but actually receiving only $40 and a note stating that the bank imposed an adminstrative fee of $60. In Japan, by way of contrast, legal fees consume only about 2 percent of compensation payments.[2] In addition to being costly, our system is cumbersome, inconsistent, and unpredictable.[3]

Still, the inefficiencies of our tort system might be tolerable if it had a deterrent effect and efficiently promoted injury avoidance. Although this is a matter of faith for tort lawyers and most torts scholars, the empirical evidence is at best weak, if not to the contrary. In a recent article, Professors Steven Shavell of Harvard Law School and A. Mitchell Polinsky of Stanford Law School, leading law and economics scholars, surveyed the empirical evidence supporting the widely held view by courts and torts scholars that product liability litigation induces manufacturers to improve product safety.[4] Noting that product liability proponents "rarely provide meaningful justification for [this] view,"[5] they conclude that the deterrent value is "problematic for a wide range of products"[6] and "that the case favoring product liability is weak for products from which market forces and regulation are strong, because the benefits of product liability are then likely to be outweighed by its costs."[7] They found "no statistical evidence suggesting that product liability has in fact enhanced product safety for three widely sold products ... studied: general aviation aircraft, automobiles, and the DPT vaccine."[8] Although they note that manufacturers have increased investment in product safety and products are safer, they do not attribute this to the threat of liability. Instead, they contend that manufacturers are primarily motivated by (1) the desire to avoid significant declines in product sales that would result if products were perceived by the public as causing injury; and (2) government regulations mandating safety standards for automobiles, pharmaceuticals, aircraft, consumer products, and toys.[9] Similar views have been expressed, attributing most improvements to product safety to market pressures and third-party evaluators such as *Consumer Reports* and the Underwriters Laboratories.[10]

Other commentators have also expressed great skepticism about any claimed deterrent effect of the tort system. Professor Gary T. Schwartz

believes that "there is substantial doubt about the actual deterrence efficacy of tort law."[11] Professor Stephen D. Sugarman of the UCLA School
of Law states that "theorists who defend torts on deterrence grounds
have no convincing empirical support for their position."[12] Likewise,
Donald Gifford of the University of Maryland School of Law doubts
the tort system's effectiveness in deterring manufacturers' negligence.[13]
George Priest of the Yale Law School, a leading critic of the modern
tort system,[14] notes that although there has been a substantial increase
in manufacturers' liability for defective products and product liability
litigation, these increases "appear to have no significant effect ... [in]
establishing incentives for the manufacture of safer products."[15] Finally,
Professor Kip Viscusi of the Vanderbilt University Law School, reaching the same conclusion as Professors Shavell and Polinsky, advocates
a diminished role for the tort system because "[m]arkets and government regulations generally can create more efficient risk-reduction
incentives."[16] These minority views are buttressed by aggregate statistics
that show no substantial reduction in product-related accidents associated with marked increases in the volume of product liability litigation.[17]
Professor Alfred E. Conard, who taught at the University of Michigan
Law School, reaching the same conclusion as Professors Shavell and
Polinsky, went even further, stating that tort law "imposes burdens on
innocent individuals that are greater in the aggregate than the benefits
that it delivers to injury victims."[18]

B. Contingency Fees and the Development of the Modern Tort System

How did we come to develop a tort system that, in the words of John
Fabian Witt, professor of law and history at Columbia University, "is
characterized by relatively greater reliance on costly tort litigation [than
other Western nations] ... leaves victims undercompensated, does a
poor job of deterring accidents, and satisfies few of its constituencies
other than the lawyers who profit from it?"[19] When tort law originated

in England almost a millennium ago, it was so that plaintiffs could receive compensation for harms caused by the criminal misconduct of the defendant.[20] The current tort system, however, is a far cry from the tort system of even 150 years ago. As John Fabian Witt explains, our "[m]odern accident law is a remarkably recent development. Indeed, the American system of accident law is almost entirely a product of the late nineteenth and early twentieth centuries ... [when] the accident rates of an industrializing economy required the development of new institutions."[21] The Industrial Revolution caused an increase in industrial accidents and injuries, which gave rise to the development of a "number of alternative institutional mechanisms for dealing with the problem of industrial accidents."[22] Tort law was one of these mechanisms. (Others included cooperative insurance societies and private employer compensation programs.) Other Western nations that experienced similar growth in accident and injury rates adopted administrative social insurance programs to compensate accident victims;[23] however, in America, the tort compensation system ultimately prevailed.[24] But as Witt explains, this contingency-fee-financed tort system "failed to contain the late-nineteenth century accident crisis [in America, in part] because it was an immensely inefficient and costly mechanism for resolving accident cases – a mechanism that proved inadequate to compensate accident victims and their families."[25]

In the early twentieth century, states enacted workers' compensation statutes to provide scheduled compensation for work-related injuries; many of these statutes limited the amounts that lawyers could charge. To combat the double threat of limited damages and fees, tort lawyers lobbied against the further encroachment of expanding bureaucracy.[26] Witt explains that, ironically, after the Great Depression, tort lawyers used the same New Deal rhetoric that paved the way for the expansion of the administrative state – including "economic freedom" and "security with freedom" – to successfully fend off attempts to create an administrative compensation system.[27] The plaintiffs' bar also capitalized on the country's nationalist impulses to urge resistance to foreign systems of government, labeling the European administrative compensation systems as "exotic theories" of administrative law "recently imported from continental Europe."[28] Through these methods, tort lawyers managed to curtail the adoption of other administrative social insurance programs that could threaten their profits.

Tort lawyers were again successful in the 1950s and 1960s in protecting their contingency fee franchise by successfully resisting the enactment of automobile no-fault plans and other proposals that would have replaced common-law tort litigation with more efficient and predictable alternative compensation mechanisms.[29]

Thus, from the formation of the tort system in the late nineteenth and early twentieth centuries to the present day, tort lawyers have played a crucial role in molding the tort system to maximize their financial interests.[30] Through their self-interested efforts, tort lawyers secured their position as commanders over their own "private bureaucracy" – the tort system – ultimately amassing vast profits.[31]

C. The Deterrent Effect of Medical Malpractice Litigation

The tort system's dysfunction is on full display in medical malpractice litigation. Medical malpractice is a serious societal problem. According to an Institute of Medicine report in 2000, 98,000 deaths occur annually as the result of medical error.[32] In 2004, Healthgrades, Inc. – a company that rates hospital quality for medical insurers and health plans – estimated 195,000 deaths annually – double the Institute's estimate.[33] In America, we resolve claims of compensation for injury due to medical error through litigation, but the merits of this system are disputed. Several studies indicate that medical malpractice litigation directed against deep-pocket physicians and hospitals is often based on the occurrence of adverse outcomes rather than negligent acts by health care providers. These studies conclude that most tort claims are not related to negligent adverse events and that most negligent adverse events do not result in tort claims; moreover, the care provided in almost half of a set of malpractice cases where payments were made was none-theless determined to be appropriate.[34] Other studies conclude that malpractice claims and payments actually do correlate with incidents in which malpractice has occurred.[35]

Even if the latter studies were valid, our reliance on juries to deter-mine whether a negligent act occurred imports uncertainties about the issue of causation. Lacking the technical competence to determine which of two (or more) competing experts has presented the most medi-cally plausible explanation, jurors tend to side with the expert they like the best. The fact that plaintiffs' lawyers get to choose where to file the action also undermines the validity of medical malpractice litigation. In many cases, instead of filing in the county where the act took place, plaintiffs' lawyers file in urban areas with large minority populations because inner city juries tend to favor plaintiffs – whom they see as fel-low "victims" – over the "establishment."[36] Evidence suggests that many of these suits would not be brought if they were restricted to the location where the alleged act of malpractice took place.[37]

In addition, substantial inefficiencies permeate the medical malprac-tice system. It is indisputable, for example, that only a fraction of patients injured by negligence obtain compensation through the tort system. For those that do, only about forty-six cents of every dollar paid in medical liability insurance premiums go to them.[38] Nonetheless, medical mal-practice costs more than doubled between 1996 and 2006.[39] Moreover, there is substantial empirical evidence that doctors practice defensive medicine – ordering unnecessary tests, diagnostic procedures, and refer-rals to specialists – in order to protect themselves in the event they are sued; these practices, as discussed in Chapter 13, Section C, add more than $100 billion annually to medical care costs.

There is more, however, at stake than the inefficiencies of the com-pensation system and whether doctors are being blamed for adverse non-negligent events so that lawyers can book profits. Medical malpractice litigation is not only intended to compensate wrongly injured parties but also to deter future acts of malpractice. Indeed, torts scholars argue that only the threat of malpractice suits keeps doctors and hospitals from subjecting even more patients to the devastating consequences of medical error.[40] However, there is little empirical support in the literature for the proposition that the threat of medical malpractice litigation deters medical malpractice. To test the "deterrence" hypothesis, two of the leading researchers in this field posited that if medical malpractice litigation were a deterrent, then tort reforms that reduce the threat of such litigation would lead to poorer patient outcomes. On the basis of their study, however, they found that "reducing the threat of tort has no effect on patient outcomes in our analysis ... [the] imposition of liability does not deter medical injuries."[41]

Undaunted, pro-tort liability expansionists continue to contend that medical malpractice litigation does have a deterrent effect and point to certain improvements to patient safety as evidence and, in particular, the experience of anesthesiologists.[42] In the 1980s, anesthesiologists were hit with disproportionately high damage awards and faced soaring insurance premiums.[43] This led the American Society of Anesthesiologists to perform a comprehensive review of practices that led to claims and to devise new practice guidelines and improvements designed to avoid simple errors in monitoring the administration of anesthesia during surgeries. These reforms led to declines in the frequency of serious injuries and in medical malpractice insurance rates.[44] Thus, there is convincing evidence that some medical malpractice litigation does motivate health care practitioners to implement procedures to prevent errors.[45] However, close examination of another example frequently cited as evidence of the efficacy of medical malpractice litigation – leaving sponges inside surgical sites – shows that the issue of deterrence is at least in doubt. Moreover, it is not at all clear that the anesthesiologists' approach can be applied to other high-risk practice specialties, such as obstetrics, surgery, and cancer detection, absent changes in the incentive system created by medical malpractice litigation as described hereinafter. [46]

The complexity and infrequency of many medical errors make it difficult for individual practitioners to identify relevant risk factors and patterns of causation and to devise systematic methods for error prevention.[47] It would be easier to find solutions to many injury-causing health care practices if health care professionals were able to work together to identify errors, the practices that lead to them, and methods for minimizing their frequency.[48] Those charged with designing new prevention methods need sufficient data to draw on. The ideal system for minimizing improper health care practices, then, is one that provides incentives for self-reporting and fosters the free exchange of ideas.[49] The current system of medical malpractice litigation not only fails to provide incentives to self-report, it goes in the wrong direction by providing health care providers with disincentives. Although no clear link between error reporting and malpractice litigation has ever been demonstrated,[50] most of the available literature suggests that health care professionals are inhibited from identifying recurring errors – a necessary step to their reduction – because of the concern that such information may be used against them in a lawsuit.[51] All sides agree that the lack of error reporting within the medical profession is a glaring failure. More than 95 percent of adverse events are never reported.[52] If the goal is to improve error reporting, we will have to alter the current mix of carrots and sticks.

Professor Jeffrey O'Connell (and others) have proposed a system that seeks to balance the patient's right to compensation for the consequences of medical malpractice with society's interest in reducing medical errors by providing doctors with incentives to report errors. Under the proposal, a defendant in a medical malpractice suit would have 180 days after the filing of a claim to offer to pay the claimant's economic losses (mostly medical care costs and lost wages in excess of collateral sources such as insurance that covers medical expenses) plus attorney's fees.[53] If the defendant does not make this offer, the claimant could file a medical malpractice suit to recover economic and noneconomic damages.[54] If an offer is made to pay all economic damages and the claimant accepts the offer, then the claimant foregoes any noneconomic damages (pain and suffering) that he could otherwise seek in the tort system. If, on the other hand, the defendant makes the offer and the claimant turns it down in favor of filing a tort claim, the claimant would have a much higher burden of proof – having to show that the defendant was grossly negligent "beyond a reasonable doubt."[55] Tilting the playing field in favor of both the care provider making the offer and acceptance of the offer by the patient increases the likelihood that doctors will more willingly disclose adverse events and the circumstances surrounding their occurrence. Whereas individual injured patients would receive less compensation, more injured patients would gain reimbursement of their essential economic losses under this proposal. And society would benefit from the increased flow of information about adverse events.[56] Professor O'Connell and other collaborators estimate that payout reductions from such a program would be quite substantial – in the 70 percent range – and that defense costs would be similarly reduced.[57]

Another reform proposal, advanced by Dr. William Sage – a professor at Columbia Law School who has degrees in both medicine and law – seeks to replace the current medical malpractice system.[58] He suggests incorporating malpractice adjudication into a systems-based approach to reduce medical error. This program would initially be tested within the Medicare system and later expanded into Medicaid and the entire health care system. Sage explains that because the Medicare program already has the infrastructure for quality assurance and error detection, it would serve as an ideal environment for the resolution of medical malpractice claims, from which error occurrence data could be analyzed to design and promulgate best practices that could decrease medical error.[59] Instead of medical malpractice litigation, cases of medical injury would be resolved within the Medicare administrative framework. Participating providers would be required to disclose medical errors, and although these providers would have immunity from suit in the tort system, their insurers would be obligated to pay damages according to scheduled amounts.[60] The administrative determination of whether the injury was caused by avoidable error would be subject to judicial review by a federal appeals court (where there is no jury trial).[61]

Sage argues that this system would create a less adversarial environment and a more proactive approach to medical error reduction. Errors could be detected earlier because the doctors would be obliged to report known errors ahead of time, rather than waiting for patients to bring claims after a discoverable injury.[62] These errors would also be recorded and analyzed to implement better practice standards, which would result in decreased incidences of medical error, benefiting both doctors and patients alike.[63] The principal losers in this proposed scheme, however, would be both plaintiff and defense lawyers.

THE NEED FOR REFORM OF MEDICAL MALPRACTICE LITIGATION IS CLEAR. The current system fails both its compensatory and deterrence functions. These failures, however, are a microcosm of the failures of the larger tort system – a system that has been shaped by lawyers' quest for profits.

NOTES

1. *See* DEBORAH R. HENSLER ET AL., TRENDS IN TORT LITIGATION 29 (1987). Plaintiffs receive only 46% of annual tort expenditures; administrative costs and lawyers' fees consume the remaining 54%. TILLINGHAST, TOWERS PERRIN, U.S. TORT COSTS: 2003 UPDATE: TRENDS AND FINDINGS ON THE COSTS OF THE U.S. TORT SYSTEM 17 (2003) (victims receive $.22 for economic losses and $.24 for noneconomic losses) [hereinafter TILLINGHAST 2003 UPDATE]; JAMES S. KAKALIK & NICHOLAS M. PACE, COSTS AND COMPENSATION PAID IN TORT LITIGATION, at ix tbl.S.3 (1986).
2. *See* KAGAN, ADVERSARIAL LEGALISM, *supra* Introduction, note 13, at 137.
3. As noted by Robert A. Kagan: "The American tort law and jury system, with its unexplained verdicts, loosely structured law of damages, and cumbersome methods of decision making, is an extraordinarily costly, inconsistent, and unpredictable way of compensating accident victims." Robert A. Kagan, *Do Lawyers Cause Adversarial Legalism? A Preliminary Inquiry*, 19 LAW & SOC. INQUIRY, 54 (1994).
4. Steven Shavell & A. Mitchell Polinsky, *The Uneasy Case for Product Liability*, 123 Harv. L. REV. 1437 (2010) [hereinafter Shavell & Polinsky, *Product Liability*].

5. *Id*. at 1489.

6. *Id*. at 1440.

7. *Id*. at 1442. This thesis is disputed in a responding article supporting product liability. See John C.P. Goldberg & Benjamin C. Zipursky, *The Easy Case For Products Liability Law: A Response to Professor Polinsky and Shavell*, 123 Harv. L. Rev. 1919 (2010). Professors Polinsky and Shavell argue in response that Goldberg and Zipursky overstate their proposition – thus attacking the proverbial straw man, that their article contains numerous distortions and errors, and that they fail to cite any study demonstrating that product liability has led to a decrease in product accident rates. A. Mitchell Polinsky & Steven Shavell, *A Skeptical Attitude About Product Liability is Justified: A Reply to Professors Goldberg and Zipursky*, 123 Harv. L. Rev. 1949, 1951 (2010).

8. *Id*. at 1473 (footnote omitted).

9. *See* Shavell & Polinsky, *Product Liability*, at 1443–59.

10. Richard Epstein, *Session One Discussion of Paper by Richard Epstein*, 10 Cardozo L. Rev. 2193, 2223, 2242–43 (1989); Paul H. Rubin & Martin J. Bailey, *The Role of Lawyers in Changing the Law*, 23 J. Legal Stud. 807, 810 (1994) [hereinafter Rubin & Bailey, *Changing the Law*]; W. Kip Viscusi & Joni Hersch, *The Market Response to Product Safety Litigation*, J. Reg. Econ. 215 (1990).

11. Gary T. Schwartz, *Empiricism and Tort Law*, 2002 U. Ill. L. Rev. 1067, 1068 (2002).

12. Stephen D. Sugarman, *Doing Away with Tort Law*, 73 Cal. L. Rev. 555, 587 (1985). Two leading law and economics scholars, Professor William Landis and Judge Richard Posner, agree that the empirical evidence is weak but conclude that what evidence exists indicates that tort law does have a deterrent effect. William M. Landis & Richard A. Posner, The Economic Structure of Tort Law 10 (1987).

13. Donald G. Gifford, *The Peculiar Challenges Posed by Latent Diseases Resulting from Mass Products*, 64 Md. L. Rev. 613, 697 (2005).

14. *See generally* George L. Priest, *The Culture of Modern Tort Law*, 34 Val. L. Rev. 573 (2000); George L. Priest, *The Invention of Enterprise Liability: A Critical History of the Intellectual Foundations of Modern Tort Law*, 14 J. Legal Stud. 461 (1985); George L. Priest, *The New Legal Structure of Risk Control*, 119 Daedalus 207 (1990); George L. Priest, *Strict Products Liability: The Original Intent*, 10 Cardozo L. Rev. 2301 (1989).

15. George L. Priest, *Products Liability Law and the Accident Rate* in Robert E. Litan & Clifford Winston, Eds. Liability: Perspectives and Policy 194 (1988).

16. W. Kip Viscusi, *Toward a Diminished Role for Tort Liability: Social Insurance, Government Regulation, and Contemporary Risks to Health and Safety*, 6 Yale J. Reg. 65, 65 (1989).

17. *See* JEFFREY O'CONNELL, THE LAWSUIT LOTTERY: ONLY THE LAWYERS WIN 23–25 (1979); Priest, *Products Liability and the Accident Rate, supra*, at 211; DONALD N. DEWEES, DAVID DUFF & MICHAEL TREBILCOCK, EXPLORING THE DOMAIN OF ACCIDENT LAW: TAKING THE FACTS SERIOUSLY 202–05 (1996); Mark Geistfeld, *Products Liability* in MICHAEL FAURE ED., 1 ENCYCLOPEDIA OF LAW AND ECONOMICS § 11.11 (2d ed. 2009); Daniel P. Kessler & Daniel L. Rubinfeld, *Empirical Study of the Civil Justice System*, in A. MITCHELL POLINSKY & STEVEN SHAVELL EDS., 1 HANDBOOK OF LAW AND ECONOMICS 343 (2007); *see also* Paul Rubin & Joanna Shepherd, *Tort Reform and Accidental Deaths*, 50 J.L. & ECON. 221 (2007) (estimating that product liability has increased accidental deaths by raising the prices of safety-enhancing goods and services).

18. Alfred F. Conard, *Who Pays in the End for Injury Compensation? Reflections on Wealth Transfers from the Innocent*, 30 SAN DIEGO L. REV. 283, 305–06 (1993).

19. Witt, *History of American Accident Law, supra* Introduction, note 13, at 697 (emphasis added); *see also* KAGAN, ADVERSARIAL LEGALISM, *supra* Introduction, note 13, at 103 (2001).

20. *See* David J. Seipp, *The Distinction Between Crime and Tort in the Early Common Law*, 76 B.U. L. REV. 59, 59 (1996) (observing that under the early common law, "[i]n most instances the same wrong could be prosecuted either as a crime or as a tort"). Over time, tort law and criminal law grew apart, and it was no longer necessary to show criminal misconduct in order to prevail in a tort action.

21. Witt, *History of American Accident Law, supra* Introduction, note 13, at 699–704.

22. *Id.* at 695.

23. *See* JOHN G. FLEMING, THE AMERICAN TORT PROCESS 26–27 (Oxford Univ. Press, 1988).

24. Witt, *History of American Accident Law, supra* Introduction, note 13, at 696–97, 708.

25. *Id.* at 696.

26. For an historical account of the role of the plaintiffs' bar in the formation of the present-day tort system, see John Fabian Witt, *Bureaucratic Legalism, American Style: Private Bureaucratic Legalism and the Governance of the Tort System*, 56 DEPAUL L. REV. 261, 261–67 (2007) [hereinafter Witt, *Bureaucratic Legalism*]; JOHN FABIAN WITT, PATRIOTS AND COSMOPOLITANS: HIDDEN HISTORIES OF AMERICAN LAW 209–78 (2007) [hereinafter WITT, PATRIOTS].

27. Witt, *Bureaucratic Legalism, id.* at 266–67; WITT, PATRIOTS, at 262 (quoting Roscoe Pound, former Harvard Law School Dean and intellectual champion of the early plaintiffs' bar).

28. *See* WITT, PATRIOTS *supra* note 26, at 257 (quoting Roscoe Pound).

29. WITT, PATRIOTS, supra note 26, at 253–57.

30. In an influential article, Professors Paul H. Rubin and Martin J. Bailey concluded that "the shape of modern product liability law is due to the interests of tort lawyers." Rubin & Bailey, *Changing the Law, supra* note 10, at 808. Todd Zywicki of the George Mason University School of Law has also noted that our tort system "has been shaped primarily by the self-interests of lawyers and judges, rather than by improvements in the law." Todd Zywicki, *Public Choice and Tort Reform*, George Mason Law and Econ. Res. Paper No. 00–36, at 4, last revised Jan. 20, 2005, *available at* ssrn.com/abstract=244658 [hereinafter Zywicki, *Public Choice*].

31. *See* Witt, *Bureaucratic Legalism, supra* note 26, at 290–91.

32. *See* LINDA T. KOHN ET AL. EDS., COMMITTEE ON QUALITY OF HEALTH CARE IN AMERICA, INST. OF MED., TO ERR IS HUMAN: BUILDING A SAFER HEALTH CARE SYSTEM 1 (2000), *available at* http://books.nap.edu/catalog/9728.html?onpi_newsdoc112999 [hereinafter KOHN, BUILDING A SAFER HEALTH CARE SYSTEM]; Lucian L. Leape, *Institute of Medicine Error Figures Are not Exaggerated*, 284 JAMA 95, 95 (2000).

33. PATIENT SAFETY IN AMERICAN HOSPITALS, JULY 2004, HEALTHGRADES, INC., *available at* www.healthgrades.com/media/english/pdf/HG_Patient_Safety_Study_Final.pdf.

34. *See, e.g.*, PAUL C. WEILER ET AL., A MEASURE OF MALPRACTICE 71 (1993) (finding that twenty-six out of forty-seven malpractice claims studied showed no evidence of malpractice); William B. Weeks et al., *Tort Claims Analysis in the Veterans Health Administration for Quality Improvement*, 29 J.L. MED. & ETHICS 335, 335 (2001) (citations omitted) ("[s]everal studies have found that most tort claims are not related to negligent adverse events and most negligent adverse events do not result in tort claims"); Frederick Chancy et al., *Standard of Care and Anesthesia Liability*, 261 JAMA 1599, 1601 (1989) (a study of lawsuits filed against anesthesiologists found nearly half to be without merit and that payments were nonetheless made in 42% of cases in which the care provided was determined to be appropriate); David M. Studdert et al., *Claims Errors and Compensation Payments in Medical Malpractice Litigation*, 354 NEW ENG. J. MED. 2024 (May 11, 2006) (a review of closed claims showed that no injury had occurred in 3% of claims, and that in another 37%, there had been no error; 27% of claims involving error were uncompensated and the same percentage of compensated claims did not involve any error) [hereinafter Studdert et al., *Claims Errors*].

35. *See, e.g.*, TOM BAKER, THE MEDICAL MALPRACTICE MYTH (2005); David A. Hyman & Charles Silver, *Medical Malpractice Litigation and Tort Reform, It's the Incentives, Stupid*, 59 VAND. L. REV. 1085, 1106 (2007) ("[P]ayment and injury are closely correlated – but injured patients often do not get what

they deserve because the malpractice system is stingy."); Neil Vidmar, *Medical Malpractice Lawsuits: An Essay on Patient Interests, The Contingency Fee System, Juries and Social Policy*, 38 LOY. L.A. L. REV. 1217 (2005) [hereinafter Vidmar, *Medical Malpractice Lawsuits*].

36. *See* Arthur S. Hayes, *Inner-City Jurors Tend to Rebuff Prosecutors and to Back Plaintiffs*, WALL ST. J., Mar, 27, 1992, at A1.

37. Pennsylvania's experience is indicative of how this phenomenon can affect medical malpractice litigation. In 2002, Pennsylvania adopted medical malpractice reforms, including a law banning what lawyers call "venue shopping," by requiring that lawsuits be filed in the county where the alleged malpractice took place. *See* Medical Care Availability and Reduction of Error Act, 40 P.S. §1303.101 *et seq*. This Act also requires attorneys to obtain a certificate of merit from a medical professional establishing that the medical procedures complained of fell below the applicable standard of care. *See id*. Before passage of the law, malpractice lawsuit filings gravitated to Philadelphia courtrooms where, as in many urban centers, juries and sometimes judges have strong pro-plaintiff proclivities. Since passage of the law, however, Pennsylvania medical malpractice filings have decreased by an astonishing 41%. Press Release, *Governor Rendell Says Medical Malpractice Insurance Continues to Show Signs of Significant Improvement*, Pennsylvania Governor's Office, Apr. 23, 2009.

38. *See* Studdert et al., *Claims Errors*, *supra* note 34, at Abstract.

39. Tillinghast, 2007 update, *supra* Chapter 2, note 29.

40. Doctors in New Zealand are not subject to damages when they err, and yet there is no evidence that New Zealand doctors are materially more careless than U.S. doctors. So then, how well does our medical malpractice system function as a deterrent? Marie Bismark et al., *Accountability sought by patients following adverse events from medical care: the New Zealand experience*, 175 CAN. MED. ASS'N J. 889 (2006).

41. Frank A. Sloan & John H. Shadle, *Is there empirical evidence for "Defensive Medicine"? A reassessment*, 28 J. HEALTH Econ. 481, 490 (2008). Other studies of the empirical literature conclude that the deterrence impact of medical liability is difficult to measure. Michelle M. Mello & Troyen A. Brennen, *Deterrence Medical Errors: Theory and Evidence for Malpractice Reform*, 80 TEX. L. REV. 1595 (2002).

42. TOM BAKER, THE MEDICAL MALPRACTICE MYTH 98–105, 108–10 (2005); David A. Hyman & Charles M. Silver, *The Poor State of Health Quality in the U.S.: Is Malpractice Part of the Problem or Part of the Solution?*, 90 CORNELL L. REV. 893 (2005).

43. Anthony J. Sebok, *Dispatches From the Tort Wars*, 85 TEX. L. REV. 1465, 1481 (2007).

44. Sebok, *Dispatches From the Tort Wars, supra*, at 1482–83.
45. Liz Kowalczyk, *Surgical Mistakes Persist in Bay Area: Still a Fraction of Total Procedures*, BOSTON GLOBE, Oct. 26, 2007, at A1 (hereinafter Kowalczyk, *Surgical Mistakes*); (noting that after "several high-profile wrong-site surgery cases," hospitals implemented procedures by which surgery sites were marked, procedures were verified, and patient identities were checked prior to the commencement of surgery).
46. Consider protocols to count sponges prior to and during surgery to reduce the frequency of gossypiboma (surgical sponges that remain in patients after surgery). *See Recommended Practices for Sponge, Sharps, and Instrument Counts*, AORN J., Feb. 1, 2006, at 418. These recommendations specify when sponge counts should occur, how the counts should be completed, and how they should be recorded. *Id.* The introduction to recommendations reminds its target audience (operating room nurses) that the "doctrine of *res ipsa loquitor*" renders litigations over retained surgical instruments "nearly indefensible," and that "members of the entire surgical team can be held liable." *Id.* Due to the dearth of information about surgical sponge retention, it is impossible to determine how many sponge retentions are actually prevented by the practice. Verna C. Gibbs & Andrew D. Auerbach, *The Retained Surgical Sponge*, in U.S. DEPT. OF HEALTH AND HUMAN SERVICES, MAKING HEALTH CARE SAFER: A CRITICAL ANALYSIS OF PATIENT SAFETY PRACTICES 255, 256–57 (2001). Moreover, a study of sponge retentions concluded that a surgical team's failure to count sponges was not a significant factor accounting for sponge retention. (In a study of fifty-four patients who had a total of sixty-one retained "foreign bodies" [sponges accounted for 69%], a team of researchers identified three significant risk factors whose presence indicated a higher chance of retention. Surprisingly, the surgical teams' failure to follow counting procedures was not one of those factors. Atul A. Gawande et al., *Risk Factors for Retained Instruments and Sponges after Surgery*, NEW ENG. J. MED., Jan. 2003, at 229, 234. According to the researchers' multivariate analysis, the three most significant risk factors were the emergency nature of the procedure, unexpected changes in the procedure, and a patient's elevated body-mass index. *Id.* The study did stress, however, the importance of sponge and instrument counts throughout the surgical process. *Id.* The authors suggest that a large-scale study of sponge retention would allow health care providers to identify a set of factors, which when present would indicate when a patient faces a heightened risk of retaining a surgical sponge. The identification of these risk factors may help health practitioners devise additional procedures that would lead to the prevention and detection of sponge retention in high-risk patients. Gawande et al., *Risk Factors, id.* at 234. The researchers suggest that "routine intraoperative radiographic screening in selected, high-risk categories of operations could prove to

be a useful measure for detecting foreign bodies that have been inadvertently left behind." *Id.* They go on to make a rather apropos observation: "[G]iven costs of more than $50,000 per case for malpractice-claims expenses alone, a $100 plain film could prove a cost-effective intervention." *Id.* Of course, the success of the large-scale study will depend on the willingness of health care practitioners to voluntarily report both incidences of sponge retention and the circumstances present in the operating room when retention occurs. So long as the "fear of litigation associated with iatrogenic foreign bodies" compels health care providers to remain silent, success on this front is unlikely. Gibbs & Auerbach, *The Retained Surgical Sponge, id.* at 257.

47. Gawande et al., *Risk Factors, id.* at 229.
48. *See* Maulik Joshi et al., *A Systems Approach to Improve Error Reporting*, 16 J. HEALTHCARE INFO. MGMT. 40, at Abstract (2002) (citing the efforts of the Baylor Health Care System to implement cooperative systems involving the self-reporting of error in order to improve patient care) [hereinafter Maulik, *Systems Approach*].
49. *See* KOHN, BUILDING A SAFER HEALTH SYSTEM, *supra*, note 32, at 86–87. The Institute of Medicine identifies these as voluntary reporting systems that exist primarily to foster attempts to improve patient safety. *Id.* Voluntary reporting systems help practitioners identify "types of errors that occur too infrequently for an individual health care organization to readily detect based on their own data, and patterns of errors that point to systemic issues affecting all health care organizations." *Id.* at 87.
50. Lucian L. Leape, *Reporting of Adverse Events*, 347 NEW ENG. J. MED. 1633, 1635 (2002).
51. U.S. DEPT. OF HEALTH AND HUMAN SERVICES, CONFRONTING THE NEW HEALTH CARE CRISIS: IMPROVING HEALTH CARE QUALITY AND LOWER COSTS BY FIXING OUR MEDICAL LIABILITY SYSTEM (2002), at 5–6, *available at* http://aspe.hhs.gov/daltcp/reports/litrefm.pdf. This conventional wisdom has been challenged by Professors David A. Hyman of the University of Illinois College of Medicine and Charles Silver of the University of Texas School of Law who argue that health care error rates are high, not because providers do not report their errors out of fear of medical malpractice liability, but because they are not subject to *enough* medical malpractice suits. David A. Hyman & Charles Silver, *The Poor State of Health Care Quality in the U.S.: Is Malpractice Liability Part of the Problem or Part of the Solution?*, 90 CORNELL L. REV. 893 (2005).
52. *See* Maulik, *Systems Approach*, *supra* note 49, at 40; *see also* Kowalczyk, *Surgical Mistakes, supra* note 46. In this article, Diane Rydrych, Assistant Director of Health Policy, Minnesota Department of Health, is quoted as saying that "hospital analyses reveal that someone knew something was wrong but didn't speak up."

53. Jeffrey O'Connell, *The Large Cost Savings and Other Advantages of a "Crimtorts" Approach to Medical Malpractice Claims*, 17 WIDENER L.J. 835, 839 (2008).

54. *Id.*

55. *Id.*

56. O'Connell's proposal could be strengthened by adding an inducement to medical care providers to report a medical error even in advance of litigation. However, the cost of adding such a provision is undeterminable and could be substantial.

57. *See* Joni Hersch, Jeffrey O'Connell & W. Kip Viscusi, *An Empirical Assessment of Early Offer Reform for Medical Malpractice*, 36 J. LEGAL STUD. 231 (2007); *see also* Jeffrey O'Connell & Patricia Born, *The Cost and Other Advantages of an Early Offer Reform for Personal Injury Claims Against Business, Including for Product Liability*, 208 COLUM. BUS. L. REV. 423 (2008); JEFFREY O'CONNELL & CHRISTOPHER J. ROBINETTE, A RECIPE FOR BALANCED TORT REFORM (2008). These estimations are disputed in a study that concludes that the reduction in payout would be only in the range of 20%. Bernard Black, David A. Hyman & Charles Silver, *The Effects of "Early Offers" in Medical Malpractice Cases: Evidence from Texas*, 6 J. EMPIRICAL LEGAL STUD. 723 (Dec. 2009), *available at* http://ssrn.com/abstract=1112135. O'Connell and his collaborators, in turn, criticize the assumptions that underlie the Black-Hyman-Silver critique. *See* Joni Hersch, Jeffery O'Connell & W. Kip Vicusi, *Reply to the Effects of 'Early Offers' in Medical Malpractice Cases: Evidence for Texas*, 7 J. EMPIRICAL LEGAL STUD. (2010), *available at* http://ssrn.com/abstract=1487681. Black, Hyman and Silver reply to this reply. *See* Bernard S. Black, David A. Hyman & Charles Silver, *O'Connell Early Settlement Offers: Toward Realistic Numbers and Two-Sided Offers*, 7 J. EMPIRICAL LEGAL STUD. (2010).

58. William M. Sage & Eleanor D. Kinney, *Medicare-Led Malpractice Reform*, in WILLIAM M. SAGE & ROGAN KERSH, EDS., MEDICAL MALPRACTICE AND THE U.S. HEALTH CARE SYSTEM 318 (2006).

59. *Id.* at 322.

60. *Id.* at 337, 342–43.

61. *Id.* at 330–34.

62. *Id.* at 340.

63. *Id.* at 325–26.

9 Lawyers' Role in the Expansion of Tort Liability

IN CHAPTER 8, I EXAMINED HOW TORT LAWYERS' QUEST FOR profits influenced the development of a tort system that neither efficiently compensates injured victims nor meaningfully deters the production of unsafe services and products. In this chapter, I continue the systemic focus by addressing the most far reaching effect of contingency fees on the tort system: the expansion of the scope of liability of the tort system over the past five decades. By expansion of the scope of liability, I mean the enlargement – mainly by judicial action – of the range of acts that make someone liable to another for causing injury.

When courts create new bases for awarding compensation by expanding the range of acts that give rise to liability, they typically apply those decisions retroactively, thus accentuating the effects of the expanded liability. This is especially true for individual or corporate acts that were lawful when they occurred in the 1940s and 1950s but were later considered wrongful after the expansion of liability that began in the late 1960s and quickened in the 1980s. Indeed, thousands of tort claims from the 1980s onward were the result of defendants' retroactive inculpation for acts committed decades earlier that were not wrongful at the time. Today, as Professors James A. Henderson and Aaron D. Twerski have stated, "a manufacturer can wake up one morning and find itself confronted with the very real possibility that all the products it has sold for the past [twenty] years (all 450 billion of them) are legally defective."[1]

Asbestos litigation is a quintessential example of the expansion of the scope of liability by retroactive inculpation. Manufacturers of asbestos-containing products and those who mined asbestos were aware that exposing their workers to raw asbestos in friable form through these activities was hazardous because of its carcinogenic and lung-scarring properties. (Despite this awareness, several major manufacturers suppressed this information and subjected their workers to lethal doses of asbestos.[2]) However, at the time of the production and sale of most asbestos-containing products, manufacturers had no reasonable basis for knowing that installation or use of their products – as in the construction or shipbuilding trades – could cause injury. Thus, no tort liability was attached to their actions.[3] In 1965, however, Dr. Irving Selikoff published the results of a study showing that insulators, who had the highest exposures of any occupational group to asbestos-containing products, were at severe risk.[4] Thereafter, manufacturers of asbestos-containing products were on notice of the possibility that users of their asbestos-containing products could be harmed. Nonetheless, in 1973 in the landmark case of *Borel v. Fiberboard Paper Products Corp.*,[5] courts began to *retroactively* impose tort liability on these manufacturers and sellers for the failure to warn construction and shipyard workers, and others, *decades earlier*, of the harmful characteristics of their products.[6]

Although the scope of tort liability has been expanding for over a century,[7] beginning in the 1960s, the pace of expansion began to quicken.[8] George Priest has analyzed the transformation of our tort system from one that provided damages for personal injury through negligence law into one of the most pervasive regulatory systems of societal behavior ever adopted by a democratic society. In 1993, he wrote: "[In] the past three decades ... courts have significantly expanded standards of tort and environmental liability, increasing the liability exposure of virtually everyone in the society but especially of manufacturers, insurers and governmental entities."[9]

One of the leading causes of this expansion has been judges' desire to enlarge the range of acts for which compensation can be awarded and to effectuate their policy judgments about the fundamental purposes of the tort system. Judges accomplished this goal by: (a) contracting traditional defenses to tort claims[10]; (b) expanding rights to recover tort damages from governmental and charitable institutions, doctors, property owners, and out-of-state businesses[11]; (c) developing the legal doctrine of "strict liability" for product manufacturers – a reconceptualization of tort law as not only a compensatory system but one designed to maximize social welfare by imposing the cost of injury on manufacturers so that they would have the incentive to minimize the costs of accidents[12]; (d) using "strict liability" to allow the retroactive inculpation of product manufacturers for acts done decades earlier[13]; (e) adopting procedural rules, which enabled plaintiffs' lawyers to expand the scope of discovery in civil litigation[14]; (f) changing other procedural rules to allow aggregation of large numbers of claims, especially the 1966 amendment to Rule 23 of the Federal Rules of Civil Procedure, which ushered in the modern era of class actions[15]; and (g) creatively interpreting business liability insurance policies to read exclusions out of the policy, hugely increasing the potential insurance assets available to plaintiffs in tort actions.[16]

Additional factors contributing to the expansion include large increases in asset pools available to plaintiffs seeking compensation for tortious injury, including auto, homeowner, and business liability insurance[17]; and changes in social, industrial, and economic conditions, which have facilitated the growth of mass tort litigation and the evolution of law firms with expertise in aggregative litigation.[18]

But one additional factor looms at least as large as any of those listed and that is the efforts of tort lawyers – driven by powerful financial incentives – to engage in what are essentially collaborative efforts with judges to enlarge the scope of tort liability. As detailed in Chapter 2, tort lawyers have experienced increases in their effective hourly rates of more than 1,000 percent during the course of this expansion. It may seem logical to attribute this substantial increase in their incomes to the great expansion and the consequent increase in the volume of tort litigation. In turn, we might attribute the increased volume of tort litigation to increased rates of injury and changes in tort doctrine. However, I reject both of these explanations.

First, I contend that the rise in profits is not primarily the result of expanded liability; rather, it is the substantial increase in profits that has driven expanded liability. Second, I further contend that the increased volume of tort litigation that we have experienced is not the result of increases in prevailing injury rates; in fact, as I explain in Chapter 14, occupational injury rates and accident rates have declined. Nor are changes in legal doctrine directly driving the increase. Rather, it is increased profits that have driven the increased volume of tort litigation and incentivized lawyers to successfully lobby judges – already, in many cases, so predisposed – to expand tort doctrines.[19] In a significant subset of cases, increased profit levels also have come to determine the outcomes of tort litigation. Put simply, it is the fee tail that wags the tort dog.

Plaintiffs' lawyers and lawyer-judges who, as explained later in this chapter, have accorded themselves increased regulatory powers, are the chief beneficiaries of the vast expansion of the tort system. Lawyers empowered by their increased financial strength have developed cooperative structures to further aggrandize their power.[20] Moreover, they continuously press the courts for expansionary changes.[21] No rational person believes that the substantial changes in doctrine, claim valuation, or evidentiary standards and procedure, which have been integral parts of tort liability expansion, "simply happened." The process of enlargement is the complex product of social, economic, political, and financial trends, as well as the collaborative efforts of judges and tort lawyers.

Legal scholars contributed significantly to that expansion by developing the theory of enterprise liability, which several influential judges began to adopt in the 1960s. The theory is based on the view that turning manufacturers into insurers and holding them strictly liable for product injuries, irrespective of whether they acted negligently, reduces accident costs. Manufacturers would be expected to react to the imposition of liability by (1) incorporating liability costs into the prices of their products, thus socializing the cost of injury; and (2) by efficiently increasing investment in product safety.[22] In fact, as previously pointed out, although manufacturers have substantially increased investments in product safety, these investments are not due to litigation risk but rather to avoid being punished in the marketplace and to comply with government safety regulations.[23] Though these market and regulatory forces have resulted in significant declines in product-related injuries, product liability litigation – because it is driven by the pursuit of profits – has not declined. In fact, it has increased.[24]

Many commentators have added to our understanding of the effects of lawyers' profit-driven efforts to expand the scope of tort liability. Robert A. Kagan attributes the expansion to the development of "adversarial legalism," which he defines as legal structures and rules that foster an adversarial and legalistic style of policy making, policy implementation, and dispute resolution, by means of lawyer-dominant litigation.[25] Robert Prichard, former president of the University of Toronto and dean of its law school, also explains the role that lawyers play in influencing courts to expand tort liability by creating new or expanded legal doctrines:

> Courts are both limited to and driven by the cases that litigants put before them: Their understanding of legal problems is limited to the cases before them. At the same time, however, courts are driven to develop substantive doctrines to respond satisfactorily to the full array of cases they are called upon to decide.... As the valid claims emerge doctrinally, the incentive to sue and to expand the range of claims is correspondingly increased. As lawyers press these newly encouraged claims, the doctrinal law must be further elaborated, specified, and developed. The process feeds on itself so that the likelihood and importance of cross-fertilization are increased. Thus the increased pace and complexity of doctrinal evolution in the American system owes its origin to the initial incentive structure.
>
> ...

[Also] incentives for lawyers under the American system provide a spur for bringing provocative and novel claims. If one were to ask English or Commonwealth lawyers to describe what they find most remarkable about American litigation, a common response would identify the startling or provocative or novel extension of existing principle: "Can you imagine arguing that?" captures the type of reaction.... [T]he origin of these novel developments lies in the incentive structure.[26]

Expansionary changes in tort liability, once adopted by courts, tend to be maintained and further expanded – a process called "path dependence." Robert A. Kagan explains that

[t]he basic idea is that existing institutional arrangements generate patterns of activity that continuously reinforce the attitudes and interests of those who benefit from those arrangements, producing an institutional "stickiness" that deflects and/or resists pressures for change. Laws and legal institutions, with their characteristic semi-autonomy, dominance by specialists with similar legal training, and emphasis on tradition, are strong candidates for such path-dependent trajectories. The U.S. tort system falls in this category.[27]

Critics of the proposition that lawyers have been instrumental in enlarging the scope of tort liability abound.[28] One criticism is that strategic actions by plaintiffs' attorneys seeking to expand tort liability in litigation have been and continue to be countered by symmetrically countervailing efforts by the defense bar. As Professor George Priest explains, "in an adversary system, each case involves two parties presenting opposing theories of decision. By definition, therefore, judges are presented theories that would expand the law equal in number to theories that would restrict it."[29] This conventional wisdom, however, fails to adequately address defense attorney agency costs.

The financial benefits of the expansion of the tort system do not redound exclusively to plaintiffs' attorneys. Expansion of liability also increases the demand for defendants' lawyers, which results in higher earnings. In addition, as plaintiffs' lawyers' effective hourly rates of return increase, defendants seeking to retain comparable quality counsel must raise the rates they pay. A rising tide of tort litigation lifts all lawyers' boats. Conversely, tort reform measures that contract tort liability harm both plaintiffs and defendants' lawyers. The president of the Defense Research Institute – the largest association of defense lawyers – acknowledged that many defense lawyers "think reforms aren't in the best interests of defense trial lawyers because it reduces litigation."[30] Indeed, there is a plethora of evidence to support the consonance of interests of plaintiffs' and defendants' lawyers.[31]

Insurance companies also contribute to tort system expansion by providing asset pools that attract plaintiff lawyers' interest. At first blush, we would expect that insurance companies would strongly resist attempts to expand tort liability. In fact, insurance companies are schizophrenic about expansion. In the short term, insurance companies oppose expansions of tort liability, especially when they have failed to anticipate an increase in the cost of liability and build that into their premiums. In the long term, however, insurance companies benefit from expansion of tort liability.[32] The more expansive the tort system, the higher the price insurers can charge for insuring against liability risk.[33] Higher premiums create higher potential profits and, therefore, higher salaries for CEOs. Of course, it is essential that insurance companies accurately assess the level of liability that will prevail through the duration of an insurance policy when they set the price of risk. In the interest of increasing the predictability of the level of damages awarded in tort litigation, insurance companies typically favor such tort reforms as damage caps and shortening of statutes of limitation. Some insurance companies, however, tend to take a dim view of tort reforms that would reduce the volume of litigation.

Strategic actions by plaintiffs' lawyers, supported by the efforts of legal scholars and influential judges, are not limited to protecting the expansionary changes from the efforts of tort reformers to scale them back. Plaintiffs' lawyers are proactively seeking to enlarge the scope of liability. Indeed, as set forth in Chapter 11, Section D, perhaps at no time in our history have tort lawyers been in a more politically advantageous position than the present to legislatively advance their interest in expanding tort liability. Again we turn to Robert A. Kagan for an explanation of the relationship between lawyers' profits and expansion of tort liability in this context:

> [T]ort litigation has generated increasing returns to the plaintiffs' bar, which has grown in size, sophistication, and resources. It has learned to litigate strategically to establish precedents that make future cases easier to win, to disseminate techniques for identifying and proving liability, and to influence judicial appointments and legislative policymaking ... [S]teady and substantial funding from the plaintiff's bar has succeeded, by and large, in lining up Democratic politicians as reliable opponents of conservative tort reforms. The ideal interests of the legal profession, too, work to resist major changes in the tort system. Legal elites – law professors, judges, lawyers in the legislatures and on legislative staffs – still tend to *support* the doctrinal changes of the 1960s and 1970s. Wedded to the ideology of adversarial legalism, they defend the distinctive features of the American tort system – large contingency fees (to ensure access to lawyers and courts); class actions (to control corporate malfeasance); trial by jury (as a check on the power of judges); and wide jury discretion in assessing noneconomic damages. Plaintiffs' lawyers regularly challenge the constitutionality of conservative tort legislation they opposed, and at least a dozen state supreme courts have struck down key aspects of such laws, inhibiting more far-reaching conservative reform proposals.[34]

NOTES

1. JAMES A. HENDERSON JR. & AARON D. TWERSKI, PRODUCTS LIABILITY: PROBLEMS AND PROCESS 159 (5th ed. 2004). Professor Adam Scales of the Washington and Lee University School of Law, in referring to the "profound expansion in tort liability that has occurred during the past few decades," conjures up a Rip Van Winkle-like "individual from the 1950s" who time-travels to the present and is "amazed to learn that she had acquired obligations to protect criminal trespassers from harming themselves on her property, warn neighbors of the sexual predations of her spouse, or prevent people from misusing purchases so as to harm themselves." Adam F. Scales, *Against Settlement Factoring? The Market in Tort Claims Has Arrived*, 2002 WIS. L. REV. 859, 874–75 n.56 (2002).

2. *See generally* PAUL BRODEUR, OUTRAGEOUS MISCONDUCT (1985).

3. *See* Richard A. Epstein, *Manville: The Bankruptcy of Product Liability Law*, AEI J. GOV'T & SOC'Y REG., Sept./Oct. 1982, at 14, 17–18 ("[A]t the time that [Johns] Manville [the leading manufacturer of asbestos-containing products in the mid-twentieth century] and other corporations sold asbestos, right up to the 1960s, they were subject to no discernable risk of tort liability.").

4. *See* I.J. Selikoff et al., *The Occurrence of Asbestosis Among Insulation Workers in the United States*, 132 ANNALS N.Y. ACAD. SCIS. 139 (1965).

5. 493 F.2d 1076 (5th Cir. 1973).

6. The "failure to warn" strategy reached its zenith in the "property damage" cases, brought by building owners against the manufacturers of asbestos-containing products used in construction. These owners incurred substantial expenses for removing asbestos-containing products (though the better option, in most cases, would have been to properly maintain the asbestos in place – a course of action that would have protected the structure's occupants or users from injury). In prevailing in their suits against the manufacturers for the costs of removal, building owners advanced the legal argument that the manufacturers failed to warn purchasers that their products were sufficiently dangerous that they should not have purchased the products. *See* Lester Brickman, *The Asbestos Litigation Crisis: Is There a Need for an Administrative Alternative?*, 13 CARDOZO L. REV. 1819, 1851–52 nn.131–36 (1992) [hereinafter Brickman, *Asbestos Litigation Crisis*].

7. The increase in the scope of liability has not been confined to the United States. A justice of the high court of Queensland, Australia, recently opined: "The generous application of [negligence] rules is producing a litigious society and has already spawned an aggressive legal industry. I am concerned that the common law is being developed to a stage that already inflicts too great a cost upon the community both economic and social.... [I]n recent times its development has been all in one direction – more liability and more damages." *Lisle v. Brice* [2002] 2 Qd. R. 168 paras. 4–5 (Thomas, J., concurring). For further discussion of the expansion in the scope of liability of the tort system, popularly known as "the litigation explosion" see sources cited in Herbert M. Kritzer, *Seven Dogged Myths Concerning Contingency Fees*, 80 WASH U. L.Q. 739, 739 n.1 (2002) [hereinafter Kritzer, *Seven Myths*].

8. It is at least of passing interest that others have noted a transformation of the three legs of the legal profession – the bar, the bench, and the academy – that also began in the 1960s. In A NATION UNDER LAWYERS: HOW THE CRISIS IN THE LEGAL PROFESSION IS TRANSFORMING AMERICAN SOCIETY (1994), Mary Ann Glendon, a professor at Harvard Law School, describes recent changes in the legal profession that have had a transformative effect on American society. Since 1960, litigation has become a much larger proportion of law practice leading

to a "litigation explosion," commercialization of the bar, and a more merce-
nary and unscrupulous bar. Glendon, *id*. at 35–84. The bench has succumbed to
"[a]n adventurous concept of judging," *id*. at 130, where self-aggrandizement
has crowded out judges' traditional reticence to use their powers to remake
society in their own images. Finally, the legal academy has devolved into
schools of esoteric scholarship that have little relevance to the practice of law.
Judge Richard Posner, in reviewing her book, agrees "that the legal profession
in all its branches has changed greatly since the 1950s and in approximately
the ways described by Glendon" and that "judges [have become] too aggressive and intrude too deeply into the activities of other branches of government,
acting all too often as ignorant policy czars." Richard A. Posner, *A Nation
Under Lawyers*, THE NEW REPUBLIC, Oct. 31, 1999 at 40. He counters, however,
that "these things do not have the significance that Glendon ascribes to them."
Moreover, "[t]he profession was not as wonderful in 1960 as Glendon makes
out" [and m]any of the changes since then are improvements or are inseparable
from improvements." *Id*.

9. *See* George L. Priest,*Lawyers, Liability and Law Reform: Effects on American
Economic Growth and Trade Competitiveness*, 71 DENV. U. L. REV. 115, 115
(1993) [hereinafter *Priest, Lawyers, Liability and Law Reform*].

10. *See* Stephen C. Yeazell,*Re-financing Civil Litigation*, 51 DEPAUL L. REV. 183,
2190–92 (2001), [hereinafter Yeazell, *Civil Litigation*] (At the beginning of the
twentieth century, tort liability expansion was largely a function of the contraction of traditional defenses to tort claims, especially defenses available
to employers, municipalities, and charities, as well as the replacement of the
absolute defense of contributory negligence by comparative fault.); *see also*
LAWRENCE M. FRIEDMAN, AMERICAN LAW IN THE TWENTIETH CENTURY 349–50
(2002).

11. Yeazell, *Civil Litigation, id*.; *see also* Robert A. Kagan, *How Much Do
Conservative Tort Tales Matter?*, 31 LAW & SOC. INQUIRY 711, 715–16 (2006)
[hereinafter Kagan, *Conservative Tort Tales*].

12. W. PAGE KEETON ET AL., PROSSER AND KEETON ON THE LAW OF TORTS § 2, at 7
(5th ed. 1984) (Tort law's "primary purpose is to compensate [the victim] for
the damage suffered, at the expense of the wrongdoer."). Tort law also seeks
to reduce the volume of injury, socialize injury cost, and maximize the gross
social product. GUIDO CALABRESI, THE COST OF ACCIDENTS: A LEGAL AND
ECONOMIC ANALYSIS 26 (1970) (It is "axiomatic that the principal function of
accident law is to reduce the sum of the costs of accidents and the costs of
avoiding accidents."). The classical view understood tort liability as a speci-
fication of what fundamental fairness requires between two interacting legal
persons. Calabresi's innovation was to reconceptualize tort law as one part of
a wider "public law" of accidents, where the salient feature about accidents

(the fact about them that calls for a public, legal response) is that they involve "costs" – a squandering of social resources. Thus, Calabresi postulates that the master-goal of any public law of accidents is to minimize the costs of accidents. This encompasses a number of sub-goals, including deterrence (preventing accidents from happening in the first place, when prevention is cheaper than their expected costs) and compensation (reducing the burden of accidents even after they have occurred by shifting the costs to deep pockets or spreading them via insurance or market prices). *See also* WILLIAM L. PROSSER ET AL., CASES AND MATERIALS ON TORTS 1 (8th ed. 1988).

13. In the case of asbestos litigation, retroactive inculpation and the development of legal doctrines that allowed plaintiffs to effectively circumvent state workers' compensation systems enabled hundreds of thousands of industrial and construction workers to sue manufacturers and sellers of asbestos-containing products. *See* Brickman, *Asbestos Litigation, supra* note 6, at 1824. Another example of retroactive inculpation is the use of a newly fashioned public nuisance theory to inculpate manufacturers of paint containing lead for acts done scores of years earlier. *See infra* Chapter 11, § B(2).

14. *See* Yeazell, *Civil Litigation, supra* note 10, at 194–95 (2001) (Pretrial discovery rules resulted in increased "expectable returns" on plaintiffs' lawyers' investment in litigation.).

15. For an historical analysis of the effect of the 1966 amendment to Rule 23 of the Federal Rules of Civil Procedure, see Lester Brickman, *Lawyers' Ethics and Fiduciary Obligation in the Brave New World of Aggregative Litigation,* 26 WM. & MARY ENVT'L. L. & POL'Y REV. 243, at App. (2001) [hereinafter Brickman, *The Brave New World*].

   For an analysis of the development of the theory of "aggregative torts" and how that is being used to justify massive but "lawless" judicial reallocations of economic resources, see James A. Henderson Jr., *The Lawlessness of Aggregative Torts,* 34 HOFSTRA L. REV. 329 (2005); Chapter 11, § A.

16. *See, e.g., Keene Corp. v. INA,* 667 F. 2d 1034 (D.C. Cir. 1981, *cert denied,* 456 U.S. 951 (1982)); *Morton Int'l Inc., v. General Accident Ins. Co.,* 629 A.2d 831, 871–72 (N.J. 1993); *Shell Oil Co. v. Winterhur Swiss Ins. Co.,* 15 Cal. Rptr.2d 815, 841 (Ct. App. 1993); *see also* Katherine T. Eubank, Note, *Paying the Costs of Hazardous Waste Pollution: Why is the Insurance Industry Raising Such a Stink?,* 1991 U. ILL. L. REV. 173, 185 (1991); Jim L. Julian & Charles L. Schlumberger, Essay, *Insurance Coverage for Environmental Clean-Up Costs Under Comprehensive General Liability Policies,* 19 U. ARK. LITTLE ROCK L.J. 57 (1996).

17. *See* Yeazell, *Civil Litigation, supra* note 10, at 189–94.

18. *See* Deborah R. Hensler & Mark A. Peterson, *Understanding Mass Personal Injury Litigation: A Socio-Legal Analysis,* 59 BROOK. L. REV. 961, 1013–14 (1993) [hereinafter Hensler & Peterson, *Mass Litigation*].

19. For an examination of the role of legal doctrine in tort law that omits any discussion of the effect of plaintiffs' lawyers' financial incentives on the development of tort doctrine, see MARSHALL S. SHAPO, TORT LAW AND CULTURE (2003). *See also* Joel Levin, *Tort Wars*, 39 TORT TRIAL INS. PRAC. L.J. 869 (2004) (critiquing Professor Shapo's book as "complete[ly] irrelevan[t] because it "fail[s] to shed a clear light on the dynamics of tort law," *id.* at 870, and ignores the two specific engines that have driven tort law in the twentieth century: the contingency fee and the American jury. *Id.* at 874).

20. *See* Yeazell, *Civil Litigation, supra* note 10, at 216 ("Both the plaintiffs' and defense bars have reorganized themselves, the former more profoundly than the latter. Compared to the world before the Great Depression ... the plaintiffs' bar is better capitalized, both in intellectual and financial terms."); Jack B. Weinstein, *Ethical Dilemmas in Mass Tort Litigation*, 88 NW. U. L. REV. 469, 480, n.43, 524 (1994) ("The speed with which the number of breast implant cases exploded on the scene is attributable in part to a well-organized plaintiffs' bar, which now has the capital, organizational skills, and advertising techniques to seek clientele."); Robert England, *Congress, Nader and the Ambulance Chasers*, THE AM. SPECTATOR, Sept. 1990, at 18; Carolyn Lochhead, *The Growing Power of Trial Lawyers*, THE WEEKLY STANDARD, Sept. 23, 1996 (reporting the "astonishing extent of political giving by trial lawyers" and the enormous political power of trial lawyers); Richard B. Schmitt, *Trial Lawyers Glide Past Critics with Aid of Potent Trade Group*, WALL ST. J., Feb. 17, 1994, at A1; Stuart Taylor Jr., *Greedy Lawyers Cheat Real Asbestos Victims*, THE NAT'L JOURNAL, September 28, 2002 ("ATLA [Association of Trial Lawyers of America, now the AAJ, American Association for Justice] is a huge campaign donor to congressional Democrats, and [its] members ... are the biggest donors to many of the elected state court judges whose sometimes-shocking rulings have helped make the lawyers so rich.").

21. *See* Hensler & Peterson, *Mass Litigation, supra* note 18, at 1033, 1043, 1045 (1993) (discussing interests of the plaintiffs' bar in maximizing returns through increasing the number of claims).

22. *See supra* note 12; *see also* George L. Priest, *The Modern Transformation of Civil Law*, paper presented at Common Good/AEI-Brookings conference on "Lawsuits and Liberty," Phil., Pa., June 27–28, 2005.

23. *See* Shavell & Polinsky, *Product Liability, supra* Chapter 8, note 4, at 2.

24. In the 1996–2005 period, as reported by thirty state courts, products liability filings increased by 26%. NATIONAL CENTER FOR STATE COURTS, EXAMINING THE WORK OF STATE COURTS, 2006 (Robert C. La Fountain et al. eds. 2007), *available at* http://www.ncsconline.org/D_Research/csp/CSP_Main_Page.html; see *also* George L. Priest, *Products Liability Law and the Accident Rate* in ROBERT E. LITAN & CLIFFORD WINSTON, LIABILITY: PERSPECTIVES AND

POLICY 184 (Brookings Institution 1988) (examining the relationship between injury rates and the 861% growth in products liability litigation from the period 1974 to 1986).

25. *See* KAGAN, ADVERSARIAL LEGALISM, *supra* Introduction, note 13, at 231–32. As evidence of this enlargement, he cites examples of substantial expansion in the number of lawyers per unit of population; expenditures on lawyers; the number of federal court appellate cases involving constitutional issues; and of state appellate and federal court cases involving schools. *Id.* at 36–37. Additional examples he lists include an unprecedented wave of regulatory statutes concerning pollution control, land use, consumer protection, and nondiscrimination in employment and education. *Id.* at 38.

26. J. Robert S. Prichard, *A Systemic Approach to Comparative Law: The Effect of Cost, Fee, and Financing Rules on the Development of the Substantive Law,* 17 J. LEGAL STUD. 451, 464–66 (1988) (citations omitted) [hereinafter Prichard, *A Systemic Approach*].

27. *See* Kagan, *Conservative Tort Tales, supra* note 11, at 727 (footnotes omitted).

28. Professor Frank Cross argues on theoretical and empirical grounds that "lawyer interests definitely will not produce doctrinal expansion in products liability or tort law." Frank B. Cross, *The Role of Lawyers in Positive Theories of Doctrinal Evolution,* 45 EMORY L.J. 523, 587 (1996). However, Cross's reliance on doctrinal development as a surrogate for tort liability is misplaced. Tort lawyers' efforts to expand tort liability extend far beyond the doctrinal. Indeed, the proposition that lawyers' efforts have significantly influenced the recent expansion in the scope of tort liability – just as they significantly influenced the development of our modern accident law – seems hardly debatable. Moreover, Cross's understanding of how lawyers function is, at least, inadequate. For example, he argues that "no individual lawyer would have much incentive to bear the costs of doctrinal expansion when he or she can reap only a fragment of the benefits." *Id.* at 549 (footnote omitted). Again, this is economic theory masquerading as fact. The evidence is clear that tort lawyers are willing to, and do, make substantial investments in enlarging tort liability, which are open to all lawyers to exploit. See Rubin & Bailey, *Changing the Law, supra* Chapter 8, note 10, for the theoretical response to Cross. Indeed, mass tort lawyers invested millions of dollars to expand tort liability in asbestos, tobacco, and breast implant litigations – to name a few – even though they knew that other lawyers would also benefit from their efforts. In return, they and other lawyers garnered billions of dollars in fees.

29. *See* Priest, *Lawyers, Liability and Law Reform, supra* note 9, at 125 (footnotes omitted).

30. Amy Stevens, *Lawyers and Clients: Corporate Clients, Some Lawyers Differ on Litigation Reform,* WALL ST. J., Mar. 17, 1995, at B6.

31. A Texas defense lawyer acknowledged that because of tort reforms enacted in Texas in 2003, his health care industry clients don't get sued nearly as much as before and that as a consequence his firm has shrunk to half its former size. *See* Terry Carter, *Tort Reform, Texas Style*, A.B.A.J., Oct. 2006, at 30, 33. A former president of the Texas Trial Lawyers Association observed that tort reform "hit the defense side harder first. Their practices are drying up." *Id.* at 33. A prominent Texas plaintiff's lawyer put it plainly: "[Defense attorneys] wouldn't be able to live nicely and send their kids to private school ... if we didn't sue their clients." Andrea Gerlin, *Personal Injury: For a Texas Lawyer, Misfortune's Big Bucks May Take a Big Dive – State's Tort Reform Cramps John Cracken's Style, So He Looks to Diversify – How to Buy a Speedy Trial*, WALL ST. J., Oct. 3, 1995, at A1.

The consonance of interests of plaintiff and defendant tort lawyers is nowhere better illustrated than in a letter from California and Los Angeles trial lawyers' associations to California business lawyers soliciting funds for a campaign to oppose three initiatives that appeared on the March 1996 California ballot. One of the initiatives would have created a true no-fault system for automobile injury compensation; under it, injured persons would collect for injuries to person and property from their own insurance companies rather than by suing the other driver. The other initiative was a variant of the "early offer" proposal described in the Introduction. This proposal would have benefited Mary Corcoran and other victims of tort lawyers' zero-based accounting scheme by limiting contingency fees to the value added by lawyers when there are early settlement offers. (A third sought to limit class actions). The solicitation letter stated that passage of the no-fault initiative would eliminate a large portion of automobile accident litigation and that passage of the contingency fee limitation would drastically reduce the number of tort filings. And *that* would harm the interests of defense lawyers. The letter went on to instruct the defense lawyers how they could make non-"public record" contributions so that their clients would be unaware of their doing so. *See* Brickman, *Money Talks, supra* Chapter 3, note 9, at 258 n.31. This illustration of the convergence of plaintiffs' *and* defendants' lawyers' financial interests should make us wary of the public policy choices that emanate from that convergence. *See* Richard A. Epstein, *The Unintended Revolution in Product Liability Law*, 10 CARDOZO L. REV. 2193, 2219 (1989) (arguing that the defense bar's interest in not limiting liability is as strong as the plaintiff bar's interest because if whole classes of claims imposing retroactive liability were removed, the business of defending clients on the merits of individual cases would no longer be of any consequence); Rubin & Bailey, *Changing the Law, supra* Chapter 8, note 10, at 808–09 (discussing that whereas it is plaintiffs' lawyers who engineer the expansion of tort law, "defendants' lawyers also have an interest in complex tort law"); Amy Stevens,

Corporate Clients, Some Lawyers Differ on Litigation Reform, WALL ST. J., Mar. 17, 1995, at B6 (stating that defense lawyers oppose tort reform because "legislative change could deliver a big blow to the bottom line"). *Cf.* Eric Helland and Alexander Tabarrok, *Exporting Tort Awards*, 23 REGULATION 21, 22 (2000) ("Defense and plaintiff's lawyers will both prefer that the more generous judge be elected because generous judges increase the demand for both plaintiff and defense lawyers."); John Fabian Witt, *State Constitutions and American Tort Law*, at 31–32, *available at* http://ssrn.com/abstract=515662 (last visited May 25, 2004) (noting that "[p]laintiffs' lawyers, insurance lawyers, and the bar associations to which they belonged 'vociferously opposed'" a plan to replace tort liability with limited, scheduled liability for motor vehicle owners who caused damage with their automobiles).

32. Rubin & Bailey, *Changing the Law*, Chapter 8, note 10, at 812.
33. *See* W. Kip Viscusi, *The Dimensions of the Product Liability Crisis*, 20 J. LEGAL STUD. 147, 148 (1991) ("[I]n the long run the insurance industry will profit from a high level of liability since that will increase the degree of coverage it can write.").
34. Kagan, *Conservative Tort Tales, supra* note 11, at 717 (footnotes omitted).

10 The Role of the Judiciary in Tort System Expansion

ROBERT KAGAN'S EMPHASIS OF THE ROLE OF STATE supreme court judges in the tort reform wars is spot on. Lawyers and judges share a mutual interest in expanding the scope of liability of the tort system. By facilitating the expansion of tort liability, judges not only support the interests of lawyers, but also increase their own regulatory role and their ability to impose their policy preferences onto society. This chapter explores the judicial role in the expansion of the tort system through analysis of state supreme court invalidations of tort reform laws and other collaborative efforts of lawyers and judges to expand tort liability.

Nowhere do the bare knuckles of state supreme court judges show through their black robes more plainly than when they invalidate legislative efforts to contract previous judicial expansions of tort liability. These frequent invalidations often violate basic constitutional principles. Unlike the U.S. government, which only has the powers granted to it under the Constitution, state governments have broad general powers, limited only by their state constitutions and the powers they have ceded to the United States. The broadest state power is the police power, which empowers state legislatures to enact legislation to advance the health, safety, morals, and general welfare of the populace.[1] Though common law courts are largely responsible for developing contract, tort, and property law, legislatures have always retained the power to create, modify, or repeal these rules.[2]

Despite state legislative authority to regulate the tort system, state supreme courts have nullified more than one hundred tort reforms since 1983.[3] Perhaps the most egregious invalidation of legislation occurred in 1997, when the Illinois Supreme Court, in *Best v. Taylor Machine Works*,[4] essentially declared the state legislature's constitutional power to change the state's common law[5] null and void by prohibiting the state's General Assembly from enacting any tort reforms to roll back judicial expansions of the tort system. This action was disguised as constitutional interpretation when, in fact, it was a constitutional *putsch*.[6]

Another prime example of judicial disenfranchisement of legislative authority to regulate the tort system is a 1999 ruling of the Ohio Supreme Court. After days of hearings and two years of study, the Ohio legislature concluded that large tort awards were driving up the cost of malpractice insurance for doctors and liability insurance for businesses to the detriment of the state's interest. In response, it enacted a series of provisions to improve the civil justice system in Ohio, which included caps on damage awards.[7] The Ohio Supreme Court struck down the legislation, stating that the damage cap was not "rationally related" to the goal of reducing costs.[8] The court's rationale does not withstand scrutiny. When California enacted the Medical Injury Compensation Reform Act (MICRA) in 1975, capping pain and suffering damages at $250,000 in medical malpractice cases, medical malpractice premium increases were thereafter significantly lower than in comparable states. Moreover, well-designed empirical studies prove that damage caps do, in fact, reduce liability insurance premium increases.[9] Thus, the Ohio Supreme Court's invalidation of this legislative effort to reform the tort system demonstrates the proclivity of some state supreme courts to violate the constitutional boundaries of the judicial branch by substituting their policy judgments for that of their legislatures in order to further the expansion of the tort system.

It is also noteworthy that an injured claimant did not initiate the Ohio lawsuit – Ohio's tort lawyers did, claiming that the legislation would injure them by resulting in lower levels of litigation and therefore less fee income and fewer tort lawyers. The pretextual nature of the court's decision is made clear by the way it described the contending parties. Ignoring the fact that Ohio's trial lawyers had initiated the lawsuit *on their own behalf*, the Ohio Supreme Court stated that "this conflict reflects a power struggle between those who seek to limit their liability and financial exposure for civil wrongs and those who seek compensation for their injuries."[10]

A third example of egregious judicial nullification occurred in 2004, when the Florida Supreme Court – one of the most pro-plaintiff-lawyer courts in the nation – stated its intention to nullify the rights of the Florida electorate. That year, Florida voters, by a two to one margin, approved a constitutional amendment effectively limiting lawyers' contingency fees in medical malpractice actions to 30 percent of the first $250,000 and 10 percent of any additional recovery.[11] This overrode the Florida Bar rule adopted by the court, limiting all contingency fees in personal injury litigation to between 33⅓ percent and 40 percent of the first $1 million in recovery, 30 percent at of any recovery between $1 million and $2 million, plus 20 percent of any recovery exceeding $2 million.[12] Despite the huge majority in favor of the amendment lowering attorney's fees, about two years later, the Florida Supreme Court declared that it would vitiate the amendment by allowing medical malpractice plaintiffs to waive this constitutional right to a lower attorney's fee.[13]

Why would a plaintiff choose to waive the right to pay a lower fee? Some plaintiffs with clear-cut liability but claims worth less than about $100,000 – not enough in most cases to gain representation – might be willing to do so in order to attract a lawyer to take their case. However, in the face of an open invitation from the Florida Supreme Court to Florida malpractice lawyers to insist on client waivers, what is the likely outcome? Anecdotal evidence from trial lawyers is that they are seeking waivers in any case where the constitutional fee cap would erode their financial incentive to take the case; moreover, no client asked to sign a waiver has failed to do so.[14]

The Florida Supreme Court's declaration that it will nullify the decision of Florida's voters is but one of many current battles in the tort reform wars. Florida's voters' only alternative to the rule of lawyers is to use the electoral process to take the state supreme court back from the tort lawyers, as business interests have convinced voters to do in Texas, Mississippi, Alabama, and Ohio.

Invalidating legislation and constitutional amendments that seek to curtail tort liability on largely pretextual grounds is merely the tip of the iceberg. Beneath the surface lies hundreds, even thousands, of judicial decisions in cases brought by tort lawyers meant to expand the scope of liability of the tort system. As noted, some expansions shrink traditional defenses to tort liability; others occur when courts rewrite insurance policies to extend insurance coverage beyond the terms of the policy by essentially nullifying limitations on coverage stated in the policy. These decisions add tens of billions of dollars to the assets available to tort plaintiffs, thus making litigation more profitable and therefore more probable.[15]

Some expansions, however, simply reflect a collaborative effort between state supreme court judges and tort lawyers to expand both the tort system and lawyers' fees. To fatten the purses of Florida lawyers, the Florida Supreme Court has held that even though an injured driver – seeking damages from an automobile manufacturer for allegedly failing to design the vehicle to minimize injuries – was drunk or on drugs at the time of the accident, that information may not be disclosed to the jury.[16] The overwhelming majority of courts, however, allow the jury to hear this evidence and apportion fault among those who share responsibility for the accident.

To fatten the purses of Texas tort lawyers, the Texas Supreme Court invited citizens from around the world to bring their tort cases to Texas. It began when eighty-two Costa Rican residents, alleging injury from exposure to a pesticide manufactured by Dow Chemical Company and Shell Oil Company at a Standard Fruit plant in Costa Rica, were searching for a place in the United States to file their claims. They struck out three times but hit pay dirt when the trial-lawyer-dominated Texas Supreme Court ruled in *Dow Chemical Company v. Alfaro*[17] that (because of some obscure legislative enactment) foreign nationals (Costa Ricans) who claim to have been injured in their own country had an absolute right to sue for damages in Texas courts.[18] The decision made Texas "the world's forum of final resort."[19] In 1993, a Republican legislature enacted a statute that overturned the decision by allowing courts to dismiss cases that could be tried in another more appropriate court.[20] The expansionary practices of the Texas Supreme Court finally ended when control of the court was wrested from pro-tort-lawyer judges in hard-fought judicial election campaigns.[21]

The decision by the Texas Supreme Court to expand tort liability went well beyond the bounds of the law-making activity of courts, called the "common law," that is, judge-made law. As discussed in the previous chapter, the modern expansion of tort liability reflects more than the ordinary process of common law making.[22] Quite apart from the obvious motivation of the Texas Supreme Court, there has been a fundamental change in the way judges see their role. As Todd Zywicki explains:

> Traditionally, common law judges and lawyers saw themselves as playing the modest role of maintaining the rules of an ongoing spontaneous order framework of law, society, and the market. In this regime, the role of judges and lawyers was to clarify the law, vindicate reasonable expectations, and preserve a system of private ordering. Change was slow, gradual, and at the margin. It is this bias in favor of private ordering, stability, and gradualism that led Tocqueville to remark on the conservative bias of lawyers in a common law system.
>
> The demise of this traditional view of judging has left judges largely unconstrained in their willingness to use the bench as a vehicle for pursuing their self-interest. ... It has been suggested by at least one notable judge, [Judge Richard Posner] however, that [this pursuit is reflected in] ... the desire for power and status.
>
> ...
>
> Judges will be interested in increasing their power in two ways: (1) relative to the power of the legislative and executive branches, and

(2) over society as a whole. In this sense, the invitation by lawyers that greater judicial activity will also further the public good is one that judges would be expected to receive favorably. Expanding the reach of tort liability, expanding the discretion of judges to redistribute wealth according to their preferences, and giving judges the power to remake tort law so as to accomplish desired ideological and policy goals are consistent with judges' desires to increase their power.[23]

Because it enlarges judicial control over society and the economy, many judges are naturally predisposed to enlarging the scope of tort liability. Their rulings reflect an inherent bias in favor of lawyers' interests over those of other occupational groups, businesses, and the rest of society. This bias is reflected in a host of special rules for lawyers that exempt them from liability for acts that are grist for tort lawyers' mills when committed by other professionals or provide them with powers, which are not extended to other professions, to protect their financial interests. For example, judges largely absolve lawyers of the consequences of mistakes made in the course of a trial but hold surgeons who make mistakes during an operation liable. Even the basic rules that judges have constructed for establishing legal and medical malpractice strongly favor lawyers – both in limiting lawyers' liability and expanding doctors' liability.[24]

Benjamin Barton of the University of Tennessee College of Law ratifies the point, arguing that "if there is a clear advantage or disadvantage to the legal profession in any given question of law ... judges will choose the route (within the bounds of precedent and seemliness) that benefits the profession as a whole."[25] Likewise, Chief Judge Dennis Jacobs of the U.S. Second Circuit Court of Appeals has gone where few judges ever have by acknowledging the existence of an inherent bias and calling for "self-restraint" among the judiciary.[26] He states that judges have an "inbred preference for outcomes controlled by proceduralism, the adversary system, hearings and experts, representation by lawyers, ramified complexity of doctrine and rules, multiple prongs, and all things that need and use lawyers, enrich them, and empower them vis-à-vis other sources of power and wisdom."[27] In the area of social change and public policy cases, Judge Jacobs observes:

> [P]ublic interest litigation greatly enhances lawyer influence and – not at all incidentally – increases the influence and power of judges. Judges love these kinds of cases. Public interest cases afford a judge sway over public policy, enhance the judicial role, make the judge more conspicuous, and keep the law clerks happy.
>
> Whether fee-paid or pro bono publico, when lawyers present big issues to the courts, the judges receive big issues with grateful hands; the bar patrols against inroads on jurisdiction and independence and praises the expansion of legal authority; and together we smugly congratulate ourselves on expanding what we are pleased to call the rule of law.
>
> Among the results are the displacement of legislative and executive power, the subordination of other disciplines and professions, and the reduction of whole enterprises and industries to damages.[28]

The consequences of this bias in mass tort cases can be profound. There, Judge Jacobs states, "judges hold in their hands the fate of vast enterprises and can cause their extinction, with capitalization forfeit to distribution between lawyers and plaintiffs and workers let go."[29] As a result, Judge Jacobs concludes that "our highly ramified litigation system imposes vast costs on other fields of endeavor, on our democratic freedoms, and on the unrepresented and the non-litigious."[30]

The connection Judge Jacobs' draws between major public policy cases and judges' influence and power bears further analysis. Judge Richard Posner argues that "some judges ... want to impose their policy preferences on society" at the expense of legislatures' authority.[31] A substantial body of literature supports the view that judges do in fact make decisions in furtherance of their ideological leanings.[32] Some judges, though, have a much greater propensity than others to use cases that may present public policy issues to seek to remake the world in their own ideological image. They have gone further than simply favoring lawyers' interests. This cadre of judges launched the products liability revolution in the 1960s. In the early 1980s, U.S. District Court Judge Jack Weinstein, who sits in downtown Brooklyn, launched the modern era of mass tort litigation when he presided over the *Agent Orange* litigation.[33] The case was a consolidation of actions brought on behalf of 2.4 million veterans of the Vietnam War[34] alleging numerous severe injuries from exposure to Agent Orange, an herbicide sprayed on vegetation in Vietnam to destroy the Vietcong's hiding places. Because the government was immune from suit, the plaintiffs sued Dow Chemical Company, the manufacturer of the defoliant. Though Judge Weinstein agreed that the claim lacked any scientific evidence of causation,[35] he nonetheless made it clear that Dow Chemical would have to pay $180 million to settle the case – at the time, the largest tort settlement in history.[36] As intended by Judge Weinstein, *Agent Orange* marked, not only the beginning of mass tort litigation, but of a heightened role for judges in regulating corporate activity as well.

Lawyers and judges share a mutual interest in expanding the scope of liability of the tort system. That mutual interest is cemented by the judiciary's bias in favor of lawyers' interests and the desire of some judges to imprint their policy preferences on society. This, in turn, has resulted in increased income for tort and defense lawyers, which assures a steady source of advocacy for further expansion. This view is complemented by Zywicki's observation:

> [T]ort reforms that enlarge liability and increase damages generally have been brought about by judicial action ... [whereas] liability and damage-decreasing reforms were almost always brought about by legislative activity. This tends to suggest that the directional evolution of tort doctrine in the courts is in one direction and that the development of tort law is not likely to be self-correcting.[37]

By expanding tort liability and thus their power to regulate society, judges have, in the words of George Priest, made our civil courts into "the most powerful regulatory institution of the modern state."[38]

NOTES

1. State legislatures first invoked this police power when they first became states of the United States and enacted "reception statutes." *See* Charles A. Bane, *From Holt and Mansfield to Story to Llewellyn and Mentschikoff: The Progressive Development of Commercial Law*, 37 U. MIAMI L. REV. 351, 363 (1983) ("[R]eception statutes were the mechanism for transferring the common law of England to the new United States."). These statutes "received" the common law of England at the time of statehood and delegated the power to judges to modify those laws. *See* Kent Greenawalt, *The Rule of Recognition and the Constitution*, 85 MICH. L. REV. 648–49 (1987).

2. The most prominent legislative change to the common law of torts was the adoption of workers' compensation statutes, which made fundamental changes to tort law. These laws eliminated injured workers' rights to (1) sue their employer; (2) elect to have a trial by jury; (3) seek pain and suffering damages; and (4) seek punitive damages. Instead, injured workers were provided with fixed levels of recovery that, though substantially less than the amounts the workers could have received in a common law suit, were not dependent on the injured worker being able to show that his employer was at fault. *See* ARTHUR LARSON, WORKERS' COMPENSATION FOR OCCUPATIONAL INJURIES AND DEATH (Desk ed. 1991). Another change was made in the 1930s, when about one-third of state legislatures exercised their constitutional authority to regulate the tort system by enacting antiheart balm statutes, which abolished tort damages for claims of sexual fraud based on promises of marriage. *See* Brian Donovan, *Gender Inequality and Criminal Seduction: Prosecuting Sexual Coercion in the Early 20th Century*, 20 LAW & SOC. INQUIRY 61, 82 (2005); *see also* Kyle Graham, *Why Torts Die*, 35 FLA. ST. U. L. REV. 359, 406–30 (2008) (describing the two major antiheart balm legislative movements in the 1930s and 1960s).

3. *See* Victor E. Schwartz & Leah Lorber, *Judicial Nullification of Civil Justice Reform Violates The Fundamental Federal Constitutional Principle of Separation of Powers: How To Restore The Right Balance*, 32 RUTGERS L. J. 907, 939 (2001) (listing ninety judicial invalidations of state tort reform statutes in the period 1983–2001).

4. 689 N.E.2d 1057, 1069–72 (Ill. 1997).

5. 5 ILCS 50/1 (West 2008).

6. In *Best*, the Illinois Supreme Court classified the tort reform at issue a "special law" and reasoned from the state constitution that this designation gave it the authority to invalidate the law. Originally, the Illinois 1870 Constitution, Article IV, Section 22, prohibited the legislature from passing any "local or special law" and included a laundry list of special laws that would, inter alia,

grant divorces; change the names of persons or places; regulate the rate of interest on money; remit fines; or grant any specific corporation, association, or individual any special or exclusive privilege, immunity, or franchise. The provision
further provided that no special law could be enacted by the legislature if a
general law could be made applicable. In 1970, when the Illinois Constitution
was revised, the laundry list was omitted, but the general prohibition against
"special" legislation remained. *See* Ill. Const. 1970, art. IV, § 13. The Illinois
Supreme Court interpreted this no-longer-adorned provision as granting it the
last word on whether the legislation was "special" or "general." The purpose for
this interpretation became clear when in 1997 the court used it to strike down
tort reforms enacted by the legislature. *See Best*, 689 N.E.2d at 1069–72. By
interpreting all tort reform legislation as "special," the court has stripped the
legislature's power to repeal or change tort law. In a 2010 case, *Lebron v. Gottlieb
Memorial Hospital* et al., 930 N.E. 2d 895 (Ill. 2010), declaring a legislative cap
on noneconomic damages in medical malpractice cases as unconstitutional, the
Illinois Supreme Court reaffirmed its position denying the state's legislature of
its constitutional power to change the common law.

7. *See Morris v. Savoy*, 576 N.E.2d 765, 768 (Ohio 1991).

8. *State ex rel. Ohio Academy of Trial Lawyers v. Sheward*, 715 N.E. 2d 1062 (Ohio 1999).

9. *See, e.g.*, Leonard J. Nelson III, *Damage Caps in Medical Malpractice Cases*, 85 Milbank Q. Rev. 259 (2007). Richard Biondi and Arthur Gurevitch published a study in 2003 based on extensive data that showed that dam-age caps on noneconomic damages reduced both claim frequency and mal-practice premiums. Richard S. Biondi & Arthur Gurevitch, *The Evidence is in: Noneconomic Damage Caps Help Reduce Malpractice Insurance Premiums*, Contingencies, Nov.-Dec. 2003, at 30, 32. figs. 3, 5, 32–33. Other studies confirm these results. *See* Daniel P. Kessler & Daniel L. Rubinfeld, *Empirical Study of the Civil Justice System* § 3.2.1 (Nat'l Bureau of Econ. Research, Working Paper No. 10825, 2004), *available at* http://www.nber. org/papers/w10825; Congressional Budget Office Paper, The Effects of Tort Reform: Evidence from the States 11 (2004), *available at* www.cbo. gov; Kenneth E. Thorpe, *The Medical Malpractice "Crisis": Recent Trends and the Impact of State Tort Reform*, Health Affairs – Web Exclusive (Jan. 21, 2004), *available at* http://content.healthaffairs.org/cgi/reprint/hlthaff. w4.20v1.pdf; W. Kip Viscusi, *Tort Reform and Insurance Markets* 12 n.11 (Harvard John M. Olin Ctr. for Law, Econ. and Bus., Discussion Paper No. 440, 2003), *available at* http://www.law.harvard.edu/programs/olin_ center/; Patricia Born, W. Kip Viscusi & Tom Baker, *The Effects of Tort Reform on Medical Malpractice Insurers' Ultimate Losses* (Harvard John M. Olin Discussion Paper 554, July 2006), *available at* http://ssrn.com/abstract=921441

(concluding that caps on noneconomic damages and limits on joint and several liability are associated with lower levels of reported losses by insurance companies and have the intended effect on the overall level of awards and settlements that insurers pay, *id.* at 13, and summarizing the results of prior studies, which conclude that caps on damages reduce mean payments in medical malpractice cases, *id.* at 2.).

10. 715 N.E. 2d at 1071.

11. Fla. Dep't of State Div. of Elections, The Medical Liability Claimant's Compensation Amendment 03–34. http://election.dos.state.fl.us/initiatives/initdetail.asp?account=37767&seqnum=1 (last visited Apr. 16, 2008).

12. Fla. Bar Reg. R. 4–1.5(f)(4)(B)(i)(a)-(b) (2007).

13. *In re Amendment to the Rules Regulating the Fla. Bar – Rule 4–1.5(f)(4)(B) of the Rules of Prof'l Conduct*, 939 So. 2d 1032 (Fla. 2006). To justify its position, the Florida court asserted that it was standard practice to allow parties to waive their constitutional rights, such as the right to a speedy trial or the right to remain silent when questioned by police. But imagine the *geshrai* that would be raised, and appropriately so, if all health care providers required women to waive their right to an abortion in order to receive medical care. Consider how this same Florida Supreme Court would react if doctors required *all* their patients to agree to binding arbitration of disputes, including malpractice claims, thus waiving the right to a trial by jury. Without hesitation, the court would declare that provision unenforceable. It would uphold the same provision, however, if lawyers included such an arbitration clause in their retainer agreements. This simply reflects the fact that the Florida Supreme Court is made up of lawyers, not doctors, engineers, architects, or businessmen and women. Pro-tort-lawyer lawyers at that.

14. Mary Coombs, *How Not To Do Medical Malpractice Reform: A Florida Case Study*, 18 HEALTH MATRIX 373, 390–91, n.78 (2008).

15. *See supra* Chapter 9, text at notes 9–15.

16. *See D'Amarto v. Ford*, 806 So. 2d 424 (Fla. 2002). This holding applies to "crashworthiness" cases in which a driver or passenger seeks to hold an automobile manufacturer liable for "enhanced injuries" – those that are in excess of what he would have incurred if the car had greater safety features.

17. 786 S.W.2d 674 (Tex. 1990).

18. In 1913, the Texas legislature statutorily abolished the "*forum non conveniens*" doctrine in personal injury actions. *See* TEX. CIV. PRAC. & REM. CODE § 71.031. This doctrine allows courts to refuse to hear cases that could be brought in other more appropriate courts. In 1990, the Texas Supreme Court concluded that the 1913 statute eliminated a judge's discretion to dismiss cases brought by citizens of foreign countries who were not injured in Texas. But as Chief Justice Thomas Phillips convincingly argued in his dissenting opinion, the intent of

the statute was to protect citizens of Texas who may be injured in a foreign country. *Alfaro*, 786 S.W.2d at 692–93. The majority's misreading of the statute simply reflected the pro-plaintiff-lawyer majority on the court.

19. *Alfaro*, 786 S.W.2d at 680; *see also* Michael D. Weiss, *America's Queen of Torts*, Pol'y Rev., Fall 1992, at 82.

20. Tex. Civ. Prac. & Rem. Code § 71.051 (2003).

21. This change in control, as well as enactment of substantial tort reforms by the legislature, appear to be reflected in changing win-loss rates. "[P]laintiffs won more than 60 percent of cases in the 1980's," but later, "the defendants were winning 83 percent by the 1995–96 court term." *See* Jim Yardley, *Bush's Choices For Court Seen As Moderates*, N.Y. Times, July 9, 2000, at 1.1; *see also* Mark Arend, *Texas' Turn*, Site Selection, March 2005.

22. *See supra* Chapter 9, notes 8, 26.

23. Zywicki, *Public Choice*, *supra* Chapter 8, note 30 at 11, 13, (citations omitted).

24. For discussion of special rules benefitting lawyers, see Appendix J.

25. Benjamin Barton, *Do Judges Systematically Favor the Interests of the Legal Profession?*, 59 Ala. L. Rev. 453, 454–55 (2008).

26. *See* Dennis Jacobs, *The Secret Life of Judges*, 75 Fordham L. Rev. 2855, 2863 (2007); *see also* Adam Liptak, *With the Bench Cozied Up to the Bar, the Lawyers Can't Lose*, N.Y. Times, Aug. 27, 2007, at A10.

27. Jacobs, *Secret Life of Judges*, at 2855.

28. *Id.* at 2857.

29. *Id.* at 2857–58.

30. *Id.* at 2858.

31. Richard A. Posner, Economic Analysis of the Law 543 (6th ed. 2003).

32. *See, e.g.*, Frank B. Cross, *The Role of Lawyers in Positive Theories of Doctrinal Evolution*, 45 Emory L.J. 523 at 569 (1996); Richard L. Revesz, *Environmental Regulation, Ideology, and the D.C. Circuit*, 83 Va. L. Rev. 1717 (1997).

33. *See In re 'Agent Orange' Product Liability Litigation*, 597 F. Supp. 740, 857 (E.D.N.Y. Sept. 25, 1984) (No. MDL 381); Peter H. Schuck, Agent Orange on Trial 7 (1986) [hereinafter Schuck, Agent Orange].

34. *See* Schuck, Agent Orange, *supra* note 33, at 4.

35. At the Fairness Hearing, Judge Weinstein approved the $180 million, "[e]ven though the evidence presented to the court to date suggests that the case is without merit." *In re 'Agent Orange' Product Liability Litigation*, 597 F. Supp. at 857; *see also* Schuck, Agent Orange, *supra* note 33, at 179.

36. *See* Schuck, Agent Orange, *supra* note 33, at 160–61 ("Weinstein, many of the lawyers felt, had somehow fixed on $180 million as the right amount and was simply immovable."). *Id.* at 161. An article in the *New York Times* reported that "[s]ome lawyers say that Judge Weinstein wades in and coerces defendants and injury victims to reach what he thinks is the best result." William

Glaberson, *Dressing Down Lawyers, and Dressing Up Gigante*, N.Y. TIMES, July 20, 1997, at 1.21.

37. Zywicki, *Public Choice, supra* Chapter 8, note 30 at 19, citing Thomas J. Campbell et al., *The Causes and Effects of Liability Reform: Some Empirical Evidence* (NBER Working Paper No. W4989 Jan. 1995), *available at* http:// papers.nber.org/papers/W4989); *see also* Paul H. Rubin, *Public choice and tort reform*, 124 PUBLIC CHOICE 223, 231 (2005); Paul H. Rubin et al., *Litigation versus legislation: Forum shopping by rent seekers*, 107 PUBLIC CHOICE 295, 304 (2001) (finding that all of the cases he examined that expanded the scope of tort liability resulted from judicial decisions in state courts; conversely, all of the restrictions of liability were adopted through legislation).

38. George L. Priest, *The Modern Expansion of Tort Liability: Its Sources, Its Effects, and Its Reform*, 5 J. ECON. PERSPECTIVES 31, 39 (1991).

11 Current and Future Expansions of Tort Liability

ARTICLES HAVE RECENTLY APPEARED IN THE MEDIA declaring that conservative business interests have triumphed over tort lawyers in the tort reform wars.[1] This is palpable nonsense. True, comprehensive tort reform legislation has been enacted in many key states, business interests have gained victories in state supreme court races in Ohio, Illinois, Mississippi, Michigan, and Texas – without which their legislative achievements would have been nullified – and Congress passed the Class Action Fairness Act. Although business interests achieved these highly visible victories, tort lawyers continue to expand the scope of liability of the tort system in other ways.

Perhaps the greatest expansion has resulted from tort lawyers' successful efforts to redefine "injury." To bring a suit in tort, a plaintiff must show that a defendant has injured him and that this conduct was wrongful.[2] Tort lawyers have been trying to replace the requirement of "injury" (as a layperson would use the term and as courts have traditionally required for the filing of a tort claim)[3] with the more pliable concept of the "legally cognizable claim." In modern tort litigation, actual injury is no longer a required component of a legally cognizable claim. Freed from the restraint of showing actual injury, the number of potential claims is limited only by the capital costs of recruiting claimants, the creativity of tort lawyers, and the complicity of courts.[4]

In five mass tort litigations – asbestos, silica, silicone breast implants, fen-phen (diet drugs), and welding fumes – lawyers have largely dispensed with the need to show actual injury. In these litigations, mass tort lawyers hired screening companies to amass huge numbers of claims and litigation doctors to manufacture hundreds of thousands of mostly bogus medical reports in return for millions of dollars in fees.[5] As noted by U.S. District Court Judge Janis Jack in a proceeding involving 10,000 mostly bogus claims of silicosis, litigation screenings are an entrepreneurial means of claim generation that seek

> to inflate the number of Plaintiffs and claims in order to overwhelm the Defendants and the judicial system. This is apparently done in hopes of extracting mass nuisance-value settlements because the Defendants and the judicial system are financially incapable of examining the merits of each individual claim in the usual manner.[6]

The strategy of using mass filings to compel defendants to settle thousands of claims without having any real opportunity to contest them in trials has been a huge success. No bar association, lawyer disciplinary agency, court, or prosecutor has attempted to intervene and either sanction or prosecute the use of litigation screenings to generate massive numbers of specious claims.[7] Indeed, it is plausible to conclude that courts, prosecutors, and disciplinary agencies have given lawyers in these litigations (and the doctors they hire) a special dispensation to commit fraud.

A. Dispensing with the Requirement of Injury

Lawyers are also advancing new or refashioning old theories of tort liability to further dispense with proof of injury and causation requirements. The biggest payoffs come from aggregating the claims of tens of thousands, even millions, of consumers into class actions. To create a class action based on personal injuries suffered from using a product, the lawyer must not only show that the product caused an actual injury to each member of the class but also that the similarities in how the injuries are caused significantly outweigh the individual differences of class members with respect to injury causation. To overcome this often insurmountable task, lawyers seek to convert masses of personal injury claims – which are largely uncertifiable as class actions – into pure economic loss claims that members of the victim group share in common. These tort claims do not allege harm to a person or his property, but instead assert a financial loss from overpaying for a product or service.[8]

Normally, contract law applies to transactions in which one party claims that the purchased goods or services were defective or not as represented. From the lawyer's perspective, contract law is problematic because losses suffered by consumers are usually too small to justify a suit and punitive damages are not usually allowed. But when lawyers bring defective product suits on behalf of thousands or millions of consumers of the products, contract law transmogrifies into tort law. This fundamentally reorders the legal regime governing the sale of products – not by an act of the legislature, but by lawyers' pursuit of profits. Professor James A. Henderson Jr. of the Cornell Law School has sounded the alarm that these "aggregative torts," as he refers to these economic torts, are "inherently lawless and unprincipled."[9]

B. "Lawless" Economic Torts

An example of this new genre of "lawless" economic torts, generated by the quest for contingency fees, is the class action suit claiming that the purchasers of products or pharmaceutical drugs were deceived by the manufacturers as to the quality, efficacy, or side effects of the product and are therefore entitled to refunds of the purchase price. Although some of these suits are based on alleged civil RICO violations, most are based on state consumer protection laws banning deceptive acts or practices in the sale of products and services and variously providing remedies of statutory damages ranging from $25 to $2,000 per violation, trebling of actual damages, return of the purchase price, punitive damages, and an award of attorneys' fees.[10] Most of these statutes were enacted in the 1960s to supplement the Federal Trade Commission's mission of protecting consumers from "unfair or deceptive acts or practices."[11] The perception was that the balance of power in the marketplace had shifted in favor of merchants, and consumers needed increased legal protection to bring the marketplace back into balance.[12] This protection included the creation of private rights of action, empowering lawyers to act as private attorneys general to enforce these statutes. Unlike FTC enforcement actions, which have a number of constraints, such as being limited to only those in the public interest, private enforcement is bounded only by the creativity of lawyers and the actions of judges with whom, as set out in Chapter 10, the lawyers share common interests. It took a while, but lawyers saw the opportunity to turn these statutes into gold mines by bringing class actions that mostly have little to do with consumer protection and much to do with creating wealth for themselves.[13]

The great attraction of consumer protections laws for lawyers is fourfold. First, the term "deceptive sales practice" and other vague terms used in the statutes are amorphous and can be easily read to include many of the standard sales practices used by manufacturers and sellers. Second, many of these state laws permit recovery even when there is no tangible injury; a plaintiff can prevail merely by virtue of the defendant's alleged bad behavior.[14] Third, although the FTC requires reasonable reliance to find a practice deceptive and common law fraud actions require an injury to result from reliance on the misrepresentation,[15] suits based on state consumer protection statutes typically do not need to show reliance on a manufacturer's "misleading" statements in purchasing the product or actual harm to a consumer – only that a statement was misleading.[16] Even when some state consumer protection laws require that consumers must have relied on a deceptive act in purchasing the product to be eligible for compensation, courts often vitiate the requirement by simply ignoring any reliance requirement or presuming reliance.[17] Finally, some state courts have stripped defendants in consumer protection suits of defenses that are available to them at common law, including the statute of frauds (requiring certain contracts to be in writing to be enforceable), warranty disclaimers, the parol evidence rule (prohibiting the introduction of prior or contemporaneous evidence that contradicts the written terms of a contract), and contractual limitations on liability or remedies.[18]

The effect of the inapplicability of the FTC requirement of reasonable reliance has been demonstrated empirically. A study of a sample of consumer protection act lawsuits found that 78 percent would not constitute legally unfair or deceptive conduct under FTC policy statements and that, of the remainder, more than half would not result in FTC enforcement.[19]

In addition to vitiating many of the common law restrictions and FTC safeguards, suits based on consumer protection statutes promise much greater returns on investment. Damages can amount to billions of dollars when these claims are allowed as class actions. In addition, some statutes allow for punitive damages, and virtually all allow substantial attorneys' fees to be tacked onto the statutory damages. The Vioxx litigation is an example of the enormous scale of potential damages. Vioxx is a nonsteroidal anti-inflammatory drug that was manufactured by Merck. When it became known that long-term use of Vioxx increased the risk for heart attack and stroke, Merck withdrew the product from the market, unleashing a tidal wave of personal injury litigation. Merck vigorously defended the lawsuits and ultimately agreed to settle for $4.85 billion, to be paid to about 50,000 personal injury claimants.

Another group of lawyers separately sued Merck, alleging that Merck committed an economic tort of the type that Professor Henderson termed "inherently lawless and unprincipled." These lawyers claimed that the purchasers of Vioxx would not have purchased the drug if they had been properly informed of the increased risks. A New Jersey trial court certified a nationwide class of Vioxx purchasers seeking to recover the $20 billion paid by purchasers of Vioxx.[20] To satisfy the New Jersey statutory requirement that consumers have relied on the alleged deceptive act, the court found that reliance could be presumed. Merck dodged this $20 billion bullet when the New Jersey Supreme Court reversed the certification. Had it not, lawyers could have easily anticipated a billion-dollar payday.[21]

Stephen Tillery, a class action plaintiffs' lawyer at Korein Tillery in St. Louis, Missouri, realized a smaller (but still substantial) payday based on the same theory. Dubbed as "perhaps the most famous class action lawyer in the most famous pro-plaintiff jurisdiction," his firm has amassed around $600 million in fees and more than $1.8 billion in settlements of class actions against such companies as IBM, AT&T, Ameritech, Xerox, MCI, GlaxoSmithKline, Allstate, and SBC.[22] Most of Tillery's cases were filed in Madison County, Illinois, and presided over by Judge Nicholas Byron. The Byron-Tillery tandem played a major role in securing for Madison County its justly deserved reputation – shared with Beaumont, Texas – as the Barbary Coast for class action litigation. Indeed, Judge Byron has probably certified more class actions than any judge in the nation. To capture a piece of the huge profits resulting from Judge Byron's rulings, class action lawyers from around the country have trooped into Madison County to file their class actions, and, in some cases, have formed alliances with Tillery. I examined Judge Byron's rulings in a single class action, imported into Madison County on behalf of elderly Americans who were the victims of a mass-marketing scheme involving the sale of interests in lottery pools conducted from boiler rooms in Barbados and Canada. After determining that these people were victimized a second time by their lawyers and Madison County justice, I concluded that the settlement Judge Byron provisionally approved was "so abusive of the class's rights that it can only gain final judicial approbation from a court oblivious to the need to protect class members from self-interested behavior by its self-appointed class lawyers. Indeed, if there was an award for the most abusive class action settlement of the decade, if not the century, this settlement would be an odds-on favorite to gain the prize."[23] A unique confluence of events in this case shed national attention on Judge Byron and the self-dealing lawyers that represented the class, resulting in the later rejection of the settlement.

More typically, the principal victims of class actions in Madison County are defendants. Indeed, Madison County's well-deserved reputation as a speed trap, standing aside the nation's litigation highways – able to reach out, ensnare, and extract ransom from virtually every large American corporation providing goods or services to consumers[24] – helped convince Congress to enact the Class Action Fairness Act, described in Chapter 18, Section E, which allowed defendants to move most of these abusive class action filings out of state courts and into federal courts.

In one case, Tillery brought suit in Madison County on behalf of those who purchased the drug Paxil for use by someone under the age of eighteen. The suit did not allege that Paxil injured its users. Instead, Tillery alleged that SmithKline Beecham, the makers of Paxil and Paxil CR, withheld and concealed negative information about the safety and effectiveness of the drug[25] and thus violated both the Illinois Consumer Fraud Act and the Uniform Deceptive Trade Practices Act.[26] The suit claimed that the company deceived purchasers, who were therefore entitled to economic damages based on the price they paid for the drug. SmithKline Beecham denied the allegations but, when faced with the prospect of Madison County justice, agreed to create a $63.8 million fund to be paid to class members, with $16.6 million of that to be paid to class counsel – a sum that Judge Ralph J. Mendelsohn, the presiding judge, approved.[27]

1. The "Light" Cigarette Class Action

Tillery came very close to a billion-dollar payday when he filed a class action against Philip Morris, the manufacturer of Marlboro Lights and Cambridge Lights. Again, he did not allege that the users of the product had suffered any disease or bodily injury. Rather, Tillery claimed that the manufacturer's advertisements that "light" cigarettes had "lower tar and nicotine" than full-flavored cigarettes were deceitful under the same Illinois Acts on which the Paxil litigation was based. The manufacturer's claims of lower tar and nicotine were based on a machine test approved by the FTC. Tillery alleged, however, that smokers of light cigarettes unconsciously compensate by puffing harder or smoking more, exposing them to as much tar and nicotine as regular cigarettes deliver. Had the suit been brought to recover for personal injuries caused by smoking the light cigarettes, Tillery could not have shown the factual commonality required for class certification.[28] By focusing on a claimed economic injury, however, Tillery was able to bypass this requirement.

Judge Byron found that the defendant was liable for misrepresentation under the Illinois statutes.[29] He awarded the class – which consisted of an estimated 1.14 million statewide purchasers – their economic loss, which he determined as the difference in value between the product at the time of sale if the representations were true and the actual value to consumers. He calculated these compensatory damages at $7.1 billion, including prejudgment interest. He also awarded $3 billion in punitive damages, payable to the State of Illinois. Additionally, Judge Byron decreed that the Tillery firm would receive a fee of $1.775 billion, 25 percent of the compensatory damage amount. The case was appealed to the Illinois Supreme Court, which reversed Judge Byron's holding in a 4–2 decision, finding that Federal Trade Commission actions had exempted the defendant from liability under the Illinois statutes.[30]

Lawyers have brought similar class actions across the country. The first case that used a nationwide class to recover economic damages arising from alleged light-cigarette fraud was filed in the Eastern District of Brooklyn, presided over by the founding father of mass tort litigation, U.S. District Court Judge Jack Weinstein.[31] This light-cigarette class action is one of many examples of plaintiffs' lawyers deliberately seeking out Judge Weinstein, not least because of his propensity to expand liability and approve large-scale aggregations. In the light-cigarette litigation, Judge Weinstein certified a class action to determine whether the light-cigarette manufacturers had violated the Racketeer Influence and Corrupt Organizations (RICO) Act[32] by deceiving smokers into believing that light cigarettes were less harmful than full flavored ones.[33] The Second Circuit Court of Appeals reversed Judge Weinstein, agreeing with the manufacturers that the issues of reliance, injury, damages, and the statute of limitations, which Judge Weinstein had dismissed, had to be determined for each member of the class, and thus these issues did not lend themselves to collective resolution in a class action.[34]

Judge Weinstein was again reversed when he certified a RICO-based class action brought by third-party payors (TPPs) who underwrite the purchase of prescription drugs by their members or insureds, against Eli Lilly and Company, for allegedly misrepresenting the efficacy and side effects of Zyprexa, an antipyschotic drug.[35] The appellate court found that class certification was not appropriate because the TPPs were too diverse, individual physicians prescribing Zyprexa may have relied on Lilly's alleged misrepresentation to different degrees or not all, and excess prescribing of Zyprexa may not have caused the TPPs to suffer losses because of the likelihood that even if doctors had decided not to prescribe Zyprexa, they might have prescribed substitute drugs.

Although the Second Circuit appears to have blocked the RICO route to riches, class action lawyers have achieved a significant victory in the U.S. Supreme Court. In *Altria Group, Inc. v. Good*,[36] the U.S. Supreme Court, in a 5–4 decision, declared that a class action based on Maine's Unfair Trade Practices Act[37] was not preempted by either federal cigarette labeling law or the FTC's actions. This decision appears inconsistent with the federal labeling act that provides in part: "No requirement or prohibition based on smoking and health shall be imposed under State law with respect to the advertising or promotion of any cigarettes."[38]

The consequences of this holding will remain unclear for years. Although *Altria* does not disturb the Illinois decision – which was based on a statutory exemption specific to Illinois – lawsuits brought under other state's laws may be sustained under the Supreme Court's holding. If that occurs, awards could amount to tens of billions of dollars – enough to put the economic viability of cigarette companies at risk.[39] The principal losers would be the states that share in the revenues from the sale of cigarettes, as well as the investors and pension funds that own shares of the tobacco companies or who have purchased municipal bonds collateralized by tobacco company payments to the states.[40]

"RETURN OF THE PURCHASE PRICE" CLASS ACTIONS ARE MERELY ONE OF several devices invented by lawyers to extract contingency fees without having to show tangible injury or actual causation. The extent of the assault on American business in the form of "return of the purchase price (and more)" class actions is yet unclear. What is clear, however, is that before the right judge and right jury, manufacturers and sellers of virtually all mass produced products – soft drinks, bottled water, cell phones, video games, pharmaceutical drugs, alcoholic beverages, fast food, and more – can be found to have violated states' deceptive practices acts by failing to disclose information about their products' defects or deficiencies or by overstating their products' benefits. Ironically, the very fact that this theory to expand tort liability threatens to let loose a veritable tidal wave of tort litigation is what may most inhibit courts from further opening this floodgate. Even so, a single state court has the power to essentially set national policy by giving its imprimatur to such an action – an imprimatur that will be heard as a clarion call to lawyers to "come and get it."

2. Medical Monitoring

The class action for "medical monitoring" is another recent theory of liability that dispenses with the requirement to prove injury. These suits, ostensibly brought on behalf of persons who were exposed to harmful substances to obtain payment for periodic medical examinations to detect the onset of any physical harm or disease,[41] are actually brought mostly to benefit the lawyers who file the actions. The real money to be made in bringing these suits lies in invoking the class action mechanism. Most courts have denied certifying medical-monitoring class actions because of wide differences in the degree and circumstances of individual exposures and the unique medical histories of those exposed.[42] Some courts, however, have found enough commonality to justify certifying medical-monitoring claims as class actions.[43] The genius of the medical-monitoring claim is that in some jurisdictions, claimants need neither show any present physical injury nor any substantial likelihood that they will sustain such an injury in the future as a consequence of the inhalation, ingestion, or exposure to an alleged harmful substance.[44] Moreover, some states allow a present lump sum award for future medical-monitoring costs based solely on exposure.[45]

When brought as class actions, these claims can generate an enormous pot of money against which lawyers can levy contingency fees. In jurisdictions that allow medical-monitoring class actions, lawyers can, in theory, aggregate hundreds of thousands and even millions of consumers into class actions based solely on exposure to alleged toxic substances and seek a lump sum of billions of dollars for medical testing and commensurate contingency fees. For example, in the fen-phen (diet drugs) litigation, thousands of personal injury claims were filed against the pharmaceutical manufacturer, Wyeth, claiming that the diet drugs caused injury to heart valves. In addition to these personal injury claims that cost Wyeth upwards of $20 billion, several courts certified state and nationwide medical-monitoring class actions despite the medical evidence that on cessation of use of the drugs, the medical condition of those adversely affected by the drugs actually improved.[46] These actions could have cost Wyeth as much as $18 billion – a prospect that drove the company to shovel out billions of dollars to settle tens of thousands of highly dubious claims.[47]

No state has gone as far as West Virginia in approving medical-monitoring damages.[48] In *Bower v. Westinghouse*,[49] the West Virginia Supreme Court not only did not require actual injuries to sustain a medical-monitoring claim but also refused to limit recovery to diseases that could be detected and treated prior to the appearance of physical symptoms.[50] Moreover, the court appears to have rejected requiring any sort of cost/benefit analysis demonstrating that such awards serve health promotion goals in a cost effective manner.[51] The court further provided that medical-monitoring awards are possible even where medical professionals do not find monitoring advisable, stating that "[t]he requirement that diagnostic testing must be medically advisable does not necessarily preclude the situation where such a determination is based, at least in part, upon the subjective desires of a plaintiff for information concerning the state of his or her health."[52] Finally, the court allowed for the award of lump sum medical-monitoring damages for future medical monitoring with no guarantee or mechanism to ensure that the money would actually be spent on medical costs.[53] It is difficult to see how the decision would have been any different if it were ghost-written by the West Virginia plaintiffs' bar.

Recognizing the dangers posed by these suits, the U.S. Supreme Court rejected a medical-monitoring claim in *Metro-North Commuter R.R. Co. v. Buckley*, concerned that allowing such claims from potentially "tens of millions of individuals" would create "unlimited and unpredictable liability."[54] Whereas most courts, thus far, have denied certification, future medical-monitoring class actions based on allegations of harm from talking on a cell phone, drinking coffee or alcohol, or eating fast food remain within the realm of possibility. Even if only a few courts join West Virginia and certify medical-monitoring class actions based solely on exposure without any need to show any actual harm and irrespective of any recognized medical benefit or wide differences in the circumstances of exposure, the financial consequences could be immense. Moreover, this result could put enormous pressure on courts in other states to legitimate medical-monitoring suits so as not to deprive their own mass tort lawyers from sharing in the bounty.

3. Lead Paint as a "Public Nuisance"

Lawyers are also seeking to reformulate the ancient tort of public nuisance to apply to product manufacturing to get around limitations imposed by product liability law.[55] The doctrine empowers government to stop quasi-criminal conduct that unreasonably interferes with the public's ability to exercise a public right. Both injunctive relief and damages can be awarded for such "public nuisances" as blocking a public roadway, contaminating public drinking water, emitting plumes of smoke that cause widespread discomfort, releasing noxious odors, or making excessive noise.[56] This concept of public nuisance, however, is a far cry from the all-consuming tort that plaintiffs' lawyers currently advance.

These profit-seeking lawyers, who have convinced state attorneys general and local and state governments to hire them, have instigated suits against the companies that manufactured and sold lead paint thirty to fifty years ago. These suits claim that the companies created a public nuisance by selling paint containing lead pigment, even though the acts took place decades earlier and the companies have had no control over the structures to which the lead paint was applied. To eliminate this public nuisance, the suits seek to recoup the costs to abate the presence of the lead paint in thousands of buildings where it is flaking off, usually because of improper maintenance by property owners.[57] Abatement involves removing the lead paint, probably hidden under many subsequent coats of paint – an expensive procedure – and then repainting the cleaned surfaces. Courts in Illinois, Missouri, New York, and New Jersey have rejected public nuisance as a theory of relief in this context.[58] A Rhode Island trial court, however, entered judgment against lead paint manufacturers,[59] which would have cost the companies an estimated $2.4 billion dollars.[60] The suit was instigated by one of the leading class action/mass tort law firms, Motley Rice, which had lobbied the state's attorney general to hire them on a 16.5 percent contingency fee.[61]

The trial court found that use of public nuisance theory, as redefined, relieved the plaintiff of the burden of showing that the defendant's products were responsible for causing the alleged harm.[62] In plain terms, the court instructed the jury that the state did not have to show that a specific defendant manufactured a particular product, which a particular homeowner purchased and used; that any of the defendants' products caused injury; or that the manufacturers' actions proximately cause an injury – a core requirement of an action in tort.[63] By adopting this public nuisance theory, the court effectively repealed the state's statute of limitations as it applied to the actions in question; that is, it ruled that the action could be brought no matter how many years had elapsed since the lead paint had been purchased. No wonder the U.S. Circuit Court of

Appeals for the Eighth Circuit called this theory a "monster that would devour in one gulp the entire law of tort."[64] Fortunately, the Rhode Island Supreme Court unanimously overturned the trial court's decision, holding that the state had failed to establish that the paint companies had interfered with a public right or controlled the premises where the lead paint still remained.[65] However, this ruling has not prevented tort lawyers from continuing to assert the "monster" public nuisance theory in other jurisdictions as well as novel variations, as discussed in the next section.

4. Global Warming as a "Public Nuisance"

Tort lawyers have also sought to convert public nuisance theory into a basis for suits against power-generating companies and chemical manufacturers, alleging that their carbon dioxide emissions contribute to global warming (also referred to as "climate change") and thus are "public nuisances." Dubbed the hot new litigation frontier, global warming has reached the U.S. Supreme Court, which has opened the door for future claims by recognizing that climate change caused by carbon dioxide emissions can result in a compensable injury.[66]

Global warming as a public nuisance has also been combined with the tort of "civil conspiracy" in a direct assault on the First Amendment. Civil conspiracy is an intentional tort in which two or more persons agree to and do commit an unlawful act, which damages the plaintiff.[67] It is important to note that unlike criminal conspiracy, which only requires an agreement to commit a criminal act, civil conspiracy is a tort that requires an actual injury.

Civil conspiracy was the basis for a case filed in federal court in the Northern District of California. An Alaskan native village with approximately 400 inhabitants sought up to $400 million from twenty-four of the leading energy companies (including oil, power, and utility companies) for relocation costs, claiming that their village was being destroyed by increasingly violent storm surges that are caused by global warming.[68]

The suit alleged that the energy companies participated in a coordinated "civil conspiracy" to mislead the public by "creating a false scientific debate on global warming."[69] This misleading information, the village argued, portrayed climate change as mythical in order to delay political pressure to regulate carbon dioxide. These allegations seek to make corporate communications about the environment generally and climate change specifically a basis for civil liability (and contingency fees). If ever sustained, the nonprofit public advocacy groups, think tanks, and public interest law firms that are contesting the prevailing view on climate change and its causes could be deemed "coconspirators." Tort lawyers have lost round one of what will be, however, a many-round championship fight. The California federal court dismissed the case as not within the power of courts to decide because it required "a policy decision about *who* should bear the cost of global warming," requiring "a political judgment" that the two dozen power companies named as defendants should be singled out as having to bear the cost of global warming "that virtually everyone on Earth is responsible [for]."[70]

Two U.S. Courts of Appeals, however, have rejected this reasoning and allowed public nuisance global warming cases to proceed. The first case, filed by eight states and the city of New York, sought injunctive relief against five major power companies that operate fossil-fuel-fired power plants in twenty states. In *State of Connecticut et al. v. American Electric Power Co., Inc. et al.*, the Second Circuit reversed a trial court's decision dismissing their global warming lawsuit because it was a "non-justifiable political question."[71] In a 139-page ruling, the Second Circuit found that the states and city have standing to bring a lawsuit and that the court did have the power to decide whether the power plants' carbon dioxide emissions sufficiently contributed to global warming as to constitute a public nuisance. Following the Second Circuit's reasoning, the U.S. Court of Appeals for the Fifth Circuit reinstated a lawsuit filed by Hurricane Katrina victims seeking compensation and punitive damages from energy, power, and chemical companies that were alleged to have caused the emission of greenhouse gases that contributed to global warming.[72] The suit alleges that these emissions caused a rise in sea levels and added to the ferocity of Hurricane Katrina – thus injuring the plaintiffs.

Legitimizing public nuisance suits based on global warming transfers enormous regulatory power to the courts to decide critical political issues that have been consigned to Congress. As the U.S. Fourth Circuit of Appeals recently observed: "[W]e doubt seriously that Congress thought that a judge holding a twelve-day bench trial could evaluate more than a mere fraction of the information that regulatory bodies can consider. 'Courts are expert at statutory construction, while agencies are expert at statutory implementation'."[73] To that same end, Professor Lawrence Tribe of Harvard Law School, long associated with liberal causes and a proponent of tort system expansion, recently wrote: "[W]hatever one's position in the ... debate over the extent or ... reality of anthropogenic climate change, one thing is clear: legislators, armed with the best economic and scientific analysis, and with the capability of binding or at least strongly incentivizing, all involved parties, are the only ones constitutionally entitled to fight that battle."[74] This view is endorsed by Carol M. Browner, senior advisor for energy and climate change to President Obama.[75]

To say, as did the Second Circuit in the *American Electric Power* case, that this was an "ordinary tort suit" no more complex than the localized discharge of raw sewage into a river or a lake,[76] is sophistry or worse. The complexity of this "ordinary tort suit" is mind numbing. How does a court go about distinguishing between the power companies' contributions to global warming from that of vehicular traffic and the contributions of other U.S. industries, as well as industrial and deforestation activities in other countries and volcanic activity? What is the body politic's recourse if courts decide that injunctive relief, raising the cost of power by billions of dollars and forcing the closure of many businesses and the loss of thousands of jobs, is appropriate? Posing these questions highlights the absence of judicial standards to be applied if the rulings of the Second and Fifth Circuits are not reversed by the U.S. Supreme Court. Allowing such suits to proceed will substantially widen the scope of tort liability and allow contingency fee lawyers to seek profit from hurricanes, rising sea levels, and other disasters that may be linked to global warming. Any company with a sizable carbon footprint and deep pockets would be fair game. Swiss Re, a giant reinsurance company with an obvious interest in future litigation trends, recently concluded that "the frequency and sustainability of climate change-related litigation could become a significant issue within the next couple of years."[77] The determination of whether the costs of global warming should be imposed on corporate actors or others is quintessentially a decision for Congress, not the courts. Moreover, many of these suits promise little or no public benefit and will merely transfer wealth from consumers' pockets to contingency fee lawyers' coffers. Modest amounts, however, may eventually trickle down to those claiming that they have been injured by climate change.[78]

OVER THE YEARS, TORT LAWYERS HAVE LAUNCHED MANY LITIGATIONS TO expand the tort envelope, which have failed to live up to their promise of generating huge profits and have instead imposed heavy costs – and there are certainly more to come.[79] Whether global warming product liability claims will find a toehold in the pantheon of established tort theories remains to be seen. Tort lawyers and their political allies, allying with populist movements, have the winds in their sails as they pursue the use of this theory to dramatically rewrite traditional common law rules and create another multibillion-dollar fee generator. If they succeed, public nuisance lawsuits based on global warming will vie with refund-the-purchase-price lawsuits for maximum destructive power.

C. New Frontiers

Because the profit potential of new tort liability expansions is virtually unlimited, tort lawyers are continuously seeking to expand the tort envelope. One new area of expansion involves the consumption of high-fat foods, which has attracted national attention because of the obesity epidemic.[80] Obesity claims come in varying forms, including personal injury suits for eating fatty foods and consumer fraud claims for alleged insufficient disclosure of the nutritional impact of junk food.[81] Notably, these claims have been analogized to those waged against tobacco manufacturers. The tobacco suits have also been cited as a paradigm of litigation against alcohol manufacturers. Some scholars posit that suits for alcohol-related diseases and injuries – which may include claims for consumer recovery for disease and injury caused by alcohol, taxpayer reimbursement for government expenses created by such products, and bystander recovery for injuries caused by such products – may follow the trajectory of tobacco suits and result in huge damages against manufacturers and sellers of alcoholic beverages.[82]

Finally, any discussion of efforts to expand the tort envelope would be incomplete without mentioning cell phone litigation. Cell phone suits, still in their infancy, may include: claims for product liability (radiation exposure); claims by drivers and others against manufacturers, blaming accidents on cell phone use distractions; and claims of liability for consumer and business losses caused by flaws in the service provider infrastructure.[83] Given the incentives for lawyers to expand the scope of tort litigation, virtually all products that factor into our everyday lives may come to provide fresh grist for tort lawyers' mills.

Tort lawyers' efforts to expand the tort envelope are augmented by the fact that lawyers often have a wide range of choices of where to file claims under our federal system. Not surprisingly, they are drawn, like iron filings to a magnet, to states where the judges have a greater propensity for adopting new legal theories that expand liability, opening up new vistas for lawyers. This "forum shopping" phenomenon can exert a powerful influence on other state courts to adopt these theories in order to preserve a share of the tort loot for their own lawyers.

D. "The Lawyers Are Coming ... The Lawyers Are Coming"

Another tort lawyer expansionary wave is flooding the halls of Congress and state legislatures. Until very recently, the AAJ – formerly

ATLA – was content to play defense, blocking most attempts to legislate tort reforms that cut back on the judicial expansion of tort liability. No longer. Tort lawyers – substantial contributors to the Democratic Party – are actively seeking to take advantage of the decline in the political fortunes of Republicans by lobbying lawmakers to enact legislation that will enlarge the scope of tort liability and the ability of tort lawyers to file lawsuits.

For example, tort lawyers are lobbying for federal legislation to prohibit and retroactively eliminate arbitration provisions that appear in hundreds of millions of consumer contracts. These clauses are prevalent in brokerage, credit card, and software company contracts with consumers.[84] They apply only to financial injury – claims that products or services are defective – not to claims of personal injury. Ironically, lawyers are increasingly including mandatory arbitration clauses in their own retainer agreements with clients.

Tort lawyers and their supporters in the House and Senate claim that elimination of these clauses – which would allow consumers to sue for alleged defects in products or services – would bring greater fairness to the legal system. In fact, it would bring greater profits to lawyers. Businesses have, in the past, included abusive provisions in arbitration clauses, such as requiring consumers invoking the arbitration clauses to pay a substantial upfront cost or journey to a distant place. These unconscionable provisions should be declared invalid by courts, and indeed, that has occurred.[85] The solution to unfair provisions, however, is state and federal regulation setting minimum standards of protection for consumers.

Underlying the proposals to ban all mandatory arbitration clauses in consumer contracts is the assumption that litigation benefits consumers whereas arbitration benefits business. This assumption, however, is not supported by the empirical evidence. Litigation is expensive and may take years. Arbitration allows consumers to resolve disputes with companies inexpensively and relatively quickly. For example, the American Arbitration Association limits consumers' fees to $125 for claims less than $10,000.[86] A study showed that, in fact, in cases with claims of

$10,000 or less, consumer claimants paid an average of $96 in fees.[87] Moreover, as U.S. Supreme Court Justice Stephen Breyer has recognized, arbitration helps level the playing field between consumers and big business. In 1995, Breyer wrote that "the typical consumer who has only a small damages claim (who seeks, say, the value of only a defective refrigerator or television set)" would be left "without any remedy but a court remedy [if arbitration were eliminated], the costs and delays of which could eat up the value of an eventual small recovery."[88]

Furthermore, as for the claim that arbitration stacks the deck against consumers, research also shows otherwise. Generally, consumers do at least as well in arbitration as they would in court.[89] A November 2009 study by the Searle Center at Northwestern University School of Law examined comprehensive data sets of consumer arbitrators and found that after controlling for variations in case characteristics, consumers were more likely to prevail in arbitration than in court and that there was "no statistically significant difference between creditor recovery rates in arbitration and in court."[90] Another recent study by the American Arbitration Association showed that consumers won or accepted a settlement in about 80 percent of arbitrations they initiated.[91] In addition, a 2004 study by the National Workrights Institute concluded that employees prevailed in 62 percent of employment cases brought in arbitration, as opposed to 43 percent of cases filed in a court.[92] Proposals to prohibit mandatory arbitration provisions are based on advancing the interests of lawyers, not consumers.

Tort lawyers are also seeking to enact laws that would make it illegal for corporate executives to "knowingly" produce or sell products that cause injury. On its face, this proposal appears to make sense. Why shouldn't company executives be subject to criminal penalties when they knowingly manufacture products – such as pharmaceuticals – that injure people? But consider that most pharmaceutical drugs are capable of causing injury to some users. We have established a regulatory system to determine whether the positive benefits sufficiently outweigh the negative effects to allow for the carefully controlled sale of drugs and to prescribe the warnings that must be listed. The real purpose of the proposed law is not to improve product safety but to force corporate officers to settle personal injury litigation – no matter how lacking in merit – for fear of a local jury finding that they intentionally inflicted injury and thus subject these officers to criminal prosecution. One likely cost of such legislation will be the development of fewer life-saving products.

Tort lawyers are also deeply involved in the health care reform legislation that is being proposed by the Obama administration. A provision slipped into the House bill in August 2009 would have drastically widened the scope of lawsuits against Medicare "third-party defendants." When Medicare pays the bills for an injured person who prevailed in a suit against a third party based on the injury, Medicare seeks reimbursement of its medical outlays from the proceeds of that lawsuit (and sometimes directly from the injurer). The inserted provision would allow lawyers to file suits against third parties on behalf of Medicare and collect substantial rewards (30% plus expenses). Even more expansively, the provision permitted lawyers to file Medicare recovery actions based "on any relevant evidence, including but not limited to relevant statistical or epidemiological evidence, or by other similarly reliable means."[93] This language would allow lawyers to gin up Medicare recovery actions against new classes of defendants who did not cause the injury but who, they claim, are responsible in a "statistical" sense, such as manufacturers or suppliers of such products as alcohol, high-calorie foods, and guns.[94]

Although the provision was omitted when Republicans raised a hue and cry, other tort lawyer "earmarks" were included in the final version of the health care overhaul bill passed by the U.S. House of Representatives in November 2009. One provision gives state attorneys general broad powers to enforce provisions outlined in Title II of the proposal law: "Protections and Standards for Qualified Health Care Benefits Plans." Under section 257, which was inserted into the bill without benefit of any hearing, state attorneys general would be able to pursue monetary damages on behalf of private plaintiffs for even technical violations of a complicated and ambiguous set of rules.[95] Victor Schwartz, a products liability defense lawyer who closely follows congressional legislation on behalf of business interests and who is also an author of one of the leading law school casebooks on torts, believes this section would effectively grant state attorneys general the authority to hire private lawyers who contributed substantial sums to their campaigns, on a contingency fee basis, to target practically anyone – small and large employers, health care providers, insurers, and so forth, for any violation of any one of thousands of regulations that will flow from the bill.[96]

The power of the tort bar is more overtly reflected in section 2531 of the bill, which authorizes the Secretary of Health and Human Services to provide grants to states that adopt "alternative medical liability" laws. The provision specifically prohibits any grants to states that limit attorneys' fees or impose caps on medical malpractice damages.[97] The provision can be interpreted to require the thirty states that cap damages in medical malpractice suits and the sixteen states that limit attorneys' fees to repeal those laws in order to be eligible to receive federal subsidies.

At the state level, tort lawyers have advanced an unprecedented number of proposals designed to benefit their financial interests. In 2008 alone, more than one hundred bills were considered in twenty-five states that would have this effect.[98] This number will likely double, if not triple, in the next year or two. On the procedural side, the tort bar is seeking to liberalize discovery rules and reverse the effects of the U.S. Supreme Court decision in *Daubert v. Merrel Dow*,[99] which commanded federal courts to reject expert testimony that was untrustworthy and lacked scientific validity – a standard that only some state supreme courts have adopted. Examples of substantive changes being sought include creating new types of rights that can be enforced by lawsuits; raising the caps on previously enacted noneconomic damages to make litigation more profitable; repealing reforms of joint and several liability laws so that if a deep-pocketed defendant is found 1 percent liable, it can be forced to pay the remaining 99 percent of the damages attributed to others who

have no assets; creating new classes of damages in wrongful death lawsuits by adding grief, sorrow, mental suffering, and hedonic damages
to noneconomic damages; allowing pet owners to collect unbounded
pain and suffering damages for injuries to their pets; and expanding the
scope of consumer deceptive practices laws to allow more such suits.
A notable illustration of the nearly unlimited opportunities that state
consumer protection laws already confer on plaintiffs is the suit by a customer of a dry cleaner in Washington, D.C., alleging that the store lost
a pair of his suit pants and claiming damages under the D.C. Consumer
Protection Procedures Act of $67 million. Despite the absurdity of this
failed lawsuit, the Korean owners of the mom-and-pop dry cleaners that
allegedly lost the pants incurred $100,000 in legal fees and lost two of
their three shops.[100]

Tort lawyers are also lobbying for legislation that would give state
attorneys general federal law enforcement powers. They could then hire
tort lawyers to represent the state in suits against big businesses, cutting
them in for tens and hundreds of millions of dollars in contingency fees.
To secure these lucrative appointments, tort lawyers would "pay to play"
by contributing to the AGs' political campaigns and parties.

Another major lobbying objective of tort lawyers is the inclusion of
language in state and federal regulatory legislation designed to expand
their opportunities to act as "private attorneys general" and file lawsuits to enforce the legislation. Typically, regulatory commissions or law
enforcement officials enforce state and federal statutes or regulations
enacted to protect the public. In some instances, however, a legislature will include a provision conferring a "private right of action." This
empowers a consumer who falls under the statute's protection to sue a
manufacturer or seller of goods and services for violating the standard
created by the regulatory legislation. In some cases, however, even without an explicit provision conferring a private right of action, given the
nature and intent of the legislation in question, a court may conclude –
at the urging of a plaintiff and her lawyer – that there is an "implied"
private right of action. This allows private individuals to sue to enforce

legislation, thus creating a whole new avenue of relief, which may extend the scope of the legislation far beyond what the legislature contemplated or intended. Implied private rights of action have the potential to produce prodigious contingency fees for lawyers.[101]

To create new sources of contingency fees, the AAJ is actively lobbying to enlarge private rights of action – the equivalent of "lawyers' earmarks." They are seeking to place innocuously appearing – but carefully crafted – words into regulatory statutes, the significance of which will be missed in the legislative debate but which can be used by some judges to justify the creation of a private right of action. For example, consider legislation that would require auto manufacturers to provide a device in all new cars, alerting drivers when tire pressures fall below a preset amount. The debate in the legislature is likely to focus on whether the cost is justified by the benefits to drivers, which regulatory agency should be tasked with enforcement of the new law, how quickly the new requirement should be phased in, and the penalties to be assessed for violation of the new standard. This debate is unlikely to focus on whether a new private right of action should be created. Supporters of the bill, however, might reject it if it *expressly* creates a new private right of action in addition to delegating enforcement power to a regulatory agency. Once enacted, however, a court may find that the seemingly innocuous language inserted into the bill indicates a legislative intent to create just such a private right of action.

An even subtler strategy of self-promotion is revealed in the Consumer Product Safety Act (CPSA), which President Bush signed into law on August 14, 2008. This legislation was spurred by concerns about the importation of unsafe products from China and was nearly unanimously approved by both houses of Congress. It addresses several product safety issues, including the safety of children's products, the regulation of imported consumer goods, and third-party testing requirements. The Act imposes civil penalties for each violation ranging from $5,000 to $100,000. Tort lawyers' and business interests squared off on the issue of empowering state attorneys general to play a role in enforcement of the Act. Although the AAJ sought wider enforcement powers for the state attorneys general, it was content with the inclusion of a provision permitting them to seek injunctive relief on behalf of a state's residents if a product threatened citizens' safety. On its face, this is an innocuous and justifiable provision. In reality, however, it was not about ensuring product safety but rather simply another means of cutting in contingency fee lawyers for additional fee opportunities, who would then lobby for these appointments by contributing to AGs' campaigns.

Here is a plausible scenario based on this legislation: Tort lawyers are representing purchasers of a product who claim to have been injured because of an inadequate warning label. The product manufacturers or sellers believe that their warning label was adequate and resist the lawyers' demands for substantial compensation. The lawyers believe the litigation to be very promising, but they need to enlist the media and the AG to ensure its profitability. Their aim is to pressure the manufacturer into settling with the lawyers by focusing public attention on the alleged infirmities of the product, thereby increasing public awareness of the threat and the number of people who will come forward to join the litigation. This will soften up the defendants and make them more amenable to settling the claims on favorable terms. To that end, the lawyers pay a call on the AG – to whom they have contributed campaign funds – to point out how the product is causing injury. The AG is convinced that taking action is politically expedient, thumbs through her file of campaign contributors, and hires private lawyers to bring suit to ban the sale of the product. The AG's action is front-page news. Local television stations start off their newscasts with an "alert," informing consumers about the public safety threat posed by the product. Soon thereafter, the seller, eager to eliminate this bad publicity, does a deal with the lawyers and adds minor changes to the warning label. The AG then proudly announces that due to her efforts, the seller has agreed to make important changes to protect public safety and the matter drops from public view.

NOTES

1. Michael Orey, *How Business Trounced the Trial Lawyers*, Bus. Week, Jan. 8, 2007, at 44; Alison Frankel, *It's Over: Tort reformers, business interests, and plaintiffs lawyers themselves have helped kill the mass torts bonanza – and it's not coming back*, Am. Law., Dec. 12, 2006, at 78; Paul Davies, *Lawsuits Against Companies Sharply Decline*, Wall St. J., Aug. 26, 2006, at A1.

2. *See* Michael J. Saks, *Do We Really Know Anything About the Behavior of the Tort Litigation System – And Why Not?*, 140 U. Pa. L. Rev. 1147, 1174 (1992) [hereinafter Saks, *Do We Really Know Anything*] ("Tort law *defines* the base of actionable injuries." [emphasis in original]).

3. *See, e.g., Janmark, Inc. v. Reidy*, 132 F.3d 1200, 1202 (7th Cir. 1997) (holding that "[t]here is no tort without injury").

4. Consider the thousands of claims that have been brought by tort lawyers for hearing loss under the Longshoreman's and Harbor Workers Compensation Act. 33 U.S.C. § 901 (2006). Occupational hearing loss, which is compensable under this act, is indistinguishable from presbycusis – hearing loss due to age. Lawyers go from plant to plant, sign up current and former workers and provide them with a medical examination that virtually always shows hearing loss. They then file hearing loss claims on their behalf. *See* Brickman, *Asbestos Litigation Crisis, supra* Chapter 9, note 6, at n.144. Because it is usually impossible to determine the source of hearing loss and because, under the law, the employer is liable for a workers' total hearing loss even if part of it is caused by presbycusis, *id.*, simply filing these claims en masse assures payment.

5. *See* Chapter 7, § F.

6. *In re Silica Prods. Liab. Litig.*, 398 F. Supp. 2d 563, 676 (S.D. Tex. 2005).

7. *See* Brickman, *Litigation Screenings, supra* Chapter 7, note 61, at § VIII. The lone exception is Judge Jack, who determined that the litigation screenings that generated 10,000 claims of silicosis were part of a "scheme" in which "lawyers, doctors and screening companies were all willing participants … to manufacture [diagnoses] for money." 398 F. Supp. 2d 635.

8. Richard A. Posner, *Common Law Economic Torts: An Economic and Legal Analysis*, 48 Ariz. L. Rev. 735, 735 (2006).

9. James A. Henderson Jr., *The Lawlessness of Aggregative Torts*, 34 Hofstra L. Rev. 329, 337 (2005).

All but the most ardent antibusiness advocates cannot help but wince, way down inside, at the prospect of courts reallocating potentially billions of dollars in the name of physically uninjured consumers, many of whom continue to demand the very same products and services paternalistically deemed by judges and juries to be against consumers' best interests. The only interest group that would clearly benefit from the wide acceptance of aggregative torts would be those plaintiff's lawyers who are conceiving, funding, and bringing these actions on a contingency fee basis. Surely their clients, many of whom never receive anything from the recoveries and most of whom end up paying higher prices for consumer goods and services, are not benefiting in the same way as their lawyers.

Instead, the lawlessness of aggregative torts inheres in the remarkable degree to which they combine sweeping, social-engineering perspectives with vague, open-ended legal standards for determining liability and measuring damages. In effect, these new torts empower judges and triers of fact to exercise discretionary regulatory power at the macroeconomic level of such a magnitude that even the most ambitious administrative agencies could never hope to possess. In exercising these extraordinary powers, courts arguably exceed the legitimate limits of both their authority and their competence. Regarding the limits of judicial authority, it is commonly understood that, in a representative democracy, macroeconomic regulation is accomplished most appropriately by elected officials and their lawful delegates. Of course, traditional tort law unavoidably involves economic regulation to some extent. But these new aggregative torts involve self-conscious judicial regulation on such a breathtaking scale, abstracted from any commitment to the individual rights of individual victims, that they clearly exceed the political boundaries of judicial authority.

Id. at 337–38 (footnotes omitted).

10. For a compendium of state consumer protection laws, see Debra P. Stark, *Does Fraud Pay? An Empirical Analysis of Attorney's Fees Provisions in Consumer Fraud Statutes*, 56 CLEVELAND ST. L. REV. 483, 518 (2008).

11. 42 U.S.C. § 45(a)(1) (2006).

12. State Consumer Protection Acts, An Empirical Investigation of Private Litigation, Preliminary Report at 1, Searle Center on Law, Regulation, and Economic Growth, Northwestern Univ. School of Law (Dec. 2009) [hereinafter Searle Report].

13. *See* Henry N. Butler, and Jason S. Johnston, *Reforming State Consumer Protection Liability: An Economic Approach*, 2010 COLUM. BUS. L. REV. (2010), *available at* http://ssrn.com/abstract=1125305.

14. *See* Ted Frank, *A Taxonomy of Obesity Litigation*, 28 U. ARK. LITTLE ROCK L. REV. 427, 440 (2006).

15. W. PAGE KEETON ET AL., PROSSER AND KEETON ON THE LAW OF TORTS § 105, at 728 (5th ed. 1984).

16. *See* Victor E. Schwartz & Cary Silverman, *Common-Sense Construction of Consumer Protection Acts*, 54 KAN. L. REV. 1, 7 (2005); Sheila B. Scheuerman, *The Consumer Fraud Class Action: Reigning in Abuse by Requiring Plaintiffs*

to Allege Reliance as an Essential Element, 43 HARV. J. ON LEGIS. 1, 5–8, 21–23 (2006).

17. Schwartz & Silverman, *id*. at 28–30.

18. Searle Report, *supra* note 12, at 11.

19. *Id*. at 39.

20. *See, e.g., International Union of Operating Engineers Local No.68 Welfare Fund v. Merck & Co.*, 929 A.2d 1076 (N.J. 2007).

21. Still another action against Merck based on the sale of Vioxx is pending. In this securities class action seeking billions of dollars in damages, lawyers are contending that Merck knowingly misrepresented the safety of Vioxx when it announced the results of a comparison study of Vioxx and naproxen. Shareholders, it is alleged, were harmed by this misrepresentation because Merck stock significantly declined when Merck later withdrew the product because of the increased risk for heart attack and stroke. *See Merck & Co., Inc. et al. v. Reynolds et al.*, 130 S. Ct. 1784 (2010). Securities class actions are discussed in Chapter 19.

22. *See* Braggin' Rights, THE (MADISON COUNTY) RECORD, Dec. 16, 2007, *available at* www.madisonrecord.com/arguments/205280-braggin-rights.

23. *See* Lester Brickman, *Anatomy of a Madison County (Illinois) Class Action: A Study of Pathology*, Civil Justice Rep. No. 6, Center For Legal Policy at the Manhattan Institute, Aug. 2002 at iii.

24. *See* Alison Frankel, *Class Actions: New Field, Same Game?* AM. LAW., Apr. 15, 2005, at 18; Jessica Davidson Miller & John H. Beisner, *They're Making a Federal Case of It ... in State Court*, Civil Justice Report, No. 3, Center for Legal Policy at the Manhattan Institute, Sept. 2001; John H. Beisner & Jessica Davidson Miller, *Class Action Magnet Courts: The Allure Intensifies*, Civil Justice Report, No. 5, Center for Legal Policy at the Manhattan Institute, July 2002.

25. *See* Settlement Agreement, *Hoorman et al. v. SmithKline Beecham Corp.*, No. 04-L-715, ¶1, (Ill. 3d Jud. Cir. Madison County Oct. 6, 2006), *available at* http://www.paxilclaims.com/. [hereinafter Settlement Agreement].

26. 815 ILCS § 505/1 *et seq. See* Order Approving Settlement, *Hoorman et al. v. SmithKline Beecham Corp.*, No. 04-L-715, ¶1, (Ill. 3d Jud. Cir. Madison County May 17, 2007) *available at* http://www.paxilclaims.com [hereinafter Order Approving Settlement]. Specifically, the complaint alleged that the drug company failed to disclose that it knew from its own research that the drug produced the same results as a placebo and could even cause adolescents to have suicidal tendencies. *See* Aruna Viswanatha, *Big Suits: Hoorman et al. v. GlaxoSmithKline*, AM. LAW., Jan. 2007, at 49.

27. *See* Order Approving Settlement; Settlement Agreement, at 2, ¶7; *see also* Brian Brueggmann, *Lawsuit details remain secret, Parties in Paxil case mum on payments*, BELLEVILLE NEWS-DEMOCRAT, Oct. 21, 2007, at B1.

28. This is so because each individual smoker in the class would have to show reliance on the defendants' misrepresentations or that he or she would have suffered the same physical harm if the cigarettes were as represented.

29. *See Price v. Philip Morris Inc.*, No. 00-L-112, 2003 WL 22597608 (Ill. Cir. Ct. Mar. 21, 2003).

30. *Price v. Philip Morris Inc.*, 219 Ill.2d 182 (2005).

31. For discussion of Judge Weinstein's role in launching mass tort litigation, see *supra* Chapter 10.

32. 18 U.S.C. § 1961 *et seq.* (2006).

33. *Schwab v. Philip Morris USA, Inc.*, 449 F. Supp. 2d 992 (E.D.N.Y. 2006).

34. *McLaughlin v. Am. Tobacco Co.*, 522 F.3d 215 (2d Cir. 2008).

35. *UFCW LOCAL 1776 et al. v. Eli Lilly & Co.*, No. 09–0222-cv, 2d Cir. Ct. App., Sept. 10, 2010.

36. 129 S. Ct. 538 (2008).

37. ME. REV. STAT. ANN. tit.5, § 207 (2002).

38. 15 U.S.C. § 1334(b) (2006). The sophistry of the Court's opinion is made clear by an editorial in the *Los Angeles Times*, a newspaper not noted for a pro-business slant: "In ruling that Altria could be sued, the court bypassed that plain [statutory] language and engaged in some legal hair-splitting. Writing for the majority, Justice John Paul Stevens concluded that the federal monopoly on warning labels about 'smoking and health' doesn't prevent state lawsuits accusing tobacco companies of making fraudulent statements. As we have argued before, that is a distinction without a difference. If the label 'light' was deceptive, it was because it underestimated the health dangers." Editorial, *Opening Pandora's Pack*, L.A. TIMES, Dec. 20, 2008, at A30.

39. A critical issue that will determine the potential consequences of class actions against the tobacco companies based on various states' deceptive trade practices acts will be how to measure damages if a suit is successful. The issue of damages in light-cigarette suits is discussed by Judge Weinstein in *Schwab v. Philip Morris USA., Inc.*, 449 F. Supp. 2d 992 (E.D.N.Y. 2006). Class action lawyers contend that the proper measure is that used in suits for breach of contract. Under this measure of economic loss, the plaintiffs are entitled to the "benefit of the bargain" with the seller, which is the difference in value between the product at the time of the sale if the representation about the product were true and the actual value of the product. Unlike its use in contract disputes, this measure of damages in the context of "economic injury" class actions against the tobacco companies is open-ended and, in theory, could even exceed the total amounts paid by all members of the class for light cigarettes. Though the U.S. Supreme Court did not reach the issue of the proper measure of damages, the Second Circuit Court of Appeals, in reversing Judge Weinstein, addressed the question. That court determined that various measures of damages it

considered were too speculative, and that differences in how the allegedly deceitful advertising by the tobacco companies affected individual smokers precluded their being lumped together as a class. *McLaughlin v. Am. Tobacco Co.*, 522 F.3d 215, 227–34 (2d Cir. 2008). The court went on to state that the tobacco companies' "misrepresentation could in no way have reduced the value of the cigarettes that plaintiffs actually purchased; they simply could have induced plaintiffs to buy Lights instead of full-flavored cigarettes." *McLaughlin*, 522 F.3d at 229. Put plainly, this court's demolition of the rationale adopted by Judge Byron in the Madison County, Illinois, action lets most of the air out of the class lawyers' balloons. Other courts, however, are free to be much more plaintiff-lawyer friendly by selecting a measure of damages that could generate billions of dollars in contingency fees for lawyers in addition to refunds to smokers that would enable them to purchase additional packs of cigarettes.

40. For a discussion of the revenue sharing partnership between the states and the tobacco companies see Chapter 22 § A.

41. *See* Victor E. Schwartz, et al., *Medical Monitoring – Should Tort Law Say Yes?* 34 WAKE FOREST L. REV. 1057, 1058 (1999).

42. *See, e.g., Wilson v. Brush Wellman, Inc.*, 817 N.E. 59, 66 (Ohio 2004); *Lockheed Martin Corp. v. Superior Court*, 63 P.3d 913, 921–22 (Cal. 2003); *Baker v. Wyeth-Ayerst Laboratories*, 992 S.W.2d 797, 802 (Ark. 1999); *In re St. Jude Medical, Inc.*, 522 F. 3d 836, 840 (8th Circ. 2005).

43. *See, e.g., Meyer v. Fluor Corp.*, 220 S.W. 3d 712, 719 (Mo. 2007); *Olden v. LaFarge Corp.*, 383 F. 3d 495, 508 (6th Cir. 2004); *Mejdrech v. Met-Coil Systems, Corp.*, 319 F. 3d 390, 911–12 (7th Cir. 2003).

44. Whereas about fifteen states require the existence of present physical harm caused by exposure to alleged toxic substances in order to award plaintiff medical-monitoring damages, at least twelve states allow the damages despite the lack of a present injury. *See* Scwartz *Medical Monitoring, supra* note 40, at 1059–71; Victor E. Schwartz, et al., *Medical Monitoring: The Right Way and the Wrong Way*, 70 Mo. L. REV. 349, 361 n.70, 71 (2005); Scott Aberson, Note, *A Fifty-State Survey of Medical Monitoring and the Approach the Minnesota Supreme Court Should Take When Confronted with the Issue*, 32 WM. MITCHELL L. REV. 1095, 1114–17 (2006). Several of the states that allow for the recovery of damages without present injury place a higher burden on the plaintiff, such as requiring the use of expert testimony to establish there is a reasonable degree of medical certainty that future medical expenses will be incurred as a result of exposure to a toxic substance. *See, e.g., Patton v. General Signal Corp.*, 984 F. Supp 666, 673 (W.D.N.Y. 1997).

45. Some states, however, do not permit the award of a lump sum for future medical-monitoring costs but rather require the creation of a court-administered fund ensuring that any damages awarded are spent appropriately. *See Petito v. A.H.*

Robins Co., Inc., 750 So. 2d 103 (Fla. Dist. Ct. App. 1999); *Burns v. Jaquay's Mining Corp.*, 752 P.2d 28 (Ariz. Ct. App. 1987).

46. *See* Brickman, *Litigation Screenings, supra* Chapter 7, note 61, at 1247.

47. *See id.* at 1249–50.

48. Louisiana previously allowed plaintiffs to recover medical-monitoring costs despite lacking a present illness. *See Bourgeois v. A.P. Green Industries, Inc.*, 716 So. 2d 355 (La. 1998). However, the legislature amended the civil code following that decision with the express intention of limiting medical monitoring damages to cases where the costs of future medical treatment are directly related to a present injury or disease. LA. CIV. CODE ANN. art. 2315 (1999).

49. 522 S.E.2d 424 (W. Va. 1999).

50. *Id.* at 433.

51. *Id.*

52. *Id.*

53. *Id.* at 434.

54. 521 U.S. 424, 441 (1997) (internal citations omitted).

55. *See* Donald G. Gifford, *Public Nuisance as a Mass Products Liability Tort*, 71 U. CIN. L. REV. 741, 791 (2003) [hereinafter Gifford, *Public Nuisance*] ("[T]he law of nuisance in a form that is identifiable today first began to appear during the reign of Henry II in the last half of the twelfth century.").

56. 4 REST. (SECOND) TORTS § 821B, cmt.b (1979).

57. *See, e.g.*, Amanda Bronstad, *Lead Paint Litigation is Beginning to Fade*, NAT'L L.J., Aug. 20, 2007, at 1.

58. *See St. Louis v. Benjamin Moore Co.*, 226 S.W.3d 110 (Mo. 2007); *In re Lead Paint Litig.*, 191 N.J. 405 (2007).

59. *See* Trial Order, *Rhode Island v. Lead Indus. Ass'n, Inc.*, 2007 WL 711824 No. 99–5226 (Super. Ct. R.I. Feb. 26, 2007) [hereinafter Trial Order]; *see also* Julie Creswell, *The Nuisance That May Cost Billions: How Decades-Old Lead Paint Becomes a Brand-New Problem for Companies*, N.Y. TIMES, Apr. 2, 2006, at 3.1.

60. *See* Abha Bhattarai, *State Court Throws Out Jury Finding in Lead Case*, N.Y. TIMES, July 2, 2008, at C4.

61. *See* Creswell, *The Nuisance That May Cost Billions*, at 3.6.

62. *See* Trial Order, at II.C.1.

63. *See* Jury Instructions at 13–14, *Rhode Island v. Atlantic Richfield Co. et al.*, No. 99–5226 (Super. Ct. R.I. 2007).

64. *Tioga Pub. Sch. Dist. #15 v. U.S. Gypsum Co.*, 984 F.2d 915, 921 (8th Cir. 1993).

65. *Rhode Island v. Lead Indus. Ass'n*, 928 A.2d 428 (R.I. 2008).

66. *Massachusetts v. EPA*, 127 S. Ct. 1438, 1446 (2007) (holding inter alia that plaintiffs had standing to petition review of the EPA's decision not to regulate

carbon dioxide because the three standing requirements – injury, causation, and redressability – had been satisfied).

67. *See Tri v. J.T.T.*, 162 S.W. 3d 552 (Tex. 2005); *Lloyd v. General Motors Corp.*, 397 Md. 108, 916 A. 2d 257 (2007).

68. Complaint, *Native Village of Kivalina and City of Kivalina v. ExxonMobil Corp., et al.*, No. 08CV1138-SBA (N.D. Cal. Feb. 26, 2008).

69. *Id.* at 2.

70. *Native Village of Kivalina et al. v. ExxonMobil Corp. et al.*, 2009 WL 3326113 at *10 (N.D. Cal. 2009). *See also California v. General Motors Corp.*, No. C06–05755MJJ, 2007 WL 2726871 (N.D. Cal. Sept. 17, 2007) (order granting defendants' motion to dismiss lawsuit filed by the California Attorney General against six auto manufacturers for damages in connection with the nuisance of global warming, on the grounds that this was a "political question" and therefore unsuitable for a court to decide. This case is on appeal).

71. 582 F.3d 309, 330–31 (2d Cir. 2009).

72. *Comer v. Murphy Oil USA*, 585 F.3d 855 (5th Circuit 2009), *vacated by* 607 F.3d 1049 (May 28, 2010). The decision was vacated by a vote of the full Fifth Circuit. 598 F.3d 208 (Feb. 26, 2010). However, because eight of the court's judges recused themselves on the grounds that each owned stock in at least one of the 150 companies targeted in the litigation, the court was unable to muster a quorum, and the appeal was dismissed. Presumably, the plaintiffs will seek review by the U.S. Supreme Court.

73. *North Carolina v. TVA*, 2010 WL 2891572, at *11 (quoting *Negusie v. Holder*, 129 S. Ct. 1159, 1171 (2009)).

74. Laurence H. Tribe et al., *Too Hot for Courts to Handle: Fuel Temperatures, Global Warming, and the Political Question Doctrine*, WASH. LEGAL FOUND. CRITICAL ISSUES SERIES (Jan. 2010) at 23.

75. See John Schwartz, *Courts Emerging as Battlefield for Fights Over Climate Change*, N.Y. TIMES, Jan. 27, 2010, at 1A.

76. 582 F. 3d at 330–31.

77. Focus Report, The Globalization of collective redress: consequences for the insurance industry at 3, Swiss Re (2009).

78. Harvard University's Kennedy School of Government energy expert Henry Lee told *Time* magazine that the cost of climate change adaptations would absorb 2% to 3% of the nation's $13 trillion GDP per year for the foreseeable future. Bryan Walsh, *How to Win the War on Global Warming*, TIME, Apr. 16, 2008, at 57. According to Lee, "[t]he plaintiffs' bar is following the litigation strategies developed in the tobacco and asbestos mega-lawsuits. The difference is that the plaintiffs' bar is now adopting questionable science to prove that American industry is responsible for global-climate change." *The Coming Global-Warming Litigation Onslaught*, DIRECTORSHIP, June/July 2008, at 35.

79. In the 1990s, suits against electric power companies claiming injury from electromagnetic field radiation (EMF) emitted by power lines was a prolific source of litigation that some lawyers thought would be the "asbestos of the nineties." By the turn of the century, however, this litigation had lost its sizzle. Nonetheless, despite the absence of any conclusive evidence that EMF, generated mainly by power lines in urban areas, causes any of the injuries attributed to it (and some evidence suggests that it does not), the cost to the electric industry had exceeded $23 billion by 1994, due mostly to the cost of moving high-voltage power lines and transformer substations. *See* William A. Bennett Jr., *Power Lines Are Homely, Not Dangerous*, WALL ST. J., Aug. 10, 1994, at A8; Stanley Pierce & Charlotte A. Biblow, *Electromagnetic Fields Attract Lawsuits*, NAT'L L.J., Feb. 8, 1993, at 20. Another litigation that has had much success but has not lived up to its expected potential is mold litigation. After a $32 million verdict in Texas in 2001, followed by a number of successful lawsuits that resulted in payments in the range of $250,000, "mold is gold" became a byword for tort lawyers who anticipated a big payday. *Ballard v. Fire Ins. Exchange*, No. 99–05252, 2001 WL 883550 (Tex. Dist. Ct. Aug. 1, 2001). The litigation was able to proceed because a small number of experts, paid millions of dollars in fees for advancing theories that were rejected by medical science, regularly testified that mold causes a terrifying array of diseases. *See* Brickman, *Litigation Screenings, supra* Chapter 7, note 61, at 1351. Although these lawsuits have been highly profitable – an estimated $3 billion in mold claims were paid out in 2002 – mold litigation has not fulfilled its early promise of being "the next asbestos." *See* Daniel Fisher, *Dr. Mold; Why Sketchy Science Doesn't Stop Medical "Experts,"* FORBES, Apr. 11, 2005, at 100.

80. *See* Ted Frank, *A Taxonomy of Obesity Litigation*, 28 U. ARK. LITTLE ROCK L. REV. 427 (2006). Proponents of fast-food industry liability have launched their first assault on the citadel of the "Big Mac." *See Pelman v. McDonald's Corp.*, 237, F. Supp. 2d 512 (S.D.N.Y. 2003) (dismissing complaint involving both intentional and negligent torts), *amended complaint dismissed by* No. 02 Civ. 7821, 2003 U.S. Dist. LEXIS 15202, at 42 (S.D.N.Y. Sept. 3, 2003) (dismissing an amended complaint based on the New York Consumer Protection Act), *vacated and remanded by* 396 F.3d 508 (2d Cir. 2005). Professor John Banzhaf, the most visible proponent of fast-food liability, stated that the Second Circuit's decision "opens the door not only to many more obesity law suits, but also to unearthing previously secret documents which may help plaintiffs persuade juries to hold fast food companies liable for their fair share of the expenses of the obesity to which they contribute." Press Release, Professor John F. Banzhaf III, Appeals Court Upholds Obesity Law Suit Against McDonald's – Decision Opens Door For More Suits and Discovery of Secret Documents (Jan. 25,

2005), *available at* http://banzhaf.net/mcback.html. Despite this optimism, some contend that obesity suits have not been well-received, and their serious flaws present an example of "why tort suits die." *See* Kyle Graham, *Why Torts Die*, 35 Fla. St. U. L. Rev. 359, 400–05 (2008).

81. *See* Frank, *Obesity Litigation, supra*, at 433. Frank's article also catalogues the various other claims launched in the obesity suits.

82. Robert F. Cochran Jr., *Hedonic Product Liability: Will Alcohol Follow the Tobacco Road?* The Brief, Fall 2002, at 12; *see also* Robert F. Cochran Jr., *From Cigarettes to Alcohol: The Next Step in Hedonic Product Liability?* 27 Pepp. L. Rev. 701 (2000). Cochran's articles detail the similarities and differences between alcohol and tobacco litigation, ultimately concluding that there is strong support that alcohol litigation suits will follow the tobacco model of litigation. Despite this theoretical potential, alcohol suits have generally not fared well. *See* David G. Owen, *Inherent Product Hazards*, 93 Ky. L.J. 377, 390, 390 n.56 (2005) (concluding that "generally, manufacturers of alcoholic beverages are not liable for injuries resulting from their consumption," and citing cases where no liability has been imposed on manufacturers of uncontaminated alcoholic beverages in claims of negligence, implied warranty, or strict liability for harm from their consumption; also concluding that claims of contamination and fraudulent advertising should still be available).

83. *See* Michael Leventhal, *Litigation Issues Likely to Confront the Wireless Industry*, http://www.wiredlaw.com/articles/wireless.html (last visited Mar. 1, 2009). Litigation over radiation has taken a tumultuous journey through the courts, which is far from complete. In 2005, the Fourth Circuit reversed a district court judgment and reinstated five class actions against manufacturers and distributors of wireless telephones in state courts alleging claims such as products liability, violation of state consumer protection laws, fraud, negligence, breach of implied warranty, and civil conspiracy related to radiation emissions. *See Pinney v. Nokia Inc.*, 402 F.3d 430 (4th Cir. 2005). The Supreme Court denied review to the appealing defendants. However, the Fourth Circuit did not completely clear the road for plaintiffs. On remand, one district court has declined to be bound by the Fourth Circuit decision based on a procedural technicality and dismissed the case as federally preempted, barring plaintiffs from advancing such claims. *See Farina v. Nokia*, 578 F. Supp.2d 740 (E.D. Pa. 2008).

84. Karen Donovan, *The Fight Is On*, Registered Rep. 55, Dec. 1, 2007, *available at* http://registeredrep.com/advisorland/regulatory/fight_on_arbitration.

85. *See, e.g., Tillman v. Commercial Credit Loans, Inc.*, 655 S.E.2d 362, 368 (N.C. 2008) (holding arbitration clause in subprime mortgage contract unconscionable "due to prohibitively high arbitration costs," including travel expenses plaintiffs faced in pursuing their claim); *Vasquez-Lopez v. Beneficial Oregon, Inc.*,

152 P.3d 940, 952 (Or. 2007) (holding a cost-sharing provision in an arbitration clause unconscionable because it was "sufficiently onerous to act as a deterrent to plaintiffs' vindication of their claim"); *Scott v. Cingular Wireless*, 161 P.3d 1000 (Wash. 2007) (holding that a clause that prohibited class action arbitration while compelling individual arbitration substantively unconscionable).

86. For claims less than $75,000, the consumer pays a maximum of $375. Businesses are required to pay the remainder plus the administrative filing fee. Consumers in California, who make less than 300% of federal poverty rates, per section 1284.3 of the California Code of Civil Procedure, do not have to pay arbitration fees and costs. *See* AMERICAN ARBITRATION ASS'N, CONSUMER ARBITRATION COSTS, EFFECTIVE JULY 1, 2003, *available at* http://adr.org/sp.asp?id=22039.

87. *See* Christopher R. Drahozal & Samantha Zyontz, *An Empirical Study of AAA Consumer Arbitrations* at 2 (Mar. 13. 2009), *available at* http://papers. ssrn.com/sol3/papers.cfm?abstract_id=1365435. For the next category of claims ($10,000–$75,000) the average amount of fees paid by consumers increased to $219. *See id.*

88. *Allied-Bruce Terminix Cos., Inc. v. Dobson*, 513 U.S. 265, 281 (1995).

89. Christine Varney, *Arbitration Works Better Than Lawsuits*, WALL ST. J., July 14, 2008, at A17.

90. *See Interim Report on Creditor Claims in Arbitration and in Court*, Searle Center on Law, Regulation, and Economic Growth at Northwestern Law 4 (2009), *available at* http://www.law.northwestern.edu/searlecenter/uploads/ Creditor%20Claims%20Interim%20Report%2011%2019%2009%20 FINAL2.pdf.

91. *Id.*

92. *See* EMPLOYMENT ARBITRATION: WHAT DOES THE DATA SHOW?, THE NATIONAL WORKRIGHTS INSTITUTE, 2004, *available at* http://www.workrights.org/current/ cd_arbitration.html (noting that the employment arbitrations studied have mostly consisted of contract disputes).

93. Walter Olson, *Inside the Health Care Bill*, FORBES.COM, July 22, 2009 *available at* http://www.forbes.com/2009/07/22/medicare-republicans-reform-bill-opinions-contributors-walter-olson.html.

94. *Id.*

95. Affordable Health Care for America Act, H.R. 3962, 111th Cong. 257 (2009).

96. Chris Rizzo, *House health care bill expands state AGs' powers*, LEGAL NEWSLINE, Nov. 30, 2009, *available at* http://legalnewsline.com/news/224232.

97. *Id.*

98. Civil Justice Reform *Outlook* at 11, American Tort Reform Ass'n, Jan. 2009.

99. 509 U.S. 579 (1993).

100. In this suit, the plaintiff, Roy L. Pearson, a D.C. administrative law judge, sued a dry cleaner for $54 million, alleging that Soo and Jin Chung, the Korean

mom-and-pop owners of the dry cleaning business, misplaced his suit pants. Henri E. Cauvin, *Court Rules for Cleaners in $54 Million Pants Suit*, WASH. POST, June 26, 2007, at A1. As part of his lawsuit, Pearson alleged that the Chungs violated the D.C. Consumer Protection Procedures Act that provides, in part, that it is a violation to "represent that ... services have a ... characteristic ... that they do not have," or to "represent that ... services are of a particular ... quality, if in fact they are of another." D.C. CODE § 28–3904(a), (d); *see also* Amended Verified Complaint for Violation of Consumer Protection Procedures Act, and Other Claims at ¶ 27, *Pearson v. Soo Chung*, 2007 WL 1972026, No. 4302–05, (Sup. Ct. D.C. July 18, 2005). Because the Chungs posted a sign in the shop saying "Satisfaction Guaranteed," Pearson contended that the Chungs misrepresented the quality of their services because Pearson was obviously not satisfied. Pearson sought statutory damages as provided by the statute from each of the three Chungs (mother, father, and son) of $1,500 per violation per day over a period of several years – adding up to $67 million. *See Pearson v. Soo Chung*, No. 07-CV-872, slip op. at *1 (D.C. App. Ct. Dec. 18, 2008); D.C. CODE § 28–3905(k)(1)(A). Even though the judge ruled for the defendants and Pearson's appeal has been denied, the family-owned dry cleaner incurred $100,000 in legal fees and lost two dry cleaning shops, leaving the Chungs with only one small shop. *See id.*; CNN.COM, *The $54 million pants suit unravels again*, Dec. 18, 2008, *available at* http://www.cnn.com/2008/CRIME/12/18/pants.lawsuit/index.html. Although they may eventually recover some of their legal fees, for the Chungs, this lawsuit has turned their American dream into a nightmare.

101. A notable example is the shareholder suits against corporations for materially misleading communications, which generate approximately $9 billion annually for lawyers. *See* infra Chapter 19.

12 The "Litigation Explosion"

Fact or Fiction?

N THIS CHAPTER, I REVIEW THE EMPIRICAL ARGUMENTS OVER
whether we have experienced a period of explosive growth in
tort litigation. Pro-tort reformers refer to this expansion as
a "litigation explosion." Growth – even explosive growth – in tort litigation is not necessarily an adverse development. The issue is whether
the increased litigation generates social costs that exceed the resulting
benefits. Steven Shavell argues that the socially optimal level of suit is
the perfect balance between social benefits (in the form of deterrence
of injurers) and the social costs of litigation (the administrative costs of
courts and judges).[1] At some level, he states, an increase in the marginal
cost of litigation may exceed the marginal deterrence benefit. In other
words, if there are too many lawsuits, the public costs may outweigh the
benefits of deterrence. On the other hand, if there are not enough lawsuits, product manufacturers may not sufficiently intensify precautions
against harm.

Professor Shavell's theoretical model assumes that all tort litigation
has a deterrent effect – an assumption that he has come to doubt[2] –
and that the social costs of litigation are purely administrative. In fact,
many costs exist outside of Professor Shavell's model. For example, as I
explain in Chapter 20, Section B(1), there was neither real compensation
nor deterrence when tort lawyers came within an eyelash of enriching themselves by more than $100,000,000 at the expense of the State

Farm Insurance Company and its policyholders. Neither does Professor Shavell's model capture the costs of tort lawyers inflating the costs of medical care in auto accidents by at least $30 billion annually in order to increase their contingency fees,[3] nor doctors running up "defensive medicine" costs (additional tests performed in order to avoid medical malpractice liability, which do not result in any additional benefit to patients) by more than $100 billion annually.[4] The model also neglects the use of litigation screenings to generate as many as one million mostly bogus claims resulting in contingency fees of approximately $14 billion.[5] The point I seek to advance is that, in the real world, some types of litigation do not advance compensation or deterrence objectives but rather tort lawyers' profits.

Whether increased litigation is a function of increased levels of injury or a need for increased deterrence are important subjects for inquiry – ones that I address in subsequent chapters. In this chapter, I focus solely on three questions: whether there has been explosive growth; if so, what accounts for it; and the political dimensions of the debate.

The dispute over the growth of tort liability and whether this has resulted in a litigation explosion transcends mere statistical jousting. Invariably, those who conclude that there has been explosive growth in tort litigation support reforms to roll back excessive tort liability expansion. Conversely, those who reject the explosive growth thesis also reject tort reforms as unnecessary and unwise. For example, Herbert M. Kritzer, an empirical researcher whose writings are frequently relied on by tort reform opponents, argues that "those considering major reforms need to obtain reliable, systematic information on the routine operation of the civil justice system generally and the contingent fee specifically before instituting significant changes."[6] He goes on to conclude that "reliable, systemic information" does not exist, and therefore, there is no demonstrated need for tort reform. In the tort reform wars, the battle over whether there has been a substantial increase in the scope of tort liability and resulting "explosion" in litigation, as measured by the volume of tort litigation, looms large.

No one disputes that tort litigation first experienced explosive growth during the last quarter of the nineteenth century – at the time of our industrial revolution. The cause is a matter of debate, however, as is the role that contingency fees played. Judge Richard Posner, one of the founders of the law and economics movement,[7] notes that there was an 800 percent increase in negligence cases in the Gilded Age of 1857–1905, which he attributes to "greater economic activity, growing hostility to big business, the population movement to the west ... [and] the rising level of education, which may have made individuals more aware of their legal rights."[8]

Randolph E. Bergstrom, who teaches in the Department of History of the University of California at Santa Barbara, has done an extensive study on the subject. He also finds that there was a personal injury litigation explosion in the 1870–1910 period, but he disagrees with part of Judge Posner's explanation.[9] He attributes the litigation explosion to changes in the populace's expectation of care from fellow citizens. "That the exercise of care remained constant (or even improved) in these forty years, but the public's expectation for care rose ahead of that exercise, is consistent with the constant incidence of injury over time and accounts for the rise in injury suits amidst the steady number of injuries."[10] Most importantly, Bergstrom rejects any significant role for contingency fees in the 1870–1910 litigation explosion.[11] He notes that although "the contingency retainer was available to attorneys in 1870" (having been legitimated when New York enacted the Field Code in 1848),[12] it did not come into widespread use until 1890.[13] "Its availability did not incite the populace to inundate the Supreme Court with injury suits."[14]

Although Bergstrom's analysis sheds much light on the explosion in personal injury litigation in the period between 1870 and 1910, he considerably understates the role of contingency fees. It is likely that the volume of contingency fee agreements was a lagging – not a leading – indicator of expansion of tort liability during this time.[15] Lawyers in the 1870s would no doubt have been reluctant to enter into the heretofore largely untried contingency fee agreements until it became clear that they were financially rewarding. From that perspective, Bergstrom is right that contingency fee financing did not *initiate* the personal injury tort explosion. His conclusion, however, that they were not a major contributor does not follow from the evidence presented. First, according to a contemporary account, the contingency fee had become an "all but universal custom of the profession" by 1881.[16] Moreover, as John Fabian Witt observes: "What evidence exists makes it fairly clear that many suits were brought [in the late 1800s and early 1900s] that would not otherwise have been filed but for the encouragement of lawyers seeking contingent fees."[17] Witt notes that, in pursuit of profits, the plaintiffs' personal injury bar established "intricate networks of 'runners' including members of the police and railroad workforces" to report accident claims in return for a percentage of the lawyer's profit on the case[18] – a practice that became known as "ambulance chasing" (discussed in Chapter 7, Section E).

The influence of contingency fees on our tort system has greatly expanded beyond the level that Witt identifies in the nineteenth-century litigation explosion. As I set out in Chapter 2, beginning in about 1960, tort lawyers' effective hourly rates began to greatly increase, contributing to the large-scale expansion of tort liability that was underway. If the resulting volume of tort litigation has "exploded," it may justify efforts to enact tort reforms to restrain "excessive" litigation. Conversely, denying that there has been any explosion of litigation obviates the need for such tort reforms.

In his book, *The Litigation Explosion, What Happened When America Unleashed the Lawsuit*,[19] Walter Olson contends that there has indeed been a litigation explosion. Such leading scholars as George Priest, Judge Richard Posner, and W. Kip Viscusi concur.[20] This is a distinct minority view, however. The dominant view of scholars is to the contrary.[21] Such leading law professors as Arthur Miller of Harvard Law School, Marc Galanter of the University of Wisconsin Law School, Theodore Eisenberg of Cornell Law School and Michael Saks of the

Arizona State University College of Law, either deny altogether[22] or cast doubt on the presence of any litigation explosion.[23] Their arguments run the gamut from Miller's assertion that "the supposed litigation crisis is the product of assumption"[24] and his claim that "reliable empirical data [is] in short supply,"[25] to Galanter and Saks's outright denial that any explosion in tort lawsuits has taken place.[26] These litigation explosion deniers mostly rely on empirical data on the numbers of tort lawsuits filed, collected by the National Center for State Courts[27] or found in annual reports issued by the federal judiciary,[28] as well as studies by the RAND Institute of Civil Justice.[29]

A. The Ineffectiveness of Case Filings as Measures of Changes in the Scope of Tort Liability

There are multiple reasons why these scholars' reliance on the cited data is misplaced. To begin, the data on tort filings in state and federal courts is more ambiguous than these litigation explosion deniers acknowledge. Federal court tort filings, for example, have fluctuated widely throughout the last fifteen years, as the following chart indicates[30]:

Federal Court Tort Filings	
1990	44,041
1995	53,986
2000	36,586
2005	51,335[31]
2006	68,804[32]

Swings in product liability filings relating to asbestos, silicone breast implants, and various diet drugs largely account for the fluctuation in tort filings.[33]

Over the fifteen-year period beginning from 1975 through 1999, sixteen state courts reported that tort filings increased by 39 percent.[34] In the 1996–2005 period, however, thirty state courts reported that tort filings decreased by 21 percent – a decrease that has been attributed in some measure to tort reform efforts. In these states, during this time period, auto tort and medical malpractice filings decreased by 29 percent and 8 percent, respectively, but products liability filings increased by 26 percent.[35]

Based solely on this published data, there is no factual basis for a litigation explosion. The published data suffers from many infirmities, however. First, the system for counting the number of case filings is flawed. The Federal Bureau of Justice (BJS) compiles one set of data, consisting of case filings in courts of general jurisdiction in the seventy-five largest counties in the U.S. The BJS, however, only counts the number of civil cases that end in a trial and thus omits the vast majority of civil cases – *approximately 97 percent* – that end in settlement before trial.[36]

In addition, the National Center for State Courts, which compiles state litigation filings, relies on the states to supply accurate and uniform data. However, states do not follow a uniform procedure for counting cases filed.[37] For example, in 2001, of the fifty states, the District of Columbia, and Puerto Rico, thirty-five counted a case as one filing if the jury or first witness were sworn, whereas seventeen required a verdict or decision.[38] Moreover, some states do not have automated or uniform systems of case management, which raises additional questions concerning the reliability of their data.[39]

Another source of inaccuracy is the periodic increase in the dollar thresholds for bringing suit in state court. Consider the 45 percent decrease in tort filings that the state of Michigan reported during these years.[40] Rather than indicating a drastic decrease in the number of tort claims filed, the data reflect the results of an increase in the minimum damage amount required to file a case in a court of general record from $10,000 to $25,000. Cases based on lower amounts had to be filed in a court of more limited jurisdiction.[41] However, filings in these lower courts are not included in the count.

Furthermore, the tort filing statistics measure ignores increases in tort claim valuation and the total amounts of wealth transferred through the tort system and, as a result, does not a provide a meaningful account of what is occurring in the tort system. Consider, for example, the experience of New York City. While the number of tort claims filed against the city grew by 50 percent between 1984 and 1994, the dollar value of the settlements and judgments in the same time period increased by more than twice that amount, from an average of $14,386 per claim to $29,894, up 108 percent.[42] Even when the aggregate number of tort claims filed against the city dropped by 18.5 percent between 1995 and 2004, the dollar amount of settlements and judgments *increased* by 122 percent, from $241.5 million to $536.8 million.[43]

These inadequacies pale when compared to the most glaring defect, set forth below, in case filing statistics: the omission of millions of tort claims that have resulted in tens of billions of dollars in wealth transfers. Relying on case filings as a measure of what is going on to the tort system is like relying on U.S. census data, which omits California, New York, and Texas, to measure the nation's population growth.

B. "Cases," Consolidations, Class Actions, and Bankruptcy Trusts

There are somewhere between 15,000,000 and 20,000,000 civil cases filed annually in state courts, including divorce, property, contracts, torts, and landlord-tenant cases.[44] An estimated 1,000,000 to 1,500,000 of these civil suits are tort cases.[45] In addition, there are approximately 50,000 to 70,000 tort filings a year in federal courts.[46] However, the actual number of plaintiffs who become claimants in state and federal courts is actually far higher than these numbers suggest. Here is why: Each time a lawyer files a tort case, he pays a filing fee to the court. In mass tort litigations – such as asbestos – tort lawyers came up with a clever ruse, which both saved money and materially increased the pressure on defendants to settle large numbers of claims, irrespective of their merits. In states such as Texas, Mississippi, West Virginia, and Illinois, lawyers filed complaints against dozens, if not hundreds, of asbestos defendants on behalf of a single plaintiff, let's say John Smith. They then added ten to fifty additional plaintiffs to the case. However, the title of the case remained *John Smith v. [one hundred defendants listed by name]*, so the lawyer paid one filing fee. For purposes of counting the number of case filings, John Smith and fifty other plaintiffs versus one hundred defendants – which added up to more than 5,000 claims – counted as one filing! As many as 100,000 asbestos plaintiffs who filed suit against scores of defendants totaling millions of claims were thus omitted from case filing statistics.

A similar process occurred when asbestos and other mass tort cases were consolidated in state courts. Consolidations are a more formal way of joining multiple plaintiffs together in suing one or more defendants. Here too, lawyers saved money on filing fees by listing only a handful of plaintiffs in a consolidated case and paying their filing fees, even when there were actually thousands of plaintiffs.

Another source of vastly undercounting civil case filings is the virtual omission of class actions and the substantial omission of bankruptcy trust claims filings. These constitute an enormous and growing number of claims, generating billions of dollars in wealth transferred through the tort system and hundreds of millions of dollars in contingency fees for lawyers. As set out in Chapter 19, shareholder class actions seek reimbursement of stock losses because of failure to disclose material information. These are tort actions created by courts to aid in the enforcement of securities laws. Leaving out five mega settlements of shareholder class actions in 2006 (each in excess of $1 billion), the average settlement in 2006 was $45 million. Multiplying this figure by the approximately 200 shareholder class actions that are filed annually and omitting mega settlements, these suits generate approximately $9 billion in wealth transfers.[47] Nonetheless, the thousands of shareholders in each of the several hundred shareholder class action suits brought each year in federal courts are virtually entirely omitted from case filings data.

This vast undercounting is not limited to securities class actions and mass tort joinders and consolidations. The number of other class actions alleging personal or financial injuries has increased dramatically over the past three decades.[48] A substantial number of these actions were disproportionately filed in a small number of state courts, where judges were predisposed to approving lawyers' requests to certify the class.[49]

Since the passage of the Class Action Fairness Act in 2005, however, the number of class actions being tried in state courts has decreased.[50]

A single class action can have a class size in the hundreds of thousands and even millions,[51] yet these millions of class action claimants who become eligible for billions of dollars of compensation annually are invisible when it comes to counting tort case filings. When a case is filed seeking a court's approval to certify the action as a class action, the lawyer will typically list the action as being brought by a few plaintiffs whom the lawyer claims are representative of the putative class. These lawyers will then pay filing fees only for each of these lead plaintiffs. Because the number of civil cases filed is determined on the basis of the number of filing fees paid, the putative class action counts for statistical purposes as one or perhaps two or three civil actions. This accounting is unchanged by the fact of certification of a class. In addition, some states do not count a civil action as filed until a jury or first witness is sworn at the commencement of a trial – events that rarely occur in class actions.

Mass tort class action filings have a double-barreled effect on the accuracy of tort filing data. Untold thousands of mass tort claimants who would have filed claims in courts do not add to the filing count when they become part of a class action. Whereas some class action settlements incorporate thousands of individual claims filed in courts, other class action settlements include claims that are filed after a settlement has been reached and a trust or other mechanism has been created for payment of the settlement funds. For example, when the silicone breast implant litigation settlement was reached, approximately 440,000 women filed claims to be paid out of the settlement.[52] The vast majority of these claimants were recruited by lawyers *after* the settlement was reached and had not previously filed suit in a court. Accordingly, these hundreds of thousands of claims were not counted in case filing compilations.[53]

Another area of large-scale undercounting involves trusts or similar mechanisms for the payment of claims, which are created in the course of certain bankruptcy proceedings. Assets are transferred from the debtor in bankruptcy to the trust for the payment of current and, in the case of latent injuries, future tort claimants. Though many of those filing claims with the trust have previously filed tort actions in federal or state court, filing a tort action in a court is typically not a prerequisite for filing a claim with the trust. As many as hundreds of thousands of asbestos claimants, mostly generated by litigation screenings, who presented claims to the trusts and received and continue to receive, in the aggregate, billions of dollars of compensation, may never have brought suit in a court and are, therefore, not counted in tort claim filing data.[54]

If joined cases, consolidated cases, class action, mass tort settlements, and bankruptcy trust filings were included in tort claims filing data – as they properly should be – then there has indeed been a second litigation explosion. Setting aside the issue of whether counting case filings is a valid measure of tort system activity, the conclusion that there has been a litigation explosion does not lead to the conclusion that there is an excess of litigation that imposes social costs without offsetting benefits. To consider this issue, we need to further explore the effects of financing tort litigation with contingency fees on our civil justice system.

NOTES

1. *See* STEVEN SHAVELL, FOUNDATIONS OF ECONOMIC ANALYSIS OF LAW 391–93 (2004); Steven Shavell, *"The Level of Litigation: Private versus Social Optimality of Suit and of Settlement,"* 19 INT'L REV. L. & ECON. 99 (1999).
2. *See* Chapter 8, note 4.
3. *See* Chapter 15, § B(2).
4. *See* Chapter 13, § C.
5. *See* Brickman, *Litigation Screenings, supra* Chapter 7, note 61.
6. *See Contingent Fee Abuses: Hearing Before the S. Judiciary Comm.*, 104th Cong. 39 (1997) (statement of Herbert M. Kritzer).
7. *See* WILLIAM M. LANDES & RICHARD A. POSNER, THE ECONOMIC STRUCTURE OF TORT LAW (1987).
8. Richard A. Posner, *A Theory of Negligence*, 1 J. LEGAL STUD. 29 (1972).
9. *See* RANDOLPH E. BERGSTROM, COURTING DANGER: INJURY AND LAW IN NEW YORK CITY, 1870–1910 (1992). Bergstrom considers and rejects all of the following explanations for the explosion: rapid industrialization in that period, *id*. at 25–29; increased danger and resultant changes in accidental death rates,

id. at 41, as accident rates were not rising, *id.* at 55; increased population, *id.* at 31–34; easier access to courts and changes in laws, *id.* at 58–86; increases in the number of lawyers, *id.* at 88–94; changes in the advocacy or practices of lawyers, *id.* at 114; and changes in the need for compensation of the populace and the likelihood of gaining it, *id.* at 145–66.

10. *Id.* at 185.

11. *Id.* at 88–94.

12. *See* Chapter I.

13. Bergstrom, Courting Danger, at 89–91.

14. *Id.* at 91.

15. *Id.* at 91, 94.

16. *See Current Topics*, 13 Cent. L. J. 381 (1891); *supra* notes 9–13.

17. Witt, *History of American Accident Law, supra* Introduction, note 13, at 765.

18. *See* Witt, *History of American Accident Law, supra* Introduction, note 13, at 764–65; *see also In re O'Neil*, 171 N.Y.S. 514 (App. Div. 1918) (concerning allegations that a plaintiffs' personal injury attorney hired people to generate claims that would otherwise not be brought); *In re Newell*, 174 A.D. 94 (N.Y. App. Div. 1916) (per curiam) (disbarring a personal injury attorney for paying a railroad worker to report accidents to him).

19. *See* Walter K. Olson, The Litigation Explosion, What Happened When America Unleashed the Lawsuit (1991).

20. *See, e.g.,* George L. Priest, *The Culture of Modern Tort Law*, 34 Val. U. L. Rev. 573 (2000); W. Kip Viscusi & Patricia Born, *The National Implications of Liability Reforms for General Liability and Medical Malpractice Insurance*, 24 Seton Hall L. Rev. 1743 (1994); W. Kip Viscusi, *The Dimensions of the Product Liability Crisis*, 20 J. Legal Stud. 147 (1991); George L. Priest, *The Invention of Enterprise Liability: A Critical History of the Intellectual Foundations of Modern Tort Law*, 14 J. Legal Stud. 461 (1985); Richard A. Posner, The Federal Courts: Crisis and Reform 76–93 (1985); *see also* Kenneth S. Abraham, *What is a Tort Claim? An Interpretation of Contemporary Tort Reform*, 51 Md. L. Rev. 172, 203 (1992); Gary T. Schwartz, *The Beginning and the Possible End of the Rise of Modern American Tort Law*, 26 Ga. L. Rev. 601 (1992); Charles R. Tremper, *Compensation for Harm from Charitable Activity*, 76 Cornell L. Rev. 401, 422 (1991); Robert G. Berger, *The Impact of Tort Law on Insurance: The Availability/Avoidability Crisis and its Potential Solutions*, 37 Am. U. L. Rev. 285, 312 (1988); Jerry J. Phillips, *Comments on the Report of the Governor's Commission on Tort and Liability Insurance Reform*, 53 Tenn. L. Rev. 679, 699 (1986).

21. *See, e.g.,* Deborah Rhode, *Frivolous Litigation and Civil Justice Reform: Miscasting the Problem, Recasting the Solution*, 54 Duke L.J. 455, 456 (2004); Herbert M. Kritzer, *Seven Dogged Myths Concerning Contingency Fees*, 80

WASH. U.L.Q. 739, 739 n.1(2002); Theodore Eisenberg, *Lessons in State Class Actions, Punitive Damages, and Jury Decision-Making Damage Awards in Perspective*, 36 WAKE FOREST L. REV. 1129 (2001); Deborah Jones Merrit and Kathryn Ann Barry, *Is the Tort System in Crisis? New Empirical Evidence*, 60 OHIO ST. L.J. 315 (1999); Michael J. Saks, *Do We Really Know Anything About the Behavior of the Tort Litigation System – And Why Not?*, 140 U. PA. L. REV. 1147, 1158 (1992); Randy M. Mastro, *The Myth of the Litigation Explosion*, 60 FORDHAM L. REV. 199 (1991) (reviewing WALTER K. OLSON, THE LITIGATION EXPLOSION: WHAT HAPPENED WHEN AMERICA UNLEASHED THE LAWSUIT); David M. Engel, *The Oven Bird's Song: Insiders, Outsiders, and Personal Injuries in an American Community*, 18 LAW & SOC'Y REV. 551 (1984); JETHRO K. LIEBERMAN, THE LITIGIOUS SOCIETY (1981).

22. *See, e.g.*, Marc Galanter, *The Day After the Litigation Explosion*, 46 MD. L. REV. 3, 7 (1986) [hereinafter Galanter, *The Day After*]. Galanter goes further in his article, however, and acknowledges that there may be a "general, uneven spread of higher expectations of justice and the growth of a sense of entitlement to recompense for many kinds of injury." *Id.* at 28; *see also* Marc Galanter, *An Oil Strike in Hell: Contemporary Legends About the Civil Justice System*, 40 ARIZ. L. REV. 717 (1998); Marc S. Galanter, *Reading the Landscape of Disputes: What We Know and Don't Know (and Think We Know) About Our Allegedly Contentious and Litigious Society*, 31 UCLA L. REV. 4 (1983).

23. Arthur Miller, *The Pretrial Rush to Judgment: Are the "Litigation Explosion" "Liability Crisis," and Efficiency Clichés Eroding Our Day in Court and Jury Trial Commitments?*, 78 N.Y.U. L. REV. 982, 996 (2003) [hereinafter Miller, *The Pretrial Rush*].

24. Miller, *The Pretrial Rush, id.*

25. *Id.*

26. Galanter, *The Day After, supra* note 22; Saks, *Do We Really Know Anything, supra* note 21, at 1196–1205. Thomas Geoghegan, in a book that garnered much attention when it was published, acknowledged that there has been a litigation explosion and that it has harmed America but blames it on right-wing policies, including deregulation, deunionization, and the right's putative dismantling of the legal system and Rule of Law. THOMAS GEOGHEGAN, SEE YOU IN COURT: HOW THE RIGHT MADE AMERICA A LAWSUIT NATION, (2007). Geoghegan's "facts" and arguments are meticulously dissected and discredited in a review by Ted Frank, then the director of the AEI Legal Center for the Public Interest. Ted Frank, *Did the Right Make America a Lawsuit Nation?*, 12 TEXAS REV. OF L. & POLITICS 477 (2008).

27. Galanter, *The Day After, supra* note 22, at 6–8; Miller, *The Pretrial Rush, supra* note 23, at 992–95.

28. Galanter, *id.* at 15–17.

29. Miller, *The Pretrial Rush*, *supra* note 23, at 995.

30. For annual compilations of federal litigation filings, see THE ADMINISTRATIVE OFFICE OF THE UNITED STATES COURTS, FEDERAL JUDICIAL CASELOAD STATISTICS (includes statistical compilation of tort actions commenced in U.S. District Courts). Although the data for 2007 has yet to be categorized, according to the nature of the suit, the Southern District of New York reported 6,500 personal injury suits filings that stem from the terrorist attacks of September 11, 2001. THE THIRD BRANCH (Newsletter of the Federal Courts), Vol. 39, No. 1., Jan. 1, 2008. The Middle District of Florida also saw 6,200 personal injury/product liability filings under a multidistrict litigation concerning allegations that Seroquel, an antipsychotic drug, caused injuries related to diabetes. *Id.*

31. U.S. DISTRICT COURTS CIVIL CASES FILED BY NATURE OF SUIT, *available at* http://www.uscourts.gov/judicialfactsfigures/Table404.pdf; *see also* Deborah R. Hensler, *Reading The Tort Litigation Tea Leaves: What's Going on in the Civil Liability System?*, 16 JUST. SYS. J. 139, 142 n.5 (1993) (federal case filings declined by as much as 20% between 1985 and 1990). Federal filings then increased by 18% in the 1991–1995 period and decreased by 3.7% between 1996 and 2000. JUDICIAL BUSINESS OF THE UNITED STATES COURTS, 1995 REPORT OF THE DIRECTOR, STATISTICS DIVISION ADMINISTRATIVE OFFICE OF THE UNITED STATES COURTS, 141 tbl.C-2A. *See* THE THIRD BRANCH (Newsletter of the Federal Courts), Mar. 2002, at 6, *available at* http://www.uscourts.gov/ttb/mar02ttb/mar02.html (discussing possible reasons for a slight decrease in federal personal injury filings in federal courts). JUDICIAL BUSINESS OF THE UNITED STATES COURTS, 2000 ANNUAL REPORT OF THE DIRECTOR, tbl.C-2A, *available* at www.uscourts.gov/judbus2000/contents.html. Between 1995 and 2005, there was a 5% total increase in the amount of civil cases filed in federal courts, with a 10% increase occurring between 2001 and 2005. JUDICIAL BUSINESS OF THE UNITED STATES COURTS, 2005 REPORT OF THE DIRECTOR, STATISTICS DIVISION ADMINISTRATIVE OFFICE OF THE UNITED STATES COURTS, p. 11, *available at* http://www.uscourts.gov/caseload2005/front/mar05JudBus.pdf.

32. U.S. DISTRICT COURTS, CIVIL CASES FILED BY NATURE OF SUIT, http://www.uscourts.gov/judicialfactsfigures/2006/Table404.pdf; *see also* THOMAS H. COHEN, FEDERAL TORT TRIALS AND VERDICTS, 2002–03 at 2, *available at* http://www.ojp.usdoj.gov/bjs/abstract//fttv03.htm.

33. *See supra* 2005 REPORT OF THE DIRECTOR, at 11.

34. For annual compilations of state litigation filings, see NATIONAL CENTER FOR STATE COURTS, STATE COURT CASELOAD STATISTICS, 2006, *available at* http://www.ncsconline.org/D_Research/csp/CSP_Main_Page.html (includes statistical compilations of tort filings in trial and appellate courts). For recent trends in tort case filings within thirty U.S. states, see NATIONAL CENTER FOR STATE COURTS, EXAMINING THE WORK OF STATE COURTS, 2006 (Robert C. La Fountain

et al. eds. 2007), *available at* http://www.ncsconline.org/D_Research/csp/CSP_Main_Page.html [hereinafter EXAMINING THE WORK OF STATE COURTS 2006]. *See* THE NATIONAL CENTER FOR STATE COURTS, EXAMINING THE WORK OF STATE COURTS, 1999–2000, at 25, *available at* http://www.ncsconline.org/D_Research/csp/1999–2000_Files/1999–2000_Civil_Section.pdf [hereinafter EXAMINING THE WORK OF STATE COURTS 1999–2000].

35. *See* EXAMINING THE WORK OF STATE COURTS, 2006, at 13.

36. BUREAU OF JUSTICE STATISTICS, CIVIL JUSTICE ROUNDTABLE DISCUSSION (Apr. 22, 2004), *available at* http://www.ojp.usdoj.gov/bjs/pub/ascii/cjrd.txt.

37. *See* CIVIL JUSTICE ROUNDTABLE DISCUSSION, at 3.

38. *See* NATIONAL CENTER FOR STATE COURTS, STATE COURT CASELOAD STATISTICS, 2001 at 204, *available at* http://www.ncsconline.org/D_Research/csp/CSP_Main_Page.html.

39. *See* CIVIL JUSTICE ROUNDTABLE, *supra*, at 3; *see also* NATIONAL CENTER FOR STATE COURTS, EXAMINING THE WORK OF STATE COURTS, 2004, at 74 (Richard Shauffler et al., eds. 2004) (discussing the methodology of the Court Statistics Project), *available at* http://www.ncsconline.org/D_Research/csp/2004_Files/EW2004_Main_Page.html.

40. EXAMINING THE WORK OF STATE COURTS 1999–2000, at 26.

41. *See id.*

42. *See* Richard Miniter, *Under Siege: New York's Liability Ordeal*, Civil Justice Memorandum, Manhattan Institute (Jan. 1996) (citing FY 1994 Report on Claims: "The Deep Pocket").

43. FY 2004 REPORT ON CLAIMS, *available at* http://www.comptroller.nyc.gov/bureaus/bla/pdf/2004_claims_ report.pdf. In 2008, the city paid out $513.7 million in settlements and judgments for personal injury claims – more than it spent on parks, transportation, homeless services, or the city university system. *See* John P. Avlon, *Sue City*, Forbes, July 14, 2009; FY 2008 REPORT ON CLAIMS, *available at* http://www.comptroller.nyc.gov/bureaus/bla/pdf/2008_Claims_Report.pdf; Press Release, Office of the New York City Comptroller, Thompson: City Paid More Than $560 million to Settle Claims in Fiscal Year 2008, Mar. 12, 2009, *available at* http://www.comptroller.nyc.gov/press/2009_releases/pr09–03–063.shtm.

44. EXAMINING THE WORK OF STATE COURTS, 2006, at 27 (estimating the 2005 number of civil case filings at 16.6 million).

45. *See* Ted Schneyer, *Legal-Process Constraints on the Regulation of Lawyers' Contingent Fee Contracts*, 47 DEPAUL L. REV. 371, 371 (1998). Another estimate puts the number of tort cases filed as approximately 10% of civil litigation suits filed. STEVEN K. SMITH ET AL., CIVIL JUSTICE SURVEY OF STATE COURTS, 1992: TORT CASES IN LARGE COUNTIES 2 (1995).

46. *See supra* note 30. An untold number of additional disputes occur but are resolved in some way prior to a formal filing in a court. *See* William L.F. Felstiner et al., *The Emergence and Transformation of Disputes: Naming, Blaming, and Claiming*, 15 LAW SOC'Y REV. 631 (1980–81); Marc Galanter & Mia Cahill, *"Most Cases Settle": Judicial Promotion and Regulation of Settlements*, 46 STAN. L. REV. (1994).

47. *See* INSURANCE INFORMATION INSTITUTE INSURANCE FACT BOOK, *Shareholder Lawsuits*, citing to Cornerstone Research (on file with the author); SECURITIES CLASS ACTION FILINGS – 2007: A YEAR IN REVIEW (Cornerstone Research 2007), *available at* http://securities.stanford.edu/clearinghouse_research.html; NERA, 2007 YEAR END UPDATE: RECENT TRENDS IN SHAREHOLDER CLASS ACTIONS 2 (2007). The average settlement has risen to $40.2 million, influenced by nine mega-settlements of more than $1 billion. *Id.* at 11. Certain pending settlements would raise the 2007 average to approximately $55 million. *Id.* The median settlement averaged $6.8 million in the 2002–2007 period but rose to an all-time high of $9.6 million in 2007. *Id.*

48. For a survey of class action filings, see generally CLASS ACTION REPORTER (Beard Group, Inc.), *available at* http://litigationdatadepot.com/ClassActionReporter. php. A survey done by the Federalist Society found that between 1988 and 1998, class action filings increased by 338% in federal courts, while the increase in state courts was more than 1,000%. *See Analysis: Class Action Litigation, a Federalist Society Survey, Part II*, CLASS ACTION WATCH (Federalist Society for Law & Public Policy Studies, Washington, D.C.) Vol. 1, no. 2 (1999), at 3. Beisner and Miller report that Palm Beach (Florida) and Jefferson County (Texas) have had a respective 34% and 82% increase in filings between 1998 and 2001, while Madison County (Ill.) has had an incredible 1,850% increase. John H Beisner & Jessica Davidson Miller, *They're Making a Federal Case Out of It … In State Court*, 25 HARV. J.L. & PUB. POL'Y 143, 161 (2001); *see also* Carlyn Kolker, *Madison County's Litigation Machine*, AM. LAW.: LITIG. 2004, Dec. 2004 (supp.) at 37 (recounting large awards for class actions in the plaintiff friendly jurisdiction of Madison County, Illinois).

49. These courts included some in large population centers, such as Los Angeles County (California), Cook County (Illinois), and Dade County (Florida). The real action, however, was in Madison County (Illinois), Jefferson County (Texas), and Palm Beach County (Florida). *See* John H. Beisner & Jessica D. Miller, *Class Action Magnet Courts: The Allure Intensifies, Civil Justice Report*, Center for Legal Policy at the Manhattan Institute (June 2002). Virtually every large American corporation has been sued in these courts and forced to pay a form of tribute to the class action lawyers to secure their release.

50. The Act is discussed in Chapter 18, § E.

51. *See* DEBORAH R. HENSLER, ET AL., CLASS ACTION DILEMMAS: PURSUING PUBLIC
GOALS FOR PRIVATE GAIN, RAND INSTITUTE (2000). For example, as many as 6
million homeowners were eligible to collect from a $950 million settlement of
a class action suit against the makers of allegedly defective plastic pipes used
in home plumbing systems. *See* Bill Rumbler, *Judge Gives Homeowners $950
Million For Bad Pipes*, CHICAGO SUN-TIMES, Nov. 10, 1995, at 28. About 4.2
million claimants were eligible to receive $408 million in discount coupons
from airline companies accused of price fixing. *See In re Domestic Air Trans.
Antitrust Litig.*, 148 F.R.D. 297 (N.D. Ga. 1993). And as many as 700,000 homeowners were eligible to participate in a $350 million settlement of class action
suits against a manufacturer of defective siding. *See* Bill Richards, *Louisiana-
Pacific Agrees to Settlement Of Class Action Suits Linked to Product*, WALL ST.
J., Oct. 18, 1995, at A8.

52. *See In re Dow Corning Corp.*, 86 F.3d 482, 486 n.2 (6th Cir. 1996).

53. Another example involves the fen-phen (diet drug) litigation. When the fen-
phen settlement was approved, tens of thousands of claims were pending in
state courts. *See Up to 90,000 Opt Out of AHP Settlement; 61,000 File Claims*,
6 MEALEY'S LITIGATION REPORT: FEN-PHEN/REDUX 8 (June 2003). After a
$3.75 billion settlement trust was established, lawyers conducted litigation
screenings and recruited tens of thousands of additional claimants. A substantial number of these claimants filed claims in state courts under an unusual
provision in the settlement that allowed them to opt out later in the process.
See Brown v. Am. Home Prods. (In re Diet Drugs Prods. Liab. Litig.), MDL
Docket No. 1203 Pretrial Order No. 1415, 2000 WL 1222042 (E.D. Pa., Aug.
28, 2000) at *21. However, thousands of claimants recruited through litigation
screenings did not exercise this later opt out right and only submitted claims
against the settlement trust. Accordingly, none of these claimants are counted
in the compilations of tort filings.

54. *See* Brickman, *Ethical Issues, supra* Chapter 7, note 69, at 862–70.

13 Measures of the Rate of Expansion of Tort Liability

I F THE OBJECTIVE OF COMPILING TORT FILING DATA IS TO measure tort system activity and changes in the scope of liability of the tort system, then even accurate filing data would be, at best, a highly imperfect measure.[1] What we would want to measure, instead, are the amounts defendants pay to insure against tort risk and the wealth transferred from defendants to plaintiffs (plus administrative and transactional costs). Counting tort filings provides little meaningful information as to what is going on in the tort system. Better to heed the advice that Deep Throat gave to Washington Post reporters Bob Woodward and Carl Bernstein in a dimly lit underground garage that enabled them to unravel the Watergate conspiracy: Follow the money trail.

True, plaintiffs entering the tort system often insist that "it's not about the money"; rather, they say that they sue because they seek an admission of fault, retribution for a defendant's conduct, or to prevent recurrences.[2] But it is about the money. Even if plaintiffs' assertions accurately reflect their motivations, it is the lawyer who decides whether to file a lawsuit. Lawyers only open the gate to the tort system for that minority of claims that will adequately reward them for venturing their time and money.

A. Tort System Costs

The tort system contributes to social welfare in many ways.[3] In addition to providing compensation to injured parties – albeit inefficiently – the tort system allows victims to gain vindication – a critical component of a just society.[4] We can all agree that the tort system should play a significant role in preventing unnecessary deaths and serious injuries. In addition, tort litigation can alert the public and regulatory agencies to the dangers of certain products and drive them off the market, as in the case of the Dalkon Shield. But the Ford Pinto, which was driven off the market by tort lawyers and the media campaign they launched, was the victim of misinformation and phony allegations. In fact, the Pinto had a better safety record than other compact cars at the time, including the Toyota Corolla, the Volkswagen Beatle, and the Datsun.[5] Nonetheless, the tort system produces some clear-cut benefits, including accelerating the development of safety improvements and technological advances in the automobile and chemical industries (among others[6]) and compelling the redesign of step ladders, farm machinery, lathes, and a variety of other products to reduce safety risks – albeit at costs that are far in excess of efficient levels.[7] Tort lawyers and many torts scholars contend, almost as a matter of faith, that the tort system is effective in deterring the sale of defective and dangerous products. As noted in Chapter 8, however, there is no convincing empirical support for this proposition, and several notable scholars believe this proposition is not just open to substantial doubt but is actually disproved by the available data.

As with all compensation systems, the tort system also imposes costs. Some of these costs are apparent, but many are underappreciated, and others simply go unnoticed.[8] These costs have burgeoned, especially when we include the direct and indirect costs that are not included in the available metrics. In determining whether the benefits provided justify the costs imposed, we need a clearer picture of the costs of the tort system and the rate of increase of those costs than is currently available. I mean to provide that enhanced view.

Although American consumers undoubtedly pay billions of dollars a year in higher costs for goods and services because of the tort system, we have no reliable measure of those costs. As an alternative, we can identify another comprehensive measure of the direct costs of the tort system, which is the level of premiums firms pay for liability insurance coverage – that is, the cost of insuring against risk. Unsurprisingly, expansions in the scope of tort liability have caused sharp increases in the cost of insuring against risk. In 1984, the total premiums paid for general liability and medical malpractice insurance amounted to $6.5 billion and $2.4 billion, respectively.[9] By 2002, the premium level for general liability insurance rose to $29.5 billion and $7.5 billion for medical malpractice. By 2004, the premium level of general liability insurance increased by 38 percent to $40.7 billion, and medical malpractice insurance premiums increased by 21 percent to $9.1 billion.[10] This amounts to more than a six-fold increase in general liability premiums and almost a four-fold increase in medical malpractice premiums – suggesting a drastic increase in tort system costs over the course of a decade.

Another measure of the costs of the tort system and changes in those costs over time takes into account the costs borne by defendants and their insurers. The Tillinghast practice of the Towers Perrin Company (Tillinghast), which provides consulting services to the insurance industry, compiles an annual measure of "tort system costs." These "costs" include the amounts that insurance companies and self-insured entities pay for liability claims (which are not a cost, from an economic perspective, but a wealth transfer to make accident victims whole) and insurance companies' administrative costs.[11] The majority of the costs Tillinghast identifies are for expenses to run the tort system rather than for compensation paid to tort claimants.[12] The Tillinghast data is subject to a number of infirmities, which lead to both the overstatement and understatement of tort system costs.[13] Caution is therefore required in using the data. Nonetheless, the data provides a useful measure of changes in tort system costs over time.

According to Tillinghast, tort system costs increased from $1,809,000,000 in 1950 (in 1950 dollars) to $247,009,000,000 in 2006.[14] On an inflation-adjusted per capita basis, tort costs, so defined, increased more than eight-fold in that period and, for much of that period, far exceeded GDP and population growth. Most of the growth took place in the 1951–1990 period and was especially pronounced during 1980–1990. Thereafter, the rate of growth mostly declined, and tort costs actually declined 5.5 percent in 2006.[15]

B. A Comparison of U.S. Tort Costs as a Percentage of GDP with Those of Other Industrialized Countries

While U.S. tort system costs – as defined by Tillinghast – were only 0.62 percent of GDP in 1950, they increased to 1.34 percent in 1970 and began to grow more rapidly in 1975.[16] In 1987, the percentage rose to a fifty-six-year high of 2.33 percent.[17] Tort costs as a percentage of GDP remained in the 2.23 percent range in 2003–2004, fell to 2.10 percent in 2005, and then decreased to 1.87 percent of GDP in 2006, as tort costs actually declined.[18]

The magnitude of the growth of tort system costs can be seen by comparing tort costs in the United States, as a percentage of GDP, with those of other industrialized countries. First, it is important to note that most industrialized countries have agency-run compensation structures for accident victims and provide some form of national health insurance as well as no-fault wage replacement systems. Thus, the same injury that may generate tort system costs in the United States would show up as a social welfare system cost in another country. Another factor affecting the comparison is that medical care costs in the United States – which drive tort system costs – are considerably higher than in other counties.[19] Even so, the data presents a compelling case that tort costs in the United States are considerably larger as a percentage of GDP than in other industrialized countries. This does not exclude the possibility, however, that some of these higher costs generate greater benefits.[20]

In a study done in the early 1980s, Professor P.S. Atiyah of Oxford University concluded that "American tort costs are at least *ten* times higher per capita than those of the United Kingdom."[21] Furthermore, on a population adjusted basis, U.S. medical malpractice costs were roughly thirty to forty times greater than in the United Kingdom.[22]

A more recent twelve-country comparative study[23] of tort costs, measured as a percentage of GDP, indicates that while U.S. tort costs were 2.2 percent of GDP in 1994,[24] the average 1994 tort costs of the other countries was 0.9 percent of GDP – nearly two and half times less than U.S. tort costs.[25] The study also reported that, at 76 percent, the relative growth of U.S. tort costs as a percentage of GDP for the period 1973–1993 was far greater than most of the other countries studied.[26] The study concluded that the U.S. tort system is "by far the most expensive in the industrialized world."[27] These findings were confirmed by a 1998 study and a study of 2003 data.[28]

Robert Kagan argues that the reasons for the discrepancies between the United States and Western European democracies in tort system costs include the unwillingness of Western European democracies to adopt key structures of American-style adversarial legalism, such as

> an overtly politically appointed judiciary; a mode of legal education and practice that, rather than mostly emphasizing black letter law, strongly endorses adversarial lawyering and lawyerly and judicial creativity; wide-ranging judicial powers to mandate and monitor institutional reforms; trial by jury and open-ended rules for calculating damages in tort cases; judge-made constitutional rules and intensive use of the exclusionary rule as principal modes of regulating police behavior.[29]

Furthermore, Kagan asserts that the political structure in the United States encourages more adversarial legalism as compared to the political structures in Western Europe.[30]

C. Indirect Costs of the Tort System

All tort system costs metrics, including Tillinghast's, fail to include billions of dollars of indirect costs, though functionally they are tort system costs. Disability costs are one example. For a brief period at the beginning of the 1990s, carpel tunnel syndrome claims grew exponentially and promised a big payday for tort lawyers. By the beginning of the new millennium, however, the number of new claims had declined.[31] Persons claiming a repetitive stress injury and seeking compensation through the tort system impose costs that are reflected in tort system cost data. However, if instead of, or in addition to, a tort claim, they present disability claims, as is often the case, the latter payments will not be reflected in tort system costs.

Another disability-type cost that is not included in tort system costs is the cost of providing alternative employment opportunities to employees who claim they cannot continue performing their current jobs due to a disability. For example, an affliction known as Multiple Chemical Sensitivity Syndrome (MCSS) has recently emerged.[32] Claimants allege that exposure to various chemicals in the workplace causes them to experience adverse, often debilitating, acute and chronic health effects.[33] Symptoms commonly begin following a single substantial exposure to a substance, with recurrences triggered by lower levels of the same substance or seemingly innocent or related substances, such as odors or fragrances; but there is no standard test to explain what triggers the symptoms of MCSS.[34] Many courts have granted motions to exclude evidence regarding the syndrome because scientists and doctors dispute its existence,[35] but a number of courts have become receptive to MCSS.[36] Following a 1991 declaration by the Equal Employment Opportunity Commission, MCSS can qualify as a disability under the Americans with Disabilities Act (ADA).[37] As a consequence, a growing number of MCSS claimants have succeeded in requiring their employers to provide alternative employment opportunities. No estimate exists of the cost of doing so, but it may be substantial.

A similar circumstance is posed by claims of allergic reactions to workplace paraphernalia. For example, health care workers may allege allergic reactions to rubber latex, a substance found in 40,000 products, including gloves and pencils. Symptoms of latex allergic reactions range from "simple rashes, itchy skin and hives to asthma to severe anaphylactic shock, which can cause ... death if not treated immediately."[38] Lawyers expected a big payday from latex allergy litigation.[39] In 1997, more than 400 federal court cases were consolidated into a federal multidistrict litigation for pretrial proceedings.[40] In the first latex glove allergy case to be tried in federal court, a Minnesota jury absolved Baxter Healthcare Corporation of any liability for the plaintiff's allergy – an outcome that appears to have taken the wind out of the sails of this litigation.[41] Nonetheless, there are substantial additional costs imposed by claims of latex allergies,[42] which are not included in tort system costs. This is especially the case in the medical profession, where the prevalence of latex allergies is much higher than in the general population.[43]

In addition to disability claims, another expense that is not captured in the measures of the cost of the tort system is the practice of defensive medicine in order to avoid medical malpractice claims. (Medical malpractice litigation is discussed in Chapter 8, Section C). Defensive medicine involves both assurance and avoidance behaviors (also known as positive and negative defensive medicine). Assurance behaviors seek to generate evidence that will defeat future malpractice actions, such as prescribing unnecessary medications and ordering unnecessary tests, diagnostic procedures, and referrals to specialty doctors. Avoidance behaviors may involve not caring for high-risk patients or performing high-risk procedures.[44] The existence of assurance behaviors is documented by Daniel Kessler and Mark McClellan in a study of elderly Medicare patients hospitalized for serious heart disease in 1984, 1987, and 1990. Kessler and McClellan found that the intensity of hospital treatment correlated with state tort laws.[45] The less tort reform that had been enacted, the greater the cost of hospital treatment;[46] conversely, the more tort reform that had been enacted (thereby lowering a physician's potential liability), the lower the cost of the hospital treatment.[47] Patients receiving the additional services at higher cost did not experience "any consequential effects on mortality or the rates of significant cardiac complications."[48]

Although the existence of defensive medicine practices and their role in substantial regional variations in the utilization of specific medical services is widely reported,[49] supporters of medical malpractice utilization, such as Tom Baker, conclude that "the overall impact ... on health care costs is not large" and that extrapolations from individual studies are "speculative."[50] The empirical evidence, however, including several recent studies, supports the conclusion that defensive medical costs are substantial and are estimated to run between $100 billion and $124 billion annually.[51] These health care costs translate into higher insurance premiums and result in fewer Americans being able to afford insurance. In 2002, The U.S. Department of Health and Human Services estimated that between 2.4 million and 4.3 million more Americans could afford health insurance if limitations were placed on noneconomic damages awards, which are one of the major motivators of defensive medicine.[52]

In addition to the increased costs of defensive medicine, the fear of litigation impedes health care providers' collaborative efforts to improve the quality of health care and reduce the number of medical errors. As explained in Chapter 8, under the current medical malpractice system, the fear of lawsuits deters doctors from acknowledging errors. This inhibits data collection, which is necessary for devising protocols and other systemic procedures for reducing the frequency of medical error. This cost also does not appear in any of the available metrics.

Another uncaptured cost imposed by the enlargement of the scope of tort liability is a decrease in worker productivity. An empirical study of CEOs concludes that in a broad range of industries, enactment of laws that decreased the scope of tort liability is associated with increases in worker productivity and employment; whereas the enactment of laws that increased tort liability is associated with decreases in worker productivity and employment.[53] For example, in the construction industry, the enactment of liability-increasing laws corresponded with a 21 percent reduction in productivity and a 22 percent reduction in employment; whereas the enactment of liability-decreasing reforms corresponded with a 3 percent increase in productivity and a 17 percent increase in employment.[54] Similar correlations occurred in the majority of the industries studied,[55] suggesting a significant link between tort reform and the economy.[56]

Finally, other indirect costs include the benefits foregone because the tort system has driven useful products from the marketplace or thwarted products from being introduced because of actual or potential liability costs.[57]

Thus, an enhanced view of tort system costs and their increases over time, which takes indirect costs into account, reveals the true magnitude of tort system costs. I now turn to potential explanations for these increasing costs.

NOTES

1. *See generally* MARK PETERSON & MOLLY SELVIN, RESOLUTION OF MASS TORTS: TOWARD A FRAMEWORK FOR EVALUATION OF AGGREGATE PROCEDURES (1988); DEBORAH N. HENSLER ET AL., TRENDS IN TORT LITIGATION: THE STORY BEHIND THE STATISTICS (1987); JAMES S. KAKALIK & NICHOLAS M. PACE, COST AND COMPENSATION PAID IN TORT LITIGATION (1986).

2. *See* Tamara Relis, *It's Not About the Money!: A Theory on Misconceptions of Plaintiffs' Litigation Aims*, 68 U. PITT. L. REV. 341 (2007).

3. *See* Gary T. Schwartz, *Mixed Theories of Tort Law: Affirming Both Deterrence and Corrective Justice*, 75 TEX. L. REV. 1801 (1997).

4. *See, e.g.*, Marc Galanter, *News from Nowhere: The Debased Debate on Civil Justice*, 71 DENV. U. L. REV. 77, 89 (1993).

5. Gary T. Schwartz, *The Myth of the Ford Pinto*, 43 RUTGERS L. REV. 1013 (1991). A Pulitzer Prize winning article titled, "Pinto Madness," published in *MotherJones*, labeled the car as a "death trap." Mark Dowie, *Pinto Madness*, MOTHER JONES 18 (Sept./Oct.1977), *available at* http://www.motherjones.com/politics/1977/09/pinto-madness. But as Ted Frank, a Fellow at the American Enterprise Institute for Public Policy Research, has pointed out, despite the car's reputation, the riskiness of the Ford Pinto is almost entirely an urban legend. *See* Ted Frank, *Rollover Economics: Arbitrary and Capricious Product Liability Regimes*, AEI Liability Outlook, Jan. 2007, *available at* http://www.aei.org/

publication25395. In fact, the Pinto was safer than other subcompact cars. In 1975–1976, the Pinto averaged 310 fatalities per year per million cars in operation while the Toyota Corolla averaged 313, the Volkswagen Beatle, 374, and the Datsun 1200/210 averaged 405. Schwartz, *The Myth of the Fort Pinto, supra*, at 1028 n.62. Because of the location of its gas tank behind the rear axle of the car, the tank was more vulnerable to rear-end impacts, which could cause explosion of the tank, igniting car fires. *Id*. at 1015. Whereas the Pinto performed poorly in rear-end collisions, fires in such collisions comprised only 0.6 percent of all automobile fatalities. Moreover, the Pinto had a lower fuel-fed fire fatality rate than the average compact or subcompact car of the time. Schwartz, *The Myth of the Ford Pinto, supra*, at 1028–32.

6. PETER W. HUBER AND ROBERT E. LITAN, THE LIABILITY MAZE: THE IMPACT OF LIABILITY LAW ON SAFETY AND INNOVATION 120, 180, 367 (1991).

7. *See* Michael Rustad, *In Defense of Punitive Damages in Products Liability: Testing Tort Anecdotes with Empirical Data*, 78 IOWA L. REV. 1, 80 (1992).

8. WILLIAM M. LANDES & RICHARD A. POSNER, THE ECONOMIC STRUCTURE OF TORT LAW 10 (May 20, 1987).

9. *See* W. Kip Viscusi & Patricia Born, *The National Implications of Liability Reforms for General Liability and Medical Malpractice Insurance*, 24 SETON HALL L. REV. 1743, 1744 (1994).

10. INSURANCE INFORMATION INSTITUTE, THE INSURANCE FACT BOOK 2006, 34–35.

11. Tort system costs as calculated by Tillinghast include: (1) insured costs; (2) medical malpractice costs; and (3) self-insured costs. Insured costs include: (1) first-party benefits, including the cost of legal defense and claims handling; (2) benefits paid to third parties, both claimants and plaintiffs; and (3) insurance company administrative costs. The Tillinghast figures are for all claims and are not restricted to those in which an action was filed. Also excluded from its compilation of tort system costs are the costs incurred by federal and state court systems in administering actual suits, as well as other indirect economic costs such as those associated with litigation avoidance measures. TILLINGHAST, TOWERS PERRIN, U.S. TORT COSTS: 2000, UPDATE, TRENDS AND FINDINGS OF THE COSTS OF THE U.S. TORT SYSTEM 18, at 12–14. (2000) [hereinafter TILLINGHAST, 2000].

12. *See* TILLINGHAST, 2003 UPDATE, Chapter 8, at note 1. Tillinghast estimates that 54% of total tort costs are expenses rather than payments to injured persons: 16% goes to claimants' attorney as fees, 14% for defense costs, and 24% to defense administrative costs; of the 46% that goes to injured persons, 24% is for economic losses – most notably, medical expenses and lost wages – and 22% is for pain and suffering.

13. Tillinghast's estimates are overstated because they are based, in part, on insurance companies' financial reports to state regulatory commissions, which are used to assess insurance company solvency. To be on the safe side, regulators insist on high-end estimates. In addition to this public data, Tillinghast uses proprietary methods and data for its estimates of medical malpractice and self-insured costs, making it impossible to gauge the accuracy of this data. For these and other reasons, Judge Richard Posner concludes that the Tillinghast estimates are "almost certainly exaggerated, given the financial connection between the firm and the insurance industry." *See* Richard Posner, "Is the Tort System Costing the United States $865 Billion a Year?", *available at* http://www.becker-posner-blog.com/archives/2007/04 is the tort sys.html (last visited Aug. 12, 2008). The Tillinghast data also significantly undercounts wealth transferred because it omits several substantial parcels of tort system transfers: uninsured punitive damages; aviation accident litigation; shareholder litigation, which amounts to more than $9 billion annually; and the $246 billion settlement in the state tobacco litigations (described in detail in Chapter 22, § A.).

14. *See* TILLINGHAST, TOWERS PERRIN, 2007 UPDATE ON U.S. TORT COSTS TRENDS 15 (2007) [hereinafter TILLINGHAST 2007].

15. *See* TILLINGHAST 2007, *id.* at 5. Average growth in the 1950–2006 period was 9.2%, which far exceeded annual population growth (1.2%), Consumer Price Index (CPI) growth (3.9%), the medical care component of the CPI (5.7%), and average annual Gross Domestic Product growth (7.0%). *See* TILLINGHAST 2007, *supra.* Much of that occurred in the 1951–1990 period, when tort system costs growth averaged 11% annually – far in excess of annual increases in GDP in most of those years. TILLINGHAST, 2006 UPDATE ON U.S. TORT COSTS 3, TABLE 1 (2006) [hereinafter TILLINGHAST 2006]. In that period, the annual increase in tort system costs exceeded the growth in GDP by 2.8%–5.6% except for the 1971–1980 period when the average annual increase in tort costs was only slightly greater than GDP growth. *Id.* The most rapid period of growth came in the 1950–1985 period. TILLINGHAST, U.S. TORT COSTS: 1995 UPDATE, TRENDS AND FINDINGS ON THE COSTS OF THE U.S. TORT SYSTEM 3 (1995) [hereinafter TILLINGHAST 1995]. From 1980 to 1990, tort system costs increased by approximately 95% and exceeded total inflation for that period by almost 47%. *See* TILLINGHAST, TORT COSTS TRENDS: AN INTERNATIONAL PERSPECTIVE A2-A3 (1992). Tort costs during this period also increased in excess of the costs of three major social welfare systems that also included wealth transfers: workers' compensation, public welfare, and social security. *Id.* at 13. The rate of growth declined in the 1990–2000 period to below GDP growth, see TILLINGHAST, U.S. TORT COSTS: 2003 UPDATE, TRENDS AND FINDINGS ON THE COSTS OF THE U.S. TORT SYSTEM 13 (2003), accelerated again in 2001–2002 (when tort costs

exceeded GDP growth by 10%), and then slowed in 2003–2006. TILLINGHAST 2007, *supra*, at tbl.1, 13. Changes in asbestos litigation partly accounts for the decline in tort costs in 2006. While insured asbestos losses increased approximately $1.9 billion in 2006, this was lower than the comparable increases in 2003, 2004, and 2005 ($10.2 billion, $7.3 billion, and $7.0 billion, respectively). *Id*. at 6. In 2006, tort costs decreased 5.5% from $261 billion in 2005 to $247 billion; this was the first decrease in tort costs since 1997 and was the largest percentage decrease in the fifty-six-year period covered by Tillinghast. *Id*. at 3.

16. TILLINGHAST 2007, *id*. at 13.

17. *Id*.

18. TILLINGHAST 2006, *supra* note 15, at 11; TILLINGHAST 2007, *id*. at 11. Tillinghast estimates that the percentage of GDP will be approximately 1.83% in the years 2007–2009. TILLINGHAST 2007, *id*.

19. *See* Tom Baker, Herbert Kritzer and Neil Vidmar, *Jackpot Justice and the American Tort System: Thinking Beyond Junk Science*, at 8, *available at* http://www.ssrn.com/abstract=1152306.

20. *See* Posner, *Tort System*, *supra* note 13.

21. P.S. Atiyah, *Tort Law and the Alternatives: Some Anglo-American Comparisons*, 1987 DUKE L.J. 1002, 1012.

22. The differences between the U.S. and the U.K. are especially telling in two areas of tort practice: medical malpractice and products liability. In 1983, there were 2,000 claims for medical malpractice in England versus 40,000 in the United States (which had five times the population of England). *Id*. at 1014. The total amount paid out for malpractice claims in the United Kingdom was $26.5 million per annum, versus $2 billion to $4 billion in the United States; adjusting for population, the total costs in the United States were roughly thirty to forty times greater than in the United Kingdom. *See id*. at 1014–15. Finally, while there were approximately 200 products liability suits brought annually in the United Kingdom, the comparable number in the United States was 70,000. *See id*. at 1013.

23. TILLINGHAST 1995, *supra* note 15, at 14. The twelve countries studied were Australia, Belgium, Canada, Denmark, France, Germany, Italy, Japan, Spain, Switzerland, United Kingdom, and United States.

24. Tillinghast 1995, *id*. App. 1.

25. This figure was calculated using the following tort costs data, as measured as a percentage of GDP, provided by Tillinghast: Australia (0.7%); Belgium (1.4%) Canada (0.8%); Denmark (0.4%); France (0.8%); Germany (0.8%); Italy (1.3%); Japan (0.5%); Spain (1.2%); Switzerland (0.9%); and United Kingdom (0.8%). *Id*. at 15 and App. 9. Had U.S. tort costs approximated the average tort costs of the other countries studied in 1994, the average real income of each

U.S. household would have risen about $900. *See* Paul H. Rubin, *The High Cost of Lawsuits*, Investor's Business Daily, Mar. 4, 1996 at A2.

26. Tillinghast 1995, *id*. at 15. Only Spain and the United Kingdom experienced greater growth in tort costs as a percentage of GDP than the United States, at 200% and 100% respectively. The relative growth of tort costs of the other nine countries studied averaged 12% in the same period.

27. Tillinghast 1995, *id*. at 3. This is illustrated by the experience of the Dow Chemical Corporation. In 1996, the company spent one dollar on litigation expenses in U.S. courts for every $160 of U.S. sales, whereas in Europe, Dow spent one dollar on litigation expenses for every $40,000 in sales. As a percentage of sales, Dow was spending 250 times as much on litigation expenses in the United States, despite the absence of any difference in the types of products sold in the United States and Europe. *See* Stephen B. Presser, *How Should the Law of Products Liability be Harmonized? What Americans Can Learn from Europeans*, 2 Global Liab. Issues 1, 12 n.8 (2002).

28. A 1998 twelve-country comparative study of tort costs, measured as a percentage of GDP, indicated that the U.S. tort system was still "the most expensive in the industrialized world." Tillinghast 2000, *supra* note 11, at 3. The twelve countries studied were Australia, Belgium, Canada, Denmark, France, Germany, Italy, Japan, Spain, Switzerland, United Kingdom, and the United States. Italy moved up in rank to be a close second to the United States. *Id*. at 19. Though tort system costs had fallen to 1.8% of GDP in 1998, Tillinghast 2000, *supra* note 11, at 19, the average 1998 tort costs of the other countries studied remained at 0.9% of GDP. This figure was calculated using the following tort cost data, as measured as a percentage of GDP, provided by Tillinghast: Australia (1.1%); Belgium (1.1%); Canada (0.8%); Denmark (0.4%); France (0.8%); Germany (1.3%); Italy (1.7%); Japan (0.8%); Spain (1.0%); Switzerland (0.9%); and United Kingdom (0.6%). Tillinghast 2000, *id*. at 19 App. 6. The study also reported that the relative growth of U.S. tort costs as a percentage of GDP for the period 1973–1993 was far greater at 32% than most of the other countries studied. *Id*. at 19. Spain, Australia, Italy, and the United Kingdom all experienced greater growth in tort costs as a percentage of GDP than did the United States, at 132%, 97%, 55%, and 49%, respectively. The relative growth of tort costs of the other nine countries studied averaged 3% in the same period. From 1994 to 1998, the percent GDP for U.S. tort costs decreased 5%, while it increased for most other countries, with Australia having the greatest increase at 41%. Spain had the greatest decrease from 1994 to 1998 of tort costs as a percentage of GDP at 22%. A study of 2003 data similarly calculated tort costs as a percentage of GDP for ten countries besides the United States. Tillinghast, U.S. Tort Costs and Cross-Border Perspectives: 2005 Update 12 (2005). The countries

studied were Belgium, Denmark, France, Germany, Italy, Japan, Poland, Spain, Switzerland, and the United Kingdom, and found that, while U.S. tort system costs increased to 2.23% of GDP in 2003, TILLINGHAST, U.S. TORT COSTS AND CROSS-BORDER PERSPECTIVES: 2005 UPDATE, *supra*, at 13, the average 2003 tort costs of the other countries remained at 0.899% of GDP. This figure was calculated using the following tort cost data, as measured as a percentage of GDP, provided by Tillinghast: Belgium (0.96%); Denmark (0.58%); France (0.74%); Germany (1.14%); Italy (1.70%); Japan (0.80%); Poland (0.59%); Spain (1.04%); Switzerland (0.75%); and United Kingdom (0.69%). *Id.* at 12.

29. Robert Kagan, *On Surveying the Whole Legal Forest*, LAW & SOC. INQUIRY 28 (3) 842–44 (2003).

30. *Id.* at 844.

31. From 1989 to 1994, carpel tunnel syndrome disability claims grew by 467%, far eclipsing the growth in all other disability claims. *See* Michael Quint, *Bane of Insurers: New Ailments*, N.Y. TIMES, Nov. 28, 1994, at D1. According to the U.S. Department of Labor Bureau of Labor Statistics, newly reported incidence of carpal tunnel was on the rise from 1992–1994. There were 332,100 new cases of occupational repetitive stress injuries filed in 1994. That turned out to be the pinnacle, however, as employers and computer manufacturers were able to beat back the push to establish a new mass tort. By 2001, the number of new cases fell to 216,400. U.S. DEPARTMENT OF LABOR, BUREAU OF LABOR STATISTICS, OCCUPATIONAL INJURIES AND ILLNESSES: INDUSTRY DATA (1989–2001), *available at* http://data.bls.gov/cgi-bin/surveymost.

32. Ruby Afram, Note, *New Diagnoses and the ADA: A Case Study of Fibromyalgia and Multiple Chemical Sensitivity*, 4 YALE J. HEALTH POL'Y L. & ETHICS 85, 91 (2004) [hereinafter Afram, *New Diagnoses and the ADA*].

33. *Salmon River Concerned Citizens v. Robertson*, 32 F.3d 1346, 1359 (9th Cir. 1994).

34. Afram, *New Diagnoses and the ADA, supra* note 32, at 99 (quotations omitted).

35. *See, e.g., Bradley v. Brown*, 42 F.3d 434 (7th Cir. 1994); *Gabbard v. Linn-Benton Hous. Auth.*, 219 F. Supp. 2d 1130 (D. Or. 2002); *Gits v. 3M*, No. 99–1925, 2001 U.S. Dist. LEXIS 20871, at *20 n.6; *Coffey v. County of Hennepin*, 23 F. Supp. 2d 1081 (D. Minn. 1998); *Sanderson v. Int'l Flavors & Fragrances*, 950 F. Supp. 981 (C.D. Ca. 1996); *Wroncy v. Oregon Dep't of Trans.*, No. 02–35809, 2004 U.S.App.LEXIS 6558 (9th Cir. April 2, 2004); *Summers v. Missouri Pac. R.R. Sys.*, 132 F.3d 599, 603 (10th Cir. 1997).

36. *See, e.g., Treadwell v. Dow-United Techs.*, 970 F. Supp. 962, 971 (M.D. Ala. 1997) (finding a triable issue as to whether MCSS is a disability and noting that although MCSS "is generally not recognized ... such an argument does not terminate the court's inquiry") (quotations omitted); *Theresa Canavan's Case*,

733 N.E.2d 1042 (Mass. 2000) (affirming the admission of expert testimony concluding that a nurse's exposure to chemicals caused MCSS).

37. *See* Dennis M. Blank, *What's in the Office Air? Workers Smell Trouble*, N.Y. TIMES, Feb. 22, 1998, at C11.

38. *See* Joe Manning, *The Latex Menace*, MILWAUKEE SENTINEL, Mar. 18, 1996, at 1.

39. By 1996, there were cases pending in various federal district courts listing many different causes of action, including strict product liability for defective design; failure to warn; negligence; intentional and negligent infliction of emotional distress; willful misrepresentation of material facts; negligent misrepresentation; and fraudulent concealment. *See* Lynn Cherne-Breckner, *The Latex Allergy Crisis: Proposing a Healthy Solution to the Dilemma Facing the Medical Community*, 18 J.L. & HEALTH 135, 147 (2004) [hereinafter Cherne-Breckner, *Latex Allergy Crisis*].

40. *See supra* Cherne-Breckner, *Latex Allergy Crisis*. Similarly, most of the companion state court cases are subject to state-wide coordination as ordered by the highest court of that state, and so most state latex cases are assigned to one state judge for overall case management.

41. *See* Allison Fashek, *Kennedy v. Baxter Healthcare*, AM. LAW., Aug. 2002, at 49; *see also Kennedy v. Baxter Healthcare Corp.*, 348 F.3d 1073 (8th Cir. 2003).

42. The aggregate costs imposed on employers would be even more substantial if latex allergies were to be sustained as a disability under the ADA, as was MCSS. 42 U.S.C. § 1201 (2006). However, the U.S. Supreme Court favors a case-by-case analysis for most impairments and appears unlikely to declare latex allergy a disability per se. *See, e.g., Albertson's, Inc. v. Kirkingburg*, 527 U.S. 555 (1999) (rejecting a lower court's conclusion that monocular vision was a disability per se, without regard to the extent of a particular individual's impairment). Generally, it is difficult for health care workers who develop latex allergies to meet the disability standards established by ADA guidelines and the courts. *See* Cherne-Breckner, *Latex Allergy Crisis*, *supra* note 39, at 163.

43. After the Centers for Disease Control issued universal precautions in the early 1980s to prevent the spread of HIV and other blood-borne pathogens, there was a dramatic increase in the use of powdered latex gloves – from 12 billion pairs in 1987 to more than 200 billion pairs a decade later. *See* Cherne-Breckner, *Latex Allergy Crisis*, *supra* note 39, at 138 (2004). This has resulted in a large increase in the number of those claiming allergic reactions. By some estimates, about 30% to 40% of these allergy sufferers have to be relocated into other areas of health care. *Id.* Hospitals are also attempting to find substitutes for latex medical products. *See* Lara Landro, *Hidden Hazard: Hospitals Target Working Latex*, WALL ST., J., Feb. 20, 2008, at D1.

44. *See* Troyen A. Brennan et al., *Liability, Patient Safety, and Defensive Medicine: What Does the Future Hold?* in WILLIAM M. SAGE & ROGAN KERSH, EDS., MEDICAL MALPRACTICE AND THE U.S. HEALTH CARE SYSTEM 102 (2006).

45. *See* Daniel Kessler & Mark McClellan, *Do Doctors Practice Defensive Medicine?*, 111 QUARTERLY J. ECON. 353 (1996) [hereinafter Kessler & McClellan, *Defensive Medicine*]; Daniel Kessler & Mark McClellan, *Malpractice Law and Health Care Reform: Optimal Liability Policy in an Era of Managed Care*, 84 J. PUBLIC ECON. 175 (2002) [hereinafter Kessler & McClellan, *Optimal Liability Policy*]; *see also* Katherine Baicker & Amitabh Chandra, *Defensive Medicine and Disappearing Doctors?*, REGULATION, Fall 2005, at 30 [hereinafter Baicker & Chandra, *Defensive Medicine*].

46. Kessler and McClellan, *Defensive Medicine, id.* at 377–78, tbls. III, IV, 380–81, tbls. V–VI. Hospital expenses were compared for states that placed no direct limits on rights to sue with states that had enacted such tort reforms as caps on either noneconomic damages (pain and suffering) or total damages, abolition of punitive damages in medical malpractice litigation or collateral service rule reform. *Id.* at 386. Hospital expenses were higher by a statistically significant amount in the nonreform states indicating that physicians were providing patients in such states with additional and unneeded services not provided in states where potential legal liability was lower. States that had restricted physician tort liability by enacting reforms in the period 1985–1987 had a 16.6% increase for the average heart attack patient in inflation-adjusted dollars for the period 1984–1990, whereas in states without those restrictions, expenditures increased 24%. *Id.* at 376 tbl. III. For ischemic heart disease (coronary artery disease), the results were even more dramatic. Over the same seven-year period, states that had restricted physician liability saw real costs increase 16.8% as compared with 28% for the states without such restrictions. *Id.*

A more recent study published in 2005 found that a 10% increase in malpractice cases increased total Medicare expenditures by 1.3%, specifically increasing imaging spending by 2.9%, due to the increased use of testing procedures such as CT scans and cardiac catheterization. Baicker & Chandra, *Defensive Medicine, supra* note 45, at 24, 30.

47. Kessler and McClellan, *Defensive Medicine, id.* Among the same group of elderly heart disease patients, it was found in another study that a tort reform proposal that would reduce the legal defense burden on physicians and hospitals by 25% could be expected to reduce medical treatment intensity by 6%, without any increase in adverse health outcomes. Daniel P. Kessler & Mark B. McClellan, *How Liability Law Affects Medical Productivity*, J. HEALTH ECON. (2002), at 21. The study also found that a policy that expedited claim resolution by six months could be expected to reduce hospital treatment costs by 2.8%, again without an increase in adverse outcomes. *Id.*

48. Kessler and McClellan, *Defensive Medicine, id.* at 383.
49. The fear of malpractice lawsuits is one of several factors accounting for substantial regional variations in the utilization of cardiac services in every step of cardiac care. Frances L. Lucas et al., *Variation in Cardiologists' Propensity to Test and Treat: Is it Associated with Regional Variation in Utilization?*, Circulation, Apr. 13, 2010, *available at* http://circoutcomes.ahajournals.org/cgi/content/abstract/CIRCOUTCOMES.108.840009. Between regions, rates of stress testing, cardiac catherization, and revascularization have been shown to differ from three- to eight-fold, depending on the procedure under examination. *Id.*

    A study survey of nearly 600 cardiologists found that those cardiologists who were more likely to recommend a cardiac catherization that was not clinically indicated were also more likely to indicate that fear of malpractice suits and what they thought their peers would do influenced their decisions. *Id.*
50. Tom Baker, The Medical Malpractice Myth 134, 128 (2005).
51. *See* Massachusetts Medical Society, Investigation of Defensive Medicine in Massachusetts (2008), *available at* http://www.massmed.org/AM/Template.cfm?Section=Research_reports_and_Studies2TEMPLATE=/CM/ContentDisplay.cfm&CONTENTID=27797 (citing to empirical studies estimating the nationwide annual cost of defensive medicine as between $100 billion and $124 billion); *see also* Kessler & McClellan, *Defensive Medicine, supra* note 45 (providing empirical proof of defensive medicine and its high cost); Kessler & McClellan, *Optimal Liability Policy, supra note* 45 (providing updated empirical data confirming the 1996 Kessler & McClellan study). Based on the work of Kessler and McClellan, Price Waterhouse Coopers estimates that defensive medicine costs range from 5% to 9% of medical costs. The Factors Fueling Rising Healthcare Costs 2006, at 7. (Price Waterhouse Coopers 2006). A study published in 2005 estimates the cost of defensive medicine to be 5% of the $1.5 trillion the United States spends on health care annually. *See* Baicker & Chandra, *Defensive Medicine, supra* note 45, at 30. A 1989 American Medical Association study estimated that doctors spend $2.70 performing unnecessary tasks for every $1 they spend on medical malpractice insurance premiums, resulting in a $30 billion cost to the economy.
52. U.S. Dept. of Health and Human Services, Confronting the New Health Care Crisis: Improving Health Care Quality and Lower Costs by Fixing Our Medical Liability System (2002), *available at* http://aspe.hhs.gov/daltcp/reports/litrefm.pdf; *see also* Baicker & Chandra, *Defensive Medicine, supra* note 46, at 30 (concluding that to the extent malpractice payments are associated with significant increases in health insurance premiums, the cost is borne primarily by workers by way of decreased wages for employees with employer-sponsored health insurance and the movement of such workers to part-time uninsured positions).

53. Thomas J. Campbell, Daniel P. Kessler, and George B. Shepard, The Causes and Effects of Liability Reform: Some Empirical Evidence (National Bureau of Economic Research Working Paper No. 4989, 1995). The industries studied were construction; local and interurban passenger transit; transport services; electric, gas, and sanitary services; wholesale trade; retail trade; insurance agents, brokers, and services; hotel and lodging places; personal services; business services; auto repair, services, and garages; miscellaneous repair services; motion pictures; amusement and recreation services; health services; legal services; and manufacturing. The study examined six reforms enacted by states between 1969 and 1990 that decreased the level of tort liability: (1) caps on contingency fees; (2) reform of the collateral source rule; (3) damage caps; (4) periodic rather than lump-sum payments; (5) reform of joint and several liability; and (6) punitive damages reform. *Id*. at 3–6. It also examined two reforms enacted by states between 1969 and 1990 that increased the scope of tort liability: comparative negligence and prejudgment interest. *Id*. at 5–6.

54. *Id*. at 18–22, 34 tbl.3, 36 tbl.5, 34 tbl.3, 36 tbl.5, 34 tbl.3, and 36 tbl.5.

55. In association with the enactment of liability-decreasing reforms, fourteen of seventeen industries experienced employment growth and thirteen of seventeen industries experienced growth in productivity. *Id*. at 34 tbl.3, 36 tbl.5. In association with the enactment of liability-increasing reforms, fourteen of seventeen industries experienced decreases in productivity and fourteen of seventeen industries experienced decreases in employment. *Id*. Nine of seventeen industries exhibited all of the correlations. *Id*.

56. The authors of the study acknowledge that the results of the study may have been influenced by three other factors. *Id*. at 28. First, state-level public policies may be responsible for the correlation between liability law and productivity and employment. *Id*. Second, the results may be due to a "Delaware effect," whereby capital flows from high-liability to low-liability states. Liability reforms would thus redistribute wealth rather than increasing or decreasing it. *Id*. Third, firms from states with relatively low levels of liability may have relatively lower costs because they do not bear the true costs of production. *Id*. For a discussion of critical reaction to the study, see Richard B. Schmitt, *Study of States Finds Tort Reform Sparked Economic Growth, Jobs*, WALL ST. J., Sept. 18, 1995, at B8.

57. George Priest, *The Modern Expansion of Tort Liability: Its Source, Its Effects, and Its Reform*, 5 J. ECON. PERSP. 31 (1991).

14 The Relationship between Injury Rates and Tort System Costs

I HAVE ATTRIBUTED THE EXPANSION OF THE SCOPE OF TORT liability and the consequent increase in tort system costs to the exceptional contemporary increases in tort lawyers' effective hourly rates. In this chapter, I consider two alternative explanations for the increases in tort system costs: an increase in injury rates, resulting in increased numbers of tort claims; and an increase in the propensity of injured persons to sue.

A. Propensity to Sue

Only a small percentage of the acts that could give rise to tort liability actually result in formal claims being made. One study indicates that 5 percent or less of those who believed they were victims of another's wrongdoing filed lawsuits.[1] Another study indicated that only one out of every twenty-five patients with a negligent or preventable medical injury brought a medical malpractice claim.[2] Thus, an increase in the propensity of injured parties to bring suit could account, at least in part, for increased tort system costs. With the exception of auto accident litigation, however, there is little data available on whether the propensity to sue for tortious injury has increased. There is, however, circumstantial data that is relevant. For example, tort lawyers engage in substantial advertising efforts to drum up business, which likely increases the public's propensity to sue. They spend hundreds of millions of dollars to advertise their ability to get accident victims "the money they deserve" or are "entitled to" and to convey the message that signing up with the lawyer is risk-free because "no recovery, no fee."[3] Lawyers also sponsor Web sites designed to look like "medical" Web sites in order to attract potential litigants who have ingested or been exposed to substances that are alleged to be toxic, informing them of the dangers of these substances and providing a phone number to call for "more information." One such for-profit Web site is WhoCanISue.com, which was launched in 2008 and advertises extensively in Florida, California, New York, Pennsylvania, and Texas. An aspiring plaintiff can select from among a menu of injuries, such as "accidents," then a subcategory, such as "slip-and-fall." The Web site visitor is then provided with the phone number and email address of a nearby lawyer to contact. Personal injury lawyers, who pay a minimum of $1,000 annually to appear on the Web site, report that phone traffic has doubled.[4] Still another example is lawyers' use of litigation screenings to manufacture hundreds of thousands of mostly bogus cases in some mass tort litigations.[5]

Almost certainly, these advertisements and other more targeted efforts to attract tort claimants have impacted the public's propensity to sue for a claimed injury. The lure of "free money" can prove irresistible.[6] Lawyers devote substantial efforts to recruiting clients because of the increased profitability of tort litigation (in the form of increased effective hourly rates). The greater the profits from contingency fees, the greater incentive there is to invest the requisite capital to increase the propensity of the population to sue.

As for auto accident litigation, there is a considerable body of data indicating that the propensity to sue has substantially increased over the past three decades. Here, it is even clearer that the increased propensity is lawyer-driven and the result of the increased profitability of tort claims. Every auto accident gives rise to one or more (potential) claims for property damage (PD) and bodily injury (BI).[7] Whereas the vast majority of auto accidents give rise to PD claims, many do not involve BI. BI claims, on their face, are a function of the severity of auto accidents; the more serious the accident, the greater the likelihood of BI; likewise, the more severe the BI, the greater the propensity to sue. In view of increased safety features in automobiles, lowered accident rates per number of miles driven, and substantial declines in the number of deaths per 100 million vehicle miles traveled,[8] we would expect that the number of BI claims per auto accident would also have decreased in the past several decades. We would also expect that BI claiming rates would be lower in urban areas than in rural areas because driving speeds in the former are well below those in the latter. In fact, the converse is true. Logic cannot stand up to the effects of increasing profits from contingency fees. Studies indicate that the propensity to sue for BI more strongly correlates with lawyer activity than with the severity of the accident. In fact, the ratio of BI to PD claims is a useful measure of litigiousness in that it is a measure of the propensity to engage in tort claiming activity, largely independent of the severity of the accident.

Consider that the 1989 ratio of BI to PD claims was less than 13 per 100 in Harrisburg, Pennsylvania, less than 16 per 100 in Pittsburgh, but 75 per 100 in Philadelphia.[9] In Los Angeles, the ratio was 98.8 per 100, 2.2 times more than the rest of California. Why do auto accidents in Philadelphia result in nearly five times the number of BI claims as in Pittsburgh, Pennsylvania's second largest city? And why do auto accidents in Los Angeles result in double the number of BI claims as the rest of the state? Lawyers. The high percentages of attorney representation of BI claims account for the higher BI:PD ratios in Philadelphia and Los Angeles. In 1997, 84 percent of BI claimants in Philadelphia were represented by lawyers, compared to 44 percent in Pittsburgh. And lawyers represented 72 percent of BI claimants in Los Angeles, as compared to 49 percent and 48 percent for San Francisco and San Diego, respectively.[10]

In 1997, the national average for lawyer representation in auto accident claims was 38.8 percent, but it climbed to 61 percent in Maryland, 70 percent in the District of Columbia, and 86 percent in New Jersey.[11] These are not simply statistical aberrations. Attorney involvement in auto accident claims has increased markedly over the years. In 1977, attorneys were involved in 18.6 percent of auto claims, but this rose to 40 percent in 1998.[12] The greater the percentage of auto accident claims with lawyer representation, the higher the number of BI claims filed per accident and the more expensive the average cost to insurance companies.[13]

More lawyer representation also means higher settlements and greater medical costs for the same accidents – facts that I address in Chapter 15. The greater the frequency and the higher the settlement value of claims, the higher lawyers' contingency fee profits.[14] Not surprisingly, higher lawyer representation also increases insurance company payouts and therefore increases the cost of auto insurance.[15]

New Jersey has the highest percentage of lawyer representation of auto accident claims in the nation – 86 percent. Unsurprisingly, New Jersey has also had the highest auto insurance rates in the country for many years – a factor that played a large role in several gubernatorial campaigns, nearly unseating a governor up for reelection.[16] An article in *The New York Times* attributes the high cost of auto insurance in New Jersey to the density of auto traffic in that state.[17] It is not the density of New Jersey traffic; rather it is the density of New Jersey lawyers in auto accident claiming that drives New Jersey's insurance cost to its pinnacle.

Further evidence of the relationship between lawyer representation and the frequency of automobile accident litigation is provided by a recent study of auto accident litigation in Texas.[18] In that state, Stephen Daniels and Joanne Martin found a general decline in the rate of automobile accident tort filings for every 1,000 accidents involving injury or death from 1985 to 2000. Daniels and Martin conducted a mail survey of Texas plaintiffs' lawyers, giving them a hypothetical case and asking if they were more or less willing to take the case at the time of the survey (1999–2000) than they would have been five years prior. The hypothetical case was "a simple car wreck with only soft tissue injuries worth $3,000, minimal PD, and with liability running to the other party who was adequately insured."[19] Results showed that 55.1 percent of "Auto Specialist" attorneys would have taken the case at the time of the survey, whereas 89.1 percent would have taken the case five years earlier. Daniels and Martin posit that the decrease in litigiousness is attributable to changes "in the market environment in which plaintiffs' lawyers do business, making it harder, in the lawyers' estimation, to stay profitable."[20] These changes include (1) Texas juries' decreased willingness to find for tort plaintiffs; and (2) the plaintiffs' bar's perceived existence of jury "reluctance to award noneconomic damages [pain and suffering] ... [which is the] damage component of the award ... where the lawyer is likely to cover his out-of-pocket expenses for the case ... and to gain whatever profit there will be."[21] Diminished profitability and Texas lawyers' decreased willingness to accept auto accident cases have resulted in a decrease in the rate of auto accident tort filings for every 1,000 accidents involving injury or death. The correlation between lawyers' profit levels and the frequency of auto accident tort filings far outweighs the "only weak relationships" that Daniels and Martin found between "injuries and accidents on the one hand and tort filings on the other."[22]

This data demonstrates that lawyers' pursuit of profits drives the propensity to sue in auto accident litigation. Increased profits result in an increase in the propensity to sue and auto insurance costs. Decreased profitability, on the other hand, results in lowered amounts of litigation.

B. Injury Rates and Tort Litigation

A second plausible alternative explanation for large increases in tort system costs is an increase in the rate of injury. Indeed, because the principal purpose of the tort system is to provide compensation to those who have been wrongfully injured, increases in tort litigation frequency and the rate of wealth transfer would appear to be a function of increases in the frequency of injury. However, the data indicates that injury and work-related and auto-accident-related accidental death rates have actually steadily declined since 1900.[23] Stephen Sugarman of the University of California at Berkeley School of Law chronicled this substantial decline in accidental death rates.[24] In 1900, when the population was 75 million, there were 100,000 accidental deaths; in 2000, after the population had almost quadrupled to 275 million, there were only 92,000 accidental deaths.[25] Michael Saks suggests that the deterrent effect of the tort system may account for the decline in injury rates:

> The number of workplace deaths and injuries are down in both absolute terms and as a population-adjusted rate. How much of this decline can be attributed to the deterrent effects of the tort system, how much to government regulation, how much to the regime of worker's compensation, and how much to changes in managerial or technological culture and practices is interesting and important to know. Something is causing it.[26]

But even as he acknowledges that the evidence to support this hypothesis is at least questionable, he fails to recognize that the beginning of the decline in accident rates (both in "absolute terms and as a population-adjusted rate") predated the rise of product liability litigation.[27]

Moreover, the empirical data indicate that accidental injury and death rates have been largely unaffected by product liability litigation. As previously noted, two leading law and economics scholars, Steven Shavell and A. Mitchell Polinsky, have studied the literature and have concluded that the empirical evidence suggests that product liability has had little influence on product safety for certain widely sold products.[28] A study by Professor John Graham of whether the increase in automobile-related product liability litigation between 1950 and 1988 led to a reduction in the automobile accident fatality rate found no statistically discernable relationship.[29] A study by George Priest found that there was no "sharp decrease in accident rates after 1970 [when modern products liability law was created] that might be attributed to the deterrent effect of products liability law," from which he concluded that "there is no evidence ... of a reduction in the injury rate of a magnitude corresponding with the expansion of products liability."[30]

Thus, we can reject the alternative explanation that increased rates of accidental injury and death have led to large increases in tort system costs. Injury rates – both in terms of the raw numbers and population-adjusted rates – have fallen. Furthermore, the surge in products liability litigation has had no discernable effect on the steady decline of accidental injury and death rates, which began at the turn of the twentieth century.

Accordingly, the case for attribution of the expansion of tort liability and the growth of tort litigation to increased lawyers' profits remains intact. In the next chapter, I further address arguments supporting such an attribution.

NOTES

1. THOMAS F. BURKE, LAWYERS, LAWSUITS, AND LEGAL RIGHTS 3 n.14 (2002) (referencing a study conducted by the Civil Litigation Research Project).
2. TOM BAKER, THE MEDICAL MALPRACTICE MYTH 37 (2005).
3. *See* Maria Aspan, *Getting Law Firms to Like Commercials*, N.Y. TIMES, June 19, 2007 ("Advertising within the legal services industry generated more than $575 million in 2006 [with] the top 10 spenders [being] personal-injury or plaintiff-related law firms."); The Florida Bar Department of Public Information & Bar Services, *Bar Issue Paper – Attorney Advertising*, § IV (1995), *available at* http://www.floridabar.org/DIVCOM/PI/BIPS2001.nsf/1119bd38ae090a74 8525676f0053b606/4acd3c2f497de74b8525669e004f5c28?OpenDocument. In a few states, the "no recovery no fee" mantra is misleading at best. In these states, if a client switches contingency fee lawyers because the first one was not doing a good job and later recovers nothing, he may still have to pay the first lawyer a substantial fee. *See* Lester Brickman, *Setting the Fee When the Client Discharges a Contingent Fee Attorney*, 41 EMORY L.J. 367 (1992). If lawyers in these states were held to a "truth in advertising" standard, they would have to say instead: No recovery, no fee – unless you become dissatisfied with my services and hire another lawyer.
4. *See* Bridget Carey, *Lawsuits Made Simple? Website Makes the Claim*, MIAMI HERALD, Aug. 7, 2008, at C1; Siobhan Morrissey, *Who Can You Sue? Click Here*, TIME, Aug. 6, 2008, *available at* http://www.time.com/time/nation/ article/0,8599,1829725,00.html; Missy Diaz, *'Whocanisue.com' Aggressively Seeks Plaintiffs*, S. FLA. SUN SENTINEL, Oct. 12 2009, *available at* http:// www.sunsentinel.com/news/palm-beach/boca-raton/sfl-who-can-i-sue-p100409,0,4368025.story.

5. *See* Brickman, *Litigation Screenings, supra* Chapter 7, note 61.
6. In 2002, lawyers sponsored an asbestos screening at a union hall in Hazelwood, Missouri, for workers who had been on the assembly lines at the local Boeing, Ford, and General Motors plants. *See* Brickman, *Asbestos Litigation*, Chapter 2, note 16, at 68 n.105. A reporter at the screening described the hundreds who turned up as appearing healthy and showing no outward signs of disease. He reports on several interviews:

   I saw the notice in the union newsletter and said, Why not?" said an automotive worker from Ford. Sitting on the tailgate of his shiny, new Chevy pickup and lighting a fresh cigarette off the one he had just finished, he added: "It's better than the lottery. If they find something, I get a few thousand dollars I didn't have. If they don't find anything, I've just lost an afternoon." Standing nearby, a Boeing worker ten days from retirement volunteered, "The lawyers said I could get $10,000 or $12,000 if the shadow is big enough, and I know just the fishing boat I'd buy with that." Asked if he'd ever worked with asbestos, he said, "No, but lawyers say it's all over the place, so I was probably exposed to it.

   Andrew Schneider, *Asbestos Lawsuits Anger Critics*, St. Louis Post Dispatch, Feb. 9, 2003, at A1.
7. For the underlying data on which the statements in this paragraph are based, see Brickman, *Effective Hourly Rates, supra* Introduction, note 4, at 671–74.
8. The number of highway deaths fell 9% in 2009. Indeed, the number of deaths per 100 million vehicle miles traveled fell to the lowest level since recordkeeping began in 1954. The fourth quarter 2009 decline was the 15th consecutive quarter of a falling highway death rate. The reasons given are more crashworthy cars, the use of seat belts, and efforts to prevent drunk driving. *Highway Deaths on the Decline*, N.Y. Times, March 12, 2010, at B4, *available at* http://www.nytimes.com/2010/03/12/business/12traffic.html.
9. Ins. Research Council, Trends in Bodily Injury Claims 17–18 (1990).
10. Ins. Research Council, Injuries For Auto Accidents at 63, 64 fig. 6–10 (June 1999).
11. *Id.* at 69–70.
12. *Id.* at 45 & fig. 4–1.
13. *See* Brickman, *Effective Hourly Rates, supra* Introduction, note 4, at 680–81.
14. *Id.* at 681.
15. *See id.*
16. *See* Jennifer Preston, *New Jersey Tackles Geographical Limits for Auto Insurance*, N.Y. Times, Mar. 27, 1998, at B9 (stating that "voter anger over paying the highest auto insurance rates in the nation nearly cost ... [the incumbent New Jersey governor] a second term"); Joseph B. Treaster, *An Escalating*

Blame Game Ensues Over the High Price of Auto Insurance, N.Y. TIMES, June 1, 2001, at B2.

17. *See* Steve Raynor, *Auto Insurance 'Reform' Really Isn't*, N.Y. TIMES, Apr. 22, 1990, at Sec. 12 NJ, p. 24.

18. *See* Steven Daniels & Joanne Martin, *The Strange Success of Tort Reform*, 53 EMORY L.J. 1225 (2004).

19. *Id*. at 1237, 1256.

20. *Id*. at 1228.

21. *Id*. at 1244, 1249.

22. *Id*. at 1233.

23. *See* Stephen D. Sugarman, *A Century of Change in Personal Injury Law*, 88 CAL. L. REV. 2403, 2417–19 (2000). Work-related accidental deaths also decreased by 90% between 1912 and 1998. *Id*. at 2420. Even the number of traffic injuries and deaths relative to the number of miles traveled and relative to the number of licensed drivers has decreased. *See* NATIONAL HIGHWAY TRAFFIC SAFETY ADMINISTRATION, TRAFFIC SAFETY FACTS: 2006 DATA 1 (2006). From 1996 to 2006, the fatality rate per 100 million vehicle miles of travel decreased from 1.69 to 1.41 and the injury rate per 100 million vehicle miles of travel decreased from 140 to 85. *Id*.

24. *See* Sugarman, *id*.

25. *Id*. at 2417–19.

26. *See* Michael J. Saks, *Do We Really Know Anything About the Behavior of the Tort Litigation System – and Why Not?*, 140 U. PA. L. REV. 1147, 1178 (1992).

27. *See* Sugarman, *supra* note 23, at 1178.

28. *See* Shavell & Polinsky, *Product Liability*, *supra* Chapter 8, note 4, at 1440–42.

29. John D. Graham, *Product Liability and Motor Vehicle Safety*, in PETER W. HUBER & ROBERT E. LITAN EDS., THE LIABILITY MAZE 182–83 (1991).

30. George L. Priest, *Products Liability Law and the Accident Rate* in ROBERT E. LITAN & CLIFFORD WINSTON, EDS., LIABILITY: PERSPECTIVES AND POLICY 184, 187–94 (1988).

15 The Impacts of Substantial Increases in Tort Lawyers' Effective Hourly Rates

IN THIS CHAPTER, I LAY BARE THE RELATIONSHIP BETWEEN the increased profitability of contingency fees and increases in the frequency of tort litigation. The greater the flow of capital to lawyers from their portfolios of cases, the greater their ability to invest in expansion of the tort system. Moreover, increased profits also result in increases in tort claim valuation. To demonstrate, I examine the ways that lawyers have driven up medical expenses and noneconomic damages (pain and suffering) in order to increase their contingency fees. Nowhere is the effect of inordinately high contingency fee profits more evident than in claims of soft-tissue injury (mostly caused by auto accidents). The leading soft-tissue claim is whiplash – a syndrome caused when the head snaps forward in an auto accident. In Appendix K, I examine the empirical evidence that whiplash is not a medical event but rather a function of contingency fees and the compensation system they generate.

A. The Relationship between Effective Hourly Rates and the Frequency of Tort Claims

As lawyers' contingency fee profits increase, the volume of tort litigation also increases.[1] This relationship is the basis for federal fee-shifting statutes in such areas as consumer credit,[2] copyright,[3] antitrust,[4] securities,[5] the environment,[6] and especially civil rights.[7] Fee-shifting statutes mostly allow or direct courts to award reasonable attorneys' fees to prevailing plaintiffs. This raises the amount of a plaintiff's recovery and, therefore, the fee that a contingency fee lawyer can realize for her representation. A congressional report states that the legislative purpose of fee-shifting provisions is "to [e]nsure that reasonable fees are awarded to attract competent counsel in cases involving civil and constitutional rights, while avoiding windfalls to attorneys."[8]

The statutes raise lawyers' fees in two ways. First, certain claims seek injunctive rather than monetary relief. The imposition of a reasonable attorney fee on losing defendants enables claimants who cannot afford the cost of such litigation to proceed if their claims appear viable. Thus, fee income is generated from claims that would not otherwise be brought. This is also true for claims for money damages in which attorney fee costs would exceed monetary relief. A claimant may nonetheless bring suit because the shifted attorney fee cost is not limited by the amount of money damages obtained.[9] Second, when representation is on a contingency fee basis and monetary damages are obtained, the lawyer can structure the contingency fee to apply to the total award (damages plus the attorney fee award), thereby raising the amount of her fee. Or, the lawyer can provide in the retention agreement that she is to be paid whatever attorney's fees the court awards and can further provide that she is also to get a percentage of the base recovery.[10] In both instances, more claims attract lawyer representation than in the absence of the fee-shifting provision. Indeed, raising lawyers' yields has generally been effective in increasing the number of claims filed in the statutorily designated areas.[11] For example, between 1961 and 1979, the number of civil rights suits filed in federal courts grew from 296 to 24,951 – a growth of nearly one-hundred-fold.[12] In 2002, 40,549 civil rights cases were filed.[13]

Just as increasing lawyers' fees increases litigation, lowering tort litigation profits decreases litigation. The latter assumption underlies states' adoption of limits on contingency fees[14] and damage awards, particularly in medical malpractice litigation. In order to reduce tort litigation, thirty-six states have enacted legislation to limit noneconomic damages[15]; whereas twenty-two states have also placed caps on punitive damages.[16] Statutory limitations on either tort damages or contingency fees reduce lawyers' projected effective hourly rates. At the margin, cases that would be considered sufficiently profitable to lawyers at a 33⅓ percent or 40 percent contingency fee will not be sufficiently profitable if these caps are imposed.

At first blush, some might expect direct and indirect constraints on lawyers' fees to increase the frequency of tort litigation because lawyers would seek to counter the diminution in fee income by taking on more cases.[17] Economic theory[18] and lawyers' actual practices, however, indicate the contrary. When lawyers' fees are limited – either directly by caps on fees or indirectly by caps on damages – lawyers react by accepting fewer cases. Empirical confirmation of this assertion is robust.[19] Among the empirical support is the study of auto accident litigation in Texas by Daniels and Martin, which was discussed in Chapter 14, Section A.[20] This study found that in the period 1985–2000, the rate of auto accident tort filings per every 1,000 accidents had declined – not because of a decline in actual injuries but because of a decline in the profitability of auto tort litigation. Lower profits for attorneys resulted in *fewer* claims.

The litigation-lowering effects of caps on fees and damage awards explain why trial lawyers, torts scholars, and consumer advocates, who favor expansion of the tort system, oppose damage and fee caps. One of the reasons advanced for imposing caps is that they will reduce the rate of increase in doctors' medical malpractice premiums. This is what occurred when California enacted a law imposing limits on pain and suffering damages and a sliding cap on contingency fees, resulting in a decrease in the rate of increase in malpractice premiums. Pro-tort expansionists, however, who argue that damage caps and other tort reforms have no effect on medical malpractice premiums, attribute the decrease to other legislation regulating insurers. However, their arguments are belied by the data showing that the California statute has resulted in a substantial lowering of doctors' malpractice premiums from the levels in comparable states and a significant decline in attorneys' fees as well.[21]

The empirically supported direct correlation between tort lawyers' profits and tort claim frequency supports the broader thesis that I am advancing: The substantial increases in tort lawyers' effective hourly rates account for the substantial increases in the scope of liability of the tort system, as well as the concomitant substantial increases in the volume of tort claims (as more accurately measured) and in the costs of the tort system.

Thus, there is a direct correlation between tort lawyers' profits and tort claim frequency. In the next section, I will demonstrate that there is a similar correlation between tort lawyers' profits and tort claim valuation.

B. Effects of Contingency Fees on Tort Claim Valuation

In addition to increasing the volume of tort litigation, the substantial increases in effective hourly rates account for additional increases in the value of tort claims. Tort claim valuation generally consists of two elements: economic losses – mostly lost wages and medical expenses – and noneconomic damages – mostly "pain and suffering."[22] The greater the value of tort claims, the greater the profits lawyers realize. Further, lawyers have also had enormous success in increasing jury awards for pain and suffering apart from the effect of increased medical care costs. Moreover, by driving up medical care costs, lawyers increase both economic damages and noneconomic damage awards, which are usually a multiple of medical expenses. I explain both of these assertions next.

1. Noneconomic Damages ("Pain and Suffering")

Noneconomic damages – mostly "pain and suffering" – have hugely increased over the past forty-five years,[23] to the point that they account for approximately half of tort damage awards.[24] In the aggregate, such payments may amount to as much as $50 billion a year – roughly twice the size of the entire tort systems of Germany and Japan.[25]

Whereas recovery for intangible loss dates back to Roman Law,[26] in their modern form, courts initially accepted (if not favored) noneconomic damages to reimburse claimants for the share of the recovery that they had to pay to tort lawyers and to compensate these contingency fee lawyers.[27] As noted by Charles Wolfram, the author of one of the leading texts on legal ethics, "inflated elements of general damage such as pain and suffering are tolerated by courts as a rough measure of the plaintiff's attorney fees."[28] Richard Abel notes that pain and suffering damages "are necessary to make cases profitable to plaintiff's lawyers, especially when liability is uncertain, the defendant intransigent and specials [economic damages] low."[29]

One hundred years ago, however, pain and suffering damages were a relatively insignificant part of American tort practice and were under the tight control of courts.[30] How then did pain and suffering damages skyrocket to become such a substantial component of the tort system? Lawyers. One, in particular, led the way: Melvin Belli – a flamboyant, self-promoting, and "ethically challenged" lawyer.[31] Belli published a law review article in 1951, which aimed to raise the value of personal injury cases.[32] Although he conceded that "pain is not a readily measurable commodity,"[33] Belli argued that tort law was about a "man's right to live out his life free from pain and suffering, with his mind and body intact."[34] The lawyer's job was to devise creative ways to vindicate that right. He showed how tort lawyers could increase the value of pain and suffering and raise the yield from the one-third contingency fee by using the courtroom for the theatrical reconstruction of the victim's pain and suffering, including displaying gruesome imagery of "badly burned hands and mangled bodies."[35] Indeed, the sky was the limit.

Belli's enormous success in raising pain and suffering damages has generated billions of dollars for plaintiffs and their lawyers. In inflation-adjusted terms, pain and suffering awards grew 300 percent between the 1960s and 1980s[36] and accelerated even faster in the next two decades.[37] Increases in pain and suffering are the principal drivers of increases in tort awards. From 1994 to 2001, average jury awards rose from $187,000 to $323,000 in auto accident cases and from $1.4 million to $3.9 million in medical malpractice cases.[38]

A number of commentators have criticized pain and suffering awards as being inappropriately large.[39] But how would a court go about determining whether a jury's award was "too high"? The difficulty is that these damages are formulaically unbounded and highly variable. As stated by a U.S. District Court Judge, "the law ... dictates no method of calculating pain and suffering damages."[40] U.S. Circuit Court Judge Paul Niemeyer notes that the impact of there being "no rational, predictable criteria for measuring [pain and suffering] damages" is that "there are also no criteria for reviewing pain and suffering awards by the presiding judge or the appellate court."[41] Another author notes that:

> Unlike economic damages, for which all information required to enable the jury to reach a just, meaningful, and informed decision will be contained in the trial record, noneconomic damages necessarily involve consideration beyond the facts of a given case. Juries are therefore left without any real guidance, aside from their own personal sensibilities and experiences, regarding how to value intangible harms.[42]

Lawyers have an additional incentive to persuade juries to award higher pain and suffering damages. In recent years, the U.S. Supreme Court has been troubled by huge punitive damages awards. After many attempts, the Court has found a basis for concluding that "excessive" punitive damages violate the Due Process Clause of the Fourteenth Amendment and for limiting punitive damages, in most cases, to the amount of compensatory damages.[43] In response, tort lawyers have urged jurors to use pain and suffering damages as a way of punishing defendants. Some juries have responded by awarding vast sums for pain and suffering, which appear to be prompted by a desire to punish, not compensate. Victor Schwartz and his law firm associate, Leah Lorber, note that recent cases have "twisted" pain and suffering damages "into a covert punitive damages substitute."[44] As examples, they cite a 2001 verdict of $41 million awarded for noneconomic damages (out of a total award of

$49.85 million in compensatory damages) and another 2001 verdict for $115 million, of which $100 million was for pain and suffering.[45]

Judge Paul Niemeyer of the Fourth Circuit Court of Appeals has called on state legislatures to regulate and rationalize pain and suffering damages in light of the U.S. Supreme Court's Due Process jurisprudence. The amorphous character of pain and suffering damages, however, lends itself to this use despite the Supreme Court's curtailment of excessive punitive damages awards. True, the business community has succeeded in enacting limits on pain and suffering damages in a number of states, but given the current political climate, there is little likelihood that additional states will be added.[46]

Joseph H. King Jr., professor at the University of Tennessee College of Law, advocates the complete elimination of pain and suffering damages in personal injury cases. King's fundamental concern is that uncertainty of valuation fosters unpredictability of outcomes, undercutting optimal deterrence and rational experience ratings.[47] Correspondingly, uncertainty promotes wide disparity among recoveries, violating fairness notions of like treatment for like cases. These consequences are unavoidable, he argues, because of the incommensurability between psychic harm and pecuniary redress. Thus, he concludes that from any widely accepted perspective on the goals of tort law – compensation, deterrence, corrective justice, fairness, administrative cost concerns, and the like – pain and suffering recovery ought to be eliminated, and recovery should be limited to economic loss suffered as a consequence of personal injury.[48]

Increases in noneconomic damages have been a driving force in expanding the value of tort claims and, therefore, raising lawyers' effective hourly rates. Stephen Sugarman observes that "lawyers are often the main beneficiaries … of large payments nominally intended for pain and suffering."[49] More pain and suffering damages mean more income for lawyers. And because tort litigation is then more profitable, tort lawyers bring more cases. This is further corroborated by a recent study that shows that the amount of tort litigation correlates with the recoverability of noneconomic loss: the lower the noneconomic loss, the less the amount of litigation.[50]

2. Medical Expense "Buildup"

Lawyers are also increasing pain and suffering awards by driving up medical expenses. Increasing medical costs boosts lawyers' fees because pain and suffering damages are usually valued for settlement purposes as a multiple of medical costs. At the beginning of the period of rapid expansion of the scope of tort liability, the ratio of pain and suffering damages to medical costs was approximately 3:1.[51] A recent U.S. Department of Health and Human Services study of medical malpractice data on closed claims from Texas and Florida indicates that the ratio of pain and suffering to economic damages is 2.6:1.[52] Another recent study indicates that the multiplier for products liability litigation is 3.35.[53] In auto accident litigation, the multiple declined to approximately 2:1 in the 1970–1990 period and has further declined to a current ratio of approximately 1.5:1.[54] Although auto accident litigation accounts for approximately 53 percent of all tort claims filed in courts,[55] average verdicts in medical malpractice and products liability litigation are approximately twenty-eight times higher than those in auto accident cases.[56] Taking this data into account, a multiple of 2.5:1 for tort claims appears reasonable.

To illustrate how this works in a typical case, assume that medical care costs are $6,000 and there is no wage loss. The pain and suffering component would be approximately $15,000, and the settlement value of the case would be $21,000. The lawyer charging a standard contingency fee of one-third would get $7,000 (plus reimbursement of expenses). Now assume that medical costs are $9,000 – a 50 percent increase. Pain and suffering would total about $22,500, and the settlement value of the case would be $31,500. The lawyer's fee – $10,500 – would also be 50 percent higher.

Given the operative mathematics of the contingent-fee-driven personal injury tort system, plaintiffs' lawyers have a clear incentive to "build up" medical costs. "Build up" is a euphemism for not just inflating medical expenses but also directing clients to doctors who will submit inflated and even fraudulent bills. Professor Jeffrey O'Connell also believes that calculating pain and suffering awards as a multiple of economic loss "promotes bill-padding, which, by inflating economic accident costs, can raise proportionate compensation for intangible injury."[57] Indeed, the empirical data demonstrate a higher incidence of medical care costs when claimants hire lawyers, as compared to claimants who do not hire lawyers. For example, a 2004 study by the Insurance Research Council indicates that average economic losses for represented claimants were about 4.7 times higher than unrepresented claimants ($33,195 for represented claimants versus $7,857 for unrepresented claimants).[58]

Tort expansionists will no doubt argue that the reason for the differential is that more seriously injured persons are more likely to hire a lawyer and run up higher medical costs. But this explanation is belied by the data. Even when the injuries are of the same type and degree of severity, those who hire lawyers still incur substantially higher medical costs than those who do not.[59] Tort system expansionists counter that this can be explained by the fact that the more severely injured within each injury category are more likely to hire lawyers and therefore run up higher medical expenses. Published studies, however, directly address this issue and reject this possibility.[60]

Recent data comparing economic losses for represented and nonrepresented back sprain claimants, using days of restricted activity as a control for variations in injury severity, show that attorney-represented claimants had, in total, average economic losses of $5,208, whereas nonrepresented claimants had average economic losses of $1,541, a 3.3:1 ratio.[61] Similar disparities in economic loss are evidenced by comparing represented and nonrepresented employed claimants whose most serious injury was a back sprain or strain with and without lost work time. Represented claimants reported, in total, average economic losses of $6,271, whereas nonrepresented claimants reported economic loss of $1,768, a 3.54:1 ratio.[62] This was the case even though there was little difference in terms of hospitalization between represented and nonrepresented claimants who had lost no time from work and reported a back sprain or strain as their most serious injury (about two-thirds received no hospital treatment).[63] Moreover, this phenomenon is not restricted to the United States. A recent study in Australia of factors affecting health care utilization by patients admitted to a trauma center found a significantly higher rate of health care utilization by those patients who hired a lawyer that was not accounted for by differences in injury severity.[64]

The conclusion that attorneys cause these increases in medical costs seems inescapable.[65] Attorney involvement is associated with higher auto injury costs, in part, because claimants with attorneys report more different types of injuries and more frequent medical visits than claimants without attorneys.[66] In states with less than 40 percent of claims involving attorneys, claimants reported an average of 1.70 different types of injuries per person in 1992. In states with attorneys involved in 40 to 49 percent of claims, there were 1.78 types of injuries per person. States with at least 50 percent of claims involving attorneys had an average of 1.94 injury types per claimant.[67] Yet, in states with higher incidence of multiple types of injury per person, the claimants were not involved in more serious crashes, on average, and were not more seriously injured.[68]

In states where attorney representation was 50 percent or more, utilization of chiropractors and physical therapists was highest. In fact, the median number of visits to chiropractors (twenty) and physical therapists (fifteen) in these states was higher than the median number of visits to medical doctors.[69] Interestingly, 18 percent of claimants reported in 1992 that their attorney advised them which doctor, chiropractor, or clinic to use for treatment.[70] In addition, a larger percentage of attorney-represented claimants used diagnostic procedures than did nonrepresented claimants.[71]

Even as profit-maximizing attorneys generate substantial increases in medical care costs in order to generate higher contingency fees in auto accident cases, these increased costs do not typically improve the net financial position of their clients in auto accident cases. Data comparing represented and nonrepresented claimants who suffered weight-bearing bone fractures in 1992 reveal that claimants who did not hire lawyers netted, on average, $5,866 more than those who did.[72] Claimants reporting sprains or strains as their most serious injury – 55 percent of those injured in auto accidents – received an average payment of $4,548 in the 1995–1998 period; those with lawyers received $9,401; and those who handled their own claims received $2,106. The unrepresented claimant had $1,688 in economic losses and received $418 more than his expenses. In contrast, whereas the represented claimant incurred $5,981 in economic losses – more than triple the expenses of those without lawyers – legal expenses consumed $3,102, leaving the claimant with a net payment of $318 – $100 less than the victim without a lawyer. But an extra $7,395 had been spent on medical services, attorney fees, court costs, and other legal expenses.[73]

The only time a claimant is substantially better off with an attorney in auto injury claims is when he is able, under the tort system, to obtain a double recovery for medical expenses – once from his medical or auto insurance and once from the jury or by settlement to cover the identical expenses. The net benefit to a claimant here, however, is offset by the strain on our medical care reimbursement systems and the increased cost borne by society for medical and automobile insurance.[74]

As for the societal costs of contingency-fee-financed auto accident claiming, according to The RAND Institute for Civil Justice, 35 to 42 percent of claimed medical costs in automobile accident claims generated in 1993 were fraudulent or the result of contingency-fee-induced medical care cost buildup.[75] The total monetary cost to society was as much as $17 billion to $22 billion.[76] In 2008 dollars, this amounts to $25 billion to $32 billion.[77]

Thus, the empirical evidence demonstrates that (1) lawyer representation in auto accident cases not only adds substantially to medical care costs but often fails to improve a client's net financial position; and (2) lawyers impose such higher costs on society in order to substantially increase their contingency fee income.

3. The Ultimate Medical Expense "Buildup": Whiplash

Medical expense buildup is typically present when the alleged injuries are subjective, such as headaches, psychological disorders, nausea, and soft-tissue injuries (mostly neck and back sprains). These are usually associated with auto accidents. In fact, one-half to two-thirds of auto accident claims involving bodily harm are for back and neck sprains.[78] More than 75 percent of bodily injury claimants in urban centers and their suburbs claimed sprains or strains as their most serious injuries, compared to 71 percent in medium cities, 65 percent in small towns, and 55 percent in rural locations.[79] Higher percentages of lawyer representation of bodily injury claims in urban areas account for this seemingly anomalous disparity between the prevalence of soft-tissue injuries in urban versus rural areas. These soft-tissue injuries cannot be detected by X-rays or magnetic resonance imaging (MRI) scans and are diagnosed solely on the basis of the symptoms reported by the injured person. The National Insurance Crime Bureau estimates that half of the amount paid out in fraudulent auto injury claims is for "exaggerated soft-tissue claims."[80] That is, it is the availability of compensation that drives soft-tissue injury claiming activity.

In Appendix K, I examine the most common soft-tissue injury claimed by auto accident victims: chronic whiplash. The evidence I present supports the conclusion that claims of whiplash provide further compelling evidence of medical cost buildup by lawyers to increase contingency fee income.

I HAVE THUS LAID BARE HOW CONTINGENCY FEE LAWYERS' INCREASED profits impact tort litigation and impose substantial costs on society. In the next chapter, I introduce class actions – the *ne plus ultra* money-making machine yet devised by contingency fee lawyers.

NOTES

1. *See* Thomas D. Rowe Jr., *American Law Institute Study on Paths to a "Better Way": Litigation, Alternatives, and Accommodation*, 1989 DUKE L.J. 824, 851–52; Thomas D. Rowe Jr., *The Legal Theory of Attorney Fee Shifting: A Critical Overview*, 1982 DUKE L.J. 651, 661 [hereinafter Rowe, *Attorney Fee Shifting*]. *Cf.* David A. Root, *Attorney Fee-Shifting in America: Comparing, Contrasting, and Combining The "American Rule" and "English Rule,"* 15 IND. INT'L & COMP. L. REV. 583, 595 (2005) (The use of contingency fee agreements has increased the amount of litigation.) (citing *Deposit Guaranty Nat'l Bank of Jackson, Miss. v. Roper*, 445 U.S. 326, 338 (1980)); Samuel R. Gross, *We Could Pass a Law ... What Might Happen if Contingent Legal Fees Were Banned*, 47 DEPAUL L. REV. 321, 341 (1998) (Banning contingency fees would result in a decrease in the total number of claims, regardless of merit.). *But cf.* Keith N. Hylton, *Fee Shifting and Incentives to Comply with the Law*, 46 VAND. L. REV. 1069, 1072 (1993) (arguing that for personal injury claims, fee shifting in favor of prevailing plaintiffs diminishes litigation because such fee shifting generates the highest level of policy compliance and therefore leads to the lowest accident frequency).

2. 15 U.S.C. § 1640(a)(3) (2006).

3. 17 U.S.C. § 505 (2006).

4. 15 U.S.C. § 15(a) (2006).

5. Securities Act of 1933 § 11(e), 15 U.S.C. § 77k(e) (2006). As originally enacted, § 11(e) of the 1933 Act did not authorize attorney's fees. Recovery of attorneys' fees in cases involving a false registration statement under the Securities Act was first authorized in 1934. Securities Exchange Act of 1934, Ch. 404, § 206(d), 48 Stat. 881, 908 (amending Securities Act of 1933, ch. 38, § 11(e), 48 Stat. 74, 83).

6. Clean Air Act, 42 U.S.C. §§ 7413(b), 7604(d), 7607(f), 7622(b)(2)(b), 7622 (e)(2) (2006); Ocean Dumping Act of 1972, 33 U.S.C. § 1415(g)(4) (2006); Endangered Species Act, 16 U.S.C. § 1540(g)(4) (2006).

7. *See, e.g.*, Age Discrimination Act of 1975, 42 U.S.C. § 6104(e) (2006); Age Discrimination in Employment Act of 1967, 29 U.S.C. § 626(b) (2006); Civil Rights Act of 1964, 42 U.S.C. § 2000a-3(b) (2006); Civil Rights Act of 1964, 42 U.S.C. § 2000e-5(k) (2006); Equal Access to Justice Act, 5 U.S.C. § 504 (2006), 28 U.S.C. § 2412 (2006); Fair Housing Act of 1968, 42 U.S.C. § 3612(p) (2006).

8. H.R. REP. No. 94–1558, at 1 (1976).

9. *See Riverside v. Rivera*, 477 U.S. 561 (1986); *see also Farrar v. Hobby*, 113 S. Ct. 566, 573, 575 (1992) (holding that a plaintiff who wins only nominal damages may nonetheless be eligible for a fee award under 42 U.S.C. § 1988, but denying this plaintiff who won only nominal damages any fee award).

10. *Gisbrecht v. Barnhart*, 535 U.S. 789, 806 (2002).

11. *See* Eric Beal, *It's Better to Have Twelve Monkeys Chasing You Than One Gorilla: Humana Inc. v. Forsyth, the McCarran-Ferguson Act, RICO, and Deterrence*, 5 CONN. INS. L.J. 751, 789–90 (1999) (By offering fee shifting and multiplied damages, plaintiffs have more incentive to pursue risky claims, leading to an increase in the number of suits.).

12. *See* Alexander H. Schmidt, Comment, *Federal Court: The Second Circuit Permits States to Recover Attorney's Fees When Prevailing as Plaintiffs in Civil Rights Actions*, 50 BROOK. L. REV. 685, 687 n.6 (1984); *see also Maine v. Thiboutot*, 448 U.S. 1, 28 n.16 (1980) (Powell, J., dissenting).

13. *See* FEDERAL JUDICIAL CASELOAD STATISTICS Table c-3: cases commenced by nature of suit and district, www.uscourts.gov/statisticsalreports.html. (The data for each year is for a twelve-month period ending March 31st of that year). *But cf.* Theodore Eisenberg & Stewart Schwab, *The Reality of Constitutional Tort Litigation*, 72 CORNELL L. REV. 641 (1987) (concluding that the promise of fee awards has not increased the rate of filing of civil rights suits).

14. For discussion of medical malpractice fee caps, see Brickman, *Contingent Fee Market, supra* Chapter 6, note 14, at 92 n.105; *see also* Richard M. Birnholz, Comment, *The Validity and Propriety of Contingent Fee Controls*, 37 UCLA L. REV. 949, 950 n.6 (1990).

15. *See* NATIONAL ASS'N OF MUTUAL INSURANCE COMPANIES, NAMIC ON-LINE, NONECONOMIC DAMAGE REFORM, *available at* http://www.namic.org/reports/tortreform/noneconomicdamage.asp (last visited Sept. 25, 2008).

16. *See* AMERICAN TORT REFORM ASS'N, TORT REFORM RECORD, Dec. 19, 2007, *available at* http://www.atra.org/files.cgi/8140_Record_12–07.pdf.

17. *Cf.* Charles Silver, *Does Civil Justice Cost Too Much?*, 80 TEX. L. REV. 2073, 2088 (2002) [hereinafter Silver, *Civil Justice*].

18. *See* Patricia M. Danzon, *Contingent Fees for Personal Injury Litigation*, 14 BELL J. ECON. 213, 222 (1984) ("The reduction in expected payoff will reduce the number of claims filed."); *Boivin v. Black*, 225 F.3d 36, 45 (1st Cir. 2000) (recognizing that fee caps reduce contingency fee litigation by "forc[ing] both lawyer and client, out of self interest, to assess likely outcomes with greater care before filing a suit that, even if nominally successful, might leave them holding a nearly empty bag"); James H. Stock & David A. Wise, *Market Compensation in Class Action Suits, A Summary of Basic Ideas and Results*, 16 CLASS ACTION REPORTER 584, 601 (1993). Stock and Wise studied the connection between the level of compensation and the level of risk that plaintiffs' lawyers are willing

to undertake. *Id.* at 584–85. Their economic analysis demonstrated that that "the 'market price' for litigation increases [and decreases] with the risk," and that "the relationship between risk and compensation ... establishes in part the cases that are litigated." *Id.* at 601.

19. *See* Daniel P. Kessler & Daniel L. Rubinfeld, *Empirical Study of the Civil Justice System* § 3.2.1, Nat'l Bureau of Econ. Research, Working Paper No. 10825 (2004), *available at* http://www.nber.org/papers/w10825; CONGRESSIONAL BUDGET OFFICE PAPER, THE EFFECTS OF TORT REFORM: EVIDENCE FROM THE STATES 11 (2004), *available at* www.cbo.gov; Kenneth E. Thorpe, *The Medical Malpractice 'Crisis': Recent Trends and the Impact of State Tort Reform*, HEALTH AFFAIRS – WEB EXCLUSIVE (Jan. 21, 2004), *available at* http://content.healthaffairs.org/cgi/reprint/hlthaff.w4.20v1.pdf; W. Kip Viscusi, *Tort Reform and Insurance Markets* 12 n.11 (Harvard John M. Olin Ctr. for Law, Econ. and Bus., Discussion Paper No. 440, 2003), *available at* http://www.law.harvard.edu/programs/olin_center/; Patricia Born, W. Kip Viscusi & Tom Baker, *The Effects of Tort Reform on Medical Malpractice Insurers' Ultimate Losses*, Harvard John M. Olin Discussion Paper 554, July 2006 *available at* http://ssrn.com/abstract=921441 (concluding that caps on noneconomic damages and limits on joint and several liability are associated with lower levels of reported losses by insurance companies and have the intended effect on the overall level of awards and settlements that insurers pay, see *id.* at 13, and summarizing the results of prior studies that conclude that caps on damages reduce mean payments in medical malpractice cases, *see id.* at 2.). This relationship has been questioned. *See* Lucinda M. Finley, *The Hidden Victims of Tort Reform: Women, Children, and the Elderly*, 53 EMORY L.J. 1263, 1272 (2004) (noting that there is "no data to establish that damage cap laws have an effect on claims frequency") (citing GENERAL ACCOUNTING OFFICE, MEDICAL MALPRACTICE INSURANCE: MULTIPLE FACTORS HAVE CONTRIBUTED TO INCREASED PREMIUM RATES (2003), *available at* http://www.gao.gov/new.items/d03702.pdf. *Cf.* Ronen Avraham, *An Empirical Study of the Impact of Tort Reforms on Medical Malpractice Payments*, 36 J. LEGAL STUD. S183 (June 2007 Supplement) (This study of effects of six types of tort reforms on the frequency, size, and total annual settlements in medical malpractice cases between 1991 and 1998 indicates that three of the reforms had no statistically significant effect but that three other reforms did have an effect.).

20. *See* Chapter 14 § A, text at nn.18–22.

21. In 1975, California enacted the Medical Injury Compensation Reform Act (MICRA), capping pain and suffering damages at $250,000, Civ. Code § 3333.2, and in 1987, imposing a sliding scale cap on attorney fees. *See* CAL. BUS. & PROF. CODE § 6146. An obstetrician in Los Angeles paid about $60,588 in 2002 for malpractice insurance, whereas an obstetrician in New York City paid $89,317 and

in Miami, a staggering $201,376. *See* Richard S. Biondi and Arthur Gurevitch, *The Evidence Is In*, Contingencies, Nov./Dec. 2003, at 31–32. The anti-tort reform contingent argues that California's significantly lower premiums for OBs is not due to MICRA. Instead, they argue that California's lower rates are a consequence of subsequently imposed insurance regulation. However, the AMA reports that medical liability premiums in California have increased only 167% since MICRA as opposed to a 505% increase across the rest of the country. American Medical Association, MICRA vs. Prop. 103: Why are Medical Liability Premiums Stable and Competitive in California?, http://www.amaassn.org/ama/pub/upload/mm/399/micraprop.pdf (last visited Oct. 29, 2008). Finally, another study shows that malpractice premiums per physician in states without caps are 33% higher than in states with caps. *Id.* at fig.5. Moreover, claim frequencies are 15% lower in states with caps. *Id.* at fig.3. Finally, a 2004 study found that MICRA's damage caps alone resulted in a 30% decrease in attorney fees, while MICRA's fee limits alone resulted in a 46% decrease in attorney fees. *See* Nicholas M. Pace et al., Capping noneco-nomic Awards in Medical Malpractice Trials: California Jury Verdicts Under MICRA, Rand Inst. for civil Justice, at 36 fig.4.1 (2004), *available at* http://www.rand.org/pubs/monographs/2004/RAND_MG234.pdf. In total, MICRA's damage caps and fee limits resulted in a 60% decrease in attorneys fees. *See id.*

22. Other noneconomic damages include loss of consortium and disfigurement.

23. *See* Victor E. Schwartz & Leah Lorber, *Twisting the Purpose of Pain and Suffering Awards: Turning Compensation Into "Punishment,"* 54 S.C. L. Rev. 47, 64 (2002) [hereinafter Schwartz & Lorber, *Turning Compensation Into "Punishment"*] ("Recently, pain and suffering awards and other noneco-nomic damages in asbestos, pharmaceutical, and other personal injury cases have been increasing. They have reached hundred-million dollar levels."). The average award for pain and suffering experienced before death increased from $48,000 in 1960–1969 to $147,000 in 1980–1987, adjusted for inflation – almost 300%. David W. Leebron, *Final Moments: Damages for Pain and Suffering Prior to Death*, 64 N.Y.U. L. Rev. 256, 345 (1989).

24. *See, e.g.*, Mark Geistfeld, *Placing a Price on Pain and Suffering: A Method for Helping Juries Determine Tort Damages for Nonmonetary Injuries*, 83 Cal. Rev. 773, 777 (1995) [hereinafter Geistfeld, *Placing a Price on Pain and Suffering*]; Ronen Avraham, Pain-and-Suffering Damages in Tort Law: Revisiting the Theoretical Framework and the Empirical Data 7 (Feb. 2003), *available at* http://papers.ssrn.com/sol3/papers.cfm?abstract_id=382120; P.C. Weiler, Medical Malpractice on Trial (1991), at 55 n.36; *see also* Steven P. Croley & Jon D. Hanson, *The Nonpecuniary Costs of Accidents: Pain-and-Suffering Damages in Tort Law*, 108 Harv. L. Rev. 1785, 1789 (1995).

25. TILLINGHAST, TOWERS PERRIN, 2002 UPDATE ON U.S. TORT COSTS TRENDS (2002) [hereinafter TILLINGHAST 2002]; TILLINGHAST, TOWERS PERRIN, 2005 UPDATE ON U.S. TORT COSTS TRENDS (2005) [hereinafter TILLINGHAST 2005].

26. *See* Jeffrey O'Connell & Theodore M. Bailey, *The History of Pain & Suffering*, in Jeffrey O'Connell & Rita James Simon, *Payment for Pain & Suffering: Who Wants What, When & Why?*, 1972 U. ILL. L.F. 1, 883 App. 5.

27. Mark Geistfeld, *Placing a Price on Pain and Suffering, supra*, at 801.

28. CHARLES WOLFRAM, MODERN LEGAL ETHICS 528 n.21(1986).

29. Richard Abel, *General Damages Are Incoherent and Incalculable, Incommensurable, and Inegalitarian (But Otherwise A Great Idea)*, 55 DEPAUL L. REV. 253, 323 (2006) (footnotes omitted) [hereinafter Able, *General Damages*].

30. *See* John Fabian Witt, *The Political Economy of Pain* 2, Paper Delivered at Brookings Institution Forum on "The Boundaries of Litigation," Apr. 15, 2008; *infra* note 39.

31. John Fabian Witt described Belli as

a flamboyant, decadent, embarrassing, self-promoting and ethically challenged showman lawyer. The King of Torts, as *Life Magazine* dubbed him in 1954, was a man of scarlet silk-lined suits, of multi-colored Rolls Royces, of courtroom theatrics and Hollywood high-jinks. He was the oafish lawyer to Jack Ruby in the murder of Lee Harvey Oswald, and he was the crass ambulance chaser who landed in Bhopal, India, to sign up plaintiffs while people were still dying of exposure to the poisonous cloud at the Union Carbide plant. As early as the middle of the 1960s such behavior by Belli caused the trial lawyers' organization to distance itself from him. But the early Belli, the Belli of the 1940s and 1950s, had been a dynamo, a man who almost single-handedly galvanized the trial lawyers and reoriented them away from the administrative bureaucracy of workmen's compensation back toward the courts, where the cases were more lucrative and more congenial to Belli's brand of showmanship.

Id. at 24–25 (footnote omitted).

32. Melvin M. Belli, *The Adequate Award*, 39 CAL. L. REV. 1 (1951).

33. *Id.* at 1.

34. *Id.* at 37.

35. Witt describes Belli's technique:

Illustrating pain and suffering played to the strong suit of charismatic mid-century trial lawyers like Belli. They liked to farm out the doctrinal niceties to specialist brief writers. Courtroom theatrics, by contrast, were their specialty, and this is where Belli excelled. In packed lecture halls and in best-selling books he taught overflow audiences and tens of thousands of readers how to describe and (better yet) reconstruct pain for a jury. The per-diem method was among his best known contributions to the art of presenting pain. How much money would it take, Belli liked to ask his juries, to make you whole for even a day of the pain of the plaintiff? Take that number and multiply it by the plaintiff's life expectancy, and the pain and suffering damages seemed sure to be higher than the defense would like ...

Belli's multi-volume book, *Modern Trials*, published at the height of his powers in the late 1950s and early 1960s ... showed trial lawyers ... the myriad ways to dwell on and describe pain in the courtroom. Pictures, he wrote, were worth a thousand words. And photographs that sought to capture his clients' pain were one of Belli's calling cards. The more gruesome the imagery, the better the photo. Badly burned hands, mangled bodies, and more – all featured in Belli's photographic shop of horrors ...

What Belli called "demonstrative evidence" was sometimes even better. One of Belli's best known courtroom tricks was the prosthetic limb hidden in thickly wrapped butcher paper in a case involving an amputated leg. In another case, he used a crane to lift a 600-pound bedridden client through the window of a second-floor courtroom. One way or another, Belli explained, the trial lawyer needed to get the jury to try to "picture" the pain of the plaintiff. The more lurid the picture the better. But in a pinch even the accumulated prescription slips for pain medication would do.

Words were good, too, of course. Belli talked about pain like the apocryphal Eskimo talks about snow. There were at least forty different kinds of pain, he asserted, and he proceeded to instruct his audiences in an elaborate taxonomy of kinds and types of pain their clients might be suffering. He distinguished "physical pain and suffering" from "mental pain and suffering," which in turn he distinguished from "embarrassment, ridicule, and humiliation," each of which he insisted could be an independent basis for intangible damages without an impermissible double counting.]

John Fabian Witt, *The Political Economy of Pain* 2 at 28–31, paper delivered at Brookings Institution Forum on "The Boundaries of Litigation," Apr. 15, 2008 (footnotes omitted).

36. *See* David W. Lebron, *Final Moments: Damages for Pain and Suffering Prior to Death*, 64 N.Y.U. L. REV. 256, 301 (1989).

37. In 1999, the average pain and suffering award had increased by almost 4.5 times the average in 1989. *See* Kim Brimer, *Has "Pain and Suffering" Priced Itself Out of the Market*, INS. J., Sept. 8, 2003, *available at* http://www.insurancejournal.com/magazines/southcentral/2003/09/08/partingshots/32172.htm.

38. *See* Robert P. Hartwig, *Liability Insurance and Excess Casualty Markets: Trends, Issue & Outlook*, at 51 (Ins. Info. Inst., Oct. 2003), *available at* http://server.iii.org/yy_obj_data/binary/686661_1_0/liability.pdf.

39. *See, e.g.*, 2 AM. LAW INST., REPORTERS' STUDY: ENTERPRISE RESPONSIBILITY FOR PERSONAL INJURY 199 (1991); Ronald J. Allen & Alexia Brunet, *The Judicial Treatment of Non-economic Compensatory Damages in the 19th Century*, 4 J. EMP. LEGAL STUD. 365 (2007) [hereinafter Allen & Brunet, *Noneconomic Damages*] (indicating that whereas high verdicts for noneconomic compensatory damages have accelerated and proliferated, there is no historical precedent for these high verdicts; that in the past, judges tightly controlled awards of noneconomic damages and uniformly reversed high awards so much that only two cases affirmed on appeal prior to 1901 involved noneconomic compensatory damages "in which the total damages ([noneconomic] and economic combined) exceeded $450,000 in current dollars." *Id.* at 397; Mark Geistfeld, *Placing a Price on Pain and Suffering, supra*; Louis L. Jaffe, *Damages for Personal Injury: The Impact of Insurance*, 18 LAW & CONTEMP. PROBS. 219 (1953); Jeffrey O'Connell & Rita James Simon, *Payment for Pain & Suffering: Who Wants What, When & Why?*, 1972 U. ILL. L.F. 1 (1972).

40. *Donahoo v. Turner Const. Co.*, 833 F. Supp. 621, 623 (E.D. Mich. 1993).

41. Paul V. Niemeyer, *Awards for Pain and Suffering: The Irrational Centerpiece of Our Tort System*, 90 VA. L. REV. 1401, 1401, 1418, 1420–21 (2004).

42. Paul DeCamp, *Beyond* State Farm: *Due Process Constraints on Noneconomic Compensatory Damages*, 27 HARV. J.L. & PUB. POL'Y 231, 235, 257 (2003) (arguing for the regulation of noneconomic damages to ensure that such awards comport with the Due Process Clause); *see also* Mark A. Geistfeld, *Due Process and the Determination of Pain and Suffering Tort Damages*, 55 DePaul L. Rev. 331 (2006).

43. *See State Farm Mut. Auto. Ins. Co. v. Campbell*, 538 U.S. 408, 416 (2003); *see also Cooper Indus., Inc. v. Leatherman Tool Group, Inc.*, 539 U.S. 424 (2001); *BMW of N. Am. v. Gore*, 517 U.S. 559 (1996).

44. Schwartz & Lorber, *Turning Compensation Into "Punishment," supra* note 23, at 64, 68 (discussing verdicts that appear to be prompted by a desire to punish rather than to compensate including *Lampe v. Cont'l Gen. Tire, Inc.*, No. BC 173567, slip op. at 6 [L.A. Super. Ct. Apr. 20, 2001]) (jury awarded $41 million for noneconomic damages out of a total award of $49.85 million in compensatory damages); *Brown v. Berdex*, No. 120595/00, 2002 WL 481102, at *1 (N.Y. Sup. Ct. Feb. 8, 2002) (total award of $53 million; $17 million for pain and suffering damages); *Evans v. St. Mary's Hosp. of Brooklyn*, No. 4038/91, slip op. at 1 (N.Y. Co. Super. Ct. [Nov. 9, 2001]) (total award of $115 million; $100 million for pain and suffering damages); *see also* David W. Clark, *Life in Lawsuit Central: An Overview of the Unique Aspects of Mississippi's Civil Justice System*, 71 MISS. L.J. 359, 389 (2001) ("Allowing juries to use noneconomic damages to 'punish' defendants would defeat the purpose of limiting punitive damages."); Allen & Brunet, *Non-Economic Damages, supra*, at 2

("[Noneconomic] compensatory damages are ... virtually identical to punitive damages in the risks they pose for rational decision making.").

45. *See* Schwartz & Lorber, *id.*

46. *See American Tort Reform Association, State and Federal Reforms, available at* http://www.atra.org/reforms/ (last visited Nov. 20, 2008).

47. Professor King's point about "uncertainty of valuation" is well taken. Jury determinations of damages including pain and suffering vary widely. In a multiparty product liability case tried in Texas before five separate juries, each jury reached substantially different verdicts despite hearing the same facts. *See* KAGAN, ADVERSARIAL LEGALISM, *supra* Introduction, note 13, at 127; *see also* Randall R. Bovbjerg et al., *Valuing Life and Limb in Tort: Scheduling "Pain and Suffering,"* 83 Nw. U. L. REV. 908, 924–27 (1989); Oscar G. Chase, *Helping Jurors Determine Pain and Suffering Awards,* 23 HOFSTRA L. REV. 763, 768–69 (1995); Shari Seidman et al., *Juror Judgments About Liability and Damages: Sources of Variability and Ways to Increase Consistency,* 48 DEPAUL L. REV. 301, 313–17 (1998); Frederick S. Levin, *Pain and Suffering Guidelines: A Cure for Damages Measurement "Anomie,"* 22 U. MICH. J.L. REFORM 303, 307–11 (1989); Frank A. Sloan & Chee Ruey Hsieh, *Variability in Medical Malpractice Payments: Is the Compensation Fair?,* 24 LAW & SOC'Y REV. 997, 997–99 (1990); W. Kip Viscusi, *Pain and Suffering in Product Liability Cases: Systematic Compensation or Capricious Awards?,* 8 INT'L REV. L. & ECON. 203 (1988); Joseph Sanders, *Why Do Proposals Designed to Control Variability in General Damages (Generally) Fall on Deaf Ears? (And Why This Is Too Bad),* 55 DEPAUL L. REV. 489, 494 (2006).

48. Joseph H. King Jr., *Pain and Suffering, Noneconomic Damages, and the Goals of Tort Law,* 57 SMU L. REV. 163, 205–08 (2004).

49. Stephen D. Sugarman, *A Comparative Law Look at Pain and Suffering Awards,* 55 DEPAUL L. REV. 399, 401 (2006).

50. *See* Junda Woo & Charles Goldsmith, *Injury Awards in Europe,* WALL ST. J., Mar. 22, 1994, at B5 (citing a study by Davies Arnold Cooper, a British Law Firm, which looked at estimated compensation for fourteen types of injuries in the European Union).

51. WOLFRAM, MODERN LEGAL ETHICS, *supra*, at 528 n.21 ("Pain and suffering and similar nonmonetary damages probably average three times the monetary damages in personal injury claims."). Other legal scholars have suggested that the multiple may be higher. *See* H. LAURENCE ROSS, SETTLED OUT OF COURT: THE SOCIAL PROCESS OF INSURANCE CLAIMS ADJUSTMENTS 107–08 (1970) (stating that the multiple is an "arbitrary coefficient – typically from two to five, depending on the practice area"); JEFFREY O'CONNELL, ENDING INSULT TO INJURY: NO-FAULT INSURANCE FOR PRODUCTS AND SERVICES 51 (1975)

(stating that the multiple is between two and ten); Neil Vidmar & Jeffrey J. Rice, *Assessments of Noneconomic Damage Awards in Medical Negligence: A Comparison of Jurors with Legal Professionals*, 78 IOWA L. REV. 883, 894 (1993) ("Judges and attorneys in North Carolina frequently speak of an informal guideline that suggests that noneconomic damages should be between three and seven times the amount of economic damages."); Daniels & Martin, *The Strange Success of Tort Reform, supra*, at 1249–50 (based on a survey of 408 plaintiffs' lawyers in Texas, conducted in late 1999 through 2000, the "average multiplier ... was 1.7 times" economic damages and that five years earlier, the average multiplier was 3.3).

52. *See* Jeffrey O'Connell, *The Large Cost Savings and Other Advantages of a "Crimetorts" Approach to Medical Malpractice Claims*, 17 WIDENER L. J. 835, tbl.1, pan.A (2008).

53. *See* Jeffrey O' Connell & Patricia Born, *The Cost and Other Advantages of Early Offers Reform for Product Liability Claims*, 2008 COLUM. BUS. L. REV. 423 at tbl.1, pan.A (2008).

54. *See* INS. RESEARCH COUNCIL, AUTO INJURY INSURANCE CLAIMS: COUNTRYWIDE PATTERNS IN TREATMENT, COST, AND COMPENSATION, 72, fig. 6–3 (2003) (The data from this 2002 study show an average bodily injury (BI) payment of $8,245 and an average economic loss, i.e. mostly medical expenses and lost wages, of $5,520, a payment-to-loss ratio of 1.49. Previous studies from 1977, 1987, 1992, and 1997 showed ratios of 2.29, 2.11, 1.87, and 1.65, respectively.) Whereas ostensibly the most current ratio indicates that for every $1 of economic loss, $0.49 is paid for general damages (pain and suffering), there is considerable evidence that the ratio understates actual payment experience. In one-third of cases where BI payment values were less than losses, Personal Injury Protection (PIP) benefits paid basic economic loss, thus lowering the actual amount paid and increasing the amount of general damages paid. *Id.* at 70. Moreover, medical charges were reduced or disallowed in 41% of cases in which payment was less than loss, again decreasing the amount of economic loss reimbursed and increasing the amount of general damages paid. *Id.* In addition, the ratio is skewed downward in more severe cases as measured by higher economic loss, which may reflect exhaustion of insurance coverage. *Id.* at 81. Because economic losses may have been paid from other sources or not paid in full, and actual payments may not have reimbursed all losses, the actual amount paid for noneconomic losses (pain and suffering) was in fact higher than reflected by the ratio. *Id.* at 75 fig.6–6 (on average, 59% of total actual payment represents general damages [noneconomic damages]). Based on the data that payment for noneconomic damages constitutes 59% of the actual amounts paid, the amount of noneconomic loss paid per one dollar of economic loss paid is actually 1.44:1. *Id.*

My conclusion that this ratio understates actual payment experience is buttressed by accounts of settlement practices at firms specializing in high-volume, low-value automobile accident cases. There, settlements clustered in the area of three to four times medical bills. *See* Nora F. Engstrom, *Run-of-the-Mill Justice*, 22 GEO. J. LEGAL ETHICS 1485, 1507–08 (2009).

55. THOMAS H. COHEN, BUREAU OF JUSTICE STATISTICS, TORT TRIALS AND VERDICTS IN LARGE COUNTIES, 2001, at 2, *available at* http://www.ojp.usdoj.gov/bjs/pub/pdf/ttvlc01.pdf [hereinafter TORT TRIALS AND VERDICTS 2001].

56. Median final award amounts to plaintiffs for automobile, product liability, and medical malpractice cases were $16,000, $450,000, and $422,000, respectively. TORT TRIALS AND VERDICTS 2001, at 4 tbl. 4.

57. Jeffery O'Connell, *Blending Reform of Tort Liability and Health Insurance: A Necessary Mix*, 79 CORNELL L. REV. 1303, 1306–07 (1994) [hereinafter O'Connell, *Blending Reform*]; *see also* Stanley Ingber, *Rethinking Intangible Injuries: A Focus on Remedy*, 73 CAL. L. REV. 772, 779 (1985).

58. *See* INS. RESEARCH COUNCIL, PAYING FOR AUTO INJURIES, at 43 (2004). A 1994 study by the IRC indicates that average economic losses for represented claimants were about 3.6 times higher than unrepresented clients. IRC, AUTO INJURIES: CLAIMING BEHAVIOR AND ITS IMPACT ON INSURANCE COSTS at 3, 31–32, 61 (1994). A 1999 study showed a rate of 2.7 ($14,165 for average economic loss for represented claimants versus $5,228 for unrepresented claimants). INS. RESEARCH COUNCIL, PAYING FOR AUTO INJURIES, at 51 (1999).

59. In a 1989 study, the average economic loss for a claimant with a weight-bearing bone fracture who was represented was $13,275 versus $8,464 for unrepresented claimants, a 1.56:1 ratio; and the average economic loss for a claimant with a back sprain or strain who was represented was $7,534 versus $2,198 for one who was not represented, a 3.43:1 ratio. ALL INDUS. RESEARCH ADVISORY COUNCIL, COMPENSATION FOR AUTO INJURIES IN THE U.S. 103–05 (1989) [hereinafter AIRAC, Compensation for Auto Injuries].

60. *See* IRC, AUTO INJURIES: CLAIMING BEHAVIOR, *supra* note 58, at 62–63; INS. RESEARCH COUNCIL, INJURIES IN AUTO ACCIDENTS: AN ANALYSIS OF AUTO INSURANCE CLAIMS 91 & Figs. 7–14, 7–15, 7–16, and 7–17.

61. IRC, AUTO INJURIES: CLAIMING BEHAVIOR, *supra* note 58, at 62–63.

62. *Id*. at 64.

63. *Id*. at 66.

64. Ian H. Harris et al., *The Effect of Compensation on Health Care Utilization in a Trauma Cohort*, 190 MED. J. AUSTR. 619, 622 (June 2009).

65. Consider the following additional data. After Massachusetts amended its no-fault law in 1988 to raise the threshold level of economic damages for bringing a lawsuit from $1,000 to $2,000, the median number of claims-related medical treatment visits per claimant rose immediately from thirteen to thirty.

See SARAH S. MARTER & HERBERT I. WEISBERG, *Medical Expenses and the Massachusetts Automobile Tort Reform Law: A First Review of 1989 Bodily Injury Liability Claims*, 10 J. INS. REG. 462, 488 tbl. 12 (1992). Although the increase in the number of doctor visits could be the natural result of raising the tort threshold (i.e. as the threshold dollar amount rises, the average number of doctor visits of those whose injuries are valued at greater than the threshold amount will necessarily rise also), evidence strongly suggests that lawyer-driven forces played a significant part in that increase. *See* Richard A. Derrig et al., *Behavioral Factors and Lotteries Under No-Fault with a Monetary Threshold: A Study of Massachusetts Automobile Claims*, 61 J. RISK & INS. 245 (1994). For example, in one study, before the increase of the damages threshold, the percentage of bodily-injury claims that involved medical cost buildup was approximately 33%; after the threshold increase, nearly 47% appeared to involve buildup. A study of the distribution of total claimed medical charges for strain/sprain claims also supports the conclusion that the increased medical charges were due to lawyers seeking to ensure that clients reached the $2,000 threshold. The distribution of these types of claims was highly bimodal and not typical of natural economic phenomena. Instead of the expected high number of small-valued claims and a small proportion of high-valued claims, there was a second peak just above the $2,000 threshold and very few claims between $1,000 and $2,000. This indicates that claims, which normally would have resulted in less than $2,000 in medical charges, were artificially inflated to achieve this level. *Id.* at 258. The study also found that the presence of a lawyer was one of the strongest predictors of who would file a claim and who would reach the threshold. This factor, more than the injury itself, determined whether the threshold would be reached.

66. *See* Derrig et al., *id.*

67. *Id.* at 56–57.

68. *Id.* at 57–58.

69. IRC, AUTO INJURIES: CLAIMING BEHAVIOR, *supra*, at 67; IRC, PAYING FOR AUTO INJURIES, *supra*, at 8 & tbl. 2–21. A study of auto tort claims in Hawaii in 1990 indicates that the median number of treatment visits by claimants visiting chiropractors was fifty-eight and that one-quarter of such claimants have more than eighty-four visits! *See* INSURANCE RESEARCH COUNCIL, AUTOMOBILE INJURY CLAIMS IN HAWAII, at 2, 26–27 (May 1991); Derrig et al., *supra*, at 67. Not only did chiropractors average a greater number of visits in general, but they had a much higher number of visits than did medical doctors when the same type of injuries were reported as the most serious. *Id.* at 10.

70. IRC, PAYING FOR AUTO INJURIES, *supra* note 58, at 29 & tbl. 4–2; *see also* IRC, AUTO INJURIES: CLAIMING BEHAVIOR, *supra*, at 68, for variations by state; Derrig et al., *supra*, at 67.

71. For example, 68% of represented BI claimants in California used at least one procedure, compared to only 45% of nonrepresented claimants. IRC, Auto Injuries: Claiming Behavior, *supra* note 58, at 69.

72. IRC, Auto Injuries: Claiming Behavior, *supra* note 58, at 60–61; *see also* IRC, Paying For Auto Injuries, *supra* note 58, at 30–32 (showing that for all injuries, attorney-represented claimants suffered an average net loss of $1,665, whereas the nonrepresented claimants suffered an average net loss of $144). The disparity in net payments favoring unrepresented auto accident claimants over represented claimants may, in part, be attributable to a higher frequency of recovery for represented claimants. The IRC data assumes that claimants did not obtain double recoveries by also being reimbursed by health care insurance or auto insurance medical payment coverage and that legal expenses included a 31% contingency fee and 2% court costs. No data is presented with regard to the validity of the assumption that claimants did not obtain double recoveries.

73. IRC, Paying For Auto Injuries, *supra* note 58, at 32.

74. For example, the cost to society in 1992 from a represented BI claimant was the average payment ($11,939) plus average medical expense ($4,579) twice, resulting in a gross payment of $21,097. The nonrepresented claimant would receive payments totaling $6,036 ($3,262 average payment plus average medical expense [$1,387] twice), a spread of $15,061. Yet the attorney-represented claimant received a $6,187 average net payment ($1,608 average net payment plus $4,579 average medical expense), and the nonrepresented claimant received $2,894 average net payment ($1,507 average net payment plus $1,387 average medical expense), a spread of $3,293 in favor of attorney involvement. IRC, Auto Injuries: Claiming Behavior, *supra*, at 60–62.

75. Excess medical claiming includes claims "based on staged or nonexistent activities, claims for nonexistent injuries when the accidents were real, and buildup of claims for real injuries to leverage a settlement from the insurance company." Stephen Carroll, Allan Abrahamse, Mary Vaiana, RAND, The Costs of Excess Medical Claims for Automobile Personal Injuries 3–4, 23 (1995).

76. As a consequence of excess medical claims, about $4 billion in health care costs were consumed in 1993 at a cost of $9 billion to $13 billion to insurers in compensation for noneconomic loss and other costs. If insurers passed these costs onto insurance premiums, then excess medical claims cost insurance purchasers $13 billion to $18 billion in 1993. Rand, *supra*, at 3, 23.

77. *See* Consumer Price Index (CPI) Conversion Factors *available at* http://oregonstate.edu/cla/polisci/faculty-research/sahr/cv2008.pdf (last visited Nov. 20, 2008).

78. Denise Grady, *In One Country, Chronic Whiplash Is Uncompensated (and Unknown)*, N.Y. Times, May 7, 1996 at C3 [hereinafter Grady, *Whiplash Is*

Uncompensated]; *see also Saving Our Necks in Car Crashes*, CONSUMERS' RES. MAG., DEC. 12, 1995, at 28 (66% of auto injury claims for bodily injuries include neck sprains).

79. *See* INSURANCE RESEARCH COUNCIL, TRENDS IN AUTO INJURY CLAIMS (2000), at 32.

80. Grady, *Whiplash Is Uncompensated, supra* note 78.

16 Class Actions

NOTHING MORE EPITOMIZES THE ASCENDANCY OF THE contingency fee into the pantheon of elemental forces driving our legal and political systems than the contingency-fee-driven class action. In a class action, a lawyer representing a single person or a small handful of people – who claim to stand for hundreds, thousands, or even millions of similarly situated persons – asserts that the defendant caused the entire "class" physical or economic injury.

A change in procedural law forty years ago transformed class actions from a sleepy backwater of legal activity into one of the greatest money-making mechanisms ever invented. A 1966 amendment to Rule 23 of the Federal Rules of Civil Procedure, which initiated this change, allowed lawyers to assemble huge numbers of consumers into a collective (class) action, subject to the right, in most class actions, of anyone so conscripted to "opt out" by filing with the court.[1] Prior to the amendment, class actions could only be formed if claimants opted in – that is, affirmatively elected to join the litigation. After 1966, those conscripted into the class formed by a plaintiff's lawyer remain included in the litigation unless they affirmatively take steps to exclude themselves.

The rule makers responsible for the change saw it as modest procedural reform and did not expect it to profoundly affect the litigation landscape.[2] In particular, they did not view the changes as affecting such large-scale personal injury litigation as mass torts. In a note accompanying the proposed rule, they stated:

> A "mass accident" resulting in injuries to numerous persons is *ordinarily not appropriate* for a class action because of the likelihood that significant questions, not only of damages but of liability and defenses to liability, would be present, affecting the individuals in different ways. In these circumstances an action conducted nominally as a class action would degenerate in practice into multiple lawsuits separately tried.[3]

Those who wrote the rule, however, could not foresee how lawyers' financial incentives in the form of contingency fees would interact with this rule change and the great expansion of the scope of tort liability that began in the 1960s. Lawyers were able to turn the "ordinarily not appropriate" language on its head as their opportunistic quest for profits overwhelmed the cautionary stance of the drafters. The "modest procedural reform" has empowered courts and lawyers to exercise significant regulatory control over large parts of our economy and has created a class of lawyer "sheiks" able to extract hundreds of millions of dollars for volunteering their services as bounty hunters. Even if the great majority of the many thousands conscripted into a putative class would oppose the action if they were polled, a lawyer need only find one person to act in a representative capacity in order to proceed. As for the rest of the class, consumer inertia coupled with paltry benefits assures that few – less than 0.2 percent according to a study – have the interest or the incentive to file with the court to opt out of the action.[4] Were the pre-1966 law still in force, this same inertia would result in few consumers electing to join most class actions, especially given the sparse or nonexistent benefits that many provide. In effect, the 1966 amendment gave lawyers a giant vacuum to suction up consumers by the thousands, and even millions, to provide the leverage that has compelled virtually every major corporation in the land to pay a negotiated tribute.

A. Social Benefits versus Costs

Class actions are intended to be an efficient and fair mechanism for the resolution of claims because they allow aggregation of large numbers of factually similar claims of compensation for injury to the person or pocketbook into a single lawsuit.[5] In addition to this compensatory function, class actions also provide a means of dealing with claims that are too small to justify the expense of individual litigation. For these "negative-value" cases, the principal purpose of allowing an aggregated action is not compensation for individuals' small losses but rather to force the defendant to cough up its ill-gotten gains.

The benefits that flow from providing incentives for class action lawyers to act as "private attorneys general"[6] in negative-value cases, however, comes at a considerable cost. First, as detailed in these four chapters, many class actions are based on highly dubious claims of wrongdoing and do far more to advance lawyers' interests than those of consumers. Second, the amendment to Federal Rule 23 allowing for the modern day class action was enacted under a statute that allowed the U.S. Supreme Court to promulgate procedural rules so long as they did not abridge, enlarge, or modify substantive law.[7] The distinction between procedural and substantive rules is one of the great mysteries in the legal literature. Often, the choice of whether the rule is deemed to be one or the other is based on which best advances the agenda of the advocate. Even so, few can deny that the amendment to Rule 23 of the Federal Rules of Procedure has effected profound changes in substantive law.[8] Whether or not consumers are better off because lawyers have been empowered to roam the land looking for opportunities to file class actions is a task I leave to others.

The dominant view of legal academics is that class actions are socially beneficial because (1) they are often the only way by which certain injured or defrauded victims can obtain compensation; and (2) punishing corporations that engage in wrongful conduct deters the future commission of wrongful acts, and thus advances social welfare.[9] Indeed, the more money corporations have to cough up because of class actions, the greater the claimed deterrent effect.[10]

The deterrence argument is fundamentally flawed because deterrence can only occur if the entity to be deterred can reasonably anticipate that a particular act may result in liability. Plausibly, corporations can be expected to exercise more care to avoid causing injury to consumers if the financial penalties are increased. However, many class actions are no more than inventions of fertile lawyers' minds. Businesses can hardly anticipate when they will be subject to liability for performing or not performing an act when the law they are alleged to have violated is amorphous or the alleged injury is mostly pure invention.

Moreover, there is little, if any, empirical evidence that class actions deter fraudulent practices such as those engaged by corporate officers at Enron and WorldCom Companies.[11] It is impossible to determine whether and to what extent corporate officers in other contexts who had intended to defraud investors have been deterred from doing so by fear of class action lawsuits. Anecdotal evidence suggests, however, that the rewards of fraud outweigh the fear of class action lawsuits that, in any event, virtually never target those responsible for defrauding investors. Scholars' belief in deterrence is an article of faith – a conviction that if corporations pay billions to settle class actions and enrich lawyers by commensurate amounts, then that *must* be good for society. As for the evidence that lawyers often wield class actions as cudgels to extract bountiful fees without any remotely commensurate benefit to society, that evidence is simply dismissed as a "mirage."[12]

Finally, the assumption that payment to settle a class action equates with deterrence is an assertion without foundation. The fact that a corporation agrees to settle a class action by making a substantial payment does not mean that a wrong has been righted. Although there is no shortage of wrongful conduct committed by corporations, the dynamics of the class action apparatus confer an awesome power on lawyers to extract wealth from corporations on the basis of even the flimsiest claims of wrongdoing.[13] Virtually all companies agree to settle class actions once certain procedural requirements have been met, irrespective of the merits of the suits. This is because lawyers can impose formidable costs on the companies they sue. Besides legal fees, these costs include producing the thousands and even millions of documents sought by the plaintiffs' lawyers during discovery. As noted by the U.S. Supreme Court, "the threat of discovery expense will push cost conscious defendants to settle even anemic cases" during the pretrial stage.[14] Even if there is no compelling evidence of fraud or other wrongful conduct, given these substantial costs, most companies are willing to settle a class action for an amount that approximates the cost they would have incurred if they had defended the action. In addition, when it comes to class actions, corporate CEOs are risk-averse. Even if the prospect of losing the litigation is remote, when damages alleged are substantial, CEOs would rather agree to pay what is required to extricate the company from a lawyer's snares than take the remote risk that a jury, spellbound by an accomplished orator decrying how companies put "profits over people," could levy huge damages that because of certain procedural requirements could not realistically be appealed. The specter of a bet-the-company scenario, which might lead to bankruptcy or otherwise cost the CEO his job, leads CEOs to invariably elevate their own short-term interests over the long-term interests of their companies and agree to settle.

Some commentators argue that settlements are merits-driven rather than products of the dynamics of class action litigation.[15] It is certainly the case that some corporations have defrauded or inflicted harm on large numbers of consumers. But no effective means has been devised to restrict the use of class actions to these instances. Proof of this proposition can be found in the anomaly that virtually all securities class actions that have received judicial approval to proceed and all mass tort class actions that have been found to have met the procedural requirements for class certification are settled. George Priest observes that "[f]or any subset of cases, uniform settlement and zero litigation is an extraordinary empirical fact, neither predicted by nor consistent with *any* current economic model of litigation and settlement."[16] The argument that the merits are determinative of class action outcomes is further belied by the settlement of some mass tort litigations that were based mainly on phony causation theories and bogus medical evidence.[17]

B. Regulation for Profit

Entrepreneurial lawyers have expanded the domain of the class action to encompass virtually every area of tort liability and beyond. According to U.S. Court of Appeals Judge Richard Posner, class action lawyers have even been empowered to place "the fate of an industry in the palm" of "[o]ne jury, consisting of six persons."[18] Though this regulatory power towers over the regulatory powers consigned to various federal and state agencies through political processes, it has neither been conferred by Congress nor the electorate. Rather, it is the product of the subterfuge described previously: the use of a procedural device to create substantive laws that bypass the political process, thus undermining democratic precepts.[19] Judicial endorsement of this expansion of the domain of the class action and the ever-increasing amounts of fees paid to lawyers assures a continuous supply of class action filings.

With rare exception, the motivation for exercise of this regulatory power is the pursuit of profit. The pursuit of profit is the touchstone of a capitalist society. But as the economic debacle that began unfolding in 2007 with the subprime mortgage crisis, followed by the near bankruptcy of virtually all major financial institutions, the freezing up of credit, and the painful deleveraging of derivatives and commercial real estate loans makes clear, unbridled capitalism contains the seeds of its own destruction. Yet, class action lawyers, quintessential capitalists, operate in a world devoid of regulatory oversight, save that of courts and, on rare occasions, Congress. Judicial oversight, however, is tempered by the judiciary's inclination to advance its influence over the private sector and the distribution of wealth.[20] Todd Zywicki observes that judges are interested in increasing their power in two ways: (1) relative to the power of the legislative and executive branches, and (2) over society as a whole... Expanding the reach of tort liability, expanding the discretion of judges to redistribute wealth according to their preferences, and giving judges the power to remake tort law so as to accomplish desired ideological and policy goals are consistent with judges' desires to increase their power.[21]

Class actions are the *ne plus ultra* vehicle for courts to redistribute wealth while also increasing their power. Recall the uncommon candor of Chief Judge Dennis Jacobs of the Second Circuit Court of Appeals when he acknowledged:

> [W]hen lawyers present big issues to the courts, the judges receive big issues with grateful hands; the bar patrols against inroads on jurisdiction and independence and praises the expansion of legal authority; and together we smugly congratulate ourselves on expanding what we are pleased to call the rule of law.
>
> Among the results are the displacement of legislative and executive power, the subordination of other disciplines and professions, and the reduction of whole enterprises and industries to damages.[22]

Nothing more epitomizes the "big issues" to which Judge Jacobs is referring than the class action. The symbiotic relationship between the class action bar and the judiciary is one of the most underappreciated political forces in our society. The political system, in the succinct words of Harold Lasswell, one of the most preeminent political scientists of the twentieth century, determines "who gets what, when, [and] how."[23] Class actions have come to play a significant role in determining the outcomes of the political process.

Few jurists would acknowledge that courts have – let alone seek – this level of regulatory power. They, along with the legal academy, acknowledge and endorse the policy of providing lawyers with sufficient incentives to pursue class actions in order to supplement government regulatory agencies that are insufficiently funded or have been captured by the industry being regulated. For both the courts and the legal academy, the effectiveness of this supplemental regulatory function is borne out by the settlement of the vast majority of class actions, once courts have given their imprimatur to the formation of a class of plaintiffs. Settlements are viewed as an acknowledgment of wrongful conduct by corporations. The payments they make contribute to social welfare by creating incentives for class action lawyers to file the actions and by reimbursing victims of the wrongdoing.

The empirical evidence, however, belies this regulatory function of the class action. Professors Eric Helland of Claremont McKenna College and Jonathan Klick of the University of Pennsylvania Law School have undertaken a study of the relationship between regulation and class actions.[24] In their study, they hypothesized that if regulation has deterrent value, the probability that a company will commit a wrongful act is a function of the level of regulation in a jurisdiction (measured by the size of the regulatory budget). We would expect that higher regulatory budgets would be associated with less harm in those jurisdictions and therefore less opportunity or need for class actions.[25] Conversely, where regulatory budgets are tighter, we would expect class actions to occur more frequently. But, in fact, when states provide more resources to regulators, more class actions are filed.[26] In other words, the available empirical evidence is contrary to the claim that class actions are brought to fill gaps in regulatory enforcement.

Moreover, deputizing class action lawyers to enforce laws by extracting payments from corporations represents a fundamental change from the original purposes of the class action. This change is not the result of a congressional policy but rather is the result of class action lawyers seeking fees. The ease with which this change has come about – from providing compensation to a law enforcement function – attests to the power that the class action bar has amassed with the support of the judiciary (which has an interest in expanding its regulatory power) and the cottage industry of law professors and other experts who also have a financial stake in the expansion of class actions.

Proponents of the regulatory function of class actions liken the class action lawyer to the bounty hunter,[27] but this view of the lawyer as bounty hunter is incomplete and misguided. In the Old West, law enforcement staffs were inadequate to handle the level of criminal activity. To supplement these resources, public authorities offered rewards for the apprehension of wanted criminals. Motivated by these financial incentives, bounty hunters set out to capture the fugitive identified by the "wanted" poster and claim the reward. The modern-day class action bounty hunter, however, comes with its own printing press. Driven by the opportunity to obtain millions of dollars in fees, the class action lawyer decides who the wrongdoer is and then proceeds to file a class action based on that belief. Some of the "wanted" posters correctly identify corporate wrongdoers. Given the amorphousness of many state and federal laws, however, many of the claims of corporate wrongdoing are dubious. These alleged acts of wrongdoing are, at best, technical violations of statutes; at worst, they are lawless aggregations of claims of economic loss or fabricated charges. All of these features are on vivid display in the class action ginned up against the Toshiba computer company.

In the 1990s, most laptop computers had a glitch: a flawed microcode in the internal floppy disc controller (FDC), which could result in data loss – a problem that was made potentially worse with the advent of multitasking computers. In plain English, stored data could be corrupted without the user's awareness.

A class action was filed against Toshiba, a leading manufacturer of laptop computers, seeking damages under a federal statute designed to combat computer crime.[28] The case, *Shaw v. Toshiba*,[29] did not allege that any of the several million Toshiba laptop purchasers had actually suffered data losses. Indeed, according to U.S. Senator Jeff Sessions of Alabama, who commented on the case, "[n]ot a single one of [Toshiba's] users had ever reported a problem due to this defect."[30] Moreover, the defect could be resolved with a software patch.

The case was filed in federal court in Beaumont, Texas. (Beaumont's reputation as a class action mecca is well deserved because of its state and federal jurists' bias in favor of the plaintiffs' lawyers' interests and the handsome ransoms that have been extracted from corporate America.) After robust litigation and adverse rulings on its motions, Toshiba agreed to settle the case by offering cash rebates, extended warranties, discount coupons, and other benefits, announced as valued at $2.1 billion but likely costing Toshiba about $1 billion. Toshiba also provided a software patch that would fix the problem to all who requested it.

How many of the laptop owners who received the patch were sufficiently concerned about the glitch that they actually installed the patch? We have no way of knowing, but anecdotal evidence suggests that many recipients of the patch felt no need to install it. The entrepreneurial lawyers who filed the action, however, were rewarded with a fee of $147.5 million, which was paid in addition to the settlement.[31]

The *Shaw v. Toshiba* story, however, is not yet complete. There is a doppelganger. Some of the class lawyers, seeing an opportunity to turn the case into a franchise, filed a nearly identical action in the same federal court against another laptop manufacturer, the Compaq Computer Corporation (now a part of Hewlett Packard), titled *Thurmond v. Compaq*.[32] Whereas in *Shaw v. Toshiba*, Judge Heartfield denied Toshiba's motion to dismiss the case, this time, the same judge granted Compaq's motion to dismiss, saying that the plaintiffs could not show they had suffered sufficient damages under the federal statute to maintain their action.[33]

What accounts for these different outcomes? Did Judge Heartfield have an epiphany? Or were there differentiating facts? Should the outcome have been affected by the fact that Toshiba was an American subsidiary of a Japanese company, whereas Compaq was a Texas corporation with its headquarters in Houston, Texas? Reports indicate that Toshiba's decision to agree to pay an announced $2.1 billion to escape from Beaumont justice was prompted by fear of a jury verdict that could have amounted to as much as $9.5 billion – putting the company at risk.[34] But without a single claim that any Toshiba laptop computer user had suffered any harm and that the problem could be easily fixed by a patch, was this fear rational? During the course of the proceeding, Judge Heartfield made it abundantly clear to Toshiba that it would be wise to settle the case and repeatedly issued rulings against Toshiba. Moreover, Toshiba may well have had reason to fear that a Beaumont jury, egged on by a contingency fee lawyer urging that the jury punish an out-of-state company and a Japanese one to boot for its reckless actions, might have rendered a verdict that could have led to bankruptcy.

The *Toshiba* case illustrates how class actions have become one of the most lucrative methods of wealth creation ever devised. After this tale of two laptop manufacturers, can there be any doubt as to the awesome unchecked power reposed in the hands of the judiciary and class action lawyers to place at risk even the largest companies in the world to compel them to transfer enormous wealth to lawyers?

C. The Unintended Consequence of Consumer Protection Laws

Class actions are facilitated by our complex state and federal regulatory systems, which provide multiple underlying statutory bases for bringing class actions. Among them are claims brought on behalf of consumers of products and services, claiming personal injury (mass torts) or economic loss resulting from sales practices that are claimed to be deceptive and therefore violate state consumer protection laws. Other class actions are based on violations of a wide range of federal and state statutes to protect investors, consumers, employees, and others. The more complex and prolix state and federal regulatory laws, the more uncertain their application and the more they are, therefore, grist for class action lawyers' mills. Lawyers are constantly trolling for opportunities to find technical statutory violations on which to base a class action. As discussed in Chapter 11, a practically unlimited amount of class action lawsuits can be brought alleging that consumers suffered an economic loss – not a personal injury – because a company allegedly violated a state's deceptive sales practices act. These acts variously allow consumers to seek the return of the purchase price or statutory damages ranging from $25 to $2,000 per violation or even treble damages, and of course, attorney fees.[35] Under these laws, if a company sells a product that it claims is better than competing products, and a million or more consumers have bought the product priced at $18.99 on multiple occasions, a class action alleging that the company's claims are deceptive can easily amount to more than $1 billion in alleged damages.

Another major target area for class actions lawyers is the wide variety of laws enacted by Congress to protect consumers in areas such as credit reporting, telephone and cable services, misuse of personal data, employment discrimination, and wage and hour law violations.[36] To encourage these laws' enforcement in judicial proceedings – even where consumers cannot show that they suffered actual injury – Congress has provided for damages from $100 to $1,000 per violation.[37] Congress's good intentions have been captured by entrepreneurial class action lawyers who have converted some of these consumer protection statutes into massive money-making machines that provide little or no benefit to consumers, penalize businesses, and fill lawyers' coffers. These statutory damage laws lend themselves to unintended consequences because they do not distinguish between real injury and technical violations with little or no harmful effect. Apparently unintentional violations, such as in the two examples discussed next – one a failure to include certain disclosures on offers of credit, the other a failure to delete customers' credit card expiration dates from receipts – render businesses vulnerable to multibillion-dollar class actions, which get settled by substantial payments to the lawyers and paltry or nonexistent benefits to consumers.

A prime example is the *Finance America* litigation. Finance America is a lending company that uses mass mailings to attract business. It purchases lists from consumer credit reporting agencies that are then used to contact targeted individuals.[38] The Fair Credit Reporting Act (FCRA) requires that lenders gaining such access to consumer credit reports may not simply solicit consumer interest, but must extend a "firm offer of credit" to the consumer,[39] which is a loan offer that will be honored, provided the consumer meets the specific criteria used.[40]

Lawyers filed a class action against Finance America, alleging that the company violated this provision because a mass mailing was a mere solicitation of interest, not a firm offer of credit, and lacked information about the interest rate, amount of credit, the loan terms, and other required disclosures;[41] the letter only informed consumers that they prequalified for a home loan and provided a phone number to discuss the details.[42] FCRA provides for damages of between $100 and $1,000 per violation. Because the solicitations were sent to sixteen million consumers, potential damages ranged from $1.6 billion to $16 billion.[43]

The settlement provided that those who received a solicitation from the company were to (1) be offered a home mortgage loan at the lower rate available from a mortgage broker, but without having to pay a broker's fee; and (2) receive an educational brochure, which encouraged consumers to apply for a free credit report.[44] In approving the settlement, the judge accepted the uncontested expert reports of class counsel, estimating the value of this settlement as in excess of $80 million.[45] This is a highly dubious proposition. The discounted loan offers made by Finance America were a way of attracting additional business without the bank paying a commission to mortgage brokers. As for the educational brochure, it is improbable that class members even read the brochure, let alone gained any valuable information from it. In other words, the settlement was simply a way to dress up a no-significant-value settlement as having great value in order to justify class counsel's demand for a multimillion-dollar fee. In an all-too-rare display of judicial vigilance, the presiding judge rejected the request for a percentage fee based on the highly dubious ascribed value of $80 million to the settlement and awarded a mere $552,231 fee – little more than pocket change when compared to many other class actions.[46]

Consumer class actions brought under the Fair and Accurate Transactions Act (FACTA) provide another example. FACTA requires businesses to delete all but the last five digits of a credit card number and the expiration date on a customer's credit card receipt; it also imposes statutory damages of $100-$1,000 per violation.[47] FACTA has been a goldmine for class action lawyers because it enables them to threaten a business' very existence unless it agrees to pay tribute to the lawyers. For example, a class action brought against Ikea, the Swedish furniture company – because costumers' credit card expiration dates were included on 2.4 million receipts for a period of less than two months – could have resulted in statutory damages of $240 million to $2.4 billion.[48] U.S. District Court Judge James Selna certified the class, rejecting Ikea's contention that the disproportionate damages violated the business's due process of law right not to be charged with excessive statutory damages, especially when there was no actual injury to the class. Ikea quickly took steps to correct its credit card processing machines to comply with the statute.[49]

Class action lawyers' exploitation of the FACTA statute was so egregious that Congress amended the Act to extend the grace period for businesses who had failed to delete the customer's credit card expiration date from receipts.[50] As a result, the class action against Ikea was dismissed.[51] A critical part of Judge Selna's ruling remains intact, however. Judge Selna ruled that Ikea's claim of a denial of due process of law should not be addressed unless and until the class was certified and damages had been assessed.[52] Judge Frank Easterbrook of the Seventh Circuit Court of Appeals has ruled likewise, holding that the appropriate role of the judicial branch is to enforce the statute as written – no matter how absurd and disproportionate the damages awarded – and then determine whether constitutional issues are raised.[53] Although there is legal authority for first resolving the certification issue before tackling any other issues,[54] these rulings by Judges Selna and Easterbrook as well as by other federal judges[55] are unnecessarily naïve. Once a court has certified a class action based on technical statutory violations with potential damages amounting to billions of dollars, defendants have little choice except to settle the case. By settling, however, they forever foreclose any possibility of raising the denial of due process of law claim. To preserve the right of a defendant to raise the denial of due process issue, federal courts should consider the issue at the class certification stage.[56]

THE EFFECTS OF LAWYERS' ROBUST FINANCIAL INCENTIVES TO FILE CLASS

actions are shrouded in a foggy mist, which serves the interests of lawyers but often leaves us blinded to the possibility that the costs imposed exceed the benefits realized. There has never been a systematic study of the aggregate social effect of class action litigation — that is, of the direct and indirect costs imposed by class actions, who pays these costs, the benefits realized, and who receives these benefits. I will leave the Herculean task of weighing the costs and benefits to others. Even without such an attempt, a thorough discussion of class actions would require volumes.

Here, I am limiting my focus to the effects of the pursuit of prodigious contingency fees through class actions. In Chapter 17, I examine how fees are set in class actions and whether these fees are reasonable. Following that chapter, I explain how lawyers have gamed this process to produce unearned windfall fees. Finally, I examine how lawyers have turned securities class actions into a multibillion-dollar scheme that targets investors.

NOTES

1. *See* FED. R. CIV. P. 23(b)(3). Rule 23 also provides that in some types of cases, members cannot opt out to bring the same action independent of the class. *See* FED. R. CIV. P. 23(b)(1)(A), (b)(1)(B), and (b)(2).
2. *See* Brickman, *The Brave New World*, *supra* Chapter 9, note 15, at App.
3. FED. R. CIV. P. 23, Advisory Committee's Note, 39 F.R.D. 69, 98–107 (1966) (emphasis added). In considering whether to certify mass torts as class actions, some courts have noted that the advisory committee's note does not mention or refer to mass torts, only "mass accidents." *See* Patricia Rimland, *National Asbestos Litigation: Procedural Problems Must Be Solved*, 69 WASH. U.L.Q. 899, 903 n.35 (1991).
4. *See* Theodore Eisenberg & Geoffery Miller, *The Role of Opt-Outs and Objectors in Class Action Litigation: Theoretical and Empirical Issues*, 57 VAND. L. REV. 1529, 1532 (2004).

5. Class Action Fairness Act, 28 U.S.C. § 1711(a)(1) (2006).

6. *Deposit Guar. Nat'l Bank of Jackson, Miss. v. Roper*, 445 U.S. 326, 338 (1980).

7. Rules Enabling Act, 28 U.S.C. §§ 2071–2077 (2006).

8. *See* Stephen B. Burbank, *The Costs of Complexity*, 85 MICH. L. REV. 1463, 1472–73 (1987).

9. *See, e.g.*, JACK B. WEINSTEIN, INDIVIDUAL JUSTICE IN MASS TORT LITIGATION 1–14, 163–71 (1995) (emphasizing the need for the tort system to compensate harmed plaintiffs and to provide an indirect deterrent effect as well); David Rosenberg, *Class Actions for Mass Tort: Doing Individual Justice By Collective Means*, 62 IND. L. J. 561, 567 (1987) (arguing that "bureaucratic justice implemented through class actions provides better opportunities for achieving individual justice than the tort system's private law, disaggregate processes").

10. *See, e.g.*, Myriam Gilles & Gary B. Friedman, *Exploding the Class Action Agency Costs Myth: The Social Utility of Entrepreneurial Lawyers*, 155 U. PA. L. REV. 103 (2006); William B. Rubenstein, *Why Enable Litigation? A Positive Externalities Theory of the Small Claims Class Action*, 74 U. MO. KAN. CITY L. REV. 709 (2006); Samuel Issacharoff & Geoffrey P. Miller, *Will Aggregate Litigation Come To Europe?*, (NYU Law & Econ. Research Paper No. 08–46, 27), *available at* http://ssrn.com/abstract=1296843.

11. *See, e.g.*, Alexei Barrionuevo, *Two Enron Chiefs Are Convicted in Fraud and Conspiracy Trial*, N.Y. TIMES, May 26, 2006, at A1; Ken Belson, *Ex-Chief of Worldcom Is Found Guilty in $11 Billion Fraud*, N.Y. TIMES, Mar. 16, 2005, at A1; Richard A. Oppel Jr., *Enron's Collapse: The Overview; Wide Effort Seen in Shredding Data on Enron's Audits*, N.Y. TIMES, Jan. 24, 2002, at A1.

12. Gilles & Friedman, *Entrepreneurial Lawyers, supra* note 10, at 104–05.

13. *See* Phyllis Korkki, *The Count: Going to Court After Stocks Take a Dive*, N.Y. TIMES, Feb. 15, 2009, at BU.2; *see also* SECURITIES CLASS ACTION FILINGS 2008: A YEAR IN REVIEW 16, CORNERSTONE RESEARCH (2009), *available at* http://securities.cornerstone.com.

14. *Bell Atl. Corp. v. Twombly*, 550 U.S. 544, 559 (2007). As more fully discussed in Chapter 19 on securities class actions, in the case of a multinational company with offices and plants in many countries, the requirement to turn over vast numbers of documents including e-mails and internal reports can require the expenditure of millions of dollars to gather the documents, determine their relevance, and identify those that may be privileged from disclosure. In addition, by taking the depositions of corporate officers, the lawyers bringing the action can tie up these officers for weeks and even months as they prepare to be deposed.

15. *See, e.g.*, Charles Silver, *"We're Scared to Death": Class Certification and Blackmail*, 78 N.Y.U. L. REV. 1357, 1359 (2003) (claiming that class action

settlements are merits-driven and citing a Federal Judicial Center study that doubts that "the certification decision itself, as opposed to the merits of the underlying claims, coerce[s] settlements with any frequency"). *See* Thomas E. Willging et al., Empirical Study of Class Actions in Four Federal District Courts: Final Report to the Advisory Committee on Civil Rules 61 (1996).

16. George L. Priest, What We Know and What We Don't Know About Modern Class Actions: A Review of the Eisenberg-Miller Study, Civil Justice Report (2005) No. 9, at 4. (emphasis in original, citations omitted).

17. A prime example is the silicone breast implant litigation in which a \$4.2 billion class action settlement was agreed to by the defendant manufacturers even though the scientific evidence – as conclusively as epidemiological evidence can demonstrate – indicated that implants did not cause the diseases claimed. *See* Brickman, *Litigation Screenings, supra* Chapter 7, note 61, at 57–71. The settlement later imploded when tort lawyers launched a massive effort to generate bogus medical evidence for tens of thousands of claimants that they recruited by using litigation screenings. *See id.* at 67–70. Another example is the diet drugs (fen-phen) class action litigation in which bogus medical evidence led to the payment of billions of dollars to claimants who had not been injured by the use of the drugs. *See id.* at 29–55.

18. *In the Matter of Rhone-Poulenc Rorer, Inc.*, 51 F.3d 1293, 1300 (7th Cir. 1995).

19. A more detailed account of how modern-day class actions undermine democratic precepts is set out in Appendix F.

20. This is discussed in Chapter 10.

21. Zywicki, *Public Choice, supra* note Chapter 8, note 30, at 13.

22. *See* Dennis Jacobs, *The Secret Life of Judges*, 75 Fordham L. Rev. 2855, 2857 (2007).

23. Harold D. Lasswell, Politics: Who Gets What, When, How (1936).

24. Eric Helland & Jonathan Klick, *To Regulate, Litigate, or Both*, (U. Pa. Inst. for Law & Econ. Research Paper No. 09–13, 2009), *available at* http://ssrn.com/asbstract=1375522.

25. *See id.* at 6.

26. *See id.* at 19.

27. *See, e.g.*, John C. Coffee, *Rescuing the Private Attorney General: Why the Model of Lawyer As Bounty Hunter Is Not Working*, 42 Md. L. Rev. 215 (1983).

28. *See* Counterfeit Access Device and Computer Fraud and Abuse Act of 1984, 18 U.S.C. § 1030 (2006).

29. *Shaw v. Toshiba Am. Info. Sys., Inc.*, 91 F. Supp. 942 (E.D. Tex. 2000).

30. Statement of Sen. Sessions, 149 Cong. Rec. S12423 (Daily ed. Oct. 3, 2003).

31. *Shaw*, 41 F. Supp. 2d at 946.

32. *Thurmond v. Compaq Computer Corp.*, 171 F. Supp. 2d 667 (E.D. Tex. 2001).

33. *Id.*

34. Kelly Holleran, *Toshiba 10 years later: A look back at a Texas city's big settlement*, LEGAL NEWSLINE, Oct. 26, 2009, *available at* http://legalnewsline.com/news/223638-toshiba-10-years-later-a-look.

35. For a discussion of state consumer protection laws, see Chapter 12, Section B.

36. *See* Fair Credit Reporting Act, 15 U.S.C. §§ 1681(a)(1), 1681n(a)(1)(A)-(3) (2006) (establishing rules for credit reporting agencies to ensure accurate credit reporting and fair credit reporting methods and allowing statutory damages of $100 to $1,000 for willful violations, punitive damages, and successful plaintiffs' attorneys' fees and costs); Telephone Consumer Protection Act, 47 U.S.C. §§ 227(b)(1), 227(b)(3) (2006) (prohibiting inter alia the use of automated dialing systems to call cell phone users and the sending of any unsolicited advertisements by fax and allowing statutory damages of the greater of actual damages or $500; treble damages available for willful or knowing violations); Cable Communications Policy Act, 47 U.S.C. §§ 551(a)-(e), 551(f) (2006) (establishing rules to protect cable services subscribers' privacy and allowing statutory damages of greater of actual damages or $100 to $1,000 per day of violation, punitive damages, and successful plaintiffs' attorneys' fees and costs).

37. For example, the Truth in Lending Act (15 U.S.C. §§1601–1667f) includes statutory damages because, as stated in the senate report, "it is difficult to prove any actual monetary damage arising out of a disclosure violation." *See* S. REP. NO. 93–278, at 14. A limited number of these statutes limit the amount of statutory damages in class actions. For example, the Electronic Funds Transfer Act (15 U.S.C. § 1693m(a)(2)(B)(ii)), Consumer Leasing Act (15 U.S.C. §§ 1640 (2)(B)), Truth in Lending Act (15 U.S.C. §§ 1640 (2)(B), Fair Debt Collection Practice Act (15 U.S.C. § 1693m(a)(2)(B)(ii)), and the Equal Credit Opportunity Act (15 U.S.C. § 1691e(b)) limits class action damages to the greater of 1% of the creditor's net worth or $500,000.

38. First Amended Class Action Complaint of Plaintiff at 2, *Fisher v. Finance America, LLC*, No. SACV 05–0888 CJC (RNBx) (C.D. Cal. Jan. 30, 2006) [hereinafter First Amended Complaint].

39. 15 U.S.C. § 1681b(c)(1)(B) (2006).

40. 15 U.S.C. § 1681a(l) (2006).

41. First Amended Complaint at 5. Such disclosures must inform the consumer that information in the consumer report was used in connection with the transaction, the consumer received the offer based on fulfilling certain criteria, the offer may not be extended if the consumer does not continue to meet certain criteria or does not provide collateral, and the consumer has the right to opt out of future offers. *See* 15 U.S.C. § 1681m(d) (2006). In 2003, Congress amended

the "clear disclosure" requirement, abolishing private remedies. *See* 15 U.S.C. § 1681m(h)(8), Pub. L. No. 108–59, 117 Stat. 1952.

42. First Amended Complaint at 5.

43. Order Granting Final Settlement Approval and Awarding of Attorneys' Fees at 7, *Fisher*, No. SACV 05–0888 CJC (RNBx) (C.D. Cal. Feb. 11, 2008).

44. *Id.* at 3.

45. *Id.* at 11.

46. *Id.* at 18. To his credit, Judge Cormac J. Carney saw that the class action was predicated on "a purely statutory violation which caused no harm or injury," *id.* at 6, and therefore declined to allow class counsel to calculate fees as a percentage of the (highly uncertain) benefit received by the class. *Id.* at 13–15. Instead, he awarded class counsel $552,231.50, based on the time and expenses claimed by class counsel. *Id.* at 18. It is interesting to note that the parties spent three weeks negotiating this fee but settled the underlying claims for the class members after a single day of mediation. *Id.* at 17. Given the absence of any substantial benefit for the class, however, here is a case where a judge, instead of awarding class counsel its hourly rate fee, should have at least halved that to reflect the lack of any substantial benefit for the class.

47. 15 U.S.C. § 1681c(g)(1) (2006). For a brief summary of FACTA and the issues being discussed, *see* Ted Frank, *Omission in FACTA Might Be Windfall for Plaintiff's Bar*, AEI, Sept. 1, 2007, *available at* http://www.aei.org/article/26879.

48. *Kesler v. Ikea U.S. Inc.*, No. SACV 07–568 JVS (RNBx), 2008 WL 413268, *1–2 (C.D. Cal. Feb. 4, 2008), *superseded by statute*, Credit and Debit Card Receipt Clarification Act of 2007, Pub. L. No. 110–241, 122 Stat. 1565 (2008). Other defendants that have been caught in this FACTA class action trap include Applebee's, Jewel Supermarkets, Wendy's, InterPark Garages, Balducci's, FedEx Kinko's, Frederick's of Hollywood, Chuck E. Cheese, Avis Rent-A-Car, Burberry, Vitamin Shoppe, U-Haul, KB Toys, Costco, Gymboree, and Toys "R" Us. For citations to these cases, see Sheila B. Scheuerman, *Due Process Forgotten: The Problem of Statutory Damages and Class Actions*, 74 Mo. L. Rev. 51, nn.56–71 (2009).

49. *Kesler, id.* at *1–2, *7.

50. Credit and Debit Card Receipt Clarification Act of 2007, Pub. L. No. 110–241, 122 Stat. 1565.

51. *See* Stipulation of Dismissal with Prejudice, *Kesler v. Ikea U.S. Inc.*, No. SACV 07–568 JVS (RNBx), 2008 WL 4197218 (C.D. Cal. July 18, 2008).

52. Kesler, *supra* note 48 at *8.

53. *Murray v. GMAC Mortgage Corp.*, 434 F. 3d 948, 954 (7th Cir. 2006). Judge Easterbrook's holding appears inconsistent with the view he expressed *In re Bridgestone/Firestone, Inc.*, 288 F. 3d 1012, 1015–16 (7th Cir. 2003), where he

recognized that the possibility of an astronomical but erroneous verdict would force a defendant to settle an unmeritorious case.

54. In some measure, these rulings stem from a misguided 1974 U.S. Supreme Court decision holding that judges determining whether to certify class actions must wear blinders and may not conduct a preliminary inquiry into the merits of a proposed class action in determining whether to grant certification. *Eisen v. Carlisle and Jacquelin*, 417 U.S. 156, 177–78 (1974). The unintended consequence of this decision was to empower plaintiffs' lawyers to file actions of dubious merit and, by meeting the procedural requirements for class certification and forming a class of tens or hundreds of thousands of claimants, pose a sufficient economic threat to a business to compel settlement irrespective of the merits of the case (as explained in Chapter 16, § A). (These requirements are set out in Fed. Rule 23(a) and are referred to as the numerosity, commonality, typicality, and adequacy tests. To meet the numerosity requirement, the lawyer must show that the persons included in the putative class are so numerous that their joinder as individual plaintiffs in a lawsuit would be impractical; for commonality, the required showing is that there are questions of law and fact common to the class; for the typicality prong, the showing required is that the representative plaintiff's claims are typical of the claims and defenses of the class; and for adequacy, that the representative plaintiff's interests are aligned with those of the class, and that the class's interests will be fairly and adequately protected. The threshold for meeting these requirements is not demanding. Once these requirements have been met, the class action must be maintainable under either Rule 23(b)(1), (b)(2) or (b)(3). The rule 23(b)(3) class action, which most merits our attention, imposes the additional requirements that questions of law and fact common to the members of the class predominate over any questions affecting only individual members – a more demanding requirement than the similar commonality threshold requirement; and that the class action mechanism for resolving the disputed claims must be found to be superior to other available methods for adjudicating the controversy.)

Over time, however, a judicial consensus has emerged that *Eisen* is flawed and should be chipped away. *See e.g., Szabo v. Bridgeport Machines, Inc.*, 249 F.3d 672 (7th Cir. 2001); *In re Initial Public Offerings Securities Litigation*, 471 F.3d 24 (2d Cir. 2006) (chronicling the emergence of the view that some scrutiny of the merits at the time of certification is permissible, *see id.* at 32–42). A recent Second Circuit Court of Appeals case promises to winnow *Eisen* to half size. The case holds than "to certify a class, the district court must find that the evidence more likely than not establishes each fact necessary to meet the requirements of Rule 23." *In re Hydrogen Peroxide Antitrust Litigation*, 552 F.3d 305, 320 (3d Cir. 2008). The dilution of *Eisen* and the approach taken in

Public Offerings was presaged by Geoffrey P. Miller in *Review of the Merits in Class Action Certifications*, 33 HOFSTRA L. REV. 51, 87 (2004).

55. *See, e.g., Parker v. Time Warner Entertainment Co., L.P.*, 331 F.3d 13, 22 (2d Cir. 2003) (reversing lower court's denial of class certification stating that a disproportionate damage award may present due process concerns but that these concerns would not "prevent certification, but [might] nullify ... and reduce the aggregate damage award").

56. For an extensive discussion of due process concerns raised by aggregated statutory damages, see Sheila B. Scheuerman, *Due Process Forgotten: The Problem of Statutory Damages and Class Actions*, 74 MO. L. REV. 51(2009).

17 Fees in Class Actions

A. How Fees Are Set

The driving force behind class actions is lawyers' fees. Even so, there is no reliable record of the contingency fees that class action lawyers have garnered. Federal court filings and settlements are usually published, but most class actions have been filed in state courts where a record of decisions is not readily available. One study of a selected sample of 1,120 class actions in the period 1973–2003 found that fees in common-fund class actions totaled $7.6 billion.[1] Another study of all class action settlements approved by federal judges in 2006–2007 indicated that the announced value of the settlements totaled $33 billion and that judges awarded nearly $5 billion in fees and expenses in these cases to the class action lawyers.[2] I estimate that over the past thirty-five years, federal and state courts have awarded class action lawyers well in excess of $50 billion. This estimation does not include the fees generated by the states' suits against the tobacco companies, which were functional equivalents of class actions, brought mostly by state attorneys general in partnership with private contingency fee lawyers. When the suits were settled for $246 billion, the fees for the private lawyers – more than $15 billion payable over a twenty-five-year period – were so enormous that the private lawyers and the attorneys general, fearing a political uproar, sought to keep the fees from public view by creating a secret arbitration process to which the public was denied access.[3]

Ostensibly, class action fees are awarded according to whether (1) the case is initiated under a statute with a fee-shifting provision which authorizes the prevailing plaintiff in an action for damages or injunctive relief to also be awarded its reasonable attorney fees[4]; or (2) a common fund has been created. Where the plaintiff or class has prevailed and there is a fee-shifting statute, the court will award attorney fees, calculated according to the reasonable amount of hours spent on the litigation, multiplied by the attorney's allowed hourly rate, plus litigation expenses (such as travel, copying costs, and expert witness fees).[5] The U.S. Supreme Court has held that attorneys' fees awarded under federal fee-shifting statutes may be enhanced by the use of "multipliers" but only in "exceptional" circumstances that are so "rare" as never to have yet been encountered by the Court.[6] As discussed later, however, this restriction, which does not apply in common-fund cases, is easily evaded in practice.

A common fund occurs when a claimant protects a fund or property that also benefits others or when a defendant in a class action pays a sum of money (by settlement or judgment), which is to be allocated for the benefit of all the members of the class.[7] In such cases, the common-fund doctrine provides that the lawyer who devoted time and money to the successful attempt to secure a benefit for the class is entitled to a reasonable attorney's fee and reimbursement of costs from the common fund.[8] The courts use two methods to set the fee: the lodestar and the percentage fee. The lodestar method is a fee calculation based on the amount of hours worked by the attorneys, multiplied by the prevailing hourly rates allowed by the courts.[9] Courts may then apply a multiplier to adjust the lodestar up (or, rarely, down) to reflect the risk involved, the quality of representation, delay in payment, or exceptional results obtained.[10] Multipliers typically range from 3 to 4.5 in common-fund cases[11]; where the recovery exceeds $100 million, the average multiplier is 4.5.[12] In some cases, however, multipliers have reached into double digits.[13]

The percentage method is much like the contingency fee in other civil litigation – the class attorney gets a percentage of the recovery for the class. In the early days of class actions, the percentage method was used to determine attorney's fees; but during the 1970s, the lodestar method gained favor because it appeared to more accurately measure the attorney's earned wages than the percentage fee, which was, at that time, perceived as "excessive and unrelated to the work actually performed."[14] The pendulum swung back to the percentage method in the 1980s, however, because the lodestar method seemed ineffective at aligning class counsel and class members' interests and conserving judicial resources.[15] The lodestar method, its opponents argued, resulted in a misalignment of the class lawyers' and class members' interests because lawyers have the incentive to invest more hours or inflate the actual number of hours worked when paid by the hour.[16] The percentage method was believed to cure this problem by removing the incentive for the lawyers to delay resolution of the case until they could run up their hours, thereby promoting a more efficient resolution of the class action.

Another major factor accounting for the shift toward the percentage method was the burden that lodestar requests place on courts. As class actions proliferated and lawyers sought, in the words of Derek Bok, "cumulative damage awards of awesome proportions,"[17] the size of the fees burgeoned. To justify these fees, lawyers devised ways to increase the number of hours claimed in these actions from the thousands to the hundreds of thousands.[18] In large-scale class actions, a detailed compilation of the hours worked by each lawyer in each participating firm could run hundreds and thousands of pages. Judges, of course, would not review these detailed compilations. Instead, they would look at summaries showing the numbers of hours devoted by each attorney, the amount of time spent on various legal tasks, and the hourly rate each attorney was seeking. Even then, however, determining whether 4,000 hours for discussions between the attorneys or 50,000 hours for document review is appropriate is not susceptible to any kind of realistic review unless a judge is willing to invest substantial amounts of time.[19]

If a judge does assiduously devote the time to thoroughly review a fee request, an appellate court might render that effort for naught. This is what occurred when U.S. District Court Judge John F. Grady – one of a handful of federal judges acutely concerned with contingency fee billing abuses – carefully reviewed the fee request in a securities class action against Continental Bank.[20] In a detailed opinion, Judge Grady lowered the $9 million fee request by roughly one-half by substantially reducing the number of hours the attorneys claimed to have invested in the litigation, which he found were "excessive or ... did not significantly benefit the class";[21] capping the attorneys' hourly rates; applying a formula to determine the fee allowable for paralegal work (as opposed to the "market" rate); and refusing to apply a risk multiplier to the lodestar.[22] Even though Judge Grady examined numerous sets of "hundreds of pages of time entries [along with] the 16-volume set of appendices" submitted by the class attorneys to substantiate the 41,955 hours they claimed to have worked, he acknowledged that it was "impossible to tell, except in the most general way, what was done."[23] Judge Grady concluded: "Whether the description of the work is general or specific, acceptance of the proposition that the time spent was no more than necessary, and that it produced something useful for the client, is often an act of faith."[24]

When the attorneys appealed to the Seventh Circuit Court of Appeals, Judge Posner slapped down Judge Grady's attempt to exercise his responsibility to carefully review the fee request, concluding that Judge Grady's effort was a "futile expenditure of judicial time."[25] Judge Posner stated that when Judge Grady adjusted the lawyers' and paralegals' hourly rates, he erred because "[h]e thought he knew the value of the class lawyer's legal services better than the market did."[26] The judges' task is not "to determine the equivalent of the medieval just price ... [but] to determine what the lawyer would receive if he were selling his services in the market rather than being paid by court order."[27] Judge Posner misses the mark in asserting that there is a "market rate" for plaintiffs' lawyers' services in class actions. What Judge Posner calls the "market" is, in fact, little more than the penumbras of the shadows cast by previous jurists' decisions that approved fees in class actions.[28] The "market" is what courts award as fees.

Today, to avoid the abuses that Judge Grady (and others) identified, most federal courts use the percentage method to calculate attorney fee awards in common-fund cases. The switch from a lodestar calculation to the percentage fee method has resulted in a major increase in the fees awarded, however. For example, in a class action based on the "junk bond" scam in the 1980s, the class action counsel, Milberg Weiss Bershad Hynes & Lerach, sought a fee of $13.5 million – 25 percent of the $54 million settlement. The trial court instead awarded a lodestar-based fee that, after reductions for excessive charges, amounted to $865,326.68 – a decision the Second Circuit Court of Appeals affirmed.[29] The appellate court acknowledged that, despite the absence of any appreciable risk, most federal courts would likely have approved the 25 percent fee request.[30] Courts that have adopted the percentage fee method sometimes "cross check" these awards to determine whether they are excessive by comparing that result to the lodestar amount.[31] When the percentage of the fund award substantially exceeds the lodestar, however, many of these courts nonetheless approve the percentage fee and assign a sufficient multiplier to the lodestar to reduce the disparity to acceptable levels.[32]

There is another unspoken reason that may account for the triumph of the percentage fee over the lodestar: the recognition that some class action lawyers abuse the honor system by grossly inflating (if not extensively padding) their time records. A long-held secret of the legal profession has seeped out in recent decades. Some lawyers in major law firms have padded their bills by substantially overstating their hours, thus overcharging their clients.[33] Press accounts of lawyers' billing and expense fraud are legion.[34] A veteran practitioner contends that whereas "billing abuses are widespread and are not confined to the few who have been prosecuted for fraudulent billing," a careful examination of billing statements can uncover the fraud.[35] In fact, in large-scale civil litigations, clients increasingly hire specialists in auditing lawyers' fees and billing practices who frequently find significant overcharges.[36] Nonetheless, courts routinely deny the requests of class members who object to the settlement or the requested fee to examine billing records. Some judges have gone to great extremes to protect class action lawyers from scrutiny of their fee request.[37]

A few judges in class actions have appointed special masters, as authorized under the Federal Rules of Civil Procedure,[38] to conduct an independent review of attorneys' fee requests.[39] The results reflect the wisdom of these albeit rare appointments. For example, in one class action, a special master appointed by a federal judge conducted "an exhaustive review," and after reducing the claimed lodestar for various charges he found excessive, recommended a lodestar award of $1,416,572.[40] The presiding judge, however, citing inter alia "over 80 instances where the time records of Milberg Weiss [the class counsel] indicating meetings and telephone conferences with co-counsel, do not correspond with the time records of other counsel," reduced the amount to $1,284,704.[41] A second special master later issued a report, approved by the court, recommending that additional excessive charges be deleted and that the lodestar award should be reduced to $865,326.[42]

Despite the substantial reductions recommended by special masters appointed to review lodestar fee requests, most courts summarily deny requests for appointment of a special master or fee auditor.[43] For example, in the *Enron* case, U.S. District Court Judge Melinda Harmon approved a $688 million fee and denied a request to appoint a special master to review the attorney fee request – emphatically defending the court's territorial rights over the fee determination. Because the court had exercised "personal oversight over all aspects of [the] case," the judge held that the appointment of an independent party to review the fee request would be redundant, costly, and a cause for delay of distribution to the class.[44] An independent review would also "undermine the Lead Plaintiff by empowering someone else to second guess its judgments."[45] This contention bears further review.

B. The Role of "Pay to Play" in Fee Setting

The judge's implicit suggestion that lead plaintiffs – such as state pension funds – are zealous guardians of the class's interest is open to question. In the recent class action against Xerox on the basis of accounting irregularities, the class attorneys sought a fee of $150 million, 20 percent of the $750 million settlement.[46] Evidence was presented to the court (discussed in detail in Chapter 19) that tens of thousands of hours included in the lodestar were improperly accounted for. A zealous lead plaintiff might well have sought the appointment of a special master to investigate the matter because payment of a grossly inflated fee would come at the expense of the class. But the lead plaintiff, the Louisiana State Employees' Retirement System, not only did not seek further proceedings with regard to the overbilling issue, it filed a brief to support the fee request, thus arguing that its pension owners should get less so that the lawyers could get more.[47]

The status of the Louisiana State Employees' Retirement System as the lead plaintiff in the *Xerox* class action is a direct result of the Private Securities Litigation Reform Act of 1995 (PSLRA).[48] Before the PSLRA, the leading securities class action law firms maintained a stable of "professional plaintiffs" – people who bought a token number of shares in many companies so that they were ready, willing, and able to lend their names as plaintiffs when the price of a company's stock declined and firms rushed to file securities class actions.[49] As noted in the Senate Report, these "investors in the class usually have great difficulty exercising any meaningful direction over the case brought on their behalf. The lawyers can decide when to sue and when to settle, based largely on their own financial interests, not the interests of their purported clients."[50] To counter this practice, the PSLRA directs courts to select the investors "most capable of adequately representing the interests of class members" and who have "the largest financial interest in the relief sought by the class" as lead plaintiffs.[51]

The leading securities class action firms have adapted to the PSLRA by courting state and union pension funds, because they often have the largest financial interests in leading companies. These are, indeed, lucrative appointments. For example, lawyers representing New York State's $116.5 billion pension fund have received more than a half-billion dollars in contingency fees over the past decade.[52] To secure these lucrative

appointments as class counsel, securities law firms "pay to play" by
contributing to the election coffers of union officers and public officials
who select the trustees of state and union pension funds or who are
themselves the trustees – even when they are running unopposed.[53]

The last three New York State Comptrollers have received more
than one million dollars in political contributions from law firms
seeking – and usually getting – a good-sized piece of this pie.[54] Norfolk
County, Massachusetts, has only a small pension fund but has been a
big player in securities class actions. Early in 2010, the fund joined in a
lawsuit against drugstore chain CVS Caremark Corp., whose stock had
fallen. Since 2006, in ten of the twelve times that the fund filed securities class actions, it hired the New York law firm of Labaton Sucharow
LLP. Attorneys at the firm and their relatives have reportedly made
sixty-eight separate donations of the maximum $500 apiece to Norfolk
County Treasurer Joseph A. Connolly, who heads the pension fund's
board.[55]

In some cases, the law firms direct their spending to "middle men"
who influence the counsel selection decision and who take a share of the
money passing through their hands. In return for these payments, union
officers and trustees look favorably on the law firm's pitch to hire them
to bring a securities class action.[56] If the pension fund is selected as one
of the lead plaintiffs by the court, the law firm that paid to play is usually
designated as lead counsel. Being thus designated allows the firm to capture the largest share of the fee and to control how much fee-generating
work is allocated to other firms.[57]

Another gambit that the firms use to secure business is to enter into
"monitoring agreements" with pension fund administrators, which provide that the law firm will monitor the fund's portfolio for securities
litigation prospects at no cost, taking payment only if it brings a successful suit. U.S. District Judge Ted S. Rakoff concluded that this arrangement creates a "clear incentive ... [for the firm] to discover 'fraud' in
the investments it monitors and to recommend ... that the Fund, at no
cost to itself, bring a class action. In other words, the practice fosters

the very tendencies toward lawyer-driven litigation that the PSLRA was designed to curtail."[58]

Entering monitoring agreements and paying to play contravene one of the auxiliary purposes of the PSLRA – to promote price competition and thus lower class action fees.[59] In a study published in 2006, James D. Cox and Randall S. Thomas concluded that whereas the proposition that institutional investors serving as lead plaintiffs will be more effective monitors of class counsel is "intuitively appealing," it "remains unproven."[60] In fact, they found "institutional lead plaintiffs have the lowest average and median recovery percentages of any group."[61] In the same year, Michael Perino published the results of his study, which found that when public pensions serve as lead plaintiffs, settlements are larger, recoveries are a greater percentage of the stakes at issue, and fee requests are lower than in cases with other types of lead plaintiffs.[62] Two years later, Cox and Thomas returned to the fray and, concurring in part, found a positive and significant impact on settlement size from the presence of public pension funds as lead plaintiffs in securities class actions.[63]

It is too early to give conclusive effect of these studies. It is plausible that a tainted lead plaintiff/lead counsel selection process provides a public (albeit lesser) benefit. When it comes to fee setting, however, the evidence is less ambiguous. When pay to play is taken into account, any fee savings realized by class members when state pension funds serve as lead plaintiffs vanish. According to a recent study, the negative effect of pay to play on shareholders is most pronounced in the case of state pension funds that receive the largest campaign contributions and associate repeatedly as lead plaintiffs with a single securities class action law firm.[64]

An illustration of the phenomenon is presented by the *Cendant Corporation Securities Litigation.*[65] In this case, the New York State Common Retirement Fund and the California Public Employees' Retirement System, lead plaintiffs, failed to object to a request for a $262 million attorney's fee, which amounted to $7,485 per hour.[66] On appeal,

the Third Circuit Court of Appeals termed the fee "staggering," noting
that it was based on "an astonishing hourly rate [and] an extraordinarily
high lodestar 'multiplier'," and instructed the lower court to award a
more reasonable fee.[67] In the end, the class lawyers were awarded $55
million – still more than $1,500 an hour,[68] but a savings of $207 million
for the class.

Why did the lead plaintiff pension fund trustees apparently show
greater fidelity to the law firms that paid to play rather than to the pension fund holders they represented by failing to object to the "staggering"
fee request? Perhaps it was just coincidence, but around the time of the
litigation, H. Carl McCall, state comptroller and sole trustee of the New
York State Common Retirement Fund, received $140,000 in campaign
contributions from two of the law firms appointed as lead counsel.[69]

C. How Reasonable Are Class Action Fees?

In determining a reasonable fee for class counsel, courts declare that
they seek to provide lawyers with sufficient financial incentives to induce
them to invest the necessary time and money to file class actions but not
so much as to constitute a windfall.[70] Nonetheless, courts routinely award
windfall fees, which are often grossly disproportionate to the benefits
actually conferred on consumers and well beyond the amounts required
to incentivize lawyers to make the necessary investments to bring class
actions. The evidence for this conclusion is both convoluted and controversial: convoluted because there is no reliably complete compendium of
fees approved in class actions or of the benefits actually received by class
members; controversial because what is a "reasonable fee" versus what
is a "windfall" is often in the eye of the beholder. And the beholder's eye
can be influenced by her politics and whether she is part of the cottage
industry that thrives on class action litigation.

Geoffrey Miller and Theodore Eisenberg have published a study,
which was featured on the front page of the *New York Times* Business
section, purporting to show that fees in class actions are reasonable.[71]

Analyzing class action recoveries and attorney fees from 370 published court opinions and comparing their data with more than 600 cases analyzed in a previous *Class Action Reports* study,[72] they concluded that attorney fees and settlement values have remained steady between 1993 and 2002.[73] During that time, they found that the mean class recovery was $100 million[74] and that the mean attorney's fee award constituted 21.9 percent of client recovery.[75] They also discovered a scaling effect of attorneys' fees: The higher the client recovery, the lower the percentage.[76] These study results, however, are open to serious question for four reasons.

First, in order to compute the percentages that fees represented of settlements, the Miller/Eisenberg study assumed that the announced values of the settlements available to the class were the actual amounts paid to the class. But as discussed in Chapter 18, Section F, many announced settlement values deliberately and substantially overstate the amount to be received by class members in order to justify inflated attorney fees – fees that may equal or even exceed the actual value realized by class members. A RAND study of class actions against insurance companies in the period 1993–2002 indicated that the median fee award to class counsel was 30 percent of the common fund. However, when calculated as a percentage of the actual monetary distribution to the class rather than as a percentage of the amount theoretically available, the median fee climbed to 47 percent. In a quarter of the cases, the effective percentages were 75 percent or higher, and in five cases, they were over 90 percent.[77] Accordingly, the mean attorney fee computed by Miller and Eisenberg substantially understates the percentage of the class's actual recoveries that fees represent in many class actions.

Second, as the authors acknowledge, the study is limited to published court opinions and does not include substantial numbers of class actions filed and settled during the 1993–2002 period, particularly in state court, where many settlements do not result in published opinions.[78] By some estimates, approximately 60 percent of all class actions filed in 2000 were filed in state court.[79] The 2008 RAND Institute study on class actions noted that "state courts are where the bulk of consumer class actions ... are litigated ... [and] [u]nfortunately, only a very small number of state courts make an attempt to track class actions to any degree."[80] As the RAND study acknowledges, many – if not most – class actions filed in state courts during that time period were not included in the study.

Third, as George Priest has indicated, the study is deficient because the cases in its database do not represent the typical mix of class action litigation.[81] Instead, the study heavily tilts toward securities class actions; more than one-half of the federal cases they report (157 of 303) are securities class actions. Mass torts (7), civil rights actions (9), and employment class actions (23) were all underrepresented in the study. Accordingly, Priest concludes that it is "simply implausible" that the study captured anywhere near "the full volume of class action litigation."[82]

Finally, even accepting Miller and Eisenberg's mean attorney fees in class actions as 21.9 percent and mean class recovery of $100 million, their assumption that these fees are reasonable is flawed. By preparing a table that they termed the "presumptively valid range of fees," which they then pronounced to be a "guide [for] courts in assessing the size of the fees in class action cases," Miller and Eisenberg implicitly endorse the reasonableness of their reported fees.[83] They further endorse the reasonableness of fees in class actions by stating that they are "well below the widely quoted one-third figure."[84] But this is a straw man argument. The fact that mean percentage fees in class actions are less than the standard one-third fee in personal injury litigation – if that be so – provides no basis for concluding that prevailing fees in class actions are reasonable. First, as I indicate in Chapter 3, the standard one-third fee significantly overcompensates tort lawyers and frequently leads to windfall fees. Even if the standard rate in personal injury cases were the product of a competitive market, however, that does not justify a 21.9 percent fee in cases with vast economies of scale and little risk of nonpayment for the millions of hours that class lawyers have run up *after* a court has certified the class.

The American public views fees in class actions differently than Professors Miller and Eisenberg. In a 2003 poll conducted by the

U.S. Chamber of Commerce, 61 percent of respondents believed that "consumers and class members benefit the least from the class action system," and 47 percent said that "plaintiffs' lawyers – those bringing the lawsuits – benefit the most."[85] The survey also found that 74 percent of Americans believed "the current class action system drives up prices and should be restrained."[86] Other polls indicate that a majority of Americans do not believe class actions are socially useful.[87]

The chief reason for the public's displeasure is the belief that, too often, consumers' benefits are paltry, whereas the class lawyers' fees are prodigious. There is much truth in this belief. Many class actions are ginned up by lawyers using their positional advantages to extract substantial fees. Often, the modest benefits that a class receives for an alleged harm do not justify the assault launched by the lawyers. Yet most courts routinely approve the settlements and fees requested in these cases, no matter how devoid the outcome is of social benefit or how excessive the fees.[88] Even in the minority of class actions that do provide substantial benefits to consumers of products and services and serve a useful social function, the courts have often significantly overcompensated these lawyers. Columbia Law School Professor John C. Coffee, the leading commentator on class actions, has long railed against the failure of judges to carefully scrutinize settlements. "[J]udicial scrutiny," he says, "of the settlement's adequacy has proved to be a weak reed on which to rely."[89] Noting that reforms are needed, he states that "only one is sure to fail: reliance on trial court scrutiny of the settlement."[90] Coffee, who has filed many declarations in support of class counsels' fee requests, does not level the same criticism of fee awards. Nonetheless, his critique extends to substantial fee awards in class actions in which settlements are the product of collusion.

The surest test of whether lawyers are being substantially over-compensated in class action litigation is to look at the lengths that the class action law firms are willing to go to in order to be able to bring these suits. Class action law firms, apparently oblivious to the great risk that courts believe they are undertaking, vigorously compete with one another to be selected as lead counsel or to have substantial participation in a class action. That competition appears unbounded by ethics or law. For example, as discussed in Chapter 19, Section A, the leading securities class action law firm illegally paid professional plaintiffs kickbacks of a percentage of the fee so that the firm could be the first to bring suit when a company's stock price precipitously declined, and thus claim the mantle of class counsel. The firm's principal explained that the firm had to pay kickbacks because other firms were doing so.

Another indicator of how lucrative class actions are for lawyers is the millions of dollars the firms pay to play, that is, "contribute" to political and union races where the elected officials receiving the funds either appoint pension fund trustees who make the decision as to which firm to hire in securities class actions or are themselves trustees or directors of pension funds by virtue of their office. (This scheme was described in Section B.)

The vigorous competition among law firms to bear the "risk" as lead counsel in a class action does not square with the view that the high level of the fees being awarded is necessary to attract lawyers to undertake complex and costly litigation. The traditional view, as expressed by a federal judge in a securities class action, is that "[a] large segment of the public might be denied a remedy for violations of the securities laws if contingent fees awarded by the courts did not fairly compensate counsel for the services provided and the risks undertaken."[91] However, Melvyn Weiss and William S. Lerach, the principals of the once leading class action law firm, stated that their losses in the cases they brought were "few and far between," and that they achieved "a significant settlement although not always a big legal fee, in 90 [percent] of the cases [they] file[d]."[92]

That same federal judge also stated that the policy of "fairly compensating" class action counsel further "support[ed] the award of a multiplier of counsel's lodestar fee."[93] This propensity to award multipliers is inconsistent with courts' frequent professions of an allegiance to "market" rates in setting fees in class actions. It is remarkable, therefore, how little attention courts pay to the "market" when awarding lodestar multipliers in common-fund cases. Here, the talk of "markets" recedes in favor of the mantra of awarding lawyers multipliers for mythical risks.

There are many other reasons why courts frequently fail in their self-professed mission to achieve that "delicate balance" between providing lawyers adequate financial incentives and overcompensating them with windfall fees. Any exploration of the reasons why windfall fees have become commonplace in class actions requires some understanding of how lawyers game the system and induce courts to rule favorably on their fee requests.

NOTES

1. *See* Stuart J. Logan et al., *Attorney Fee Awards in Common Fund Class Actions*, 24 CLASS ACTION REP. 167 (2003).
2. Brian T. Fitzpatrick, *An Empirical Study of Class Action Settlements and their Fee Awards* (Feb. 12, 2010) at 4, *available at* http://ssrn.com/abstract=1442108 [hereinafter Fitzpatrick, *Fee Awards*].
3. *See* Chapter 22, § A(2).
4. I discuss the origin of these fees in Chapter 2. There are well over 150 federal fee-shifting statutes. *See* MANUAL FOR COMPLEX LITIGATION (FOURTH) § 14.11 (2004). Notable examples include the Freedom of Information Act, 5 U.S.C. §§ 552(a)(4)(E) and (F); Securities Exchange Act of 1934, 15 U.S.C. §§ 78i(e) 78r(a); Endangered Species Act of 1973, 16 U.S.C. § 1540(g)(4); Interstate Commerce Act, 49 U.S.C. §§ 11705(d)(3), 11710(b); Truth in Lending Act, 15 U.S.C. § 1640(a); The Civil Rights Attorney's Fees Awards Act of 1976, 42 U.S.C. § 1988.
5. For an example of an award of attorney's fees based on a fee-shifting statute in a Civil Rights Claim, see *Am. Civ. Liberties Union of Ga. v. Barnes*, 168 F.3d 423, 427 (11th Cir. 1999) (discussing the legal standard governing attorney's fee awards in a § 1988 claim).
6. *Perdue et al., v. Kenny A.*, S. Ct. Slip. Op. at 8, 10 (Apr. 21, 2010); *see also City of Burlington v. Dague*, 505 U.S. 557 (1992).
7. *See* 7B CHARLES ALAN WRIGHT & ARTHUR R. MILLER, FEDERAL PRACTICE & PROCEDURE § 1803 (3d ed. 2008); MANUAL FOR COMPLEX LITIGATION (FOURTH) § 14.11 (2004).
8. *See Boeing Co. v. Van Gemert*, 444 U.S. 472, 478 (1980); *see also* 4 NEWBERG ON CLASS ACTIONS § 14:6 (4th ed. 2008).

9. *See Bowling v. Pfizer, Inc.*, 922 F.Supp. 1261, 1277–80 (S.D. Ohio 1996) (discussing the evolution of the alternative methods of computation of attorney's fees in common-fund class actions).

10. *See Grendel's Den, Inc. v. Larken*, 749 F.2d 945, 951(1st Cir. 1984) ("Once the basic lodestar figure is calculated, the court must consider whether an upward or downward adjustment should be made to reflect the contingent nature of any fee (if such is not reflected in the hourly rate), delay in payment, quality of representation (i.e. an unusually good or poor performance above or below the skill already reflected in the hourly rates), exceptional (and unexpected) results obtained, etc.").

11. *See, e.g., In re NASDAQ Market-Makers*, 187 F.R.D. 465, 489 (S.D.N.Y. 1998) ("multipliers of between 3 and 4.5 have become common"); *Vizcaino v. Microsoft Corp.*, 290 F.3d 1043 (9th Cir. 2002) (listing an appendix of multipliers in common-fund cases, with an average of 3.43).

12. *See* Stuart J. Logan et al., *Attorney Fee Awards in Common Fund Class Actions*, 24 CLASS ACTION REP. 167, 169 (2003) [hereinafter *Attorney Fee Awards*]. A study of all federal class actions settled in 2006–2007 indicated that fees in 444 of the 688 settlements were calculated as a percentage of the announced value of the settlement and that in 204 of these settlements, where a lodestar could be calculated so as to do a lodestar cross-check, the lodestar multiplier median was 1.34 and the mean was 1.65. Fitzpatrick, *Fee Awards, supra* note 2, at 30.

13. *See, e.g., In re Standard Oil Co./British Petroleum Litig.*, No. 126760 (Ohio Ct. C.P. Cuyahoga Co. July 2, 1987) (multiplier of 21.8), cited in *Attorney Fee Awards*, at 169; *In re Merry-Go-Round Enter., Inc.*, 244 B.R. 327 (2000) (multiplier of 19.6); *In re Rite Aid Corp. Securities Litigation*, 146 F. Supp. 706 (E.D. Pa. 2001) (multiplier of 10.73), cited in *Attorney Fee Awards*, at 169; *Wilson v. Bank of America Nat'l Trust & Sav. Ass'n*, No. 643872 (Cal. Super. Ct. Aug. 16, 1982) (multiplier of 10), cited in 3 Newberg & Conte, NEWBERG ON CLASS ACTIONS, § 1403, at 14–5 n.21; *In re Epson Ink Cartridge Cases*, JCCP No. 4347 (Cal. Super. Ct. L.A. County, Oct. 23, 2006) (multiplier of 7).

14. *Bowling*, 992 F.Supp. at 1278.

15. *See* COURT AWARDED ATTORNEY FEES, REPORT OF THE THIRD CIRCUIT TASK FORCE, 108 F.R.D. 237 (1985); *see also* William B. Rubenstein, *Why the Percentage Method?*, CLASS ACTION ATTORNEY FEE DIGEST, March 2008, at 93.

16. *See* COURT AWARDED ATTORNEY FEES, 108 F.R.D. at 248 (noting that the lodestar method encourages lawyers to "engage in duplicative and unjustified work, inflate their 'normal' billing rate, and include fictitious hours or hours already billed on other matters").

17. DEREK BOK, THE COST OF TALENT: HOW EXECUTIVES AND PROFESSIONALS ARE PAID AND HOW IT AFFECTS AMERICA 391 (1993).

18. *See, e.g., Carlson v. Xerox Corp.*, No. 3:00-CV-1621 (AWT), *19 (D. Conn. Jan. 14, 2009) (290,759 hours); *In re Tyco Int'l, Ltd.* MDL, 535 F. Supp.2d 249, 270 (D. N.H. 2007) (488,000 hours); *In re WorldCom, Inc. Securities Litig.*, 388 F. Supp.2d 319, 354 (S.D.N.Y. 2005) (277,862 hours); *In re Lease Oil Antitrust Litigation (No. II)*, 186 F.R.D. 403, 443–449 (S.D. Tex. 1999) (132,000 hours); *In re NASDAQ Market-Makers Antitrust Litigation*, 187 F.R.D. 465 (S.D.N.Y. 1998) (129,629 hours); *In re Antibiotics Antitrust Litigation*, 410 F. Supp. 680, 704 (D. Minn. 1975) (115,150 hours).

19. A judge may instead appoint a fee auditor to review the billing records. As discussed infra, at note 43, however, this is rarely done.

20. In this case, lawyers alleged on behalf of shareholders that Continental officers made misleading statements about the bank's financial condition before its collapse. *In re Continental Ill. Sec. Litig.*, 750 F. Supp. 868 (1990) *rev'd In the Matter of Continental Ill. Sec. Litig.*, 962 F.2d 566 (1992). After the parties settled, the class attorneys requested $9 million in fees and costs (20% of the $45 million common fund).

21. *See Continental*, 750 F. Supp. at 872.

22. *Id.* at 878–85, 889, 892, 896; 962 F.2d at 568.

23. *Id.* at 878–79.

24. *Id.* at 879–80.

25. *Continental*, 962 F.2d at 571–72.

26. *Continental*, 962 F.2d at 568.

27. *Id.* Judge Posner additionally insisted on the "acute" need of a risk multiplier of at least 2 because the lawyers were paid on a contingent basis with a 50/50 chance of failure in the litigation despite Judge Grady's conclusion that the "risk of non-payment ... was not sufficient to warrant a contingency multiplier." *Continental*, 750 F. Supp. at 896; 962 F.2d at 569. Judge Posner also disapproved of Judge Grady's reduction of attorney hours, stating: "[a] judge is not permitted to destroy substantial entitlements to attorneys' fees on the basis of his inarticulable and unsubstantiated dissatisfaction with the lawyers' efforts to economize on their time and expenses." *Continental*, 962 F.2d at 570.

28. The U.S. Court of Appeals for the Ninth Circuit, which typically champions the interests of class action lawyers, has expertly pricked Judge Posner's market balloon. That court said: "The 'market' is simply counsel's expectation of court-awarded fees." It characterized the Seventh Circuit's effort to construct a market for such cases by determining what counsel "would have received had they handled a similar suit on a contingent fee basis, with a similar outcome, for a paying client" as "a unhelpful measure in many cases, and certainly an inappropriate measure to apply to all cases." Unlike commercial litigation where the fee is determined by application of the negotiated contingency percentage to the amount of the recovery, in class action litigation the fee is determined

on the basis of what a court finds to be reasonable. An attempt to "estimate the terms of the contract that private plaintiffs would have negotiated with their lawyers ... had bargaining occurred at the outset of the case strikes us as entirely illusory and speculative." *Vizcaino v. Microsoft*, 290 F.3d 1043, 1049 (9th Cir. 2002) (citations omitted).

29. *Goldberger v. Integrated Resources, et al.*, 209 F. 3d 43, 46 (2d Cir. 2000).

30. *Id*. at 51–52.

31. *See, e.g., Goldberger v. Integrated Resources, Inc.*, 209 F.3d 43, 50 (2d Cir. 2000) (encouraging the lodestar method as a cross-check on the reasonableness of the requested percentage); *see also* MANUAL FOR COMPLEX LITIGATION (FOURTH) § 14.11 n.484 (2004).

32. For example, in the *Rite Aid Corporation Securities Litigation*, the lower court awarded the class attorneys their requested fee of 25% of the fund created, which amounted to a lodestar multiplier of 4.07. *See In re Rite Aid Corp. Sec. Litig.*, 269 F. Supp. 603, 611 (2003). The Third Circuit Court of Appeals vacated the judgment and remanded the case because the district court had arrived at this multiplier by using an inflated hourly rate – that of the most senior attorneys in the litigation, and not the customary blended rate of all attorneys and paralegals. *See In re Rite Aid Corp. Sec. Litig.*, 396 F.3d 294, 306 (2003). If the calculation had been arrived at in the correct way, the Third Circuit stated, "the multiplier would have been a higher figure, alerting the trial court to reconsider the propriety of its fee award." 396 F.3d 294 at 306. The District Court apparently did not catch the hint, though, and merely adjusted the multiplier upward to 6.96 in order to reinstate the 25% attorneys fee award stating that "our recalculation of the multiplier does not alter our original conclusion." *In re Rite Aid Corp. Sec. Litig.*, 362 F. Supp. 2d 587, 589–90 (2003).

33. *See* Lisa G. Lerman, *Blue-Chip Bilking: Regulation of Billing and Expense Fraud by Lawyers*, 12 GEO. J. LEGAL ETHICS 205 (1999) (detailing sixteen cases of billing and expense fraud); *see also* WILLIAM G. ROSS, THE HONEST HOUR: THE ETHICS OF TIME-BASED BILLING BY ATTORNEYS 265–66, 269–70 (1996) (reporting that nearly two-thirds of the 106 outside counsel and nearly three-quarters of the 91 inside counsel who responded stated that they personally knew about some instances in which attorneys had padded their timesheets to record time that they had not actually performed).

34. *See* Douglas R. Richmond, *For a Few Dollars More: The Perplexing Problem of Unethical Billing Practices by Lawyers*, 60 S.C. L. REV. 63, 64 n.9 (2008).

35. Gerald F. Phillips, *The Bandits: Attempts by Lawyers to Pad Hours can Often Be Uncovered by a Careful Examination of Billing Statement*, 29 W. ST. U. L. REV. 265–81 (2002).

36. *See* James P. Schratz, *Cross-Examining a Legal Auditor*, 20 AM. J. TRIAL ADVOC. 91, 101 (1996) (concluding that "[g]iven the apparent frequency of

overbilling by a significant percentage of the legal profession and the corresponding belief of clients that they are being overcharged, the need for legal auditing is likely to increase").

37. A plausible explanation of judicial reluctance to allow scrutiny of time records is that there is much in those records that courts would regard as embarrassing if they were to see the light of day. For example, in a class action involving the distribution of cosmetics by department stores accused of price fixing, which is more fully discussed later in this chapter, the court went to great lengths to shield the time records from public view. *See* Chapter 18, § C. Lawyers attempting to horn in on the $24 million fee awarded for the cosmetics giveaway managed to let slip out that there were many billings of 24-hour days and even 72-hour days as well as other abusive billing practices. An even more disturbing example of judicial complicity is described by Judge Posner when he reversed the lower court's approval of a class action settlement and award of attorneys' fee in *Reynolds v. Beneficial National Bank*, 288 F. 3d 277 (2002). The case involved a class action against H&R Block, the tax preparer, and the Beneficial Bank. When Block filed a refund claim with the IRS, it offered its customers the opportunity to advance the payment by borrowing that amount from Beneficial Bank at an annual interest rate often exceeding 100%. *Reynolds*, 288 F.3d at 280. Block did not disclose that Beneficial paid Block a fee for arranging each loan. Judge Posner found the settlement inadequate but reserved his full fire power for the action of the trial judge in approving the fee request of more than $2 million, stating: "[A]fter approving the settlement, the district judge encouraged the ... [class action lawyers] to submit their fee applications in camera [i.e. privately to the judge], lest the paucity of the time they had devoted to the case (for which the judge awarded them more than $2 million in attorneys' fee) be used as ammunition by objectors to the adequacy of the representation of the class. There was no sound basis for sealing the fee applications, let alone for sealing the number of hours each of the settlement class counsel had devoted to the case. The applications are not in the appellate record and we do not know what the total number of hours devoted by the class counsel to this litigation was, but apparently it was a small number. This is not surprising, since the lawyers' efforts between the filing of the complaint and the settlement negotiations were singularly feeble." *Reynolds*, 288 F.3d at 284.

38. *See* Fed. R. Civ. Pro. 53 and 54(d)(2)(D).

39. *See, e.g., Gunter v. Ridgewood Energy Corp.*, 223 F.3d 190, 201 n.6 (3d Cir. 2000) (noting that if the "court ... suspects that the plaintiffs' rights in a particular case are not being adequately vindicated, [it] may appoint counsel, a special master, or an expert to review or challenge the fee application filed by plaintiffs' attorneys"); *In re AOL Time Warner Sec. & ERISA Litig.*, 2006 WL 3057232 (S.D.N.Y. Oct. 26, 2006) (adopting special master's report of attorney fees).

40. *Goldberger v. Integrated Resources, et al.*, 209 F.3d 43, 46 2d Cir. (2000).

41. *Id.*

42. *Id.* at 46–47.

43. *See, e.g., In re WorldCom, Inc. Sec. Litig.*, 2004 WL 2591402, *22 (S.D.N.Y. Nov. 12, 2004) (denying request for appointment of a special master); *In re Intelligent Electronics Sec. Litig.*, 1997 WL 786984, *10 (E.D. Pa. Nov. 26, 1997) (denying request for appointment of special master because it would "needlessly complicate the procedures"); *In re NASDAQ Market-Makers Antitrust Litig.*, 187 F.R.D. 465, 481 (S.D.N.Y. 1998) (denying request for appointment of a special class guardian).

44. *See In re Enron Corp. Sec.*, Derivative & ERISA Litig., 2008 WL 4178130, *59 (S.D. Tex. Sept. 8, 2008).

45. *See id.* at *59.

46. *See* Ruling on Motion for Award of Attorneys' Fees, at ex.2, *Carlson v. Xerox Corp.*, No. 3:00-cv-1621, (D. Conn. Jan. 14, 2009).

47. *See* Lead Plaintiffs' Second Supplemental Response to Objections, *Carlson v. Xerox Corp.*, No. 3:00-cv-1621, (D. Conn. Oct. 9, 2008).

48. Pub. L. No. 104–67, 109 Stat. 737 (1995) (codified as amended at 15 U.S.C. § 77z-1 [2006]).

49. *See* 15 U.S.C. § 78u-4(a)(3) (2006).

50. S. REP. No. 104–98, at 6 (1995).

51. *See* 15 U.S.C. § 78u-4 (a)(3)(B)(ii) and (iii)(I)(bb) and (cc) (2006). This provision is further analyzed in Chapter 18 § (I). According to a 2007 report, as a result of this PSLRA requirement, public and union pension funds are being selected as the lead plaintiff in 40% of securities class action cases. Grace Lamont, ed., 2007 SECURITIES LITIGATION STUDY, PricewaterhouseCoopers, Apr. 8, 2008, *available at* http://10b5.pwc.com/PDF/2007%20SECURITY%20 LIT%20STUDY%20W-LT.PDF.

52. Kenneth Lovett, *Pension Pay-to-Play: Law Firms Gave Canholders Big Bucks, Then Got $518M in Fees from State Fund*, N.Y. DAILY NEWS, Oct. 8, 2009.

53. Editorial, *Pay-to-Play Torts*, WALL ST. J. Oct. 31–Nov. 1, 2009 at A18. The pay-to-play firms are not only seeking – and obtaining – designation as lead counsel, they are also requesting the public officials to allow them to direct which other law firms are to be selected to join in sharing the fees generated. Drew T. Johnson-Skinner, *Paying-to-Play in Securities Class Actions: A Look at Lawyers' Campaign Contributions*, 84 N.Y.U. L. REV. 1725, 1751 (2009).

54. Lovett, *supra* note 52.

55. Mark Maremont, Tom McGinty & Nathan Koppel, *Trial Lawyers Contribute, Shareholder Suits Follow*, WALL ST. J., Feb. 3, 2010, at A1.

56. The blatant nature of this exchange of cash for selection is made apparent in an e-mail from one partner in a major securities class action firm to another.

This e-mail was sent in response to a demand from a state attorney general, conveyed through the firm's lobbyist, that the firm contribute $20,000 to the attorney general's campaign in order to be retained by the attorney general in a particular class action. *See* Mar. 7, 2008 e-mail on file with the author, quoting from Aug. 3, 2004 e-mail. The e-mail instructed the other partners how to raise the required $20,000 payment. After listing those law firm partners who had already contributed the maximum allowed amount of $1,000 each, the e-mail listed other partners, who had not maxed out and the amount of money each was to contribute to make up the $20,000 "pot."

57. As described in an article in *Forbes*:

Plaintiff lawyers give handily to the politicians who hire them. They hire ex-insiders to woo pension funds, fete clients at cushy conferences and pay referral fees to powerbrokers who hook them up with new pension plaintiffs. None of this is illegal per se; nor does it violate existing rules of legal ethics.

Neil Weinberg and Daniel Fisher, *The Class Action Industrial Complex*, FORBES, Sept. 20, 2004, at 152.

58. *Iron Workers Local No. 25 Pension Fund v. Credit-Based Asset Servicing and Securitization, LLC, et al.*, 08 Civ. 10841, at 5 (S.D.N.Y. May 26, 2009).

59. *Id.* at 153.

60. James D. Cox & Randall S. Thomas, *Does the Plaintiff Matter? An Empirical Analysis of Lead Plaintiffs in Securities Class Actions*, 106 COLUM. L. REV. 1586, 1589 (2006).

61. *Id.* at 1627.

62. Michael A. Perino, *Institutional Activism through Litigation: An Empirical Assessment of Public Pension Fund Participation in Securities Class Actions* (St. John's University School of Law Legal Studies Research Paper Series, Paper No. 06–0055, 2006), *available at* http://papers.ssrn.com/abstract=93872.

63. James D. Cox, Randall S. Thomas & Lynn Bai, *There Are Plaintiffs and … There Are Plaintiffs: An Empirical Analysis of Securities Class Action Settlements*, 61 VAND. L. REV. 355, 378–79 (2008).

64. *See* Stephen J. Choi, Drew T. Johnson-Skinner & Adam C. Pritchard, *The Price of Pay to Play in Securities Class Actions* (Dec. 22, 2009), *available at* http://ssrn.com/abstract=1527047.

65. *See In re Cendant Corp. Sec. Litig.*, 264 F.3d 201 (3d Cir. 2001); *In re Cendant Corp. Sec. Litig.*, 243 F.Supp.2d 166 (D.N.J. 2003); *see also* Neil Weinberg and Daniel Fisher, *The Class Action Industrial Complex*, FORBES, Sept. 20, 2004, at 150.

66. *In re Cendant Corp. Sec. Litig.*, 243 F.Supp.2d 166, 173 (D. N.J. 2003).

67. *See In re Cendant Corp. Sec. Litig.*, 264 F.3d 201, 285–86 (3d Cir. 2001).

68. *In re Cendant Corp. Sec. Litig.*, 243 F.Supp.2d 166, 173 (D. N.J. 2003).

69. *See* Neil Weinberg & Daniel Fisher, *The Class Action Industrial Complex*, FORBES, Sept. 20, 2004, at 152.

70. The Second Circuit in *City of Detroit v. Grinnell Corp.* cautioned: "For the sake of their own integrity, the integrity of the legal profession, and the integrity of Rule 23, it is important that the courts should avoid awarding 'windfall fees' and that they should likewise avoid every appearance of having done so." 495 F.2d 448, 470 (2d Cir. 1974). *See also Rawlings v. Prudential-Bache Prop., Inc.*, 9 F.3d 513, 516 (6th Cir. 1993).

71. Geoffrey P. Miller & Theodore Eisenberg, *Attorney Fees in Class Action Settlements: An Empirical Study*, 1 J. EMPIRICAL LEGAL STUD. 27 (2004) [hereinafter Miller & Eisenberg]; *see also* Jonathan D. Glater, *Study Disputes View of Costly Surge in Class-Action Suits*, N.Y. TIMES, Jan. 14, 2004, at C1.

72. *See* Miller & Eisenberg, *id.* at 46; *see also* Stuart J. Logan et al., *Attorney Fee Awards in Common Fund Class Actions*, 24 CLASS ACTION REP. 167 (2003). This study of attorney's fees in a selected sample of 1,120 class actions in the period of 1973–2003 done by *Class Action Reports* found that the average percentage of attorney's fees was 18.4%, totaling $7.6 billion in fees.

73. *See* Miller & Eisenberg, *supra* note 71, at 28.

74. *Id.* at 47.

75. *Id.* at 27.

76. *Id.* at 27.

77. Research Brief, *Anatomy of an Insurance Class Action*, RAND 2007, *available at* http://www.rand.org/pubs/research_briefs/RB9249/.

78. *Id.* at 45–46. The authors state that "[a]lthough published opinions are not necessarily representative of the universe of all cases, they can lead to important insights." *Id.* at 46.

79. *See* Warren H. Harris & Erin G. Busby, *Highlights of the Class Action Fairness Act of 2005*, 72 DEF. COUNS. J. 228, 228 (2005).

80. PACE ET AL., HOW TRANSPARENT ARE CLASS ACTION OUTCOMES?, at 16–17. The Federal Judicial Center has also noted: "reliable data on class action activity in most state court systems simply do not exist." *See* PROGRESS REPORT TO THE ADVISORY COMMITTEE ON CIVIL RULES ON THE IMPACT OF CAFA ON THE FEDERAL COURTS FEDERAL JUDICIAL CENTER, 4 (Nov. 2007), *available at* http://www.fjc.gov/public/pdf.nsf/lookup/cafa1107.pdf/$file/cafa1107.pdf.

81. GEORGE L. PRIEST, WHAT WE KNOW AND WHAT WE DON'T KNOW ABOUT MODERN CLASS ACTIONS: A REVIEW OF THE EISENBERG-MILLER STUDY, CIVIL JUSTICE REPORT, (2005) No. 9.

82. *Id.*

83. *See* Miller & Eisenberg, note 71 at 78.

84. *Id.* at 27.

85. Press Release, U.S. Chamber of Commerce, Chamber Poll Shows Americans Want Class Action Reform: Almost Half Believe Plaintiffs' Lawyers Benefit More than Consumers (Mar. 5, 2003), *available at* http://www.uschamber.com/press/releases/2003/march/03–40.htm.

86. *Id.*

87. *See* John H. Beisner, Matthew Shors, & Jessica Davidson Miller, *Class Action "Cops": Public Servants or Private Entrepreneurs?*, 57 STAN. L. REV. 1441, 1444 (2005) (referring to polls showing that "Americans do not trust the class action system, do not think that consumers benefit from class actions, and believe that lawyers take home all the money recovered in such cases").

88. *See* Theodore Eisenberg & Geoffrey Miller, *Attorneys' Fees and Expenses in Class Action Settlements*: 1993–2008, 7 J. EMPIRICAL LEGAL STUDIES (2010), *available at* ssrn.com/abstract=1497224 (finding that state and federal judges awarded the fees requested by class counsel in 72% of settlements); Theodore Eisenberg, Geoffrey Miller & Michael A. Perino, *A New Look at Judicial Impact: Attorneys' Fees in Securities Class Actions after* Goldberger v. Integrated Resources, Inc., 29 WASH. U.J.L. & POL'Y 4 (2009), *available at* ssrn.com/abstract=1244322 (finding that mean and median fee awards in securities class actions hovered around 90% of what class counsel requested).

89. John C. Coffee, *Rescuing the Private Attorney General: Why the Model of Lawyer As Bounty Hunter Is Not Working*, 42 MD. L. REV. 215, 237 (1983).

90. John C. Coffee, *Class Action Accountability: Reconciling Exit, Voice, and Loyalty in Representative Litigation*, 100 COLUM L. REV. 370, 438 (2000).

91. *In re Union Carbide Corp.*, 724 F. Supp. 160, 169 (S.D.N.Y. 1989).

92. Quoted in *In re Quantum Health Resources, Inc. Sec. Litig.*, 962 F. Supp. 1254, 1258 (C.D. Cal. 1997).

93. *Id.*

18 How Class Action Lawyers Game Fee Setting

IN COMMON-FUND CLASS ACTIONS, THE INTERESTS OF THE lawyers who bring the class action diverge from those of the class when it comes time to set the fee. Because the fee comes from the common fund, a zero-sum game prevails: The more the lawyers are awarded, the less there is available for the class.

A similar conflict of interest arises in cases initiated under a statute with a fee-shifting provision, which allows the court to order a settling defendant to pay the plaintiffs' attorneys fee and costs in addition to the settlement amount. In these cases, defendants are concerned about the total payment required to settle the action, which consists of the payment to the class plus the payment of the class lawyer's fee. For this reason, the parties often simultaneously negotiate the settlement amount and the fee so that the defendant has a fix on the total cost of the settlement. But this presents the parties with the opportunity to trade a higher fee for a more-than-offsetting lower settlement amount for the class. Even when the shifted fee is negotiated after the settlement is reached, the defendant takes the expected fee reimbursement into account in agreeing to the terms of the settlement. Courts are well aware of the incentives for collusion in these circumstances and maintain that they carefully scrutinize such settlements. Even so, many collusive settlements gain approval.

A. "Clear Sailing" Provisions

Lawyers protect their fees from careful scrutiny by requiring that, as part of any settlement, the defendant agrees not to contest their fee request to the court and instead gives it "clear sailing."[1] In fee-shifting cases that settle without the creation of a common fund, this means that the defendant agrees not to contest a fee request up to a certain amount. When a common fund is created, the clear-sailing clause typically provides that the defendant will not contest the percentage or the lodestar plus multiplier-based fee request that class counsel will present to the court (up to a certain amount). Class counsel and the defendant thus present a united front to the court, seeking approval of both the settlement and the agreed upon fee. At this point, as Judge Henry Friendly observed, "[a]ll the dynamics conduce to judicial approval of the settlement."[2]

The intended effect of a clear-sailing agreement is further made manifest by the U.S. Supreme Court's decision to refuse to hear a case contesting an attorney's fee that was more than double the total payout to the class. Justice Sandra Day O'Connor recognized that the fee was "by any measure ... extraordinary"; but because of the clear-sailing agreement, she concluded that the Court could not entertain the objection to the fee by the defendant because "the parties agreed that ... [class counsel] would apply for attorney's fees in an amount up to one-third of the reversionary fund, and ... [the defendant] expressly pledged not to 'directly or indirectly oppose [respondents'] application for fees'."[3]

It is common practice for class counsel to hold the settlement hostage to defendant's acquiescence to the fee request and a clear-sailing provision. The Ninth Circuit Court of Appeals prohibited this practice in *Staton v. Boeing*,[4] noting that this inflates attorneys' fees.[5] Judge Jon Newman of the Second Circuit Court of Appeals also criticized the use of clear-sailing agreements, stating:

> [W]hen a "clear sailing" clause is used and the fee application is not challenged by the defendant, the figure allowed by a trial court will

tend to be very close to, and frequently precisely at, the negotiated ceiling, as occurred in this case.

A "clear sailing" clause has two adverse effects that cast substantial doubt on the legitimacy of its use. First, it deprives the trial court and a reviewing court of the certainty of having the propriety of the fee request tested in the adversary process ... [It] creates the risk that a fee request within the negotiated ceiling will not be challenged, placing upon the courts the burden of examining the basis for the fee, unaided by the challenges of an adverse party. Second, the clause creates the likelihood that plaintiffs' counsel, in obtaining the defendant's agreement not to challenge a fee request within a stated ceiling, will bargain away something of value to the plaintiff class. It is unlikely that a defendant will gratuitously accede to the plaintiffs' request for a "clear sailing" clause without obtaining something in return. That something will normally be at the expense of the plaintiff class.[6]

Courts that talk the talk about clear-sailing provisions increasing lawyers' fees at the expense of the class, however, do not walk the walk. No court has ever invalidated a settlement because of a clear-sailing provision. In fact, these provisions are now routinely used in class actions.

B. The Experts Who Bless the Fees

After a settlement has been reached, the court must hold a hearing to determine the "fairness" of the settlement for the class, hear any objections from members of the class, and set a reasonable fee for class counsel. Only a handful of class members out of even hundreds of thousands have enough interest in these proceedings to object to some settlements or fee requests. Moreover, many courts look on these objections as attempts to "hold up" approval of the class lawyer's fee so as to coerce a payment to the objectors and their counsel and therefore give these fee objectors short shrift.

Class counsels buttress their fee requests by obtaining declarations from "experts" – often law school professors and former judges – to support their fee requests. Prominent legal academics and retired judges who appear frequently to endorse class counsels' fee requests and the value of settlements announced as being made available to the class – often vastly inflated – include Professors John Coffee, Theodore Eisenberg, Arthur Miller, Geoffrey Miller, William Rubenstein, Charles Silver, and former Judges Lee Sorokin and Arlin Adams.[7] The more prominent the law professor's academic credentials and the more prestigious his academic institution, the more influential the endorsement and the greater the fee that the academic can charge. Furthermore, because these declarations are rarely viewed by the public and are never subjected to challenge before the court, the financial incentives to endorse class counsels' fee requests often predominates over other considerations.

"Bless the fee" experts' willingness to endorse improbable if not purely fictitious settlement values is on particular display in settlements where the sole or principal relief is injunctive – that is, a promise enforceable in court that the defendant will or will not take certain actions in the future that are alleged to benefit consumers or shareholders. These types of relief are inherently difficult to value and particularly susceptible to abuse in determining the settlement value. Many of these and other settlement values announced as being made available to the class are vastly inflated in order to justify even more inflated fee requests.

An example of such an abusive settlement and a fee request, nonetheless endorsed by a fee expert, is the Automotive Directions class action,[8] which was based on marketing schemes that allegedly violated the Driver's Privacy Protection Act (DPPA).[9] That act regulates the obtainment, use, and disclosure of personal information from state motor vehicle records. Because the class size exceeded 200 million persons and the DPPA provides for statutory damages of $2,500 per violation, damages could have amounted to $500 billion. Instead of paying statutory damages, however, the defendant agreed to settle the case for a payment of $25 million to the lawyers and nothing to the class. To justify the fee, the settlement included a scheme that would provide more privacy protection than the regulations set out in the DPPA – though there was no evidence that any licensed drivers were seeking this added protection.

To obtain this "relief," class counsel said they worked a total of 20,311 hours over a six-year period and asserted a lodestar of $8,786,928.75. Professor Geoffrey Miller, who has provided declarations and affidavits to support fee requests in more than twenty class actions, supported the request for a $25 million fee – a multiplier of 2.78 of the claimed lodestar. As for the value of the settlement to licensed automobile drivers, he said that "[i]t is clear that this relief ... would have very significant value ... [which if] quantified ... would easily justif[y]" the requested fee.[10] But the elaborate enforcement scheme appears to have been simply a fig leaf used to hide the fact that the "relief" was largely illusory. The only ones who realized "significant value" were the class lawyers and the experts who supported the fee requests.

Courts frequently rely on and cite these expert recommendations in granting fee requests as if they were the product of unbiased academic scholarship rather than financial self-interest. Courts could appoint a guardian for the class, at the class's expense, to argue in favor of the class and thus balance the recommendations of the "bless these fees" experts hired by the class lawyers, but they virtually never do. Instead, courts denominate themselves as the guardians for the class to assure that the fee is reasonable, often emphasizing their "fiduciary role."[11] In reality, however, fee determinations are essentially *ex parte* proceedings – that is, ones in which only one side of the issue is represented: those of class counsel. The absence of an adversarial process makes it much easier for the large majority of courts to award class counsel the fee that it has negotiated with the defendant or, if there is no agreement, the amount the attorney is seeking. In fact, in a 2008 study of 730 securities class actions, Michael Perino of the St. John's University School of Law found that "plaintiffs' lawyers received approximately 90% of their requested fee."[12]

Another device class action lawyers use to bolster their fee requests involves hiring former federal judges to render an "independent" analysis of the reasonableness of the fee request in a legal memorandum. Not surprisingly, these memoranda, which are received with great deference by courts, invariably support the fee requests.[13] The intent of hiring former judges is apparently to lend gravitas to fee requests. However, because the class lawyers hire and pay these former judges, it is difficult to regard their declarations as anything more than self-serving declarations, bought and paid for by class counsel and perhaps even charged to the class.[14]

C. Time Records and the Lodestar Process

As discussed earlier, some class action fees are set by a court using a lodestar method: the number of hours worked by each attorney multiplied by the prevailing hourly rate for those attorneys (usually in the $300–$900 range). Even here, however, I contend that effective hourly rates are much higher than these lodestar calculations reflect. First, the numbers of hours claimed to have been expended (which can range as high as 400,000 or more) are virtually never subject to any meaningful audit and are almost certainly overstated. As noted, courts' audit phobia has led them to mostly deny fee objectors who seek to get further information through discovery of class counsels' time records. In one such case, the Ninth Circuit Court of Appeals upheld the denial of a fee objector's discovery request in a cellular phone antitrust case in the face of evidence that class counsel overstated its hours in other cellular phone antitrust cases and could easily have logged hours spent on these other cases to the one in contention.[15] The court reasoned on the "catch 22" grounds that "there was no showing of any overstating of hours in this case."[16] In other words, you can't use legal processes to uncover evidence of billing fraud unless you have clear evidence of billing fraud.

Furthermore, even when class counsel submit their fee requests using the lodestar method, no attempt is made to cross-check this request with fee requests submitted by that law firm in other class actions. Such a cross-check would show how many hours each of the firms' lawyers had listed for *all* of the class actions that they had participated in during the same time period. If class action law firms, when seeking fees, were subject to an audit of each lawyer's time records in that and other contemporaneous class actions, some of these attorneys' hourly totals and the fees they generate would be out of this world – literally.[17]

Though courts routinely deny fee objectors and others the opportunity to use discovery to uncover bill padding, if not billing fraud, three class actions – all involving a falling out among the lawyers about how millions of dollars in fees should be divided – provide us with a rare view into the underworld of lawyers' time records in class actions. In the first, Dexter and Gretchen Kamilewicz, mortgage holders with BancBoston, were two out of 715,000 plaintiffs conscripted into an Alabama state court class action involving the timing of BancBoston's crediting of certain amounts of escrow surplus to each mortgage holder's account.[18] The relief ranged from a mere $0.00 to $8.76 per mortgage holder.[19] Class counsel and BancBoston agreed to a fee of $8.5 million, which bore no relationship to the paltry relief secured.

To come up with the $8.5 million, class counsel and BancBoston agreed on a scheme to mulct the mortgage holders by charging their accounts for the lawyer's fee. Though the Kamilewiczes were credited with $2.19 as their share of the settlement, their account was debited $91.33 to pay the purloined fee.[20] When the Kamilewiczes sued the class counsel that had scooped them up,[21] they were denied all relief. Once the Alabama state court approved the settlement and fee,[22] it was over. No matter how egregious and self-serving their class lawyer had been, once the judge in the class action gives his approval, there can be no subsequent attack on the settlement or lawyer's fee.[23]

However outrageous this outcome, it is eclipsed by class counsel's own claims of a record-keeping scam. Our insight is purely accidental, the result of a fee dispute between two sets of plaintiffs' lawyers, one from Alabama and the other from Chicago, who had agreed to split their fees 60/40, respectively. The Chicago lawyers believed they had been shortchanged and sought an accounting from the Alabama lawyers who had actually collected the fee. The latter refused to provide an accounting but did send a copy of IRS Form 1099 provided by BancBoston, showing a total fee payment of $7.18 million. When the Chicago lawyers went to BancBoston, they learned that the bank had actually paid $8,556,201. The Chicago lawyers then sued the Alabama lawyers with regard to the fee split. During the fee fight, both sides testified to the amounts of time they had worked on the case. The Alabama firm stated that it worked about 2,000 hours on the case and that the Chicago lawyers worked, at most, 335 hours. Together, this totaled 2,335 hours.[24] At the hearing several years earlier to determine the fairness of the settlement and approve the fee, however, the lead Alabama lawyer testified that he and two other members of his firm worked between 5,500 and 7,500 hours – about 60 percent of the work done on the case – and that the Chicago lawyers did the other 40 percent, for a total of about 10,000 hours. Thus, we learn from the fee fight that the 10,000 hour total reported to the court to justify the $8.5 million fee request was more than four times the 2,335 hours the lawyers later claimed to have actually worked.[25]

There was a similarly informative fee fight in a class action filed against various department stores and cosmetics manufacturers, charging that they had fixed the prices of certain cosmetics products.[26] The suit, brought on behalf of nearly 40 million purchasers of cosmetics between May 1994 and July 2003,[27] alleged violations of both state and federal antitrust laws, which provided for tripling the damage award plus an award of attorneys' fees.[28] Although potential damages could have run into the billions of dollars, the suit was ultimately settled with no monetary payment to any class member. Instead, the settlement agreement stated that defendants would provide $175 million worth of department store cosmetics to members of the settlement class.[29] These products could come from the manufacturers' existing stock or be specially manufactured for the settlement.[30] In fact, the products made available – which the manufacturers or stores claimed were worth $18 to $25[31] – were chosen by the manufacturers and made specifically for the giveaway.[32]

Consumers had to sign a form attesting that they qualified as class members and were entitled to one product only.[33] By the end of the first day of distribution, however, supplies at many stores were completely cleaned out, as consumers simply ignored the "one claim per customer" limit.[34] Many of those who came the second day to claim their "compensation" were sent away empty-handed. Although the judge overseeing the case stated that "[t]here is no dispute as to the serious weakness of plaintiffs' case,"[35] he approved the lawyers' $24 million fee request. Moreover, despite paying this hefty fee,[36] the stores believed the "giveaway" might have paid for itself in increased business.[37]

During the proceedings, a group of lawyers, who became known as the "coordinated objectors," tried to cut themselves in for a share of the fees, claiming that they contributed to the settlement.[38] Because many firms were involved in bringing the class action, the court appointed a special master to recommend how the fees should be allocated among them.[39] The special master required the firms to submit their time records. When the coordinated objectors sought those records, however, the firms refused to produce them.[40] After the coordinated objectors filed a motion to compel production of the records, and the special master indicated that he would be inclined to order the production of the records, class counsel tendered the records to the objectors.[41]

These billing records were designated "confidential" by class counsel when they were provided to the objectors.[42] However, after the special master recommended that counsel for the coordinated objectors receive no part of the legal fees,[43] they filed the records publicly as exhibits attached to a motion for reconsideration of the fee award.[44] Although the court removed those exhibits from public access ten days later,[45] a motion filed by the coordinated objectors provides some snapshots of the firms' billing practices.[46]

For example, the objectors indicated that one of the firms representing the class had eleven instances in which a single individual billed between forty-eight and seventy-two hours in a single day.[47] That same firm had approximately seventy-three other instances in which its lawyers and staff had twenty-four-hour billable days. One of the other firms provided time sheets for paralegals that indicated more than 7,000 hours of paralegal time. However, more than 5,000 of those hours were only supported by time sheets that did not reference the Cosmetics litigation. That firm also billed between 4,700 and 7,350 hours for contract staff. Although most of the amounts billed by and paid to these workers were redacted, there were at least two time sheets that the firm failed to redact. These sheets showed that one firm charged $195 per hour for a contract worker, while paying her at a rate of $30 per hour. Other billing records for this firm indicated an attorney billing a one-and-a-half-hour conference with himself and more than 500 hours billed that remained completely undocumented. A third firm submitted bills, at rates ranging from $90 to $195 per hour, for such tasks as moving boxes, cleaning desks, filing, copying, and placing a deposition transcript in a room. Finally, a fourth firm submitted billing records that documented a total lodestar of nearly $3.3 million, but when the records were produced, it reduced its total to $1.5 million with no documentation or explanation.

In a third fee fight over payments from settlements of an antitrust class action, substantial evidence indicated that the 97,000 hours claimed by the lawyers were vastly inflated. In fact, the class lawyers had "worked backwards" by selecting a desired percentage of the $50.65 million settlement fund as their requested fee and then simply inflated their hours to justify the fee.[48]

Unfortunately, these fee fights, which one of the attorneys in the antitrust action characterized as "sharks in a feeding frenzy,"[49] are the only glimpses provided to us of the practices that lawyers use to compile time records in class actions. Despite the evidence that class action lawyers engage in extensive bill padding, some courts go to great lengths to protect class action lawyers from having their time records scrutinized. One plausible explanation is that they are concerned that this scrutiny would reveal a regular pattern of outright padding of law firms' lodestar submissions in class actions – thus perhaps undermining the regulatory power conferred by courts on themselves by empowering and enriching class action lawyers.

In addition to these instances of padding of the hours in the lodestar and overstating the number of hours productively invested in cases, class lawyers have developed a number of other practices to raise their fees and avoid close scrutiny of their fee requests. In the following sections, I address some of these practices.

D. The Reversionary Settlement Ploy

As noted, a practice that class action lawyers use to game the system and obtain excessive fees involves trading a higher fee for the lawyer for a more-than-offsetting lower payment to the class. Generally, class action monetary settlements are of two types: pro-rata and reversionary. In a pro-rata settlement, any amount of the settlement not claimed by class members is redistributed to those class members who file qualifying claims. In a reversionary settlement, however, any amount of a settlement not claimed by class members reverts to the defendant.[50]

Here is an illustration of how class lawyers and defendants can use a reversionary settlement to inflate fees for their mutual benefit at the expense of the class. Assume that the class action lawyer and defendant have decided to settle the class action for a payment by the defendant of $20 million. Out of this sum, the lawyer may anticipate that the court will approve an attorney's fee of 25 percent of the recovery – that is, $5 million. By colluding with the defendant at the class's expense, however, both the class lawyer and the defendant can improve their respective positions. Instead of a $20 million pro-rata settlement, the parties agree to a $40 million reversionary settlement. This increases the lawyer's anticipated 25 percent fee to $10 million. To make it palatable to the defendant, the defendant must be reasonably assured that in addition to paying the $10 million fee, it will not actually pay out the full additional $30 million; in fact, this additional payment will be far less than $10 million, bringing the total bill to well below the previous $20 million amount. Here is how this is done. First, the class lawyer agrees to a less than robust notice process so that fewer class members are put on notice of the settlement than would otherwise be the case. Second, the class lawyer agrees to claim filing requirements that are so onerous that few class members are able to file a claim or have the incentive to do so. For example, to recover her share of the settlement amount, a class member may be required to provide copies of credit card receipts for purchases made five years earlier or other evidence of a purchase that few consumers retain for any length of time. So structured, both parties reasonably predict that, at most, 20 percent of the class will actually file valid claims – a number consistent with the reality of many reversionary settlements. Therefore, of the $30 million available for payment to class members after deducting the lawyers' fee (and ignoring expenses), $6 million (20% of the $30 million) will actually be paid to class members. Thus, the lawyers' fee actually amounts to 62.5 percent of the total recovery and is 167 percent of the class's actual recovery. The total payment of $16 million constitutes a 20 percent savings for the defendant when compared to the cost of a $20 million pro-rata settlement. This math may explain the popularity of reversionary settlements.

E. Coupon Settlements and the Class Action Fairness Act

Another ploy class action lawyers have used to generate unearned fees is the "coupon" settlement. Coupon settlements occur when the defendant settles the class action by agreeing to issue coupons, or some variant, to class members who submit the required paperwork, entitling them to purchase the defendant's products or services at a discount.[51] The defendant also agrees to pay the class lawyer a cash-on-the-barrelhead fee, typically calculated as a percentage of the face value of the coupons. For example, a coupon settlement providing 1,000,000 class members with the right to apply for coupons giving them a $500 discount off the purchase of a car could be valued for fee-setting purposes at $500,000,000. The lawyer's fee in such a scenario could range from $5 million to

$50 million and would be payable in cash, not in coupons. Indeed, the only cash payment made by the defendant is the payment to the attorney. For purposes of this fee computation, the fact that car makers frequently offer far more substantial discounts to entice purchasers and that only 1,000 of the 1,000,000 class members actually redeemed the coupons, is irrelevant.

To stem these corrupt settlements that were rarely rejected by courts, Congress enacted the Class Action Fairness Act (CAFA) in 2005.[52] A specific provision dealing with coupon settlements requires courts to make a written determination that "the settlement is fair, reasonable, and adequate for class members."[53] Although this standard imposed by CAFA on courts for approval of coupon settlements is the same standard that courts purported to apply pre-CAFA, courts have interpreted "the statutory directive to imply the application of a greater level of scrutiny to the existing criteria than existed pre-CAFA."[54] As a consequence, coupon settlements face a far higher level of scrutiny than in the past, resulting in fewer such settlements.

Another feature of CAFA, which mitigates abuse of coupon settlements, is the requirement that "the portion of any attorney's fee award to class counsel that is attributable to the award of the coupons shall be based on the value to class members of the coupons that are redeemed."[55] Thus, at least in coupon settlements, courts may no longer use the face value of largely worthless coupons as the basis for fee setting. Instead, they are directed to base any percentage fee on the actual value of redeemed coupons. However, a provision no doubt inserted by supporters of the class action bar allows the attorney to forgo seeking a fee based on the actual coupon value to the class and instead seek a lodestar-based fee, that is, a fee based on the number of hours expended and the hourly rates allowed by a court.[56] This provision allows a court to ignore the underlying objective of CAFA and award a class action lawyer in a coupon settlement a lodestar-based fee running into the millions of dollars. It remains to be seen whether this loophole will be used to an extent that it undermines CAFA.

Another sizeable loophole in CAFA is the ease with which class action lawyers can restructure what would have been a coupon settlement pre-CAFA into injunctive relief (which is specifically excluded from the CAFA provision regulating fees).[57] Injunctive relief can be as worthless as coupon settlements, as illustrated by a proposed settlement on behalf of Costco members who purchase motor fuel from Costco. Though labeled as "injunctive relief" to avoid CAFA's strictures, the settlement requires Costco to install a device on its gas pumps, which may or may not benefit class members. Costco's undertaking is contingent on class counsel thereafter applying for approval and paying the necessary regulatory fees to convert the pumps (which it is not obligated to do) and further contingent on whether Costco decides that it can secure the equipment affordably and without disrupting its business. This economically worthless (or worse) settlement includes $10 million to be paid to class counsel.[58]

CAFA asserts that a primary purpose of the statute is to "provid[e] for federal court consideration of interstate cases of national importance under diversity jurisdiction."[59] This is an implicit reference to state courts that routinely certified class actions of nationwide importance where the law of one state would be imposed on the nation even if contrary to other states' laws. Presumably, these abusive holdings will be largely precluded by the leading provision of CAFA, which allows any defendant in most class actions filed in state court that have nationwide application to be removed to federal courts.[60] The assumptions on which this provision was based – both expressed and implicit – are that federal judges are far less likely than state court judges to (1) certify baseless class actions or class actions that impose one state's laws on all of the other states; and (2) approve abusive settlements and outlandish fees for mostly low-worth or worthless settlements.[61] Even so, there are wide differences in the propensity of federal judges to certify class actions filed in or removed to their courts.[62]

CAFA, however, has a mandatory carve-out from the removal provision for actions filed in state courts where two-thirds or more of the members of all proposed plaintiff classes in the aggregate and the primary defendants are citizens of the State in which the action was originally filed.[63] Class action lawyers, therefore, may be able to circumvent CAFA's removal provisions by filing the same class action in several of the most populous states, limiting their reach in each filing to mostly in-state residents.

Experience to date with CAFA, enacted in 2005, appears to indicate a mixed picture as to whether the objectives of the legislation are being met, though the data is not yet robust and is available only as to filings and not actual litigation practices. Although class action filings in federal courts based on diversity have substantially increased, this increase appears not to have been driven by removal of actions filed in state courts.[64] There is no data yet on whether CAFA has had any discernable impact on the rate of certification of class actions. The limited pre-CAFA information available for federal courts indicates that the rate of class certification was falling at the turn of the millennium.[65] Likewise, a study of California state court class actions for the period 2000–2005 also showed a substantial decline in the frequency of certification, suggesting a pre-CAFA increased scrutiny of the merits of filings.[66] Even if post-CAFA data emerge indicating a further decline in the percentage of class certifications, which is an intended effect of CAFA's passage, it will still have to be determined whether this is attributable to CAFA or simply a continuation of pre-CAFA trends. Thus, the effect of CAFA on class action abuse remains uncertain. However, there are many other areas of class action abuse, such as inflated settlement values, that CAFA does not address.

F. Inflated Settlement Values

Grossly inflating settlement values enables lawyers to obtain grossly inflated fees. Only on rare occasions have judges refused to ratify the use of inflated settlement values in order to justify unearned attorney fees. In one such instance, plaintiff lawyers brought parallel class actions

against BellSouth in four different federal courts, alleging that customers were misled into paying for the telephone carrier's inside wire
service maintenance plan.[67] In three of the proceedings, each class lawyer requested and was awarded a $1.5 million fee, which was based on an
announced total settlement value of $64 million.[68] In the fourth proceed-
ing, however, U.S. District Court Judge F.A. Little took a different tack.
He denied the requested $1.5 million attorney's fee (which would have
brought the total fee to $6 million) because the class had only received
$2 million, not the claimed $64 million.[69] He stated:

> In this case, I could hold my nose and accept the settlement, after
> all, it is said that a bad settlement is better than a good trial. When
> it comes to the approval of attorney fees under the circumstances
> presented in this case, the court is the gatekeeper. We will not allow
> to pass that which reeks with impropriety and overreaching.[70]

Judge Little, insisting that the actual class benefit "was essential to the
final determination of attorneys' fees,"[71] minced no words in refusing to
go along with the typical scheme of vastly inflating settlement values to
justify unearned fees for attorneys. He stated:

> [I]t is clear that the $64 million figure is a phantom … A request for
> $6 million in attorneys' fees where counsel has provided no more
> than $2 million in benefits to the class is astonishing. It is a sad day
> when lawyers transmogrify from counselors into grifters. Suffice it
> to say that we find the request unreasonable.[72]

Despite Judge Little's condemnation of the lawyers' actions, the total
fee paid to the class counsels was still two-and-one-half times the actual
benefit received by the class. Judge Little's refusal to "pass that which
reeks with impropriety and overreaching," is an anomaly. The standard
practice is for courts to approve such fee requests.

G. The Irrelevance of Response Rates

One of the principal reasons why many settlement values announced as
being made available to the class are, in reality, highly inflated is that

the figures are based on 100 percent of class members applying for and obtaining the benefit. However, as is well understood, class members' response rates are frequently far lower than 100 percent. Although class actions lawyers and (usually) defendants have access to the data on how many class members actually submit claims and what they receive, they not only remain mum, but also vigorously oppose efforts to bring such data into public view. These attempts to keep the public in the dark are often supported by the judges presiding over the class actions. Why this reluctance from bar, bench, and defendants to allow this information to be released to the public? Because the data would frequently show that the value of the settlement announced as being made available to the class is a phony number, ginned up to justify a substantial attorneys' fee. All parties involved in the settlement process are aware that low response rates and deceptive claims as to the value of settlements will lead to realization of only a small fraction of the announced value of the settlement by class members.[73]

Consider the RAND study data reported in Chapter 17, Section C, that the median effective fee in the class actions studied increased from 30 percent of the announced value of the settlement to 47 percent of funds actually distributed to class members, and in one quarter of the cases, it was over 75 percent.[74]

Consider further the class action against Intel, the computer chip manufacturer. In 1996, Intel announced that it had overstated the results of speed tests of two of its Pentium microprocessors by about 10 percent.[75] Almost immediately, lawyers filed a class action, claiming that Intel had engaged in false advertising and unfair business practices in violation of the California Consumer Legal Remedies Act.[76] In the ensuing settlement, Intel agreed to include some essentially meaningless disclaimers in its claims about microprocessor performance and to provide the 600,000 customers who bought the Pentium chips in question with a $50 rebate coupon on request. Based on the announced settlement value of $25 million, Intel agreed to pay a $1.5 million attorney's fee. Not surprisingly, the number of class members who took advantage of the coupon rebate offer fell short of what the attorneys had predicted.

In fact, only 156 of the 600,000 purchasers of the chips applied, so the total payment was less than $8,000.[77]

One of the class members who objected to the requested fee was represented by Larry Schonbrun, a California lawyer who has devoted much of his practice to representing class members objecting to abusive settlements and excessive fee requests. Schonbrun has been much maligned by some class action lawyers and judges for this activity.[78] Though criticizing the actions of the attorneys and complementing the actions of Schonbrun, the judge nonetheless approved the fee.[79]

The *Sears Automotive* class action is an even more egregious example. For approximately ten years, Sears Automotive charged car owners for a pricier four-wheel alignment on cars that could only be serviced with less expensive, two-wheel alignments.[80] Although the inflated charge amounted to only a few dollars per customer, Sears made millions of dollars from the alleged scheme.[81] Sears settled the nationwide class action, filed in state court in Illinois, by agreeing to compensate class members with $10 cash payments and $4 coupons and to pay class counsel $1.1 million.[82] To justify the fee request, lead class counsel claimed that as many as 1.5 million motorists were defrauded by Sears, estimated that 30 percent of class members would file claims, and asserted (falsely) that 1,900 claims had already been filed by the hearing date.[83] In fact, after the settlement was approved, only 317 valid claims were filed.[84] Based on this number, the entire nationwide class ultimately received only $2,402 in cash and coupons.[85] In other words, class counsel's initially approved fee was almost 500 times greater than the real benefit realized by the class.

This dismal record and the actions of lead class counsel and the presiding judge do not make the Sears settlement unique. What does is the careful examination of the proceedings by another judge, in a different state, who was presiding over a separate and parallel state class action. In a rare moment of candor from a judiciary that has frequently aligned itself with class action lawyers, North Carolina Judge Ben Tennille expressed strong disapproval of class counsel's actions, finding that "[t]he shocking incongruity between class benefit and fees afforded counsel and the representative leave[s] the appearance of collusion [between class counsel and defendant] and cannot help but tarnish the public perception of the legal profession."[86] Judge Tennille is also responsible for revealing that only 317 valid claims were filed.[87] Were it solely up to the presiding judge in Illinois (as is usually the case in class actions), this information would never have come to the light of day.[88]

Even in treatises and other official reports, response rates from class actions are veiled in secrecy. In the 1992 edition of *Newberg on Class Actions*, a leading class action treatise, only four class actions from the period 1971–1975 are listed in a table recording response rates.[89] In that table, the average response rate was 3.75 percent where settlement funds were paid out to only those class members filing claims.[90] Even the meager information available in 1992 was no longer available ten years later: in the 2002 edition, there is no table with response rate information. A 1996 Federal Judicial Center study of class action litigation found that "parties generally did not report the number of claims received."[91] A 2008 Rand Institute study confirms that there is a "veil of secrecy" about "how many class members actually received compensation and to what degree."[92] Despite expending "significant time and effort," the RAND researchers were able to find claims filing information in only seventeen of the eighty-eight class actions that were included in their first sample. Of those cases, 23 percent had payout rates of 5 percent or less.[93] RAND posits several explanations of why judges, lawyers, and settlement administrators refused to disclose "anemic distribution rates."[94] One explanation that RAND did not offer appears most compelling. Some judges align themselves with the interests of class action lawyers and reject compiling the information on actual payouts to class members because that information is inimical to lawyers' interests.

Judges also routinely reject requests from class members to delay awarding part or the entire fee until the payout or benefit actually realized by the class can be ascertained so that the fee can be based on this actual benefit. This is especially the case when the settlement values announced as being made available to the class are, in reality, vastly inflated to justify exorbitant and largely unearned fees. This occurs frequently in cases of dubious merit.

Consider, by way of example, the Epson printers case. When the "replace [ink] cartridge" indicator light came on in Epson inkjet printers, the printers displayed an on-screen message that the ink supply was out and printer function was suspended, even though some ink actually remained in the cartridges.[95] Epson maintained that "the cartridges must contain a safety reserve to protect the reliability of Epson's permanent printheads."[96] Lawyers brought a class action alleging that Epson's message violated California's Business and Professions Code and the California Consumers Legal Remedies Act, which prohibits "any unlawful, unfair or fraudulent business act or practice,"[97] and making a statement about a product that is "untrue or misleading."[98] In the settlement, Epson agreed to (1) change its disclosures to consumers regarding its ink technology in its packaging and marketing; and (2) change the on-screen message from "ink out" or "empty" to "a variable amount of ink remains in the cartridge."[99] Epson made no changes to the printer or ink technology. Thus, Epson printers continue to cease operation when the new display message is shown.

In addition to this "relief," class members were given a choice of receiving a $45 credit at the Epson E-Store; a $25 check and $20 E-Store credit; or a 25 percent discount off an E-Store purchase of up to $100. Those who had not registered their printers with Epson and those who wanted any benefit other than the $45 credit would have to send in a claim form with the date and place of purchase of the printer. Some class members objected to the settlement because no changes were to be made to the printer technology. The court, however, rejected this and similar arguments, reasoning that "judicial relief requiring [Epson] to change its patented technology would be difficult to obtain."[100]

So, how much was the Epson settlement worth to Epson printer users? How much value is there in being informed that some ink remains in the printer when the replace cartridge light comes on even though the printer no longer functions? I daresay that most computer users continue to press the print button despite the appearance of messages in the printer that the ink cartridge is low or has to be replaced. Consumers replace the cartridge only when the print quality is unacceptable or when the printer ceases to operate. Some judges, apparently appear oblivious to this consumer practice.[101] As for the coupons, how many were actually used and what were they really worth? Certainly, coupons that allow the consumer to purchase the defendant's products at a discount may have some value, but many businesses routinely offer such discounts on their products in the expectation that they will induce sales that would not have otherwise occurred.[102] Courts' reasoning that discount coupons are a benefit to consumers justifying an award of substantial counsel fees would also justify the IRS in counting the value of grocery coupons, mailed to or otherwise made available to consumers, as taxable income.

Class counsel claimed that, at a minimum, the benefits to the 4.8 million registered printer owners were worth more than $200 million.[103] In support of their request for $35 million in fees, class counsel retained Professor Theodore Eisenberg, one of the leading empirical scholars of the civil justice system. Professor Eisenberg supported the claim that the value of the settlement to Epson printer customers was at least $220 million. Although class counsel's claimed lodestar fee (hours worked times the hourly rate) was $5.1 million, Professor Eisenberg declared that $35 million – a fee seven times higher or 15.9 percent of the low-end settlement value of $220 million – was appropriate.[104] The court agreed, holding that the quantifiable value of the settlement was between $200 million and around $300 million and also that an attorneys' fee of $35 million was reasonable, even though this required a multiplier of 6 to 7 to the lodestar calculation.[105] Further, requests by some class members to wait a year before setting the fee, so that the actual cash benefit realized by the printer owners from the coupons could be first determined, were denied.[106]

Ostensibly, the reason for the denial is that it is the availability of the benefit created that counts, not its utility from the point of view of class members. Indeed, the majority of courts have held that the fact that a majority of class members regard the available benefit as not worth applying for is irrelevant.[107] Allowing fees to be based on the announced value of the settlement incentivizes class lawyers to announce settlement values that are – however much blessed by former judges and law professor fee experts – pure fantasy. Courts that routinely reject attempts to delay awarding fees until the actual amount of benefit realized by the class becomes known and to base fees on that actual amount exhibit a "public be damned" attitude that leaves little doubt as to who are the principal beneficiaries of class actions.[108]

H. Other Ways Lawyers Game Class Action Fees

Other fee ploys that class action lawyers employ to increase their fees are discussed in Appendix G. These include how lawyers: (1) easily evade a U.S. Supreme Court ruling that prohibits applying a multiplier to fees in class actions where a fee-shifting provision applies; (2) structure common-fund settlements so that any reduction in the agreed on fee ordered by a court will revert to the defendant rather than the class, thereby reducing the court's incentive to cut the fee – no matter how inflated; and (3) combine both of these strategies so that they gain both inflated fees and reduced judicial inclination to subject their fees to scrutiny.

I. The Rise and Fall of the Use of Auctions to Set Fees

The most effective fee-setting mechanism that has been devised for combating excessive fees is the use of auctions in which potential class counsels submit "bids" to the presiding judge, who then selects a lead class counsel based on the proposed fee and the quality of representation the candidate firm can provide.[109] In response to another judge's lament over the one-sidedness of fee applications, U.S. District Court Judge Vaughn Walker for the Northern District of California introduced auctions to set class action fees in 1990 in *In re Oracle Securities Litigation*.[110] He provided that law firms interested in being lead counsel would independently submit "bids," consisting of their qualifications, the contingency percentage of recovery they will assess against the common fund, and their "contribution ... to the welfare of class plaintiffs."[111]

Auctions have resulted in lower fees, not only in securities class actions, but in antitrust class actions as well. *In re Auction Houses Antitrust Litigation* marked the zenith of the auction procedure, resulting in a 5 percent award of attorneys' fees – only about a third of the percentage typically awarded by courts in settlements of this magnitude.[112] Indeed, the court noted that "[a]s a percentage of the recovery, this is among the lowest fee awards ever in comparable litigation."[113] In that case, Judge Lewis Kaplan of the Southern District of New York required lead counsel-candidates to submit their qualifications along with an "X" factor, representing the amount of the settlement that would be paid entirely to the class free from fees; class counsel would receive one-third of any recovery above that amount.[114] When the parties settled, the court approved the creation of a class fund of $512 million ($100 million of which was discount coupons on future commissions).[115] In approving the attorneys' fee of $26.75 million, Judge Kaplan also required that class counsel receive the same amount of discount certificates as the class in payment for their services, so that they would have "the same proportionate stake in the value of the certificates as the class they represent."[116]

The fee-setting process used in the *Auction Houses* litigation was so successful in eliminating excessive fees that it set off alarms throughout the class action community. Because the volume of class action litigation is dependent on the quantum of plaintiffs' lawyers' profits, not only were plaintiffs' lawyers' fees at stake, but so too were defendants' lawyers' incomes. Joining forces to combat this insidious threat to the overcompensation routinely awarded by most courts, the lawyers convinced the U.S. Third Circuit Court of Appeals to appoint a task force to examine the use of auctions in class action fee setting. The task force concluded that "class recovery generally can be maximized more effectively by using the traditional methods of appointing counsel" and that the auction method could only be used "in certain limited situations."[117] The report argued that auctions resulted in negative incentives for the lowest bidder, such as the risk that the lowest bidder would provide the lowest quality legal services and would have the incentive to settle prematurely at a lower amount.[118] The report also claimed that because low bidders may invest fewer resources in litigating the case, class recovery might not be maximized.[119] As for attorneys' fee awards, the report concluded that auctions do not necessarily guarantee that the fees will be reasonable.[120]

Professor Michael Perino's study of 244 post-PSLRA securities class actions resolved between 1997 and 2005, however, found that lead counsel auctions resulted in significantly lower fee requests and awards.[121] Contrary to the criticisms of the Third Circuit task force, Perino found little evidence of low-quality representation that auctions could induce.[122] Additionally, Perino found no statistical variation in case age between cases with and without auctions, which undermines the argument that low-bidding firms have a greater incentive to settle the case quickly and at a lower settlement value.[123] In fact, adapting the correlations to a hypothetical $25 million settlement, Perino found that the use of auctions resulted in a 55 percent reduction in fees from cases that did not use an auction procedure in selecting lead counsel.[124] As a result, Perino concludes that auctions are beneficial and useful, making it "far too early to abandon courts' experimentation with the auction procedure."[125]

The task force's report has had the intended effect of putting the kibosh on the use of auctions to set fees in class actions. When auctions proved a threat to the financial interests of the class action industry, the empire struck back and routed the meager forces that were attempting to limit fees in class actions to "reasonable" amounts.

The Private Securities Litigation Reform Act (PSLRA) has also had a negative impact on the use of auctions. As noted in Section B of this chapter, the Act directs courts to select the investors "most capable of adequately representing the interests of class members" and investors "who have the largest financial interest in the relief sought by the class" as lead plaintiffs.[126] Once the lead plaintiff has been appointed, the statute provides that the lead plaintiff "shall, subject to the approval of the court, select and retain counsel to represent the class."[127] How this language bears on the use of auctions in securities class actions is addressed in the *Cendant* case, a securities fraud class action brought against the Cendant Corporation (owner of Avis, Century 21, and the Ramada and Howard Johnson hotel franchise chains) and its auditors, Ernst & Young, and settled for $3.2 billion.[128] After the District Court selected three pension funds as lead plaintiffs (the CalPERS Group), the lead plaintiffs asked the District Court to appoint as lead counsel two law firms with which it had previously negotiated a retainer agreement. The court declined to do so and instead conducted an auction to select lead counsel and gave the CalPERS Group counsel the option to match the lowest qualified bid. These firms exercised that option and, after the settlement, were awarded $262 million in counsel fees — anomalously, an amount at least $76 million higher than that provided in their retainer agreements with the CalPERS Group.[129] The Third Circuit Court of Appeals, however, reversed the lower court's decision to hold an auction as inconsistent with the PSLRA provision granting to the designated lead plaintiff the power "subject to the approval of the court, [to] select and retain counsel to represent the class."[130] According to the court, setting the fee via an auction process would be too much of an interference with the lead plaintiff's selection right. In addition, the court held it would conflict with one of the policy bases for the PSLRA, which is that institutional investors would likely do a better job than courts in not only selecting and monitoring counsel but also in negotiating the fee agreements (over which the court retains final approval).[131]

The assumption, however, is at least questionable. As previously discussed,[132] the selection process appears to have been influenced by the pay to play practices of leading class action law firms. Though the *Cendant* court did acknowledge that one of the class counsel selected had made substantial contributions to the reelection campaign of the New York State Comptroller who was the sole trustee of the New York

State pension fund – one of the three funds in the CalPERS Group – both the trial court and appellate court concluded that there was no basis for concern because no proof had been offered in support of the claim that the counsel selection was influenced by pay to play.[133] Because it is highly unlikely that either counsel or pension fund trustees would acknowledge that pay to play influenced counsel's selection, proof of the kind demanded by the courts can virtually never be obtained. Thus, the court has effectively given its imprimatur to the practice of pay to play as a way of securing appointment as class counsel.

It is thus safe to say that class action counsel, including those who engage in pay to play, are safe and secure from the most effective mechanism ever devised for combating excessive fees in class actions.

NOTES

1. *See Weinberger v. Great N. Nekoosa Corp.*, 925 F.2d 518, 520 n.1 (1st Cir.1991) ("In general, a clear sailing agreement is one where the party paying the fee agrees not to contest the amount to be awarded by the fee-settling court so long as the award falls beneath a negotiated ceiling."); *see also* William D. Henderson, *Clear Sailing Agreements: A Special Form of Collusion in Class Action Settlements*, 77 TUL. L. REV. 813 (2003).

2. *Alleghany Corp. v. Kirby*, 333 F.2d 327, 347 (2d Cir. 1964) (J. Friendly, dissenting).

3. *See Int'l Precious Metals, Corp. v. Waters*, 530 U.S. 1223 (2000).

4. 327 F.3d 938, 972 (2003) (disapproving of conditioning the settlement on a set amount of attorneys' fees based on an actual or putative common fund).

5. *Staton*, 327 F.3d at 972–73.

6. *Malchman v. Davis*, 761 F.2d 893, 907 (2d Cir. 1985) (J. Newman, concurring).

7. *See, e.g.*, Declaration of Theodore Eisenberg, *In re Epson Ink Cartridge Cases*, JCCP No. 4347 (Cal. Super. Ct. L.A. County Oct. 23, 2006); Declaration of Charles Silver In Support Of Lead Counsel's Motion For An Award Of Attorney Fees, *In re Enron Corp. Sec. Litig.*, No. H-01–3624 (S.D. Tex. 2008); Declaration of Lucian Bebchuk In Support Of Lead Counsel's Motion For An Award Of Attorney Fees, *In re Enron Corp. Sec. Litig.*, No. H-01–3624 (S.D. Tex. 2008); Declaration of John C. Coffee, Jr. In Support Of Lead Counsel's Motion For An Award Of Attorney Fees, *In re Enron Corp. Sec. Litig.*, No. H-01–3624 (S.D. Tex. 2008); Declaration of Professor William B. Rubenstein In Support of Plaintiffs' Motion For Order Approving Award of Attorneys'

Fees, *In re Dep't of Veterans Affairs (VA) Data Theft Litigation*, MDL No. 1796 (U.S.D.C., D.D.C., Aug. 7, 2009). Lawyers also hire former judges to give their blessing as well. *See, e.g.*, Declaration of H. Lee Sarokin In Support Of Lead Counsel's Motion For An Award Of Attorney Fees, *In re Enron Corp. Sec. Litig.*, No. H-01–3624 (S.D. Tex. 2008).

8. *Fresco v. AUTOMOTIVE DIRECTIONS, INC.*, No. CIV-03–61063 (S.D. Fla. Oct. 8, 2007).

9. 18 U.S.C. §§ 2721–25 (2006).

10. Declaration of Professor Geoffrey P. Miller, *Fresco v. AUTOMOTIVE DIRECTIONS, INC.*, Case No. 03-cv-61063-JEM (S.D. Fla. Oct. 3, 2007).

11. *See, e.g., Bowling*, 922 F.Supp. at 1277 (noting that "[t]he divergence of interests requires a court to assume a fiduciary role in reviewing fee applications ... because 'there is often no one to argue for the interests of the class'") (quoting *Rawlings v. Prudential-Bache Prop., Inc.*, 9 F.3d 513, 516 (6th Cir. 1993)).

12. Michael A. Perino, *The Milberg Weiss Prosecution: No Harm, No Foul?* (St. John's U. School of Law Legal Studies Research Paper Series No. 08–0135, 2008).

13. For example, in the *Xerox* securities litigation, former Federal District Court Judge Alfred Wolin was hired to prepare a "Private Memorandum" to support the 20% fee request. *See* Lead Plaintiffs' Memorandum Summarizing The Background Of The Wolin Report, *Carlson v. Xerox Corp.*, No. 3:00-cv-1621 (D. Conn. Sept. 22, 2008). Judge Wolin resigned from the federal bench after being disqualified by the Third Circuit Court of Appeals from presiding over several asbestos bankruptcies because it was discovered that he had selected advisors that had a financial interest in the decisions he was making and he had private ("ex parte") conversations with a number of plaintiffs' lawyers. *See* Brickman, *Ethical Issues, supra* Chapter 7, note 69, at nn.19, 26. He then joined the firm of one of the lawyers that he had hired to advise him. Judge Wolin stated in his "Private Memorandum" that it was not necessary for the court to order a lodestar cross-check because Judge Wolin's own "general consideration of lodestar factors ... confirms the reasonableness of the requested fee." *See* Lead Plaintiffs' Memorandum Summarizing The Background Of The Wolin Report, ex.1 at 35, *Carlson v. Xerox Corp.*, No. 3:00-cv-1621 (D. Conn. Sept. 22, 2008). U.S. District Court Judge Alvin Thompson cited to Wolin's "Private Memorandum" throughout his order in which he approved a 16% fee that amounted to $120 million of the $750 million settlement fund. *See* Ruling On Motion For Award Of Attorney Fees, *Carlson v. Xerox Corp.*, No. 3:00-cv-1621 (D. Conn. Jan. 14, 2009). Additionally, Judge Wolin, along with Judge Abner J. Mikva, former Chief Judge of the Court of Appeals for the D.C. Circuit, was retained by class counsel in the *Tyco* securities litigation to "evaluate"

the fee request. *See In re Tyco Int'l, Ltd.* MDL, 535 F. Supp. 2d 249, 269 (D. N.H. 2007); *see also* Joint Declaration of Richard S. Schiffrin, Jay W. Eisenhofer and Sanford P. Dumain In Support of Proposed Class Action Settlement, Plan of Allocation and Petition for an Award of Attorneys' Fees and Reimbursement of Expenses at ex.6, *In re Tyco Int'l, Ltd. Multidistrict Litigation,* 535 F.Supp.2d 249 (D. N.H. Oct. 22, 2007). Judge Wolin's endorsement of the fee request was embraced by the court, which adopted his recommendation. *See In re Tyco Int'l, Ltd.* MDL 535, F. Supp.2d 249, 274 (D. N.H. 2007).

14. It is possible that the millions of dollars paid to these academics and former judges to endorse class counsels' fee requests may be being billed to the class. If so, the class is then being required to pay for testimony to support reducing its recovery. Because courts do not require detailed expense accountings and do not review the minimal accounting that is provided to justify millions of dollars in expenses, it is impossible to determine whether class lawyers are lumping these expert fees together with other expert fees as part of the expenses incurred by class counsel, which are charged against the class's recovery or reimbursed by the defendant. No one should be surprised, however, if this is the case.

15. *Havird, et al. v. U.S. West Cellular of California, Inc.*, 222 F.3d 1142 (9th Cir. 2000).

16. *Id.* at 1148–50.

17. Whereas an Earth day is 24 hours long, a day on Saturn is 244.8 Earth hours.

18. *See Hoffman v. BancBoston Mortgage Corp.*, No. 91–1880 (Ala. Cir. Ct. Jan. 24, 1994).

19. *See Kamilewicz v. Bank of Boston Corp.*, 92 F.3d 506, 508–09 (7th Cir. 1996), *reh'g denied*, 100 F.3d 1348, *cert. denied*, 520 U.S. 1204 (1997). For an extensive analysis of the Kamilewicz facts, see Susan P. Koniak & George M. Cohen, *Under Cloak of Settlement*, 82 VA. L. REV. 1051, 1056 (1996).

20. *See Kamilewicz*, 92 F.3d at 508–09.

21. *See Kamilewicz*, 92 F.3d at 509. The causes of action included: violations of the Racketeer Influenced and Corrupt Organizations Act, 18 U.S.C. 1962; violations of the Civil Rights Act, 42 U.S.C. 1983; common law fraud; negligent misrepresentation; attorney malpractice; breach of fiduciary duty; and conversion. *See id.*

22. *See Kamilewicz*, 92 F.3d at 508–09.

23. *See* Brickman, *The Brave New World, supra* Chapter 9, note 15, at 302–04.

24. *See* Eddie Curran, *You Win, You Pay*, MOBILE REGISTER, Dec. 30, 1999, at A1.

25. *See id.*

26. *Azizian v. Federated Dept. Stores*, No. 403CV03359 (N.D. Cal. July 18, 2003).

27. Notice of Settlement at 1, *Azizian v. Federated Dept. Stores*, No. 403CV03359 (N.D. Cal. July 16, 2003).

28. 15 U.S.C §15 (2006); CAL. BUS. & PROF. CODE §16750(a) (Deering 2009).

29. Settlement Agreement at 5, *Azizian v. Federated Dept. Stores*, No. 403CV03359 (N.D. Cal. July 16, 2003). In addition, the defendants agreed to various conditions of injunctive relief, prohibiting them from fixing, establishing, controlling, or maintaining resale prices of their products. Stipulated Order at 3–6, *Azizian v. Federated Dept. Stores*, No. 403CV03359 (N.D. Cal.). The defendants did not admit that they engaged in any of the prohibited activities or violated any laws. *Id.* at 1.

30. Distribution Plan at 1, *Azizian v. Federated Dept. Stores*, No. 403CV03359 (N.D. Cal. July 16, 2003).

31. Distribution Plan at 1.

32. Jen Aronoff, *Get a free beauty product, thanks to legal settlement: 4 local stores giving away high-end cosmetics; lawsuit accused manufacturers and store chains of price-fixing*, CHARLOTTE OBSERVER, Jan. 17, 2009. These brands and products included Chanel, Dior, Calvin Klein, Clinique, Coco Mademoiselle body wash, Dior J'Adore eau de parfum, Estee Lauder advanced night repair cream, and Lancome Cils Design Pro mascara. *Id.* The settlement Web site, www.cosmeticssettlement.com, is no longer available, but a full listing of participating retailers and available products can be found at http://www.meilily.com/2009/01/beauty-and-the-law-class-action-cosmetic-cases-settlement-consumers-get-one-free-product/ (last visited Mar. 18, 2009).

33. *See* Aronoff, *supra.*

34. Susan Taylor Martin, *Putting Lipstick on a Lawsuit*, ST. PETERSBURG TIMES, Feb. 1, 2009. As noted by the author, it appeared many people ignored the "one item per customer," to the point that class members, such as her, were shut out of the distribution. *Id.* She adds, "a Lancome representative merely chuckled when I asked where I should go to get my free product. 'We were all out the first day,' she said. 'I think Macy's is out, too.'" *Id.*

35. Josh Gerstein, *Antitrust Suit Over Pricing of Cosmetics Hits a Snag*, N.Y. SUN, Jan. 12, 2005, at 4.

36. Final Judgment Granting Final Approval to the Class Action Settlement with All Defendants Awarding Attorneys' Fees and Costs at 7, *Azizian v. Federated Dept. Stores*, No. 403CV03359 (N.D. Cal. Mar. 30, 2005).

37. Mary Flood, *Giveaway a win-win case; Consumers got cosmetics, stores got advertising, lawyers got cash*, HOUSTON CHRONICLE, Jan. 27, 2009, at B3.

38. Their claim was that their objections led to (1) limiting the number of products that could be claimed by each class member from nine to one; (2) creating a Product Review Committee to monitor the settlement; and (3) requiring stores to post the notice of the settlement at cosmetics counters. Coordinated

Objectors' Motion to Compel Class Counsel's Time Sheets and Expense Summaries, *Azizian v. Federated Dept. Stores*, No. 403CV03359 (N.D. Cal. May 17, 2005).

39. Final Judgment at 7.

40. Class Counsel's Opposition to Coordinated Objectors' Motion to Compel Class Counsel's Time Sheets and Expense Summaries, *Azizian v. Federated Dept. Stores*, No. 403CV03359 SBA, (N.D. Cal. May 19, 2005); *see also* Letter from Francis O. Scarpulla to Michael A. Caddell dated May 3, 2005, Coordinated Objectors' Motion to Compel Class Counsel's Time Sheets and Expense Summaries at ex.H, *Azizian v. Federated Dept. Stores*, No. 403CV03359 (N.D. Cal. May 17, 2005) ("Class Counsel declines to provide time records to Coordinated Objectors, noting that time records contain attorney-client and work-product privileged information.").

41. Coordinated Objectors' Amended Motion for Reconsideration of Total Fee Award and Opposition to Class Counsel's Petition for Attorney Fees and Expenses at 3, *Azizian v. Federated Dept. Stores*, No. 403CV03359 (N.D. Cal. Mar. 31, 2006).

42. Special Master's Report and Recommendation at 2, *Azizian v. Federated Dept. Stores*, No. 403CV03359 (N.D. Cal. May 18, 2006).

43. Amended Recommendation of the Special Master as to the Allocation of Awarded Fees and Costs to Counsel for the Coordinated Objectors and State Objectors at 9–10, *Azizian v. Federated Dept. Stores*, No. 403CV03359 (N.D. Cal. Mar. 29, 2006).

44. Coordinated Objectors' Amended Motion for Reconsideration at 4–5; *see also* Josh Gerstein, *Quite a Legal Brawl Emerges Over Cosmetics Pricing*, N.Y. Sun, May 3, 2006.

45. Special Master's Report at 2.

46. Coordinated Objectors' Amended Motion for Reconsideration, *supra* note 46.

47. *Id*. at 6. All of the following statements in this paragraph come from the Amended Motion at 6–8. Contract lawyers are discussed in Chapter 19 § (B).

48. *See In re Fine Paper Antitrust Litigation*, (MDL 323), 98 F.R.D. 48, 68–69, 77–78 (E.D. Pa. 1983) *aff'd in part, rev'd in part by* 751 F.2d 562 (3d Cir. 1984); John C. Coffee Jr., *Rescuing the Private Attorney General: Why the Model of the Lawyer As Bounty Hunter Is Not Working*, 42 Md. L. Rev. 215, 260 (1983) (citing to the Weil, Gotshal Report).

49. 98 F.R.D. at 77 n.8.

50. Reversionary settlements are common in class actions, but not in securities class actions, most likely due to a provision in the PSLRA that requires that the attorneys' fee be based on the damages "actually paid to the class." 15 U.S.C. § 78u-4(a)(6) (2006).

51. *Fleury v. Richemont North America, Inc.*, No. C-05–4525 EMC, 2008 WL 3287154, at *2 (N.D. Cal. Aug. 6, 2008).
52. Pub. L. No. 109–2, 119 Stat. 4 (codified as amended at 28 U.S.C. § 1711 *et seq.* (2006).
53. CAFA, 28 U.S.C. §1712(e) (2006).
54. The heightened judicial scrutiny that Congress mandated is on full display in *True and Delgado v. American Honda Motor Co.*, 2010 WL 707338 (C.D. Cal. 2010); *Figueroa and Dixie M. Garner v. Sharper Image Corp.*, 517 F. Supp. 2d 1292, 1321 (2007).
55. 28 U.S.C. § 1712(a) (2006).
56. 28 U.S.C. § 1712(b) (2006).
57. 28 U.S.C. § 1712(c) (2006).
58. *See* Proposed Settlement, *In re Motor Fuel Temperature Sales Practices Litigation*, MDL No. 1840 (D. Kan. 2009). The basis for the claim is that Costco gas pumps are set to measure the quantity of fuel dispensed at 60°F. Because motor fuels expand and contract volumetrically in hot and cold temperature, gas sold at 75°F has about 1% less value than gas sold at 60°F. Some gas pumps have automatic temperature compensation devices that adjust the gallonage to take ambient temperature into account. The claim is that Costco, over about an eight-year period, overcharged members who purchased fuel when the temperature exceeded 60°F. The settlement provides no payment to these purchasers, which could have been calculated and automatically credited to affected members' accounts or which could have been secured in the form of coupons to be used to offset future purchases. Instead, the settlement provides what it calls "Injunctive and Other Relief," specifically that Costco will equip its gas pumps with automatic temperature compensation (ATC) in fourteen of the states where it operates. There is far less here, however, than meets the eye.

According to the Objection To Proposed Settlement by Amy Alkon and Nicholas Martin, represented by The Center for Class Action Fairness (directed by Theodore H. Frank), the settlement provides that if regulatory approval is required under state laws for this conversion of its gas pumps, that class counsel will undertake to secure that approval. *See* Objection to Proposed Settlement by Amy Alkon and Nicholas Martin, represented by The Center for Class Action Fairness, *In re Motor Fuel Temperature Sales Practices Litigation*, MDL No. 1840 (D. Kan. Mar. 1, 2010). And if class counsel is unable or unwilling to do so (why would it expend any such effort?), then Costco has no further obligation. If regulatory approval is not needed or is secured, then Costco is obligated to go forward only if it can secure the equipment affordably and without disrupting its business – a determination that is in Costco's sole discretion. However, regulatory agencies have concluded that ATC would yield no economic benefit to consumers. Indeed, the National Conference of Weights and Measures

(NCWM), composed of state and local weights and measures officials, has rejected the use of ATC at retail for several reasons, including lack of benefit to consumers. Going beyond NCWM, the California Energy Commission, in response to a legislative directive to do a comprehensive survey and cost-benefit analysis of ATC, found that the "cost-benefit analysis ... [indicates] that the results are negative or a net cost to society under all the options examined." Quoted in Objection to Proposed Settlement at 9. For these reasons, some of the fourteen settlement states prohibit the use of ATC at retail. Additionally, the proposed injunctive relief is also economically worthless because Costco can freely adjust the posted price of motor fuels to counteract any temperature correction. Moreover, some class members who frequently purchase fuel when the ambient temperature is under 60°F would end up paying more for fuel. For this "injunctive relief," Costco has agreed to pay class counsel $10 million, and any reduction in the fee ordered by a court will revert to Costco – a ploy discussed in § H of this chapter and Appendix G.

59. Pub. L. No. 109–2, § 2, 119 Stat. 4 (2005).

60. Pub. L. No. 109–2 (2005), (codified as amended at 28 U.S.C. § 1453 (2006)).

61. Pub. L. No. 109–2, § 2, 119 Stat. 4 (2005).

62. A study indicates that federal courts in the Second, Third, and Ninth Federal Circuits (comprising New York, Pennsylvania, New Jersey, California, and other states) are more likely to certify class actions, whereas courts in the Fourth, Fifth, and Seventh Circuits (comprising Virginia, Maryland, Florida, Texas, Illinois, Indiana, and other states) are least likely to certify a class. John C. Coffee Jr. & Stefan Paulovic, *Class Certification: Developments Over the Last Five Years 2002–2007*, 8 CLASS ACTION LITIG. REP. (BNA) S-787, S-819 (Oct. 26, 2007).

63. 28 U.S.C. § 1332 (d)(4)(B) (2006). Where between one-third and two-thirds of the class members, as well as the primary defendants, are citizen of the state in which the action is filed, a federal court may decline to exercise CAFA jurisdiction. *See* S. REP. NO. 109–14, at 136 (2005).

64. EMERY G. LEE III & THOMAS E. WILLGING, THE IMPACT OF THE CLASS ACTION FAIRNESS ACT OF 2005 ON THE FEDERAL COURTS (FOURTH INTERIM REPORT, APRIL 2008), at 1, 12–13. The data on removals of diversity-based class actions from state to federal courts is mixed; whereas there were increases in removals, there was some indication of a more recent decline as well. *Id.* at 2, 6. Because there is no reliable data on class activity in state courts, it is not possible to "determine whether the declining number of removals indicates that there are fewer class actions filed in the state courts and thus fewer to remove, or whether the declining number of removals indicates that class action defendants in the state courts are choosing to remove fewer cases to federal court." *Id.* at 7.

65. *See* Thomas E. Willging & Shannon R. Wheatman, *Attorney Choice of Forum in Class Action Litigation: What Difference Does it Make?*, 81 NOTRE DAME L. REV. 591, 606 (2006) (Frequency of certification of federal court class actions terminated pre-CAFA declined approximately one-third in 1999–2002 compared to an earlier study of class actions terminated in 1992–1994.).

66. ADMINISTRATIVE OFFICE OF THE COURTS, CLASS CERTIFICATION IN CALIFORNIA (SECOND INTERIM REPORT, FEBRUARY 2010), at 6 (reporting a more than 50% decline in class certifications from 2000–2005, observing that this trend mirrors the federal court experience and offering as an explanation that "evolving California and federal case law has narrowed the standards for a class certification." *Id.* at 10–11).

67. *Strong v. BellSouth Telecomm., Inc.*, 173 F.R.D. 167 (W.D. La. 1997) *aff'd by* 137 F.3d 844 (5th Cir. 1998).

68. *Id.* at 172.

69. *Id.* at 172–73.

70. *Id.* at 172.

71. *Id.*

72. *Id.* at 172.

73. The RAND Institute for Civil Justice studied what actually happened after settlements of class actions and concluded that "aggregate payments in class settlements sometimes constitute a mere fraction of the compensation fund extolled by the parties at the time of settlement review." *See* NICHOLAS M. PACE & WILLIAM B. RUBENSTEIN, HOW TRANSPARENT ARE CLASS ACTION OUTCOMES? EMPIRICAL RESEARCH ON THE AVAILABILITY OF CLASS ACTION CLAIMS DATA, RAND INSTITUTE FOR CIVIL JUSTICE, at v (2008).

74. Research Brief, Anatomy of an Insurance Class Action, RAND Inst. (2007).

75. *Judge OKs Settlement with Fee Restrictions*, SAN FRANCISCO DAILY J., Oct. 6, 1997, at 1.

76. *Judge Approves Intel Fee Pact But Lauds Objector*, SAN FRANCISCO DAILY J., June 24, 1998, at 1.

77. *Id.*

78. *See, e.g.*, Edward Brunet, *Class Action Objectors: Extortionist Free Riders or Fair Guarantors*, U. CHI. LEGAL F. 403, 438 nn.155, 175, 185 (2003).

79. *Id.*

80. *Moody v. Sears, Roebuck & Co.*, No. 02 CVS 4892, 2007 WL 2582193, at * 3 (N.C. Super. Ct. May 7, 2007) (*Moody I*).

81. *See id.*

82. *Id.* Both parties subsequently agreed to reduce counsel fees to $950,000 in response to the results of an accounting of the actual benefits paid to class members. *See id.* at ¶2 n.1.

83. *Moody v. Sears Roebuck and Co.*, 664 S.E.2d 569, 573 (N.C. Ct. App. 2008) (*Moody II*).
84. *Moody I*, 2007 WL 2582193, at *5.
85. *Id.* at *4.
86. *Id.* ¶2.
87. *See id.* at *1. To prevent this disclosure, which was mandated by Judge Tennille, class counsel unsuccessfully petitioned the North Carolina Court of Appeals to prohibit Judge Tennille from obtaining an accounting. *See id.* at *11.
88. Another insight into redemption rates is provided by the class action against the Ford Motor Co. Ford agreed to provide $500 discount coupons toward the purchase of a new SUV to Ford Explorer owners because rollover problems diminished the resale value of their vehicles. The lawyers, touting the availability of a benefit as much as $500 million for the one million Explorer owners, were awarded $25 million in fees and expenses. In another rare occurrence, however, the judge required the lawyers to report the redemption rate. Just 75 out of one million coupons were redeemed for a total benefit of $37,500. Paul Elias, *In Ford Settlement, Lawyers Emerge as the Winner*, ASSOC. PRESS, Aug. 3, 2009.
89. *See* ALBA CONTE & HERBERT B. NEWBERG, NEWBERG ON CLASS ACTIONS, tbl. II: Response Rates, Appendix 8–4 (3d ed. 1992).
90. *See id.*
91. THOMAS E. WILLGING ET AL., EMPIRICAL STUDY OF CLASS ACTIONS IN FOUR FEDERAL DISTRICT COURTS: FINAL REPORT TO THE ADVISORY COMMITTEE ON CIVIL RULES, FEDERAL JUDICIAL CENTER, 55 (1996).
92. *See* PACE, ET AL. HOW TRANSPARENT ARE CLASS ACTION OUTCOMES?, at *v*.
93. *Id.* at 34.
94. To obtain a portion of the case data, the RAND study authors contacted all of the judges (both state and federal), defense counsel, plaintiffs' counsel, and the settlement administrators (private companies hired by the class lawyers to administer the notice to class members and distribute benefits to class members) in fifty-seven cases. *See* PACE, ET AL. HOW TRANSPARENT ARE CLASS ACTION OUTCOMES?, at 31. Only five of the fifty-seven judges, seven of the plaintiffs' counsel, one defense attorney, and one settlement administrator sent data. Overall, only 6% of the 222 participants contacted responded with pertinent data. *See id.* Although not drawing conclusions of motivations of the respective groups, the study authors identified several factors that incentivize silence. First, "anemic distribution rates ... make class counsel look simultaneously incompetent and greedy," *id.* at 35, whereas for defense counsel, these low response rates threaten the goal of "finality for their client at as low a price as possible." *Id.* at 36. Settlement administrators, which are for-profit companies hired by class counsel, virtually always refuse to provide response rate data, though they have

it all at their fingertips, saying that it is the property of their clients (the class lawyers) and thus not open to the public. *Id.* at 38. The RAND Institute authors explain that "judicial actors are situated in a context that also makes them averse to publicizing the actual claiming rates in class cases" for four reasons: (1) judges are busy and a settlement clears what often is a large complicated case from their dockets; (2) judges have little information of the actual case before them; (3) judges get some "reputational boost" from presiding over a large class action; and (4) judges have little information on comparative response rates due to the veil of secrecy in other class actions. *Id.* at 36–37. For these reasons, the study concludes, judges have thus far failed to bring these low response and distributional rates into public view.

95. Order Granting Final Approval of Settlement at 2, *In re Epson Ink Cartridge Cases*, JCCP No. 4347 (Cal. Super. Ct. L.A. County Oct. 23, 2006) [hereinafter Final Approval Order].

96. *Id.* at 19.

97. *See id.*; CAL. BUS. & PROF. CODE § 17200 *et seq.*

98. CAL. CIV. CODE § 1750 *et seq.*

99. *See* Final Approval Order, *supra* note 96, at 12–13.

100. *Id.* at 11–13, 19.

101. The success in the Epson printers case has made suing printer manufacturers into a cottage industry. In a class action involving similar claims against Canon, the judge dismissed the claim that Canon's "low ink" warning when there was still usable ink in the cartridge violated California's false advertising law but allowed the claim based on the state's unfair competition law to proceed because "members of the public are likely to be deceived by the representations made by their printer that the ink cartridge is 'empty' when in fact it is not." Order denying in part and granting in part Defendant's Motion To Dismiss The Second Amended Complaint, Pursuant to Fed. R. Civ. P. 12 (b) (6), *Shein et al. v. Canon USA, Inc.*, CV 08–07323 CAS (EX) (C.D. Cal. June 22, 2009). The judge's conclusion is dubious at best.

102. In one class action settlement involving "port charges" by a cruise line that went out of business, another cruise line that had not been sued and had no liability agreed to offer discount coupons to class members as a promotional opportunity. *Premier Cruise Lines Reaches Settlement*, MEALEY'S LITIGATION REPORT: CLASS ACTIONS, July 17, 2003.

103. *See* Plaintiff's Response to Objections to Settlement at 1, *In re Epson Ink Cartridge Cases*, JCCP No. 4347 (Cal. Super. Ct. L.A. County Oct. 23, 2006).

104. *See* Declaration of Theodore Eisenberg at 2, 5–6, *In re Epson Ink Cartridge Cases*, JCCP No. 4347 (Cal. Super. Ct. L.A. County Oct. 23, 2006).

105. *See* Order Granting Final Approval of Settlement, at 12, 31.

106. *See* Order Granting Final Approval of Settlement, at 37–38.

107. Federal appellate courts mostly agree that lawyers' fees should be awarded "on the basis of the total funds made available, whether claimed or not." *See Masters v. Wilhelmina Model Agency, Inc.*, 473 F.3d 423, 437 (2d Cir. 2007); *see also Williams v. MGM-Pathe Comm. Co.*, 129 F.3d 1026, 1027 (9th Cir.1997) (holding that the district court abused its discretion by basing attorneys' fees on the class members' claims against the fund rather than on a percentage of the entire fund or on the lodestar); *Waters v. Int'l Precious Metals Corp.*, 190 F.3d 1291, 1295 (11th Cir.1999) (declining to consider only the actual pay-out in determining attorneys' fees). Even the U.S. Supreme Court appears to have adopted this pro-class lawyer view in *Boeing v. Van Gemert*, 444 U.S. 472, 481–82 (1980), though its holding is limited to cases where the defendant's liability is fixed and is not contingent on the quantity of claims filed. Professor William B. Rubenstein of Harvard Law School, who writes about class actions and serves as an expert witness in class actions to support attorneys' fee requests, concurs with the reasoning of these courts. It makes "perfect sense," he says, to award a fee based on a percentage of the total fund made available because "[i]t captures the fact that the defendant has been disgorged of this amount of money regardless of where the funds end up." William B. Rubenstein, *Percentage of What?*, CLASS ACTION ATTORNEY FEE DIGEST, Mar. 2007, at 63. This "form of litigation," he continues, "primarily serves deterrent rather than compensatory purposes." *Id.* at 64. The Private Securities Litigation Reform Act, enacted by Congress rejects this policy in securities class action litigation and requires that the percentage awarded as attorneys' fees be based on the damages "actually paid to the class." 15 U.S.C. § 78u-4(a)(6) (2006). Likewise, the Class Action Fairness Act requires that in class actions where coupons are the basis for the fee request, any percentage attorneys' fee be based on the actual value of the redeemed coupons. 28 U.S.C. § 1712(a) (2006). CAFA is discussed in § E of this chapter.

108. This public-be-damned attitude is well reflected in the rulings of Judge Richard Kramer of the Superior Court of California, San Francisco County. Judge Kramer presided over a class action brought on behalf of Sears credit card customers in California, who alleged that Sears sold their private information to third parties without their consent. Order Approving Settlement, *Utility Consumers' Action Network v. Sears, Roebuck & Co.*, No. 306232, at 1 (Sup. Ct. Cal. San Francisco County Aug. 18, 2004). The settlement he approved (1) required the essentially useless modification of the Sears Financial Information Privacy Notice; and (2) provided the class a benefit of either a $10 certificate to be used at Sears and a 15% discount voucher on Sears merchandise or a $15 certificate. Order Awarding Attorneys' Fees & Expenses & Award to Plaintiff James C. Cox, *Utility Consumers' Action Network v. Sears, Roebuck & Co.*, No. 306232, at 1 (Sup. Ct. Cal. San Francisco County Aug. 18, 2004). The class

attorneys were awarded a fee of $1,575,000. *Id.* The total value of the settlement was apparently so modest that Judge Kramer did not even include a statement as to the announced value in his orders approving the settlement and attorney fees. In response to the request that the number of class members who actually returned claim forms indicating their choice of coupons be reported to the court, Judge Kramer replied:

Regarding the reporting, I am not going to require it. There's no purpose for it. Having found that the settlement is reasonable, fair, and adequate, having found that the coupons are going to people who, if they want to, and in accordance with their already demonstrated proclivities given that they've got credit cards from Sears, are going to go to Sears and spend their coupons, that's fine. If they don't, that does not, in my mind, take away from the fairness or strengthen or weaken the value of the settlement. It's their choice. End of story. So I don't see any practical reason for getting a report on a regular basis. It would add expense to counsel. It would add a business expense to Sears, and it would add an expense to the court system. I would have to look at this and figure out what to do with it, if anything; and frankly, I have plenty of other things to do, and there's just no need to do it.

Transcript of Hearing, Final Approval of Class Settlement, *Utility Consumers' Action Network v. Sears, Roebuck & Co.*, No. 306232, at 39 (Sup. Ct. Cal. San Francisco County July 8, 2004). Judge Kramer's assertion that providing a report on the number of claims filed and how many of the coupons were used would be a business expense of substance to either Sears or the court system is sheer nonsense. What Judge Kramer was worried about – probably with good cause – was that reporting would show that only a small or, more likely, a tiny percentage of Sears credit card holders would use the coupons, and that the class lawyer fee might then be a substantial percentage of, if not well in excess of, the actual benefit realized by Sears credit card holders. This is presumably what Judge Kramer meant when he said that if he directed that the outcome of the settlement be reported to the court, then he "would have to look at this and figure out what to do with it, if anything." Judge Kramer further stated that as for purposes of determining the fee, he was utterly disinterested in whether class members would regard the coupons as worth applying for. The fact that consumers do not regard the benefit as worth applying for or using (in the case of coupons) is irrelevant. The purpose of the class action is mostly to benefit lawyers – a view that Judge Kramer evidently shares along with a majority of the public.

109. *See* Jonathan R. Macey & Geoffrey P. Miller, *The Plaintiffs' Attorney's Role in Class Action and Derivative Litigation: Economic Analysis and*

Recommendations for Reform, 58 U. Chi. L. Rev. 1, 105–16 (proposing the use of auctions as a measure of class action reform and discussing the advantages and disadvantages of auctions).

110. 131 F.R.D. 688 (1990).

111. *Oracle*, 131 F.R.D. at 697.

112. 2001 WL 17092 at *17 (S.D.N.Y. Feb. 22, 2001). This low contingency fee percentage may be explained, in part, by indictments during the litigation by the Department of Justice of Christie's, Inc., and Sotheby's, Inc., for fixing the seller's commissions and buyer's premiums in its auctions. *Id*. at *1.

113. 2001 WL 17092 at *17 (S.D.N.Y. 2000).

114. *See In re Auction Houses Antitrust Litig.*, 197 F.R.D. 71, 74 (S.D.N.Y. 2000).

115. *See* 2001 WL 170792 at *2.

116. 2001 WL 17092 at *17 (S.D.N.Y. 2001).

117. Third Circuit Task Force on the Selection of Class Counsel, Final Report 61–62 (Jan. 2002).

118. *Id*. at 45–46, 48.

119. *Id*. at 41–42.

120. *Id*. at 43. A more balanced consideration of the positive and negative attributes of using auctions to set fees in class actions is set forth in *In re Cendant Corp. Litig.*, 264 F.3d 201, 258–60 (2001).

121. *See* Michael A. Perino, *Markets and Monitors: The Impact of Competition and Experience on Attorneys' Fees in Securities Class Actions*, Legal Studies Research Paper Series, Paper No. 06–0034 (Jan. 2006) [hereinafter Perino, *Markets and Monitors*].

122. *See id*. at 26.

123. *See id*.

124. *See id*. at 25.

125. Perino, *Markets and Monitors*, at 26 (Jan. 2006). As of August 2001, the Federal Judicial Center found only fourteen cases in which the auction method was used to select class counsel. *See* Laurie L. Hooper & Marie Leary, Auctioning the Role of Class Counsel in Class Action Cases: A Descriptive Study (Federal Judicial Center 2001).

126. 15 U.S.C. §78U-4(a)(3)(ii) and (iii) I(bb) and (cc) (2006).

127. *Id*.

128. *In re Cendant Corp. Litigation et al.*, 264 F.3d 201 (2001).

129. *Id*. at 219–20.

130. *Id*. at 220, 271–79.

131. *Id*. at 276.

132. *See* Chapter 17, § B, text at notes 46–49.

133. *Id*. at 269, 280.

19 Securities Class Actions

SUITS ALLEGING SECURITIES FRAUD ARE A SPECIALIZED form of class action brought on behalf of shareholders against the company issuing the purchased securities and its officers and directors (and sometimes the company's auditor and attorney). They are typically brought under section 10(b) of the Securities Exchange Act, which Congress enacted in 1933 following the stock market crash of 1929. The Act prohibits deception in the "purchase or sale of any security."[1] Pursuant to this section, the Securities and Exchange Commission (SEC) promulgated Rule 10b-5, which makes it unlawful to make any material misrepresentation or omission that would mislead investors.[2] Under the Act, enforcement was delegated to the SEC; there was no explicit provision allowing for a private right of action. Just over ten years after enactment, however, individual investors were given the right to directly sue companies for violating Rule 10b-5. This right was created by judicial fiat in a 1946 federal district court opinion, which was later accepted as a fait accompli by the U.S. Supreme Court in a decision devoid of recognition of the probable consequences.[3] The creation of a private right of action was based on the belief that private actions are an "effective weapon" of enforcement and a "necessary supplement" to limited SEC resources.[4] These suits, which most large businesses have been subjected to, typically allege that the corporation failed to disclose material information in a timely manner. This failure is alleged to harm shareholders who purchased or held the shares because, at that time, the share price was inflated by the failure to disclose this information and plunged when the information was belatedly revealed.

To further facilitate shareholder class actions, the Supreme Court has allowed plaintiffs to sidestep the daunting task of proving that each investor claiming a loss relied on a public misrepresentation in purchasing or selling a security.[5] The "fraud on the market" theory, which is the mechanism for this maneuver is based on the idea that because stock prices react automatically to public information, whether true or false, an investor who purchases or sells a security affected by the fraud is presumed to have relied on the false information.

Entrepreneurial lawyers have capitalized on the Supreme Court's actions to protect investors and maintain investor confidence in our stock markets by creating a multibillion-dollar business that burdens markets far more than it benefits them. Indeed, investors, as a whole, are being scammed by class action lawyers. Because corporate assets are depleted to pay the settlements, gains realized by shareholders at the time of the failure to provide the material information are at the expense of current shareholders. Thus, as engineered by class action lawyers, one group of shareholders is being compelled to pay another group of shareholders. Because many investors are diversified, and over time are both present and previous owners of stocks of various corporations, however, the net aggregate effect of most shareholder class actions is to transfer wealth from all shareholders' left pockets to their right pockets, less the billions of dollars in fees paid to the class action lawyers. As stated by Professor John Coffee, securities class action litigation "benefits corporate insiders, insurers and plaintiffs' attorneys, but not investors."[6] Despite the compelling evidence, most academics writing on the subject, though acknowledging the existence of some problems, defend securities class actions as necessary for policing the securities market, improving corporate governance, and because of what they claim is their deterrent effect.[7]

Recognizing that the class action bar has extracted billions of dollars from investors and corporations without commensurate benefit to investors and the securities market, Congress enacted the Private

Securities Litigation Reform Act (PSLRA).[8] In addition to changing the process federal courts use to select the lead plaintiff,[9] the PSLRA increases pleading requirements in securities class actions, requiring plaintiffs (1) to state with particularity both the facts constituting the alleged violation; and (2) to prove "scienter," that is, the defendant's intent "to deceive, manipulate or defraud."[10] When plaintiffs' lawyers sought to evade the heightened pleading requirements imposed by the PSLRA by filing securities class actions in state courts, Congress passed the Securities Litigation Uniform Standards Act (SLUSA).[11] SLUSA prevents most securities-fraud-based class actions from being filed in state courts. Even so, SLUSA has not closed all of the loopholes that plaintiffs' lawyers are likely to exploit.[12]

The U.S. Supreme Court has supported the congressional objectives and, in its own right, having recognized that the private right of action it created had been captured by lawyers to advance their own financial interests at the expense of shareholders, has placed significant restrictions on bringing securities class actions.[13] Nonetheless, few if any securities class action lawyers can be found on unemployment lines as the recent subprime mortgage crisis, which has enveloped virtually all financial institutions, is providing numerous targets for class action lawyers. Indeed, experts who serve as consultants or witnesses in litigation, including securities litigation, have noted an uptick in demand for their services in 2009–2010.[14]

A. Milberg Weiss

The Milberg law firm, formerly Milberg Weiss Bershad Hynes & Lerach (Milberg Weiss),[15] was once the most feared securities class action firm in the country. In the early 1990s, Milberg Weiss perfected the class action "strike suit," an immediate filing of a dubious class action lawsuit against a publicly traded company, alleging securities fraud a day or two after the company's stock significantly declined. By transferring billions of dollars from corporate tills (and their insurers) to investors, the firm won hundreds of millions of dollars for itself. In 1995, Congress enacted the Private Securities Litigation Reform Act (PSLRA)[16] – aimed primarily at the firm – which directed judges to select investors with the highest financial stakes to control the litigation and to select the lead counsel.

Prior to passage of the PSLRA, class action firms vied to be appointed as lead counsel by being the first to file suit when a company's stock price fell precipitously. Milberg Weiss perfected this "race to the courthouse" by maintaining a stable of paid professional plaintiffs who prepositioned themselves as suit-ready by buying a small number of shares in virtually all of the large corporations.[17] When a company's stock price declined substantially, the firm would immediately file a class action in the name of one of the prepositioned plaintiffs and, after settlement, kick back about 10 percent of its fee to that plaintiff.[18] Sharing fees with these plaintiffs, by prearrangement, while expressly denying to courts that it was doing so, however, violated a number of ethical and statutory prohibitions.[19] Both the firm and its former lead partners, Melvyn Weiss and William Lerach – who claim that the other securities class action firms were doing the same thing – pled guilty to paying secret kickbacks to their stable of professional plaintiffs and received prison terms.[20]

Securities class action lawsuits are typically triggered when a company's stock suffers a substantial decline. That decline could be because evidence has surfaced that the company engaged in fraud – as was the case with Enron and WorldCom – or because negative information regarding a company's products or earnings becomes known. In the latter case, lawyers sue, claiming that the information should have been disclosed earlier and that shareholders who bought or owned the stock in the absence of such disclosure were defrauded. The damages sought are the product of the number of shares outstanding at the time of the violation – which for large corporations could total hundreds of millions of shares – and the amount of the stock's decline. Because stocks decline for a variety of reasons, including a broad decline or sector decline in the stock market, class action lawyers hire damage experts to testify as to the part of the decline attributable to the failure to disclose material information. Lawyers are prohibited from paying these expert witnesses fees that are contingent on the outcome of the case because giving the experts a stake in the litigation improperly incentivizes them to alter their testimony.

John Torkelson was the leading damage expert in securities class actions, and his testimony has been instrumental in securing billions of dollars in settlements. But Torkelson's testimony was bought and paid for – at a very high price – by Milberg Weiss and other securities class action firms.[21] In a plea agreement with federal prosecutors, Torkelson admitted to lying in court when he denied being paid on a contingency fee basis for his "independent" expert testimony.[22] In fact, Torkelson had a financial incentive to maximize claimed losses from allegations of securities fraud because greater shareholder losses increased the judgment or settlement amount, which in turn increased the attorneys' fees and Torkelson's cut. If class counsel did not prevail in the action, Torkelson got nothing; if class counsel prevailed, Torkelson inflated his fees to make up for previous losses. In total, Torkelson submitted more than $60 million in expert witness fees between 1993 and 1996, inflated more than $7 million in fees ($4 million alone for Milberg Weiss), and wrote off another $7 million when class counsel did not prevail.[23]

The *Wall Street Journal* characterized the Milberg operation as a

> ... corrupt enterprise that perpetrated a vast fraud on our system of justice. Legitimate tort claims involve injured individuals who need a lawyer to seek redress. Milberg paid stockbrokers to recruit plaintiffs who weren't injured to sue companies that weren't guilty. Then it paid off to those plaintiffs and the "expert" witnesses who would inflate the amount of injury, thereby raising the value of damage settlements and the riches the firms lawyer received.[24]

Joe Nocera, a columnist for the *New York Times*, added the sobering note that, although Milberg violated the law, under our system, securities class action lawyers "have the right to file bogus suits and extract what they can from them."[25]

How did the Milberg firm know that the companies in which its stable of professional plaintiffs invested would fail to timely disclose material information? Because violations of the law rarely had anything to do with bringing these suits! A share price decline triggered a suit. For large companies, it is always possible to find some information that had a negative impact on share prices and was not disclosed as early as it might have been. These cases virtually always settle for a very small fraction – 2 percent to 3 percent – of the claimed damages once the class has been certified.[26]

Payment often does not equate with the merits of the litigation, however. Rather, as previously discussed in this chapter, payment is mostly a function of the dynamics of class action litigation – the ability of the lawyers to inflict substantial costs and the risk, however improbable, that a jury will be persuaded to find billions of dollars in damages. Moreover, if there has been wrongdoing and shareholders receive some compensation for their losses, these suits virtually never result in any monetary sanction against the corporate officers or directors who were responsible for misleading and therefore defrauding investors.[27] The deterrence value, therefore, is zilch.

B. Use of Contract Lawyers

Another artifice, involving the widespread use of "contract lawyers," may account for billions of dollars improperly charged against the settlement funds generated for shareholders. Contract lawyers are fully licensed lawyers who are hired on a temporary basis to perform work, such as reviewing millions of documents that are routinely subpoenaed in large-scale litigations.[28] The practice of using contract lawyers originated in 1978 when Harold Kohn, a noted plaintiffs' antitrust lawyer, decided to employ recent law school graduates instead of paralegals to perform basic discovery tasks.[29] Kohn wrote to a law school placement director: "We do want people who have some common sense and make a good appearance but we don't need top scholars."[30] Kohn made this decision after courts changed the rules for setting the attorneys' fee in class actions from a percentage of the common fund to the attorneys' lodestar.[31] At that time, charges for paralegal services could not be inflated by a multiplier as could lawyers' time. By substituting contract lawyers to do the same work, Kohn was able to circumvent this preclusion and substantially increase his fees.

Today, new layers of sophistication have been added to this subterfuge, elevating its value to lawyers by billions of dollars. The scheme involves assigning contract lawyers hundreds of thousands of hours, much of it make-work, to review the thousands of documents subpoenaed by class counsel, including e-mails, spreadsheets, reports, letters, photos, and any electronically stored communications or information. The process of discovery of electronically stored information (ESI) is complex and involves sophisticated electronic search methods.[32]

When faced with a daunting discovery demand, defendants usually hire a vendor who specializes in this document gathering process. The vendor, or the defendant's law firm, codes each document so that it can be searched in a database. "Objective coding" involves indicating the nature and reference number of each document, the author, its recipients, date, subject, and other data indicated on the face of the document. To maintain cost effectiveness, vendors usually assign objective coding to data processors and clerical personnel to be done electronically. "Subjective coding," which follows, involves attorneys making notes on the relevance of the document, whether it is privileged against disclosure because it contains confidential communications with the defendant's lawyers or because it is "work product," and whether it involves sensitive business information and should be protected by requiring some degree of confidentiality.

Defendants have a greater burden with respect to document review than plaintiffs' counsel, especially with regard to the issues of whether documents are privileged from discovery. Nonetheless, document review, as carried out by plaintiffs' counsels in class actions, is far more labor-intensive because plaintiffs' counsel use document review to increase their lodestars to justify their multimillion-dollar fee requests. Indeed, document review is often the major time component in their lodestars. For example, in the *Tyco* securities litigation,[33] of the 423,380 hours that the class lawyers claimed to have worked (not including clerical staff), 290,552, or 69 percent, of those hours were accounted for by contract lawyers reviewing 83.5 million documents.[34] Likewise, in the *Xerox* securities litigation,[35] of the 290,759 hours claimed to have been worked by the plaintiffs' attorneys, 201,506, or 69 percent, of those hours were by contract lawyers reviewing four million pages of documents.[36] For one of the firms in the *Xerox* litigation, contract attorneys represented 98 percent of its 15,300.50 claimed hours, making it essentially a supplier of contract attorneys with no other substantive role in the litigation.[37]

Three issues are raised by the document review performed by the plaintiffs' lawyers:

(1) Whether the payments to the contract lawyers (or the agencies that hire them) are either (a) expenses, which the firms can then submit for reimbursement at cost when the class action is settled; or (b) billable hours, which the firm can charge to its lodestar at "market rates" that are multiples of the actual costs to the firm.

(2) Assuming that the contract lawyers' time can be included in the billable hours totals, whether objective coding, if done by the contract lawyers, is clerical work to be billed at paralegal rates or legal work to be billed at (a) contract lawyer rates; or (b) at a much higher associate lawyer rate.

(3) Whether the subjective coding is undertaken to further the litigation strategy of the plaintiffs' lawyers or whether "writing extensive attorney notes on documents of little or no evidentiary value"[38] is undertaken principally to run up the billable hours.

1. Contract Lawyer Wages: Expenses or Billable Hours?

The decision whether securities class action law firms can count contract lawyer time as billable hours and mark them up to "market rates" or whether firms must treat them as expenses, which are then reimbursable at settlement, has profound economic consequences. As indicated previously, contract lawyers' hours in some major securities class actions account for nearly 70 percent of the hundreds of thousands of hours "billed" to the class.

Law firms pay contract lawyers $35 to $40 an hour. If they go through an agency to hire these lawyers, firms pay $55 an hour, of which about $35 is paid to the contract lawyers. When class action lawyers submit their request for fees and reimbursement of expenses, they do not list the payments to contract lawyers as an expense. Instead, they list them in their lodestar as "project associates" or a similar non-informative title and "bill" their time at about $300 an hour. Is this legal? Absolutely. Phillip Crawford Jr., a contract lawyer who worked for the leading securities class actions firm, wrote a "whistle-blower" letter to the judge in the *Tyco* securities litigation[39] in which he alleged that in another litigation, *In re Oxford Health Plans, Inc. Securities Litigation*,[40] Milberg Weiss had misidentified the contract attorneys as "associates" (full-time firm lawyers).[41] In fact, this mislabeling of contract lawyers' time in securities class actions is common. Crawford then requested appointment of a special master by the court to review possible billing irregularities. Judge Barbadoro chose not to directly respond. He made clear in his decision, however, that he regarded the issue of how the contract lawyers were identified in the firm's billing summary as irrelevant, stating:

> An attorney, regardless of whether she is an associate with steady employment or a contract attorney whose job ends upon completion of a particular document review project, is still an attorney. It is therefore appropriate to bill a contract attorney's time at market rates and count these time charges toward the lodestar.[42]

Judge Barbado's decision is in accord with the prevailing judicial view that contract lawyer time may be billed at "market rates."[43]

Judges' infatuation with "market rates" has created an opportunity for securities class action law firms to pocket huge profits from document review. Based on lodestar submissions by plaintiffs' firms in securities class actions, the "market rate" they claim for contract lawyers is $300 an hour or more.[44] This is the "market rate" because judges accept the rates that the law firms use in the lodestar calculation without making any attempt to verify their accuracy.

But these overcharges are small potatoes when viewed in the larger context of "expense" versus "billable hour." Consider what occurs on the defense side. First, clerical or technical personnel – not contract lawyers – mostly perform the objective coding electronically. Contract lawyers may then be used to do a first cut review of the documents for relevance and privilege. About a decade ago, with legal fees in large-scale litigations rising exponentially, corporate clients began to carefully scrutinize their outside counsel fees. This scrutiny and increased competition among law firms for selection in large-scale litigations led law firms to relinquish abusive billing practices that had become routine.[45] One consequence is that in large-scale securities litigations, clients have come to insist that payments to contract lawyers, whether by the vendor or by the law firm, be treated as an expense and reimbursed at cost rather than treated as a profit center. There is much variation here, however. In some cases, for example, bargaining with the client allows the firm to add a comparatively modest overhead component – around 20 percent. On the plaintiffs' side, however, there is no client to demand cost efficiencies and no court to insist on the same cost efficiencies as clients impose on defense firms.

2. Which Billable Hour Rate: Paralegal, Contract Attorney, or Associate?

Even if contract lawyer hours are permissibly billed to the lodestar rather than accounted for as an expense, the issue remains as to how this work is to be characterized for purposes of determining the rate: as a paralegal, contract lawyer, or associate. The answer should be that it depends on the nature of the tasks they are performing. It is improper for a law firm to bill for clerical tasks at paralegal rates – let alone at associate or part-ner rates – even if the work is done by a paralegal, associate, or partner rather than by clerical staff.[46] Likewise, it is improper to bill for objective coding of documents – which is clerical work – at contract lawyer rates.[47] These unexceptionable propositions, however, do not apply to securities class actions. Here, the prevailing standard appears to be that whatever billing practice maximizes lawyers' profits is permissible.

This billing issue was raised in the *Xerox* securities litigation. Two contract lawyers, Stephen Vasil, a Yale Law School graduate, and Andrew Gilman, a New York University School of Law graduate, were hired for $35 and $40 an hour, respectively, by a securities class action firm to do both objective and subjective coding of documents in the *Xerox* litigation.[48] After concluding that the document review process was "ineffective and wasteful," and having done document review for defense firms where the focus was on efficiency and controlling costs,[49] they came up with a business plan for a more efficient process, which they presented to a partner in the firm. In their words, the reaction to their "observations and proposed solutions led [them] to suspect that the systematic inefficiencies [they] ... pointed out were not mere unintended consequences of poor managerial decisions" and that "maintaining significant personnel costs associated with document review work was essential to justifying requests for large fees in class action lawsuits."[50]

After concluding their work in the litigation, they read a newspaper article reporting the proposed settlement and the attorney's fee request. After unsuccessfully presenting their ethical concerns of improper bill-ing for their work to the law firm that hired them, Vasil and Gilman submitted a letter to presiding Judge Alvin Thompson, stating that the 4,169 hours of document review work they performed – billed at $300 an hour – was misrepresented as legal work. They also claimed that 2,877 hours or 69 percent of their work was clerical, as defined by the coding manual provided to them by the law firm, and involved objective coding of documents with minimal supervision.[51]

Even though the class counsel's expert retained to endorse their fee request acknowledged that outsourcing the objective coding task to third-party clerical service providers is "typically done in class actions,"[52] class counsel in the *Xerox* litigation maintained that the decision had been made not to outsource the "objective coding" portion of the document review (recording the type of document, who wrote it, its recipients, etc.) in order to "maximize the integrity of future database searches."[53] If this coding were outsourced to paralegals, they argued, the work would have to be cross-checked by attorneys.[54] They further argued that outsourcing would delay the review process and that, due to the complexity of the documents, the firm chose to hire attorneys to perform both the objective data entry and fill in the "attorney notes."[55] At the Fairness Hearing, class counsel also argued that they "were very concerned that highly relevant documents could easily be mischaracterized and missed from the analysis if we engaged in a review that was led by nonlawyers."[56] Thus, the firm hired contract lawyers to perform both the objective, data entry aspects of the document review as well as the subjective or legal relevancy analysis.

On the basis of Gilman and Vasil's calculations, using contract lawyers to perform the clerical task of objective coding of documents accounted for approximately 135,000 – nearly half – of the 290,759 hours in the *Xerox* litigation lodestar. These are hours that the defendants' vendors or law firms do not incur. Perhaps the defense firms do not believe that using contract lawyers for objective coding is necessary to "maximize the integrity of future database searches." As for the 67,000 hours of contract lawyer time included in the lodestar for subjective coding, Gilman and Vasil further allege that much of the subjective coding they did was "an unnecessary task which certainly contributed to the inefficiencies of the document review."[57]

3. Subjective Coding by Contract Attorneys: Benefit to the Litigation or to the Lodestar?

Vasil and Gilman also claimed that the firm – whose work in the litigation was almost entirely (98%) done by contract attorneys – functioned like a "quasi-employment agency"[58] because the firm "failed to provide them with any meaningful supervision, offering them neither payroll services nor employment benefits."[59] Vasil and Gilman expressed the concern that they "may have been unknowingly participating in a scheme to pad the hours of temporary document review staff by assigning them burdensome clerical tasks and other such busy work."[60]

Judge Thompson dismissed the contract lawyers' assertions, finding that an early e-mail sent by Gilman to a supervisor undermined their argument that they spent a majority of their time performing clerical tasks without supervision.[61] Moreover, he found that "it is not objectionable per se in this case to apply a multiplier to a lodestar that includes work performed by contract attorneys, even though the profit margin for the firms employing them was greater than the profit margin the firms would have had for work done by full-time employees."[62]

In the end, Judge Thompson awarded an attorneys' fee of 16 percent, or $120 million, of the $750 million settlement.[63] This award meant that the lodestar of roughly $96 million was augmented by a multiplier of 1.25.[64] Thus, class counsel was awarded $375 per hour for contract lawyer work. Given Vasil's hourly rate of $35, plus the agency costs of approximately $20 an hour,[65] the profit for each contract attorney hour was $320 – a profit margin of nearly 600 percent. Considering the total contract attorney hours of 201,506.77 in this one litigation, the firms profited, at the class's expense, by $64,482,166.40 through their use of contract attorneys, who spent two-thirds of their time engaged in clerical data entry and a portion of the other third, according to Vasil and Gilman, "writing extensive 'attorney notes' on documents of little or no evidentiary value."[66]

4. Use of Contract Lawyers: A Summing Up

There is no conclusive evidence by which to sort out the conflicting claims of class counsel and those of the "whistle-blowers." Class counsel vigorously deny Vasil and Gilman's claims that they were assigned to do mostly clerical work and that one-third of their work was writing notes on documents of "little or no evidentiary value" to the litigation.[67] Class counsel also vigorously maintain that the document review – performed entirely by contract attorneys – was a "strategic decision," essential to the successful conclusion to the litigation.[68] Judge Thompson took the law firms at their word and dismissed Vasil and Gilman's assertions. Perhaps Judge Thompson peered into Pandora's box and decided to keep it sealed. Perhaps it was simply unthinkable that a judge would jeopardize billions of dollars in fees for lawyers by limiting or eliminating hundreds of thousands of hours from securities class action law firms' lodestars or by drastically lowering the billing for those hours to clerical rates.

In assessing the firm's contention that it had a valid reason to assign contract lawyers to do clerical work and that the "attorney notes" work was properly supervised and not undertaken to run up the hours to be billed at "market rates," it is instructive to consider the financial incentives to run up hundreds of thousands of contract lawyer hours. An e-mail sent in 2001 from one partner to another in a securities class action firm sets out the incentives in stark form:

> I am not satisfied that we are logging enough hours in the cases that we see as big $$ cases to justify a big fee at the end. I am not commenting on whether we are doing what we need to do in the cases from quality of litigation standpoint to drive a big result ... What I'm talking about is whether we should simply commit to having a temp or staff atty putting in a certain # of hours each week (like 20–40 hours) no matter what ... The cases that arguably justify the time (subject to everyone's thoughts) include ... [list of cases omitted]. The associate on the case would be in charge of directing the staff/ temp atty on what they should be doing. However, there are a thousand and one things that can be done, from internet research, to creating bios on individual defs, to identifying customers, etc., etc. One temp atty billed @ $225/hour, working 30 hours a week for 45 weeks per year generates a lodestar of $303,750. A 3X [multiplier] lodestar on that # generates revenues of $1.0 million in revenue. If we have 4 attys doing this, we generate potential revenues of close to $4 million for their work for that year. Obviously, each case is unique

and our fee may or may not depend directly on our lodestar. We need to consider for each case how direct we think the relationship will be between lodestar and fee. The cost of doing one atty for one year is $50/hour times 30 hours times 45 weeks, or $67,500. For 4 attys for one year, the cost is $270,000.[69]

Updating the hourly rates indicated in this e-mail to those being paid and billed in 2008 would result in the following calculus:

> One temp atty billed @ $300/hour, working 30 hours a week for 45 weeks per year generates a lodestar of $405,000. A 3X lodestar on that # generates revenues of $1.215 million in revenue. If we have 4 attys doing this, we generate potential revenues of close to $4.86 million for their work for that year ... The cost of doing one atty for one year is $35/hour if hired directly or $55/hour if through an agency, times 30 hours times 45 weeks, or an average of $60,750. For 4 attys for one year, the cost is $243,000.

Thus, the yearly net profit from the use of one contract attorney, based on this scenario, is $1.15 million. Multiplying that by the number of contract attorneys hired by plaintiffs' law firms in securities class action litigations yields staggering profits, which courts have mindlessly approved because they are the "market rate." But there is only one market in which the "market rate" of $300 or more an hour for contract lawyers prevails: federal courtrooms.

NOTES

1. 15 U.S.C. § 78j (2006).
2. 17 C.F.R. § 240.10b-5 (2008).
3. *Superintendent of Ins. of N.Y. v. Bankers Life & Casualty Co.*, 404 U.S. 6, 13 n.9 (1971).
4. *Stoneridge Inv. Partners, LLC v. Scientific-Atlanta*, 128 S. Ct. 761, 779 n.10 (2008).
5. *Dura Pharmaceuticals, Inc. v. Broudo*, 544 U.S. 336, 341–42 (2005).
6. *Id.* at 1534.
7. *See, e.g.*, Symposium, *The Continuing Evolution of Securities Class Actions*, 2009 Wis. L. Rev. 151 (2009).

8. Private Securities Litigation Reform Act of 1995, Pub. L. No. 104–67, 109 Stat. 737 (1995) (codified as amended at 15 U.S.C. § 77z-1 (2006).

9. *See* Chapter 17, § B.

10. *Ernst & Ernst v. Hochfelder*, 425 U.S. 185, 194 (1976).

11. Pub. Law No. 105–353, 112 Stat. 3227 (1998) (codified as amended at 15 U.S.C. § 78 u-4(b)(1), (b)(2) and (b)(4) (2006).

12. Matthew O'Brien, *Choice of Forum in Securities Class Actions: Confronting "Reform" of the Securities Act of 1933*, 28 REV. LITIG. 845 (2009).

13. *See Stoneridge Investment Partners, LLC. v. Scientific-Atlanta, Inc.*, 128 S. Ct. 761 (2008) (holding that a private plaintiff, as opposed to the Securities and Exchange Commission, may not maintain a securities fraud action against those who have merely aided and abetted a primary violation of the securities act); *Bell Atlantic Corp. v. Twombly*, 550 U.S. 544 (2007) (raising the standard for bringing a claim alleging an antitrust violation of the Sherman Act by requiring "enough factual matter to suggest that an agreement [to fix prices] was made"); *Tellabs, Inc. v. Makor Issues & Rights, Ltd.*, 551 U.S. 308 (2007) (holding that in determining whether a defendant acted knowingly (with "scienter"), "plausible nonculpable explanations" must be considered).

14. Robert Ambrogi, IMS Expert Services BullsEye Bulletin, April 2010, *available at* http://www.ins-expertservices.com/newsletters/april/2010.ql-litigation report.

15. The firm was known as Milberg Weiss Bershad Hynes & Lerach before William Lerach left the firm in 2004 to form his own firm, Lerach Coughlin Stoia Geller Rudman & Robbins. *See* Peter Elkind, *The fall of America's meanest law firm*, FORTUNE, Nov. 3, 2006, at 155–56.

16. *See supra* note 8.

17. *See* Peter Elkind, *The fall of America's meanest law firm*, FORTUNE, Nov. 3, 2006, at 155.

18. *See id.* at 163.

19. *See* Editorial, WALL ST. J., June 18, 2008, at A14 ("Milberg now admits that, over 30 years, seven former partners (three remain unnamed) paid secret kickbacks to plaintiffs in 165 suits. Those suits earned the firm some $240 million in fees.... In addition to paying plaintiffs, Milberg was also funneling kickbacks to New York-area stockbrokers who referred clients for Milberg suits.").

20. In 2008, the Milberg law firm settled with federal prosecutors for $75 million, and key partners were sentenced for their roles in an illegal kickbacks scheme spanning twenty-five years: Melvyn Weiss (thirty months), William Lerach (twenty-four months), David Bershad (six months), and Steven Schulman (six months). *See* Edvard Pettersson, *Ex-Milberg Partners Bershad, Schulman Get 6-Month Prison Terms*, BLOOMBERG.COM, Oct. 28, 2008, *available at* http://www.bloomberg.com/apps/news?pid=20601127&sid=a2b8e5SfdqRc#.

21. *See* Nathan Koppel, *Filing Shines Light on Expert-Witness Payments – Torkelson Says Firm Was Aware He Padded Costs*, WALL ST. J., Mar. 5, 2008, at B10; *see also* Guilty Plea Agreement, *U.S. v. John B. Torkelson*, at ex.A (Feb. 28, 2008).

22. Press Release No. 08–020, U.S. Attorney's Office, Central District of California, New Jersey Man Who Served as Expert Witness in Numerous Class Actions Agrees to Plead Guilty to Perjury for Concealing Arrangement with Law Firms (Feb. 28, 2008), *available at* http://www.usdoj.gov/usao/cac/pressroom/pr2008/020.html; *see also* Guilty Plea Agreement, at ex.A.

23. *See* Press Release, at 2.

24. Editorial, WALL ST. J., June 18, 2008, at A14.

25. Joseph Nocera, *Serving Time But Lacking Remorse*, N.Y. TIMES, June 7, 2008, at C1.

26. *See* Elaine Buckberg et al., RECENT TRENDS IN SHAREHOLDER CLASS ACTION LITIGATION: ARE WORLDCOM, AND ENRON THE NEW STANDARD? 6 (NERA Econ. Consulting 2005).

27. *See* John C. Coffee Jr., *Reforming the Securities Class Action: An Essay on Deterrence and Its Implementation*, 106 COLUM. L. REV. 1534 (2006).

28. *See* Anonymous, *Down in the Data Mines*, A.B.A. J., Dec. 2008, at 32.

29. *See* Connie Bruck, *Harold Kohn Against the World*, AM. LAW., Jan. 1982, at 30.

30. *See id.* (quoting Kohn's letter).

31. *See* Chapter 17, § A.

32. In Appendix C, I provide a more detailed analysis of electronic discovery, the extensive use of contract lawyers by class counsel, and the sources on which my analysis is based.

33. *In re Tyco Int'l, Ltd. Multidistrict Litigation*, 535 F.Supp.2d 249 (D. N.H. 2007).

34. *See* Securities Plaintiffs' Counsel's Memorandum of Law in Support of Petition for an Award of Attorneys' Fees and Reimbursement of Expenses at 18, *In re Tyco Int'l, Ltd. Multidistrict Litigation*, 535 F.Supp.2d 249 (D. N.H. Oct. 22, 2007); *see also* Joint Declaration of Richard S. Schiffrin, Jay W. Eisenhofer and Sanford P. Dumain In Support of Proposed Class Action Settlement, Plan of Allocation and Petition for an Award of Attorneys' Fees and Reimbursement of Expenses at exs.19–26, *In re Tyco Int'l, Ltd. Multidistrict Litigation*, 535 F.Supp.2d 249 (D. N.H. Oct. 22, 2007).

35. *Carlson v. Xerox Corp.*, No. 3:00-cv-1621 (D. Conn. Jan. 14, 2009).

36. *See* Lead Plaintiffs' Second Supplemental Response to Objections at ex.2, *Carlson v. Xerox Corp.*, No. 3:00-cv-1621 (D. Conn. Oct. 14, 2008); Fairness Hearing Transcript at *27, *Carlson v. Xerox Corp.*, No. 3:00-cv-1621 (D. Conn. Oct. 7, 2008).

37. *See* Fairness Hearing Transcript at *42, *Carlson v. Xerox Corp.*, No. 3:00-cv-1621 (D. Conn. Oct. 7, 2008); *see also* Joint Declaration of Richard S. Schiffrin, Jay W. Eisenhofer and Sanford P. Dumain In Support of Proposed Class Action Settlement, Plan of Allocation and Petition for an Award of Attorneys' Fees and Reimbursement of Expenses at 68, *In re Tyco Int'l, Ltd. Multidistrict Litigation*, 535 F.Supp.2d 249 (D. N.H. Oct. 22, 2007).

38. *See* Supplemental Objection To Motion For Award Of Attorneys' Fees at ex.B, *Carlson v. Xerox Corp.*, No. 3:00-cv-1621 (D. Conn. Nov. 5, 2008).

39. *In re Tyco Int'l, LTD., Securities Litigation*, MDL Docket No. 02–1335-B.

40. 244 F. Supp.2d 247 (S.D.N.Y. Feb. 11, 2003).

41. *See* Letter from Phillip Crawford Jr., at 5, *In re Tyco Int'l, Ltd.* Multidistrict Litigation, No. 02–1335-PB, Doc. # 1161, 535 F.Supp.2d 249 (D. N.H. Oct. 31, 2007). Associates are full-time employees of a law firm. Major firms in large cities were paying first-year associates a starting salary of $160,000 a year in 2008 and multiples of that for more experienced associates.

42. *See In re Tyco Int'l, Ltd. Multidistrict Litigation*, 535 F.Supp.2d 249, 272–73 (D. N.H. 2007).

43. *See Missouri v. Jenkins*, 491 U.S. 274 (1989) (fees for legal assistants, paralegals, investigators, and nonsecretarial support staff are included in the lodestar at market rate rather than at their cost to the attorneys); *In re Enron Corp. Securities, Derivative & ERISA Litigation*, 586 F.Supp.2d 732, 785 (S.D.Tex. 2008) (concluding based on the Supreme Court's reasoning in *Jenkins*, that counsel can recover fees for contract attorney services at market rates rather that at their cost to the firm); ABA Formal Opinion 00–420, Nov. 29, 2000 (stating that contract attorneys' work may be charged to the client as fees rather than costs when "the retaining lawyer has supervised the work of the contract lawyer or adopted that work as her own").

44. In fact, there is evidence that law firms bill contract lawyer time at much lower rates in other forms of litigation. A 2006 article in the *American Lawyer* stated that: "The American Bar Association's committee on ethics and professional responsibility concluded in a formal 2000 opinion that firms could bill temporary attorneys at triple the rate they pay the agency [tripling $55/hour equals $165/hour]. In our survey, though, only a handful of firms using temps reported triple-billing; a third reported a 0–25 percent markup over the role the firm pays its agencies; and another third reported a 20–100 percent markup." Julie Triedman, *Temporary Solution: Law firms say they don't like using contract attorneys. Yet, more and more, they're hiring hundreds of temps at a time*, AM. LAW., Sept. 1, 2006, at 96; *see also* Anonymous, *Down in the Data Mines*, A.B.A. J. Dec. 2008, at 32. Using an average markup of 50%, this differential amounts to much more than $100,000,000 in just the *Tyco* and *Xerox* securities litigations.

45. *See* Susan Beck & Michael Orey, *Skaddenomics: The Ludicrous World of Law Firm Billing*, AM. LAW., Sept. 1991, at 3.

46. *Missouri v. Jenkins*, 491 U.S. 274, 288 (1989).

47. The issue was raised by Phillip Crawford in the *Tyco* securities case when he wrote to the judge that much of the work that he and the other contract attorneys did was "non-legal work ... billed as legal work," and could have been done by "paralegals or data entry processors" because the firm "collapsed together both the objective and subjective coding components of the document review." *See* Letter from Phillip Crawford Jr., at 2, 5, *In re Tyco Int'l, Ltd. Multidistrict Litigation*, No. 02–1335-PB, Doc. # 1161, 535 F.Supp.2d 249 (D. N.H. Oct. 31, 2007). Judge Barbadoro dismissed this argument stating: "[A]s the Supreme Court has noted, there are many types of work that lie "in a gray area of tasks that might appropriately be performed either by an attorney or a paralegal." Depending on the particular circumstances, it may or may not be cost-efficient to preclude attorneys from doing such work, particularly if it is intermingled with work that only an attorney can perform." *See In re Tyco Int'l, Ltd. Multidistrict Litigation*, 535 F.Supp.2d 249, 272–73 (D. N.H. 2007) (citing *Missouri v. Jenkins*, 491 U.S. 274, 288 n.10 [1989]).

48. *See* Daniel Fisher, *Nice Work If You Can Get It*, FORBES, Dec. 8, 2008, at 44; *see also Carlson v. Xerox Corp.*, No. 3:00-cv-1621 (D. Conn. Jan. 14, 2009).

49. *See* Supplemental Objection to Motion for Award of Attorneys' Fees at ex.B, *Carlson v. Xerox Corp.*, No. 3:00-cv-1621 (D. Conn. Nov. 5, 2008).

50. *See id.* at ex.A.

51. *See id.*

52. Lead Plaintiffs' Memorandum Summarizing the Background of the Wolin Report, at 8, 37, *Carlson v. Xerox Corp.*, No. 3:00-cv-1621 (D. Conn. Sept. 22, 2008).

53. Supplemental Objection to Motion for Award of Attorneys' Fees at ex.A, *Carlson v. Xerox Corp.*, No. 3:00-cv-1621 (D. Conn. Nov. 5, 2008).

54. *Id.*

55. *See* Joint Declaration of Glen DeValerio, Brad N. Friedman, and Dennis J. Johnson in Support of Final Approval of Class Action Settlement, Plan of Allocation, Award of Attorneys' Fees and Reimbursement of Expenses at ¶ 47, *Carlson v. Xerox Corp.*, No. 3:00-cv-1621 (D. Conn. Sept. 22, 2008).

56. *See* Fairness Hearing Transcript at *27, *Carlson v. Xerox Corp.*, No. 3:00-cv-1621 (D. Conn. Oct. 7, 2008).

57. E-mail from Stephen Vasil, Jan. 19, 2009 (on file with author).

58. *See,* Supplemental objection, *supra* note 49.

59. *See id.*

60. *See id.*

61. *See* Ruling on Motion for Award of Attorney Fees at 14, *Carlson v. Xerox Corp.*, No. 3:00-cv-1621 (D. Conn. Jan. 14, 2009). Gilman sent the e-mail in response

to a conference call from the supervising attorney to a group of contract attorneys, setting benchmarks for the number of documents that they were to review daily. *See* Lead Plaintiffs' Second Supplemental Response to Objections at ex.3, *Carlson v. Xerox Corp.*, No. 3:00-cv-1621 (D. Conn. Oct. 14, 2008). In the e-mail, Gilman expressed concern that he had not been coding enough documents and described the time required to code each document as including "5 minutes reading and interpreting" the document and another "5–10 minutes filling in the fields (most of it spent writing my attorney notes)." *See* Lead Plaintiffs' Second Supplemental Response to Objections at ex.3, *Carlson v. Xerox Corp.*, No. 3:00-cv-1621 (D. Conn. Oct. 14, 2008). According to Judge Thompson, this e-mail supported class counsel's contention that the attorneys were properly supervised and performed enough legal work to justify a billing rate of $300 an hour. Vasil maintains that Judge Thompson's reliance on Gilman's e-mail is misplaced. He argues that the e-mail shows that the contract attorneys were required to write "attorney notes" on vast numbers of documents regardless of their relevance and questions whether a field labeled "attorney notes" ipso facto makes such descriptions "legal work." E-mail from Stephen Vasil, Jan. 19, 2009, on file with author. Based on the work that he and Gilman did, he concludes that this portion of the subjective coding was "an unnecessary task which certainly contributed to the inefficiencies of the document review." E-mail from Stephen Vasil, Jan. 19, 2009 (on file with author).

62. *See* Ruling On Motion For Award Of Attorney Fees at 17–18, *Carlson v. Xerox Corp.*, No. 3:00-cv-1621 (D. Conn. Jan. 14, 2009).

63. *See id.* at 27.

64. *See* Lead Plaintiffs' Second Supplemental Response to Objections at ex.2, *Carlson v. Xerox Corp.*, No. 3:00-cv-1621 (D. Conn. Oct. 14, 2008).

65. *See* Anonymous, *Down in the Data Mines*, A.B.A. J. Dec. 2008, at 32.

66. *See* Supplemental Objection, *supra* note 49.

67. *See id.*

68. *See* Joint Declaration of Glen DeValerio, Brad N. Friedman, and Dennis J. Johnson in Support of Final Approval of Class Action Settlement, Plan of Allocation, Award of Attorneys' Fees and Reimbursement of Expenses at ¶47, *Carlson v. Xerox Corp.*, No. 3:00-cv-1621 (D. Conn. Sept. 22, 2008). Class Counsel also stated in the fairness hearing: "We were very concerned that highly relevant documents could easily be mischaracterized and missed from analysis if we engaged in a review that was led by nonlawyers." Fairness Hearing Transcript at *27, *Carlson v. Xerox Corp.*, No. 3:00-cv-1621 (D. Conn. Oct. 7, 2008).

69. E-mail from one partner in a securities class action law firm to another, 2001.

20 Regulation through Litigation

COURTS CREATED THE TORT SYSTEM TO PROVIDE compensation for injury and to deter injurious conduct.[1] Two distinctive but related types of recent litigation, however, depart from this traditional compensation-deterrence model in favor of a regulatory model. In one set of litigation, the primary goal of the litigation is to prohibit certain business practices or restrict the manufacture or sale of goods or services in the same way as if there had been legislation or administrative rule making; here, redress for injury is secondary to obtaining a settlement, monetary judgment, or injunctive order issued by a court. This use of litigation is described as "regulation through litigation."[2] To be sure, in addition to injunctive relief, such suits may seek substantial monetary damages. The dominant purpose of the damage claim, however, is to pose a sufficient financial threat to manufacturers and sellers as to induce them into settling the claims by agreeing to change their product or their method of conducting business.[3] The second type of litigation that falls under "regulation through litigation" aims to generate substantial contingency fees through effectuation of a wealth transfer. What is distinctive about this type of litigation is that the wealth transfer is linked to a regulatory outcome. Indeed, the regulatory outcome is the means of gaining the wealth transfer.

Most conventional tort litigation is not intended to (and does not have) a significant regulatory effect beyond general deterrence. However, tort litigation can function in a regulatory manner when class actions or other aggregations, repetitive suits, or large punitive damage awards force a producer of goods or services to change its business practices; restrict or discontinue the manufacture or sale of one of its products; or cause changes in professional practices. Where lawyers seek compensation for alleged harm done to large numbers of claimants, the attainment of a significant regulatory outcome may become a deliberate part of the litigation strategy.

States' attorneys general (AGs) play a significant role in regulation through litigation by bringing *parens patriae* litigation against product manufacturers. In this type of litigation, the AG sues on behalf of the state as a collective plaintiff, seeking tort-type damages, such as reimbursement for the costs of treating or preventing injuries resulting from product use.[4] These collective actions leap over legal barriers that would otherwise effectively preclude alleged victims from prevailing if they sued individually. As discussed in this chapter, through these actions AGs frequently seek to supplant regulatory regimes enacted by Congress, federal agencies, or state legislatures and substitute their policy preferences.

This expansion of the power of the AGs at the expense of legislatures is facilitated when they retain private lawyers to represent the state on a contingency fee basis. Contracting out the use of a state's police power has produced enormous profits for lawyers and political benefits for the AGs. In these instances, wealth-generating litigation also produces a significant regulatory outcome. As Wendell Gauthier, a class action lawyer who represented the City of New Orleans in its litigation against gun manufacturers, boasted, the plaintiffs' bar has become a "de facto fourth branch of government."[5]

In the following sections, I expand on and provide examples of how certain fee-seeking litigation produces regulatory outcomes. To illustrate how conventional but repetitive tort litigation can produce regulatory outcomes, I provide two contrasting examples. One is medical malpractice litigation based on the occurrence of cerebral palsy that has enriched lawyers and induced deleterious changes in physician's practices. A second example is sexual abuse litigation against clergy, which has had a salutary impact on the hidden practices of the Catholic Church that have been exposed largely by this use of litigation.

I also present two examples of litigation that more directly sought a significant regulatory outcome as the means of effectuating a substantial wealth transfer. One is a class action suit against the State Farm Insurance Corporation – ostensibly on behalf of its policyholders – to force the company to change its policy of using non-original equipment automobile parts. In Appendix D, I discuss another litigation of this type brought against health maintenance organizations (HMOs), attacking their core business plan.

In Chapter 21, I discuss another distinctive form of regulatory litigation that is brought primarily for the purpose of generating substantial fees by obtaining substantial punitive damages awards.

Finally, in Chapter 22, I use the tobacco litigation that contingency fee lawyers ginned up against the states to illustrate the perverse policy effects of regulation through litigation. I conclude that chapter by examining the effects of contingency fee lawyers entering into de facto partnerships with states' AGs to bring regulatory litigation and the perverse impacts of these partnerships on the process by which our society allocates authority among the legislative, judicial, and executive branches of government; distributes resources; and establishes policies, including tax and regulatory policies.

A. Conventional Tort Litigation

1. Cerebral Palsy Suits

Medical malpractice lawsuits against doctors on behalf of children born with cerebral palsy are an example of contingency-fee-driven litigation that has produced an unsound and potentially harmful regulatory effect on the medical profession. Because of the substantial medical and custodial care that can be required for a child with cerebral palsy over an extended period and the likelihood that a jury will be sympathetic to the parents of an infant born with cerebral palsy, these suits are often lucrative, generating contingency fees in the millions of dollars. The theory usually advanced in these cases is that (1) obstetricians act negligently when they do not use fetal heart monitors to detect fetal distress; (2) as a consequence, they fail to, or delay in, advancing Cesarean delivery of the infant; and (3) that delay results in intrauterine hypoxia (shortage of oxygen in the womb), which causes cerebral palsy.[6] However, use of a fetal heart monitor has not been proven an effective tool to detect fetal distress.[7] Nonetheless, in reaction to plaintiffs' lawyers' success in bringing these claims, doctors have increasingly resorted to Cesarean deliveries whenever an anomaly appears on a fetal heart monitor. In fact, the number of Cesarean deliveries has increased from 6 percent in 1970 to 26 percent in 2004[8] and is associated with an increase in infant mortality.[9] Despite this sharp increase in Cesarean deliveries, the incidence of cerebral palsy has remained constant at 1 in 500 births.[10] Indeed, there are no data that support the contention that Cesarean delivery on the basis of any single or combination of fetal heart rate patterns reduces the rate of cerebral palsy.[11] As stated in a recent article in a medical journal, "the continued presentation of claims that cerebral palsy would have been prevented by an earlier Cesarean delivery are clear evidence that the policy of judicial policing of junk science has not been as effective as had been hoped."[12]

2. Clergy Sexual Abuse Litigation

By contrast, sexual abuse litigation against the Catholic Church has not only compensated hundreds of victims of clergy abuse, but also forced the Catholic Church to acknowledge the existence of a massive failure and to ultimately address it forcefully. The first suit, filed in 1983, attracted national attention to the problem[13] and encouraged others who were similarly abused to come forward.[14] When the diocese of Fall River,

Massachusetts, settled claims of sexual abuse by more than one hundred victims, widespread media attention led to a dramatic increase in the number of victims coming forward. The litigation against the Boston archdiocese revealed the widespread scope of the abuse and cover-up by the church. Though many issues remain unresolved, this litigation has forced the Catholic Church to begin to confront the problem and make significant personnel and institutional changes.[15]

B. Seeking Contingency Fees by Effectuating a Regulatory Outcome

1. The State Farm Litigation: Seeking Profit by Banning the Use of Non-original Equipment Automobile Parts

Avery v. State Farm Mutual Automobile Insurance Co.[16] is an example of an opportunistic scheme to extract substantial contingency fees by forcing a change in business practice. This national class action, filed in a small community in Illinois, although later overruled as an improper certification of the class,[17] effectively sought to require automobile insurance companies to use or pay for original equipment manufacturer (OEM) parts (marketed by General Motors, Ford, Chrysler, Toyota, Honda, etc.) when making repairs. The trial court effectively found that non-OEM parts were inferior to OEM parts and required the use of OEM parts nationwide, despite the fact that (a) State Farm's policies stated that it would provide replacement parts "of like kind and quality"; (b) a majority of states specifically do not require the use of OEM parts; and (c) some states mandate use of non-OEM parts.[18] The $1.2 billion judgment would have provided an enormous payday for the contingency fee lawyers who brought the action – in the range of $200 million to $350 million. In addition, the court would have set a nationwide standard for auto insurance companies, thus usurping the authority of state legislatures and the insurance commissions they created.[19]

a. Regulation of the Use of OEM Parts

There are more than 30,000 automobile accidents in the United States every day.[20] Whereas many of these accidents do not result in personal injury, there may be massive vehicular damage. For most damages to hoods, fenders, and grills, repairs can be made at a lower cost using less expensive non-OEM parts. Moreover, numerous studies have generally found that non-OEM parts differ only cosmetically from OEM parts and create little to no safety risk.[21]

Up until the late 1980s, auto manufacturers had a monopoly on the supply of auto parts, allowing them to set prices as high as they wished.[22] Non-OEM manufacturers then began to vigorously compete and drove prices down by an average of 60 percent.[23] The auto manufacturers then lobbied Congress to maintain their former monopoly for a ten-year period, but this effort failed.[24]

Defeated in Congress, the OEMs attempted to influence state legislators by demanding prohibitions on the use of non-OEM parts in repair estimates. Nonetheless, the OEMs were defeated in the 1990s, failing to convince a single state to adopt their proposed legislation. The OEMs then tried to control use of non-OEM parts by targeting the insurance regulators, but in 1987 the National Association of Insurance Commissioners adopted model regulation that rejected any proposal to prohibit use of non-OEM parts in cars manufactured in the current or preceding model year.[25] In fact, some states specifically allow or require insurance companies to use non-OEM parts when available because extensive use of OEM parts increases the cost of accidents and therefore the costs of insurance coverage.[26] The Alliance of American Insurers calculated that building a 1996 Chevy Lumina from OEM parts would cost $72,600, more than triple the sticker price of the car.[27] Although use of OEM parts is not completely unregulated,[28] for the most part, state legislatures and insurance regulators have consigned the issue of OEM versus non-OEM to the highly competitive marketplace for auto insurance.

b. The Avery Class Action

The *Avery* action arose from State Farm's practice of specifying use of non-OEM parts on repair estimates for policyholder's damaged vehicles. State Farm was not alone in this practice; many insurers followed this policy to create a competitive market with OEM parts, insurance premium rates, and repair costs. The class action was brought on the theory that State Farm's policy of using non-OEM parts was a violation of the terms of the insurance agreement in which State Farm promised to replace damaged parts with parts of "like kind and quality."[29] The plaintiffs also alleged that that State Farm had breached its contractual obligation to them by specifying use of these parts and that the parts did not restore the insured vehicle to "pre-loss condition," as provided by the policy. Finally, the plaintiffs alleged that State Farm violated the Illinois Consumer Fraud and Deceptive Business Practices Act[30] because it knew that non-OEM parts could not restore the vehicle to "pre-loss condition" and had not so notified policyholders.[31] In awarding a $1.2 billion judgment against State Farm, the court ruled that non-OEM parts are inferior to OEM parts, thus effectively overruling the laws and regulations of other states and their insurance commissions with regard to the use of non-OEM parts.[32]

c. The Effect of the Avery Trial Court Decision

The *Avery* class, which was certified as a nationwide class action, included approximately 4.7 million State Farm policyholders, who were "awarded" $1.2 billion (reduced on appeal to approximately $1 billion).[33] To reach this result, the court applied Illinois consumer fraud law to the entire class, even though most of the class members were citizens of other states. The court argued that, because the "of like kind and quality" language appeared in most of State Farm's contracts nationwide, its interpretation of this contractual language was consistent with the laws of all the states. However, states interpreting the identical language in a contract or statute can and do differ as to the meaning or effect of the words. Had the court applied the law correctly, it would have created numerous subclasses so that each of the State Farm policyholders in the class would be subject to the law of their own state. Of course, this would likely have so complicated the litigation as to render it untriable. For this reason, a Maryland state court refused to certify a nearly identical class action brought against the Geico Corporation.[34]

Because State Farm is a mutual insurer, owned by its policyholders, savings on the cost of repairs are passed on to the policyholders in the form of dividends and lower premiums. Conversely, increased costs are borne by the policyholders.[35] The outcome of this case was that State Farm had to pay "damages" of $1 billion to its policyholders, which it would recoup as higher premiums, lower dividends, or both from its policyholders. The recoupment would not be revenue neutral, however, because the lawyers bringing the action would likely have been awarded a fee of approximately $200 million to $300 million for their services.

Before *Avery* was overruled,[36] it had a profound effect on the insurance and OEM markets. Though brought by a law firm for profit, the trial court's ruling also rewarded the OEM manufacturers who had been unable to recapture their monopoly through lobbying regulators or legislators. Several other automobile insurers also began using OEM parts after facing their own threat of lawsuit.[37] If the Illinois Supreme Court had not struck down the class certification, this case could have meant the end of the non-OEM market. This, in turn, would have lead to increased consumer costs, both by increasing the price of replacement parts and increasing insurance premiums. It would have also resulted in a Williamson County, Illinois, court and jury – convened by lawyers for the sole purpose of seeking substantial contingency fees – regulating the auto insurance industry for the entire country.

Avery's reversal came on a 4–3 vote. Because the Illinois Supreme Court had been firmly in the pro-plaintiff lawyer camp, and had a record of invalidating legislative tort reforms,[38] the business community had made a concerted effort to wrest control of the court from the trial lawyers. This resulted in a hotly contested election contest between Justice Lloyd Karmeier and Judge Gordon Maag; between them, they raised a record-setting $9.3 million. Karmeier received $2.3 million from the U.S. Chamber of Commerce and $415,000 from the American Tort Reform Association; Maag benefited from $2.8 million contributed by trial lawyers to the state Democratic Party and $1.2 million from an ad hoc coalition of trial lawyers and labor leaders.[39] Justice Karmeier prevailed in the election and provided the deciding vote in *Avery*, averting a billion-dollar scam. If Justice Maag had won, it is a virtual certainty that the *Avery* decision would have been upheld and "me-too" cases brought against other auto insurers, driving up auto insurance rates all over the country.

2. The HMO Litigation

Before he headed to the hoosegow for bribing a judge, Richard "Dickie" Scruggs, a leading mass tort lawyer, pioneered the use of asbestos litigation screenings to generate hundreds of thousands of bogus claims[40] and was one of the initiators of the states' tobacco litigation.[41] Scruggs devised a scheme to extract substantial contingency fees from HMOs, which, had it fully succeeded, would have forced the industry to abandon its business model, if not cease operation. As described in Appendix D, he sought to shake down the HMOs for a substantial payment by filing a class action alleging a "'nationwide fraudulent scheme' to enroll members by promising quality health care and then denying needed services – all in the name of corporate profit."[42]

The early effects of *Avery* and the precipitous multibillion-dollar decline in the value of HMO stocks demonstrates the serious nature of the threats posed by the State Farm and HMO suits. That both suits failed is not, however, a basis for complacency. Contingency fee lawyers constantly prowl the consumer economy in search of opportunities to launch raids on businesses that they consider vulnerable. Until changes are made to reduce their unearned profits and to require that they bear the costs that they now can freely impose on others when their suits fail, entrepreneurial lawyers will continue to have high incentives to seek out opportunistic litigations based solely on projected profits. Businesses' moderate success in reversing the control exercised by trial lawyers over state supreme courts may counter plaintiffs' lawyers' efforts to preserve and extend tort liability. But in a possible harbinger of what is to come, in the 2008 election, a perfect storm engulfed the Republican Party in Michigan, and tort lawyers succeeded in unseating Michigan Supreme Court Justice Clifford Taylor, thereby shifting control of that court on tort liability issues back to tort lawyers. If a few more state supreme court seats similarly change hands in forthcoming elections, opportunistic litigation will materially increase and succeed.

NOTES

1. By the "tort system," I mean the process of creating and applying doctrines and public policies to determine, through judicial adjudication, whether someone has sustained an injury, whether someone else should be held responsible for causing that injury, and if so, the damages to be assessed. Robert Kagan has called this process a model of governance by private adversarial litigation. *See* KAGAN, ADVERSARIAL LEGALISM, *supra* Introduction, note 13.

2. *See, e.g., Regulation By Litigation: The New Wave of Government-Sponsored Litigation*, Manhattan Institute, Transcript of Conference, June 22, 1999, *available at* http://www.manhattan-institute.org/html/mics_1_a.htm [hereinafter New Wave Transcript]; *Regulation through Litigation: Assessing the Role of Bounty Hunters and Bureaucrats in the American Regulatory Regime*, Manhattan Institute, Transcript of Conference, Feb. 23, 2000, *available a*t http://www.manhattan-institute.org/html/mics2a.htm; W. KIP VISCUSI, ed., REGULATION THROUGH LITIGATION, (AEI-Brookings Joint Center, 2002) [hereinafter VISCUSI, REGULATION]; *see also* Robert B. Reich, *Regulation is out, litigation is in*, USA TODAY, Feb. 11, 1999, at 15A ("The era of big government may be over, but the era of regulation through litigation has just begun.").

3. An example is a suit by a city against gun manufacturers, sellers, and distributors, seeking to compel the industry to incorporate certain safety features such as trigger locks in the design of handguns or to adopt restrictions on gun distribution practices. *See, e.g., City of Gary v. Smith & Wesson Corp.*, 801 N.E. 2d 1222 (Ind. 2003); *City of Cincinnati v. Beretta U.S.A. Corp.*, 768 N.E. 2d 1136 (Ohio 2002); *City of Philadelphia v. Beretta Corp.*, 277 F.3d 415 (3d Cir. 2002); *see also* Philip J. Cook & Jens Ludwig, *Litigation as Regulation: Firearms* in Viscusi, REGULATION at 67. Another example is a suit against McDonald's or Burger King seeking to use the threat of substantial damages for causing

obesity to compel them to change their products or advertising methods. See *supra* Chapter 11, § C for discussion of obesity suits.

4. *See generally* Donald G. Gifford, *Impersonating The Legislature: State Attorneys General and Parens Patriae Product Litigation*, 49 B.C. L. Rev. 913 (2008).

5. Douglas McCollam, *Long Shot*, 21 Am. Law. 86 (June 1999).

6. *See* Walter Olson, *Curing Health Care: Delivering Justice*, The Wall St. J., Feb. 27, 2003, at A12 (recent Brooklyn, New York, juries gave verdicts of $94 million, $90 million, and $62 million).

7. Since its introduction in the 1970s, the fetal heart monitor has proven no more effective than periodic auscultation (listening to fetal heartbeat sounds by stethoscope). *See* Alastair MacLennan, M.D., et al., *Who Will Deliver Our Grandchildren? Implications of Cerebral Palsy Litigation*, 294 J. Am. Med. Ass'n 1688 (2005) [hereinafter MacLennan, *Who Will Deliver Our Grandchildren*]; *see also* Z. Alfirevic, et al., *Continuous Cardiotocography (CTG) as a Form of Electronic Fetal Monitoring (EFM) for Fetal Assessment During Labour*, Cochrane Database of Systematic Rev. Issue 3. Art. No. CD006066 (2006) (use of fetal heart monitoring showed no decrease in incidence of cerebral palsy but is associated with an increase in Cesarean deliveries). Moreover, studies have concluded that fewer than 10% of cerebral palsy cases are linked to an oxygen shortage at birth; in most cases, the damage occurred long before labor. *See* Adam Liptak & Michael Moss, *In Trial Work, Edwards Left a Trademark*, N.Y. Times, Jan. 31, 2004, at A1; *see also* MacLennan, *Who Will Deliver Our Grandchildren, supra* (Most brain damage results from factors far removed from the control of delivering obstetricians such as genetic predisposition, intrauterine infections, blood clotting, and premature birth.).

8. MacLennan, *Who Will Deliver Our Grandchildren, supra*.

9. The infant mortality rate for Cesarean deliveries is twice that of vaginal births. *See* Nicholas Bakalar, *Voluntary C-Sections Result in More Baby Deaths*, N.Y. Times, Sept. 5, 2006, at F6 (Citing Marian F. MacDorman, Ph.D., et al., *Infant and Neonatal Mortality for Primary Cesarean and Vaginal Births to Women with "No Indicated Risk," United States, 1998–2001 Birth Cohorts*, Birth 33:3 at 175 (Sept. 2006) (The study examined low-risk mothers with no medical reason to have a Cesarean delivery and found that, even when controlling for risk factors such as intrauterine hypoxia and congenital malformation, neonatal mortality for Cesarean deliveries was twice the rate for vaginal deliveries.).

10. *Id.*

11. Steven L. Clark & G.D.V. Hankins, *Temporal and Demographic Trends in Cerebral Palsy – Fact and Fiction*, 188 Am. J. Obstetrics & Gynecology 628 (2003).

12. Steven L. Clark et al., *Improved Outcomes, Fewer Cesarean Deliveries, and Reduced Litigation: Results of a New Paradigm in Patient Safety*, 199 Am J. Obstetrics & Gynecology 105 (2008).

13. *See* Jason Berry, Lead Us Not Into Temptation: Catholic Priests and the Sexual Abuse of Children 14–26 (1992).

14. *See* Timothy D. Lytton, *Using Tort Litigation to Enhance Regulatory Policy Making: Evaluating Climate-Change Litigation in Light of Lessons from Gun-Industry and Clergy-Sexual-Abuse Lawsuits*, 86 Tex. L. Rev. 1837, 1850 (2008).

15. *Id*. at 1850–58.

16. *Avery v. State Farm Mut. Automobile Ins. Co.*, 1999 WL 955543 (Ill. Cir. 1999); *see also Avery v. State Farm Mut. Automobile Ins. Co.*, 1999 WL 1022134 (Ill. Cir. 1999).

17. *Avery v. State Farm Mut. Automobile Ins. Co.*, 216 Ill. 2d 100, 835 N.E.2d 801 (Ill. 2005) (holding that the class was too broad and the plaintiffs failed to show either breach of contract or consumer fraud). The Illinois Supreme Court's decision is further discussed in §§ C and D of this chapter.

18. *See* Eric Helland & Jonathan Klick, *The Tradeoffs between Regulation and Litigation: Evidence from Insurance Class Actions*, 1J. Tort L. at *12 (2007) [hereinafter Helland & Klick], *available at* http://mailer.fsu.edu/~jklick/research.html. ("According to the GAO [report *MOTOR VEHICLE SAFETY: NHTSA's Ability to Detect and Recall Defective Replacement Crash Parts Is Limited* at page 28] 40 states have enacted some form of legislation governing the use of OEM parts. Of these, 36 states require companies to identify aftermarket crash part used in the repair. A warranty is required by 27 states and 23 states require a manufacturer's ID for tracking purposes on any OEM parts.").

19. Victor Schwartz & Leah Lorber, *State Farm v. Avery: State Court Regulation through Litigation Has Gone Too Far*, 33 Conn. L. Rev. 1215, 1224, n.38 (2001) [hereinafter Schwartz & Lorber, *State Farm*] (The McCarran-Ferguson Act provides that the business of insurance is be subject to the "laws of the several States." 15 U.S.C. § 1012 (1994). "That means that one state cannot regulate insurance transactions and claims procedures that take place entirely in another state." *Prudential Ins. Co. v. Benjamin*, 328 U.S. 408, 431 & n.39 (1946) (When Congress enacted the McCarran-Ferguson Act, it eschewed uniformity of regulations for insurance by leaving regulation to each state.).

20. Schwartz & Lorber, *State Farm*, *supra*, at 1222.

21. *See* GAO Report *MOTOR VEHICLE SAFETY: NHTSA's Ability to Detect and Recall Defective Replacement Crash Parts Is Limited*, GAO-01–225, at 12 (2001) [hereinafter GAO report] (Studies by the Insurance Institute for

Highway Safety determined that, with the possible exception of the hood, there
is no crash safety difference between OEM and non-OEM parts).

22. During the 1970s, OEM parts were the only source of replacement parts. This
gave the OEM parts manufacturers an effective monopoly over the crash part
market, allowing them to set prices as high as they wished. *See* Schwartz &
Lorber, *State Farm, supra* note 19, at 1222. During Congressional Oversight
Hearings in 1976, Owen M. Johnson Jr., Director of the FTC Bureau of
Competition, testified:

In November 1971 the Commission's task force concluded that the
underlying competitive problems in the "crash parts" aftermarket derived
from the monopoly power possessed by the automobile manufacturers,
that each vehicle manufacturer possessed a de facto monopoly in the manufacture, sale, and distribution of such parts, and that there was every indication that these monopolies had been maintained by the affirmative acts
and practices of the vehicle manufacturers.

(citing *Cost of Automobile Crash Parts: Hearing Before the Subcomm. for
Consumers of Senate Comm. on Commerce* 94th Cong., 2d Sess., at 7 (1976)).

23. The availability of cheaper parts – non-OEM parts were on average 60%
cheaper than OEM parts – caused the non-OEM market to surge. Schwartz &
Lorber, *State Farm, supra* note 19, at 1222 (citing *Mandating A Car Parts
Monopoly*, CHI. TRIB., Oct. 10, 1999, at H16). "The Alliance of American
Insurers studied the price differences between OEM crash parts and non-
OEM crash parts for thirteen different 1994–1999 models and found OEMs
charged an average of sixty percent more than distributors selling non-OEM
crash parts." *Id.* (citing ALLIANCE OF AMERICAN INSURERS, COST COMPARISON,
OEM VS. NON-OEM (AFTERMARKET) (1999); *see also* John C. Bratton & Stephen
M. Avila, *After Market Crash Parts: An Analysis of State Regulations*, J. INS.
REG. 150, 168, tbl.7 [quoting information from AAI]). Because of the competition from the aftermarket suppliers, the price of OEM parts dropped in
response. For example, in 1982, a 1983 Chevrolet Camaro front nose cover
made by GM cost $325. In 1988, as aftermarket replacement parts began to
appear, the same GM part cost only $225. No competing replacement parts
existed for a door shell for the same Camaro, however, and its price continued
to increase. In 1982, it cost $445; by 1988, its price had risen to $590. By the end
of the 1990s, 15% of the crash parts market consisted of aftermarket cosmetic
parts, such as bumpers, hoods, and fenders. Schwartz & Lorber, *State Farm,
supra* note 19, at 1223.

24. In response to the growing threat from the non-OEM manufacturers, automobile manufacturers attempted to persuade Congress to create a new
federal "industrial design" copyright standard that would essentially prevent

production of aftermarket sheet metal parts and give OEM manufacturers a ten-year monopoly on the market. Several hearings were held in both the House and the Senate in the 1987–1992 period. The OEMs ultimately failed to gain the passage of this proposed legislation to essentially provide them with a federally enforced monopoly. *See* Hearing on S. 791 Before the Subcomm. on Patents, Copyrights and Trademarks of the Senate Judiciary Comm., 100th Cong., 1st Sess. (1987); Hearing on H.R. 1179 Before the Subcomm. on Courts, Civil Liberties and the Admin. of Justice of the House Judiciary Comm., 100th Cong., 2d Sess. (1988); Hearings on H.R. 902, H.R. 3017, H.R. 3499 Before the Subcomm. on Courts, Intellectual Property and the Admin. of Justice of the House Judiciary Comm., 101st Cong., 2d Sess. (1990); Hearing on H.R. 1790 Before the Subcomm. on Intellectual Prop. and Judicial Admin. of the House Judiciary Comm., 102d Cong., 2d Sess. (1992).

25. Schwartz & Lorber, *State Farm*, *supra* note 19, at 1223.

26. *See* Schwartz & Lorber, *State Farm, supra* note 19, at 1254 ("Former and current representatives of state insurance commissioners testified that the laws in many ... states permit and in some cases encourage the use of non-OEM parts as an effort to encourage competitive price control."); *see also* GAO Report, *supra* note 21, at 6; *see also* Helland & Klick, *supra* note 18.

27. *See* Matthew Wald, *Suit Against Auto Insurer Could Affect Nearly All Drivers*, N.Y. TIMES, Sept. 27, 1998, at 29.

28. *See* Helland & Klick, *supra* note 18.

29. *Avery v. State Farm Mut. Automobile Ins. Co.*, 321 Ill. App. 3d 269, 746 N.E. 2d 1242, 1249 (Ill. App. Ct. 5 Dist. 2001).

30. 815 ILCS 505/1 et seq. (West 1998).

31. *Id.*; *see also* Schwartz & Lorber, *State Farm, supra* note 19, at 1226 (The policyholders were directly informed of this practice in their policies, which stated that repairs would include either parts furnished by the vehicle manufacturer or "parts from other sources including non-original equipment manufacturers." If non-OEM parts were used, a guarantee of satisfaction for the life of the automobile was given.).

32. *Avery*, 746 N.E. 2d at 1254. According to the court, "[f]ormer and current representatives of state insurance commissioners testified that the laws in many ... states permit and in some cases encourage the use of non-OEM parts as an effort to encourage competitive price control." The court, however, dismissed this evidence on the basis that the local jury had found that "inferior" aftermarket replacement parts had been used and that no state had sanctioned the use of "inferior" parts. The court appears to have used the word "inferior" to mean "non-original equipment manufacturer parts," and so they were not of "like kind and quality" as State Farm had promised in its contracts of insurance. *Id.*

at 1247. Accordingly, on the basis of this wordplay, use of non-OEM parts was, by definition, the use of "inferior" parts.

33. *Avery*, 746 N.E. 2d at 1260–61.

34. *Snell et al. v. Geico Corp. et al.*, 2001 WL 1085237 (Md. Cir. Ct., Aug. 14, 2001). Plaintiffs in Maryland argued that their case "is on all fours with [*Avery*];" although the court concurred, it found that certifying a nationwide class action could result in nullification of the laws and policies of other states with regard to the use of non-OEM parts. *Id.* at 7.

35. *See* Schwartz & Lorber, *State Farm, supra* note 19, at 1217.

36. *Avery*, 835 N.E. 2d at 801.

37. Joseph Treaster, *Generic Car Parts Makers Fighting Back*, N.Y. TIMES, July 31, 2000, at 8C.

38. *See, e.g., Best v. Taylor Machine Works*, 179 Ill. 2d 367 (1997).

39. DEBORAH GOLDBERG ET AL., THE NEW POLITICS OF JUDICIAL ELECTIONS 2004 19 (2005). A petition for rehearing in *Avery* that was filed alleging that State Farm was responsible for substantial and improper contributions to Karmier's campaign was denied. *Avery v. State Farm Mut. Auto. Ins. Co.*, 216 Ill.2d 100, 835 N.E.2d 801, 296 Ill. Dec. 448 (Ill. Aug. 18, 2005) (NO. 91494), *reh'g denied* (Sept. 26, 2005).

40. *See generally* Brickman, *Disparities, supra* Chapter 7, note 66.

41. The tobacco litigation and Scruggs' role in that litigation is discussed in Chapter 22, § A.

42. *See* Adam Bryant, *Who's Afraid of Dickie Scruggs*, NEWSWEEK, Dec. 6, 1999, at 46.

21 A New Role for Punitive Damages

Policy Making as a Profit Center

PUNITIVE DAMAGES ARE A UNIQUE FEATURE OF THE American tort system. Punitive damages are not intended to be compensatory but rather, are imposed to advance societal interests by punishing reprehensible conduct and deterring its future occurrence.[1] Continental European countries reject any form of punitive damages, and British tort law allows them sparingly.[2] This distinctive difference between the American and English legal systems has been attributed to the use of contingent fee financing of tort litigation in the United States and to the American rule, which provides that each side pays its own attorney.[3]

Punitive damages have come to play a prominent role in "regulation through litigation" and are a hotly contested issue in the tort reform wars, especially the question of whether such awards have a deterrent effect. For any award of damages to be a deterrent, those to be deterred must be aware that they will face a penalty if they act or fail to act in a certain way. Critics claim, however, that punitive damages awards are randomly assessed and lack predictability. Hence, they do little to promote investment in safer products. W. Kip Viscusi compared the incidents of risky behavior as measured by toxic accidents, toxic chemical releases, accident fatality rates, and insurance premium levels in states with punitive damages to four states that prohibit punitive damages. Viscusi found "results [that] are consistent with the views expressed by punitive damages critics, who observe that random and unpredictable awards will not have a deterrent effect."[4]

David Luban of the Georgetown University Law Center challenges Viscusi's argument and makes the case for the expanded use of punitive damages.[5] He argues that Viscusi's research design is flawed because businesses must make their risk decisions based, not merely on the law in the small number of states where punitive damages are prohibited, but on the large majority of states where punitive damages are permitted.[6] Luban further argues that deterrence is not – or at least should not be – the only goal of punitive damages. He cites other benefits including the fact that because punitive damages raise the threat level faced by defendants and their insurers, this increases the likelihood of settlement on terms advantageous to plaintiffs. In addition, multimillion-dollar punitive damages awards – one in every nine punitive damages awards exceeds $1 million – play a vital role in financing plaintiffs' lawyers. Finally, government regulation alone cannot secure safe products because there are too few regulators and special interests that often exercise undue influence over regulatory agencies. Better to sic thousands of fee-seeking lawyers to corral corporate misbehavior.[7]

Another area of controversy is whether punitive damages awards have been increasing in recent decades. Despite contrary claims from the business community, there is compelling empirical data indicating that in cases where plaintiffs prevail, neither the percentage of those with punitive damages awards (around 2%–4%) nor the median award has increased over the past two decades.[8] Reliance on median punitive damages award levels may paint a false picture, however, because such data obscures the effect of "blockbuster" punitive damages awards of $100 million or more. According to Kip Viscusi, "there has been an explosive growth in punitive damages awards of $100 million or more as well as a substantial increase in the number of billion dollar punitive damages awards."[9] As of 2008, there were sixty-four punitive damages awards of at least $100 million.[10] Offsetting this is the report by the *National Law Journal* that "total [punitive damages] awards among the top 100 verdicts in 2005 slid for the third straight year," and the "punitive damages portion of total awards over the past five years has dropped markedly" from 58 percent of the total award in 2001 to 43 percent in 2005, with a high of 87 percent in 2002 and a low of 38 percent in 2004.[11]

There is additional room for concern about the reliability of some of the data. One of the most cited statistics is issued by the U.S. Department of Justice's Bureau of Justice. It reports that the percentage of punitive damages awards in civil trials in the seventy-five largest counties has not increased and that the amounts awarded have decreased.[12] George Priest, however, found that reliance on data from the seventy-five largest counties is misleading because punitive damages are awarded more frequently in smaller counties. Indeed, he found more punitive damages claims in smaller counties than in the claimed national "handful" reported by the Bureau of Justice.[13]

Finally, some studies indicating that punitive damages awards are sparse appear misleading. Michael Rustad of the Suffolk University Law School found that there were a total of 355 punitive damages awards between 1965 and 1990 in all products liability cases.[14] Rustad cautions that the number of cases he reported was computed by verdict and not by the number of plaintiffs and that in asbestos cases, this measure understates the number of punitive damages awards.[15] Indeed it does – to the point of rendering Rustad's data meaningless.[16]

The U.S. Supreme Court has taken notice of the rise of blockbuster punitive damages awards and found that "grossly excessive" awards violate the Due Process Clause of the Fourteenth Amendment; such awards "serve no legitimate purpose and constitute[ ] an arbitrary deprivation of property."[17] "In practice," said the Court, "few awards exceeding a single-digit ratio between punitive and compensatory damages, to a significant degree, will satisfy due process."[18] This ruling is likely to curtail the incidence of new blockbuster punitive damages awards. The mitigative effect, however, may be offset by increasing attempts by plaintiffs' lawyers to induce juries to sharply increase compensatory awards by urging them to use those awards to punish defendants for their egregious behaviors – the same arguments they make when seeking punitive damages.[19]

Proponents of an expanded tort system decry these recent Supreme Court decisions applying the Due Process Clause to limit punitive damages awards. They argue that the availability of punitive damages is essential to deter harmful conduct by product manufacturers and others.[20] Two of the leading advocates for an expanded tort system, Marc Galanter and David Luban, also support an expanded role for punitive damages in policy making. They argue that punitive damages "constitute the best available means for social control and moral sanction of economically formidable wrongdoers."[21] Under the regime of punitive damages, "[p]laintiffs and their lawyers are granted authority to assume vital law enforcement functions."[22] They go on to state:

> The reason underlying the grant of enforcement endowments is essentially identical to the reason underlying the grant of regulatory endowments: a limited government is and ought to be too small and too overstretched to regulate every area of life and to enforce such regulations. It is and ought to be compelled to delegate its *regulatory* and enforcement authority to nongovernmental parties.[23]

Even while mounting an aggressive argument for extending the role of punitive damages in policy making, Luban, Galanter, and other supporters of an expanded tort system argue that punitive damages are "no big deal" because there has been no increase in the percentage of tort cases in which plaintiffs prevail and punitive damages have been awarded. But in the scheme of things, they are a "big deal." That is why the argument between the advocates of an expanded tort system and those who seek its contraction is so heated. Punitive damages would not be a big deal were it not for the contingency fee. Tort lawyers are the principal beneficiaries of the expanded role of punitive damages in our tort system and the driving force behind the growth of punitive damages.

The focus on the punitive damages awards data serves to obscure the myriad ways in which tort lawyers have used punitive damages to drive up compensatory awards and reshape the tort system in their quest for increased profits.[24] One sample used in a study published by the Insurance Services Office indicated that settlements in claims where plaintiffs sought punitive damages were nearly 150 percent higher than those in which plaintiffs did not seek punitive damages; another sample indicated that settlements were 60 percent higher due to this "shadow effect" of punitive damages.[25]

A. The Impact of Punitive Damages on Policy Making

One effect of punitive damages that is not captured in the statistical data is its impact on policy making. Punitive damages awards can have the same effect as a decision by a regulatory agency or legislature to ban the sale of a product or require changes in how the product is manufactured or distributed. Indeed, the availability of punitive damages can facilitate courts effectively overruling legislative enactments. Consider, for example, a 1993 Florida case in which a Florida Court of Appeal affirmed an $800,000 punitive damages verdict against an employer, arising out of a traffic death caused by an employee who was driving home from a business convention while legally drunk.[26] Despite the fact that the employer neither sponsored the event nor owned the premises on which the event occurred, and that a Florida statute provided that "[a] person who sells or furnishes alcoholic beverages to a person of lawful drinking age shall not thereby become liable for any injury or damage caused by or resulting from the intoxication of such person,"[27] the case was submitted to a jury that concluded that the employer was at fault because the employer – who also attended the convention – knew or should have known the employee was in no condition to drive home.[28] The court of appeal held that, unlike a social host, an employer has a far greater ability to control the actions of its employees and should exercise such control; thus, the employer can be vicariously liable for punitive damages.[29] The issue here is not whether the policy adopted by the jury and reviewing judges is more socially beneficial than the one adopted by the legislature; rather, it is one of separation of powers. The legislature had the authority to legislate and did so. This policy was overruled by profit-driven policy making.

B. Regulating the Temperature of Coffee

No extended discussion of contingency fees can fail to include the McDonald's "hot coffee" case. Over the past several decades, a vigorous debate has been carried on in the press and in scholarly articles between those that oppose tort reforms and those who believe that the tort system should be contracted. The latter argue that the McDonald's litigation was frivolous, whereas the former counter that it was meritorious, given the fact that the coffee drinker was seriously injured and that McDonald's had been informed many times that "too hot" coffee could cause injury.

Consider the differences between reliance on a jury versus legislative policy making in the context of this most famous punitive damages case of our era. In 1992, seventy-nine-year-old Stella Liebeck was a passenger in a car driven by her grandson when she purchased takeout coffee from McDonald's. After receiving the coffee in a Styrofoam cup, the grandson pulled forward and stopped so that his grandmother could add cream and sugar to her coffee. She placed the cup between her knees and, in attempting to remove the plastic lid, spilled the coffee onto her lap.[30] As a consequence, she suffered third-degree burns and incurred approximately $20,000 in medical expenses. After being offered only a nominal amount by McDonald's, she sued and was awarded $160,000 in compensatory damages and $2.7 million in punitive damages, later reduced to $480,000.[31] The case was eventually settled for an undisclosed amount.

After the verdict was handed down, one juror commented that the jury wanted to deliver a message to McDonald's that "the coffee's too hot out there."[32] Was the coffee "too hot"? Testimony indicated that it was McDonald's corporate policy to serve its coffee between 180°F and 190°F. (Water boils at 212°F.) There are conflicting accounts, however, as to the temperature of the spilled coffee. One account states that the coffee was between 165°F and 175°F;[33] other accounts indicate that the temperature of the coffee was estimated to be 180°F[34] and 180°F to 190°F.[35]

The resonating impact of the case on public opinion has stirred a fierce defense of the case by the anti-tort reform, pro-tort expansionists. Three of the leading members of this professoriate, Tom Baker, Herbert Kritzer, and Neil Vidmar, defend the outcome because "[m]ost coffee in restaurants and home coffee makers is served at 160 degrees."[36] Not so. Starbucks serves its coffee at 175°F to 185°F.[37] Additionally, the Specialty Coffee Association states that coffee should be brewed at 195°F to 205°F, and holding temperatures should be between 175°F and 185°F.[38] The American National Standards Institute standard for home coffee makers also states that brewing temperatures should be close to 200°F to properly dissolve the oils in the bean containing aromatic compounds; it requires that coffee makers "brew and hold coffee at a temperature that does not fall below 170°F."[39] Likewise, the widely read consumer products magazine, *Consumer Reports*, states that "[b]rewed coffee should stay between 170 and 185 degrees to ensure that it will remain satisfyingly hot even after milk is added."[40] A *Consumer Reports* test of twenty-eight different models of home coffee makers in 1994 indicated that most home coffee makers brew and maintain coffee at a temperature of 175°F–185°F.[41] According to the "law" of the McDonald's case, millions of home coffee makers produce coffee that is "too hot."

The McDonald's case has become a rallying cry for tort reformers who cite it as evidence of the excesses of the tort system.[42] It has even been the subject of a *Seinfeld* episode titled "The Maestro." In this episode, to avoid the high prices movie theaters charge for refreshments, Kramer smuggles a cup of hot coffee into a theatre by stuffing it into his shirt. The coffee spills, and Kramer is scalded. Kramer then consults a lawyer who assures him that he will become a "rich man" and instructs him to immediately see a certain doctor so he can incur medical expenses. Later, when Kramer meets up with Jerry and Elaine, Elaine adds her disdain to Jerry's, stating "whoever heard of ... [s]uing a company because their coffee is too hot. Coffee is supposed to be hot."

Even if one accepts the evidentially dubious proposition that the coffee was "too hot," which most jurisdictions have rejected,[43] then what temperature complies with the jury's "law"? McDonald's cannot know whether it will be insulated from future liability even if it lowers the temperature of its coffee because any jury is free to make its own determination about what temperature is "too hot."[44] Unlike a legislative enactment, the verdict provides no guidance to McDonald's or any other restaurant that serves coffee as to what temperature complies with tort law and, therefore, insulates it from liability. Nor does the judicial decision-making process allow those consumers to be heard who want their coffee served hot because they intend to add cream or because they take their coffee "to go" and do not want it to be tepid by the time they get to their offices.[45] Whatever the appropriateness of the verdict for compensatory damages, the punitive damages verdict, which was largely driven by the financial interests of contingency fee lawyers, was a dysfunctional form of policy making.

C. The GM "Side Saddle" Truck Litigation

An example of an even more dysfunctional capture of public policy-making power in order to generate punitive damages profits for tort lawyers is the General Motors "side-saddle" litigation, involving mid- and full-sized GM pick-up trucks with side-mounted gas tanks outside the frame rails. Class actions were filed on behalf of GM pick-up truck owners seeking economic damages but not a recall or a "fix." A settlement was reached in short order providing for issuance of $1,000 coupons, useable toward the purchase of any GM vehicle and an attorney's fee approximating $10 million. Numerous proceedings ensued as lawyers jockeyed with one another to claim the fruits of this venture.[46]

In addition to the class actions seeking economic damages, one lawyer filed a wrongful death action against General Motors in 1993, alleging that a GM side-saddle pick-up truck was unsafe and caused a death. In closing argument, the plaintiff's attorney urged the jury to hit GM with a huge punitive damages award to force GM to recall the five million trucks with side-saddle gas tanks still on the road. The jury complied and awarded the plaintiff $105 million, of which $101 million was for punitive damages. However, a Georgia appellate court overturned the decision.[47] Amid the flurry of litigation, the Secretary of Transportation sought to force GM to recall the truck under federal law. He withdrew his decision, however, after the Justice Department advised him that the truck complied with federal safety standards, and he settled for a tax deductible $51 million contribution by GM to a variety of unrelated safety programs. Had the jury's verdict not been overturned, GM may have been forced to undertake a massive recall even though its trucks met all federal safety requirements. The saga of the GM side-saddle truck is detailed in Appendix E.

PUNITIVE DAMAGES HAVE THUS BECOME A POLICY-MAKING FORCE WIELDED by contingency-fee-seeking lawyers and judges that displaces legislative and regulatory authority. Policy making for profit is further explored in the next chapter.

NOTES

1. As stated by Supreme Court Justice Clarence Thomas: "A jury's assessment of the extent of a plaintiff's injury is essentially a factual determination, whereas its imposition of punitive damages is an expression of its moral condemnation ... [punitive damages] are not compensation for injury. Instead, they are private fines levied by private juries to punish reprehensible conduct and to deter its future occurrence." *Cooper Indus., Inc. v. Leatherman Tool Group, Inc.*, 532 U.S. 424, 423 (2001); *see also State Farm Mut. Auto Ins. Co. v. Campbell*, 538 U.S. 408, 416 (2003). ("[G]rossly excessive" awards, the Court

stated, "further[] no legitimate purpose and constitute[] an arbitrary deprivation of property." *Id.* at 417). Courts have previously justified punitive damages
"as additional compensation for mental suffering, wounded dignity, and injured
feelings – harms that were otherwise not legally compensable at common
law." Thomas B. Colby, *Beyond The Multiple Punishment Problem: Punitive
Damages As Punishment for Individual, Private Wrongs*, 87 Minn. L. Rev. 583,
647 (2003).

2. *See, e.g.*, Ronald A. Brand, *Punitive Damages Revisited: Taking the Rationale
for Non-Recognition of Foreign Judgments Too Far* (University of Pittsburgh
School of Law, Working Paper Series #26, 2005), *available at* http://law.bepress.
com/pittwps/papers/art26.

3. J. Robert S. Prichard, *A Systemic Approach to Comparative Law: The Effect of
Cost, Fee, and Financing Rules on the Development of the Substantive Law*, 17
J. Legal Stud. 451, 463 (1988) [hereinafter Prichard, *A Systemic Approach*].

4. W. Kip Viscusi, *Punitive Damages: The Social Costs of Punitive Damages
Against Corporations in Environmental and Safety Torts* , 87 Geo. L.J. 285, 299
(1998); *see also* Kip Viscusi, *Why There is No Defense of Punitive Damages*, 87
Geo. L.J. 381 (1998).

5. David Luban, *A Flawed Case Against Punitive Damages*, 87 Geo. L.J. 359
(1998).

6. *Id.* at 362–63.

7. *Id.* at 367, 375–76.

8. *See, e.g.*, Thomas H. Cohen, *Tort Trials and Verdicts in Large Counties,
2001*, Bureau of Justice Statistics Bulletin, Nov. 2004, at 1, *available at* http://
www.ojp.usdoj.gov/bjs/abstract/ttvlc01.htm (reporting that the median punitive damages award in all tort trials had declined from $38,000 in 1991 to
$25,000 in 2001; and that "[t]he reported differences in plaintiff winners
receiving punitive damages between 1992 (4%) and 2001 (5%) were not statistically significant"); Thomas H. Cohen, *Punitive Damage Awards in Large
Counties*, 2001, Bureau of Justice Statistics Selected Findings, Mar. 2005, at
2, *available at* http://www.ojp.usdoj.gov/bjs/abstract/pdalc01.htm (comparing
civil jury trial data in the seventy-five largest counties from 1992 and 2001
and finding the percentage of punitive damages awards in general civil jury
trials and tort jury trials to have remained the same and that punitive damages award amounts have decreased); David Hechler, *Big Awards Continue
to Drop As Punitives Decline After 2003's 'State Farm,'* Nat'l L. J., Feb.
21, 2005, at 2 (comparing the Bureau of Justice Statistics [DOJ] studies with
the *National Law Journal*'s 2004 review of the one hundred largest jury
verdicts and finding "[n]either data set shows signs of rising awards").

9. W. Kip Viscusi, *The Blockbuster Punitive Damages Awards*, 53 Emory L. J.
1405, 1408 (2004).

10. Alison F. Dei Rossi & W. Kip Viscusi, *The Changing Landscape of Blockbuster Punitive Damages Awards*, 12 Am. L. Econ. Rev. 116, (2010).
11. Leigh Jones, *It's a Harder Sell: Juries Will Make the Injured Whole, But Big Punitives are History*, Nat'l L. J., Feb. 20, 2006, at 2.
12. *See supra* note 8.
13. *See* George L. Priest, *Punitive Damages Reform: The Case of Alabama*, 56 La. L. Rev. 825, 829 (1996).
14. Michael Rustad, *In Defense of Punitive Damages in Products Liability: Testing Tort Anecdotes with Tort Data*, 78 Iowa L. Rev 1 (1992).
15. *Id.* at 39, n.193.
16. In *Cimino v. Raymark Ind.*, substantial punitive damages were awarded to 3,031 plaintiffs claiming injury from exposure to asbestos despite the fact that the vast majority had no symptomatology, no impairment, and no injury. 751 F. Supp. 649 (E.D. Tex. 1990). In just this one case, the number of punitive damages awards was more than eight times the total number of *all* punitive damages in products liability cases that Rustad found in a thirty-five-year period. Though the case was overturned on appeal (*Cimino v. Raymark Ind.*, 151 F. 3d 297 [5th Cir. 1998]), case management orders issued by the trial court severely limited, if not virtually eliminated, the ability of defendants to defend themselves at trial. *See* Brief of Amicus Curiae, American Tort Reform Association, May 17, 1994, *Cimino v. Raymark Indus., Inc.*, 151 F.3d 297 (5th Cir. 1998). As a consequence, the large majority of defendants settled the cases and paid the inflated punitive damages awards. They feared an even worse outcome before a judge who epitomized the Queen of Hearts in *Alice in Wonderland* who pronounced: "sentence first – verdict afterwards." Lewis Carroll, Alice's Adventures in Wonderland ch. 12 (1865) (said by the Queen of Hearts). For them, the reversal was meaningless.
17. *State Farm Mut. Auto Ins. v. Campbell*, 538 U.S. 408, 416 (2003); *see also Cooper Indus., Inc. v. Leatherman Tool Group, Inc.*, 539 U.S. 424 (2001); *BMW of N. Am. v. Gore*, 517 U.S. 559 (1996).
18. *Campbell, id.*
19. *See* Chapter 5, § B(1).
20. *See, e.g.*, Michael Rustad, *The Supreme Court and Me: Trapped in Time with Punitive Damages*, 17 Widener L.J. 783, 785 (2008) (arguing that punitive damages fulfill a key societal purpose in constraining corporate misconduct); Thomas C. Galligan Jr., *Disaggregating More-than-Whole Damages in Personal Injury Law: Deterrence* and *Punishment*, 71 Tenn. L. Rev. 117, 117 (2003) ("Punitive damages are ... designed both to punish defendants and to deter them and others from engaging in the same or similar misconduct in the future."); Michael Rustad, *In Defense of Punitive Damages in Products Liability: Testing Tort Anecdotes with Tort Data*, 78 Iowa L. Rev 1 (1992) (arguing that "[p]unitive damages fulfill

the social functions of punishment, deterrence of the defendant, and general deterrence of the defendant's conduct which violates social mores").

21. Marc S. Galanter & David Luban, *Poetic Justice: Punitive Damages and Legal Pluralism*, 42 AM. U. L. REV. 1393, 1396 (1993).

22. *Id*. at 1445.

23. *Id*. at 1445 (emphasis added).

24. *See* Appendix L: The Effect of Punitive Damages on Compensatory Awards.

25. *See* Paul B. Taylor, *Encouraging Product Safety Testing By Applying The Privilege of Self-Critical Analysis When Punitive Damages Are Sought*, 16 HARV. J.L. & PUB. POL'Y 769, 793 n.90 (1993) (citing ISO DATA, INC., CLAIM FILE DATA ANALYSIS: TECHNICAL ANALYSIS OF STUDY RESULTS 86–87, 87–88 (1988); *see also* Janet Novack, *Torture by Tort: Tort Reform and the Growth of Punitive Damages Awards*, FORBES, Nov. 6, 1995, at 138 [hereinafter Novack, *Torture by Tort*] (quoting the general counsel of a large bank acknowledging that the threat of punitive damages results in higher settlements).

26. *Carroll Air Sys. v. Greenbaum*, 1993 Fla. App. LEXIS 91–3240 (Fla. Ct. App. Dec. 1, 1993).

27. FLA. STAT. § 768.125 (1986).

28. *Carroll Air Sys.*, at *4.

29. *Carroll Air Sys.*, at *8.

30. *See* Mark B. Greenlee, *Kramer v. Java World: Images, Issues, and Idols in the Debate Over Tort Reform*, 26 CAP. U. L. REV. 701, 718 (1997).

31. Alex Kozinski, *The Case of Punitive Damages v. Democracy*, WALL ST. J., Jan. 19, 1995, at A18. The jury's initial punitive damages award was justified by the plaintiff's attorney, who noted that McDonald's sold more than one billion cups of coffee a year, generating daily revenues of $1.35 million, and convinced the jury to award as punitive damages the equivalent of two days' worth of McDonald's gross coffee sales. S. Reed Morgan, *Verdict Against McDonald's is Fully Justified*, NAT'L L. J., Oct. 24, 1994, at A20.

32. *See* Kozinski, *supra* note 31, at A18.

33. *Jury Says McDonald's Should Pay $2.8 Million For Hot Coffee*, LIABILITY WEEK, August 22, 1994.

34. Andrea Gerlin, *A Matter of Degree*, WALL ST. J., Sept. 1, 1994, at A1.

35. *See* Greenlee, *supra* note 30, at 718 (1997).

36. Tom Baker, Herbert Kritzer, & Neil Vidmar, *Jackpot Justice and the American Tort System: Thinking Beyond Junk Science*, (Wm. Mitchell College of Law Legal Stud. Research Paper Series, Paper No. 95, 16, 2008), *available at* http://ssrn.com/abstract=1152306.

37. Matt Fleisher-Black, *One Lump or Two?*, AM. LAWYER, June 2004, at 15, 17.

38. *See* TED R. LINGLE, THE COFFEE BREWING HANDBOOK 37 (1996).

39. *McMahon v. Bunn-O-Matic Corp.*, 150 F.3d 651, 656 (7th Cir. 1998) (citing 5.2.1 and 5.2.3.2 of the ANSI/AHAM CM-1–1986 standard adopted by the

American National Standards Institute). *Id*. at 658–59 ("The smell (and therefore the taste) of coffee depends heavily on the oils containing aromatic compounds that are dissolved out of the beans during the brewing process. Brewing
temperature should be close to 200°F to dissolve them effectively, but without
causing the premature breakdown of these delicate molecules.").

40. Consumer Reports, Dec. 2002, at 44.
41. *Coffee Makers*, Consumer Reports, Oct. 1994, at 652.
42. *See* Greenlee, *supra* note 30, at 704–08.
43. Due to the notoriety of this suit, similar "copy cat" suits were filed against
McDonald's, Burger King, Hardee's, and Starbucks. *See* Mike Folks, *Suit Says
Coffee Scalded Man In Eatery*, Sun Sentinel, Palm Beach Edition, Sept. 14,
1994 at 7B; The Toledo Blade, *Woman Sues Burger King For $65,000 over
Hot-Coffee Spill, The Arizona Republic*, Sept. 1, 1994, at A11; Burke III
Koonce, *Hardee's Java Too Hot to Handle, Claims Suit*, Triangle Bus. J.,
Jan. 20, 1995, at 1; Brian Wheeler, *Burns from Hardee's Prompt $2.25 Million
Lawsuit*, The Capital, Nov. 8, 1994 at C1; *Calif. Woman Sues Starbucks Over
Spill*, UPI, Jan. 25, 1995, available in LexisNexis library, UPI file. These similar claims were denied. *See, e.g., McMahon*, 150 F.3d at 659; *Holowaty v.
McDonald's Corp.*, 10 F. Supp. 2d 1078 (D. Minn. 1998). Nearly identical claims
against McDonald's by thirty-six claimants in England were also denied in the
course of a comprehensive analysis by the court of the factual circumstances
surrounding the claims of injury. Before 1993, McDonald's coffee in England
was served at a temperature between 188°F and 194°F, and after 1993, at a temperature between 167°F and 174°F. Both pre- and post-1993 claims were before
the court. The British court concluded that McDonald's was not negligent and
did not have a duty to warn consumers that hot drinks could cause scalding injuries, stating, "I am quite satisfied that those who bought coffee and tea could
be taken to know that such drinks sometimes get spilled and are served at temperatures which cause serious and painful injury if they come in contact with
someones [sic] skin." *Sam B. v. McDonald's Rest., Ltd.*, No. HQ0005713, 2002
WL 347059 (Q.B., Mar. 25, 2002); *see also* Anthony Ramirez, *For McDonald's,
British Justice is a Different Cup of Tea*, N.Y. Times, Apr. 7, 2002, at 7.
44. *See* Kozinski, *The Case of Punitive Damages, supra* note 31.
45. *See McMahon*, 150 F.3d at 659 (noting that coffee can be cooled by the use of
cream, sugar, stirring with a metal spoon, pouring the liquid into a cooler con-
tainer, and delayed consumption).
46. *See In re General Motors Corp. Pick-Up Truck Fuel Tank Prods. Liab. Litig.*,
55 F.3d 768 (1995), same, 134 F.3d 133 (1998); *White v. General Motors Corp.*,
835 So. 2d 892 (La. App. 2002).
47. *General Motors v. Moseley*, 447 S.E.2d 302 (Ga. 1994).

22 For-Profit Partnerships between State Attorneys General and Contingency Fee Lawyers

S TATES HAVE A BROAD RANGE OF POWERS, INCLUDING the power of the legislature to enact legislation and of the executive branch to initiate litigation in a state's own courts in order to enforce its laws or protect its assets. These powers are being invoked by partnerships between states' attorneys general and private contingency fee lawyers. The purpose of these partnerships is to generate substantial wealth for the lawyers and political benefits for the attorneys general as a result of the financial benefits gained for the state and the anticipated future flow of campaign contributions from lawyers. These partnerships transfer regulatory power from the legislature to the courts, the attorneys general, and the profit-seeking lawyers. This transference and privatization of public policy making has corrupting effects on the political process.[1] The prime example of this new form of public-private partnership for mutual profit is the litigation strategy used to bring suit against the tobacco companies.

A. The Tobacco Litigation

The tobacco litigations were initiated by Michael Moore, the Attorney General of Mississippi, and Richard "Dickie" Scruggs, a prominent Mississippi tort lawyer who had earned huge profits from asbestos litigation.[2] The strategy they devised to extract money from the tobacco companies was not predicated on any tenable legal theory or precedent.

The theories of recovery sought to avoid the need for the state to prove that cigarette smoke consumption caused an individual's injury and to eliminate the traditional and effective defenses of the tobacco companies that smokers were aware of the dangers of smoking but continued to do so. In fact, these theories were simply placeholders. The real strategy was to convince enough attorneys general to bring suit so as to elevate the threat level to a point where the tobacco companies would agree to settle.[3] To be sure, had the suits come to trial, state taxpayers qua jurors would have been given the opportunity to shift the burden of revenue raising from the state's taxpayers to unpopular out-of-state deep-pocket defendants. The strategy of massing states to file suit as a way of negating the tobacco companies' legal defenses succeeded in forcing the tobacco companies to settle the litigation.

Ostensibly, the suits were predicated on reimbursing the states for medical expenses incurred in treating smokers who had become ill and lacked insurance or other means to pay for these expenses. In fact, under the settlements, there is no retroactive compensation for past harms. Instead, under the settlements – which totaled $246 billion – the states receive a share of future tobacco sales in perpetuity.[4] To pay the states, the tobacco companies, in unison, raised the price of a pack of cigarettes.

Effectively, these price increases are an excise tax levied on future sales but without state legislatures actually voting to raise cigarette taxes and facing the attendant political pain of taxing smokers, a mostly lower-income group that bears the full burden of the settlement.[5] The commissions charged by the lawyers for devising and implementing the strategy of taxing future sales were enormous and unprecedented, amounting to more than $15 billion over a twenty-five-year period[6] (capped at $1.25 billion for each of the first three years, $750 million for the next two years, and $500 million annually thereafter until fully paid).[7] To pay these commissions, the states essentially agreed to share their share of the future flow of revenue from cigarette sales with private lawyers.

Who won, who lost, and what was gained by the litigation and settlement? No smokers received even a single penny as compensation for contracting illnesses from smoking. Young adults still overwhelmingly make up the 3,000 people who start smoking daily.[8] And a recent study by Harvard's School of Public Health found that nicotine levels in major cigarette brands sold in Massachusetts had increased by about 11 percent between 1997 and 2005.[9] Cigarette companies' profits and their share prices have substantially increased since the settlement. Profits for industry leader Philip Morris increased 37 percent from 1997 to $4.5 billion in 2005 and its stock price doubled since the first tobacco suit was filed in 1994.[10] Less than 8 percent of the $61 billion thus far paid by the tobacco companies has been spent on antismoking efforts.[11] The contingency fee lawyers were awarded $15 billion in fees, payable over twenty-five years, and effective hourly rates that – at least in the Texas settlement – were well in excess of $100,000 per hour.[12] The states' attorneys general trumpeted their victory over Big Tobacco and collected millions in campaign contributions. And bringing up the rear, tobacco smokers paid for the settlement when the companies increased the price of a pack of cigarettes by forty-five cents.[13]

As damning as these facts are, they pale in comparison to the damage done to our governmental institutions. As detailed in the following sections, the tobacco litigations and resulting settlements constituted an illegitimate transference of political authority from the legislature to the courts and relegated ethical rules limiting lawyers' fees to reasonable amounts to chimerical status.

1. The Appropriations Power

The United States – and virtually all of its states – have adopted constitutions and enacted legislation that prohibits government from spending money unless the expenditure is appropriated by the legislature.[14] In the states, this rule applies equally to all state funds, regardless of the source of the funds.[15] Prevailing state and federal case law and statutes hold that the fees awarded in a litigation are the property of the client, not her attorney.[16] Thus, when states' attorneys general contracted with the private lawyers and agreed to pay them on a contingency fee basis, they committed the state to pay fees and expenses that had not been the subject of any legislative appropriation.

To avoid the public firestorm that would have resulted from the states' periodically paying lawyers billions of dollars from their share of payments from the tobacco companies, the contingency fee agreements were superseded by agreements for the fees to be set by a secret arbitration process. These fees were to be paid directly to the lawyers by the tobacco companies and were in addition to the amounts to be paid to the states under the settlements. The assertion that such fees did not fall within the appropriations power of the legislature because they were not monies belonging to the states is simply pretextual. These sums would have been available for payment to the states had the settlements been structured so that, after the fees were paid out of the settlements, the net amounts to the states would have been roughly the same. In fact, the companies were indifferent to whether they paid all of the settlement monies to the state or part of it to the lawyers and the remainder to the states.[17]

In addition, by negotiating agreements, which provided that the $15 billion in fees would not be subject to judicial scrutiny in the ordinary manner and by further providing that the settlement monies to be paid to the states would be held hostage until their lawyers' fees were approved, the contingency fee attorneys violated their fiduciary duty of loyalty to their client, the states.[18]

2. "Pay to Play"

Typically when major contracts for the purchase of goods or services are awarded by a government entity, they make a public announcement and invite bids. However, this is not the way most states' attorneys general selected their private attorneys. In fact, the selections were made in secret, and the principal criteria for selection were cronyism and campaign contributions.[19]

3. The "Sale" of the States' Legislative Authority

Another example of the corrupting influence of this for-profit public policy making was the sale of the states' legislative authority as part of the Master Settlement.[20] The settlement – negotiated in secret and not subject to public scrutiny – provided that states would either (1) enact legislation under their taxing power to require start-up tobacco companies to pay amounts (equivalent to what the settling companies were paying to the states) into a prospective damages fund to prevent start-ups from underpricing the settling manufacturers; or (2) suffer significant reductions in annual payments from the tobacco companies if they lost market share. Given the fact that under the settlement the states are dependent on the continued success of the tobacco companies (because the $246 billion settlement is substantially funded by current and future tobacco sales),[21] it is unsurprising that all of the states enacted the legislation provided for in the Master Settlement agreement to protect the revenue stream of their tobacco company partners.

4. Fee "Arbitration"

Because of the great public outcry against multibillion-dollar contingency fees, the parties to the settlement opted to forgo the contingency fees provided for in the original retainer contracts and substitute an arbitration process to set the fees. This was like no arbitration process that had ever been held, however. First, there were no rules. Second, the arbitrations were designed to be a fig leaf, enabling the lawyers to hide the unprecedented fees they were seeking, ranging from tens of millions to billions of dollars.[22] Third, as a condition of the settlement, the tobacco companies agreed not to oppose the fee requests of the first three pattern-forming arbitrations, which facilitated huge fee awards to the Mississippi, Florida, and Texas contingency fee lawyers and became a model for the subsequent arbitrations. Fourth, the outcomes of these arbitrations were never in serious doubt because the lawyers effectively controlled the selection of two of the three arbitrators.[23] Fifth, to limit public exposure, the arbitrations were carried on in secret, and members of the public and news media were excluded. In sum and substance, an illegitimate fee-setting process was used to divert public attention from contingency fee agreements that were wildly excessive and utterly incompatible with fiduciary obligation and ethical rules.

5. The Nullification of Ethical Rules Limiting Fees to "Reasonable" Amounts

The unprecedented multibillion-dollar fees in the tobacco litigation could not, in many instances, be justified by the time and limited risks that most of the lawyers undertook.[24] All states have ethics rules limiting lawyers' fees to reasonable amounts.[25] Nonetheless, these rules were effectively suspended in virtually all states. On the few occasions when judges actually applied a test of reasonableness, appellate courts rejected or overturned these attempts on procedural grounds.[26]

The chicanery and ethical obtuseness of the fee-setting practices in the tobacco litigation reached its zenith in Maryland. In March 1996, the Maryland attorney general hired the Law Firm of Peter Angelos for a 25 percent contingency fee – far in excess of what could remotely be considered as "reasonable." After Angelos brought a lawsuit on the state's behalf, a lower court held that the state was effectively limited to subrogation in its classical form; that is, the state could only recover money spent through its Medicaid program on behalf of individual program recipients who had actual pending claims against the tobacco companies. This would have doomed the state's case.[27] At the urging of Angelos, the Maryland legislature then enacted a law that stripped the tobacco companies of their defenses.[28] When the Angelos law firm sought payment of $1.2 billion (25% of the state's estimated $4 billion portion of the settlement), the Maryland general assembly cut the fee to 12.5 percent.[29]

Angelos then made a deal with the legislature in which he agreed to cut his fee in half (to 12.5%) in exchange for the legislature lifting the caps on noneconomic damage awards in asbestos cases – a statute that provided Angelos, the leading asbestos lawyer in Maryland, with many millions of dollars in increased fees.[30] Even though Angelos had used the state's money to pay for the purchase of state legislation to increase his income from asbestos litigation, in exchange for giving up one-half of his fee, Angelos reneged on the deal, insisting that he be paid the full 25 percent of the $4 billion settlement. Eventually, Angelos settled for $150 million paid over five years.[31]

B. Regulation by Litigation versus Regulation by Legislation or Rule Making

1. The Effect of Policy Making for Profit

In our system of government, public policy making is largely consigned to state legislatures, which are, in turn, responsible to the electorate. This is the core principle of our republican form of government. The tobacco settlements undermined this fundamental structure by shifting the locus of taxing policy from the legislature to the courts and the parties to the litigation. Smokers (who would be taxed an additional forty-five cents per pack by the settlement) and other interest groups were precluded from being heard on the issue[32] – a basic tenet of legitimating democratic decision making. States acted as partners in a private deal.

In reality, however, the settlements were public contracts, negotiated privately between the states, the contingency fee lawyers, and the tobacco companies, which effectuated certain public policies regarding the sale and advertising of tobacco products and, in some cases, determined how the tobacco payments were to be spent. These policies were not approved by legislatures, but by courts, which unanimously ratified the agreements with virtually no public participation. Put plainly, it was a judicial usurpation of the constitutional allocation of authority to legislatures engineered by profit-seeking lawyers.

Moreover, the litigation violated another fundamental precept. As a matter of policy, we do not allow the power of government to be used for self-enrichment, because such a power inevitably is abused. Some states specifically prohibit state employees from using their position "for private gain." Yet that is exactly what happened in Rhode Island when the law firm of Motley Rice solicited the state's attorney general to hire the firm on a contingency fee basis to sue paint manufacturers that, decades earlier, had sold paint with lead pigment. State law was simply overridden by the quest for profits.[33]

The U.S. Supreme Court has consistently held that private entities are forbidden to perform governmental functions on a contingency fee basis and that doing so constitutes a violation of constitutional guaranties of due process of law.[34] The court has further held that appointing a prosecutor who has an interest in the outcome of the proceeding fundamentally undermines the integrity of a judicial proceeding and violates due process.[35]

There are numerous policy bases for prohibiting state attorneys general and other governmental units from hiring outside lawyers on a contingency fee basis to seek damages on behalf of the state or entity.[36] When a state attorney general needs to hire private attorneys to supplement the resources of her office, the proper procedure to follow is to conduct a competitive contracting process with payment on an hourly basis. To be sure, by entering into a contingency fee arrangement, an executive branch of state government may bring litigation that it could not otherwise afford. Fiscal limitations, however, are part of the checks and balances of government and provide "budget-based political accountability."[37] Contingency fee arrangements with private counsel remove that fiscal constraint, giving the executive branch free reign to pursue any litigation that presents an opportunity for mutual profit, while at the same time depriving the legislature of its constitutional power to control state spending.

Empowering contingency fee lawyers to add a state attorney general's name to a lawsuit generates negative publicity for a defendant and increases pressure to settle the case irrespective of the merits of the litigation. The illegitimacy of this practice is accentuated when – as is often the case – contingency fee lawyers conceive of the lawsuits and then "shop" them to various attorneys general in an effort to sign up as many states as possible.

The potential for self-interested conduct is only one of several ills that result from these partnerships for profit. As indicated, contingency fee agreements also allow states' attorneys general – 85 percent of whom are elected – to institute a system of political patronage in which friends, former colleagues, and big ticket donors are awarded lucrative contracts in exchange for campaign contributions and other benefits.[38] Both of these abuses occurred in the tobacco litigations when government functions were conjoined with the profit motive. In addition to the multibillion-dollar profits for the contingency fee lawyers, the tobacco suits enabled a part of states' executive branches – with the rubber-stamp imprimatur of the judicial branch – to implement a scheme to raise revenue and impose a regulatory regime without risking the political fallout that often results from raising taxes. When public policy making is thus removed from the legislature, so too is political accountability, thus undermining the fundamental structure of our republican government.[39]

The justification advanced to support regulation through litigation is that the public will has been thwarted by private interest groups' lobbying of legislatures.[40] When interest groups, however, fail to convince voters of the merits of their position and instead resort to courts willing to impose their own political views, they deny the electorate the political accountability that our representative form of government is intended to bestow. Alliances between the power of the state and the capital base of the contingency fee bar create awesome power that is being exercised outside of the ordinary machinery of representative government.

2. Institutional Differences between Courts and Legislatures

A second reason why regulation through litigation is fundamentally inconsistent with our structure of government is the inherent institutional differences between legislatures and courts engaged in regulatory policy making. Typically, the need for regulation arises because of market failures such as impeded competition or externalities, that is, social costs, which are not internalized in the price of goods and services. Even if there is a basis for regulation, the proper role for the legislature is to then compare the costs of the proposed regulation to the benefits projected. Indeed, the legislative branch has been consigned with the authority to weigh these issues – not courts – because of the different institutional mechanisms available to legislatures and courts.

The legislative process allows for citizen participation in numerous ways. Legislative committees hold public hearings to gather information and to allow interested parties to voice their views. Because the laws apply to everyone, input is provided by a wide range of interest groups. The committee structure also allows legislators to gain expertise in particular areas and to have the assistance of professional staffs. In addition, candidates for legislative office express their views on public policy issues, allowing the electorate to influence the public policy goals of the state. Press reports on legislators' positions enable the electorate to compare what a legislator has done with what he stated while running for office and to respond via the ballot box. Further, bills are debated in committees and then on the floor of the House and the Senate and, if passed by both houses, must then be approved by the governor of the state. If a statute proves counterproductive or generates sufficient opposition from the electorate, it can be amended or repealed.

Judicial regulation, by contrast, as Robert A. Kagan has observed, is "markedly inefficient, complex, costly, punitive, and unpredictable."[41] Thomas Aquinas, in expressing a preference for legislative, as opposed to judicial, law making, cited Aristotle for the proposition that "those who make laws consider long beforehand what laws to make; whereas judgment on each single case has to be pronounced as soon as it arises; and it is easier for man to see what is right, by taking many instances into consideration, than by considering one solitary fact."[42]

Judicial policy making, which is heavily influenced by private lawyers who seek profit by partnering with states' attorneys general, is also not subject to the many procedural safeguards that have been established for rule making by administrative agencies created by legislative enactments.[43]

Finally, another infirmity of judicial policy making is that a randomly selected jury, which is reacting to specific facts in a specific case, may make rules and policies that have national impact. A single jury in a single jurisdiction should not be setting national norms. Consider the State Farm Insurance case that I described.[44] Authority to determine whether original equipment should be used exclusively to repair damaged automobiles is consigned to Congress or to state legislatures. Nonetheless, a jury in Illinois came within a whisker of, not only setting national policy, but also overturning the contrary policy of other states. To have had national policy decided by this jury, heavily influenced by profit-seeking lawyers, is more than a mere anomaly. It is a worrisome invitation to lawyers in their quest for profits to impose enormous direct and indirect costs on society.

NOTES

1. By corruption, I do not mean the payment of bribes to public officials for personal gain, though there is evidence that states' attorneys general selected law firms in the tobacco litigation on the basis of contributions by those firms to the political coffers of the attorney general. *See* Thomas B. Edsall, *Windfall in Tobacco Lawsuits*, WASH. POST, Sept. 6, 1998, at A1 (stating that it was reported that the Missouri attorney general authorized $300 million to be paid to thirty lawyers, many of whom were contributors to his campaign). I do mean the corruption of the political process resulting from the bypassing of states' statutes requiring appropriations (to pay contingency fee attorneys) to be approved by the legislature, "selling" of the states' legislative authority, and transferring legislative powers to the courts in order to direct productive resources to attorneys partnering with states' attorneys general for profit.
2. *See* Mark Curriden, *Up in Smoke*, A.B.A. J., Mar. 2007, at 27 [hereinafter Curriden, *Up in Smoke*].
3. *See* Richard Epstein, New Wave Transcript, *supra* Chapter 20, note 2 (The tobacco lawsuits skirted the subrogation claim issue by "creat[ing] an imaginary independent cause of action, one that is technically incorrect."); *see also* Hanoch Dagan & James J. White, *Governments, Citizens and Injurious Industries*, 75 N.Y.U. L. REV. 354, 374–76 (2000) ("We believe that the states had only one meritorious claim against the tobacco manufacturers, namely subrogation to the claims of their citizens against the tobacco manufacturers in tort.") Subrogation

claims, however, would be vulnerable to the same defenses that the tobacco industry had successfully raised in the context of smoker's suits. *See* William H. Pryor Jr., et al., *Report of the Task Force on Tobacco Litigation Submitted to Governor James and Attorney General Sessions*, 75 CUMB. L. REV. 577, 589–90 (1996–97). Dickie Scruggs, the lawyer most responsible for formulating the tobacco litigation strategy, stated that in light of the misconduct of the tobacco industry, "[i]t doesn't matter which legal theory you use." Quoted in Statement of Dr. Donald Vinson, New Wave Transcript, *supra* Chapter 20, note 2, at 3.

4. The settlement also included a variety of regulatory changes, including restrictions on advertising, measures designed to prevent the use of marketing practices targeting youths, and funding or antismoking efforts. For analysis of the settlement, see MARTHA DERTHICK, UP IN SMOKE: FROM LEGISLATION TO LITIGATION IN TOBACCO POLITICS (2002); Jeremy Bulow and Paul Klemperer, *The Tobacco Deal*, in Perry Brainard, ed., Brookings Papers on Economic Activity (Washington, D.C. 1998).

5. *See* Judge Stephen Williams, *The More Law, The Less Rule of Law*, 2 THE GREEN BAG 2d 403 (1999) ("As anyone who took ECON 101 in college will recognize, the settlement is the equivalent of an excise tax on cigarettes, a tax that will fall overwhelmingly on consumers.").

6. Curriden, *Up in Smoke, supra* note 2, at 27.

7. *See* Mark Curriden, *Feuding Over Fees*, A.B.A. J., Jan. 1998, at 23.

8. Curriden, *Up In Smoke, supra* note 2, at 25, 27.

9. *Id.*

10. *Id.*

11. *Id.*

12. *See* 150 CONG. REC. S5774–75 (daily ed. May 19, 2004) (statement of Senator Jon Kyl).

13. Curriden, *Up In Smoke, supra* note 2, at 32.

14. *See* US CONST., art.1, § 9, cl. 7; WIS. CONST., art.8, §2; NEV. CONST., art.4, §19.

15. 63 Am. Jur. 2d *Public Funds* §37 (1984); 81 AC.J.S. *States*, § 233 (1977).

16. *Venegas v. Mitchell*, 495 U.S. 82, 87–88 (1990); *Erickson v. Foote*, 112 Conn. 662, 666 (1931); 7A C.J.S. *Attorney and Client* § 283 (1980).

17. *Cf.* Statement of U.S. Representative Christopher Cox:

It is specious to argue that these … billions in [lawyers'] fees are not being diverted out of the funds available for public health and taxpayers. The Tobacco industry is willing to pay a certain sum to get rid of these cases. That sum is the total cost of the payment to the plaintiffs and their lawyers. It is a matter of indifference to the industry how that sum is divided – 75% for the plaintiffs and 25% for their lawyers, or vice versa. That means that every penny paid to the plaintiffs' lawyers – whether it is technically "in" the settlement or not – is money that the industry could have paid to the states or the private plaintiffs. Excessive attorneys' fees in this case will not be a victimless crime.

Testimony of the Honorable Christopher Cox, Subcommittee on Courts and Intellectual Property Hearing on Proposed Legislation to Limit Lawyers Fees Resulting from Congressionally Enacted Tobacco Settlement, at 14–15 (Dec. 10, 1997), *available at* http://www.afn.org/~afn54735/tob971210a.html.

18. *See* Affidavit of Lester Brickman on Attorneys' Fees, *Texas v. Am. Tobacco Co.*, No. 5:96-CV-91 (Mar. 11, 1998) (opining that the private attorneys retained by the Texas attorney general breached their fiduciary obligations to the client they were hired to represent [the state of Texas] by structuring a settlement for their own benefit at the expense of the client); Declaration of Geoffrey Hazard Jr., *Texas v. Am. Tobacco Co.*, No. 5:96-CV-91 (Mar. 11, 1998) (opining that the private attorneys retained by the Texas attorney general were complicit with the attorney general's breach of the fiduciary obligation he owed to the people of the state of Texas).

19. *See, e.g.*, Thomas B. Edsall, *Windfall in Tobacco Lawsuits*, WASH. POST, Sept. 6, 1998, at A1 (reporting that the Missouri attorney general authorized $300 million to be paid to thirty lawyers, many of whom were contributors to his campaign).

In 1996, then-Attorney General Carla Stovall of Kansas hired her former law partners at Entz & Chanay to serve as local counsel in the state's tobacco lawsuit. *See* Hearing on H.B. 2893, Before the Kansas House Taxation Comm., Feb. 14, 2000, *available at* http://www.kslegislature.org/committeeminutes/2000/house/HsTax2-14-00b.pdf; *see also* Testimony of Kansas Attorney General Carla Stovall at 16–17, 35–36 (discussing her decision to hire two of her previous employers, both who had contributed to her campaign in 1994, as counsel for Kansas' tobacco litigation). In addition to accepting the case that resulted in a "jackpot" fee award, Entz & Chanay performed other "favors" for General Stovall during her campaign and also contributed money to her campaign effort. John L. Peterson, *Payment for Law Firm Draws Fire; Hearing Continues In Case Involving Tobacco Litigation*, KANSAS CITY STAR, Feb. 17, 2000, at B3.

In New Jersey, a team of six lawyers, five of whom were former presidents of ATLA-NJ, the New Jersey trial lawyers' association, got the contract after ATLA-NJ's PAC contributed nearly $100,000 over six months to Republican lawmakers, including $4,350 in checks written the day after the contract was signed. Walter Olson, *Puff, the Magic Settlement*, REASON, Jan. 2000, at 66.

Then-Texas Attorney General Dan Morales also hired contingency fee lawyers to file his state's tobacco litigation in 1996. Four of the five hired firms had collectively contributed nearly $150,000 in campaign contributions to Morales from 1990 to 1995. *See* Robert A. Levy, *The Great Tobacco Robbery: Hired*

Guns Corral Contingent Fee Bonanza, LEGAL TIMES, Feb. 1, 1999, at 27. After hiring the firms, Morales reportedly asked them to make an additional political contribution of $250,000. *See* Miriam Rozen & Brenda Sapino Jeffreys, *Why Did Dan Morales Exchange Good Judgment for the Good Life?*, TEX. LAW., Oct 27, 2003. at 1.

South Carolina Attorney General Charles Condon handpicked seven law firms to represent the state in the tobacco litigation. *See* ASSOC. PRESS, *Lawyer Fees Weren't S.C.'s Official Says*, CHARLOTTE OBSERVER, May 2, 2000, at 1Y. Six of the seven firms included the attorney general's friends or political supporters. *See id.*

Missouri Attorney General Jay Nixon selected five law firms that had made more than $500,000 in political contributions over the preceding eight years, mostly to him and his party, to handle the state's participation in the multistate litigation against tobacco companies. Editorial, *All Aboard the Gravy Train*, ST LOUIS POST-DISPATCH, Sept. 17, 2000, at B2. Those firms eventually received $111 million in fees, an amount decried as "out of proportion to the work performed and the risk involved," given that Missouri was the twenty-seventh state to join the litigation, coming in only after the hard work had been done by other states and settlement was inevitable. *Id.* When Nixon ran unsuccessfully for the U.S. Senate in 1998, numerous attorneys in those firms made $1,000 contributions to his campaign, the maximum individual donations permitted by law. *See* John Fund, *Cash In, Contracts Out: The Relationship Between State Attorneys General and the Plaintiffs' Bar* at 7 (U.S. Chamber Inst. for Legal Reform, 2004), *available at* http://www.instituteforlegalreform.com/pdfs/Fund%20AG%20report.pdf.

20. *See* Margaret A. Little, *Legal Fees Awarded in the State Tobacco Suits and Other Mass Tort and Class Action Cases Face New Ethics and Legal Challenges*, 3 ENGAGE 120 (2002).

21. Michael DeBow, *The State Tobacco Litigation and the Separation of Powers in State Government: Repairing the Damage*, 31 SETON HALL L. REV. 563, 569 (citing W. Kip Viscusi).

22. *See* John Fund and Martin Morse Wooster, *The Dangers of Regulation through Litigation*, Am. Tort Reform Found. (2000), at 20–21 (stating that Wisconsin tobacco lawyers, after submitting an initial demand of $847 million in fees, or roughly $32,000 per hour, later reducing that to a mere $75 million, fought a losing battle to prevent public disclosure of their billing records, citing "ethical issues"); *see also* Mike Ivey, *Tobacco Suit Lawyers Keep Hours Secret*, THE CAPITAL TIMES, May 1, 1999, at 1A; Mike Ivey, *Tobacco Suit Lawyers Traveled In Style: Hotels, Limos, Flights Add Thousands To Bill*, THE CAPITAL TIMES, July 13, 1999, at 1A.

23. *See* Susan Beck, *The Fee Giver*, AM. LAW., Dec. 2, 2002. The real parties in interest in these "arbitrations" were not the tobacco companies but (1) the law firms that operated on a national basis and which were hired by multiple states; and (2) the local law firms hired in each state in addition to one or more national law firms. This was so because the settlement included a provision limiting the total amount paid to the lawyers to $500 million a year. The more fees awarded to the local firms, the less the annual payments to the national firms because their fees were in the aggregate, far in excess of the local lawyers' fees. Although their total fees would ultimately be paid, the time value of money would result in a significant decrease in the current value of their future flow of fees. To protect their interests, the national lawyers argued in favor of lower fees for the local law firms. Whereas the tobacco companies also argued for lower fees, they were essentially bystanders because each arbitration panel was effectively controlled by the contingency fee lawyers.

24. *See* Affidavit of Lester Brickman at 7–14, *Brown Rudnick Berlack & Israels, L.L.P. v. Massachusetts*, No. 01–5883 B.L.S. (Mar. 26, 2003) (stating that the 25% contingency fee sought by the private attorneys was not justified by the risk undertaken because the Massachusetts legislature had enacted statutes that stripped the tobacco companies of defenses that were the basis for prevailing in prior suits); Declaration of Lester Brickman at 4–9, *Wisconsin v. Philip Morris Inc.*, No. 97-CV-328 (May 14, 1999) (stating that the liability risk was considerably less than that claimed by the private attorneys at the time they contracted with the state because significant documentary evidence of an incriminating nature had already surfaced, and within two months, the idea of a global settlement was under active consideration); Affidavit of Lester Brickman on Attorneys' Fees at 6–11, *Texas v. Am. Tobacco Co.*, No. 5:96-CV-91 (Mar. 11, 1998) (opining that the contingency fee sought was not remotely commensurate with the limited risk that the attorneys undertook).

25. *See* MODEL RULES OF PROF'L CONDUCT (2006), Rule 1.5 (a); NY LAWYER'S CODE OF PROFESSIONAL RESPONSIBILITY, DR 2–106.

26. *See State v. American Tobacco Co.*, No. CL95–1466 (Fla. Cir. Ct. Nov. 21, 1997), *rev'd on other grounds sub. nom. Kerrigan, Estess, Rankin & McLeod v. State*, No. 97–4008, 1998 WL 246325 (Fla. Dist. Ct. App. May 18, 1998); *State v. Philip Morris Inc., et al.*, 308 A.D.2d 57, 65, 763 N.Y.S. 2d. 32 (NY 1st Dept 2003) (finding that Justice Charles Ramos had no authority or jurisdiction *sua sponte* to undertake an independent inquiry into the amount or method used in fixing attorneys' fees and reversing Justice Ramos' October 22, 2002, order that, in part, held that the $625 million fee awarded by the arbitrators to the attorneys that Judge Ramos calculated to amount to at least $13,000 per hour, without approval of a court, was "unprecedented" and required that the State

of New York be given an opportunity to argue that the fee was excessive and that any refund should revert to the state).

In Florida, the lawyer who negotiated a 25% contingency fee contract with the state also secured the Florida Legislature's passage of a law to allow a suit by the state against tobacco companies that not only stripped the companies of their defenses but virtually declared the outcome in the case. FLA. STAT. § 409.910 (1). He commented that enactment of that legislation made success in the state's suit "a virtual slam-dunk." 20/20 (ABC television broadcast, Mar. 16, 1998) (quoting Fred Levin, Esq.). If the "reasonable fee" mantra has any substance, then a 25% contingency fee in a virtual slam-dunk case amounting to billions of dollars is prototypically an excessive and unreasonable fee. The processes for applying ethical rules to the lawyers' fees in the tobacco litigation were, however, effectively suspended.

Likewise, in Texas, plaintiffs' lawyers hired on a contingency fee basis by Texas Attorney General Dan Morales ("private counsel"), handpicked a judge who favorably ruled on their request for a $2.3 billion fee. These lawyers filed an action against the tobacco manufacturers in federal district court in the Eastern District of Texas, Texarkana, Division, where U.S. District Court Judge David Folsom solely presided. *Texas v. Am. Tobacco Co.*, 14 F. Supp. 2d 956 (E.D. Tex. 1997). Of the approximately forty cases filed by the states against tobacco manufacturers, this was the only one filed in federal court. Although Judge Folsom did dismiss several of the claims, he sustained the critical parts of the suit and approved the proposed proof of damages by use of a statistical model, the details of which were not available to him when he made his decision. *See* Philip C. Patterson & Jennifer M. Philpott, Note, *In Search of a Smoking Gun: A Comparison of Public Entity Tobacco and Gun Litigation*, 66 BROOK. L. REV. 549, 563–64, 574–75 (2000). Most importantly, however, Judge Folsom fully merited the unusual efforts of private counsel to select him to preside over Texas' action against the tobacco companies by consistently ruling in favor of the financial interests of private counsel.

In January 1998, several Texas legislators filed a mandamus action in Texas state court challenging the authority of Attorney General Morales to bind the state to a contingency fee agreement. Private counsel removed that action to the federal court. *In re Senator Troy Fraser*, No. 5:98-CV-45 (E.D. Tex. 1998). Later, for procedural reasons stemming from an arbitration panel's award of $3.3 billion in fees over a twenty-five-year period, the challenge to Morales' action was found mooted. *Fraser v. Real Parties*, Nos. 00–40024, 00–40036, 00–40038 (5th Cir. 2000). The effect of this maneuvering was to deny to Texas state courts any role in determining the reasonableness of the fees awarded private counsel under the disciplinary standards adopted by the Texas Supreme Court. Effectively then, Judge Folsom prohibited Texas state courts and the

Texas Supreme Court from applying the Texas Rules of Professional Discipline to determine whether the fees in the tobacco litigation violated the ethical standards adopted by the Texas Supreme Court.

While these and other related proceedings were winding their way through the courts, the Texas press reported that noted Texas torts attorney, Joe Jamail, had been invited by Morales to be one of the private counsel but that as a condition of selection, he would have to pay Morales one million dollars. Jamail stated that he refused the demand and was not one of those selected. *See* Deborah Tedford, *Jury Eyes Tobacco Legal Fees*, Hous. Chron., Nov. 30, 2000, at 37. Later, in 2003, after the tobacco companies had settled the suit for $17.3 billion, Morales pled guilty to charges of mail fraud for back-dating a contract and transporting it across state lines in order to steer unearned attorney fees from the tobacco settlement to his friend, Marc Murr. *See* Ken Herman, *Morales gets four years*, Austin Am. Statesman, Nov. 1, 2003, at A1. In addition, he pled guilty to charges of tax evasion for diverting $420,000 from his campaign account for personal use without reporting it to the IRS. He was sentenced to four years in federal prison. *Id.*

27. *State v. Philip Morris, Inc.*, 1997 WL 540913 (Md. Cir. Ct. May 21, 1997).
28. 1998 Md. Law 122.
29. *See* Jonathan Shier, *Maryland Among States Targeted by U.S. Chamber of Commerce for Tobacco Fees*, Capital News Serv., Mar. 14, 2001, *available at* http://www.newsline.umd.edu/business/specialreports/tobacco/tobacco 031401.htm.
30. *See* Daniel LeDuc, *Angelos, Md. Feud Over Tobacco Fee*, Wash. Post, Oct. 15, 1999, at B1; Daniel LeDuc & Michael E. Ruane, *Maryland's Power Player; Orioles Owner Masters Political Clout*, Wash. Post, Mar. 28, 1999, at C1. "Adding to the controversy is that one member of the [Legislative] Committee ... [was] Norman R. Stone Jr., the Senate's most senior member, the Senate President Pro Tempore and a lawyer at Angelos' firm." *Id.*
31. *See* Donna M. Owens, *A Conversation with Peter Angelos*, Baltimore Sun, Nov. 18, 2002, at 2.
32. *See* Bulow & Klemperer, *The Tobacco Deal supra* note 4, at 323 ("The companies would settle lawsuits cheaply, smoking would decline because of the price increase, state governments would raise taxes under the name of 'settlement payments,' and the lawyers would be able to argue for contingency fees based on tax collections instead of the much smaller cost to companies. Only consumers, in whose name class action suits were filed, would lose out.")
33. In the Rhode Island lead paint litigation, the law firm of Motley Rice – which was awarded more than $1 billion in the tobacco litigation – approached Rhode Island Attorney General Sheldon Whitehouse and proposed that he retain the law firm to sue companies that once manufactured lead pigments

for paint used in residential applications. Whitehouse did so, agreeing to pay the firm 16⅔ percent of any recovery. The suit was to be based on an unprecedented theory, discussed earlier in Chapter 11, § B(2), that the mere presence of lead paint in Rhode Island buildings constituted a public nuisance that must be abated by the total removal of the paint. But this was exactly what Rhode Island had considered and rejected. First, in 1991, the State of Rhode Island adopted the Lead Poisoning Prevention Act, which requires that property owners maintain painted surfaces so that old lead-based paint remained covered and intact. R.I. St. T. 23, Ch. 24.6. Second, under Rhode Island law, lead-based paint that is covered by intact non-lead-based paint is not considered a hazard and need not be removed. *See* Rules & Regulations for Lead Poisoning Prevention, R23–24.6-PD, §§6.1, 11.1, 12.1 (Nov. 2001). Third, Rhode Island has rejected requiring home and building owners to remove lead paint because it would be enormously expensive and provide no increase in public health benefit over that of covering the lead paint and would create additional hazards resulting from the dust and debris generated by the removal of the lead paint. *See* Explaining Childhood Lead Poisoning in Rhode Island FY 1995 Applications Project Year Five, submitted by RIDOH Division of Family Health, Apr. 22, 1994, quoted in Brief of the Chamber of Commerce of the United States and the American Tort Reform Associate as *Amici Curie*, May 13, 2005, at 7–8, *Rhode Island v. Lead Indus. Ass'n, Inc., et al.*, No. 2004–63-M.P. (R.I. Sup. Ct.). Nonetheless, contrary to state policy, the profit-driven litigation proceeded to a verdict against the manufacturers of the lead pigments used decades earlier in paints, requiring them to bear the cost of removing all lead paint in Rhode Island residential buildings – a decision later overturned by the Rhode Island Supreme Court.

When Rhode Island Attorney General Whitehouse hired Motley Rice to bring the lead paint suit, he did so in the teeth of Rhode Island law. That law provides that the attorney general and his or her employees may not "use their position for private gain or advantages" (R.I. Gen. Laws § 36–14–1) and are forbidden to "have any interest, financial or otherwise, direct or indirect … which is in substantial conflict with the proper discharge of his or her duties or employment in the public interest." R.I. Gen. Laws §36–14–5(a). When Motley Rice was deputized by Whitehouse to prosecute the claim on behalf of the state, the same duties that state law imposed on Whitehouse also applied to the law firm. The quest for profits, however, simply overrode state law.

34. *Marshall v. Jerricho*, 446 U.S. 238, 249–50 (1980); *see also* Margaret A. Little, *Legal Fees Awarded in the State Tobacco Suits And Others Mass Tort And Class Action Cases Face New Ethics and Legal Challenges*, 3 Engage 119, 120 (Oct. 2002).
35. *Young v. United States*, 481 U.S. 808, 814 (1987).

36. In 1985, the California Supreme Court held a contingency fee arrangement for enforcing public nuisance ordinances unconstitutional because it was "antithetical to the standard of neutrality that an attorney representing the government must meet when prosecuting" such a claim. *People ex rel. Clancy v. Superior Court*, 705 P. 2d 343, 353 (Cal. 1985). That ruling, however, has been narrowed. In a case dealing with the propriety of the County of Santa Anna hiring an outside attorney on a contingency fee basis to prosecute a public nuisance lead paint abatement action, the trial court recognized the similarity found by the U.S. Supreme Court in *Young v. U.S.*, *id.*, between criminal prosecutions and civil actions to abate public nuisance. Citing to the 1985 California Supreme Court ruling, the court found that outside counsel cannot be engaged on a contingency fee basis. In upholding the reversal of this decision by an intermediate appellate court, the California Supreme Court maintained the requirement of neutrality imposed on local prosecutors but held that it was satisfied the standard had been met because the city prosecutor retained complete control over the litigation. Recognizing that that was an insufficient safeguard, however, the court also required that the retainer agreements between public entities and private counsel "specifically provide that decisions regarding settlement of the case are reserved exclusively to the discretion of the public entity's own attorneys ... [and] that any defendant that is the subject of such litigation may contact the lead government attorneys directly without having to confer with contingent fee-counsel." *County of Santa Clara et al., v. Atlantic Richfield Co.*, Case No. S163681, at 29 (Sup. Ct. Cal. July, 26, 2010); *see also* Walter Olson, *Tort Travestry* WALL ST. J., May 18, 2007, at A.17.

37. *See* Howard M. Erichson, *Coattail Class Actions: Reflections on Microsoft, Tobacco, and the Mixing of Public and Private Lawmaking in Mass Litigation* 34 U.C. DAVIS L. REV. 1, 39 (2000).

38. Stuart Taylor Jr., *How a Few Rich Lawyers tax The Rest of Us*, 31 NAT'L L.J. 1866, 1867 (1999).

39. *See* Robert B. Reich, *Don't Democrats Believe in Democracy?* WALL ST. J., Jan. 12, 2000 at A22 ("These lawsuits are end runs around the democratic process. ... This is faux legislation, which sacrifices democracy to the discretion of ... officials operating in secrecy.")

40. As expressed by a *New York Times* editorial, a resort to litigation to accomplish regulation is justified when the legislature has unjustifiably failed to act and "so far nothing else has worked." Editorial, *Lawsuits Against Handguns*, N.Y. TIMES, Nov. 14, 1998, at A12. See also Wendy Wagner, *When All Else Fails: Regulating Risky Products Through Tort Litigation*, 95 GEO. L.J. 693 (2007), which argues in favor of "regulation through litigation" because of its ability to correct the informational asymmetries that are responsible for the failure of agencies to regulate various industries sufficiently. According to

Wagner, agencies responsible for regulating risky industries are not able and, in some cases, not willing to access the information about products that is necessary for effectively regulating them. *Id*. at 698–702. Through discovery, tort litigants are more capable of wresting this information from the manufacturers of risky products and are more willing to disseminate this information to other interested parties. *Id*. at 700–01. Furthermore, whereas the goal of the agency regulatory process is the design and implementation of regulations, the goal of litigation that results in regulation is a transfer of wealth. This represents the courts' ability "to transform at least some of the public's diffuse interest in protective regulation into high stakes damages packages." *Id*. at 707. As a result of this transformation, the public has more incentive to participate in regulation when it is achieved through litigation than it does when regulation is implemented through the agency process. *Id*. at 707–08.

41. KAGAN, ADVERSARIAL LEGALISM, *supra* Introduction, note 13, at 4.

42. *See* Clarence Morris, *Liability for Pain and Suffering*, 59 COLUM. L. REV 476, 482 (1959) quoting from SUMMA THEOLOGICA, q. 95, art. 1, reply obj. 2.

43. Consider, for example, the procedures that are in place for the promulgation of federal regulations. As noted by Professor W. Kip Viscusi:

Agencies considering a proposed rule must prepare a regulatory impact analysis of the rule and submit it to the Office of Management and Budget sixty days before posting a notice of proposed rulemaking in the Federal Register. If the regulation is consistent with the priorities of the administration and is published in the Federal Register, the public has thirty to ninety days to be made aware of the regulation and provide comments. Thus there is a formal mechanism at the very early stages of the regulatory process to engage the public in providing information pertaining to the merits of the regulatory proposal. The agency then prepares the final rule and regulatory impact analysis and must send it to the Office of Management and Budget thirty days before publishing it in the Federal Register. If the regulation is approved by the Office of Management and Budget, which is guided by an executive order that establishes well-defined principles for assessing costs and benefits of regulation, then the agency will be permitted to publish the final rule in the Federal Register. At that point, Congress has an opportunity to review the regulatory proposal should it wish to do so, where the rule would go into effect thirty days after being published in the Federal Register.

Even listing these various stages of study and review does not do justice to the scrutiny that regulatory policies receive. The regulatory impact analysis process itself often involves a detailed discussion of the benefits and costs of the regulation. These assessments are often the subject of bitter battles between the Office of Management and Budget and the regulatory agency. Moreover, there are often public hearings associated with regulatory proposals to obtain detailed information and public input on these efforts. Although all regulatory proposals that emerge from this process are not always ideal, there is a much greater opportunity for informational input and for diverse points of view to be expressed than is the case with secret deals negotiated by participants in a litigation process, such as that for the tobacco settlement. Moreover, even within the overall context of this regulatory effort, there are legislative guidelines that provide additional structure to what regulatory agencies can and cannot do, when these guidelines are the results of laws enacted by Congress.

W. Kip Viscusi, *Tobacco: Regulation and Taxation through Litigation*, in W. KIP VISCUSI ed., REGULATION THROUGH LITIGATION 51 (AEI-Brookings Joint Center, 2002); *see also* Robert B. Reich, *Regulation is out, Litigation is in*, USA TODAY, Feb. 11, 1999, at 15A ("Regulating U.S. industry through lawsuits isn't the most efficient way of doing the job. Judges don't have large expert staffs for research use and analyses, which regulatory agencies posses. And when plaintiffs and defendants settle their cases, we can't always be sure the public interest is being served.").

44. *See* Chapter 20, § B.

Conclusion

I BEGAN MY DISCUSSION OF CONTINGENCY FEES BY ASSERTING that the contingency fee is the most underappreciated of all of the elemental forces that shape our legal and political systems. I then set out to raise the level of awareness by showing how contingency fees have empowered lawyers to shape our civil justice system in ways that further their financial interests while relegating the interests of the polity to secondary importance. The result, I concluded, is a loosely structured, cumbersome system for compensating accident victims, which is extraordinarily costly, inconsistent, unpredictable, and inefficient. Nor is there much solid evidence that the tort system promotes injury avoidance. What it best promotes, instead, are lawyers' fees. Under the guise of financing the system for compensating accident victims, tort lawyers have increased their effective hourly rates, adjusted for inflation, by more than 1,000 percent in the past forty-five years. This is far beyond any level needed to assure access to the civil justice system and well above the level of risk being assumed by tort lawyers.

Rent-seeking tort lawyers are able to extract productivity-unrelated gains by (1) studiously avoiding competing on the basis of price and, instead, charging standard fees of one-third or more, even where there is no meaningful liability risk and there is a high probability of a substantial recovery; (2) using the stealth sheathing that envelopes contingency fees to conceal the fact that they are routinely charging for entrepreneurial risks that they are not undertaking; (3) applying their contingency fee percentages not just to the value they add to a claim but to the entire recovery – even if their efforts generate zero additional value; (4) imposing, in the guise of ethics, prohibitions against practices and business plans that would promote price competition; and (5) benefitting from judicial protection of lawyer self-governance that enables the profession to fend off societal controls that would expose lawyers to the same rules they apply to other occupational groups.

Most importantly, tort lawyers and judges who produce the law that the lawyers invoke have been engaged in a collaborative enterprise to expand the scope of liability of the tort system. This expansion is driven by the substantial increase in tort lawyers' profits over the past fifty years – an increase that is attributable in large part to judicial approbation of various strategies employed by lawyers to increase their fees. The relationship between profits and expansion of the tort system – which has been ignored in the legal literature – should now be abundantly clear.

Lawyers' immensely successful quest for profits has had perverse effects on the tort system. The collaborative effort of lawyers and judges to increase the scope of the tort system has increased the volume of tort litigation to levels far beyond that which can be justified as contributing to injury avoidance. That quest has also driven up the awards of noneconomic (pain and suffering [P&S]) damages to levels that have no rational relationship to the objectives of a tort system. It has also driven up medical care costs in auto accidents by more than $30 billion annually. Furthermore, as Paul Rubin has noted, the increased litigation from an expanded tort system "is also a particularly virulent and costly form of rent seeking because it imposes costs on all of the economy in terms of increased uncertainty and difficulty of doing business."[1]

Lawyers have also turned the class action from a procedural device used to aggregate similar claims into a form of substantive law that tilts the playing field so far in their favor as to overwhelm defendants into settling, irrespective of the merits of the action. This coercive power has become a huge money-making machine, generating profits in the millions and hundreds of millions of dollars. The threat of these mass actions has given entrepreneurial class action lawyers unmatched regulatory power, which is often not exercised in the public interest but instead, wielded solely for the pursuit of profit. Armed with their awesome powers, lawyers increasingly use tort litigation to effectuate the kind of public policy outcomes that we have consigned to our legislative and administrative branches of government. Policy making is thus being driven by lawyers' pursuit of profit.

Having exposed some of the perverse effects of contingency fees, the logical follow-up is to present a "what do we do about it" analysis. In the saloon scenes in the old Westerns, there is a sign above the piano that reads: *Please Don't Shoot the Piano Player.* The small print at the bottom of the sign adds: *unless you can play the piano.* I did not set out to shoot down the use of contingency fees in the tort and class action systems. Even if I had, it would matter little. No proposal to abolish the use of contingency fees would gain any political or judicial traction. Nor do I espouse any such course of action. Moreover, identifying the ways that lawyers have gamed the tort and class action systems to produce inordinately high profits – which are largely unearned and mostly the result of their dominant position in the market for tort-claiming services – falls far short of shooting the piano player. Nonetheless, I recognize that it is incumbent on me to offer some courses of action to counter some of the flagrant abuses that I identify in this book.

Alas, I have no grand solution to offer – no magic bullets, no panaceas. Contingency fee financing of tort litigation is too tightly intertwined with our tort system to be either extracted whole or purged of its great excesses by any single overarching curative measure. The prime objective of most tort reformers is enactment of a "loser pays" regime in which losing parties in litigation would be responsible for reimbursing the winning party's attorney fees. After explicating the arguments in favor and in opposition, I conclude that the political calculus is not favorable to "loser pays." Instead of "loser pays" or a grand scheme, I offer targeted approaches that seek to fix specific abuses. These proposals are not the standard tort reforms, such as capping P&S and punitive damages or shortening the time in which to file lawsuits, that have been advanced by the business community and its political allies over the past thirty years.[2]

A. "Loser Pays"

The holy grail of tort reformers – the one that has so far eluded them – is the "loser pays" approach to replace or modify the American Rule. As explained in Chapter 1, the American Rule provides that, absent agreement or statutory fee-shifting provisions, parties to a litigation are responsible for their own attorney fees. Under a "loser pays" approach, the losing party in a civil litigation is required to reimburse a major part of the prevailing party's reasonable attorneys fees.

There is a vast sea of literature on the merits – or lack thereof – of changing the American Rule to some variant of the "loser pays" rules that prevail in most of Europe.[3] Advocates of "loser pays" claim that (1) it is unfair for someone who is sued and wins to still owe her attorney fees under the prevailing American Rule; (2) as a matter of policy, allowing plaintiffs to inflict attorney fees on defendants, even when defendants win, stacks the deck too strongly in favor of plaintiffs and encourages nuisance value litigation, that is, claims of little legal merit that are filed solely to induce a defendant to settle in order to avoid the expenses of litigation;[4] (3) because bringing suits *pro se* (without a lawyer) is too daunting for most, it would promote access to the legal system by allowing claimants with small but valid damage claims of a few thousand dollars, who are currently shut out of the legal system because lawyers do not find the cases sufficiently remunerative, to attract a lawyer; (4) it would limit excessive motions and discovery requests in order to impose higher costs on the other side as a way of increasing settlement pressure; and (5) it would encourage compliance by potential tortfeasors.[5] Opponents of "loser pays" counter that injured parties with valid claims may be discouraged from seeking to vindicate their right to access the courts or have to settle for less than the full value of the claim out of fear that if they lose, they would be liable for the defendant's legal fees and costs.[6]

Theoretical studies of adopting a "loser pays" rule have produced mixed results, supporting both advocates and critics. For example, studies differ on how "loser pays" would impact settlement rates.[7] One of the more recent studies attempts to account for flaws in earlier research and finds that "loser pays" would result in decreased filing of frivolous claims, higher settlement rates when damages are high, greater expenditure of resources during trial, and higher success rates for defendants.[8]

Comparisons with European countries that have "loser pays" regimes, such as England, are apt to mislead because, as Judge Richard Posner has noted, these nations have differing legal systems.[9] In the United States, even the results of two states' experimentation with forms of "loser pays" do not present a clear picture of the effects of a national adoption of the English Rule.[10]

Tort reform *proponents* favor a "loser pays" approach because they anticipate that it will reduce the volume of tort litigation. Tort reform *opponents* resist "loser pays" for precisely the same reason – the belief that fewer tort claims will be brought because injured persons will forego filing such actions out of fear of having to pay the defendant's legal fees if they do not prevail, resulting in inadequate incentives for manufacturers to invest in improving product safety.

Both proponents and opponents of a "loser pays" approach, however, fail to understand the implications of the incentives created by contingency fees. Were a substantial "loser pays" proposal to be enacted, tort lawyers would not simply accept the ensuing decrease in the volume of tort litigation. Instead, they would seek to protect their valuable franchise by guaranteeing to clients – at least in cases with low risk and high reward – that if they did not prevail, the lawyer would foot the "loser pays" penalty. Most likely this would be done by purchasing legal expense insurance, which would provide coverage against having to pay the winning party's legal fees. This type of insurance is universally available where "loser pays" rules have been adopted.[11]

Here is an example of how a "no brainer" tort case would play out under a "loser pays" regime. Assume a forty-year-old driver, married with kids, is stopped at a stop light. He is rear-ended and rendered paraplegic. The driver who hit him is driving a Fortune 500 company vehicle en route to a supplier. The lawyer visits the victim in the hospital, goes over the facts, and obtains his signature on a standard contingency fee retainer form. She explains to the victim – now her client – that the case is high-value and foolproof (which it is), but if they lose the case, he will have to pay the defendant's legal fees, which could run into the hundreds of thousands of dollars. The victim freaks out. No matter how much the lawyer reassures him that they cannot lose, the victim is so risk averse that he refuses to proceed with the suit. The defendant's insurance company, sensing the victim's risk averseness, offers a low-ball settlement offer.

Most commentators agree that this is a clear example of "loser pays" resulting in a miscarriage of justice. But they have it wrong. This is a lucrative case where a windfall fee – easily amounting to several million dollars – is highly likely. Any tort lawyer worth her salt would tell such a victim: "I will indemnify you against loss. However inconceivable, if we lose the case, I'll pay all of the legal expenses assessed against you (or advance the costs of legal expense insurance)." Tort lawyers in a "loser pays" regime would, of course, not offer this reimbursement guarantee to every potential client, but only to those with claims they would regard as sufficiently profitable to justify assuming this potential added expense. In fact, this is exactly what tort lawyers already do. As explained in Chapter 2, tort lawyers carefully screen potential clients and reject the majority of those seeking representation. If tort lawyers were made to bear the cost of insuring against liability for a portion of the defendant's legal fees in the event of a defense verdict, that would simply be added to the costs that lawyers already potentially bear in tort litigation: the investment of their time and the advancement of litigation costs such as expert witness fees, deposition transcripts, and so forth, which they do not recoup in the event of a loss. The additional insurance expense would simply shift the lawyer's calculus on her risk/reward curve. At the margins, some cases that would be perceived to be sufficiently profitable under the American Rule would no longer be sufficiently profitable if a "loser pays" regime were adopted.

Whereas most predictions of how a "loser pays" rule would affect tort litigation are apt to fall prey to the law of unintended consequences, the cost that it would add would decrease the volume of tort litigation. The current configuration of political forces, however, makes it highly unlikely that such a rule will be adopted at the federal or state level in the foreseeable future. Moreover, if there is political capital that can be amassed in support of reform of contingency fee financing of tort litigation, I believe that capital can be put to better use than pursuing a "loser pays" agenda.

B. Advancing a Consumer Protection Agenda

The political calculus in the tort reform wars plays out along well-channeled paths. Plaintiff lawyers, in collaborative efforts with judges, succeed in enlarging the scope of tort liability. The business community responds by lobbying for legislative reforms, mostly at the state level, to roll back the expansion.[12] The proposals engender a familiar chorus of opposition. Led by the editorial page of the *New York Times*, the AAJ and torts scholars decry the proposals because they will *take away* victims' right to access the courts.[13] And indeed, they will. That is precisely the purpose of the reforms: to narrow or roll back the judicial expansion of liability. On this public relations battlefield, tort lawyers and their supporters in the legal academy usually have the upper hand. To counter the simple statement that the proposal will take way victims' rights, supporters of the reform must go on at great length to explain the need for it.

1. The "Early Offer" Proposal

To counter the "take away" sound bite and push the focus toward tort lawyers' rent-seeking behavior, Professor Jeffrey O'Connell of the

University of Virginia Law School, Michael Horowitz of the Hudson Institute, and I advanced the "early offer" proposal. The proposal received front-page coverage in the *New York Times* when it was introduced in 1994,[14] has had extensive coverage in law school professional responsibility casebooks, and is widely cited in scholarly articles.[15] This proposal does *not* take away the rights of tort victims. Indeed, it protects them from the abusive fee practices routinely practiced by tort lawyers. In addition, the proposal would enforce long-dormant ethical rules by limiting personal injury lawyers from applying standard contingency fees to amounts offered in settlement before the lawyer adds any significant value. Had the "early offer" proposal been adopted by the Illinois Supreme Court, Mary Corcoran would not have been mulcted out of $140,000 by her lawyer.

The proposal is based on the supposition that an early settlement offer is a marker of the value of a claim before value-adding efforts have been made. Charging a standard contingency fee against the value of a claim that already existed before the lawyer was retained – the zero-based accounting scheme – is not just an abusive fee practice, it is a clear violation of lawyers' fiduciary and ethical obligations. As I discuss in Chapter 3, the ethical validity of charging a contingency fee depends on the presence of a meaningful risk of loss. To enforce this dormant ethical rule, the proposal prohibits plaintiff lawyers in personal injury cases from charging standard contingency fees where allegedly responsible parties make early settlement offers before the lawyer has added any significant value to the claim.[16] Instead, the lawyer is restricted to charging an hourly rate fee for the effort required to assemble the relevant details of the claim and to notify the allegedly responsible party of the claim. If an early settlement offer is rejected and a larger subsequent settlement or judgment is obtained, the lawyer then applies the contingent percentage to the amount in excess of the early offer, that is, to the value he added to the claim. He would thus be paid what he would have received had the offer been accepted plus the contingent percentage of the value he added. Our "early offer" proposal replicates the market bargain that a sophisticated client – such as a corporation hiring a lawyer for commercial litigation – would negotiate. It is the bargain that the Illinois Supreme Court said Mary Corcoran should have negotiated after she received an "early offer" of $1.4 million, even as it and other state courts prohibit insurance companies from informing injured persons of just this strategy.

To determine whether to make an early settlement offer, the alleged responsible party will first consider how it is likely to fare in the tort system. If liability is likely, the next question is how much to offer. Some of the factors that affect this calculus include (1) that each $1 offered is worth no less than 90¢ to the injured party rather than 66⅔¢ as is currently the case; and (2) an early settlement will generate substantial savings because (a) the longer a case remains in the tort system, the greater the opportunity for tort lawyers to "build up" unnecessary medical expenses in order to increase fees – a practice described in Chapter 15, Section B; and (b) defense costs will be lower – costs that currently amount to a hefty 14 percent of the monies paid out by insurance companies for tort liability.

Moreover, the dynamics of the "early offer" proposal assure that only serious offers are made. Alleged responsible parties will only make an early settlement offer of an amount that is less than its expected exposure from a full-scale tort claim if they perceive it to be in their self-interest to do so. To secure a settlement, the offer will have to be sufficient to minimize the incentive of the injured party's lawyer to counsel rejection of the offer. A "lowball" offer encourages the attorney to recommend that his client refuse the offer and seek a higher recovery so that the attorney can obtain a contingency fee on the recovery in excess of the offer. Only an offer that is a substantial percentage of the value of the claim will deprive the plaintiff's lawyer of the incentive to counsel rejection. Thus, our proposal relies on the alleged responsible party's self-interest as deterrence against "lowball" offers.

Individual claimants will benefit from early settlement offers because they will get paid sooner, avoid the inherent uncertainties posed by further litigation, and, by retaining a larger share of the settlement, many will recover as much or even more as in the current system. In fact, a recent study indicates that most plaintiffs in contingency fee cases who passed up settlement offers and went to trial ended up with at least $43,000 less than if they had taken the offer.[17] Society will also benefit from lower insurance costs.

These benefits, however, come at a cost. Doctors will be losers because this proposal will avoid tens of billions of dollars in unneeded medical care costs, which are run up solely for the benefit of the doctors and lawyers. Plaintiffs' lawyers will be net losers because the proposal will counter their zero-based accounting scheme and because they will miss out on some of the windfall fees they gain by charging a standard one-third fee (or more) in cases where there is no meaningful risk – cases that are the most likely to attract early settlement offers. Although insurance companies will have gains from lowered settlement costs, they are likely to be net losers because adoption of the "early offer" proposal would decrease the price of risk. This, in turn, would result in lower revenues to insurance companies and lower incomes for their CEOs. And defense lawyers will be losers because earlier settlements mean lower defense costs. Indeed, defense lawyers acknowledge that any reforms that reduce litigation are harmful to their financial interests.[18]

When a version of our proposal was placed on the California ballot in 1996 by initiative, Ralph Nader – at the request of tort lawyers – came out to California to campaign against it, declaring it "diabolical." Indeed it was. Usually, when tort reforms are proposed, tort lawyers and their supporters declare their opposition in a simple sound bite: The proposal will take away victims' rights to access to courts. Proponents of the reform must then devote long arguments to explain the need for the proposed reform. This proposal reverses the sound bite imbalance. In sound bite terms, the "early offer" proposal protects consumers of legal services from abusive fee practices used by their lawyers by requiring lawyers to comply with their own ethical rules.

The proposal, which failed by a narrow margin after a barrage of negative ads blanketed the airways in the weeks before the election, drew the wrath not only of tort lawyers but also defense lawyers, process servers, expert witnesses, and court reporters.[19] All are "shareholders" in Litigation, Inc. – that is, they all depend on an ever-increasing supply of litigation. What is good for purchasers of insurance and consumers of legal services is definitely not good for lawyers and the other cottage industries that are a part of Litigation, Inc.

Not a single state supreme court has adopted the "early offer" rule or any comparable rule seeking to protect consumers from price gouging by tort lawyers. The most that state supreme courts have done is to set maximum contingency fee percentages – maximums that immediately become the minimums that lawyers charge, irrespective of whether the fees are reasonable.

2. The "Auto Choice" Proposal

Another proposal that enhances consumer protection and does not fall victim to the "take away rights" sound bite is the "Auto Choice" plan, which has been advanced by Professor Jeffrey O'Connell, Michael Horowitz, and Peter Kinzler. Currently, as each motorist pays her automobile insurance premium, a tort lawyer representative helps himself to about 25 percent of the payment.[20] Here is how. All states make it mandatory for motorists to take out certain minimum levels of auto insurance. But, due to the efforts of rent-seeking lawyers, states do not allow motorists to have the choice of whether to purchase insurance to cover only their own economic losses and decline coverage for noneconomic losses (i.e. P&S). Instead, P&S coverage is bundled with economic loss protection. Mandatory P&S coverage transfers billions of dollars annually from motorists to tort lawyers.

"Auto Choice" would allow consumers to purchase unbundled auto insurance. Specifically, it would allow motorists to purchase only personal injury protection (PIP) insurance. With PIP coverage, an injured motorist would be compensated for medical bills and lost wages up to her policy limit, without having to prove fault. Injured persons could

also sue a driver at fault in an accident to recover the cost of any medical bills and lost wages beyond their policy limits. A motorist with
bodily injury who purchased only PIP coverage, however, could not
sue P&S. The motorist could also purchase pain and suffering coverage – and thus replicate her current insurance – but she would not
be compelled to do so. The average American family owning one or
more automobiles could save up to $438 a year in premium costs by
choosing only PIP coverage,[21] and the average insurance premium
would be reduced by 21 percent[22]; low-income drivers would save
even more.[23] Assuming 100 percent of insured motorists switched to
PIP coverage, annual premium savings would amount to approximately
$55.3 billion.[24]

Under "Auto Choice," motorists would have the choice of putting the pieces back together by also purchasing P&S coverage; but
how many insured motorists would do so? Professors Steven P. Croley
and Jon D. Hanson contend that consumer purchases of uninsured
motorist (UM) coverage, which includes P&S indicates consumer
demand for P&S coverage. They further argue that the unavailability of UM coverage excluding P&S coverage is evidence of consumer
choice.[25] Their argument is remarkable for how far it misses the mark.
First, motorists purchase UM coverage, not because it includes P&S
coverage, but to protect themselves because many drivers who cannot afford the high cost of bundled auto insurance are uninsured.
Uninsured low-income drivers would benefit the most in terms of premium deduction from "Auto Choice."[26] The availability of lower-cost
coverage would mean fewer uninsured drivers and, therefore, less
need for insured drivers to purchase UM coverage. Second, motorists who purchase UM coverage that includes P&S coverage are not
choosing to include P&S coverage. Tort lawyers have made the choice
for them. If you want to purchase UM coverage, it is only available
with P&S coverage.

Despite the contention of Croley and Hanson, motorists would be
unlikely to purchase P&S coverage if given the choice. Purchasing such

coverage would be a poor investment because it is expensive and there is little chance of collecting a major P&S award. But we need not rely on speculation. New Jersey motorists have been paying the highest auto insurance rates in the country.[27] Wary of voter wrath, New Jersey legislators enacted a "choice" system for motorists in 1989. Instead of bundled coverage, the standard insurance policy offered less expensive "no fault" coverage, under which injured motorists could recover from their own insurance carriers but could only sue in the tort system in cases of serious injury or death. Motorists, however, could also elect to purchase traditional and more expensive bundled insurance that allowed them to sue, at will, for P&S.[28] Ninety percent of motorists in New Jersey chose not to make the election, generating a savings per motorist of between $400 and $800 per year.[29]

In addition, Pennsylvania motorists have a statutory right to file a written form in which they can reject the traditional bundled coverage, thus foregoing P&S coverage in exchange for lower premiums.[30] Despite the additional step required of motorists seeking to choose the "limited tort" option and the fact that insurance agents have little incentive to recommend that option because most are compensated as a percentage of the premium, 71 percent of motorists in Philadelphia so elected as did 51 percent of motorists statewide, generating a savings of 40 percent on insurance premiums.[31] Contrary to the arguments of Professors Croley and Hanson in the *Harvard Law Review*, the empirical evidence indicates that if given a choice, consumers will opt for omitting P&S coverage – a rational choice given the higher cost of including P&S coverage and the unlikelihood of realizing a financial benefit from that higher cost.

"Auto Choice" will also generate substantial savings by avoiding medical cost buildup, which occurs when bodily-injury claimants retain contingency fee lawyers.[32] Finally, because under the current system part of the premium cost for (bundled) P&S coverage subsidizes contingency fee lawyers, allowing consumers to forgo such coverage would substantially reduce the volume of auto tort litigation.

"Auto Choice" was first introduced into the U.S. Senate in 1996[33] and enjoyed a brief moment in the spotlight when it was reintroduced in 1997 by Republican Senator Mitch McConnell of Kentucky[34] with the bipartisan support of Senators Daniel Moynihan of New York and Joseph Lieberman of Connecticut, both Democrats. The bill faced three major obstacles: one that it overcame, one that proved insurmountable, and one that may have been surmountable.

The first obstacle was opposition from conservative Republican senators who strongly believed in federalism and therefore objected to the displacement of state law by a federally mandated "Auto Choice" plan. This objection was overcome when Senator McConnell, the principal sponsor of the bill, added a provision to give states an "out" from the federally mandated choice. It allowed a state, which did not wish to provide motorists with a choice of unbundled coverage, to opt out from the bill by a vote of the state's legislature. But even state legislators with close ties to tort lawyers would have been reluctant to vote to opt out of a federal law that would have allowed motorists to cut their rapidly rising auto insurance bills by as much as a third, especially at a time when motorists' anger at rapidly rising auto insurance rates would later manifest in a near-political-death experience for both Senator Bill Bradley and Governor Christine Whitman of New Jersey.[35]

The second obstacle to building momentum behind the proposal could not be overcome. "Auto Choice" was a proposal to unbundle auto insurance. One key to the bill's early progress was the endorsement by the auto industry. The Ford Motor Company supported the bill, but that could not make up for the intense opposition by General Motors. The general counsel of GM, Thomas A. Gottschalk, endorsed the view, first expressed by one of his staff lawyers, that "Auto Choice" was a bad choice. If it were enacted, the GM counsels believed that tort lawyers would respond to the substantial decrease in their income from auto accident litigation by increasing product liability suits against the auto manufacturers.[36]

At the time, Detroit, Michigan, was the center of the automobile industry. GM's opposition prevented Michigan Senator Spencer

Abraham, a Republican, from announcing his support for the bill (which he did, in fact, support). This opposition proved to be a gift to tort lawyers at a time when the "Auto Choice" proposal was building steam. (Pogo had this opposition in mind when he said: "We have met the enemy and they is us.") Since then, although the bill has been reintroduced several times with additional sponsors, tort lawyers' allies in the Senate have prevented the bill from regaining the necessary momentum to command serious attention.[37] Had GM endorsed the bill, the momentum may have been sustained. Even so, getting the sixty Senate votes necessary to pass the bill would have been a daunting task, given that passage would have reduced tort lawyers' incomes by $10 billion or more annually.

3. The "Early Offer" in Medical Malpractice

The third proposal, also by Professor O'Connell (and others), deals specifically with medical malpractice litigation and was described earlier.[38] Under the proposal, a defendant in a medical malpractice suit has 180 days after the filing of a claim to offer to pay the claimant's economic losses plus attorney's fees. If such an offer is rejected in favor of litigation, then to recover P&S damages in addition to economic damages, the claimant would have to show that the defendant was grossly negligent "beyond a reasonable doubt."[39] The proposal seeks to strike a balance between the patient's right to compensation and society's interest in an efficient compensation system and in reducing the incidence of medical errors by inducing an increased flow of information about adverse events. As noted, O'Connell and his collaborators estimate that if the proposal were adopted, payouts and defense costs would each decline by 70 percent[40] – a projection that is disputed by Professors Black, Hyman, and Silver.[41]

For these tort reform proposals to attract sufficient support to become part of the national discourse on the civil justice system, they would first have to gain the support of the business community. That, however, is a tall order. Businesses view tort reform through a one-dimensional prism.

Companies tend to support only those reforms that are fully responsive to the civil justice issues that the company perceives as harmful. Put succinctly, businesses tend to only support "red meat" proposals that advance their clear specific interests. Rarely do they agree to advance a half-a-loaf agenda. The tort reform proposals that I am advocating do not qualify by that standard. They do not roll back the expanded rights to sue for injury that threaten specific corporate interests. They do, however, protect consumers of legal services from abusive fee practices at the hands of their lawyers; enforce long-dormant ethical principles by restricting lawyers' fees to reasonable amounts; promote improvements in the delivery of medical care; protect insured motorists from pick-pocketing tort lawyers by giving them a choice of whether to reduce their auto insurance costs up to $55 billion annually; reduce unnecessary and fraudulent medical care expenses by $30 billion or more; lower the cost of other liability insurance; and most importantly from the perspective of business interests, considerably lower the volume of tort litigation and promote settlements of injury claims.

C. A Proposed Exception to the American Rule for Entrepreneurial Class Actions

As noted, "loser pays" has gained the most academic and political attention of all tort reform proposals. Generally speaking, "loser pays" proposals seek to reverse the American Rule by making the loser in civil litigation responsible for a sizeable portion of the legal expenses of the prevailing party.[42] Although I remain skeptical as to whether any effective "loser pays" proposal can gain sufficient political traction, there is one circumstance in which I do endorse such an approach.

American jurisprudence has long provided that someone who accidentally confers a benefit on another may, under some circumstances, recover some of that value. The Contracts Law doctrine of "unjust enrichment" allows, for example, for someone hired to drill a well on certain land, who mistakenly drills a successful well on an adjoining piece of land, to recover the amount by which the land has increased in value because of the well (though not the cost of drilling the well). If that same well driller wanted to increase business and, unbidden, simply drilled wells on various parcels of land, he would not be able to collect anything for his work, even if the owners of the land would have been enriched. The legal maxim is that "[n]o man, entirely of his own volition, can make another his debtor."[43]

Lawyers are an exception to this rule. They can, by their own volition and for their profit, make others their debtor. This doctrine traces back to 1877 when the U.S. Supreme Court created an exception to the American Rule for those creating or preserving a common fund.[44] The Court held that anyone acting to preserve assets – such as a trust fund – who conferred benefits on other owners of the fund was entitled to be paid for his efforts.[45] This "common fund" doctrine was essentially incorporated into the 1966 amendment to Rule 23 of the Federal Rules of Civil Procedure in order to create the modern class action. Armed with the awesome – though unintended – powers conferred by Rule 23 and the doctrinal power to, by their own volition, make others their debtors, class action lawyers set out to remake the regulatory map. Seeking contingency fees of millions, tens, and hundreds of millions of dollars from receptive courts, they would, and did, roam the land searching out corporate misdeeds. And when there was not enough corporate wrongdoing to go around, they searched out situations where they could aggregate tens and hundreds of thousands, even millions, of persons into a class and use the bet-the-company threat as well as the potential imposition of substantial litigation costs to compel fee-yielding settlements.

Class action practice today is an entrepreneurial activity undertaken for profit. When the U.S. Supreme Court – wrongly, as I argue in Chapter 1 – declared the American Rule to be the law of the land, no one could have envisioned that it would come to protect class action lawyers' purely entrepreneurial activity. The policy justification for the American Rule today – to promote access to courts – simply does not justify always protecting class action lawyers from bearing any of the costs they impose on defendants. To be sure, the American Rule can be altered by fee-shifting statutes, and many have been enacted. Congress could enact a law, creating another exception to be the American Rule by allowing defendants in unsuccessful class actions to recover their legal expenses. But the rule can also be altered by the courts when there are compelling public policy reasons, such as those that were first invoked to allow those creating or preserving a common fund that benefitted others, to extract fees from those strangers.

The policy basis for such an exception was articulated by U.S. District Court Judge Vaughn Walker – who pioneered the use of auctions in setting class action fees – in the case of *Ghorbani v. Pacific Gas & Electric Co. Group Life Ins.*[46] This case involved a challenge of a denial of benefits by a disability plan beneficiary under a federal law regulating employer-provided benefit plans (ERISA). Judge Walker granted the defendant insurance company's motion for summary judgment, noting that the "plaintiff's claim was particularly anemic on the merits."[47] The prevailing insurance company then moved for attorneys' fees and costs under a section of the statute giving the court discretion to award fees to "either party."[48] Under the fee-shifting statute, Judge Walker could have held that the defendant was entitled to collect its legal expenses from the plaintiff. Judge Walker believed, however, that the plaintiff's lawyer should be on the hook – not the plaintiff. But the statute limited the court's exercise of discretion to "parties" to the action. Judge Walker, looking at the reality of the litigation – in particular, the entrepreneurial character of this venture by a contingency-fee-seeking lawyer – held that the plaintiff's lawyer was a "party."[49] On this basis, Judge Walker ordered the plaintiff's contingency fee lawyer – not the plaintiff – to pay the defendant's attorneys' fees and costs.[50]

There is a long history, however, of federal courts shielding lawyers from any liability when applying statutory fee shifting. In most of these cases, the issue of whether lawyers are to be immune from any financial responsibility arises under fee-shifting statutes that permit judges to award successful plaintiffs a "reasonable attorney's fee" but are silent about who is to pay the fee – the defendant, his lawyer, or both. Rather emphatically, the courts answer: not the lawyer.[51]

To be sure, though the *Ghorbani* case was not a class action, there was a fee-shifting statute allowing the court to require either *party* to pay the other's legal fees and expenses. Judge Walker, based on sound policies about the entrepreneurial basis for most class actions, simply rejected the weighty presumption that courts have erected to restrict lawyers' liability for the costs that they impose on others. My proposal, following in the steps of Judge Walker's decision, is that when class actions are purely entrepreneurial ventures by lawyers, courts should engraft an additional exception to the American Rule. This exception should allow for shifting fees in favor of the defendant, at the sole expense of the lawyer seeking certification of a class action, if certification is denied; the case is later dismissed; the settlement is rejected because it is essentially worthless to the class; or the defendant prevails at trial.

Examples of class actions that are purely entrepreneurial ventures bereft of social value and brought for the sole purpose of generating contingency fees are legion. Consider the filing of more than twenty identical class action lawsuits in at least sixteen states against the J.M. Smucker Co., claiming that although it markets its jams under the "Simply 100% Fruit" label, its jams contain far less than 100 percent fruit.[52] The lawyers filing the actions claim that Smucker's strawberry jam contains only 30 percent strawberries and its blueberry jam only 43 percent blueberries; however, the labels on the jars state that the product is a "fruit spread" and that it has the following ingredients, in descending order: fruit syrup, strawberries (or blueberries), lemon juice concentrate, fruit pectin, red grape juice concentrate added for color, and natural flavors. All of these are fruit products.[53] An all-strawberry product would either be whole strawberries or minced, diced, or mashed strawberries. None of these products, however, could be called strawberry jam or preserves. Despite the lack of a substantive basis for these class actions, after extensive litigation, Smucker entered into a national settlement with plaintiffs' counsels, though the terms are not known.[54]

Although my proposal to stiffen Smucker's resolve to resist settlement constitutes a great leap in view of the prevailing jurisprudence, the effect of such an exception would be uncertain. It would likely deter a small number of class action filings with weak arguments for certification. Lawyers can easily circumvent financial responsibility by negotiating settlements in losing cases that simply paper over the fact that no meaningful relief was obtained. Would the possibility of imposing a financial cost on class counsel affect defendants' clear propensity to settle all certified class actions, even those utterly devoid of merit? Given the dynamics of the class action process, I am compelled to acknowledge that judicial adoption of this proposal is unlikely to be enough to embolden CEOs to litigate, rather than settle, certified class actions where the evidence of wrongdoing is flimsy. Moreover, some courts would resist assessing any costs against class counsel out of concern that doing so would lead to fewer class action filings. Consider, for example, the decision of Kansas state court Judge Kevin P. Moriarty in a suit claiming that corporate officials breached their fiduciary duty by not getting the highest possible price when their corporation was taken over. Though the attorneys achieved nothing for the shareholders, the judge approved a $1 million fee for the "benefit" to the shareholders of learning, through the *failure* of the action, that the takeover price was fair.[55]

Given the proclivities of many courts to favor the interests of class action lawyers and the propensity of most CEOs to settle all certified class actions, the best I can offer is that imposing financial responsibility in a small number of cases could shift the dynamic at least slightly. Simply having the authority to impose fee reimbursement on entrepreneurial class action lawyers could be a catalyst for courts' rethinking the prolawyer bias that they manifest in much class action litigation.

D. The Policy Favoring Settlement versus "Just Say No"

In addition to "amending" the American Rule for purely entrepreneurial class actions, courts need to rethink their strong predisposition in favor

of approving class action settlements that provide only superficial benefits to class members. For the great majority of judges, the prevailing
view, as expressed by U.S. District Court Judge John F. Keenan is that
"[i]n deciding whether to approve ... [a] settlement proposal, the court
starts from the familiar axiom that a bad settlement is almost always better than a good trial."[56] This policy is both wrongly based and perverse.
First, only a tiny number of certified class actions are ever tried. Given
the dynamics of class action litigation, certification by a court essentially
assures settlement and the payment of a fee to the lawyer. Second, the
policy encourages lawyers to file class actions, irrespective of merit,
where they believe – as is often the case – that they can impose sufficient
litigation and other costs on the defendant as to compel settlement and
payment of a substantial fee. What appears to be simply a policy favoring settlement of class actions irrespective of the measure of benefit to
the class is, in fact, a manifestation of the judicial bias favoring lawyers
discussed in Chapter 10.

The perverse effects of the policy are exacerbated by the propensity
of many courts to refuse to dismiss class action filings, no matter how
little merit there appears on the face of the complaint or is developed in
the course of discovery. As a consequence, once a defendant determines
that there is little chance of gaining dismissal of the filing or having a dismissal sustained on appeal, the defendant has little choice but to reach a
settlement and negotiate an acceptable tribute.

These perverse effects are on full display in the twenty-seven putative class actions filed against "Bluetooth" headset marketers alleging that
use of the headsets would potentially cause noise-induced hearing loss
(NIHL). After the suits were filed, some of the defendants added various warning messages, such as "Do not use headphones/headsets at high
volumes for an extended period of time. Doing so can cause hearing loss."[57]
Not content to seek whatever minimal value this statement of the obvious could be shown to have generated, class counsel continued to pursue
the actions, finally reaching the inevitable settlement in which defendants
agreed to modify their warnings about NIHL, donate $100,000 to certain

nonprofit organizations dealing with hearing loss, and pay the attorneys $850,000 of which $50,000 was for expenses. Noting that the Ninth Circuit Court of Appeals has a "strong judicial policy that favors settlements, particularly where complex class action litigation is concerned," U.S. District Court Judge Dale Fischer approved the settlement.[58]

Judge Fischer set the bar for approval somewhat below the level of the Dead Sea, finding that the meaningless change in the warning and the $100,000 payment to a charity "provided at least minimal benefit."[59] There were compelling reasons, however, why he should have rejected the settlement as being of no value to the class and dismissed the action: (1) the class received $0; (2) the claims lacked merit and were unlikely to succeed had they gone to trial; (3) at the time of the settlement, the defendants' product manuals contained at least sufficient warnings about hearing loss; and (4) the counterproductive effect of warnings about an open and obvious danger. Product warnings compelled by class actions and tort litigation have become so ubiquitous that they are simply ignored by consumers. Instead, Judge Fischer took the position that settlements are favored outcomes, and even if the case is meritless and unlikely to succeed, it is preferable to allow defendants to escape by paying a small sum to a charity because plaintiffs would get nothing if the case were thrown out.

The defendants' agreement to pay the $850,000 fee contained the now typical condition that any amount not approved by the court would be retained by the defendants rather than benefit class members. As I discuss in Appendix G, Section 2, negotiating a settlement that compromises the right of the class to recover fees deemed excessive by a court or which inhibits a court's propensity to review the reasonableness of the fee request is a clear violation of the fiduciary duty owed by class counsel to the class. Following class counsel's script, Judge Fischer deemed it not worth his time to scrutinize the fee request because "any amount not awarded by the court would be retained by the defendants rather the benefiting class members."[60] Indeed, Judge Fischer rejected the need to even calculate the "precise lodestar amount" under these circumstances.[61]

Unfortunately, the *Bluetooth* litigation is not an outlier. "Minimal benefit" settlements are routinely approved by courts. Consider another zero-benefit settlement approved by a California appellate court. A class action was brought against Sprint relating to its practice of locking its cell phone handsets to prevent use of the phones on other service provider networks.[62] Class counsel claimed damages of $789 million but settled for zero payment to the class and a promise by Sprint to inform its customers that its handsets could be unlocked at the conclusion of a lengthy contract term or after payment of a significant termination fee.[63] Stated simply, the class got zero dollars and zero benefit. Not so the lawyers who were awarded a fee of $2.3 million plus $200,000 for expenses.

In the *Bluetooth* litigation, Judge Fischer acknowledged that under current law, class counsel are invested with the power to compel defendants to settle cases without merit. Courts are complicit in creating this power by refusing to dismiss putative class actions that have only the slightest pretense of merit and by applying the policy that "bad settlements" should be approved no matter how minimal the benefit to the class. What Judge Fischer, the California appellate judges, and indeed most judges frequently fail to acknowledge, however, is that while this policy benefits the courts by clearing its dockets, there is a high social cost. Consumer welfare would be improved if courts rejected "minimal benefit" settlements and thus stop promoting rent-seeking litigation that benefits only lawyers (including defendants' lawyers). If attorneys knew they could not profit from bringing litigation that provides no meaningful benefit to the class, they would be deterred from bringing such inefficient lawsuits that impose substantial costs ultimately borne by consumers. Indeed, abusive class action filings would be significantly curtailed if more judges were as assiduous as Charles E. Ramos, a New York State trial court judge, in ferreting out worthless settlements that reward the lawyers but do little or nothing for the class.

Judge Ramos is apparently descended from different stock than most judges. He presided over a suit brought against Citibank, its board members and officers, claiming that the board grossly mismanaged the company and wasted corporate assets by failing to implement internal controls, which in turn led to a series of improper financial arrangements with such companies as WorldCom, Inc., Enron Corp., Parmalet, S.PA., and others.[64] Similar actions previously brought in Delaware were dismissed by the courts. The settlement in the New York suit provided that the plaintiff's attorneys were to receive a fee of $3.3 million and that Citibank would adopt certain corporate governance reforms. However, according to Judge Ramos, Citibank had already instituted the reforms before the action was commenced.

Judge Ramos emphatically rejected the settlement, stating that "if this settlement is approved, it will be setting a dangerous precedent in that plaintiff's counsel with admittedly meritless claims will be using meritless litigation as leverage to negotiate large fees in exchange for illusory benefits to the corporation...."[65] But this is precisely the kind of settlement that courts routinely approve. Moreover, this characterization justifies, if not compels, requiring these entrepreneurial class action lawyers to reimburse the defendant for a substantial portion of its attorney costs. Without such authority weighing on judges, however, Judge Ramos is simply a lone wolf baying at the moon. The great majority of federal and state court judges presiding over the Citibank action would undoubtedly have approved the "bad settlement." It is high time for courts to recognize the inherent prolawyer bias that subtends the imbalances they have created in class action litigation by (1) routinely approving "minimal benefit" settlements; and (2) insulating lawyers from any liability for launching rent-seeking class action assaults on defendants for the sole purpose of extracting substantial fees.

E. The Effects of the Legal Professions' Self-Regulatory Power and How to Mount a Challenge

Although the U.S. Supreme Court has made inroads on the bar's prohibition of lawyer advertising, maintenance of minimum pricing, and restrictions on the mechanisms for delivery of legal services, it nonetheless remains the fact that no profession is as exempt from societal control as is the legal profession. Indeed, the rule of lawyers is intimately intertwined with the profession's self-regulatory status. Lawyers' self-regulatory power largely flows from the judiciary's seizure of control over the practice of law – what I have described as constitutional *putsches* to deprive state legislatures of their historic authority to regulate lawyers and to change the parameters of the civil justice system. State supreme courts effectuate exclusive control over the practice of law in concert with state bar associations and the American Bar Association (ABA). All but two state supreme courts have adopted ethical codes for lawyers that have been developed by the ABA. Thus, lawyers largely write the codes of ethics that purport to regulate lawyers, which courts mostly rubber stamp.[66]

Not surprisingly, the codes of ethics drafted by lawyers, ostensibly in the public interest, are intended to and do advance lawyers' interests. Consider the rule regulating lawyer disclosure of fraudulent conduct by a client when the lawyer learns that the client has used the lawyer's work to commit that fraud. This is what occurred in a decade-long, $225 million fraud, perpetrated by a computer leasing company called O.P.M. (Other People's Money). The scheme used phony computer leases and forged loan documents to create bogus collateral that was used to secure bank loans.[67] After learning of their client's fraud and extracting a promise from the client that it would cease defrauding banks, O.P.M.'s lawyers continued to help the company draft loan documents for three more months, during which time it obtained more than $70 million in loans. After receiving full payment for their services – which constituted a significant part of the firm's revenue – the firm quietly terminated the relationship without disclosing the fraud, which had, in fact, continued.[68]

At the time of this fraud, the prevailing ethics rule was that the lawyer could decide whether or not to make disclosure if she discovered the client was using her services to commit fraud. When a new code of ethics was drafted in 1983 – partly in response to the notoriety generated by the O.P.M. lawyers – the drafters changed the rule from "may" disclose to "must" disclose. When the proposed set of rules came before the ABA for adoption, however, a majority of delegates voted to change the proposed rule from "must" to "must *not*" disclose. The delegates resoundingly endorsed the view that confidentiality was a core value of the legal profession and had to be preserved, but underlying that professional value was professional self-interest. Both lawyers' fees and client fraud are maximized when the prevailing ethics rule is "must not" disclose.[69]

Professors Rick Abel and Deborah Rhode long ago argued that the ABA is inherently incapable of doing what it professes to do: adopt ethical rules that sublimate the parochial self-interested concerns of the bar to the public interest.[70] Many other commentators have decried the exclusive control exercised by the bar and judiciary over the practice of law.[71] Manifestations of that control include the ubiquitous "unauthorized practice of law" rules and statutes that are ostensibly enacted to protect consumers. In reality, they are intended to protect lawyers from competition that would benefit the public from businesses and insurance companies seeking to implement policies to foster early and less expensive resolution of accident claims.[72]

Just what is this "practice of law" that only lawyers can engage in? It is whatever judges say it is. The most common formulation is that it is the provision of services that require legal knowledge, skill, judgment, or ability.[73] In other words, the practice of law is what lawyers do. And what lawyers do is the practice of law. And if lawyers do it, then no one else may do it. This self-serving, circular definition is what enabled an Arkansas trial court to certify a class action accusing the Union Pacific Railroad of the unauthorized practice of law because the company is "practicing law" when it offers to settle claims directly with victims or their families before they have hired lawyers – an argument that was not rejected when the Arkansas Supreme Court overturned the certification of the class on procedural grounds.[74]

Lawyers' self-regulation also means that the fast and loose fee practice that Mary Corcoran fell victim to is a protected activity. Lawyers' codes of ethics all have a provision limiting fees to "reasonable amounts."

But as I have previously documented, the "reasonable fee" declaration is an essentially ritualistic incantation, designed to give an appearance of effective disciplinary enforcement of ethics rules, but is actually devoid of much substance. In fact, the reasonable fee invocation is nothing more than a ringing endorsement of the status quo, in which lawyers routinely charge and obtain substantial windfall fees in thousands of cases where there is no meaningful risk.[75] Even when clients initiate complaints before the authorities constituted with power by state supreme courts to discipline lawyers who violate ethical rules, these complaints virtually never result in disciplinary action.[76] Fleeced clients fare no better in the civil justice system as Mary Corcoran learned to her dismay.

The self-regulatory status of the American legal profession, secured by state supreme court edicts, and the consequences of that control are usefully contrasted with extensive reforms recently adopted in Britain. There, the British government directly intervened in the legal services marketplace, bringing the English legal profession's self-regulatory status to an end with passage of The Legal Services Act of 2007.[77] The law, which was enacted in response to widespread dissatisfaction with how lawyers and their professional bodies handled client complaints – provides unprecedented focus on consumer protection and redress to clients outside of revamped lawyer disciplinary schemes.[78] Two of the articulated goals of the legislative revamping were "protecting and promoting the interests of consumers" and "promoting competition in the provision of services."[79] To protect consumer interests, the legislation provided for a publicly accountable regulatory body, the Legal Services Board, composed of a majority of lay people appointed by the Lord Chancellor – usually an elected member of Parliament serving as the head of the Justice Ministry. Thus, regulation of the legal profession has been taken out of the hands of the bar and placed in a politically accountable body. To promote competition, the legislation opened up new avenues for the delivery of services to compete with lawyers and to allow lawyers to partner with other professionals to provide "one stop shopping" services – precisely the kind of integration that state supreme courts prohibit.[80]

The insularity and rigidity of state supreme court control over the practice of law creates many inefficiencies that burden businesses and society with higher costs.[81] Many efficient and cost-saving practices are banned simply because they pose an economic threat to lawyers. For example, computers can be programmed to provide wills for most Americans through interactive programs – which is why they are prohibited as the unauthorized practice of law. So too are ventures that the legal profession calls "multidisciplinary practice," which would allow businesses to combine strategic, engineering, accounting, and legal services to solve complex regulatory and planning problems. No matter how efficient that service would be, blatant lawyer self-interest dictates that unless lawyers head up the multidisciplinary venture and hire the others to provide a unified service, this business plan – now legitimated in England – is prohibited. For example, lawyers who specialize in drafting wills and trusts are prohibited from partnering with investment advisors so that the entity can provide clients with efficient one-stop wealth management services. Instead, this business plan can only be effectuated if lawyers run the show and hire the investment advisors. Gillian Hadfield of the USC Law School has written some of the most trenchant criticisms of lawyer self-regulation and the resultant costs imposed on society. She contends that "self-regulation stands as a tremendous barrier to innovation in legal markets and thus as a severe obstacle to the effort to develop legal mechanisms that meet the needs of a rapidly transforming, globally competitive economy."[82]

The nearly complete control exercised by the courts and the bar over the practice of law is also the greatest obstacle to curbing the inordinately high profits obtained by lawyers, which drives the expansion of the tort system. Wresting away some part of this control is a *sine qua non* for limiting lawyers' rent seeking – an activity that imposes high costs not only on consumers of legal services but also on the general economy.

At first blush, the task seems impossible. Control of the legal profession is securely ensconced in state courts that have the last word on the meaning of state constitutions and simply will not allow any dilution of the power they have appropriated. True, state constitutions can be amended, but tort lawyers wield sufficient power in state legislatures to block amendments that would dilute the power of state courts in maintaining collaborative enterprises with lawyers to elevate lawyers' interests.

Citizens of many of the western states have the constitutional power to bypass the legislature and, by initiative, propose a limited range of constitutional amendments. This is what the citizens of Arizona did when confronted with a decision by the bar and the Arizona Supreme Court to enact a tax on real estate transactions to benefit lawyers. In 1961, the Arizona Supreme Court, responding to a petition from the Arizona State Bar Association, declared that the practice of real estate brokers drafting the documents to be used in the purchase and sale of homes constituted the unauthorized practice of law.[83] In other words, the court held that anyone buying a house had to hire a lawyer to handle the transaction. In response, real estate brokers led a movement and gathered sufficient signatures to put the issue to a vote by the electorate. Torn between whom they liked least, Arizonans voted by a four-to-one margin to amend the state constitution to allow real estate brokers to fill out contracts used in real estate transactions.[84] In this battle of two of the most disliked professions, the realtors prevailed over the lawyers.

Unfortunately, there is little possibility that this direct action model can be applied outside of this precise context. Arizona real estate brokers were an organized group with a direct financial interest at stake. They had the motivation and the means to challenge lawyers and prevail. With the exception of doctors, insurance companies, and business groups, there are no other organized groups with the knowledge, interest, and means to mount a serious challenge to lawyers' rule by educating the public to understand the costs that it bears as a result of judicial control over the practice of law and lawyer self-regulation that stems from that control. This helps to explain why, without the backing of any such group, a 2007 Arizona initiative to move the authority to license lawyers from the state supreme court to its legislature failed. The proponents, citing the need for a "maximum level of competence, extreme honesty, unyielding integrity and respect for the law from those … licensed to practice law," maintained that the Arizona Supreme Court had failed "to provide that level of professionalism."[85]

Other groups that are capable of mounting and supporting such an initiative have been dissuaded or are disinterested.[86] Insurance companies are reluctant to take on the torts bar out of the (not unjustified) fear that the lawyers will turn the tables by enacting legislation or sponsoring initiatives that would increase insurers' exposure to tort liability. Though business interests support tort reforms that they see as specifically advancing their interests, they are typically uninterested in the kind of systemic reforms that I am advancing. Finally, two-thirds of the states do not have an initiative process for proposing amendments to state constitutions that bypass the legislature.[87]

With all avenues largely foreclosed, the only alternative is to bring political pressure for change at the state supreme court level. This is a tall order – perhaps an even insurmountable one. I can envision, however, that – over time – perhaps a decade – the heavy cost to the American economy of the self-regulating status of the bar will become so manifest that pressures for change will greatly intensify. Especially as other nations implement changes that allow for more efficiency in the practice of law, there will be more competition from outside the legal profession and a system of client redress that is outside the control of the bar. Professor Tom Morgan of the George Washington University Law School believes that this will disadvantage American lawyers who will have to increasingly compete with legal service providers from all over the world who are not hobbled by the American regulatory mechanisms. Even unauthorized practice of law prohibitions, he states, will fail to fully insulate American lawyers from competition because of globalization. Inevitably, he contends, the resulting economic pressures will result in state supreme courts being forced to yield some of their control.[88]

Pending that possibility, I offer another avenue for more timely change – one that emulates an available model. Most state supreme court judges are elected. Historically, these elections have been low-key affairs that largely escaped public notice. The noncontroversial nature of these elections changed in 1986, however, when an aroused electorate in a politically charged atmosphere unseated California Supreme Court Justice Rose Bird and two of her liberal colleagues for their voting records on criminal cases involving the death penalty.[89] Voters replaced them with conservative judges, who made the new court more amenable to dismantling the court's significant expansion of tort liability.[90]

The role of state supreme courts in expanding tort liability became a central focus when, in the early 1990s, business interests began to invest in state legislative races that, until that point, had been dominated by tort lawyers. After mounting expensive and effective public relations campaigns to establish the relationship between runaway jury verdicts and rising liability insurance rates, these interests succeeded in reversing tort lawyer dominance of legislatures. Business interest gains in the political process were often negated, however, when state supreme courts in Illinois, Ohio, and other states – dominated by tort lawyers – invalidated tort reforms.[91] Business interests responded to the challenge by investing heavily in state supreme courts races theretofore dominated by tort lawyers. After succeeding in changing the balance of power in the Texas Supreme Court in the mid-1990s, and reversing some of the great expansions of tort liability previously promulgated by the court, business interests saw the need for a more extended campaign. Led by the U.S. Chamber of Commerce and Steven Hantler – who worked in the legal department of Chrysler – similar successes were achieved in Alabama, Ohio, Michigan, Illinois, Mississippi, Wisconsin, and other states.[92]

Tort lawyers and their supporters, outgunned at the polls, sought to fight back by using rules regulating judicial conduct to preclude partisan campaigning for state court office. For example, Minnesota had a rule prohibiting candidates for judicial election from announcing their views on disputed legal and political issues. In a little heralded but critical decision, the conservative majority of the U.S. Supreme Court struck down this effort to restrict campaigning for judicial office by a 5–4 margin.[93]

The real issue before the Court – which it did not directly address – was tort reform.

If business interests want to challenge tort lawyer dominance of state supreme courts, they need to mount aggressive campaigns to unseat pro-tort lawyer justices in the thirty-nine states that elect judges. Most voters have little or no knowledge about candidates for these offices. Raising public awareness of expanded tort liability issues requires an extensive and expensive campaign.[94] Restricting challengers from raising tort reform issues is a way of maintaining the status quo.

Tort scholars have decried the politicization of state supreme court races. Professor George Brown of the Boston College Law School believes that the institution of the elected judiciary is "in crisis" and that the pressures of campaigning and the intensity of electioneering are damaging to the institution itself.[95] David E. Pozen also laments the fact that judicial elections have "gone wild" because forces seeking to benefit from highly politicized courts are "undermin[ing] the integrity of our democratic process."[96] The fallacy of these liberal screeds is that they are based on the conclusion that it is conservative business interests that have "politicized" state supreme court races. Politicization presumably means rendering decisions based on political rather than on legal bases. Before conservative business interests became engaged, tort-lawyer-dominated state supreme courts had already politicized the process by striking down legislative tort reforms that sought to roll back judicial expansions of the tort system. No doubt – depending on whose ox is being gored – some politicizations are good whereas others are bad. Is it good or bad politicization when (1) courts engage in a collaborative enterprise with lawyers to expand tort liability and strike down legislative tort reforms designed to roll back some of that expansion; or (2) when conservative business interests successfully challenge tort lawyer dominance of state supreme courts in order to contract tort liability?

Alas, the utility of this electoral model for changing the balance of power, which lawyer-judges have vested in the legal profession to one more congenial to the interests of consumers of legal services and society, is quite limited. Although conservative judges have upheld most legislative enactments rolling back expansions of tort liability, their decisions on client protection issues are mostly indistinguishable from those of the pro-tort lawyer-judges they replaced.

The task, then, is to make the issue of protection for consumers of legal services as visible and prominent a part of state judicial campaigns as conservative business interests have made of rolling back expanded tort liability. This is a daunting task but one deserving of effort. Educating the news media about how consumer and societal interests have been sublimated in favor of lawyers' interests is an essential starting point for refocusing the content of state supreme court election campaigns. To my knowledge, no candidate for state supreme court office has run a populist campaign, declaring herself a friend of consumers and an opponent of judicial bias favoring lawyers' interests. Is the public ready for such a candidate, running on a platform that endorses the creation of a structure outside of the control of the legal profession and the courts, to hear client complaints about lawyers, allowing nonlawyers to provide competing services to drive down prices, and approving partnerships between lawyers and other professionals to provide efficient "one stop shopping" services; and, for good measure, one that also supports adoption of the "early offer" and "Auto Choice" proposals discussed earlier in this chapter? A platform of such increased protections for clients, which would come at the expense of lawyers who profit from the judiciary's tilting the playing field in their direction, will almost certainly incur the opposition of the American Bar Association – the trade organization seeking to advance the financial and political interests of its members. Given the low esteem in which lawyers are held today,[97] however, that opposition could be turned into a political asset.

At the very beginning of this book, after describing the fate of Mary Corcoran, I posed the question: So how did we come to allow fee gouging by tort lawyers to become the law of the land? I believe I have answered that question and, at the same time, answered the question of whether there would be public support for a judicial candidate declaring herself in favor of leveling the playing field and changing the regime of self-governance. Under the new regime advocated by the candidate, drivers would be given the choice of whether to cut out the lawyers' share of their insurance premium and buy only the coverage they want; tort victims would have recourse outside the control of the legal profession when they are price-gouged by their lawyers, and, unlike Mary Corcoran, would have to pay only for the value that lawyers have added to their claims. Assuming the appropriate qualifications, I would vote for that candidate, and I believe that a majority of the electorate would as well.

NOTES

1. Paul H. Rubin et al., *Litigation versus legislation: Forum shopping by rent seekers*, 107 PUBLIC CHOICE 295, 303 (2001).
2. A fuller list of the standard tort reforms enacted by legislatures includes (1) shortening the time period in which to file a tort action in court; (2) capping the amount of damages for noneconomic losses, most notably, P&S as well as punitive damages, that can be awarded in a lawsuit; (3) limiting the liability for P&S when there are multiple defendants to the percentage of responsibility that the jury has assigned to each defendant to prevent a "deep pocket" defendant such as a city from having to pay 100% of a multimillion-dollar P&S award when the jury actually held that the city was only responsible for 1% of the injury to the defendant; (4) reversing the current prohibition in many jury trials against informing the jury that the plaintiff's medical insurance is reimbursing her for the medical expenses caused by the negligent injury and instead allowing such information to be disclosed to the jury; (5) requiring claimants in professional malpractice actions, such as medical malpractice, to file an affidavit of merit by a qualified professional verifying the merits of the claim; and (6) limiting the ability of out-of-state claimants from filing claims in "magnet" states where judges and juries have a close affinity with tort lawyers despite the fact that the places where such suits are filed have no connection with the injury to the plaintiff.
3. *See, e.g.,* Thomas D. Rowe Jr., *Predicting the Effects of Attorney Fee Shifting*, 47 LAW & CONTEMP. PROBS., Winter 1984, at 139; John A. Shannon Jr., *Let the Loser Pay Costs? That's 'English Rule,' Not American Way*, ARIZ. REPUBLIC, Sept. 24, 1993, at A22.
4. Marie Gryphon, Manhattan Inst., *Greater Justice, Lower Cost: How a "Loser Pays" Rule Would Improve the American Legal System*, CIV. JUST. REP. 11, at 4–5 (Dec. 2008) [hereinafter Gryphon, *Loser Pays*].

5. *See* Gryphon, *Loser Pays*, at 11.

6. *See* Herbert M. Kritzer, *"Loser Pays" Doesn't*, LEGAL AFF., Nov–Dec. 2005, at 20, 21; John F. Vargo, *The American Rule on Attorney Fee Allocation: The Injured Person's Access to Justice*, 42 AM. U. L. REV. 1567, 1609–10 (1993).

7. *See* Gryphon, *Loser Pays*, at 9.

8. Kong-Pin Chen & Jue-Shyan Wang, *Fee-Shifting Rules in Litigation with Contingency Fees*, 23 J.L. ECON. & ORG. 519, 522 (2007).

9. *See* RICHARD A. POSNER, LAW AND LEGAL THEORY IN THE UK AND USA 72 (1996). It is nonetheless interesting to note that a study of lawyers' fees in the Netherlands, where a change in the "loser pays" regime provided that it could apply to settled cases, found that lawyers' fees increased rather dramatically after that change. See Neils J. Phillipsen & Michael G. Faure, *Fees for Claim Settlement in the Field of Personal Injury: Empirical Evidence from the Netherlands*, 1 J. EUROPEAN TORT LAW 75 (2010).

10. Alaska is the only state with a virtually universal "loser pays" rule that provides for partial recovery of lawyers' fees. A comprehensive empirical analysis has concluded that the fee-shifting "seldom played a significant role in civil litigation." Susanne Di Pietro & Teresa W. Carns, *Alaska's English Rule: Attorney Fee Shifting in Civil Cases*, 13 ALASKA L. REV. 33, 77 (1996). This comprehensive study revealed ambiguous results but provides numerous indications that fee shifting does not produce the virtues proponents suggest. For example, Alaska's case filing rate did not substantially differ from states operating under the American Rule, though there were some variations in types of cases filed, which might be accounted for by other factors. *Id.* at 63–67. Additionally, Florida's "loser pays" statute, promoted by doctors and limited to the medical malpractice context, proved counterproductive because courts only awarded fees when doctors sued for malpractice lost but did not award fees when they prevailed. Florida's doctors ran up the white flag and succeeded in repealing the statute that they had successfully lobbied for. The legislation increased plaintiff success rates at trial, average jury awards, and out-of-court settlements; however, litigation (especially defense) expenses increased and the rule appears to have actually discouraged low-value but, high-merit suits. James W. Hughes & Edward A. Snyder, *Litigation and Settlement under the English and American Rules: Theory and Evidence*, 38 J.L. & ECON. 225, 243–46 (1995). Additionally, a major obstacle to the law's success was the inability of prevailing defendants to recover from insolvent plaintiffs. Philip Shuchman, *It Isn't that the Tort Lawyers Are So Right, It's Just that the Tort Reformers Are So Wrong*, 49 RUTGERS L. REV. 485, 537 (1997).

11. Many European countries with "loser pays" regimes and prohibitions on contingency fees have well-developed markets for legal insurance. *See* Gryphon, *Loser Pays*, at 18–19. Two kinds of insurance policies are available. Legal

expense insurance (LEI), which is purchased before potential claims arise, provides coverage against having to pay the winning party's legal fees. A plaintiff can also buy "after the event" insurance (ATE), which is done after filing suit to insure against the risk of having to pay the prevailing defendant's legal expenses. *See id.* at 16–17. English legal expense insurance allows successful claimants to recover their insurance premiums and also allows deferment of the premium payment until the conclusion of the litigation. *See* Richard Moorhead and Peter Hurst, *"Improving Access to Justice" Contingency Fees: A Study of their Operation in the United States of America,* Civil Justice Council, at 4 (Nov. 2008); *see also* Anthony Heyes et al., *Legal expenses insurance, risk aversion and litigation,* 24 INT'L REV. L. & ECON. 107 (2004) (finding, inter alia, that a higher level of legal expense insurance increases the plaintiff's negotiating leverage in settlement and increases the defendant's level of care).

12. *See supra* note 2.

13. *See* Editorial, *Bashing Lawyers,* N.Y. TIMES, Feb. 15, 1992, at A20. Traditional tort reform proposals are also criticized for being a blunderbuss approach; that is, capping P&S damages, for example, may appropriately limit damages in cases where a jury has been unduly influenced by the plaintiff's attorney into an unjustifiable level of P&S award, whereas the cap may unfairly penalize a litigant who has suffered a disastrous injury or been the victim of egregious conduct by a doctor. These objections could be met by more finely tuned sets of caps based on severity of injury, the long-term medical needs of the litigant, the degree of egregiousness of the doctor or hospital's negligence, and so forth.

14. *See* Peter Passell, *Windfall Fees in Injury Cases Under Assault,* N.Y. TIMES, Feb. 4, 1994, at A1.

15. *See* Curriculum Vitae of Lester Brickman (Feb. 2010) at 11–12, *available at* www.lesterbrickman.com.

16. For further detail, see LESTER BRICKMAN, MICHAEL HOROWITZ & JEFFREY O'CONNELL, RETHINKING CONTINGENCY FEES (1994); Michael Horowitz, *Making Ethics Real, Making Ethics Work: A Proposal for Contingency Fee Reform,* 44 EMORY L.J. 173, 207 (1995).

17. *See* Randall L. Kiser et al., *Let's Not Make A Deal: An Empirical Study of Decision Making in Unsuccessful Settlement Negotiations,* 5 J. EMPIRICAL LEGAL STUD. 551, 567 (2008); *see also* Jonathan D. Glater, *Study Finds Settling Is Better Than Going To Trial,* N.Y. TIMES, Aug. 7, 2008, at C1.

18. Amy Stevens, *Lawyers and Clients: Corporate Clients, Some Lawyers Differ on Litigation Reform,* WALL ST, J., Mar. 17, 1995, at B6.

19. Brickman, *Money Talks, supra,* Chapter 3, note 9, at 258 n.31.

20. JOINT ECONOMIC COMM., CHOICE IN AUTO INSURANCE: UPDATED SAVINGS ESTIMATES FOR AUTO CHOICE 4 fig.3 (2003) [hereinafter JOINT ECONOMIC REP.].

21. *See* JOINT ECONOMIC REP., at 7. The Joint Economic Committee Report, released in 2003, reports that the average savings per car would be $189. On average, each family owns two cars, and adjusted to 2008 dollars, this equals a savings of $219 per car and $438 per family. For conversion table, see http:// oregonstate.edu/cla/polisci/faculty-research/sahr/cv2008.pdf (last visited May 4, 2009).

22. *See* JOINT ECONOMIC REP., at 8.

23. Low-income drivers, who often can only afford to purchase liability-only insurance policies (not including comprehensive and collision coverage), but who nonetheless spend up to one-third of their income on auto insurance premiums, would benefit even more with a 37% decrease in insurance premiums. *See* JOINT ECONOMIC REP., at 8. A 1998 study of poor families with incomes below 50% of the poverty line found that one-third of their income goes to automobile insurance premiums. *Id.* at 5.

24. *See* JOINT ECONOMIC REP., at 7. The Joint Economic Committee Report, released in 2003, reports that the total savings, assuming a 100% switch to PIP-only coverage would be $47.7 billion. Adjusted to 2008 dollars, this equals $55.3 billion. For conversion table, see http://oregonstate.edu/cla/polisci/ faculty-research/sahr/cv2008.pdf (last visited May 4, 2009).

25. Steven P. Croley & Jon D. Hanson, *The Nonpecuniary Costs of Accidents: Pain-And-Suffering Damages in Tort Law*, 108 HARV. L. REV. 1787, 1863–67 (1995).

26. *See* JOINT ECONOMIC REP., at 8.

27. *See* Jennifer Preston, *New Jersey Tackles Geographical Limits For Auto Insurance*, N.Y. TIMES, Mar. 27, 1998, at B9 (stating that "voter anger over paying the highest auto insurance rates in the nation nearly cost ... [the incumbent New Jersey governor] a second term."); Joseph B. Treaster, *An Escalating Blame Game Ensues Over the High Price of Auto Insurance*, N.Y. TIMES, June 1, 2001, at B2.

28. *See* Stephanie Owings-Edward, *Choice Automobile Insurance: The Experience of Kentucky, New Jersey, and Pennsylvania*, 23 J. INS. REG. 25, 35 (2004). N.J. PERMANENT STATUTES, 39:6A-8.1(b) provides that "[i]f the named insured fails to elect, in writing, any of the tort options ... the named insured shall be deemed to elect the [limitation on lawsuit] option."

29. *See* Owings-Edward, *Choice Automobile Insurance*, at 35.

30. 75 PA. C.S.A., section 1705, requires insurance companies to send the insured a notice that provides in part: "If you wish to choose the 'limited tort' option ... you must sign this notice where indicated below and return it. If you do not sign and return this notice, you will be considered to have chosen the 'full tort' coverage ... and you will be charged the 'full tort' premium."

31. *See* JEFFREY O'CONNELL & CHRISTOPHER J. ROBINETTE, A RECIPE FOR Balanced REFORM 103 (2008). Pennsylvania's choice system was enacted on July 1, 1990,

and gives drivers the option of "full tort," which allows drivers to sue for P&S damages or "limited tort," which only allows drivers to sue for P&S damages in cases of serious injury such as death or permanent impairment and cases where the at-fault driver was drunk, uninsured, suicidal, or insured in another state. *See* Owings-Edwards, *Choice Automobile Insurance*, at 36.

32. *See* Chapter 15, § B(2).

33. The Auto Choice Reform Act was initially introduced in the Senate in 1996 by Senator Mitch McConnell of Kentucky and cosponsored by Senators Robert Dole of Kansas, Joseph Lieberman of Connecticut, and Patrick Moynihan of New York. *See* S.1860 104th Cong. (1996).

34. *See* S.625, H.R.2021 105th Cong. (1997).

35. *See* Chapter 14, § A.

36. The GM general counsel's position on "Auto Choice" was based on the assumption that tort lawyers were holding back some suits against the auto manufacturers because they already had a full plate suing drivers on behalf of other drivers. With their plate emptier because of "Auto Choice," they would increase litigation against the manufacturers. As explained in Chapter 2, however, the volume of tort litigation is a function of the profitability of litigation. When profits decline, fewer suits are filed. When profits increase, more suits are filed. "Auto Choice" would have cost tort lawyers billions of dollars in lost income. In response to this decrease in cash flow, tort lawyers would have brought fewer suits – not more as General Motors's counsel feared. *See* Letter from Lester Brickman to Thomas A. Gottschalk, June 28, 1996 (on file with author) (reviewing these arguments).

37. The Auto Choice Reform Act was last introduced into the Senate in 2004, sponsored by Senator John Cornyn of Texas and cosponsored by Senators John McCain of Arizona and Mitch McConnell of Kentucky. *See* S.2931, 108th Cong. (2004).

38. *See supra* Chapter 8, § C, text at notes 52–56.

39. Jeffrey O'Connell, *The Large Cost Savings and Other Advantages of a "Crimtorts" Approach to Medical Malpractice Claims*, 17 WIDENER L. J. 835, 839 (2008).

40. *See supra* Chapter 8, § C, note 56.

41. *See id*.

42. In an attempt to reconcile the benefits and shortcomings of a "loser pays" system, the Manhattan Institute has formulated perhaps the most detailed and carefully constructed proposal yet advanced. *See* Gryphon, *Loser Pays*, at 18–19. Under this plan, the losing party in a civil case would indemnify the prevailing party for costs of litigation and reasonable attorneys' fees, which would be set as the lesser of actual fees or 30% of the difference between the final judgment and the last offer of settlement. The proposal also requires the

plaintiff to file proof of ability to pay costs at the time of initiating the lawsuit. The authors of the Manhattan Institute report claim that the proposal would compensate winning litigants more fully; reduce the number of abusive lawsuits; ensure plaintiffs of modest means but strong cases access to the justice system; promote early and reasonable settlement; contain legal expense costs; and result in the development of a legal expenses insurance industry to facilitate meeting the requirement of reimbursing costs.

43. *Noble v. Williams*, 150 S.W. 507 (1912).

44. *See Cowdry v. Galveston, Houston, & Henderson R.R.*, 93 U.S. 352, 355 (1877).

45. *See id.; see also Trustees v. Greenough*, 105 U.S. 527, 532–33 (1881) ("[W]here one of many parties having a common interest in a trust fund, at his own expense takes proper proceedings to save it from destruction and to restore it to the purposes of the trust, he is entitled to reimbursement, either out of the fund itself, or by proportional contribution from those who accept the benefit of his efforts.").

46. 100 F. Supp.2d 1165 (N.D. Cal. 2000).

47. *Ghorbani v. Pacific Gas & Elec. Co. Group Life Ins.*, 100 F. Supp.2d 1165 (N.D. Cal. 2000).

48. *See* 29 U.S.C. § 1132(g)(1) (2000) (provides inter alia that "the court in its discretion may allow a reasonable attorney's fee and costs of action to either party").

49. As stated by Judge Walker: "When a contingent fee attorney brings a case under a statute with a bilateral fee-shifting provision ... he acquires a stake in a claim which, by statute, has both an upside and a downside. The latter is the possible claim for fees and costs of a prevailing defendant, counsel's liability for which must be viewed as part of the contingent fee bargain.

"In addition, the dominant role of counsel in the decision to bring a contingent fee case and in management of the case supports potential liability under ... [the statute]. Potential liability will, of course, affect the decision of the attorney to pursue the claim. But that is as it should be. A bilateral fee shifting provision signals legislative concern for prudent pursuit of litigation. An adverse fee award against unsuccessful contingent fee counsel, insofar as it promotes such prudence, is in keeping with the mandate of ... [the statute]." *Ghorbani*, 100 F. Supp.2d at 1167. Less than one year later, however, a different judge from the same court rejected Judge Walker's reasoning in a similar ERISA action denying the prevailing defendant's motion for attorneys' fees and costs from an unsuccessful plaintiff. *See Lessard v. Applied Risk Mgmt., Inc.*, 2001 WL 34033100, *4–5 (N.D. Cal. 2001).

50. *Ghorbani*, 100 F. Supp.2d at 1170. Other courts have also awarded attorneys' fees and costs to be paid by both the party and its counsel. *See, e.g., Baker v. Greater Kansas City Laborers Welfare Fund*, 716 F. Supp. 1229 (W.D. Mo.

1989); *Cowden v. Montgomery County Soc. for Cancer Control*, 653 F.Supp. 1072 (S.D.Ohio 1986).

51. For a summary of the case law and discussion of the policy reasons, see *In re Crescent City Estate, LLC et al. v. Draper et al.*, 588 F. 3d 822 (2009). It is notable that when the U.S. Supreme Court is so disposed, the term "party" becomes sufficiently expansible to achieve the Court's objective. *See Devlin v. Scardelletti*, 536 U.S. 1 (2002) (holding that whereas typically only "parties" to a final judgment could appeal the judgment and that whereas in class actions, only the representative ["named"] plaintiffs were considered parties, the U.S. Supreme Court nonetheless concluded that class members who filed objections to class action settlements should be considered as "parties" solely for the purpose of appealing settlements.)

52. *Smith v. J.M. Smuckers, Co.*, no. 03CH08522 (Ill. Cir. Ct. filed May 16, 2003, *noted in J.M. Smucker Co. v. Rudge*, 877 So. 2d 820, 821 (Fla. Dist. Ct. App. 2004). *See also* Sheila B. Scheuerman, *The Consumer Fraud Class Action: Reigning in Abuse by Requiring Plaintiffs to Allege Reliance as an Essential Element*, 43 Harv. J. Legis. 1 (2006).

53. *See Smucker's mistakes its spread, suit claims*, Arizona Daily Star, July 24, 2004, 2004 WLNR 11612584.

54. *See e.g.*, Docket Proceedings, *Neal Loeb v. J.M. Smucker Co.*, Case No. 2003CV002641 (Cir. Ct., Dane Cty., Wis. Oct. 14, 2004) ("[S]ettlement has been reached at the national level with counsel on this case signing off on that agreement."). An examination of the docket proceedings in the suits filed in Illinois, Wisconsin, and other states indicates that substantial litigation ensued, undoubtedly costing Smucker's hundreds of thousands, if not millions of dollars, in attorney fees. These suits illustrate how lawyers can use the legal system and the reluctance of judges to dismiss such suits at an early stage of the proceedings, to put enormous pressures on defendants to settle suits that lack a substantive basis.

55. *See* Transcript of Proceedings, at 9, 11–18, 23, 28, 49, 60, *Tyner v. Embarq Corp.*, Case No. 08CV10125 (Dist. Ct. Johnson City, Kan. Nov. 20, 2009).

56. *In re Warner Communications Securities Litigation*, 618 F. Supp. 735, 740 (S.D.N.Y. 1985).

57. Brief for Objectors – Appellants, at 7–8, *In re Bluetooth Headset Prods. Liab. Litig.*, Case No. 09–56683 (9th Cir. Apr. 26, 2010).

58. Order Granting Final Approval, *In re Bluetooth Headset Prods. Liab. Litig.*, Case No. CV 07-ML-1822-DSF (EX) (C.D. Cal. Sept. 8, 2009) [hereinafter Bluetooth Litigation] (citing to *Class Plaintiffs v. Seattle*, 955 F.2d 1268, 1276 (9th Cir. 1992)).

59. Civil Minutes – General at 5, Oct. 22, 2009, *Bluetooth* Litigation.

60. Quoted in Brief for Objectors – Appellants, *supra* at 21.

61. Civil Minutes-General, *supra* at 4.

62. *Cell Phone Termination Fee Case*, 180 Cal. App. 4th 1110 (2009).

63. *Id.* at 1126.

64. *Carrol v. Weill*, no. 0600 695/2006, 2007 WL 2175568 (N.Y. Supp.).

65. *Id.*

66. *See* Fred C. Zacharias & Bruce A. Green, *Rationalizing Judicial Regulation of Lawyers*, 70 Ohio St. L.J. 73, 92 (2009).

67. *See* Stuart Taylor Jr., *The O.P.M. Fraud: Report Faults Many*, N.Y. Times, Apr. 27, 1983, at D1.

68. *See id.*

69. Consider three legal regimes, which differ in only one respect. In one, the prevailing rule is that lawyers, on learning that their clients have used the lawyers' work to commit fraud, must disclose that fact. In the second regime, the rule is "may," and in the third regime, the rule is "must not" disclose. Now consider how these rules impact lawyers' fees. The value of a lawyer's services is maximized if the client can use those services to commit fraud and be assured that, even if the lawyer learns of the fraud, he cannot disclose it. Conversely, of the three regimes, a lawyer's services are worth least if, on discovery, the lawyer must disclose that the client has committed a fraud with the unwitting assistance of the lawyer. *See* Lester Brickman, *Keeping Quiet in the Face of Fraud*, L.A. Times, Mar. 12, 1992, at A11.

70. Richard L. Abel, *Why Does the ABA Promulgate Ethical Rules?*, 59 Tex. L. Rev. 639 (1981); Deborah L. Rhode, *Policing the Professional Monopoly: A Constitutional and Empirical Analysis of Unauthorized Practice Prohibitions*, 34 Stan L. Rev. 1 (1981); Model Rules of Prof'l Conduct, Preamble (2008).

71. *See, e.g.*, Gillian K. Hadfield, *Legal Barriers to Innovation: The Growing Economic Cost of Professional Control over Corporate Legal Markets*, 60 Stan. L. Rev. 1689 (2008).

72. Jonathan Macey notes that "legal self-regulation displays the typical self-interested behavior of a cartel without any of the concomitant benefits." Jonathan R. Macey, *Occupation Code 54110: Lawyers, Self-Regulation, and the Idea of a Profession*, 74 Fordham L. Rev. 1079, 1096 (2005).

73. Am. Bar Ass'n Task Force on the Model Definition of the Practice of Law, *Definition of the Practice of Law*, Sept. 18, 2002, *available at* http://www.aba-net.org/cpr/model-def.

74. For more discussion of this case, see the Introduction.

75. Brickman, *Disciplinary System*, *supra* Chapter 3, note 7, at 1344.

76. *Id.* at 1357–58.

77. Legal Services Act, 2007, c.29 (U.K.). *See* Paul D. Paton, *Multidisciplinary Practice Redux: Globalization, Core Values, and Reviving the MDP Debate in America*, 78 Fordham L. Rev. 2193, 2232–40 (2010).

78. Judith L. Maute, *Bar Associations, Self-Regulation and Consumer Protection: Wither Thou Goest?*, 2008 J. Prof'l Law. 53, 55, 75 (2008).

79. Legal Services Act of 2007, c. 29, pt. 1(1)(d)-(e) (U.K.).

80. Anthony E. Davis, *Regulation of the Legal Profession in the United State and the Future of Global Law Practice*, 19 Prof'l Law. 1 (2009).

81. For discussion of the costs imposed on businesses and society by lawyers' control over the practice of law, see Hadfield, *Legal Barriers to Innovation*, *supra*, at 127–39.

82. Gillian K. Hadfield, *Legal Barriers to Innovation*, 31 Regulation 14, 14 (2008).

83. *See State Bar of Ariz. v. Ariz. Land and Title Trust Co.*, 366 P.2d 1 (Ariz. 1961).

84. *See* Ariz. Const. art.XXVI, § 1; Jonathan Rose, *Unauthorized Practice of Law in Arizona*, 34 Ariz. St. L.J. 585, 588 (2002).

85. *See* Vesna Jaksic, *Some States Seek Changes in How Lawyers are Regulated*, Nat'l L.J., Jan. 21, 2008, at 16. In 2008, a South Carolina legislator introduced a constitutional amendment that would have similarly stripped that state's supreme court of its oversight of the legal profession. Although the proposed amendment generated considerable discussion, it, too, failed to pass. *See* Alex B. Long, *Attorney Deceit Statutes: Promoting Professionalism through Criminal Prosecutions and Treble Damages, available at* http://ssrn.com/abstract=1559238.

86. As for doctors, recall that even when they secured a constitutional amendment in Florida to lower the maximum fees that lawyers could charge in medical malpractice cases, the bar and the Florida Supreme Court gave lawyers permission to nullify that amendment. *See* Chapter 10.

87. Twenty-four states have the initiative process but only eighteen allow constitutional amendments by initiative. *See* Initiative & Referendum Process, Initiative & Referendum Institute at the University of Southern California, *available at* http://www.classroomlaw.org/documents/oregon_and_constitution/referendum_what_is.pdf (last visited June 1, 2009).

88. *See* Tom Morgan, *The Last Days of the American Lawyer, available at* http://ssrn.com/abstract=1543301, (Paper based on Thomas D. Morgan, The Vanishing Lawyer: The Ongoing Transformation of the U.S. Legal Profession [2010]).

89. *See* Kyle Graham, *Why Torts Die*, 35 Fla. St. U. L. Rev. 359, 379 (2008).

90. *See* Stephen D. Sugarman, *Judges as Tort Law Un-Makers: Recent California Experience with "New" Torts*, 49 De Paul L. Rev. 455 (1999).

91. *See* Chapter 10.

92. *See, e.g.*, Jonathan H. Adler & Christina M. Adler, *A More Modest Court: The Ohio Supreme Court's Newfound Judicial Restraint*, Fed. Soc. Whitepaper (Oct. 2008), *available at* http://www.fed-soc.org/doclib/20080929_OHWhitePaper.

pdf; Michael DeBow, *The Road Back from "Tort Hell": The Alabama Supreme Court 1994–2004*, Fed. Soc. Whitepaper (Oct. 2008), *available at* http://www. fed-soc.org/doclib/20070325_alabama2004.pdf.

93. *See Republican Party of Minn. v. White*, 536 U.S. 765 (2002).

94. As tort lawyers have stepped up their support of pro-tort-expansion judges and candidates in response to the campaigns run by business interests, the costs of these elections have skyrocketed. Adam Liptak, the legal affairs reporter for the *New York Times* (and now its U.S. Supreme Court reporter) has documented the substantial increases in the costs of these campaigns. Adam Liptak, *Rendering Justice, With One Eye on Re-election*, N.Y. TIMES, May 25, 2008, at A1; Adam Liptak, *Tilting the Scales?: The Ohio Experience; Campaign Cash Mirrors a High Court's Rulings*, N.Y. TIMES, Oct. 1, 2006, at A1; Adam Liptak, *Judicial Races in Several States Become Partisan Battlegrounds*, N.Y. TIMES, Oct. 24, 2004, at N1. The median amount raised in 2006 judicial campaigns was $243,910; the total raised was $34.4 million. JAMES SAMPLE ET AL., THE NEW POLITICS OF JUDICIAL ELECTIONS 2006, 15–16, *available at* www.justiceatstake. org. Some individual races, however, far exceeded the median. In a 2004 campaign in Illinois, two candidates raised $5 million; *See* Adam Liptak, *Judicial Races in Several States Become Partisan Battlegrounds*, N.Y. TIMES, Oct. 24, 2004, at N1. In 2006, three candidates for chief justice in Alabama raised $8.2 million. NEW POLITICS OF JUDICIAL ELECTIONS, at 15. The total raised that year by all Alabama state court judge candidates reached $13.4 million. NEW POLITICS OF JUDICIAL ELECTIONS, at 15.

95. *See* George D. Brown, *Political Judges And Popular Justice: A Conservative Victory or a Conservation Dilemma?* 49 WM. & MARY L. REV. 1543 (2008).

96. David E. Prozen, *The Irony of Judicial Elections*, 108 COLUM. L. REV. 265, 269, 307 (2008).

97. *See supra* Chapter 7, note 44.

Appendix A: A Critique of Alex Tabarrok

The Problem of Contingent Fees For Waiters

Alex Tabarrok has challenged the validity of my conclusion that tort lawyers' effective hourly rates have increased by more than 1,000 percent in real terms in the 1960–2002 period.[1] Using data for the *median* income of *all* lawyers in 2002 ($90,290) and the *mean* income of "deans, lawyers and judges" in 1960, Tabarrok concludes that "real income for lawyers has increased by only 59 percent since 1960."[2] On its face, this claimed increase of less than 1 percent a year in real terms flies in the face of data about real increases in tort claim values and the volume of tort litigation.

A close analysis of Tabarrok's methodology shows why he went so far off the track. First, he uses median rather than mean income. The imprecision this imports is illustrated by income data compiled by the 2000 U.S. Census, which shows that the mean income for lawyers in 1999 was nearly 50 percent more than the median.[3] This probably understates the disparity between the mean and the median because a segment of tort lawyers' annual incomes are in the multimillion-dollar range – many multiples of the median income level.

Second, Tabarrok used data on the annual earnings of *all* lawyers rather than tort lawyers. He justifies this use by arguing that "if lawyer salaries in one field were substantially larger than in another ... lawyers would switch fields."[4] Therefore, he concludes that the use of income for *all* lawyers is a reasonable substitute for tort lawyers' income because "[l]awyer salaries in different fields ... cannot depart from one another too much."[5] Balderdash. The Bureau of Labor Statistics reports, that "[s]alaries of experienced attorneys vary widely according to the type, size, and location of their employment."[6] Altman Weil, a leading authority on law firm structure and income data, reported that in 2002, average law firm income per lawyer for "plaintiffs' contingency" firms was $414,525; this was approximately 100 percent higher than the average firm income per lawyer for all firms, which was $208,490.[7]

Tabarrok has fallen prey to a form of economists' palsy, a condition that blinds them to empirical reality and substitutes a reliance on projections based on economic theory. His conclusion that lawyers' salaries for different practice fields cannot vary much because lawyers would then switch practice specialties and incomes would then be equalized ignores the substantial barriers in place to such movement and flies in the face of the fact that lawyers' incomes vary hugely. Some lawyers who specialize in class action and mass torts earn tens of millions of dollars annually. Despite the fact that there are many class action and mass tort wannabe lawyers, class action and mass tort lawyers' incomes have not declined because of a surge of lawyers switching fields. Similarly, lawyers in major law firms have incomes that far exceed average lawyers' incomes. Contrary to Tabarrok's conclusion based on economic theory, the ranks of major firm lawyers have not swelled as a consequence of lower-income lawyers leaving their practices in droves to enter the corporate field.

The most glaring defect in Tabarrok's data, however, is his critical reliance on highly imprecise data, indicating that the mean income of "deans, lawyers and judges" in 1960 (which he uses as a surrogate for tort lawyers' income) was $9,326 ($56,680 in 2002 dollars).[8] According to data published by the Treasury Department, however, tort lawyers' incomes in 1960 were about a third less than that amount.[9]

Tabarrok reasoned that because the *median* income of *all* lawyers in 2002 was $90,290 and the *mean* income of "deans, lawyers and judges" in 1960, in 2002 dollars, was $56,680 and tort lawyers' incomes were the same as all other lawyers' incomes, then the *mean* income of *tort* lawyers increased by only 59 percent in that time period. Given the number of errors in that calculation, which have a multiplicative effect when combined, it is not surprising that there is simply no data published by the Bureau of Labor Statistics, Altman & Weil, Tillinghast, or any other reputable source that lends the slightest credence to Tabarrok's calculation.

Tabarrok also advances an "economics for dummies" argument to counter my contention that the contingency fee market is not price competitive. He argues that waiters have many of the same characteristics as contingency fee lawyers: they are the "consummate contingent fee" recipients, receive uniform "fees" (tips), have an incentive to steer customers to higher-priced menu items thus maximizing the "recovery" of their principals and their own "fees" as well, and like tort lawyers do not engage in competitive fee advertising.[10] Yet everyone would regard the market for waiters as competitive. And, therefore, so too is the market for tort lawyers services.

Tabarrok's analogy is flawed because the relationship between waiters and restaurant customers is fundamentally different than the relationship between tort lawyers and clients. Many occupational groups such as realtors and insurance agents are paid commissions for their services, which are a percentage of their sales. Nonetheless, these practices are no more relevant to the practice of tort lawyers charging contingency fees against recoveries as that of waiters who receive tips that are a percentage of the check.

By contrast, there is no economic reason to expect waiters to depart from tipping norms (and how could they because waiters do not get to charge restaurant customers for their services). Waiters have no reason to compete in the market for restaurant customers. Whereas lawyers are employed by their clients, waiters are not employed by restaurant patrons but by restaurant owners. They do not control the customers they can service; the restaurants do. They do not set the tip percentage; the customers do. Moreover, customers chose a restaurant based in part on the price range of the entrées. Accordingly, they can exercise considerable control over the price of the meal and thus the amount of any tip based on a percentage of the meal check. Tort claimants, however, find it futile to shop around for lower-priced services because lawyers mostly maintain uniform pricing. Finally, waiters have no informational advantages over their customers (with the exception of how fresh the fish is) and hence no market power associated with those informational advantages. As a result, Tabarrok's analogy between lawyers and waiters, however amusing, is a bit like the proverbial bowl of soup served by the waiter: it has a fly in it.

In one respect, though, Tabarrok's comparison of the restaurant waiter with the contingency fee lawyer does have merit. Both employments generate conflicts of interest. A lawyer's incentive to minimize time and risk to maximize return may conflict with a client's interest in maximizing the lawyer's time and resulting settlement. Similarly, waiters, as Tabarrok notes, have an incentive to steer patrons to the highest-priced items on the menu to maximize the amount of their tip.[11] As with contingency fee lawyers, however, this self-interested behavior may be at odds with the interests of the restaurant owner because more expensive menu items such as Porterhouse steak and lobster are less profitable to restaurant owners. Instead, restaurant owners prefer that patrons select the less expensive items on the menu because these items usually have the highest mark-ups.[12]

Tabarrok also mistakenly asserts that I argue that the use of standard contingency fees is per se anticompetitive. I do not paint with such a broad brush. Indeed, I have acknowledged that uniform contingency fees do not, by themselves, establish the existence of noncompetitive pricing.[13] The thrust of my argument is that there are compelling economic reasons to expect lawyers to depart from the standard fee when confronted with a case that presents little risk and high reward and is likely to generate unearned windfall fees. If the market for lawyer services were competitive, lawyers would compete on price to obtain such lucrative cases. Although there are reasons for charging standard contingency fees in garden-variety tort cases, albeit at levels more commensurate with the "standard" risk level being assumed, the financial incentives for cutting fees in cases of no risk/large reward would overwhelm those reasons if the market for lawyer services were competitive. Yet we do not see competitive pricing in those cases.

Tabarrok and his coauthor, Professor Eric Helland, in *Two Cheers for Contingent Fees*,[14] a chapter in a book on American tort law from which Taborrok's article is adapted, advance a number of additional arguments regarding the effects of contingency fee financing of tort litigation. These arguments, like the summary version published in *The Green Bag*, demonstrate a fundamental lack of understanding of the dynamics, incentives, and economic considerations that apply to contingency fees. In this appendix, I address three of their arguments.

One argument they advance is that contingency fee caps enacted by states as part of tort reform measures intended to limit the volume of litigation are ineffective because lawyers respond by switching to hourly rates.[15] Tabarrok and Helland offer no empirical evidence to sustain this conclusion that they derive from economic theory.[16] Indeed, there is none – not even a scintilla. Most contingency fee lawyers refuse to even offer clients the opportunity to pay an hourly rate because this would significantly decrease their profits.[17]

Tabarrok and Helland state that they "have found no strong evidence that contingent fees harm the interest of clients."[18] Perhaps they should talk to Mary Corcoran. Apparently they do not consider that charging standard (and substantial) contingency fees in cases devoid of any realistic risk – a form of price gouging – harms the interests of clients.[19] By overcharging such clients, lawyers generate cash flow that enables them to accept riskier cases promising higher rewards.[20]

Tabarrok and Helland also argue that caps on contingency fees do not reduce tort awards, citing data indicating that "awards in the states that limit contingency fees are more than twice as high as in states without restrictions."[21] Rather than proving their contention, their data demonstrates the opposite. When contingency fees are capped, lawyers respond by declining to accept cases that would have been marginally profitable at 40 percent or 33⅓ percent contingency fee rates but which no longer appear to be profitable when rates are capped at 25 percent.

Thus, average tort awards in states that cap contingency fees are higher because lawyers in those states do not take lower value cases that they accepted before the fee caps were enacted. Fee caps thus drive up award averages but drive down the volume of litigation and the total amount of tort damages awarded. Tabarrok and Helland further argue that, when fees are capped, "lawyers [will] increase their reliance on hourly rates [and] will be more willing to take weaker cases."[22] Once again, the opposite is true. When fees are capped, lawyers are more selective in case selection and take only stronger cases.

Overall, Tabarrok and Helland fail to capture the critical economic relationship between contingency fees and tort litigation: The higher tort lawyers' effective hourly rates, the greater the amount of tort litigation; and conversely, the lower the effective hourly rate, the less the amount of tort litigation.[23] Caps on damages and contingency fees lower effective hourly rates and, as a result, lawyers decline to accept certain cases that they would have accepted in the absence of any caps because of lower profit projections.

NOTES

1. *See* Alex Tabarrok, *The Problem of Contingent Fees for Waiters*, 8 GREEN BAG 2d 377, 377 (2005) [hereinafter Tabarrok, *Waiters*].
2. *Id*. at 377.
3. U.S. CENSUS BUREAU, CENSUS 2000, PHC-T-33. EARNINGS DISTRIBUTION OF U.S. YEAR-ROUND FULL-TIME WORKERS BY OCCUPATION: 1999, *available at* http://www.census.gov/population/cen2000/phc-t33/tab01.pdf.
4. Tabarrok, *Waiters, supra* note 1, at 378.
5. *Id*.
6. BUREAU OF LABOR STATISTICS, U.S. DEPARTMENT OF LABOR, OCCUPATIONAL OUTLOOK HANDBOOK, 2004–05 EDITION, LAWYERS, *available at* www.bls.gov/oco/ocos053.htm. The Bureau indicates that the median starting salary of *all* lawyers six months after law school graduation was $60,000; for those in private practice, which includes all tort lawyers, it was $90,000, a 50% increase over *all* lawyers. *Id*. For experienced lawyers, the disparity between all lawyers and those in private practice is even greater.
7. ALTMAN WEIL, INC., SURVEY OF LAW FIRM ECONOMICS, (2002). The Altman Weil data directly contradicts Tabarrok's data, which is from Payscale.com,

a private online employee salary compiler. Payscale.com calculates that the median income for "personal injury & wrongful death" lawyers is $60,000, and the median income for "litigation & appeals" is $73,000; "corporate, business, mergers & acquisitions" is $85,000; "general" is $63,500; "real estate/construction/land use" is $65,000; "insurance law" is $70,000; "labor/employment/ERISA/benefits" is $75,000; and "family law" is $59,833.

8. Tabarrok, *Waiters, supra* note 1, at 378 (citing Edward N. Wolff, *Occupational Earnings Behavior and the Inequality of Earnings by Sex and Race in the United States*, 22 REV. INCOME & WEALTH 151, 151–66 [1976]).

9. U.S. TREASURY DEP'T, UNITED STATES BUSINESS TAX RETURNS CONTAINING STATISTICS OF INCOME, 1959–1960.

10. Tabarrok, *Waiters, supra* note 1, at 379–81.

11. *See* Tabarrok, *Waiters, supra* note 1, at 380 (suggesting that many waiters up-sell or suggestively sell the most expensive menu items because bigger bills lead to bigger tips).

12. *See* Jeff Grossman, *Writing the Recipe for a Restaurant*, N.Y. TIMES, Oct. 16, 2005, at WE 3.

13. *See* Brickman, *Contingent Fee Market, supra* Chapter 6, note 14.

14. *See* HELLAND & TABARROK, JUDGE AND JURY, Chapter 2, note 33.

15. *Id.* at 107–08.

16. Tabarrok's reliance on theory as a way of determining reality is reminiscent of the old joke about the economist who told his wife that he saw a $20 bill on the sidewalk on his way home from work but not did pick it up. When she asked why, he replied: if it were real, someone would have already picked it up.

17. For discussion of how the ABA elevated lawyers' self-interest over the interests of consumers of legal services by eliminating the ethical requirement that lawyers offer clients a choice of fee structures, see Lester Brickman, *The Continuing Assault on the Citadel of Fiduciary Protection: Ethics 2000's Revision of Model Rule 1.5*, 2003 U. ILL. L. REV. 1181 (2003) [hereinafter Brickman, *Continuing Assault*].

18. HELLAND & TABARROK, JUDGE AND JURY, Chapter 2, note 33, at 125.

19. *See* Brickman, *Effective Hourly Rates*, Introduction, note 4, at 657–61.

20. *Cf. Stuart v. Bayless*, 964 S.W. 2d 920 (Tex. 1998).

21. HELLAND & TABARROK, JUDGE AND JURY, Chapter 2, note 33, at 126.

22. *Id.* at 110.

23. This is why fee-shifting statutes are intended to and do increase the amount of litigation.

Appendix B: Calculating Tort Lawyers' Effective Hourly Rates in 1960

Although there is no data available indicating the average net income of contingency fee lawyers in 1960, a reasonable substitute is the average net income of sole practitioners in 1960. This substitute data should yield reasonably reliable equivalent data because (1) most contingency fee lawyers at that time were sole practitioners; (2) sole practitioner's incomes did not include the profit generated by associates as did law firm partners; and (3) the average net profit of a sole practitioner is a conservative substitute for the subclass of tort lawyers' incomes because tort lawyers "fared less well" income-wise than most other lawyers in 1960.[1]

The average net profit of a sole practitioner in 1960 was $7,080 (in 1960 dollars), which is 32 percent lower than Tabarrok's estimate of $9,326 (in 1960 dollars). This data is based on a compilation by the Treasury Department and is more precise data than the data that Tabarrok used, which was an estimate of the income of "deans, lawyers and judges" in 1960 ($9,326 in 1960 dollars). Using the Treasury Department-derived data and estimates of overhead and the number of hours worked, sole practitioners earned an effective hourly rate of $6.68 in 1960 dollars.

This conclusion is based on the following calculations. The average overhead for a sole practitioner in 1960 was 47 percent and can be calculated by using the following formula: Overhead = 1 − (Net Profit/Gross Profit). Accordingly, 1 − Net Profit ($877 million) / Business Receipts ($1,642 million) = 47 percent.[2] Whereas there is evidence that hourly rate lawyers in the early 1960s billed in the range of 1,200 to 2,000 hours per year,[3] Reginald Heber Smith, a leading expert on lawyers' incomes in that era, indicated that sole practitioners worked longer hours than hourly rate lawyers because of "insufficient income." According to Smith's estimation, sole practitioners worked an average of 2,000 hours per year.[4] Substituting $7,080 for net profit and 47 percent for overhead yields a gross profit of $13,359. Dividing the gross profit ($13,359) by the number of hours worked per year (2,000) yields an average hourly rate of $6.68 (in 1960 dollars). Although as indicated previously, tort lawyers earned less as a group than any other category in that time frame,[5] I have no substantial basis for estimating a lower hourly rate and so will use the average calculated hourly rate for all sole practitioners of $6.68 in 1960 dollars.

Contemporary data on hourly rates in the early 1960s mostly shows a range from $5 to $25 per hour.[6] Reports of median hourly rates for lawyers in various cities indicate a range of $10 to $30 per hour.[7] Taking into account that tort lawyers earned substantially less than other sub-groups of lawyers, these higher hourly rates are not inconsistent with my calculation of a much lower rate for tort lawyers. Finally, a brief survey of cases indicates that hourly rates in cases where lawyers' fees had to be approved by a court as "reasonable" or were contested ranged from $5 to $35 per hour.[8]

NOTES

1. *See* Robert I. Weil, Economic Facts for Lawyers; Resurvey Shows Dramatic Changes in Pennsylvania Practice, 6 LAW OFF. ECON. & MGMT. 373, 378 (1965) [hereinafter Weil, *Pennsylvania Practice*]; ("Plaintiff lawyers, a large group, fared less well [income-wise] on the whole" than attorneys practicing in other fields of law including "corporations," "probate, trust and wills," and "patent, trademark and copyright law.") *See also* Comm. on Econ. of the Bar, Benchmarks for Your Practice, 17 J. Mo. B. 13, 13 (1961) [hereinafter Benchmarks] (showing that nontimekeeping lawyers, which included tort lawyers, earned less on average than timekeeping lawyers); Samuel H. Morgan,

By Our Bootstraps – A Story of Economic Improvement, 49 ILL. B.J. 622, 626 (1960) [hereinafter Morgan, *By Our Bootstraps*].

2. *See supra* Cantor, *Ethics and Economics in Hourly Fees*, Chapter 2, note 35, at 953.

3. *See* Reginald Heber Smith, *Lawyers' Incomes: Illinois Institute Opens a New Era*, 46 A.B.A. J. 945, 948 (1960).

4. *Id.*

5. *See* Weil, *Pennsylvania Practice, supra* note 1; Benchmarks, *supra* note 1; Morgan, *By Our Bootstraps, supra* note 1.

6. *See, e.g.*, Barenbaum, *Attorney Fees*, Chapter 2, note 38, at 21, 28 tbl.1 (minimum fee schedules for office consultations across forty-seven states ranged from an hourly rate of $2 to $5). Other sources indicate that statewide fee schedules then in use set minimum hourly rates in the $12.50 to $20 range. *See, e.g.*, Cantor, *Ethics and Economics in Hourly Fees*, Chapter 2, note 35, at 951; Morgan, *supra* note 1, at 623. However, the higher hourly rates set forth in minimum fee schedules are not indicative of what lawyers actually charged, but instead were regarded as "charging the most traffic will bear." *See* Boughner, *Reasonable Fee Schedules*, Chapter 2, note 38, at 252.

7. *See, e.g.*, Weil, *Pennsylvania Practice, supra* note 1, at 379 ("median standard hourly rate reported in Allegheny County for 1965 is $25 per hour, except for partners who reported a median of $30 per hour. The median reported by Philadelphia sole practitioners, space sharers, and associates for 1965 is also $25 per hour."); Robert I. Weil, Economics Facts for Lawyers, 4 LAW OFF. ECON. & MGMT. 405, 407 (1964) ("Hourly rates [for New Jersey lawyers in 1963] range from $10 to $25 for office consultation, and are generally below those of comparable states.")

8. *See, e.g.*, *Pac. Gamble Robinson Co., v. Minneapolis & St. Louis Ry. Co.*, 134 F. Supp. 849, 853 (D. Minn. 1955) ($15 per hour was reasonable); *Cromwell Paper Co. v. Central States Paper and Bag Co.*, 162 N.E.2d 500, 502 (Ill. App. Ct. 1959) ($25 per hour); *Official Creditors' Comm. of Fox Mkts., Inc., v. Ely*, 337 F.2d 461 (9th Cir. 1964) (holding that $62 an hour is a reasonable fee imposed under section 241 of the Bankruptcy Act, and citing other cases finding rates of $18.50 an hour and $33 an hour as excessive, and $12 an hour and $5 an hour as reasonable).

Appendix C: Electronic Discovery and the Use of Contract Lawyers

To understand the scheme devised by class counsels in securities class actions to inflate their lodestars by hundreds of thousands of hours, we need to first set out the rudiments of the discovery process in class actions. Document review in securities class actions is typically not undertaken until a court first certifies that the putative class meets certain procedural requirements and denies the defendant's motion to dismiss the case because of the insufficiency of the complaint. Class certification and denial of the motion to dismiss are forthcoming in about 60 percent of all securities class actions filed; virtually all of these class actions are then settled because of the litigation dynamics discussed in Chapter 16.

As part of the dance leading up to settlement, class counsel has the power, under the Federal Rules of Civil Procedure,[1] to demand that the defendant produce a wide range of documents that may be relevant to the case, including e-mails, spreadsheets, reports, letters, photos, and any electronically stored communications or information. Defendants are required to respond to these discovery requests, though they may seek to contest their scope. Frequently, the search process is facilitated by the parties agreeing on key search terms and proposed Boolean search strings.[2] Most public companies in securities class actions hire outside law firms as soon as suit is filed to take over the defense of the action. The task of responding to the document request is especially daunting, costly, and disruptive for large and multinational companies.

These companies, or their outside law firms, often hire outside vendors to provide the necessary service.[3]

Increasingly, due to the huge volume of the documents and information demanded and the differing ways in which these are stored, parties invoke their right to obtain electronically stored information (ESI) in a usable form[4] – that is, in searchable electronic form rather than printed on paper. This allows the plaintiffs' law firms to use various electronic search methods to search word processed documents, e-mails, reports, spreadsheets, and so forth. Defendants may also prefer assembling the material by electronic searches because of the enormous cost of other forms of production.

Once the documents have been assembled, they are reviewed in a multistage process for relevance and to identify those documents that are privileged from disclosure because they contain confidential communications with the defendant's lawyers or because they are "work-product" – that is, materials prepared by or for the lawyers in preparation for defending the action. Depending on the case and the parties, documents may also be reviewed to determine if they involve sensitive business information, which would call for subjecting their production to a protective order that will maintain some degree of confidentiality.

In the initial document reviews, each document is coded so that it can be searched in a database. Coding is divided into two tasks. The first step, known as "objective coding" involves indicating the nature and reference number of the document, its author, recipients, date, subject, and other biographical data indicated on the face of the document. The second component of document review is "subjective coding" and involves what one software program template labels "attorney notes," which can include any notes on the relevancy of the document to the claims of the litigation or the privileged status of the document.[5] On the defense side, objective coding is mostly outsourced to a vendor. The vendor does an electronic search of documents, which are in "native format" and therefore are text-searchable. Native format refers to a file in its original format, meaning the format that an application normally reads and writes.[6] Examples of documents in native format include e-mails in Outlook and other documents in Word, PowerPoint, and Excel.[7]

Documents in native format are much easier to electronically code than documents not in native format. The latter include scanned documents, photocopies, and older PDF (Portable Document Format) documents. These cannot be searched electronically because a typical document scan stores an image of the document that can be viewed on the screen, but the computer does not recognize words on the document – to the computer, the image just appears as a collection of black and white dots (known as a bitmap).[8]

In recent years, optical character recognition (OCR) has been developed to convert hard-copy documents into searchable electronic documents.[9] OCR software translates the bitmap into digital text and creates a searchable full-text version of the document.[10] Using OCR software, law firms can convert thousands of pages into electronic documents relatively quickly and cheaply.[11] Once the electronic documents are created, they can be easily searched for keywords or phrases at a faster rate and significantly lower cost than manual searching.[12]

At the vendor level, to maintain cost-effectiveness, data processors and clerical personnel perform objective coding. If done by the law firm, the clerical personnel are usually paralegals. However, subjective coding, which involves some legal input as to relevancy and the privileged status of documents, is done by contract lawyers employed by the vendor or the law firm. These documentary searches and categorizations of relevance and privilege then go for a second cut, where they are examined by the associates in the law firm before the results are turned over to the class counsel. Additional reviews may also be necessary, depending on the complexities of the case.

Vendor's charges for their work varies considerably, depending on how extensive the search is and how many personnel are assigned to the task. A contract lawyer who worked for both plaintiff and defense firms reported that defense firms commonly outsourced the objective coding component of document review at $1.25 per document and hired contract attorneys only to determine the relevancy of each document.[13] It is likely that this price was being charged for paper (and thus imaged) documents. Electronic documents are less expensive, and vendors usually charge by the gigabyte rather than by the page.

NOTES

1. *See* FED. R. CIV. PRO. 26(f)(3)(C).
2. "Boolean uses keywords like *and* or *or* to find specific combinations. In more complex litigation, more sophisticated Boolean strings are often used with a fuzzy search technique, designed to account for spelling mistakes and word variations. Fuzzy search models attempt to refine a search beyond specific words, recognizing that words have multiple forms, so that even if search terms don't use the exact words, in a relevant document, the document might still be found." Jason Krouse, *In Search of the Perfect Search*, A.B.A. J., Apr. 2009, at 43. Other technologies include algebraic search, probabilistic search, alternative search, clustering, and concept and categorization.
3. For example, Kroll Ontrack states that it is available to "provide large-scale electronic and paper-based discovery and computer forensics services and software to help attorneys ... quickly, efficiently and cost-effectively recover, review, manage and produce information and documents." About Us, Ontrack Inview, Kroll, *available at* http://www.ontrackinview.com/aboutus (last visited Feb. 14, 2009). There are other similar providers.
4. *See* FED. R. CIV. PRO. 34(a)(1)(A).
5. *See* Supplemental Objection To Motion For Award Of Attorneys' Fees at ex.B, *Carlson v. Xerox Corp.*, No. 3:00-cv-1621 (D. Conn. Nov. 5, 2008).
6. *See* Shannon M. Curreri, *Developments in the Law: Defining "Document" in the Digital Landscape of Electronic Discovery*, 38 LOY. L.A. L. REV. 1541, 1548 n. 24 (2005); PCMag.com, Definition of Native Format, http://www.pcmag.com/encyclopedia_term/0,2542,t=native%20format&i=47655,00.asp# (last visited Feb. 23, 2009). There are several advantages to producing documents in native format during discovery. First, there are no additional processing charges for converting the documents into a different format (such as TIFF or PDF). Bruce A. Olson, eDiscovery: Everything You Need to Know About Review, TechnoLawyer Blog (Oct. 30, 2007), http://blog.technolawyer.com/2007/10/ediscovery-ev-2.html; Lexbe.com, e-Discovery Documents Production Formats: Native, TIFF and PDF, http://www.lexbe.com/hp/e-Discovery-production-formats-native-PDF-TIFF.aspx [hereinafter *Lexbe*] (last visited Feb. 23, 2009). Second, and perhaps most importantly, native files are searchable as is and thus don't encounter the problems with text errors found

with OCR. There are also many litigation support programs that allow native files to be stored in a central database for search and retrieval purposes. *See, e.g.*, CT Summation Produce Feature Glossary, Native Format, http://www.summation.com/Support/glossary.aspx (last visited Feb. 23, 2009). Further, some document formats are difficult to convert to other formats, and thus native format is the only practical way to view them. For example, Excel files may be difficult to view in other formats and any formulas or hidden text may not make the transition. *Lexbe, id.* Finally, native files can be easily altered, unlike a static image such as a TIFF or PDF. However, there are some draw-backs to production in native format, including the fact that Bates-stamping and redacting is difficult, if not impossible, for documents in native format. *See Lexbe, id.* Bates-stamping can be handled through including a Bates designation in the name of the file; however, this will not allow individual pages to be separately Bates-numbered. *Id.* As far as documents that require redacting, they are usually handled by converting to another format that can be redacted, such as PDF. *Id.*

7. To search these documents, it was necessary to have the software that was used to create the documents. Modern litigation support applications, however, allow most native file formats to be reviewed without installing the applications that created the file. *See* Courtney Barton, Do the New Federal Rules Require Production in Native File Format?, LexisNexis, http://law.lexisnexis.com/litigation-news/articles/article.aspx?groupid=EB5UKhAhqzA=&article=wulvHXFfx2u; *Lexbe, id.*

8. *See* Legal Scans, What is OCR, how does it work, and what should you expect from it?, http://www.legalscans.com/ocr.html (last visited Feb. 15, 2009); Sami Lais, *Quickstudy: Optical Character Recognition*, COMPUTERWORLD, July 29, 2002, *available at* http://www.computerworld.com/softwaretopics/software/apps/story/0,10801,73023,00.html

9. Although the technology is continually improving, OCR software is still not perfect at identifying the correct words from an image when the image is of poor quality. Examples in which the images are of poor quality include documents that have been faxed or photocopied multiple times. *See* STEPHEN V. RICE ET AL., OPTICAL CHARACTER RECOGNITION: AN ILLUSTRATED GUIDE TO THE FRONTIER 2 (1999) (Noting that "[a]ccuracies of 99% or more are routinely achieved on cleanly printed pages," but discussing several common problems that arise with OCR software, including imaging defects, similar-looking symbols, punctuation characters, and typographic features); Michael R. Arkfeld, *Technology & Law: Back to the Basics: Scanning, Images, OCR and Full Text*, 36 ARIZ. ATTORNEY 20 (1999) ("Depending on the type and format of the written documents, the conversion rate for documents can easily fluctuate between 70 and 99 percent accuracy per page."). The problem is most acute with handwritten

documents, which the OCR software may not read at all. Because of these potential problems, documents created using OCR software may have to be reviewed for accuracy by humans. *See* Legal Scans, What is OCR, how does it work, and what should you expect from it?, http://www.legalscans.com/ocr. html (last visited Feb. 15, 2009) ("[I]f the original documents were clean, laser printed pages, OCR should read 98+% of the words correctly ... If the original documents were faxes, or multi-generational photocopies, or were printed with a dot matrix printer, the success rate of OCR drops off quickly. These types of documents may only have a 60%–80% successful read."). Accordingly, these documents may require additional handling.

10. Fred Galves, *Where the Note-So-Wild Things Are: Computers in the Courtroom, the Federal Rules of Evidence, and the Need for Institutional Reform and More Judicial Acceptance*, 13 HARV. J. L, & TECH. 161, 195 (2000).

11. *See, e.g.*, LINDA L. EDWARDS, LAW OFFICE SKILLS 168 (2003) ("OCR programs can scan thousands of pages of text into a computer and are cheaper and hundreds of times faster than keyboard operators. Although OCR is not 100 percent accurate, its speed and financial savings are huge benefits.").

12. LegalScans, What is OCR, how does it work, and what should you expect from it?, http://www.legalscans.com/ocr.html (last visited Feb. 15, 2009) ("[The search] will find every page of every document where [the searched word] appears. The process may take some time, depending upon how many pages are to be searched, but no matter how many pages there are, there is no cost involved. No one has to dedicate any time to the process once it starts.").

13. *See* Letter from Phillip Crawford Jr., *In re Tyco Int'l., Ltd. Multidistrict Litigation*, No. 02-md-1335-PB, Doc. # 1161, 535 F.Supp.2d 249 (D. N.H. Oct. 31, 2007).

Appendix D: The HMO Litigation

Richard "Dickie" Scruggs, a leading mass tort lawyer, devised a scheme to extract substantial contingency fees from health maintenance organizations (HMOs).[1] Had his scheme fully succeeded, it would have forced the industry to abandon its business model, if not cease operation. He filed a class action against the country's HMOs, alleging a "'nationwide fraudulent scheme' to enroll members by promising quality health care and then denying needed services – all in the name of corporate profit."[2] As in the tobacco litigation, Scruggs had no intention to take the case to trial. Rather, he sought to shake down the HMOs for a substantial payment.[3]

In these suits,[4] Scruggs alleged that HMOs subjected managed care subscribers to a pattern of racketeering activity and breach of fiduciary duty under ERISA.[5] Further, he alleged that the subscribers had been defrauded into purchasing health care of lower value than promised because the HMOs had policies to reduce the amount of coverage – policies that were more restrictive than the disclosed "Medical Necessity Definition."[6] Although subscribers were told that treatment decisions would be determined by "medical necessity," he charged that the HMOs had "established a set of financial incentives for claims reviewers – including direct cash bonus payments – designed to encourage denial of claims without regard to the medical needs of patients."[7] Furthermore, Scruggs alleged that there were "risk-sharing" agreements with physicians "including without limitation so-called 'capitated payment' arrangements, that provide[d] financial incentives to treating physicians for not prescribing or recommending treatment."[8]

Scruggs' litigation strategy included a bald attempt to coerce a settlement by driving down the share prices of the HMOs[9] and appealing to financial analysts' and investors' self-interests to bring pressure on management to settle the claims. In fact, after the suits were announced, most of the managed care stocks tanked, losing billions of dollars in value as they plunged to half their 1999 highs.[10] The strategy was particularly threatening because the legal theories effectively made the HMO business plan an illegal and tortious act in and of itself.[11] Had a class been certified, the lawyers would likely have succeeded in mortally wounding or eliminating HMOs. Such an outcome would have resulted in a reversion to the health care system that existed before managed care[12] and an increase in the consumer health care costs of the very people (health care customers) in whose name the litigations were launched.[13] Ultimately, the court denied certification of the class (which would have numbered 145 million)[14] and dismissed most of the subscriber claims.[15]

NOTES

1. Traditionally, health care has operated on a "fee-for-service" model. *See* William N. Reed and Bradley W. Smith, *HMO Class Actions: How to Kill a Gnat With a Howitzer*, 69 Miss. L. J. 1181, 1181 (2000). A patient visits his doctor and the doctor renders the services he deems necessary for a price that is typically paid, in large measure, by the patient's insurer. *Id.; see also Pegram v. Herdrich*, 530 U.S. 211, 218 (2000). This system provides incentives to providers to overprescribe treatment, thus maximizing profits. Grant H. Morris, *Dissing Disclosure: Just What the Doctor Ordered*, 44 Ariz. L. Rev. 313, 344–45 (2002). If consumers of health care services had to substantially pay their own medical bills, they would certainly be more cautious in incurring costs.

   The managed care industry arose in response to health care costs rising from 5% of GNP in 1950 to 13% in 1990, with health insurance costs escalating at an annual rate of 15% to 20%. *Id.* at 345. HMOs, one popular form of managed care, operate by limiting the patient to a set of primary care physicians who agree to provide services at below-market rates and serve as gatekeepers, following strict guidelines with respect to providing additional treatments and referrals to specialists in order to prevent the excesses of the fee-for-service model. *Id.* at 346. In essence, HMOs lower the costs to subscribers by limiting choice to lower-cost providers and rationing the amount of health care dispensed presumably to what is necessary. *Pergam v. Herdrich*, 530 U.S. 211, 212 (2000) ("[I]nducement to ration care is the very point of any HMO scheme, and rationing necessarily raises some risks while reducing others"). HMOs, however, also have a financial incentive to reduce medical expenses to below what is medically necessary because such reductions redound to the benefit of the officers and shareholders of the HMOs.

2. *See* Adam Bryant, *Who's Afraid of Dickie Scruggs*, NEWSWEEK, Dec. 6, 1999, at 46; Allissa J. Rubin & Henry Weinstein, *5 Major HMOs Targeted in Class-Action Suits*, L.A. TIMES, Nov. 24, 1999, at A1 (reporting on suits filed against PacifiCare Health Systems Inc., Foundation Health Systems Inc., Cigna Healthcare, Prudential Health Care and Humana Inc.); *see also Lawyers Step Up Pressure Against HMOs*, LIABILITY WK., Nov. 29, 1999 *available at* 1999 WL 13960687 (same).

3. *See* Collin Levey, *Three Ways to Shake Down an HMO*, WALL ST. J., Jan. 3, 2000, at A19 ("Richard Scruggs hinted ... that he hopes these cases will never see the inside of a courtroom").

4. *In re Managed Care Litig.*, 150 F.Supp.2d 1330, 1334 (S.D. Fla. 2001); *see Panel Sends 50 H.M.O. Suits to One Judge*, N.Y. TIMES, Oct. 25, 2000, at C9; *see also REPAIR Team Strikes Again*, BUS. & HEALTH, Jan. 1, 2000, *available at* 2000 WLNR 1769754 (reporting on lawsuits filed in U.S. District Court in Hattiesburg, Miss., by a group of lawyers led by Dickie Scruggs).

5. Sharon King Donohue, *Health Care Quality Information Liability & Privilege*, 11 ANN. HEALTH L. 147, 153 (2002); *see also* Victor E. Schwartz et al., *Federal Courts Should Decide Interstate Class Actions: A Call for Federal Class Action Diversity Jurisdiction Reform*, 37 HARV. J. LEGIS. 483, 505–07 (2000) ("[T]he novel claims asserted in the HMO class actions are dependent on convincing a court to assume the role of regulator and to reject existing principles of law"). Similar claims were also filed on behalf of providers (doctors) alleging fraud under RICO through the use of automated client process systems. *In re Managed Care Litigation*, 430 F.Supp.2d 1336, 1340–41 (S.D. Fla. 2006). These claims actually survived longer than the subscriber claims but were also ultimately dismissed. *Id.*

6. Subscriber Track Consolidated Amended Complaint – Class Action at 5, *In re Humana Inc., Managed Care Litigation* MDL No. 1334, 150 F.Supp.3d 1330 (S.D. Fla. 2001) [hereinafter "Complaint"].

7. *Id.*

8. *Id*. at 37.

9. *See* Levey, *Three Ways to Shake Down an HMO, supra* note 3 ("[T]rial lawyers have sought to create a market selloff of managed care stocks in order to force out-of-court settlements.").

10. *See* Milo Geyelin, *Lawyer Seeks Support of Settlement With HMOs*, WALL ST. J., Nov. 22, 1999, at B2 (reporting that Scruggs "has been shuttling between Wall Street and Capitol Hill, trying to drum up support for a national settlement"); Schwartz, *supra* note 5, at 506 ("While Mr. Scruggs has claimed that his goal 'is not to simply shake a settlement out of the industry', he has counseled stock analysts and institutional investors about the potentially disastrous effect that class action litigation could have on prices of managed care stocks."); Levey, *Three Ways to Shake Down an HMO, supra* note 3 ("'If HMO investors were smart', [Scruggs] said recently, 'they'd lean on their companies to see if we can work something out'.").

11. As George Priest put it, "The basic thesis of these lawsuits is that to apply cost structures to care creates incentives that are inappropriate and therefore constitute fraud." Quoted in Levey, *Three Ways to Shake Down an HMO, supra* note 3. As put plainly by a *Wall Street Journal* reporter, "if you are an HMO, you're guilty. Case closed." *Id*.

12. Bryce A. Jenson, *From Tobacco to Health Care and Beyond – A Critique of Lawsuits Targeting Unpopular Industries*, 86 CORNELL L. REV. 1334, 1336–37 ("A plaintiff victory would thus be truly ironic because the removal of incentives that keep doctors from over treating their patients will return Americans to the system of health care that they rejected just twenty years ago.").

13. Jason A. Glodt, *Watch Out HMO: The Future of Patients' Rights Will Soon Be Determined*, 45 S.D. L. REV. 640, 654 (2000) (predicting an increase in premiums, resulting in Americans having to forgo health care and possibly returning to the high-cost situation that gave birth to the managed care system in the first place).

14. *In re Managed Care Litigation*, 209 F.R.D. 678 (S.D. Fla. 2002) (denying certification of the class for a lack of predominance of common issues of law and fact and manageability).

15. *In re Managed Care Litigation*, 150 F.Supp.2d 1330, 1347 (S.D. Fla. 2001) (finding that "the pleadings are imprecise with respect to what dates, times and places the alleged fraudulent misrepresentations were made to plaintiffs," and dismissing all but one of the subscriber claims).

Appendix E: The GM "Side Saddle" Truck Litigation

The (Short-Lived) Triumph of Litigation Over the Regulatory Process

In *Moseley v. General Motors Corp.*,[1] a case involving a death that allegedly resulted from a truck with a side-mounted gas tank outside the frame rails, a jury awarded $105 million to the plaintiff – $101 million of that award was for punitive damages. The plaintiffs' attorney had urged the jury to grant punitive damages of $100 million, $20 for each such truck on the road, to force GM to recall these five million trucks. In closing arguments, he told the jury: "We want it recalled and we want a punitive damage verdict that makes it virtually impossible not to recall it." The jurors agreed: "I hope they'll read this verdict and make it right. They need to recall the trucks," said one juror. "We added the extra million to let General Motors know how strongly we felt," said another.[2]

The Georgia Court of Appeals later overturned this verdict citing a number of instances of reversible error, including (1) plaintiff's counsel repeatedly breached the trial court's ruling on GM's motion *in limine* to exclude evidence of other cases involving GM pickup trucks and fuel tank fires by making numerous references to the other cases during the trial without first establishing the "substantial similarity" of the cases; (2) the trial court improperly allowed the jury to hear testimony regarding the redesign of the truck during the negligence phase of the trial; (3) the trial court improperly allowed in evidence of a pending NHTSA investigation (discussed hereinafter); (4) the trial court improperly denied GM's request for jury instruction on the difference between the "clear and convincing evidence" standard of proof required for punitive damages and the "preponderance of the evidence" standard for compensatory damages; and (5) the trial court improperly allowed evidence on punitive damages to influence and inflame the jury's determination of compensatory damages.[3]

Although the judgment was reversed, it is nonetheless useful to compare the outcome of the regulatory process with the tort system outcome had the case not been reversed – an outcome that may well have led General Motors to recall the truck.

Authority to recall a motor vehicle is vested in the National Highway Traffic Safety Administration (NHTSA) and the Secretary of Transportation.[4] Any decision reached by the Administration may be appealed; 49 U.S.C., section 30161 provides that

> [a] person adversely affected by an order prescribing a motor vehicle safety standard under this chapter may apply for review of the order by filing a petition for review in the court of appeals of the United States for the circuit in which the person resides or has its principal place of business.[5]

The NHTSA and the Secretary of Transportation had been advised by the Justice Department, which would have had to defend an NHTSA mandatory recall order in court, that GM would likely prevail in a suit to stop the recall. The Justice Department lawyers were swayed by three GM arguments against the recall: (1) the trucks have significantly lower crash fatality rates than many vehicles, including smaller trucks and cars; (2) the government cannot recall vehicles that complied with federal safety standards; and (3) there is little evidence that the fuel tanks leak excessively in crashes at less than forty miles per hour.[6] On October 17, 1994, however, the Secretary of Transportation decided to pursue a recall. He announced his finding that "the increased safety risk due to post-crash fires in the subject vehicles is unreasonable" and as a result made an initial determination that "pursuant to 49 U.S.C. § 30118(a) ... the subject vehicles contain a defect that relates to motor vehicle safety."[7] In making this determination, the Secretary of Transportation overruled the advice of both the Justice Department lawyers discussed previously and the technical experts at the NHTSA's Office of Defects Investigation, who advised the Secretary after extensive testing that the trucks did not pose an "unreasonable risk," nor did the trucks fail to comply with federal motor vehicle safety standard No. 301, "Fuel System Integrity."[8]

Shortly after announcing his initial decision, however, the Secretary of Transportation agreed to withdraw his finding of "unreasonable risk" and abandon the recall effort in exchange for GM's promise to contribute $51.3 million to Transportation Department motor vehicle safety programs (in cash and noncash in-kind contributions, mostly tax deductible).[9] In announcing the withdrawal of his decision to seek a recall, the Secretary conceded the strength of GM's position in a suit to prevent the recall. In a statement, the Secretary commented that his alternatives were "to close the case with no public benefit or to proceed with a forced recall, which would have involved years of litigation, an uncertain outcome, and prevented few, if any, deaths."[10]

Procedurally, GM would have had ample opportunity to defend a mandatory recall. In addition to *de novo* judicial review of a recall order, pursuant to 49 C.F.R., section 554.10,[11] GM would have been entitled to defend itself at public hearings to be held by the Secretary of Transportation prior to the issuance of a recall order. Furthermore, if the case had proceeded to trial, GM would have been able to call government employees who advised the Secretary of Transportation against a mandatory recall to so testify.[12] GM's position was also supported by the fact that the trucks complied with all applicable federal safety standards both when manufactured as well as those applicable today.[13] This fact would likely have left the government with only an untested legal argument on which to proceed – that a manufacturer's knowledge of a safety problem can make the risks "unreasonable."

Moreover, the Secretary's theory was so inclusive that it would support recall of virtually any vehicle because all vehicles are less safe in some aspect than comparable vehicles and this "less safe" aspect would be or become known to the manufacturer. The Secretary of Transportation's decision to seek a recall of the trucks would also have been frustrated by the fact that the eight-year statute of limitations on recalls would nearly be up by the time he made a final decision; GM would have been legally obligated to recall perhaps only 200,000 of the 9.2 million 1973–1987 trucks.[14] Finally, although the average resale prices of the GM trucks declined at about a 3 percent greater rate than that of comparable Ford and Chrysler trucks in a six-month period in 1994, GM trucks were still worth more than the comparable Chrysler models, which is indicative of how the market evaluated the alleged "safety defect."[15]

In contrast to the numerous procedural and substantive protections afforded to GM under the statutory scheme, and the market's response in its favor, a jury egged on by a profit-seeking lawyer and a judge strongly favoring the plaintiff essentially abrogated to themselves the effective authority to circumvent the regulatory and market processes. Although the jury could not directly order the truck off the road, they did award a verdict effectively constituting a functional equivalent of what the Secretary of Transportation ultimately decided he could not do through the processes established by Congress.

NOTES

1. Case No. 90V6276 (State Ct., Fulton Co., Ga. 1993).
2. Billy Bowles, *GM Vows to Fight $105 Million Unsafe Truck Verdict*, REUTERS, Feb. 5, 1993.
3. *General Motors v. Moseley*, 447 S.E.2d 302 (G.A. 1994).
4. *See* Recodification of Title 49, United States Code, Pub. L. No. 103–272, 108 Stat. 745 (1994) (codified as amended at 49 U.S.C. §§ 30101–30169 [2006]); *see also* 49 C.F.R § 1.50.
5. 49 U.S.C. § 30161 (2006).
6. *See* Bryan Gruley, *Case for Recalling G.M. Pickups Deemed Weak*, DETROIT NEWS, June 3, 1994, at D1.
7. General Motors Pickup Truck Defect Investigation, 59 Fed. Reg. 54025, (Dep't Trans. 1994) (notice of initial decision and public meeting).
8. *Id.*; *See* 49 C.F.R. § 571.301.

9. *See* Daniel Pearl and Gabriella Stern, *Driving a Bargain: How G.M. Managed to Wring Pickup Pact and Keep on Truckin'*, WALL ST. J., Dec. 5, 1994, at A1.

10. *See* James Bennet, *U.S. and G.M. End Truck Case Without Recall*, N.Y. TIMES, Dec. 3, 1994, at A1.

11. *See* 49 U.S.C. § 30161 (2006).

12. *See* Barry Meier, *G.M. Asks U.S. to Drop Hearing on Truck Safety*, N.Y. TIMES, Nov. 2, 1994, at A14.

13. *See* General Motors Pickup Truck Defect Investigation, 59 Fed. Reg. 54025, (Dep't Trans. 1994) (Engineering Analysis Rep-Exec. Summary).

14. *See* Max Gates, *The C/K Battle: A Litmus Test For Recalls?: Public Hearing Puts GM On Trial*, AUTOMOTIVE NEWS, Nov. 28, 1994, at 3.

15. *See* James Bennet, *U.S. and G.M. End Truck Case Without Recall*, N.Y. TIMES, Dec. 3, 1994, at A1.

Appendix F: Modern Class Actions Undermine Democratic Precepts

Professor Martin Redish of the Northwestern Law School argues that "in all too many cases, the modern class action has undermined the foundational precepts of American democracy."[1] This is so because a purportedly procedural device has been conscripted by class action lawyers for use as a means of securing bounties without the legitimacy of substantive authorization. He explains that the class action is a procedural device that allows aggregation of *existing* individual private rights created by substantive law. But this procedural rule allowing for the creation of class actions, in and of itself, is not a substantive law. The class action

> was never designed to serve as a free-standing legal device for the purpose of "doing justice," nor is it a mechanism intended to serve as a roving policeman of corporate misdeeds or as a mechanism by which to redistribute wealth. Both its structure and description, rather, make clear that it is nothing more than an elaborate procedural device designed to facilitate the enforcement of pre-existing substantive law ... If no pre-existing substantive law vests a cause of action in plaintiff class members, they cannot bring a class action suit.[2]

Nonetheless, scholars wrongly assume that the class action procedure itself provides a freestanding check on illegal corporate actions. It is the underlying substantive law – not the procedural rule – that determines whether the corporate action in question is illegal.

Redish goes on to explain that when government wishes to deter or punish certain behavior, it has a number of remedial options, including criminal enforcement, civil penalties, administrative regulation, and private enforcement. The modern-day class action, however, "permits the transformation of the remedial enforcement model expressly adopted in the underlying substantive law from a victim's damage award structure into an entirely distinct form not contemplated in the underlying substantive law."[3]

To illustrate his point, Redish compares the class action lawyer to the bounty hunter of the Old West. A critical difference that he points out is that the bounty hunter "furthered the public interest not by redistributing illegally held wealth ... but rather by apprehending those who threatened the public peace."[4] The closest modern-day legal equivalent of the bounty hunter is the *qui tam* action.[5] This statute gives whistle-blowers the right to bring suit against persons who have knowingly defrauded the government even though the whistle-blower has not suffered any harm as a consequence of that behavior.[6] A percentage of the recovery provides the incentive for bringing the action. He uses *qui tam* actions to illuminate the murky legal underpinning of the modern class action. *Qui tam* actions "have been explicitly authorized by congressional statute; class action bounty actions have not."[7] Redish elaborates that class actions are

> disguised bounty hunter actions [that] have never been authorized by the underlying substantive law that such actions purport to enforce. In effect, then, these actions constitute a form of procedural shell game, in which a procedural device that has been designed to do nothing more than facilitate the enforcement of the substantive law's authorization of private damage suits transform that private remedial model into a qualitatively different form of remedy that was never part of that substantive law. If the substantive law is to authorize a bounty hunter remedial model as a supplement to or replacement for the pre-existing private damage remedy, the change may not properly be effected through the operation of a procedural device such as Rule 23 [which authorizes class actions]. Such a dramatic modification of the substantive law through resort to an avowedly procedural device

contravenes the fundamental democratic notions of representation and accountability, because the process effectively disenfranchises the electorate.[8]

He concludes that when the class action device substitutes for substantive law,

controlling substantive law is not transformed through the democratic process of legislative amendment, where the electorate may measure its chosen representatives by how they voted on the proposed revisions for existing law. Rather, this democratic alteration in governing substantive law arises from, essentially, a form of indirection and subterfuge, by use of a procedural device whose sole legitimate function is the considerably more modest one of implementing and facilitating the enforcement of existing substantive law.[9]

NOTES

1. *See* Martin H. Redish, *Class Actions and the Democratic Difficulty: Rethinking the Intersection of Private Litigation and Public Goals*, 2003 U. CHI. LEGAL F. 71, 73 (2003) [hereinafter Redish, *Democratic Difficulty*]. Professor Redish has followed up his article with a book, MARTIN H. REDISH, WHOLESALE JUSTICE (2009).
2. Redish, *Democratic Difficulty*, at 74 (footnotes omitted). Professor Richard Epstein has taken this argument an additional step. He notes that the "aggregation of claims [through class actions] has resulted in a powerful distortion of the substantive law in ways that systematically favor plaintiffs over defendants." Richard Epstein, *Class Actions: Aggregation, Amplification and Distortion* (John M. Olin Law & Econ. Working Paper No. 182, 35–36 2003), *available at* http://ssrn.com/abstract=392520.
3. Redish, *Democratic Difficulty*, *supra* note 1, at 77.
4. *Id.* at 80–81.
5. *Id.* at 81.
6. 31 U.S.C. §§ 3729, 3730 (b) (2006).
7. Redish, *Democratic Difficulty*, *supra* note 1, at 81.
8. *Id.* at 81–82.
9. *Id.* at 73–74.

Appendix G: Other Ways Lawyers Game Class Action Fees

1. The End Run Around the "No Multiplier" Rule in Fee-Shifting Cases

If a class action is based on a federal statute to which a fee-shifting provision applies and the result is a verdict in favor of the class, the defendant is responsible for the class's attorney fee. That fee, which is then typically awarded to the class counsel, is based on the lodestar. As noted, unlike common-fund cases, multipliers of the lodestar are virtually never allowed in these fee-shifting cases.[1] This limitation, however, has been held not to apply to cases *initiated* under statutes with fee-shifting provisions and then *settled* through the creation of a common fund.[2] In such cases, lawyers are permitted to seek a percentage of the common fund created for the class. There is a simple explanation why lawyers who have strong statutory violation cases do not litigate these cases to judgment but choose to settle them by the creation of a common fund: A percentage fee awarded under common-fund principles will often amount to multiples of the unaugmented lodestar that would be awarded if the case were successfully litigated.

Because of the high probability that lawyers will settle a case to obtain a higher fee than if they litigated it to a conclusion, courts purport to subject fee applications in this context to "thorough judicial review."[3] Indeed, courts repeatedly assert that in class actions, they are the guardians of the class – assiduous protectors of the fiduciary rights of class members. Under centuries-old fiduciary principles, lawyers must advance clients' interests as the clients would define them if the clients were well-informed.[4] The requirement that lawyers act in a non-self-interested fashion, however, has largely been gutted by courts' approval of the loophole in the prohibition against fee multipliers. Class members are further shorted in these circumstances because if the litigation were successfully concluded, the class would have been eligible for an award of reasonable attorney fees on top of the damage award. Instead, the case is settled to enable the attorney to take a larger part of the class's recovery.

2. The Separately Paid Fee Ploy

Class action lawyers also increase their fees by structuring common-fund settlements so that rather than the defendants paying the entire settlement amount to class and class counsel then requesting the court to approve a percentage of that settlement as its fee, the defendants agree to directly pay a fee to the class counsel. Under this arrangement, class counsel negotiates an initial payment – which is the class's recovery – and an additional separate payment to the class counsel. Though this fee must still be approved by the court, as part of the arrangement the defendant agrees to a clear-sailing provision, binding her not to oppose court approval of the fee. In addition, the agreement with the defendant provides that, unlike a reduction in the fee request in a common-fund situation, which then benefits the class, any court-ordered reduction of the fee reverts *only* to the defendant – a provision demanded by class counsel and acceded to by the defendant.

This arrangement has two purposes: (1) to inflate the fee at the class's expense; and (2) to reduce the court's incentive to carefully scrutinize the fee for unreasonableness, because any reduction *only* benefits the defendant. This worked like a charm in the *Bluetooth* litigation (described in the Conclusion, Section D) where the U.S. District Court judge determined that it was not worthwhile to scrutinize the fee request because "any amount not awarded by the court would be retained by the defendants rather than benefiting class members."[5] Even Professor Charles Silver, who has championed the cause of tort lawyers and class counsel, acknowledges that this fee arrangement is "a strategic effort to insulate a fee award from attack."[6] Here, class lawyers are entering into settlements designed to elevate their financial interests by maximizing their fee at the expense of the class that they purport to represent. This self-interested strategy is a clear breach of class counsel's fiduciary obligation not to allow their own financial interests to take precedence over obligations to their client – the class.[7]

Class counsel's retort is that this arrangement benefits the class because the fee does not come out of the settlement but is separately paid by the defendant. However superficially appealing, in reality, this rationale is simply false. Defendants are concerned with the total cost of settling a class action. Any fee that a defendant agrees to pay directly to class counsel is an amount it would have been willing to include as part of the payment to the class.[8] It is a virtual certainty that the price the defendant will demand for agreeing to pay a fee directly to class counsel, on top of the settlement, will be subtracted from the amount it was willing to pay to the class. Moreover, because the fee thus negotiated is likely to be higher than the amount that class counsel could reasonably seek by way of a lodestar or percentage of the common fund, the net effect of the higher fee is to diminish the recovery that the class would have received if a lodestar or percentage fee were paid from the common fund. In addition, it is likely that in exchange for agreeing to such a fee structure, the defendant has extracted as a benefit a diminishment in the cost of the settlement to be paid to the class.

Courts have recognized that "such an agreement has the potential to enable a defendant to pay class counsel excessive fees and costs, in exchange for counsel accepting an unfair settlement on behalf of the class."[9] Cautionary notes are an insufficient response, however. As argued in a letter I submitted to the American Bar Association (ABA) Standing Committee on Ethics and Professional Responsibility requesting an advisory ethics opinion on the propriety of these fee schemes – which a score of prominent law professors signed onto – negotiating a settlement that elevates a lawyer's financial interests over that of the class is a breach of the lawyer's fiduciary obligation to the client not to elevate the lawyer's financial interests over that of the client and is unethical as well, no matter how much money is at stake for the lawyer. Had the ABA Committee lived up to its own professional responsibility, it would have issued an opinion articulating a brightline standard that it is both per se unethical and a violation of the fiduciary duty that class counsel owes to the class to negotiate a settlement that in any way compromises the right of the class to recover fees deemed excessive by a court or inhibits a court's propensity to review the reasonableness of the fee request.[10] Unfortunately, but not surprisingly, the ABA Ethics Committee decided to duck the issue,[11] once again illustrating that when "money talks, ethics walks."

An even bolder if not chilling illustration of the power of money coupled with the judicial bias in favor of lawyers' interests is the recent decision of the U.S. Court of Appeals for the Ninth Circuit prohibiting a class member from appealing a fee award because any reduction would only benefit the defendant.[12] In that case, a class member ("objector") appealed a fee award of $1.5 million payable directly by the defendants. Class counsel argued that the objector had no legal right to appeal the fee award because, even if the court reduced the fee, neither the objector nor any of the class members would receive any benefit. A panel of Ninth Circuit judges agreed and dismissed the appeal despite contrary authority in the Ninth Circuit.[13] Under this ruling, in order for a class member to object to the fee where it is to be separately paid by the defendant, that objector must appeal the settlement that provides for the separate payment of the fee. However, upon doing so, that class member will then be accused by class counsel of holding the settlement hostage and attempting to extort a payment from class counsel in exchange for dismissing the appeal. Even though the class member is interested only in objecting to the fee, he will be tarred by this accusation and some courts will excoriate the objector's lawyers and even require that the objector post a substantial bond in order to proceed – a requirement that effectively requires the objector to dismiss any appeal. Put simply, this decision bulletproofs attorneys' fee awards from appellate review where the fee is to be paid directly by the defendant, separately from any common fund. No court that takes even half-seriously its self-imposed obligation to protect the interests of class members could subscribe to this decision.

3. The Fee-Shifting/Common-Fund Mix-and-Match Ploy

In class actions initiated under statutes with fee-shifting provisions, lawyers avoid the prohibition against fee multipliers by settling cases under common-fund principles. In common-fund cases, lawyers are allowed to arrange for the defendant to pay their fees directly in order to reduce the court's incentive to find the fee request excessive (because any reductions revert to the defendant). The latest ploy is to combine both of these features.

This ploy was used in a class action against UBS, a financial services company. The suit claimed that UBS misclassified their securities brokers as exempt under the Fair Labor Standards Act (FSLA) and asserted claims on behalf of 13,000 current and former UBS securities brokers for unpaid overtime and unlawful wage deductions.[14] The FSLA provides that if the plaintiffs prevail, the court may additionally award reasonable attorney fees.[15] Though the U.S. Department of Labor ruled that stockbrokers were not covered under the Act and therefore had no federal right to overtime wages, the case was settled prior to that ruling; indeed, because of other developments, the case settled even before it was filed, and the lawyers did little work after they filed the action.[16]

Nonetheless, they requested a fee of 25 percent of the announced $45 million reversionary settlement. In approving the fee request, the trial court refused to require class counsel to file a billing summary so that the lodestar could be determined. It did acknowledge, however, that the percentage fee was a multiple of at least ten of the lodestar (had it been filed).[17] A petition requesting the U.S. Supreme Court to review the case states that the multiplier was actually more than forty times the lodestar.[18] But the fee-shifting and common-fund ploy included a second element. Reverting to fee-shifting principles, the agreement provided that the defendant would separately pay the 25 percent fee and that any reduction in the fee ordered by a court would revert to the defendant. If this was intended to reduce the trial court's incentive to scrutinize the fee request, it worked like a charm. Because class members submitted claims for approximately $21 million, more than half of the announced settlement was paid to class counsel or retained by UBS.

This mix-and-match ploy was nonetheless approved by the U.S. Ninth Circuit Court of Appeals in an unreported decision.[19] The court did find the provision that any reduction in attorneys' fees would revert to the defendant to be "problematic because it acts as a device to isolate fees from scrutiny."[20] The court also decided, however, that because the attorneys obtained "exceptional results for the class ... the class's interests were not compromised by the reversion clause."[21] The "exceptional results," however, were recoveries that the Department of Labor ten months later ruled that the stockbrokers were not entitled to. As observed by Judge Edward Carnes of the Eleventh Circuit Court of Appeals, "[a] result that obtains more or better relief than plaintiffs are entitled to receive under the law is, to the extent it exceeds their entitlement on the merits, analogous to relief on a meritless claim."[22]

As for the lower court's approval of the mix-and-match jumbling of common-fund and fee-shifting principles to get around the unavailability of a lodestar multiplier and to reduce the court's incentive to give the fee request careful scrutiny, the Ninth Circuit court reverted to legal mumbo-jumbo to find that the lower court had not abused its discretion.

NOTES

1. *See Purdue et al. v. Kenny A. et al.* U.S. Sup. Ct., slip op. at 8, 10 (Apr. 21, 2010); *City of Burlington v. Dague*, 505 U.S. 557 (1992).
2. *See, e.g., Staton v. Boeing*, 327 F.3d 938, 967 (9th Cir. 2003) ("[T]here is no preclusion on recovery of common-fund fees where a fee-shifting statute applies."); *Brytus v. Spang & Co.*, 203 F.3d 238, 246–47 (3d Cir. 2000)

(implying that common-fund fees would be allowed in settled cases with statutory fee-shifting provisions and stating that under certain circumstances, the common-fund doctrine could apply even if the case were litigated to judgment); *Florin v. Nationsbank of Ga.*, 34 F.3d 560, 564 (7th Cir. 1994) ("[C]ommon-fund principles properly control a case which is initiated under a statute with a fee-shifting provision, but is settled with the creation of a common fund.").

3. *Brytus v. Spang & Co.*, 203 F.3d 238, 247 (3d Cir. 2000).

4. For a discussion of the fiduciary obligation of the lawyer, see Brickman, *Contingent Fees, supra* Introduction, note 18, at 44–47.

5. *Supra* Conclusion, Section D.

6. Charles Silver, *Due Process and the Lodestar Method: You Can't Get There from Here*, 74 TULANE L. REV. 1809, 1839 (2000).

7. As the U.S. Supreme Court has held: "[A] lawyer is under an ethical obligation to exercise independent professional judgment on behalf [of] his client; he must not allow his own interest, financial or otherwise, to influence his professional advice." *Evans v. Jeff D.*, 475 U.S. 717, 728 n.14 (1986).

8. *See Johnson v. Comerica*, 83 F.3d 241 (8th Cir. 1996) ("[I]n essence the entire settlement comes from the same source. The award to the class and the agreement on attorney fees represent a package deal.").

9. *Lobatz v. U.S. West Cellular of Cal., Inc.* 222 F.3d 1142, 1148 (9th Cir. 2002).

10. *See* Letter to ABA Standing Committee on Ethics and Professional Responsibility from Lester Brickman et al., Sept. 17, 2007, *available at* http://www.lesterbrickman.com under Recent Events (seeking ethical guidance with regard to contingency fee attorneys negotiating their fees directly with settling defendants and arguing for a per se rule banning the practice when its use compromises the right of the client or class to recover fees deemed excessive or unethical upon judicial review).

11. *See* Letter from Steven C. Krane, Chairman, ABA Standing Committee on Ethics and Professional Responsibility to Lester Brickman, Feb. 27, 2008 (on file with author).

12. *In re Palm Trio 600 and 650 Litig.*, Case No. 10–15072 (9th Cir. Aug. 10, 2010).

13. *See Zucker v. Occidental Petroleum Corp.*, 192 F. 2d 1323 (9th Cir. 1999); *Lobatz v. U.S. West Cellular of Cal., Inc.*, 222 F. 3d 1142 (9th Cir. 2000).

14. *See* Order Granting Joint Motion For Final Approval Of Settlement, at 1–2, *Glass v. UBS Fin. Servs., Inc.*, No. C-06–4068-MMC (N.D. Cal. Jan. 26, 2007); *see also* 29 U.S.C. § 201 *et seq.* (2006).

15. *See* 29 U.S.C. § 216(b) (2006).

16. Order Granting Joint Motion, *supra* note 11, at 24.

17. *See* Order Granting Joint Motion, *supra* note 11, at 25; Hearing Transcript at 9:25–10:1–4, *Glass v. UBS Fin. Servs., No.* 07–15278, D.C. No. CV-06–04068-MMC (9th Cir. Jan. 19, 2007).

18. Petition for Writ of Certiorari, *D'Aria v. Glass et al. and UBS et al.*
19. *Glass v. UBS Fin. Servs.*, No. 07–15278, D.C. No. CV-06–04068-MMC (9th Cir. Feb. 9, 2009) (unpublished opinion).
20. *Id.* at *6.
21. *Id.* at *7.
22. *Kenny A. et al. v. Perdue et al.*, 532 F. 3d 1209, 1230 (11th Cir. Ct. App. 2008).

Appendix H: Nonrecourse Financing of Tort Litigation

As discussed in Chapter 6, section C(1), lawyers are prohibited by ethics rules from subsidizing clients' living expenses or otherwise advancing them a portion of anticipated recoveries. To fill this need, entrepreneurial entities have sprung up to advance nonrecourse loans (called "investments") to tort claimants in need of money in exchange for a share of the recovery. (The nonrecourse feature means that in the event of no recovery the investing entity will lose its entire investment.) Nonrecourse financing of tort litigation has burgeoned in recent years.[1] The nature of this business is described on the Web site of Injury Funds:

> Injury Funds provides nonrecourse financing and settlement advancement to Plaintiffs in pending personal injury lawsuits. In simpler terms, we purchase a small percentage of your lawsuits [sic] anticipated recovery. We do not lend money, we do not make loans, and we do not earn interest on our investment. Instead, if the case is won, we get a percentage of the total recovery. If the case is lost, the funds are yours to keep and you owe us nothing.[2]

The litigation financing business model has come under attack from some state supreme courts. In the most noted such case, *Rancman v. Interim Settlement Funding Corp.*,[3] the Ohio Supreme Court – though rejecting the lower court's reasoning for invalidating the agreement, which was that the 280 percent effective interest rate the firm charged was "usurious" – invalidated the funding agreement on the grounds that it promoted litigation.[4] This peculiar resurrection of the much-out-of-date prohibition against champerty (advancing financing for litigation for profit) probably reflected the courts' unwillingness to get into the morass of what it called determining "the threshold level of risk necessary for a contingent advance to be treated as an investment rather than a loan."[5] The court strenuously avoided examining whether the risk assumed justified the company's charges; this allowed the court to simply ignore the issue of whether charging a one-third standard contingency fee in a "sure winner" case violates the ethical requirement that fees must be "reasonable."[6]

NOTES

1. *See, e.g.*, Richard B. Schmidt, *Staking Claims*, WALL ST. J., Sept. 15, 2000, at A1 (describing the Resolution Settlement Corporation, which makes nonrecourse loans directly to plaintiffs and occasionally to their lawyers based on the firm's assessment of the strength of the case); Margaret Cronin Fisk, *Large Verdicts For Sale*, NAT'L L.J., Jan. 11, 1999, at 1 (an exploration of the range of the burgeoning business of investing in others' lawsuits and pointing out that it has now become common practice to invest in individuals' lawsuits; investors have fully covered the market, beginning with wholly speculative claims that have yet to reach the settlement table, and continuing throughout the appeals process; and that a large portion of the business involves purchasing shares in previously awarded judgments that are on appeal). Three large investment firms, each with available capital in the range of $100 million, have started up recently for the primary purpose of funding large-scale litigation. *See Third-Party Investors Offer New Funding Source for Major Commercial Lawsuits*, 26 ABA/BNA LAWYERS' MANUAL ON PROF. CONDUCT 207 (3/31/10).
2. *Available at* http://www.injuryfunds.com/about.shtm (last visited Jan. 29, 2003). A similar enterprise may be accessed at http://www.captron.com (last visited Jan. 29, 2003).
3. 789 N.E. 2d 217 (Ohio 2003).
4. In 2008, the Ohio legislature reversed the Ohio Supreme Court by passing one of the first statutes that explicitly allows litigation financing in the consumer financing context. OHIO REV. CODE ANN. § 1345.55 (LexisNexis Supp. 2009).
5. 789 N.E. 2d at 219.
6. *See Rancman v. Interim Settlement Funding Corp.*, No. CV-99–12–5160, 2001 WL 1339487, at *3 (Ohio Ct. App., 9th Dist. Oct. 31, 2001) (finding

that the trial court's judgment that the contracts were loans because "no real probability existed that non-payment would occur" was supported by competent and credible evidence). A similar result was reached in *Echeveria v. Estate of Linde*, No. 018666/2002 (N.Y. Sup. Ct., Nassau County 2005). For discussion of this decision, see Anthony J. Sebok, *A New York Decision That May Imperil Plaintiffs' Ability to Finance Their Lawsuits: Why It Should Be Repudiated, Or Limited to Its Facts*, FindLaw (2005), http://writ.news.findlaw. com/sebok/20050418.html (with hyperlink to decision); Susan Lorde Martin, *Litigation Financing: Another Subprime Industry That Has a Place in the United States Market*, 53 VILL. L. REV. 83, 93–95 (2008); *see also* Susan Lorde Martin, *The Litigation Financing Industry: The Wild West of Finance Should be Tamed, Not Outlawed*, 10 FORDHAM J. CORP. & FIN. L. 55 (2004); Julia H. McLaughlin, *Litigation Funding: Charting a Legal and Ethical Course*, 31 VT. L. REV. 615 (2007). A similar business plan involves lending money to lawyers to cover litigation expenses. Advocate Capital, for example, provides lawyers with loans to cover litigation expenses, using the "case as collateral." Whereas lawyers must repay these loans even if the case is lost, the Web site provides assurance that it is their "experience that a minimal amount of money is invested in cases that are ultimately abandoned." http://www/advocatecapital.com.

Appendix I: Political Contributions by Tort Lawyers and the U.S. Chamber of Commerce

Tort lawyers recycle a portion of their profits from contingency fees into the political process. Their trade association, with 56,000 members, formerly called the Association of Trial Lawyers of America (ATLA), has renamed itself the American Association for Justice (AAJ) – a tacit acknowledgement that the public has come to regard "trial lawyer" as a term of opprobrium. Even so, the AAJ has long been the heavyweight champion of Washington lobbying and has almost always been able to block adoption of tort reform proposals introduced in Congress. As Walter Olson, a Fellow at the Manhattan Institute who maintains a frequently visited Web site (www.overlawyered.com) and a leading critic of the legal profession, has noted: "the litigation lobby rightly boasts of its record, year in and year out, under Republicans and Democrats alike, of turning back any threats to its prosperity."[1] *Fortune*, which publishes periodic rankings of lobby clout, has ranked trial lawyers among the top half-dozen most powerful lobbies in Washington, ahead of the AFL-CIO, the Chamber of Commerce, government employees, bankers, doctors, the real estate community, organized teachers, and the entertainment industry.[2]

In addition to its lobbying efforts, the AAJ has raised substantial funds from its members to support anti-tort reform candidates. The vast majority of this support goes to Democratic Party candidates. For example, in the 2006 election cycle, the AAJ spent a total of $6.3 million on the federal election, almost entirely to support Democrats.[3]

In the 2008 federal election cycle, AAJ's political action committee provided nearly $3 million in contributions, of which 95 percent went to Democratic candidates and only 5 percent to Republican candidates.[4]

AAJ's substantial political contributions are far exceeded by contributions from individual wealthy tort lawyers to candidates and political party organizations – almost always on the Democratic side. For example, in the 2006 election cycle, AAJ's individual members contributed more than $20 million to Senate candidates.[5] In addition, *The Wall Street Journal* reported in September 2008 that the tort bar "has already thrown $107 million toward increasing Democratic majorities."[6]

Tort lawyers also increasingly use their wealth to support their own candidacies for political office. In the fall 2006 election, fourteen of eighteen tort lawyers running for seats in the U.S. House won their races.[7] John Edwards, who made millions by claiming that cerebral palsy was caused by delay in or failure to do a Cesarean delivery – contrary to epidemiological data as discussed in Chapter 20, section A(1) – was elected a U.S. Senator from North Carolina. When he ran for the Democratic nomination for the presidency, his chief fundraiser was Fred Baron. Baron's law firm, Baron & Budd, made hundreds of millions of dollars from asbestos litigation. According to the *Dallas Observer*, the firm used witness preparation techniques that journalists termed "implanting false memories."[8]

The interplay between tort lawyers, political contributions, Democratic Party policy, and tort reform is nowhere better illustrated than in the "call sheet" affair in which a slip of paper from the 1996 federal election campaign became public four years later. It set forth the script for a phone call solicitation by Vice President Al Gore of Walter Umphrey, the centi-millionaire, asbestos/tobacco attorney from Beaumont, Texas: "I know you will give $100K when the president vetoes tort reform, but we really need it now."[9] True to the scripted words of his vice president, President Bill Clinton vetoed the tort reform bill that the Republican Congress enacted.[10]

Of course, business groups – including the U.S. Chamber of Commerce's Institute for Legal Reform – have also made substantial political contributions, mostly to support Republican candidates.[11] In the period 2001 to mid-2004, it was reported that the Chamber had spent more than $100 million on television commercials and related strategies.[12] Another major participant in tort reform on the business side is the American Tort Reform Association (ATRA) with a membership of several hundred corporate and trade groups. Corporations have also contributed millions of dollars to support various tort reforms. However, corporations have a wide range of concerns, most notably tax policy, safety and environmental regulation, and trade policies – to which most of their lobbying efforts are directed. Moreover, directly comparing dollars spent can be misleading. Playing defense – the AAJ's strong suit – requires far less capital than the business community's efforts to mobilize public support for tort reform and to create the political will to garner the elusive sixty votes in the Senate needed to enact any significant legislation.

NOTES

1. Walter Olson, *The Lawsuit Lobby*, AM. SPECTATOR (Mar.–Apr. 2003).
2. *See, e.g.*, Jeffrey H. Birnbaum, *Washington's Power 25*, FORTUNE, Dec. 8, 1997, at 144; Jeffrey H. Birnbaum, *Fat & Happy in D.C.*, FORTUNE, May 28, 2001, at 94.
3. Bara Vaida, *Trial Lawyers' New Confidence*, NAT'L L.J., Jan. 27, 2007, at 39.
4. CENTER FOR RESPONSIVE POLITICS, AMERICAN ASS'N FOR JUSTICE CAMPAIGN CONTRIBUTIONS, *available at* http://www.opensecrets.org/orgs/summary. php?id=D000000065 (last visited Sept. 6, 2009).
5. Vaida, *supra* note 3. *See also* Deborah R. Hensler, *Jurors in the Material World: Putting Tort Verdicts in Their Social Context*, 13 ROGER WILLIAMS U. L. REV. 8, 14 (2008).
6. *The Tort Bar's Comeback*, WALL ST. J., Sept. 16, 2008, at A24.
7. Terry Carter, *New Names, New Strategies*, 93 A.B.A. J. 38 (Feb. 2007).
8. *See* Brickman, *Asbestos Litigation*, *supra* Chapter 2, note 16, at nn.141–157. (Baron died on October 30, 2008, from a rare cancer. *See Democratic backer Fred Baron dies*, ASSOC. PRESS, OCT. 30, 2008.)

9. Quoted in Olson, *The Lawsuit Lobby, supra* note 1.

10. On May 2, 1996, President Clinton vetoed the *Common Sense Product Liability Legal Reform Act of 1996* HR 956. On May 9th, The House of Representatives attempted to override the veto but failed on a vote of 258 for, 163 against, less than the two-thirds needed. *See* THE LIBRARY OF CONGRESS, THOMAS HOME, BILLS, RESOLUTIONS, H.R. 956, *available at* http://thomas.loc.gov/cgi-bin/bdquery/z?d104:HR00956 (last visited Nov. 20, 2008).

11. *See* Vaida, *Trial Lawyers' New Confidence, supra* note 3, at 1.

12. Shailagh Murray, *Trial-Lawyers Lobby Discovers Unlikely Friends: Republicans*, WALL ST. J., July 8, 2004, at A1.

Appendix J: Special Rules
Favoring Lawyers

Courts have constructed many rules favoring the interests of lawyers. Consider, by way of example, the different rules regulating malpractice liability for doctors and lawyers that lawyer-judges have created. If a patient has a 70 percent likelihood of dying from a certain condition and in the course of treatment his doctor fails to prescribe a drug that would have raised the odds of survival from 30 to 40 percent and the patient dies, then in a majority of states, the doctor is liable in damages for the "loss of chance," that is, the heightened risk caused by his negligence even though the patient was unlikely to survive even if the doctor had correctly treated the condition. Lawyers, however, have a special rule largely exempting them from malpractice under equivalent circumstances. When a client sues her lawyer for malpractice because the lawyer failed to file an action within the time limit for doing so, she must show that "but for" the lawyer's negligence, the client would have had a 100 percent likelihood of prevailing in the underlying action.[1] Similarly, when a surgeon makes a mistake in the course of a grueling protracted operation, the surgeon is liable. But a lawyer who errs during the course of a grueling protracted trial is exempt from liability because "tactical decisions" do not constitute grounds for legal malpractice.[2]

Lawyers are also accorded special protection from courts when instituting litigation. For example, assume that a client hires a lawyer to sue various doctors and health care providers for malpractice. The client lists five doctors as having contributed to his iatrogenic injury, including

Dr. A. Lawyer then files suit against the five doctors, the hospital, and attending nurses. Dr. A maintains that he never treated the claimant nor had any contact with him. Lawyer, however, refuses to dismiss Dr. A from the suit. Dr. A then incurs $20,000 in legal fees and expenses in order to obtain a dismissal on that ground. Had Lawyer done an even modest amount of factual investigation, he would have verified the veracity of Dr. A's claim. Dr. A then hires a lawyer to sue Lawyer for malicious prosecution. However, the uniform holding of courts throughout the land is that Lawyer is not liable to Dr. A for his lack of diligence.[3] Indeed, lawyers have been exonerated of any requirement to investigate a client's assertions unless there is "compelling evidence" that the client's statements are untrue.[4]

Lawyers also have special powers created by courts for the protection of their financial interests. Most notable are attorney's liens – which are "not strictly like any other lien known to the law."[5] The retaining lien permits a lawyer to withhold a client's papers until she gets paid.[6] The charging lien gives the attorney owed a fee a security interest in a client's monetary recovery that the attorney helped to secure.[7] No payments may be made to clients or others unless the attorney is paid. These devices that help lawyers secure payment of their fees are not available to other professionals.[8]

Consider further how court-made rules elevate the interests of lawyers above the rest of society. A corporation that suspects some of its officers have been engaged in an accounting scam to create phantom profits that will fatten their stock options may decide to hire professionals to do an internal investigation. If the company hires an accounting firm, then in an enforcement action brought by the SEC or a subsequent litigation by shareholders based on the effects of the fraud, the report prepared may have to be turned over to the SEC or the plaintiffs. If the corporation hires a law firm to do the internal investigation, however, the report will often be privileged from discovery.

Finally, it should also be acknowledged that there are statutes that specifically target lawyers. Unbeknownst to most of the public and even to most lawyers, there are at least twelve states that have enacted criminal or civil statutes specifically targeting attorney deceit and collusion.[9] These statutes descend from Chapter 29 of the First Statute of Westminster, promulgated in England, in 1273, which addressed lawyer misconduct, a severe problem at the time. The statute provided for imprisonment for a year or more for "deceit and collusion in the king's court" – a term to which it gave an expansive interpretation.[10] However, despite this ancestry, according to Professor Alex Long, "these statutes have languished in obscurity and, through a series of restrictive readings of the statutory language, have been rendered somewhat irrelevant."[11] New York, however, is a recent exception. New York first adopted its version of the Statute of Westminster in 1787 and added a provision allowing for the award of treble damages. In 2009, New York's high court, in *Amalfitano v. Rosenberg*,[12] considerably broadened the reach of the current version of its "lawyer deceit" law[13] by holding that reliance on an attorney's misrepresentation is not an essential element of the statutory claim.[14]

NOTES

1. *See* Brickman, *Continuing Assault, supra* Appendix A, note 17, at 1193 n.52.
2. *See, e.g., Simko v. Blake,* 532 N.W.2d 842, 848 (Mich. 1995) ("Perhaps defendant made an error of judgment in deciding not to call particular witnesses, and perhaps another attorney would have made a different decision; however, tactical decisions do not constitute grounds for a legal malpractice action.")
3. *See, e.g., Cottman v. Cottman,* 468 A.2d 131, 136 (Md. App. 1983) (stating that such claims are viewed with disfavor in the law and that this is "particularly true when the defendant is an attorney because of the attorney's professional duty to represent his client zealously").
4. *See Friedman v. Dozorc,* 312 N.W.2d 585, 605 (Mich. 1981); *Millner v. Elmer Fox & Co.,* 529 P.2d 806, 808 (Utah 1980) ("As a general rule, an attorney is not required to investigate the truth or falsity of facts and information furnished by his client."); *Moiel v. Sandlin,* 571 S.W.2d 567, 570 (Tex. Civ. App.-Corpus Christi 1978). ("Unless lack of probable cause for a claim is obvious from the facts disclosed by the client or otherwise brought to the attorney's attention, he may assume the facts so disclosed are substantially correct.").
5. *Estate of Clarks ex rel. Brisco-Whitter v. U.S.,* 202 F. 3d854, 856 (6th Cir. 2000) (quoting RAY ANDREWS BROWN, THE LAW OF PERSONAL PROPERTY §116, at 559 (2d ed. 1955).

6. *See Attorneys At Law* (Lester Brickman) in WARREN'S WEED NEW YORK REAL PROPERTY, vol. 1 at § 6.02 (1991).

7. *See Attorneys At Law, id.* at § 6.03.

8. Joseph M. Perillo, *The Law of Lawyers' Contracts Is Different*, 67 FORDHAM L. REV. 443, 444 (1998). *See also id.* at 448 (noting other pro-lawyer rules); Lester Brickman & Jonathan Klein, *The Use of Advance Fee Attorney Retainer Agreements in Bankruptcy: Another Special Rule for Lawyers?*, 43 S.C. L. REV. 1037, 1039 (1992).

9. *See* Alex B. Long, *Attorney Deceit Statutes: Promoting Professionalism Through Criminal Prosecutions And Treble Damages*, at 4, 30–31 (2010), *available at* ssrn.com/abstract=1559238.

10. *See* Jonathan Rose, *The Legal Profession in Medieval England: A History of Regulation*, 48 SYRACUSE L. REV. 1, 50, 56, 58 (1998).

11. *Id.* at 5; *see also id.* at 32.

12. 903 N.E.2d 265 (N.Y. 2009).

13. N.Y. Judiciary Law, § 487.

14. *Id.* at 269.

Appendix K: The Ultimate Medical Expense "Buildup": Whiplash

Soft-tissue injuries account for a majority of the bodily injury claims generated by auto accidents.[1] This is especially the case in bodily injury claims in urban areas. Soft-tissue injuries cannot be detected by X-rays or MRI scans and are diagnosed solely on the basis of the symptoms reported by the injured person.[2]

The most common soft-tissue injury claimed by auto accident victims is chronic whiplash.[3] A whiplash injury is defined as "an injury to the cervical spine resulting from acceleration and hyperextension of the head during a motor vehicle accident."[4] The diagnosis of whiplash is made primarily on the basis of subjectively reported symptoms, such as neck pain, headache, back pain, concentration, and memory difficulties, and the absence of similar pre-existing complaints.[5] Ten years ago, it was estimated that more than $29 billion was spent annually in the United States on whiplash injuries and litigation.[6] Today, that amount is undoubtedly higher.

A study conducted in Lithuania attempted to determine whether chronic whiplash was a medical event or simply a reflection of the compensation system.[7] (Lithuania was chosen because, at the time of the study, there was no financial incentive for Lithuanians to claim chronic injuries; because few automobile drivers were covered by personal-injury insurance, most medical bills were paid by the government and lawsuits were rare.) The study compared injury complaints reported by 202 individuals from Kaunas, Lithuania, who had experienced rear-end collisions with injury complaints reported by a control group of 202 individuals from the same region, who had not been involved in an automobile collision.[8] If "chronic whiplash" were a medical event, then those involved in auto accidents should have a higher prevalence of whiplash symptoms.

However, the study found "no significant differences" between the accident victims and the control group in the prevalence of chronic neck pain, headache, or any other symptom studied.[9] The study also found that "[n]one of the 202 individuals in the accident victims group stated that they had persistent or disabling symptoms caused by the car accidents." Indeed, according to the study's logistic regression models, neither neck pain nor headache was even related to the automobile accidents.[10] Moreover, neither the severity of car damage, use of headrest, use of seat belt, or collision speed had any significant impact on the frequency of claims of chronic neck pain or headache,[11] which is inconsistent with the notion that whiplash syndrome is caused by hyperextension of the neck. Though the study's authors acknowledge that "[n]o study can totally disprove that in single cases persistent symptoms can be caused by trauma," they conclude that chronic whiplash has "little validity."[12]

In another study, researchers concluded that "[t]he elimination of compensation for pain and suffering is associated with a decreased incidence and improved prognosis of whiplash injury."[13] Specifically, the researchers studied the effects of changing to a no-fault system in Saskatchewan, Canada, and found a 28 percent decrease in the incidence of whiplash and a 200-day reduction in the median time to closure of claims.[14]

NOTES

1. *See* Grady, *Whiplash is Uncompensated*, Chapter 15, note 78; *see also Saving Our Necks in Car Crashes*, CONSUMERS' RES. MAG., DEC. 12, 1995, at 28 (66% of auto injury claims for bodily injuries include neck sprains).
2. *See supra* Chapter 15, § B (3).
3. The origin of the chronic whiplash syndrome appears to have emulated the nineteenth-century claim of "railway spine," the symptoms of which were

almost identical to those that would be recognized as associated with whiplash: memory impairment, poor concentration, sleep disturbance, back stiffness and pain, headache, and so forth. *See* Ferrari, Whiplash, *supra*, at 4, 54. Like chronic whiplash, there was a lack of objective evidence for the existence of railway spine, yet the medical community cooperated with – if not supported – efforts of claimants to secure compensation for this injury. *Id.* at 3. Railway spine all but disappeared as both a compensation claim and a medical event by the turn of the twentieth century, by which time it had been established that railway spine was essentially a psychological illness. *Id.* at 3. For a further account of railway spine, see DORNSTEIN, ACCIDENTALLY ON PURPOSE, *supra*, at 209–216.

4. Simon Carette, *Whiplash Injury and Chronic Neck Pain*, NEW ENG. J. MED., Apr. 14, 1994, at 1083; *see also* Bogdan P. Radanov, GiuSeepe Di Stefano, Ayesha Schnidrig, Matthias Sturzenegger, Klaus F. Augustiny, *Cognitive Functioning After Common Whiplash: A Controlled Follow-Up Study*, ARCHIVES OF NEUROLOGY, Jan. 1993, at 87 (defining whiplash as "a musculo-ligamental sprain/strain of the cervical region without fractures or dislocations of the cervical spine or herniation of the intervertebral disks"). The term "whiplash injury" was coined in 1928 by Dr. Harold Crowe, an orthopedist. *See* DORNSTEIN, ACCIDENTALLY ON PURPOSE, *supra*, at 203. Interestingly, Dr. Crowe later regretted having used the term. In 1963 he stated: "At the time ... I used the unfortunate term 'whiplash'. This expression was intended to be a description of motion. It was not thought to be a name of a disease. The name 'whiplash', however, has been accepted by physicians, patients, and attorneys as the name of a disease and the term 'whiplash' has been published subsequently by many physicians with this unfortunate misunderstanding of the word." *Id.* at 203–204.

5. *See* Harald Schrader, Diana Obelieniene, Gunnar Bovim, Danguole Surkiene, Dalia Mickeviciene, Irena Miseviciene, *Natural Evolution of Late Whiplash Syndrome Outside the Medicolegal Context*, 347 THE LANCET, May 4, 1996, at 1207, 1209–10 [hereinafter Schrader et al., *Whiplash Syndrome*]; *see also* Robert Ferrari, Whiplash – A Review for Lawyers 43–50, 67–80 (July 18, 1996) (unpublished manuscript, on file with author) [hereinafter Ferrari, Whiplash] (describing diagnostic tools used in the last fifty years to identify chronic whiplash, and concluding that "the whiplash injury has never actually been proven to exist by means that are considered to be scientifically objective," *id.* at 56, and also noting that neurologic testing over the past forty years "has not provided medical researchers with the site of whiplash injury," *id.* at 79). *But see* Helge Kasch et al., *Handicap After Acute Whiplash Injury*, 56 NEUROLOGY 1637 (2001) (finding that whiplash injury caused chronic disability in as many as 50% of cases).

6. Michael D. Freeman, *Discrediting Defense Experts in Whiplash Cases*, TRIAL MAGAZINE 62 (Mar. 1999).

7. *See* Schrader et al., *Whiplash Syndrome, supra*; Grady, *Whiplash Is Uncompensated*, Chapter 15, note 78 (describing the Lithuanian study).

8. *See* Schrader et al., *Whiplash Syndrome, supra*, at 1207.

9. *See* Schrader et al., *Whiplash Syndrome, supra*, at 1210. For example, neck pain was reported by 35.1% of the accident victims group, but also by 33.2% of the control group. *Id.* at 1208–09 & tbl.2. Similarly, headaches of varying severity were reported by 53% of the accident victim's group and by 49.5% of the control group. *Id.* at 1209 & tbl.4. Chronic neck pain and chronic headache (i.e. more than seven days per month) were also reported in similar proportions by the two groups, 8.4% v. 6.9% and 9.4% v. 5.9%, respectively. *Id.* at 1207–09 & tbls.3–4.

10. *See* Schrader et al., *Whiplash Syndrome, supra*, at 1209–10 & tbl.7.

11. *Id.* at 1209 tbls.5–6.

12. *Id.* at 1210. Plaintiffs' lawyers have criticized this study. *See* Michael D. Freeman, *Discrediting Defense Experts in Whiplash Cases*, TRIAL MAGAZINE, Mar. 1999, at 62, 66 (contending that the sample size was inadequate and therefore, "the authors' statements regarding chronic pain after whiplash are not based on valid research results").

13. J. David Cassidy et al., *Effect of Eliminating Compensation for Pain and Suffering on the Outcome of Insurance Claims for Whiplash Injury*, 341 NEW ENG. J. MED. 1179, 1179 (2000).

14. *Id.* at 1184.

Appendix L: The Effect of Punitive Damages on Compensatory Awards

In recent years, tort lawyers have succeeded in establishing a "bad faith" cause of action against insurance companies for their failure to offer to settle certain tort claims for policy limits brought against their insured. In these litigations, large punitive damages or their functional equivalents have been assessed against insurance companies for their failure to offer policy limits.[1] This has a dual effect. First, it directly enriches tort lawyers. Second, insurance companies, fearful of punitive damages awards if they fail to make substantial settlement offers, are more likely to offer higher settlements, even when they do not believe the claim merits such an offer.

Punitive damages amounting to tens of millions of dollars have also been awarded against medical insurers and HMOs for failing to cover "experimental" treatments for life-threatening conditions. For example, a jury awarded $77 million in punitive damages to a family of a woman who died after an HMO denied her the ability to undergo an experimental bone marrow transplant.[2] In another case, a jury rendered a $116 million punitive damages award for an "HMO's refusal to authorize payment for an expensive, state-of-the-art treatment for terminal cancer that the HMO considered to be experimental."[3] No doubt, some medical insurers' denials of coverage have more to do with financial self-interest than with the medical appropriateness of the course of treatment. But it is profit-driven public policy making when juries get to decide whether medical insurance should be extended to cover a new complex procedure that an insurer claims is experimental and without proven efficacy. Juries are at least susceptible to the plea that *any* procedure that might be of benefit should be covered. The consequence is that juries are setting national health policy by effectively ordering the provision of insurance coverage for experimental procedures not now covered by insurance policies. Because a jury – not a state or national legislative body – is deciding the policy choice, the cost implications of such a decision are simply not considered or addressed.[4]

The threat of unleashing punitive damages is a weapon wielded by some courts to coerce defendants to settle large numbers of cases. This was the strategy adopted by then U.S. District Court Judge Robert Parker, in the *Cimino* case, discussed in Chapter 21.[5] Cimino was a class action brought on behalf of approximately 3,000 oil refinery workers who claimed injury from asbestos exposure. Judge Parker created a structure designed to bludgeon the defendants into settling thousands of claims of refinery workers, though most had no asbestos-related injury or lung impairment recognized by medical science. As part of that design, the jurors were to first determine the amount of damages that would be assessed if the jury later found the defendants liable. Jurors were to also determine, in advance of a trial on liability, the amount of punitive damages for each of the more than 3,000 plaintiffs. Instead of a dollar amount, the jurors were to determine a multiplier that would be applied to the damage awards if the jury later found that the defendants were liable. As a consequence, the defendants were faced with a pretrial punitive damages award that amounted to $500,000 per class member, plus substantial compensatory damages, also predetermined. For the class, this amounted to more than $1.5 billion just for punitive damages. In the face of this intended threat to their economic viability, mounted at the expense of their constitutional rights to trial by jury and due process of law, the large majority of the defendants settled the claims on terms highly favorable to the plaintiffs.

In another notorious asbestos litigation scenario, the judge's threat to allow a jury to assess punitive damages on top of substantial compensatory awards to asbestos claimants, who reported no respiratory problems and normal pulmonary function tests, compelled the defendants to settle 1,700 mostly meritless claims for tens of millions of dollars.[6]

NOTES

1. *See, e.g., Paine Webber Real Estate Securities, Inc. v. Fireman's Fund Ins. Co.*, No. CGC-88–888592 (Super. Ct., S.F. County, Cal. 1993) ($22 million punitive damages award for bad-faith failure to offer settlement in slander claim); *Hedrick v. Sentry Ins. Co.*, No. 96–128100–90 (Dist. Ct., Tarrant County, Tex. 1993) ($100 million punitive damages award for bad-faith denial of $20,000 underinsured motorist claim).
2. *See Fox v. Health Net*, No. 219692, 1993 WL 794305 (Super. Ct. Riverside County, Cal. 1993); *HMO Liable for Punitives*, NAT'L L.J., Jan. 10, 1994, at 19.
3. *See* Gail B. Agrawal and Mark A. Hall, *What If You Could Sue Your HMO? Managed Care Liability Beyond the ERISA Shield*, 47 ST. LOUIS U. L.J. 235, 240, n.16 (2003) (citing *Goodrich v. Aetna U.S. Healthcare of Cal. Inc.*, No. RCV 20499, 1999 WL 181418, at *4 (Cal. App. Dep't Super. Ct. Mar. 29, 1999).
4. *See* Ron Winslow, *How Political Pressure Pushed a U.S. Agency Back to a New Therapy*. WALL ST. J., Nov. 17, 1994, at A1, A8 (reviewing the decision of the Federal Office of Personnel Management ordering 350 health plans serving nine million federal employees and their dependents to cover an experimental breast cancer treatment that costs up to $100,000). The result is higher insurance costs without any showing of commensurate health benefits.
5. *See supra* Chapter 21, note 16.
6. For discussion of this mass consolidation of asbestos claims in Fayette, Mississippi, in 1998, known as *David Cosey*, see Brickman, *Asbestos Litigation, supra* Chapter 2, note 16, at 40 n.17. For discussion of how the credible threat of punitive damages award was used to effectively compel asbestos defendants to settle thousands of claims, many of dubious merit, see Brickman, *Asbestos Litigation Crisis, supra* Chapter 9, note 6, at 1862 n.176.

Index